Criminal Justice Ethics
Edition 2

For James

Criminal Justice Ethics

Edition 2

Theory and Practice

Cyndi Banks

Criminal Justice Department, Northern Arizona University

Los Angeles • London • New Delhi • Singapore

For information:

SAGE Publications, Inc.
2455 Teller Road
Thousand Oaks, California 91320
E-mail: order@sagepub.com

SAGE Publications India Pvt. Ltd.
B 1/I 1 Mohan Cooperative Industrial Area
Mathura Road, New Delhi 110 044
India

SAGE Publications Ltd.
1 Oliver's Yard
55 City Road
London EC1Y 1SP
United Kingdom

SAGE Publications Asia-Pacific Pte. Ltd.
33 Pekin Street #02-01
Far East Square
Singapore 048763

Printed in the United States of America.

Library of Congress Cataloging-in-Publication Data

Banks, Cyndi.
Criminal justice ethics: theory and practice/Cyndi Banks. — 2nd ed.
    p. cm.
Includes bibliographical references and index.
ISBN 978-1-4129-5832-5 (pbk.: alk. paper)
    1. Criminal justice, Administration of—Moral and ethical aspects. I. Title.

HV7419.B36 2009
172'.2—dc22   2008019312

This book is printed on acid-free paper.

08   09   10   11   12   10   9   8   7   6   5   4   3   2   1

Acquisitions Editor:	Jerry Westby
Editorial Assistant:	Eve Oettinger
Production Editor:	Karen Wiley
Copy Editor:	Cate Huisman
Typesetter:	C&M Digitals (P) Ltd.
Proofreader:	Gail Fay
Indexer:	Gloria Tierney
Cover Designer:	Gail Buschman
Marketing Manager:	Jennifer Reed Banando

Contents

Preface

This is the second edition of a text on ethics and criminal justice that seeks to examine the criminal justice system through an ethical lens, to identify ethical issues in practice and in theory, to explore ethical dilemmas, and to suggest how ethical issues and dilemmas faced by criminal justice professionals might be resolved. The first edition received positive responses from reviewers and colleagues and has proven its worth as a useful tool in the academy in the crucial task of teaching criminal justice students about ethics. The second edition contains new material, fresh case studies, and an entirely new chapter on ethics and terrorism. It also incorporates a comparative dimension, because promoting ethics in criminal justice is, or ought to be, a global endeavor. I hope readers will find that the book is challenging and informative, offers a variety of perspectives, and above all, is of value in the classroom.

The text adopts a critical perspective in the sense that each element within the criminal justice system is scrutinized within a framework where questions are raised about proper conduct or standards. Drawing on the by-now substantial literature associated with ethics in criminal justice (including classical studies and monographs as well as the most up-to-date research), this book tries to provide a context for the resolution of ethical issues. In each case, historical and social events set the context for the ethical discussions, and ethical issues are analyzed in a way that attempts to take full account of the impact of historical, social, and cultural aspects of ethical development.

The theoretical chapters draw upon a much wider range of philosophical literature than is usually the case in books of this nature, and certain ethical theories such as virtue ethics and the ethic of care have been presented in greater depth than is usual. The rationale for this approach is to recognize the importance of gender in ethics and also to reflect the topicality of virtue ethics with its emphasis on character and community.

The format of the book is unusual in the sense that instead of beginning with theoretical chapters, the book first presents the practical material on the interaction between ethics and criminal justice and then presents philosophical and ethical discourses. This inversion of the usual textual presentation is deliberate and is aimed at ensuring that students are well grounded in practical ethical issues before they are called upon to grapple with theory. In my experience of teaching criminal justice ethics, I have found that a significant percentage of students are perplexed and baffled when ethical theory is presented before practice, because they do not see themselves as philosophers, nor have most of them studied philosophy to any extent. Acquainting them with practical issues to which they can apply theory and philosophy at a later stage seems to help them to make closer linkages between theory and practice. Those who do not favor this approach to teaching ethics can of course reverse the order of the book in their classes.

Following an introduction to the study of ethics generally, Part I of the book engages with ethical issues in the criminal justice system as they affect specific institutions and the system overall. The subject areas in Part I are policing, racial discrimination, legal ethics, punishment, corrections, ethics and the War on Terrorism, and criminal justice policy making. Part II focuses on ethical theories, presenting deontology, consequentialism, virtue theory, egoism, stoicism and hedonism, social justice, and the ethic of care.

Most of all, the writing and publication of this edition owes much to James Baker, whose insightful comments and ongoing encouragement and support has, as always, sustained me and makes this work possible. I owe considerable thanks to my editor, Jerry Westby, who was instrumental in initiating the first edition and once again has given his support and encouragement for this second edition. I am also appreciative of the assistance given to me by Jennifer Curtis Wildeman, who helped locate resources for this edition. This book has grown as a result of input from the students who have studied ethics under my tuition. They have been a valuable resource and have taught me much about how to present ethics in an accessible but nevertheless sophisticated manner that captures the complexity of ethical decision making in criminal justice.

I would also like to thank the reviewers of this edition: Robert J. Diemer, Saint Leo University; Cheryl Swanson, University of West Florida; Abbe Justus, Florida State University; Price Foster, University of Louisville; Melissa Wagner, San Francisco State University; Richard Hill, University of Houston, Downtown Campus; Lee Latham, University of North Texas; Dan Ford, Cameron University; and Ted Paddack, Midwestern State University.

PART I

The Interaction Between Ethics and the Criminal Justice System

CHAPTER 1

The Importance of Ethics in Criminal Justice

To live ethically is to think about things beyond one's own interests. When I think ethically I become just one being, with needs and desires of my own, certainly, but living among others who also have needs and desires.

—Peter Singer 1995: 174

The Meaning of Ethics

Ethics, also known as moral philosophy, is a branch of philosophy concerned with the study of questions of right and wrong and how we ought to live. Ethics involves making moral judgments about what is right or wrong, good or bad. Right and wrong are qualities or moral judgments we assign to actions and conduct. Within the study of ethics, there are three branches: *metaethics,* concerned with methods, language, logical structure, and the reasoning used in the interpretation of ethical terms, for example, what exactly does the term "good" mean; *normative ethics,* concerned with ways of behaving and standards of conduct; and *applied ethics,* concerned with solving practical moral problems as they arise, particularly in the professions, such as medicine and law.

Ethics provides us with a way to make moral choices when we are uncertain about what to do in a situation involving moral issues. In the process of everyday life, moral rules are desirable, not because they express absolute truth, but because they are generally reliable guides for normal circumstances (Singer 1995: 175). The focus of this book is on normative and applied ethics, particularly the exploration and analysis of ethical dilemmas and conflict situations that arise within the criminal justice system.

The Value of Ethics

Do we need to study ethics? One view is that if we need to make a decision about a dilemma that confronts us, we can do so without any knowledge of ethics. From this perspective, ethics is too abstract and theoretical and is not related to the practical world. Another view is that we need a system of rules and principles to help guide us in making difficult decisions when moral issues arise. If we cannot draw upon an ethical framework, we have to rely on emotion, instinct, and personal values, and these cannot supply an adequate answer to moral dilemmas. Among the reasons commonly given for studying ethics are the following:

- Ethical considerations are central to decisions involving discretion, force, and due process that require people to make enlightened moral judgments.
- Knowledge of ethics enables a person to question and analyze assumptions that are typically not questioned in areas of activity like business and politics. Questioning the criminal justice system should also be encouraged. This includes raising issues regarding such topics as the relationship between crime and justice, the role of law enforcement, the place of punishment, the limits of punishment, the authority of the state, the proper function of prisons, fairness in the workplace through creating a safe working environment, and equal opportunity.
- The study of ethics increases sensitivity to issues of right and wrong and the right way to conduct oneself and aids in identifying acts that have a moral content.
- Only through studying ethics is it possible to define unethical behavior. A full understanding of ethical behavior demonstrates that it includes not only "bad" or "evil" acts, but also inaction that allows "bad" or "evil" to occur.
- It is important to have the capacity to point to moral reasoning in justifying behavior, and the study of ethics develops that capacity.
- It is crucial that ethical decisions are made, and the study of ethics enables the development of tools that enhance ethical decision making.
- Training in critical ethics helps to develop analytical skills and reasoning abilities needed to understand the practical as well as the theoretical aspects of the criminal justice system (Felkenes 1987).
- Understanding ethics enables an appreciation of the complexities of acts that involve ethical issues and dilemmas.
- Without knowledge of ethics, criminal justice professionals may be naïve about moral issues occurring within the criminal justice system.
- The study of ethics helps criminal justice professionals quickly recognize the ethical consequences of various actions and the moral principles involved.
- Within the criminal justice system, ethics is germane to most management and policy decisions relating to punishment and is the rationale used in making these decisions, such as whether to rehabilitate, deter, or impose just deserts. Examples of such management and policy issues include whether it is ethical to force someone to attend a treatment program against his or her will, and, given that the system of punishment is based on an assumption of rehabilitation, whether it is ethical to send an offender to jail and not offer treatment programs to help him or her change behavior in order to regain freedom (Felkenes 1987).

- The criminal justice system comprises professionals who exercise power and authority over others and who in some cases are authorized to use force and physical coercion against them. The law, or accepted standards of behavior, imposes ethical rules and responsibilities on these professionals. It follows that professionals in the criminal justice system must be aware of ethical standards in carrying out their functions. Ethics is crucial in decisions involving discretion, force, and due process, because criminal justice professionals can be tempted to abuse their powers (Felkenes 1987).

In this book, the value of the study of ethics by criminal justice professionals will become apparent as the criminal justice system is analyzed to reveal how decision makers sometimes fail to make the "right" choices or deliberately act unethically in carrying out their functions. It will become clear that studying and applying ethics is a prerequisite for any competent criminal justice professional. As an introduction to the kinds of ethical issues that can arise in criminal justice, two reports of criminal cases are presented in case studies 1.1 and 1.2.

CASE STUDY 1.1 POLICE BRUTALITY IN NEW ORLEANS

In March 1990 Adolph Archie, an African American, was injured in an incident in which police claimed he shot and killed a white police officer during a downtown shootout. Archie later died under circumstances that are still far from clear. Transporting Archie to the hospital after the shooting took police 12 minutes, but the distance was only seven blocks. When he arrived, about 100 officers were present, having heard about the death of their fellow officer. While Archie was being taken to the hospital, police radios were used to utter death threats against him, and those accompanying him to the hospital believed there might be a lynching if he were taken there. According to their account, they decided not to take him to that hospital, and instead of taking him to a different hospital, they took him to the police station where the deceased officer had worked. Here, officers reported there was a scuffle involving Archie and he fell, causing blood stains on the floor. However, the sergeant at the police station denied seeing either Archie or the officers and did not ask about the blood stains, but simply ordered that they be cleaned up.

When Archie finally got medical treatment, it was clear that he had been severely beaten, but no officers were held responsible. At the hospital, X-rays of Archie's injuries disappeared, and staff were unable to record details of Archie's name and background. He was injected with iodine, to which he was alleged to be allergic, for a medical test, and some concluded that this was the cause of his death. However, other accounts by pathologists reported that he had been beaten to death. Ultimately his death was reported as a "homicide by police

(Continued)

(Continued)

intervention" by the coroner. Within hours of his death, police Superintendent Warren Woodfork cleared all officers involved in the incident of any violations of conduct. Reportedly, the rookie officer who arrested Archie was denounced by fellow officers for not killing Archie on the spot.

Subsequently, in May 1993, a report by the advisory committee on human relations found that some officers had brutalized Archie and that the department had failed to hold them accountable. The committee noted the existence of a police code of silence that was supported at the highest levels within the department.

SOURCE: Human Rights Watch 1998.

It was not until 3 years after Archie was beaten to death that reports concluded that some officers had behaved brutally. Despite the extreme circumstances of this case, no police officers were prosecuted or sanctioned administratively, largely due to the police "code of silence," a part of the institutional culture of the police (see Chapter 2). However, it is significant that the officers transporting Archie did not enter the hospital but instead took him to the police station. Archie is supposed to have slipped and fallen at the police station, and by the time he did receive medical treatment, he had been severely beaten to such an extent that he died as a result of what was termed "a homicide by police intervention." Furthermore, Archie's family was compensated by the city in an out-of-court settlement. Ethical questions concerning police use of force, possible police perjury, and a police cover-up of illegal acts ultimately surfaced. These and other ethical issues in policing will be addressed in Chapter 2.

CASE STUDY 1.2   DEATH ROW INMATE SET FREE

On February 28, 2005, an Ohio judge dismissed all charges against Derrick Jamison in relation to the death of a bartender in Cincinnati. Prosecutors had elected not to retry him in the case. He had been convicted and sentenced to death in 1985 based in part on the testimony of a codefendant, Charles Howell, whose own sentence had been reduced for testifying against Jamison.

The prosecution decision not to retry him followed a finding that the prosecutor had withheld statements that contradicted the testimony of Charles Howell, would have undermined the prosecution's theory about the victim's death, and would have suggested other possible suspects for the murder. Two federal courts ruled that the prosecution's actions had the effect of denying Jamison a fair trial.

The deceased victim, Gary Mitchell, was murdered on August 1, 1984, at the Central Bar in downtown Cincinnati. He was found by customers almost dead, having received blunt-force trauma to the head. He died several days later. Several eyewitnesses gave different accounts of persons entering and leaving the bar, and a shoe print was found on top of the bar. Jamison was arrested 2 months later after robbing a restaurant. He was wearing the gym shoes that had produced the impression on top of the bar. A few months after Jamison's arrest, Charles Howell was also arrested as an accomplice in the murder, and he informed police that he and Jamison had robbed the bar and that Jamison had attacked the bartender.

Before trial, the prosecution indicated that it was unaware of any exculpatory evidence, but in fact such evidence had been excluded from the homicide book prepared by the Cincinnati police department. This is the book that is passed to the prosecutor for trial. Ultimately Jamison argued that he did not receive 35 documents from the prosecution prior to trial and that the practice of the police department and the prosecutor's office had the effect of suppressing evidence material to his defense. Jamison's conviction rested principally on the testimony of Charles Howell, the shoe print found on the bar, and the testimony of a witness who positively identified Jamison as the perpetrator. She had identified him at the trial but in the police offense report had indicated that she could not make that identification. Obviously, the offense report could have been used to challenge her identification of Jamison at the trial.

SOURCE: Death Penalty Information Center 2007.

In this report of a death row inmate released from prison after 19 years' incarceration, the state admitted there was a lack of evidence linking him to the crime for which he was convicted. His lawyers alleged prosecutorial misconduct, pointing out that the prosecution withheld critical eyewitness evidence from the defense that contradicted the main evidence used to convict him originally. This case illustrates the need for prosecutors to adhere to ethical standards of conduct, a subject that will be more fully explored in Chapter 4.

Normative Ethics

Normative ethics is fundamental to ethical decision making in the criminal justice system. A central notion in normative ethics is that one's conduct must take into account moral issues; that is, one should act morally, using reason to decide the proper way of conducting oneself. Essentially, ethics, in prescribing certain standards of conduct, gives us a way of making choices in situations where we are unsure about how to act.

What are these standards of conduct and how do we decide what is right and wrong? Some argue that because standards of conduct and ways of doing things differ from society to society, there can never be one single standard for all people everywhere, and that we must make ethical decisions based on each situation. This approach to setting standards of conduct is called *ethical relativism*. Others argue that one set of ethical standards applies across all societies, and people have an obligation to do what is "known to be right"; that is, they argue in favor of *ethical absolutism*.

Ethical Relativism

Ethical relativists argue that what is morally right or wrong may vary in a fundamental way from person to person or from culture to culture. In other words, as Arrington (1983) argues, we cannot simply say that a moral judgment is true for all purposes, persons, and cultures—we can assert only that it is true for a particular person or social group. Relativism does not mean that we cannot criticize people of other cultures on moral grounds, but it does mean that when we say that a person in another culture did wrong or acted immorally, we must judge that person by the standards of that culture and not by our own (Cook 1999: 35). In other words, there are objective moral standards as long as judgments about right and wrong are made relatively.

Holmes (1998: 163–164) discusses three forms of ethical relativism: ethical relativism, cultural relativism, and extreme or individual relativism. *Ethical relativists* agree that there is moral right and wrong but contend that what is right for one person or culture may be wrong for another. *Cultural relativism* is a form of relativism that claims that moral beliefs and practices vary from culture to culture. It is important to understand, however, that cultural relativists do not argue that certain acts or practices are right or wrong in a particular culture. They simply note the differences.

Extreme or *individual relativism* takes the position that moral beliefs and practices vary from person to person. In contrast to ethical absolutists (see the following section, Ethical Absolutism), ethical relativists draw attention to factors such as moral diversity among different cultures, the varying state of morals in a particular society at different historical periods, and the fact that at any given time there is a high degree of moral disagreement within a particular culture. One example is the moral disagreement in the United States concerning abortion (Bunting 1996: 73).

Cultural Relativism

The proponents of *cultural relativism* argue that every society has a different moral code explaining what acts are permitted or not permitted. They argue that we cannot judge one moral code as being superior to another, because there is no objective standard to apply to make such a judgment. In other words, the moral code that we, in the United States, subscribe to is not special; Accordingly, it is simply one moral code among many. If the moral code of a particular society determines that a certain act is right, then the act is right within that society. Accordingly, it is not for us to judge other people's conduct in other societies. We should be tolerant and avoid being judgmental.

At first, the notion of cultural relativism seems to reflect the way many of us see the world; for example, we believe in tolerance and understanding, and we recognize diversity in society. However, there are a number of objections to cultural relativism that show it cannot be viewed as a viable approach to ethical issues, including the following:

- There is the problem of identifying what constitutes a culture or society. For example, it is easy to imagine an isolated tribe in a far-off country as a separate culture with its own ethical standards and rules, but what of American culture? Although we may think of American culture as homogeneous, it is very diverse, because many languages are spoken within it, and the various ethnic groups that make up American society may well maintain their own ethical standards of conduct, which differ from those of the dominant culture.
- If this difficulty in identifying a culture or society exists, then it is easy to see that we may end up in a position where our own individual values, family background, education, or religion can determine ethical standards. In other words, cultural relativism can become transformed into a matter of individual ethics (individual relativism), where each person can claim that his or her moral standards are those that should apply to society and others.
- Cultural relativists are not able to explain which ethical standards should apply when cultures overlap. Cultures are no longer totally isolated from each other, and it becomes increasingly difficult to avoid interacting with other cultures. This raises the problem of deciding whose ethical standards are to apply.
- In all societies, standards of conduct change over time, and the cultural relativist is faced with the problem of acknowledging these changes while arguing that morality is relative to a culture. However, which values in which historical period should apply? On the face of it, the values applying in all periods have equal validity. For the cultural relativist, therefore, there is no overall standard to apply.
- A major problem with cultural relativism is that it operates as moral isolationism. This means that arguing that everything is relative tends to suggest this must be the end of the issue and all debate must stop. It also suggests, in the view of Carol Gilligan (in Hinman 1998: 55), an attitude of "couldn't care less," because when we say that all things are relative, we are really saying we don't care about them. Therefore, cultural relativism fails to provide us with answers to issues and in fact tends to close off debate altogether.

Cultural relativism is closely associated with anthropology, and some even refer to it as an anthropological theory. Some philosophers argue that cultural relativism is in fact a methodology that requires that they adopt a nonjudgmental framework toward the culture they study, and therefore, as a methodological practice only; cultural relativism does not involve moral relativism (Cook 1999: chap. 7; Ladd 1973: 2). However, other philosophers contend that cultural relativism contains elements of both methodology and a value system (Womack 1995: 48).

Ethical Absolutism

This view argues that there exists an eternal and unchanging moral law, the same for all people, at all times and places (Holmes 1998: 165). The absolutist believes that certain moral principles apply to all people everywhere, and that people can recognize or discover these principles and be guided by them in deciding the nature of their own conduct and in judging the conduct of others. Also, the ethical absolutist, being already aware of these principles, believes himself or herself qualified to pass judgment on anyone (Cook 1999: 7). Absolutism is considered valid regardless of thought and feeling. This position is the opposite of relativism, in that there can be no consideration of other perspectives, because it is argued that there is only one "true" perspective.

An example of an absolutist position arises in arguments about capital punishment. As Jonathan Glover (1999: 245) points out, two absolutist views prevail on this question. One is emphatic that the murderer must be given the punishment he or she "deserves," which is death, and the other can see no justification for "judicial murder" under any circumstances. An absolutist would not change his or her view with respect to capital punishment, no matter what arguments were put forward by either side. Among the questions that arise from adopting an absolutist position include, "If there are universally accepted values, what are they?" and, "If universally accepted values exist, do they remain constant or do they change over time?"

If there is disagreement about moral issues between societies, then how should we act? On the one hand, the ethical relativist will say we should not judge, and there is no single truth that applies across societies and cultures. On the other hand, the moral absolutist will argue that one single truth must be applied across all societies and cultures regardless of beliefs and values. In favor of ethical relativism, it can be said that it is correct in warning us against assuming that our ethical standards represent some absolute standard, because many, although not all, of our ethical standards apply only to our own society. Also, ethical relativism teaches us the value of an open mind, of tolerance, and of understanding. One way of resolving this disagreement about relative and absolute ethical standards is the notion of *ethical pluralism.*

Ethical Pluralism

Ethical pluralism argues that in most situations there are many truths rather than one single truth. Lawrence Hinman (1998: 67–68) contends that ethical pluralism allows us to adopt four principles to resolve conflicts between differing ethical standards. These principles are the following:

> *The Principle of Understanding.* This requires that we fully understand and appreciate the meaning of ethical standards found in another culture from the perspective of that culture. For example, before making any judgment about an issue such as female circumcision, we should possess a full understanding of the history and cultural context of this practice as it applies in the many societies in which it is performed. We should recognize that a Western response to an issue of this nature is shaped and constructed by our own cultural values.

The Principle of Tolerance. This means accepting the existence of differences as opposed to denying any diversity in ethical standards. This principle therefore rules out an approach based on ethical absolutism.

The Principle of Standing Up Against Evil. Hinman argues that understanding and tolerance ought not to lead us to a position where "anything goes," as the ethical relativists argue, but rather, we should be prepared to stand up against what he calls "egregious moral wrongdoing," especially when such conduct affects the powerless and the marginalized of the world. An example of this kind of moral wrongdoing would be the crime of genocide, which is internationally recognized as a crime against humanity.

The Principle of Fallibility. This principle argues in favor of our own fallibility. We should always be prepared to learn from other cultures and to have our own moral shortcomings exposed. Most countries have prohibited capital punishment for children (see Chapter 7). However, until recently[1] in the United States, the Supreme Court declared that states had the right to execute those as young as 16 years of age. The principle of fallibility would argue that the United States and its Court at that time did not choose the correct ethical position on the issue of capital punishment for juveniles and at that it should be prepared to listen to the reasoning and experience of the rest of the world, which has outlawed capital punishment for juveniles.

Other philosophers seem to agree with an approach that emphasizes ethical pluralism, which Kane (1996: 14–16) calls "openness." He stresses that a pluralistic point of view only suggests the possibility that other views are correct; it does not demonstrate that they are in fact correct. Pluralism challenges absolute values but does not rule out their possibility. We can be open and tolerant to other points of view while still believing that some are better than others, even while we believe that only one is correct. Openness does not imply indifference; it only indicates recognition that we do not possess the truth and are willing to learn from others and to search for truths beyond our own limited point of view. Kane advocates an approach that assumes an attitude of openness to other points of view to allow others to prove themselves right or wrong.

Cook (1999: 169) suggests an approach that sets aside an argument based on tolerance and that instead advocates taking cases one by one and examining them in light of the details of each particular case. He therefore suggests that the question of whether we ought to interfere with the practices of another culture is not a philosophical question but a practical moral one. The examination of a particular case means understanding the nature of the problem, what considerations would be relevant to a solution, and what a "right solution" would be. This seems to parallel

---

1. In March 2005, in a 5-to-4 decision in *Roper v. Simmons*, the U.S. Supreme Court abolished juvenile executions, arguing that it is unconstitutional to sentence anyone to death for a crime he or she committed while younger than 18. The court argued that teenagers are too immature to be held accountable for their crimes to the same extent as adults given the "national consensus" against executing juveniles and the medical and social science evidence demonstrating their immaturity.

Hinman's point that there must be a full understanding of the cultural context of a particular case before any attempt is made to resolve conflicts among differing ethical standards.

Religion and Ethical Standards

As discussed earlier, when societies apply normative ethics, they are prescribing ethical standards for conduct. What is the origin of these standards? Many people believe that ethical standards and religion are connected, and that ethical standards are derived from religious principles and tenets. For example, many hospitals in the United States have ethics committees that typically include representatives of the clergy as members, and when ethical issues are discussed in the media, religious representatives are often invited to comment on them. People assume, therefore, that religious representatives who interpret religion are also able to define ethical standards of conduct. The *divine command theory* expresses this view, and argues that what is morally right is what God directs, and conversely, what is morally wrong is what God prohibits.

In a famous discussion, the Greek philosopher Socrates took up the question of whether divine command theory was concerned with the power of the gods to command or the "rightness" of the gods' commands. He asked the question, "Is conduct right because the gods command it or do the gods command it because it is right?" The arguments about this question are considered in the following sections.

Conduct Is Right Because God Commands It

According to this perspective, the only issue is the simple matter of God requiring a particular kind of conduct. If God commands it, that is sufficient and the conduct is right regardless of what reason tells us. However, this raises the question of how we discover what constitutes God's will. If we argue that it is contained in religious texts, should we look to only one text, for example, the Bible; if not, how do we discover God's will from the multitude of religious texts that exist in the many religions on earth? It is also difficult to determine the exact nature of God's will. If we assume it is to be found from reading the Bible, what if we cannot find any statements there about a particular ethical issue, and what do we do if there are conflicting statements about God's will regarding a particular ethical issue? Also, if we argue that conduct is right because God commands it, this means we are giving God the power to issue whatever commands He wishes. This in turn means that God can give a different command from the one He has already given, and so His commands can be considered arbitrary. However, the notion that God's commands are arbitrary is inconsistent with the belief that God is all-powerful and all-knowing. It is obvious that this argument raises a number of complex and difficult issues.

God Commands Right Conduct Because It Is Right

This is the second option offered by Socrates, and it means that God's commands are not arbitrary, but emanate from the application of His wisdom in knowing what is best for us. However, there is a problem, because in accepting the rightness of God's commands, we must also accept that there is some standard of right and wrong outside of God's will that must exist prior to and independent of God's command. In the final analysis, therefore, we must either accept that God's commands are arbitrary or recognize that His commands have reference to a standard of rightness and wrongness independent of His will. Those who take the position that ethical standards are set by God are therefore obliged to accept arguments that tend to conflict with their fundamental religious belief in God's goodness and omnipotence. The divine command theory raises so many complex and difficult issues that it leads to the conclusion that setting ethical standards by reference only to religion is highly problematic.

Ethics and Natural Law

In looking at the origin of ethics, some ask whether natural law is the origin. The idea of natural law is that underneath the diversity of human cultures and beliefs about what is right and wrong, we can identify some factors that are common to our human nature. The notion of natural law was a favorite of ancient thinkers like Plato and Aristotle, who sought to identify universal traits of human nature, with the aim of finding common goals or ends that would bring human fulfillment or happiness (Kane 1996: 46). This pattern of looking for natural laws continued into the medieval and later periods of Western culture. Natural laws are said to be laws that govern human behavior and define the right way to live. They are said to be "natural" because they are thought of as incorporating human nature and the goals that humans naturally seek. In effect, natural law represents a search for moral absolutes that define what is "normal" and "natural." For example, despite more progressive and inclusive modern attitudes toward homosexuality, some still argue that practicing homosexuality is "unnatural," because it is contrary to human nature. Nowadays, natural law arguments have tended to gravitate toward arguments in favor of human rights.

Ethics and Law

Is law a source of ethical standards, and what is the relationship between law and ethics? It is important to understand that ethics and law are distinct categories. By *law*, we generally mean legislation, statutes, and regulations made by states and by the federal government on a host of subjects for the public good and public welfare. Laws do not, and are not intended to, incorporate ethical principles or values, but sometimes ethical standards will be reflected in laws. For example, both morality and the law prohibit the act of murdering another human being. Similarly, legislation regulating the legal profession or other professions may give legal effect to certain professional codes of conduct. It is possible to argue, therefore, that codes of conduct regulating legal practice have the force of law. However, on a whole range of subjects from business practice to driving a vehicle, laws do not set ethical standards.

It is important to appreciate, therefore, that ethical standards are not necessarily written down in the form of laws or other rules, but represent the collective experience of a society as it regulates the behavior of those who make up that society. The fact that an ethical standard is not repeated or copied in a law does not affect the validity of that ethical standard. However, where ethical standards are incorporated into law—such as a law governing the right to choose an abortion—although people must obey the law, they are not necessarily required to hold the same ethical beliefs expounded by that law.

Sometimes laws can conflict with ethical standards. For example, laws promoting apartheid in South Africa and slavery in the United States were both clearly in violation of ethical standards relating to the dignity of the person but were nevertheless lawful and were expected to be obeyed when in force. From time to time, a mass movement develops against a particular law or set of laws, reflecting a section of public opinion that claims that the law is wrong and should be repealed. Where there is a deliberate disregard of the law by those protesting its wrongness, the result can be acts of civil disobedience. For example, in India during the British colonial period, Gandhi advocated and practiced civil disobedience to British laws because he and his followers wanted an end to the colonization of their country. Similarly, in the United States, activists in the civil rights movement deliberately flouted laws that were racially discriminatory, and civil rights workers were prepared to be arrested and jailed in pursuit of equal treatment for all citizens.

Ethical Dilemmas

Ethical questions and issues arise for all people, not just for professionals in the criminal justice system, or professors who teach ethics, or members of the clergy. We may all have to make decisions involving ethical issues in our daily and professional lives, because, as we have noted, ethical issues are concerned with questions of right and wrong and how we ought to act. For example, we might apply for a job, and in order to be considered for the position, we may have to decide whether to hide the fact that we were fired from a previous job for misconduct. In other words, we have to decide whether to lie to promote our own career interests or whether to reveal the truth. Another instance may arise as we walk down the street and see a person who is apparently homeless, panhandling from passersby. The ethical dilemma here is whether we should act to help the poor and needy or just pass by and give nothing.

We will have to make ethical decisions in our day-to-day lives, so it is helpful to recognize when an issue involves ethical considerations and then have the ability to apply a knowledge of ethics, including ethical terminology and concepts, in making our decision about what to do. A number of ethical approaches can be taken in making a decision about an ethical issue, and you will see in the following chapters that no one approach is the "correct" one; rather, different approaches are equally valid in ethical terms. The approach we adopt to an ethical issue will frame and give meaning to any decision we make and can be used to justify and validate our actions. Of course, it is always possible to abandon the responsibility for making an ethical decision. We might decide that we will simply follow the dictates of others rather than applying our own minds to a particular ethical issue. For example, during World War II, many war crimes were committed by members of the Nazi Party, who claimed they were simply following orders in committing those crimes. In effect, they abandoned their responsibility to make an ethical decision not to kill or murder and opted instead to obey unethical and inhumane directions.

Similar situations may arise in the criminal justice system. For example, a prosecutor may have to decide whether to seek the maximum penalty against an accused under three-strikes legislation. If he or she does decide to seek the maximum, the result may be that the accused will be incarcerated for the rest of his or her life. A prosecutor may decide to act ethically and fully weigh this issue in light of the facts of the case and the nature of the crime committed. Alternatively, he or she may choose not to follow that process and may simply take the position that the law reflects public opinion and that he or she should always exercise discretion so as to impose the full penalty provided by the law.

When we decide to accept responsibility and make a decision involving ethical considerations, we are faced with a personal ethical dilemma. A personal ethical dilemma can be contrasted with an ethical issue. The latter is usually an issue of public policy involving ethical questions. Examples of such issues include the morality of capital punishment, whether to incarcerate more people or use alternative sanctions for convicted offenders, and other important social issues. A further distinction between ethical dilemmas and ethical issues is that an ethical dilemma is the responsibility of an individual and requires a decision to be made. Ethical issues, on the other hand, being broad issues of social policy, do not require individual decision making beyond the decision of whether one is in favor of, or opposed to, a particular social issue. However, the fact that ethical issues do not require most individuals to decide the issue does not mean that an individual is helpless to influence the public debate on a social issue.

Ethical dilemmas are important in the criminal justice system, because criminal justice professionals are often faced with having to make decisions that involve ethical issues. Much of the material in this book concerned with ethical practices in the criminal justice system will focus on ethical dilemmas faced by criminal justice professionals, and it will analyze options in light of ethical theories and any relevant rules and regulations.

How do we recognize when a dilemma is an ethical dilemma as opposed to merely a dilemma? An ethical dilemma arises only when a decision must be made that involves a conflict at the personal, interpersonal, institutional, or societal level or raises issues of rights or moral character.

What process is followed in resolving an ethical dilemma? Hare (1987) argues that we initially use an *intuitive* level of moral thinking when we consider ethical dilemmas. This provides us with relatively simple principles derived from our upbringing and past experience of decision making. *Critical thinking* is another process of thinking about moral decisions; in contrast to intuitive thinking, critical thinking applies principles established by philosophy and moral concepts, and it is therefore nonintuitive. In making moral judgments when faced with moral dilemmas, we may initially apply an intuitive form of thinking, relying on our intuition to identify possible courses of action to make the decision. However, we are likely to find that our intuitions do not adequately equip us to make moral decisions and that critical thinking is required. Consider the following scenario:

> A newly recruited correctional officer, Tom, overhears three other correctional officers, Fred, Bob, and Charlie, discussing arrangements to assault an inmate, Raymond, who has previously attacked another correctional officer, a close friend of the three officers.

Tom is faced with a dilemma: whether or not to prevent the attack on Raymond. His dilemma is an ethical dilemma, because if he does act, this will involve a conflict between himself and Fred, Bob, and Charlie. It is also an ethical dilemma because it raises issues of rights and morality; that is, the right of Raymond to safety and security even in prison, and the morality of allowing a person to be assaulted other than in an act of self-defense. In order to resolve his ethical dilemma, Tom will need to pursue a process of analysis resulting in a decision. The following process is intended to provide Tom with a method for reaching his decision:

1. He will identify the fact that he is faced with an ethical dilemma and state the dilemma clearly.

2. In his mind, he will collect the facts and circumstances of what he overheard so that he is quite clear about what he heard, the identities of those involved, and all other relevant information.

3. He will collect all the facts and knowledge relevant to the decision, including his own values about the issue and the values of his workplace. He will consider his own position at the prison as a newly trained officer and the consequences of reporting the incident and of not reporting it.

4. This is an ethical dilemma, so he will call to mind his knowledge of ethical principles and theories with the aim of applying those ethical approaches to his possible courses of action.

5. Tom will now identify his available options for action. First, he could intervene in the situation by informing his supervisor of the conversation he overheard. This action will be based on his responsibility to ensure the safety and security of all inmates and to enforce the policies and rules of the institution. Second, he could choose to ignore the conversation because of his loyalty to his fellow officers and his need in the future to receive their assistance and support when carrying out his duties. Third, he could choose to intervene by talking to the officers involved in an attempt to prevent the misconduct with the aim of minimizing the harm for all involved parties. Tom must support each alternative action with reasoning derived from ethical principles in order to give credibility to his choice of action.

6. Tom will make his decision based on his analysis of the dilemma after applying the ethical approaches to each course of action. He will choose the option that for him is the most ethically appropriate. In other words, after considering the choices according to this process, he will decide, "This would be the right

thing for me to do." He therefore resolves his ethical dilemma by making an ethical decision and acting on that decision.

Tom's process for making an ethical decision seems straightforward. However, making an ethical decision may involve factors such as personal values, personal priorities, or how a particular decision might affect friends or even strangers. Therefore, the most ethical choice is not always clear. To act ethically is not simply a matter of deciding what is right and wrong in advance and stubbornly sticking to that position. Since there are many gray areas where there are no specific rules, laws, or guidelines laid out in advance, it is not always easy to know which decision is the most ethical choice. In addition, if we are to act in an ethical way, we have to justify what we do, and the justification must be sufficient that it could in principle convince any reasonable human being. As Rachels puts it,

> A moral judgment . . . must be supported by good reasons. If someone tells you that a certain action would be wrong, for example, you may ask why it would be wrong, and if there is no satisfactory answer, you may reject that advice as unfounded. In this way, moral judgments are different from mere expressions of personal preference . . . moral judgments require backing by reasons, and in the absence of such reasons, they are merely arbitrary. (1991: 438)

Hare (1987: 218) argues that moral judgments must be able to be applied universally. According to this principle, similar actions ought to be judged similarly, unless there are morally relevant differences between them. For example, if I judge it wrong for you to cheat in examinations, I must be prepared to say that it is wrong for me as well, unless I can explain how my situation is different from yours in a morally relevant way (Holmes 1998: 151). Thus, the principle does not say whether you should cheat, but it does require that whatever you do, you must be consistent. Singer (1995: 175) expands this notion somewhat by arguing that when thinking ethically, I ought to consider the interests of my enemies as well as my friends and of strangers as well as my family. If, after I have fully taken into account the concerns and preferences of all these people, I still believe that a particular action is better than any alternative, then I can honestly say that I ought to do it.

What weight do we give to our *personal values* when making ethical decisions? By values, we mean what individuals care about and what they think is important. This can include such things as people's desires, such as social approval; what they enjoy, such as sports or music; their goals or purposes; their ideas of happiness or success; and their highest ideals. Each person develops a set of values that forms his or her value system. We often assume that our values are similar to others'; however, we may define values differently than others do. For example, we may have different definitions of what constitutes a "family," but we may all share "family" as a value. Even if we do have similar definitions of values, we often prioritize them differently. Thus, one person might give the value of "freedom" a higher priority than the value of "preservation of life." Another may prioritize the value of "loyalty" higher than "personal freedom." The fact that we may order our values differently explains why our thinking about ethical decisions differs from that of others and why we arrive at different conclusions.

Ethical Issues in Criminal Justice

In order to illustrate the relevance of the study of ethics to the criminal justice system, a number of specific ethical problems and issues that might arise for professionals in the criminal justice system are sorted into sections and listed below. These problems and issues might, for example, be concerned with how to exercise authority, with how to deal with conflicts between the personal and the professional, or with ethical issues confined within one particular part of the system, such as juvenile justice.

Ethical Problems in the Use of Authority

- The use of authority to promote personal values
- The use of authority to avoid accountability for wrongdoing
- Police gratuities, free meals, discounts on purchases, etc.

Ethical Problems in the Relationship Between Personal and Professional Interests

- Using professional status to promote personal interests (religious, philosophical, financial, etc.)
- Using institutional time and materials for personal gain unrelated to legitimate work activity
- Engaging in or promoting professional activities that are contrary to personal values
- Engaging in public or private personal activity that is contrary to professional values (use of drugs, driving under the influence of alcohol, etc.)

Ethical Problems in Personal and Professional Commitments to Clients

- Behaving unethically in personal relationships with clients
- Using relationships with clients or the public for personal gain (acquiring goods more cheaply, having work done for personal benefit, accepting gifts, etc.)

Ethical Issues in Criminal Justice and Public Policy

- The War on Drugs
- Government policies having implications for criminal justice professionals in issues such as youth confinement, fingerprinting of juveniles, and compulsory treatment such as mandatory participation in substance abuse programs or anger management

- Capital punishment
- The move away from rehabilitative juvenile justice policies toward more punitive policies
- Policies involving harsher penalties resulting in "prisoner warehousing"
- Government-imposed mandatory sentencing (three-strikes legislation, mandatory minimum sentences)
- Truth in sentencing policies
- Increased surveillance of citizens in society
- The policies implemented in the War on Terrorism

Ethical Issues Resulting From Policing Policies

- Policing policy in domestic violence cases
- Racial profiling
- Use of force
- Use of police discretion

Ethical Problems in Information Sharing

- The ethics of withholding information, for example, from a client, the court, or the police
- Problems of confidentiality and privileged communication, for example, counselor–client relationships and participation in research
- Rules or practices relating to the retention or disposal of court records, for example, in the juvenile justice system where some states are now considering making juvenile records and court hearings open to the public and the media

Ethical Problems Dealing With Human Rights Issues in the Criminal Justice System

- The administration of cruel and unusual punishment
- Human rights violations against prisoners (women, men, juveniles)
- Capital punishment

Ethical Issues in the Media Reporting of Crime

- Crime and public opinion
- Crime as entertainment
- The politicization of crime
- Representation of particular groups of offenders and of women or girl offenders

Summary

In this chapter, the role of ethics in shaping decisions has been explored. Ethics has been shown to be a central component in decisions involving ethical dilemmas, and the process of analyzing an ethical dilemma has been illustrated. Ethics is concerned with standards of conduct and with "how I ought to act," and standards of conduct may vary among different societies. Approaches to setting standards range from cultural relativism to moral absolutism; a perspective that emphasizes moral pluralism seems to offer the best hope for resolving problems of relativities. Investigating sources of ethical standards reveals that religion, natural law, and other forms of law have an influence in shaping ethical standards. An understanding of ethics is essential to competent decision making by criminal justice professionals and to the proper working of the criminal justice system. In this chapter, case studies in the form of media reports of unethical conduct by police and prosecutors have been presented. In the next chapter, ethical issues in law enforcement will be explored in depth.

DISCUSSION CASE

In November 2006, the center-right government in Holland pledged that if returned to power in the general election, it would legislate to prohibit the wearing of the *niqab* and the *burqa* in public. Holland's population includes 1 million Muslims (Bell, 2006). The *niqab* is a scarf used to cover a woman's hair, and the *burqa* covers the woman from head to toe and totally conceals the face.

In October 2006, the British foreign minister complained that the *niqab* created barriers between people and impeded communication, because a meaningful interaction "requires that both sides see each other's face" (BBC News 2006) British prime minister Tony Blair agreed that it represented a divisive "mark of separation."

In certain German states, wearing the *niqab* in schools is against the law. Similarly, in some parts of Belgium, there are bans against wearing the *niqab* in school.

In 2003 France passed legislation banning head scarves in public schools, ostensibly to protect the separation between church and state required by French law (CNN 2003). There are an estimated 6 million Muslims in France.

In France and in the rest of Europe, only a very small proportion of Muslim women wear veils. Proponents of the prohibition of veiling see wearing the veil as challenging or threatening more progressive Muslim women who refuse to wear it. However, when one asks the women who wear the veils why they wear them, they explain that the veil symbolizes modesty, humility, and devotion to their faith.

DISCUSSION QUESTIONS

1. How is *ethics* defined?

2. Why is it important for criminal justice professionals to study ethics? Explain how applying ethical approaches helps criminal justice professionals make appropriate and "correct" decisions.

3. What are the possible sources of ethical rules? Discuss the problems inherent in each source.

4. Discuss the advantages offered by ethical pluralism over ethical absolutism and ethical relativism.

5. Outline the steps involved in analyzing an ethical dilemma.

CHAPTER 2

Ethics and the Police

Ethics and Policing

The study of ethics in policing has expanded considerably over the past few years as cases of police brutality and corruption have surfaced in the media and in the courtroom. Commentators agree that three issues have shaped the role of ethics in policing: *styles of policing, the police as an institution,* and *police culture.*

Generally, we think of the police as controllers of crime; however, the original English conception of the role of the police force emphasized the need for police to obtain the goodwill of citizens in performing their policing duties. The very first set of instructions to constables, published in England in 1829, reminded the new police officer:

> There is no qualification more indispensable to a Police Officer than a perfect command of temper, never suffering himself to be moved in the slightest degree, by any language or threats that may be used; if he does his duty in a quiet and determined manner, such conduct will probably induce well-disposed by-standers to assist him should he require it. (quoted in Skolnick and Fyfe 1993: 70)

When policing came to the United States, there was little concern among police officers about adhering to legal norms, despite their formal policing role as enforcers of the law (Haller 1996: 7). In fact, police received little training in law, and most of those arrested were tried before justices who also had little legal training. Police were part of the larger political system, seen as a resource at the command of local political organizations. In the early period, it was common for police and other public officials to earn rewards by operating rackets (p. 8). Patrolmen worked on the streets with little supervision, and the main expertise a detective offered was his knowledge of the underworld. Violence was an accepted norm, because many policemen believed they were entitled to punish wrongdoers themselves and, on their patrols, were expected to be able to physically dominate the streets without resorting to arrest. Police operated in neighborhoods as authority figures, sometimes whipping delinquent boys as a more effective sanction than arrest and incarceration. Police commonly used violence to persuade suspected persons to confess, and newspapers reported interrogations of this nature without unfavorable comment (p. 22). In addition, the police culture of the time supported the use of violence in upholding the dignity of the police officer. Over time, and by the end of the 1930s, police organizations had become large bureaucratic structures organized along military lines (Walker 1996: 27).

During the 1930s era of reform, police began to narrow their functions to focus on crime control and the apprehension of criminals, and consequently police became enforcers of the law with the goal of controlling crime. Other activities that police formerly engaged in, such as solving problems in the community, became identified as "social work" and were ridiculed (Kelling and More 1996: 79). Notwithstanding the police attitude that constructs policing as crime fighting, many observers of police work regard the primary function of the police to be peacekeeping. In this view of policing, police occupy their time for the most part by attending to a range of problems that have little to do with law enforcement. In fact, they may spend as little as 10–15% of their time engaged in enforcing the law (Manning 1996: 225).

The Nature of Policing

Commentators on policing have struggled to adequately express and theorize the nature of policing in society, including its ethical base. Researchers have developed models of policing to assist in understanding the police function in society; these models are the crime fighter, the emergency operator, the social enforcer, and the social peacekeeper (Kleinig 1996: 24–29).

The *crime fighter* sees criminals as the enemy, and police and the community as the "good guys." In other words, police see their role in punitive terms, for example, treating suspects as though they were already guilty. Perceiving the policing role as crime fighting runs the risk of ends justifying means and dramatizes policing so as to condone invasions of privacy and abuse of power. This is especially the case when citizens have surrendered their right to use force to the police.

The influence of media representations of police, either through police dramas on television or in reality programming depicting police carrying out their duties, should not be underestimated. In constructing images of police as "fighters against evil" in drama and as "protectors of society against permissiveness" in police reality programs, the media reinforce the notion of the police officer as crime fighter. In terms of audience response to this entertainment, three notions emerge: that offenders are professional criminals who are clever and motivated by greed; that the interests of justice are not well served by liberal judges or lawyers who are preoccupied with defendants' legal rights; and that hardworking, dedicated cops are out there, on the streets, doing their best in the face of these constraints (Beckett and Sasson 2000: 118).

The *emergency operator* model sees the policing role as akin to that of other emergency personnel like ambulance operators and firefighters. Police offer emergency assistance, clearing the way for professionals such as social workers, who provide more substantive problem-solving services. This model emphasizes the policing mission as dealing with people rather than crime fighting; however, competence in crime control is still required in this model.

Viewing the police as *social enforcers* emphasizes coercion as the central feature of police work (Bittner 1967). This model sees the role of police as addressing many day-to-day problems whose solutions may require the use of force. The social enforcer model has been criticized for focusing excessively on coercion as a police function and for failing to recognize that other members of society may also use coercion, such as parents and schoolteachers.

In formulating the *social peacekeeper* model, Pollock-Byrne (1998) and Kleinig (1996) argue for the need to adopt a broader definition of policing, with Pollock-Byrne advocating for policing as public service rather than crime fighting and Kleinig promoting policing as social peacekeeping. For Kleinig, this characterization offers the most satisfactory definition of the actual tasks that police perform, and he locates it historically in the Anglo-Saxon notion of the King's Peace, breaches of which were considered crimes. According to Kleinig, the peacekeeper model incorporates the crime fighter and social service models and reflects the range of acts that might occupy the police in a community (1996: 28).

Skolnick (1975) noted the inherent tension between the police role of enforcing the law and at the same time protecting citizens, and he considered that tension as irreconcilable. He argued that police could reconcile this conflict by giving priority to their duty to uphold the law. Muir (1977) and Goldstein (1977) saw a need for officers to be trained properly to exercise their considerable discretionary powers, and Muir noted that because officers are free to choose their style of policing, this enables them to act ethically or otherwise according to their desires. Delattre (1989) and Sherman (1985) were concerned about issues of corruption in policing arising during the 1980s. Delattre argued that the best way to ensure ethical policing was to recruit officers with integrity. Sherman, however, saw the temptations open to police as an issue constituting a "slippery slope," where minor acts of corruption would lead to major acts, unless internal police controls and accountability sanctioned those minor acts.

Police as an Institution

The institution of policing has been perceived either as a profession or as a bureaucracy. Kleinig sees the police as possessing some of the aspects of a profession, such as discretionary authority and providing a public service, but not others, such as the possession of higher education and special expertise (1996: 30–46). The importance of the distinction between a profession and a bureaucracy for the study of police ethics is that professions emphasize ethical standards and a service ideal. Police commonly define themselves using the rhetoric of professionalism, sometimes to deflect criticism, arguing that outsiders are incapable of understanding police work and therefore should have no say in its performance (Walker 1996: 29).

Police Culture

Individuals within institutions carry out roles defined by the rules, regulations, and procedures of the institution, and these roles and their relationship to each other make up the structure of the institution. However, there is another dimension to the workings of an institution that commonly includes the attitudes, values, and norms of that institution, collectively described as the *institutional culture*. This culture largely determines the way in which institutional activity is performed, adding another layer to the official rules, regulations, and practices of the institution.

A number of commentators have attempted to analyze aspects of the police institutional culture. Manning (1997: 4) argues that it is the occupational culture interacting with regulations, policies, law, and politics that constitutes the driving force of policing. For Manning, immorality, violence, and lies are routine in policing; teamwork is essential; and secrecy is endemic. Sherman (1982) identifies a set of values that new police officers acquire through their training process, through conversations with veteran officers, and in interactions with the public. These include the notion that enforcement of the law is not limited to the question of whether an offense has been committed but also includes the nature of the suspect. Accordingly, aspects of the individual such as demeanor, the degree of cooperation with police, race, age, and social class are all significant considerations in law enforcement decision making. In a somewhat similar way, the institutional culture views any show of disrespect for police authority as a matter of great concern, and the perpetrator of such behavior is likely to be punished by arrest or use of force.

In terms of the use of force, the culture requires that police should never hesitate to use physical or deadly force against those who *deserve* it. Given that the role of police is to fight crime, police culture views due process as a process that merely protects criminals and therefore as something that should be ignored when possible. From this perspective, rules concerning the protection of suspects and accused persons should be circumvented when possible, because the function of such rules, so far as the police are concerned, is simply to handicap them in carrying out their true functions. Similarly, lying and deception are considered integral parts of the police function. Loyalty is a paramount duty, and the protection of one's colleagues, even when they perform acts of misconduct, is considered an overriding principle of police work. Finally, because the police engage in "danger work" in the protection of the public, it is considered appropriate for police to accept gifts from the public such as free meals, coffee, and Christmas gifts. Sherman (1982) contends that police culture argues in favor of taking a reward that has no impact on what a police officer would do, such as eating a meal, but he argues that the culture rejects acceptance of money that would affect the policing task itself, such as accepting money for not giving traffic tickets. Sherman judges that these values have weakened over time due to diversity within the police, the power of the police unions to defend individual officers, and the rise of investigative journalism, which has uncovered corruption in high places. Additionally, he points to the fact that police chiefs have taken significant steps to counter aspects of institutional culture.

In his explanation of police culture, Crank (1998: iii) argues that existing literature oversimplifies the police, describing them in simplistic terms and minimizing the complexities of their employment. Crank presents various themes that he argues characterize police culture, ranging from "coercive territorial control" (the notion that the police view much of their work by reference to the use of force in controlling their assigned territory), to the vision of the police as "the new warriors," to guns as the ultimate expression of police authority. Crank extends his discussion to include the importance of suspicion in police work; the theme of "turbulence and edge-control," meaning triumph over unpredictable events, and cultural themes of solidarity. Other writers have identified suspicion as a characteristic of police work and the police personality, but Crank argues that it is a feature of police culture, a characteristic of the police worldview that provides a basis for all interaction between police and citizens. Importantly, in his discussion of the construction of police morality, Crank suggests that the police perceive themselves as "representatives of a higher morality embodied in a blend of American traditionalism, patriotism and religion" (1998: 151).

Muir (1977) argues that police loyalty results in complicity. Once a police officer breaks or violates a rule or standard, he or she is bound to remain silent about other officers' violations, even if they are more serious. Scheingold (1984) asserts that there are three dominant characteristics of police culture:

1. *Cynicism.* Police view all citizens with suspicion, and all citizens are seen as a "problem," especially if they can be categorized into a "type." Those who can be categorized are to be dealt with as though they have already committed a crime, because they probably have. The very nature of police work leads police to the conclusion that all people are weak, corrupt, and/or dangerous.

2. *Force.* This is to be used in all situations where a threat is perceived. Threats can include perceived threats against the officer's authority rather than physical threats, so that anyone with "an attitude" is thought to deserve a lesson in humility. Force, then, is both expressive and instrumental. It is a symbol of the officer's authority and dominance and is seen as the most effective method of control, because it keeps all people in line.

3. *The Police Are Victims.* The idea that the police are themselves victims of public misunderstanding and scorn, recipients of low wages, and victims of vindictive administrators sets police officers apart from other people and legitimizes and rationalizes a different set of rules for them. Police perception is that the public does not mind when the civil rights of "criminal types" are violated; they are only upset when police misconduct targets "good people." A study of community policing in Seattle, observing interactions between police and the community, reveals how police see themselves as "members of a politically vulnerable group that deserves protection from ill-informed public meddling; they possess an authority to control situations to which the public should defer; they command a unique base of knowledge, and thus deserve an elevated professional status" (Herbert 2006: 86). Commentators, therefore, generally portray police culture as negative, defensive, and isolationist. In contrast to this portrayal, police often promulgate statements of values or of their policing mission that are positive in nature, as in Box 2.1.

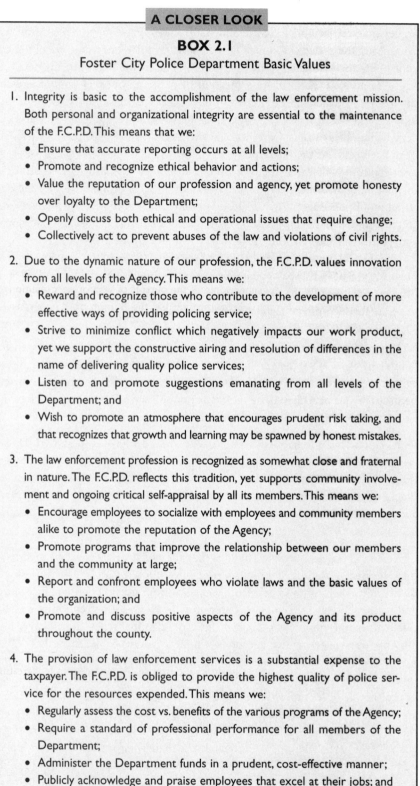

A CLOSER LOOK

BOX 2.1
Foster City Police Department Basic Values

1. Integrity is basic to the accomplishment of the law enforcement mission. Both personal and organizational integrity are essential to the maintenance of the F.C.P.D. This means that we:
   - Ensure that accurate reporting occurs at all levels;
   - Promote and recognize ethical behavior and actions;
   - Value the reputation of our profession and agency, yet promote honesty over loyalty to the Department;
   - Openly discuss both ethical and operational issues that require change;
   - Collectively act to prevent abuses of the law and violations of civil rights.

2. Due to the dynamic nature of our profession, the F.C.P.D. values innovation from all levels of the Agency. This means we:
   - Reward and recognize those who contribute to the development of more effective ways of providing policing service;
   - Strive to minimize conflict which negatively impacts our work product, yet we support the constructive airing and resolution of differences in the name of delivering quality police services;
   - Listen to and promote suggestions emanating from all levels of the Department; and
   - Wish to promote an atmosphere that encourages prudent risk taking, and that recognizes that growth and learning may be spawned by honest mistakes.

3. The law enforcement profession is recognized as somewhat close and fraternal in nature. The F.C.P.D. reflects this tradition, yet supports community involvement and ongoing critical self-appraisal by all its members. This means we:
   - Encourage employees to socialize with employees and community members alike to promote the reputation of the Agency;
   - Promote programs that improve the relationship between our members and the community at large;
   - Report and confront employees who violate laws and the basic values of the organization; and
   - Promote and discuss positive aspects of the Agency and its product throughout the county.

4. The provision of law enforcement services is a substantial expense to the taxpayer. The F.C.P.D. is obliged to provide the highest quality of police service for the resources expended. This means we:
   - Regularly assess the cost vs. benefits of the various programs of the Agency;
   - Require a standard of professional performance for all members of the Department;
   - Administer the Department funds in a prudent, cost-effective manner;
   - Publicly acknowledge and praise employees that excel at their jobs; and
   - Support and encourage employees in their pursuit of higher education.

5. Law enforcement, in the course of performing its primary mission, is required to deal with both dangerous and difficult situations. The F.C.P.D. accepts this responsibility and supports its members in the accomplishment of these tasks. This means we:

- Review and react to an individual's performance during such an event based upon the totality of the circumstances surrounding their decision and actions;
- Encourage all employees, as the situation permits, to think before they act;
- Take all available steps and precautions to protect both the City's and employee's interests in incidents that provide either danger or civil exposure;
- Keep our supervisor informed of any incident or pending action that jeopardizes either the reputation of the Agency or individual employee;
- Attempt, conditions permitting, to reason with individuals in the enforcement setting prior to resorting to the use of force; and
- Recognize that it is our duty to prevent, report, and investigate crimes, together with the apprehension and the pursuit of vigorous prosecution of lawbreakers. We also recognize that it is the domain of the court to punish individuals convicted of crimes.

SOURCE: Cited in More 1998: 48–49. Reprinted with permission from the Foster City Police Department, Foster City, California.

The study of police ethics is especially important in light of the functions and duties of the police as well as the wide powers of discretion that they enjoy. Police decisions can affect life, liberty, and property, and as guardians of the interests of the public, police must maintain high standards of integrity (Pollock-Byrne 1998: 3–4). In addition, police have assumed the right to use intrusive, covert, and deceptive methods of law enforcement and have a crucial role in protecting minority groups. Lately, they have also suffered a series of blows to their reputation for integrity through acts of corruption, incompetence, and racism (Neyroud and Beckley 2001: 38). All of these factors point to the centrality of fostering ethical standards in policing. Police discretion concerning how to act in a given situation can often lead to ethical misconduct.

Police Discretion

By law, police are given the power to deprive citizens of their freedom by arresting them and the right to use force in the performance of their policing function, including lethal force in certain situations. The police are therefore given great authority under the law, and that authority is to be employed ideally in enforcing the law and protecting the public. Police authority and power is exercised within the discretionary sphere given them; any exercise of power or authority is an exercise of discretion. As well as authority conferred by law, police have another kind of authority derived from their role as police officers and represented by their physical uniformed presence on the street. The public, therefore, tend to treat police officers with circumspection in most cases, aware in a general sense that police have specific powers, such as to arrest, but they are unclear as to the total extent of police authority. Police culture insists on the public giving the police respect and cooperation; flouting or resisting police authority can result in arrest or other consequences that may sometimes amount to misconduct; for example, threatening a future arrest or even assaulting a person to punish him or her for an attitude considered disrespectful.

In performing their policing duties, police officers are able to exercise a high degree of discretion. This means that they have broad freedom to make decisions about how to act in a given situation. For example, a police officer may decide to investigate an occurrence, or he or she may decide that it is not worthy of his or her time and effort. Officers can also decide whether or not to make an arrest, and may make decisions about the amount of force required during a confrontation. Some commentators argue that police discretion should be limited so that, for example, the rules and regulations of the police department and ethical standards circumscribe that discretion. Reiman argues even more radically that "police discretion has no rightful place in a free society" (1996: 80). Manning (1997) points out that policing guidelines themselves create uncertain circumstances and that the impact of guidelines is unclear, because cases in which the guidelines were not adhered to are never reported to supervisors. From the police patrol officer's point of view, Wilson (1968) notes that patrol officers may legitimately complain that having no agreed-upon standards for the exercise of discretion makes their task harder, especially if the existence of many procedural rules enables others to easily penalize them for acting in an allegedly improper manner. Manning (1997: 295) summarizes the issue of guidelines by noting that the solutions offered for limiting the wide powers of police discretion include judicial rule making, legislative regulation, and developing internal codes and regulations. Skolnick and Fyfe (1993: 120) point out, however, that elaborate police rule books, although purporting to be definitive, actually provide limited guidance of any worth to police, because hard and fast rules do not adequately assist police in dealing with the fluid and fast-changing situations they may be faced with.

Some police officers deliberately use their wide powers of discretion and their authority to perform acts of misconduct, as discussed in this section. Davis (in Cohen 1996: 97) argues that discretion ought to be confined, so that it is used only when truly required. In other words, where a rule, law, or policy can be applied to a situation, it should be applied. If this is not done, he argues, justice may be seen to be arbitrary or subject to inequalities. Fyfe (1996: 183) contends that police ought to enjoy some degree of discretion, but like discretion in any profession, it can be justified only to achieve a broadly agreed-upon purpose; in the case of the police, this purpose is often hard to define. Like Manning (1997), he attributes this lack of clarity about police goals to those same police chiefs who complain that discretion in police organizations is broad at the base and much narrower at the top. However, most citizens, including most police officers, support police having *wide discretion* on the basis that their hands should not be tied in their role as guardians of the public.

Many argue that if police are permitted wide discretion, a high level of accountability should match it, so that processes and machinery exist to investigate complaints of misconduct or abuse of discretion. (See section later in this chapter on

Combating Corruption.) Manning (1997: 146) notes that discretion creates uncertainty, and from the perspective of the police supervisor, creates randomness in patrol practice that makes it difficult for administrators to enforce accountability.

Kleinig (1996: 4–5) outlines a distinction between decisions about scope and decisions about interpretation in exercising discretion. In the former, police must decide whether a given situation requires them to act, and in the latter, questions of definition arise, such as "Has an offense been committed?" and "Is this a situation in which I should act at all?" Police also must consider questions of priorities and make what Kleinig calls "tactical decisions" that bear on police attitudes, such as whether to react strongly to circumstances or to follow a more mediatory role.

Ethics and Codes of Ethics

Kleinig (1996: 234) traces the history of a police code of ethics, noting that it was not until 1928 that such a code was formulated for police in the United States. Professions commonly have codes of ethics regulating standards for the protection of clients and the public, and the desire for professional status is a major rationale for the development of police codes of ethics (Kleinig 1996: 243). Within the United States, individual police departments have codes or canons of ethics, and the International Association of Chiefs of Police (IACP), which is dominated by the United States, finalized its Law Enforcement Code of Ethics in 1991 (see Box 2.2).

A CLOSER LOOK

BOX 2.2
Law Enforcement Code of Ethics*
International Association of Chiefs of Police

All law enforcement officers must be fully aware of the ethical responsibilities of their position and must strive constantly to live up to the highest possible standards of professional policing.

The International Association of Chiefs of Police believes it is important that police officers have clear advice and counsel available to assist them in performing their duties consistent with these standards, and has adopted the following ethical mandates as guidelines to meet these ends.

Primary Responsibilities of a Police Officer

A police officer acts as an official representative of government who is required and trusted to work within the law. The officer's powers and duties are conferred by statute. The fundamental duties of a police officer include serving the community; safeguarding lives and property; protecting the innocent; keeping the peace; and ensuring the rights of all to liberty, equality and justice.

(Continued)

(Continued)

Performance of the Duties of a Police Officer

A police officer shall perform all duties impartially, without favor or affection or ill will and without regard to status, sex, race, religion, political belief or aspiration. All citizens will be treated equally with courtesy, consideration and dignity.

Officers will never allow personal feelings, animosities or friendships to influence official conduct. Laws will be enforced appropriately and courteously and, in carrying out their responsibilities, officers will strive to obtain maximum cooperation from the public. They will conduct themselves in appearance and deportment in such a manner as to inspire confidence and respect for the position of public trust they hold.

Discretion

A police officer will use responsibly the discretion vested in the position and exercise it within the law. The principle of reasonableness will guide the officer's determinations and the officer will consider all surrounding circumstances in determining whether any legal action shall be taken.

Consistent and wise use of discretion, based on professional policing competence, will do much to preserve good relationships and retain the confidence of the public. There can be difficulty in choosing between conflicting courses of action. It is important to remember that a timely word of advice rather than arrest—which may be correct in appropriate circumstances—can be a more effective means of achieving a desired end.

Use of Force

A police officer will never employ unnecessary force or violence and will use only such force in the discharge of duty as is reasonable in all circumstances. Force should be used only with the greatest restraint and only after discussion, negotiation and persuasion have been found to be inappropriate or ineffective. While the use of force is occasionally unavoidable, every police officer will refrain from applying the unnecessary infliction of pain or suffering and will never engage in cruel, degrading or inhuman treatment of any person.

Confidentiality

Whatever a police officer sees, hears or learns of, which is of a confidential nature, will be kept secret unless the performance of duty or legal provision requires otherwise. Members of the public have a right to security and privacy, and information obtained about them must not be improperly divulged.

Integrity

A police officer will not engage in acts of corruption or bribery, nor will an officer condone such acts by other police officers. The public demands that the integrity of police officers be above reproach. Police officers must, therefore, avoid any conduct that might compromise integrity and thus undercut the public confidence in a law enforcement agency. Officers will refuse to accept any gifts, presents, subscriptions, favors, gratuities or promises that could be interpreted as seeking to cause the officer to refrain from performing official responsibilities honestly and within the law. Police officers must not receive private or special advantage from their official status. Respect from the public cannot be bought; it can only be earned and cultivated.

Cooperation With Other Officers and Agencies

Police officers will cooperate with all legally authorized agencies and their representatives in the pursuit of justice. An officer or agency may be one among many organizations that may provide law enforcement services to a jurisdiction. It is imperative that a police officer assist colleagues fully and completely with respect and consideration at all times.

Personal/Professional Capabilities

Police officers will be responsible for their own standard of professional performance and will take every reasonable opportunity to enhance and improve their level of knowledge and competence.

Through study and experience, a police officer can acquire the high level of knowledge and competence that is essential for the efficient and effective performance of duty. The acquisition of knowledge is a never-ending process of personal and professional development that should be pursued constantly.

Private Life

Police officers will behave in a manner that does not bring discredit to their agencies or themselves.

A police officer's character and conduct while off duty must always be exemplary, thus maintaining a position of respect in the community in which he or she lives and serves. The officer's personal behavior must be beyond reproach.

SOURCE: Center for the Study of Ethics in the Professions 2003. Copyright held by the International Association of Chiefs of Police, 515 North Washington Street, Alexandria, VA 22314, USA. Reprinted with permission. Further reproduction without express written permission from IACP is strictly prohibited.

*Adopted by the Executive Committee of the International Association of Chiefs of Police on October 17, 1989, during its 96th annual conference in Louisville, Kentucky, to replace the 1957 code of ethics adopted at the 64th annual IACP conference.

The IACP gratefully acknowledges the assistance of Sir John C. Hermon, former chief constable of the Royal Ulster Constabulary, who gave full license to the association to freely use the language and concepts presented in the RUC's "Professional Policing Ethics," Appendix I of the Chief Constable's Annual Report, 1988, presented to the Police Authority for Northern Ireland, for the preparation of this code.

What is the relationship between ethics and codes of ethics? Kleinig (1996: 239) suggests that statements of values and ethical standards generally are likely to be briefer and more general than codes, with the latter detailing what kinds of acts may or may not be performed. Most codes of ethics are directed toward an undefined client or public base, and it may be in the public interest to establish certain standards expected of a particular profession. In this external sense, codes may be seen to have a rhetorical function and can provide some assurance that police do follow standards or are being urged to follow them by the code. Kleinig (1996) says that it is increasingly common for codes to be used as internal documents, so that even when they are phrased in generalities, they at least identify issues and provide criteria for decision making.

Police academies apparently use codes of ethics as a teaching device; however, codes cannot be considered definitive and do not usually include enforcement procedures (Kleinig 1996: 248). Kleinig cautions that although police officers pledge themselves to their codes of ethics, this does not mean that they are required to sacrifice their reflexivity as individuals, and police may well find that their codes do not respond adequately to the situational demands placed upon them. In one study, more than 75% of police officers surveyed responded that they depended mostly on their own personal ethics rather than the ethics of law enforcement to guide them in their professional activities (Felknes 1984: 217).

The standards of conduct incorporated in codes of ethics are directed at each individual police officer, and therefore each officer must decide his or her own level of compliance. While some studies suggest that ethical standards held by officers during initial training diminish once they are "on the job" (Crank and Caldero, 2000; Rokeach, Miller, and Snyder, 1971; Zhao, Ni, and Lovrich, 1998), Catlin and Maupin (2004: 299) suggest that socialization within law enforcement has no effect on an officer's ethical orientation. Ultimately, compliance may become a question of character, and officers may be admonished to "do the right thing even when no one is watching." Part II of this book will explore various ethical theories, including virtue theory, which emphasizes the importance of character, and deontology, which argues that one must do the right thing even though others are not there to see simply because there is a duty to do the right thing. Clearly this theory has considerable relevance for codes of ethics regulating standards of behavior in policing.

Police Use of Force

Police use of force is a major and contentious issue in policing, because the capacity to use force or coercion goes to the very core of the police role. The police are the only authority empowered to use physical force and it is to be used only as a last resort. Further, police are to use no more force than is necessary to subdue a suspect (Skolnick and Fyfe 1993: 13). While there is general acceptance of the fact that police are entitled to use force, there is an equal degree of uncertainty as to what constitutes *excessive or unnecessary force*. For example, in the well-known Rodney King incident, although the majority of the public considered the force used in subduing King to be excessive, a jury acquitted the police officers charged for the beating.

Approximately 300 persons are shot and killed by police in the United States every year (Parent 2006: 230). This compares to a rate of about 10 a year in Canada and even lower rates in Australia, where 41 deaths occurred because of police shootings between 1990 and 1997, and New Zealand, where about 20 police shootings have occurred in the past 60 years (p. 230). In the United Kingdom, 7 incidents of police causing deaths by shooting occurred between 1991 and 1993. In the Netherlands, between 1978 and 1999, 67 fatal police shootings were recorded, and during the same period police wounded 288 persons. On average, about 70 police officers are murdered each year in the United States, and approximately 60 officers are accidentally killed through incidents involving motor vehicles and aircraft (p. 235). Compared to Canada, where there are about two murders of police each year, the risk of a police officer being murdered is about 3 times greater in the United States.

State and local law enforcement agencies employing 100 or more sworn officers received more than 26,000 complaints about officer use of force during 2002 (Hickman 2006: 1). Of this number, about 8% were sustained in the sense that there was enough evidence to justify disciplinary action. About 34% were not sustained, and 25% were unfounded. About one fifth of large municipal police departments were accountable to a civilian complaints review board, and these departments received a higher rate of complaints than those without such boards (p. 1). This compares with a smaller number of complaints in England and Wales where, during the 12-month period ending March 2003, police received 6,154 complaints alleging assault by police officers. This reveals an overall rate of 4.6 complaints of assault per 100 officers compared to the U.S. rate of 6.6 complaints per 100 officers (p. 3). In 2003, 82% of large municipal police departments in the United States had an internal affairs or similar unit with full time personnel, and 33% of such departments maintained an operational computer-based early intervention system for responding to officer conduct. As to use of excessive force, there were more than 2,000 sustained citizen complaints in the United States in 2002 (p. 6).

Skolnick and Fyfe (1993: 38–39) outline the ascending scale of action that police can draw on in handling street situations:

- *Presence.* Often the mere presence of police will produce the desired outcome, and use of force is irrelevant
- *Persuasive Verbalization.* Where the mere presence of officers has not been successful, police now speak persuasively in tones that are firm but not commanding.
- *Command Verbalization.* This is the next step up the scale from persuasive verbalization, which police call the "command voice." Here, police will use a stronger tone and tell the person with whom they are interacting what behavior they expect.
- *Firm Grips.* This is the next step beyond verbalization; it consists of police gripping parts of the body to warn the individual that he or she is to remain motionless or move in a certain direction. The objective is to guide and coax, and not to cause pain.
- *Pain Compliance.* At this next level of forcible contact, officers try to gain the cooperation of a person by inflicting pain in a way that does not cause

lasting physical injury. These contacts include holds like finger grips and hammerlocks.

- *Impact Techniques.* These actions are designed to overcome resistance that is forcible but is not life threatening. Here, police may use batons or kicks or employ chemical sprays and the like. Skolnick and Fyfe maintain that it is at this point that misunderstanding arises about police action. It should be noted that while police are obliged not to provoke confrontations, they are not obliged to use a lesser degree of force to counter the particular force used against them.

- *Deadly Force.* This is the most extreme use of force, often involving firearms and defined by law as "force capable of killing or likely to kill." Apart from firearms, some police are also trained in using neck holds intended to make a person unconscious. Under the law, police are permitted to use deadly force in order to apprehend those fleeing persons who are shown to be dangerous, such as someone who is armed or is fleeing from a violent crime. Deadly force is not limited to the use of firearms; Kleinig (1996: 117) points out that each year, police motor vehicle pursuits kill and maim more people, including innocent bystanders, than police firearms.

In what circumstances is it inappropriate for police to use force? Kleinig (1996: 99–102) identifies a number of factors that he considers relevant to assessing the use of force in ethical terms:

Intentions. Police may use force as a means of punishment rather than to contain a suspect. For example, tightening handcuffs may be employed to punish an arrested person, or police may use rough handling or an overnight stay in the lockup as punishment. Kleinig argues that measures of this kind are clearly unethical and outside the scope of the police function.

Seemliness. Force not only must be employed in good faith, but also must be seemly. When police methods shock the conscience or offend even hardened sensibilities, they are not considered seemly. In one case, for example, a suspect's stomach was pumped to recover apparently swallowed evidence of drug possession, and the court judged this as unseemly (*Rochin v. California* 1952).

Proportionality. The force used to achieve legitimate police aims ought to be proportionate to the seriousness of the offense alleged or threatened. Thus, shooting a person suspected of committing a misdemeanor would be an example of employing disproportionate force.

Minimization. This requires that police use the least means to secure their aims, and is known as the principle of the least restrictive alternative. For example, if handcuffs will do the job, they should be used rather than some more draconian method of immobilization, and deadly force should not be employed if a person can be arrested without it.

Practicability. Since there is a presumption against using force, it must be shown that its use will achieve the purpose for which it is deployed. In other words, police need to appreciate those situations in which a forceful presence is required as opposed to those in which a softer strategy is called for. This relates back to the need for police to exercise their discretion according to the demands of a particular situation rather than applying one rule, such as to intimidate or punish, in all cases.

Historically, in the early days of policing, police on the streets employed police force as a matter of course to keep order and enforce their will. Skolnick and Fyfe (1993: 24) trace police brutality back to the lynching and vigilante acts invoked against African Americans, revealing how police violence links to racism and notions of white supremacy. Studies have shown that police routinely used excessive force in the riots and disturbances of the 1960s (Ericson 1992), and Crank (1998: 72) warns of the dangers of paramilitary-type police units, often used now to perform normal police functions, whose members often perceive themselves as "warriors."

Two U.S. Supreme Court decisions are relevant in assessing use of force. In *Tennessee v. Garner* 1985 (as cited in Rahtz 2003: 21–23) the facts were that in October 1974 in the late evening, two Memphis police officers investigated a complaint about a prowler, and on arrival at the home owner's address, investigated the rear of the house. There they observed someone running away across the backyard. The suspect had to stop at a chain link fence, and one of the officers was able to see his face and hands. He was 17 or 18 years old and unarmed. The officer called out "police—halt," but the suspect began climbing the fence, and the officer, thinking he would escape, fired a shot that hit the suspect in the head and killed him. According to Tennessee law, police were permitted to use all necessary means to effect an arrest once they gave notice of their intention to arrest and consequent to the suspect fleeing or forcibly resisting. In considering the case, the Supreme Court issued guidance on police use of deadly force. They determined that whether or not deadly force was justifiable in a particular case depended upon whether or not it was "objectively reasonable." An officer might only use deadly force "if he has probable cause to believe that the suspect posed a threat of serious physical harm, either to the officer or to others."

In *Graham v. Connor* (1989, as cited in Rahtz 2003: 25) the Court applied the test of the reasonableness of the force used to all claims of the use of excessive force, noting that there is no precise definition of reasonableness but that four factors are relevant, namely, the severity of the crime, whether or not the suspect threatens the safety of the arresting officers, whether or not the suspect actively resists arrest, and whether or not he or she is attempting to evade arrest by fleeing from the scene. The Court also determined that "reasonableness" concerning the use of force must be judged after taking the perspective of a reasonable officer on the scene and must take account of the fact that police sometimes have to make split-second decisions concerning the use of force. The International Association of Chiefs of Police's Code of Conduct (1991) offers guidance on the use of force (see Box 2.3).

A CLOSER LOOK

BOX 2.3
Use of Force

A police officer will never employ unnecessary force or violence and will use only such force in the discharge of duty as is reasonable in all circumstances.

Force should be used only with the greatest restraint and only after discussion, negotiation and persuasion have been found to be inappropriate or ineffective. While the use of force is occasionally unavoidable, every police officer will refrain from applying the unnecessary infliction of pain or suffering and will never engage in cruel, degrading or inhuman treatment of any person.

SOURCE: Center for the Study of Ethics in the Professions 2003.

Writing in 2000, Lieutenant Arthur Doyle, a retired police officer with 29 years service in the New York Police Department, offers his description of the police attitude toward using force:

> A(n) . . . unwritten law covered chases as well. If an officer had to chase someone, by car or by foot, the person would invariably be beaten when captured. After a long chase, the officers would be pumped up, angry. They would want revenge for having put their lives in danger. That was the case in the Rodney King situation. It was taken to the extreme. (Doyle 2000: 174)

When faced with complaints of excessive force, police often adopt the strategy of characterizing the excess as an aberration by a particular officer, but many argue that police brutality is systemic (Lawrence 2000). Given that incidences of police abuse now often attract media attention, researchers have investigated the relationship between the media and police and have revealed that police are on intimate terms with the media in their role as providers of news, and the police have developed a high level of competence in public relations. In fact, one researcher has suggested that the police employ a media-centered framework in their work, because police believe that the public obtains its notions of acceptable police standards and conduct from television and the movies (Perlmutter 2000).

Generally, as noted earlier, the use of force in a given situation by police is nearly always ambiguous, and hence the boundary between excess and adequate force becomes difficult to establish. As an example of procedures that police must follow if force is used in an interaction with the public, the Miami-Dade Police Department requires that officers file a report in the following circumstances:

1. Force is applied that is likely to cause an injury or a complaint.

2. An injury results or may result from a struggle.

3. There is a complaint of an injury.

4. A chemical agent is discharged.

5. A baton is used.

6. The neck restraint is utilized.

7. There is an injury or complaint of an injury that results from guiding, holding, directing, or handcuffing a person who offers resistance. (Alpert and Dunham 2004: 21)

Clearly a report of this kind would be a vital document to any authority reviewing a particular instance of use of force.

Sometimes, there is a clear case of police brutality, such as that in New York involving the Haitian immigrant Abner Louima (see Case Study 2.1)

CASE STUDY 2.1 COP GETS 15 YEARS IN TORTURE CASE

A former patrolman was sentenced to more than 15 years in prison for holding down Haitian immigrant Abner Louima as he was tortured in a police station bathroom. The sentencing came after former officer Charles Schwarz delivered a vitriolic speech declaring his innocence. U.S. District Court Judge Eugene Nickerson sentenced Schwartz to 15 years and 8 months, about half of the 30-year term given to fellow officer Justin Volpe, who pleaded guilty to carrying out the attack on Louima. He also ordered Schwarz to pay Louima $227,495 in restitution.

Schwartz, 34, was convicted in 1999 of violating Louima's civil rights by holding him down while Volpe viciously sodomized the skinny, handcuffed victim with a broken broomstick in August 1997. "But for Volpe's extraordinary brutality, it is unlikely Schwartz would now face a sentence for sexual assault carried out with such force," Nickerson said.

At a second trial in March 1999, a jury found Schwartz and two other former officers, Thomas Bruder and Thomas Wiese, guilty of federal obstruction of justice charges—a cover-up prosecutors said reflected a "blue wall of silence" code observed by some officers. . . . Volpe—who is serving 30 years on his guilty plea—admitted wanting to punish Louima, because he mistakenly thought the victim had punched him as police broke up a brawl outside a Brooklyn nightclub. But he claimed Schwartz was not the officer with him in the bathroom. . . .

The attack by white officers on a black prisoner touched off protests alleging widespread police abuse of minorities. It triggered an ongoing Justice Department inquiry into whether the New York Police Department fosters brutality through lax discipline of wayward officers. Louima, who suffered internal injuries, has sued the city, the police officers union, and several individual officers for $155 million. . . . Louima insisted the second assailant—who put a foot in his mouth when he started to scream—was the same officer who drove him to the stationhouse. Records show the driver was Schwartz.

SOURCE: From "Cop Gets 15 Years in Torture Case," by Tom Hays. Associated Press, June 27, 2000. Reprinted with permission.

Fundamentally, whether or not force is excessive must depend on the context, and even witnesses often cannot resolve the issue. According to Lawrence (2000), ambiguity about the use of force has the effect of reducing or limiting media coverage of police abuse, because ultimately journalists ask for proof of abuse, and this can almost never be demonstrated. She argues that so long as much of the public is willing to give police the discretion they seek, incidents, such as the one involving Rodney King, can always be rationalized by police as "collateral damage" in the "war against crime." In the following examples of police violence (see Case Study 2.2), the first case was explained as an "unintentional outcome" and the second as violence used as punishment. Westmarland (2001: 325) witnessed these two incidents of police violence while observing general police life as part of a study into police culture in England.

CASE STUDY 2.2 BLOWING THE WHISTLE ON POLICE VIOLENCE

While driving around the city center, a crew, including a female officer, drove past a woman whose male companion seemed to be assaulting her. The police van came to a sudden halt, and the female officer jumped out to check whether the woman needed any help. At this point, it became obvious that the woman was very drunk, and she started shouting and abusing the police officer. After a warning, she was arrested and physically bundled into the back of the "cage" in the police van. Upon reaching the custody suite, she sobered up somewhat but then decided to become even more uncooperative, refusing to give her name and address. At this, the woman officer who had arrested her grabbed her in a headlock, twisted her over the bench and made her scream that she would provide the required information.

On patrol, early one morning at the end of a long night shift, some officers were dragging a "druggie" out of the back of a police van along the ground. His bare skin was being grazed along the concrete leading up to the custody suite door. He was then picked up by four of the officers, one at each "corner," and his head was used as a battering ram to attract the attention of those inside operating the automatic doors. From most people's perspective, this would be excessive, as the emaciated heroin addict did not pose a physical threat to the much larger, stronger officers who in any case outnumbered him. His "crime" had been to be "lippy" to the officers who were arresting him for suspected possession of illegal substances and a refusal to submit to a body search.

SOURCE: Westmarland 2001: 525.

Research on excessive force reveals that it is rarely used. For example, studies conducted from the 1960s to the 1990s show that in Boston, Chicago, and Washington, DC (Reiss 1971 in Alpert and Dunham 2004: 38), approximately 9%

of offenders were handled using force, and other researchers report 8% and 10% use of force (p. 38). In 2001, the Police Foundation surveyed police officers for their opinions on use of force, and after interviewing almost 1,000 officers from more than 100 agencies, the foundation reached the following conclusions:

- Most police officers disapproved of using excessive force.
- A substantial minority believed they should be permitted to use more force than the law allowed.
- A substantial minority believed that using more force than permitted by the law was sometimes acceptable.
- In the case of a physical assault on a police officer, almost 25% believed that using more force than was legally allowed in that situation was acceptable.
- More than 4 out of 10 police officers said that always following the rules was not compatible with doing police work.
- Only 7% of officers thought that police should be allowed to use physical force as a response to verbal abuse. (Alpert and Dunham 2004: 38)

In Alpert and Dunham's (2004: 66) study on the use of force in the Miami-Dade Police Department based on written reports from 1996 to 1998, they reported that almost all cases involving police use of force concerned acts of resistance by the suspect (97%), with resisting arrest (39%) and attempting to escape or fleeing the scene (26%) rating highest. In 21% of cases the police officer was assaulted, and the most common type of force was striking or hitting an officer (36%) (p. 66). In terms of force used by officers to subdue suspects, the primary method was using hands and fists (55%), but officers also used dogs, batons, other weapons, and firearms in 23% of cases (p. 68).

Internationally, excessive force is said to be prevalent in all Asian countries. Fernando (2003) comments that in these countries police officers "are expected to use coercion, including torture, in criminal investigations" (p. 30). This is justified by reference to the need to maintain order, because the maintenance of public order has a higher priority than law enforcement in Asian countries. In Nigeria, Alemika (2003) suggests that the maintenance of the colonial policing model has resulted in police–citizen interactions being largely involuntary and "characterized by, police brutality, corruption and hostility to citizens" (p. 72). Citizens see police as oppressor and repressor, and police employ various methods of torture including

whipping with electrical cables; hanging or suspending suspects from ceiling fan hooks; chaining suspects to the ground in a squatting position or against the wall in a standing position; shock batons and chairs; insertion of sharp objects into male genitals and blunt objects (such as bottles) into female organs; forceful removal of fingernails; deprivation of sleep, food and medical care; and solitary confinement and denial of access to relations, friends and attorneys. (Alemika 2003: 78)

Alemika explains that the police are primarily used to maintain order.

In Argentina, a crime survey conducted in 1998 revealed that 18.5% of those reporting believed that retired police and military personnel most frequently committed crimes and about 7% believed that active police officers committed crimes (Smulovitz 2003: 132). In Brazil, according to Mesquita Neto and Loche (2003: 191) government and police responses to crime control have been "undermined by the persistence of police brutality and the low level of respect for and cooperation with the police and the criminal justice system on the part of the community."

Associated with questions about police use of force is the notion that within police culture, there is a perspective that the ends always justify the means. This perspective is termed "*Dirty Harry*/dirty hands."

Dirty Harry/Dirty Hands

The use of *dirty hands* or *dirty means* by police to secure their goals (Kleinig 1996) has been characterized as the "*Dirty Harry* problem" (Klockars 1980). Drawing on the 1971 film, *Dirty Harry*, which shows Inspector Dirty Harry Callahan using torture to establish the whereabouts of a kidnapped girl, Klockars raises the issue of the morality of using force to extract information from suspects. Dirty means is not limited to actual torture, but it can include beating confessions out of suspects, making false arrests, stopping and searching without proper cause, and using threats and coercion to obtain evidence. An analysis of the components of the *Dirty Harry* situation reveals four conditions faced by the police officer (Miller, Blackler, and Alexandra 1997: 119):

1. The police officer has an opportunity to achieve a morally good end or outcome and intends to do so. (In the *Dirty Harry* movie, Callahan used torture to discover the location of the girl.)

2. The means used to achieve this good end are normally considered morally wrong (dirty). (In the *Dirty Harry* case, the torture included standing on the suspect's mangled and wounded leg to obtain the location of the girl.)

3. The use of these means is perceived by the police officer to be the best or only practicable means of ensuring that the good end is met.

4. The good likely to be achieved by using dirty hands far outweighs the bad consequences of using dirty means, a perspective held by utilitarianism (see Chapter 10).

The crux of the problem raised by *Dirty Harry* is whether means that are illegal and morally questionable may be used to achieve ends that may themselves be considered moral. In policing, employing dirty means to achieve moral ends is known as *noble cause corruption*. Using dirty hands is, of course, morally problematic, because it involves the use of unlawful methods. Some argue that public life necessarily involves dirtying one's hands (Walzer in Kleinig 1996: 55), whereas others like Kleinig (1996: 56) are not convinced that the scenarios usually presented justify the use of dirty hands. Others suggest that such situations should be avoided as much as possible, because the person using dirty hands will often feel moral qualms about what he or she has done, and frequent use of dirty means may induce a moral callousness in an individual (Miller et al. 1997: 123).

Klockars (1980) concludes that police officers who use dirty means should be punished, because they will grasp the wrong moral choice they have made only if this happens. Importantly, Klockars implies that so far as the public is concerned, if it fails to condemn the use of dirty means, it becomes complicit in noble cause corruption. Conversely, if the public insists on punishing police officers who use dirty means, the ironic effect is to increase our fear of crime since criminals may go unpunished.

Police abuse of their right to use force, or noble cause corruption in the form of dirty hands or dirty means, is a specific issue within policing that raises ethical questions. Ethical issues also arise in general police work, and police corruption can occur in a variety of situations involving police power or in day-to-day interactions between the police and the public.

In Europe, the European Committee for the Prevention of Torture and Inhuman or Degrading Punishment or Treatment, a body that was established by the European Convention on Human Rights which prohibits torture or inhuman or degrading treatment or punishment, can investigate the improper use of force by the police (Jobard 2003). Members of the committee have the right to visit places in which people are held against their will, including police stations, at any time. By the year 2000, the committee had visited France five times, and in 1999 the European Court of Human Rights found that France had tortured a person held in custody by its Criminal Investigation Service (p. 424). When the committee visited France, it heard accusations against the police that included punching and slaps, depriving prisoners of food and medication, and psychological pressures (p. 424).

Police Corruption

Police corruption has been variously defined as the following:

- Accepting money or its equivalent for doing something that a public official is already required to do, or not required to do, or in consideration of exercising a discretion for improper reasons (McMullan in Kleinig 1996: 165)
- Accepting goods or services for performing or not performing duties that are part of one's employment. A gift becomes a gratuity according to the reason for which it is given, and it is the reason the gift is accepted that constitutes the corruption (Cohen and Feldberg in Kleinig 1996: 165).
- The misuse of authority by a police officer in a way intended to produce personal gain for the officer or others (Goldstein in Kleinig 1996: 165).
- Actions taken by a police officer that exploit police powers in exchange for considerations of "private-regarding benefit" that violate standards governing the officer's conduct (Johnston 1995: 287). In this definition, *private-regarding benefit* means a range of rewards acquired by the officer, the officer's colleagues, family, and friends.

The above definitions do not exhaust all forms of police misconduct. For example, improperly eliciting confessions and lying to secure a conviction are distinct forms of misconduct and will be discussed later in this chapter (see Ethical Issues in Investigation, Interrogation, and Custody).

Accepting gratuities like free meals and coffee, free lunches, half price dinners, and gifts from merchants during holiday seasons is a vexed and much discussed issue within policing. In 1988 Richard Kania (in Coleman 2004: 37; also see Kania 2004) argued that under certain circumstances police ought to be encouraged to accept gratuities, because most people offering them do not have the intention of corrupting police but are expressing a debt to police for their services, which they are attempting to repay through the offer of gratuities. Kania, a former police officer from Louisiana, suggested an analogy with tipping, where the recipient is being tipped for services rendered and where no future obligations are being created by the transaction. He argued that only in situations where the provider of the gratuity was seeking to establish credit for future use were such transactions problematic and that if police did not vary the way in which they carried out their duty as a result of receiving gratuities, then receiving them was ethically appropriate.

Responding to Kania's arguments, Stephen Coleman (2004) argues that police should refuse gratuities that could in the public mind be regarded as influencing their judgment in the conduct of their duties. He argues that the practice cannot be regarded as analogous to tipping, because those who commonly receive tips come to expect them and perhaps even make a demand for them. Also, he argues that there may be a future orientation toward tipping, and he suggests that giving a generous tip may give rise to an expectation of above average service in the future. Another objection is that police regard themselves as professionals, and most professionals do not receive tips. Further, accepting gratuities may well have an effect on how police conduct themselves, even if they fail to appreciate that fact. For example, if the police patronize establishments that offer gratuities, and this causes them to visit and spend time there more often to the detriment of other establishments, the result affects the distribution of police services in the community (p. 38).

Ruiz and Bono (2004) also take issue with Kania, arguing that accepting gratuities is a harmful practice that should be actively discouraged. The authors are unable to accept that a police officer's acceptance of daily gratuities (amounting to thousands of dollars each year) will not give rise to expectations on the givers' part (p. 46). One of the authors, a former police officer, recounts that merchants who gave gratuities "were quick to remind him of their generosity when stopped for a traffic violation . . . at the very least they expected to be given special consideration when calling for service" (p. 46). Ruiz and Bono contend that the annual value of regular gratuities in the form of coffee, donuts, lunch, cigarettes, alcohol, laundry, and free movie tickets could be between $8,000 and $10,000 each year, and with an average national police gross salary of around $35,000, these gratuities comprise an increase in gross salary of more than 33% (pp. 50–51).

Feldberg (in Del Pozo 2005: 28) links gratuities with distributive justice, arguing that the effect of a gratuity is to induce a police officer to "distribute the benefit of his presence disproportionately to some taxpayers and not to others, a practice that undermines the democratic ethos of public service." Thus, if police eat lunch daily at one restaurant that offers a free or half price lunch, they are providing their presence and therefore police protection and security to one restaurant during that period. In this view, their presence skews the distribution of police service in favor of a particular restaurant. One solution to this argument about distributive justice is to follow the approach tried in England in the 1970s where all police officers were required to eat their meals in a canteen located inside the police headquarters. However, Del Pozo argues (p. 33) that this would "also have the effect of cutting off one's nose to spite one's face: were officers forced to take meals at the stationhouse, no location would benefit from their presence."

What policy should police departments follow in relation to the issue of accepting gratuities? Many departments strictly prohibit their acceptance, but because police officers are often out of direct supervision, enforcing such a policy is very problematic. As well, those giving the gratuities have no incentive to report officers for violating their departmental policy (Withrow and Dailey 2004: 174). Some departments attempt to regulate gratuities by imposing a policy that limits the amount of gratuity on the basis that the value of the gratuity is related to the level of corruption (p. 175). Arguably the most important factor in the acceptance of gratuities is the rationale for offering the gratuity. Thus a policy that merely seeks to limit the extent of the gratuity appears unrelated to the real likelihood of corruption.

An example of how those who give gratuities to police do so with an expectation of police assistance is given by Brian Withrow, as shown in Box 2.4.

A CLOSER LOOK

BOX 2.4
No More Free Meals

Withrow, while a headquarters staff officer in a state police agency, was conducting a routine inspection tour and was invited to lunch by local troopers. In the restaurant, when the bills came, the troopers argued with the waitress about the full price stated on the bills. They were regulars at the restaurant, but the waitress told them that restaurant policy had changed, and now everyone had to pay the full price. One of the troopers responded very loudly, "We never pay full price, and we are not going to start now." In order to defuse the situation, Withrow told the troopers to pay the full price plus a tip, and Withrow apologized to the waitress. He later discovered that the restaurant owner's son had recently been arrested for driving while intoxicated (DUI).

SOURCE: Withrow and Dailey 2004: 165

Kleinig (1996: 166) offers the following definition of corruption: "Police officers act corruptly when, in exercising or failing to exercise their authority, they act with the primary intention of furthering private or departmental/divisional advantage." Kleinig admits that his definition covers many acts and practices that are never explicitly revealed as corrupt—for example, ignoring small jobs for the large visible ones—but makes the point that such acts are not motivated by a spirit of corruption. The important point is that a police officer is motivated by a personal desire for gain regardless of what acts he or she actually performs to secure that gain.

It may be helpful to characterize corruption in typologies, because they explain, illustrate, and add specificity to the kinds of acts defined as corruption. The following represents a typography produced by Barker (in Kleinig 1996: 168).

Corruption of Authority. This involves authorized and unearned benefits officers are given by virtue of their employment as police officers. Included are free meals, liquor, sex, entertainment, discounts on purchases, payments for property protection extending beyond normal police duties, secret payments by property owners to arrest robbers and burglars at their places of business, and payments by bondsmen to police for the arrest and notification of those who jumped bail where the bondsmen are acting as bounty hunters. It is common practice for restaurants to offer police free or half price meals or free coffee. This raises the issue of the expectations of those businesses in giving these benefits. In one survey in Reno, Nevada, of 116 people, about half reported that if they were to run a small business like a coffee shop or movie theater, they would offer police free coffee, meals, or movie tickets (Ivkovic 2005a: 39). Significantly, one third of those who would make such offers explicitly reported that they would expect special favors in exchange. An example of this kind is shown in Box 2.5.

A CLOSER LOOK

BOX 2.5
Detectives Receive Sex Services in Antiprostitution Campaign

Undercover police detectives from Spotsylvania County in northern Virginia involved in "rooting out prostitution" in the massage parlor business received sexual services from "masseuses" (Jackman 2006: B01). According to court papers, "detectives allowed women to perform sexual acts on them on four occasions and once left a $350 tip" (p. B01).

The sheriff argued that this practice was "not new, and only unmarried detectives are assigned to such cases. Most prostitutes are careful not to say anything incriminating, so sexual contact is necessary. If I thought we could get a conviction without that, we wouldn't allow it. If you want to make them, this has to be done."

However, numerous police and experts told the reporter that they had no knowledge of any law enforcement agency in the Washington, DC, area or in the nation that permitted sexual contact in prostitution investigations. As they put it, "Police should not break the law to enforce it."

It is normal practice for a verbal agreement to provide services plus an explicit act such as undressing or producing a condom to be considered sufficient evidence in charges of soliciting prostitution.

SOURCE: Jackman 2006: B01

Kickbacks. These include goods, services, and money received for a multitude of services, such as referring business to various professionals, like lawyers and bondsmen, with whom police regularly interact in their duties. Kickbacks have been condoned within police culture, as long as the rewards are modest and the businesses legitimate, the rationalization being that businesses providing kickbacks are simply demonstrating their enterprising nature.

Opportunistic Theft. This takes a number of forms, including stealing property from those arrested, those involved in traffic accidents, and other victims; stealing money or goods left behind by a burglar when investigating a burglary; removing items from unprotected property sites, such as building materials; or stealing parts of confiscated evidence, such as drugs, drug money, or liquor.

Shakedowns. This is understood to include accepting payments for not making an arrest or issuing a summons that in the ordinary course of events would have been made or issued. Shakedowns may be protected by a police code of silence, but if revealed, they are usually strongly condemned by police supervisors.

Protection of Illegal Activities. There are many forms of protection that police may provide to those engaging in illegal enterprises so they may operate with the minimum of official harassment. Examples are payments to police by cab companies to park illegally and to operate cabs in breach of safety standards; payments by trucking firms to haul overloaded cargoes; and payments by construction companies to overlook violations of regulations. According to Roebuck and Barker (1974: 430), some of these activities, where there are no complainants, are difficult to prosecute and have the effect of causing "resignation, ritualism, inaction or corruption" in honest police officers. Kleinig (1996) proposes that selling confidential police information should also be included in this category.

The Traffic Fix. This involves taking money or other reward for disposing of traffic citations.

The Misdemeanor Fix. Here a police officer quashes proceedings for a misdemeanor by, for example, not proceeding with a prosecution, tampering with evidence, or perjuring him- or herself in proceedings.

The Felony Fix. This is the same as the misdemeanor fix, except that felonies are involved.

Direct Criminal Activities. These occur when officers commit criminal acts for personal gain as if they were themselves criminals.

Internal Payoffs. There are various forms of internal corruption where police officers may buy, barter, or sell aspects of their employment, such as off days, holidays, and promotions. Officers who administer assignments may receive rewards for assigning officers to particular divisions or for providing transfers to or from specific or preferred assignments.

The results of investigations into police corruption in Australia are shown in Box 2.6.

A CLOSER LOOK

BOX 2.6
Police Corruption in Australia

There have been two major investigations of police corruption in Australia: the Royal Commission into the New South Wales Police Service (1997) and the Fitzgerald Commission in Queensland (1989). Their findings of corruption in these two states are described below:

Royal Commission Into the New South Wales Police Service (1997) *New South Wales, Australia*	*Fitzgerald Commission (1989)* *Queensland, Australia*
A state of systemic and entrenched corruption (p. 33), well organized	Corruption by prostitutes, gambling, drug dealers
A very serious state of corruption that is widespread and of long-standing origin (p. 101)	Thefts
Types: thefts of drugs and money; shake-downs of drug dealers; regular payments from drug dealers, gambling operations, clubs, and brothels; assaults	
"Process corruption" (noble cause corruption)	
Supervisors unaware or unwilling to respond	

SOURCE: Ivkovic 2005a: 52–53.

Conditions Contributing to Police Corruption

What justifications or explanations do police and others offer to explain the existence of police corruption? This is an important issue, because an analysis of the explanations for police corruption can contribute to possible solutions. Johnston (1995: 285) argues that explanations for police corruption may be personalistic, institutional, or systemic.

Personalistic Explanations

Three major explanations emphasize the individual police officer as the ultimate cause of corruption: the rotten apple, the recruitment perspective, and the police personality explanation.

In the *rotten apple* explanation, corruption is described by police chiefs and others as merely the acts of a few rotten apples in an otherwise honest department. The aim of this explanation is to divert attention away from the possibility that corruption might be systemic. This argument may also function as an excuse for not instituting investigations that might uncover other corruption, as a way to limit investigations, or as a means to protect individuals. It implies that recruiting persons of the right character will eliminate corruption. Barker (1996: 39) asserts that police use the term *rotten apple* because they wish the public to believe that a publicly identified corrupt or racist cop is an aberration and not a departmental problem. He regards the labeling of individual police as rotten apples to be a management technique used to explain away corrupt behavior.

In the United Kingdom, investigations of corruption have revealed how close links between police and their criminal informants can result in passing information that can be used for criminal activities. Box 2.7 shows an example of this kind of individual corruption.

A CLOSER LOOK

BOX 2.7
The Rotten Apple

Local criminals regularly visit a gym that is also used by a police officer. The officer becomes friendly with some of the criminals and begins to socialize with them. As their relationship develops, they ask him to provide information from the police national computer and from the police intelligence system. In return for some favors, such as free meals or drinks, he passes this information on to them and it is used by the criminals to build up a picture of the activities of the police.

SOURCE: Miller 2003: 10.

In the *recruitment perspective,* it is argued that personal traits shared by officers recruited from similar social backgrounds make them particularly susceptible to corruption. It is true that in the early days of policing, officers tended to be recruited from certain groups. However, over the last decade, police forces have become more heterogeneous, and now it is common to see women, African Americans, Hispanics, and others in police departments. The argument is that whites with working-class, lower-status backgrounds and a lack of advanced education might harbor certain attitudes and values that could make them susceptible to corruption.

The *police personality* argument is analogous to one that asserts that the institutional police culture is responsible for creating an environment that encourages or fails to discourage police corruption. It contends that certain traits make up the police personality, including suspiciousness, authoritarianism, and loyalty. Caldero (in Crank and Caldero 2000: 58–60), in a 1997 survey of the values of police officers, found that over the past 25 years, police values have remained constant, that these values are imported from particular groups in society, and that education has had little effect on these values. This contention concerning the influence of police values or police personality suggests that corruption therefore is linked to personality and values.

The Institutional Approach

The wide discretionary powers that police officers enjoy, as well as the difficulties in supervising that discretion, are aspects of policing as an institution, and it is argued that police discretion makes corruption more likely to occur. Police discretion can be used for illegitimate purposes, and while its existence does not make corruption inevitable, it does give a police officer scope to hide unethical decisions. The problems inherent in the task of supervising officers who have wide discretionary powers mean that corruption can be allowed to go unchecked and unrevealed.

Two factors that may bear on corruption from the institutional viewpoint are the *low public visibility* of police and the issue of *secrecy* within the institution. The public has little knowledge or sense of what police officers do, and much police activity is shielded from the public. This low visibility can provide opportunities for corruption. In terms of secrecy, it is argued that the person most likely to observe corruption first hand is another police officer. Frequently, however, he or she will not reveal the corruption to anyone due to fear of retaliation, bonds of friendship, loyalty, or an institutional ideology that sets police against the public in an isolationist approach. It follows that information about corruption may be difficult to collect, and officers may refuse to testify against their colleagues.

This so-called *wall of silence* is also found in other nations as well as among U.S. police forces. For example, in the Netherlands, a survey conducted to ascertain the views of police on the seriousness of ethics violations and on their willingness to report such violations (either self-reporting or reporting others)—that is, to break the wall of silence—found that receiving free meals and discounts was seen as serious or very serious (Huberts, Lamboo, and Punch 2003: 226). Comparing these results to a similar survey in the United States, the researchers found that police in the Netherlands were significantly more ready to report receipt of such benefits than were U.S. police officers. A similar survey undertaken in Finland and Croatia revealed that while Croatian police regarded free meals and discounts as more serious than accepting occasional gifts, police in Finland took the opposite view regarding receiving free merchandise as a serious wrongdoing (Ivkovic 2005b: 557). A similar survey conducted in the United Kingdom revealed that most officers surveyed believed that accepting free meals and gifts was contrary to police policy, but only 14% thought it was very serious behavior, and 11% considered it not serious at all (Westmarland 2005: 149). Similarly, accepting gifts during holiday periods such as Christmas was not regarded as very serious, but nevertheless, 36% of respondents said they knew that it was contrary to police policy (p. 149).

A final factor is *managerial secrecy,* suggesting that those in supervisory positions who were formerly patrol officers and who have risen through the ranks share police values and culture, including those values that ensure that corruption is hidden. This kind of secrecy extends to feelings of resentment about what is perceived to be interference by outsiders in police processes, including formal inquiries like the Knapp Commission's investigation into corruption. Essentially, managerial secrecy will be strengthened by the values fostered by police culture.

Systemic Explanation

This type of explanation looks at pressures placed upon the police by society that might provoke police corruption and suggests that police corruption is rooted within the police interaction with society, rather than within the individual police officer. For example, legislation dealing with social behavior such as alcohol consumption, gambling, and prostitution is often regarded by the public as an attempt to impose moral standards and is therefore often resisted. Thus, underage persons purchase alcohol, and citizens gamble and engage in prostitution. This ambivalence in society about personal morality tends to encourage police reluctance to enforce the law and can ultimately result in those engaged in crimes of vice offering bribes and incentives to police to look the other way. From the police point of view, violations of vice laws often constitute victimless crimes, providing further encouragement toward corruption.

In developing countries, low police salaries operate as a contributing factor to police corruption. For example, in Bosnia during the postwar period, police received low salaries and were not paid consistently, rendering them vulnerable to corruption (Ivkovic and Shelley 2005: 444). Examples of police corruption in Bosnia include taking bribes and looking the other way when cars are stolen and later the thieves handing them back to their owners in exchange for a kickback to the police officers concerned (p. 445).

Drugs and Corruption

Miller et al. (1997: 105–106) single out illegal drugs as a major contributing factor to police corruption, arguing that police operate in an environment where there is a widespread use of illegal drugs and a vast amount of drug money. They describe the circumstances of enforcing antidrug laws as follows:

- There exists a large amount of money and a willingness on the part of drug users and dealers to bribe police.
- There are no complainants, because the "victims" are not likely to report that they have been the victim of a criminal act.
- In light of this victimless crime, bribes can be accepted and drugs or drug money stolen with relative impunity.
- Sections of the public see drug addiction as a medical condition rather than as a crime and therefore see corruption as less morally damning.
- Younger police officers may well share the attitudes of their peers who are not police officers and regard the use and sale of illegal drugs as a minor matter.
- Police officers working in drug investigations may, out of fear, turn a blind eye to drugs, or even take drugs themselves, entering a spiral of corruption moving from moral compromise to covert corrupt activities.

The contention that there is a relationship between drug dealing and police corruption finds support in a 1998 government report that cites examples of drug-related police corruption in a number of cities and reports that one half of all police officers convicted following FBI-led investigations into corruption cases between

1993 and 1997 were convicted for drug-related offenses. Particular forms of drug-related corruption identified in the report include stealing money and/or drugs from drug dealers, selling stolen drugs, and protecting drug operations (Government Accounting Office 1998).

In the United Kingdom, a notorious example of the linkage between police corruption and drug dealing occurred in the early 1990s; it highlights the temptations of drug dealing as a source of corrupt benefits for police as well as the dangers of consorting with informants without following police policies and procedures (see Box 2.8).

A CLOSER LOOK

BOX 2.8
Corrupt Arrangements Within the Southeast Regional Crime Squad, South London, England

---

Members of a particular team within the Southeast Regional Crime Squad, who called themselves The Groovy Gang, engaged in corrupt activities that were organized around Detective Constable Bob Clark. Clark maintained a close relationship with Evelyn Fleckney, an informant who regularly socialized with the police team. She not only joined the team for evening social occasions but was romantically connected with Clark and took several holidays with him. Senior police officers failed to properly enforce policies regulating contacts between police and informants like Fleckney.

Fleckney was a drug dealer, and in return for police protection from investigation and prosecution, she passed on information about rival drug dealers to the team, who would then be able to claim successes in arresting and prosecuting Fleckney's drug-dealing competitors. Also, drugs seized in searches could be recycled back onto the streets by Fleckney, and team members stole cash discovered during drug raids.

SOURCE: Miller 2003: 12.

Slippery Slope

An important explanation for police corruption is termed the *slippery slope*. This notion was developed by Sherman (1985) and suggests that taking rewards and money begins on a small scale and is tacitly acknowledged by other police officers. Sherman suggests that officers who become accustomed to taking small rewards will eventually develop connections to other officers involved in corruption on a grander scale. In other words, officers become desensitized to the moral implications of their acts, and the acts themselves become addictive.

According to Sherman, police officers find themselves on this slope as the result of social considerations that bind police together and because of the way in which police perceive their own behavior. He argues that young recruits learn early on that as police officers, they are bound to one social group and are alienated from others.

The pressures of the social group and the acceptance of minor perks alter the self-image of the young recruits to make them vulnerable to more substantial corruption. Sherman also suggests that the slide down the slippery slope is eased by the relatively small moral gap along the continuum of graft stages.

Sherman's solution to this problem is to decriminalize those activities that most easily tempt police into graft, and his solution finds anecdotal support from those corrupt police officers who have described their lapse into corruption. However, Feldberg (1985) disagrees, claiming that police officers can make a distinction between accepting minor perks and bribes intended to affect the performance of their duties. Fundamentally, the dispute between Feldberg and Sherman rests on a moral basis, in that Sherman believes that to accept a free cup of coffee constitutes a moral compromise, whereas Feldberg does not. Kleinig (1996) offers the opinion that people commonly offer each other cups of coffee as a gesture, not with the intention of creating any obligation, and that police supervisors who see the acceptance of such small rewards as morally compromising are likely to be seen as over-reacting and risk losing the respect of their rank-and-file officers.

Crank and Caldero (2000: 74) offer an alternative slippery slope model, describing a process of *noble cause corruption* rather than simply economic corruption. This slope begins with encouragement to accept free meals, not to test the willingness to accept graft but to establish whether an officer's loyalty to others in the squad can be relied upon. This is followed by loyalty backup, where the officer is tested for his or her own willingness to back up other officers, which may involve giving false testimony or taking part in the shakedown of a suspect. The next stage is using physical violence against citizens, involving greater risks to the officer in terms of detection, risk of injury, or retaliation. Finally, "flaking" drugs is described as a much more serious form of noble cause corruption, in which police plant drugs to enhance the seriousness of the crime. In this model, therefore, police are able to justify their progress down the slippery slope by employing the justification of noble cause.

In England, in a case involving alleged Irish Republican Army (IRA) terrorist suspects, it seems that the English police justified their actions in the noble cause of jailing IRA terrorists (Punch 2003: 185–189). Six suspects were imprisoned for up to 16 years on the basis of false confessions and doubtful evidence before they were released because of this police wrongdoing. In the early 1970s, the IRA commenced a bombing campaign in Britain, and in 1973 in Birmingham, two explosions occurred in pubs resulting in 21 deaths. This caused a national outrage, putting pressure on the police to secure convictions. A number of the suspects arrested were assaulted by police, intimidated with threats of violence, and assaulted by fellow prisoners while on remand. Doubts arose about the convictions, which were upheld by the court of appeal in 1977. Ultimately, another group of alleged terrorists were arrested and admitted the bombings for which the Birmingham Six were jailed. It emerged that the confessions were fabricated by the investigating officers, important evidence was withheld from the courts, and forensic evidence turned out to be highly questionable. According to Punch (2003: 187), the concept of noble cause corruption applied to this case, and the police involved believed that the ends justified the means, having already satisfied themselves about the prisoners' guilt.

Consequences of Corruption

One implication of corruption is that corrupters gain influence over the police, subverting police from their proper role and creating conditions that favor crime in the sense that there is an increase in public tolerance for some crimes. In the inner cities, corruption may permit crime to flourish. Most importantly, corruption undermines public trust in the police force and diminishes credibility in the integrity of individual police officers.

Combating Corruption

Some (for example, Miller et al. 1997) suggest that corruption can be reduced through examining four basic aspects of policing, namely, recruitment, reducing the opportunities for corruption, detecting and deterring corruption, and reinforcing the motivation to act morally. With *recruitment,* it is clearly essential that only those with the highest moral character be recruited into policing (Delattre 1989), as well as those capable of becoming competent police officers, because the incompetent might easily become disaffected and open to corruption. *Reducing opportunities for corruption,* for example, by regularly rotating officers employed in drug squads, may be effective, but the very nature of police work, especially the wide discretion given to police at the street level, makes opportunity reduction a daunting task. Ultimately, legislative and other policies that promote decriminalization will reduce opportunities for corruption. *Detection and deterrence* are achieved through accountability, internal and external, and through tools such as investigation, auditing, surveillance, and the use of informants.

In the United Kingdom, a number of police forces have recently established professional standards units whose task is to "proactively cultivate and analyse information or 'intelligence' on unethical police activity from a range of sources, and mount formal investigations . . ." (Miller 2003: 2). These units are divided into an intelligence cell and a number of operational teams, with the intelligence cell staffed by analysts tasked to manage a central database of information relevant to anticorruption efforts. The operational teams then conduct formal investigations into individuals. Examples of corrupt activities in the English police forces have included accepting protection money from criminals, stealing and recycling drugs to criminals, the theft of cash from crime scenes, and fabricating evidence to secure convictions (p. 6). Contemporary corruption was found in scale to be smaller than that revealed by, for example, the Knapp Commission in 1972 and the Mollen Commission in 1994 in the United States or the Fitzgerald Commission in 1987 in Australia. According to the report, the level of staff identified as potentially corrupt amounted to between 0.5% and 1% of police staff, including both police and civilian staff (p. 6). The report suggests that corruption is for the most part committed by individuals, and the passing of sensitive information from police sources to those outside the force, including criminal informers, is a significant form of corruption in the United Kingdom (p. 10). Corruption was also found to arise from interactions between police and criminals in social networks outside of work involving, for example, friends or relatives of police staff or persons using the same

gyms as police staff or the same pubs and clubs. Officers in the professional standards units believed that criminals involved in organized crime targeted police with
the aim of gaining information to assist with their criminal activities (p. 21).

Motivating police to do what is morally correct ought to reduce the temptations
for corruption. Providing a just system of rewards and penalties within the police
organization, and rejecting systems of promotion that are unjust, as well as addressing police complaints about unfair workloads, will assist in motivating police to
resist inducements to illegality. The publication and dissemination of ethical standards and an emphasis on the ethical ends of policing can contribute to the development of proper motivation, especially if such statements of ethical standards are
the subjects of ongoing discussion in training programs and supervision. Finally, an
emphasis on the collective responsibility of police for controlling corruption will
effectively assist in changing an attitude that only isolated individuals who hero-
ically blow the whistle on others reveal corruption. Whistle-blowing is discussed in
the next section.

Ensuring Police Accountability

The question of how to make police accountable is a complex one. Most police
departments employ a wide array of mechanisms like police boards and other
structures that involve the community to provide oversight and accountability.
Arguments in favor of citizen review include the following:

- Involving citizens in oversight is likely to result in more objective and
  thorough investigations.
- Involving citizens is likely to deter police misconduct; citizen involvement
  leads to a greater rate of conviction, because police are less able to conceal
  wrongdoing.
- Individual complainants and the public will have a higher level of confidence
  in the integrity of police practice. (Alpert and Dunham 2004: 33)

Citizen oversight of the police began in the 1920s and has seen a steady growth
despite consistent police resistance to the notion that outsiders should judge their
conduct (Walker 2001). The heyday of citizen oversight and review was during the
1980s and 1990s, when police ceased to be the sole judges of whether their conduct
toward citizens reached an acceptable standard (Bayley 1994: 91). In his comprehensive exploration of the "new police accountability" in the United States, Samuel
Walker (2005: 7) explains how police accountability refers both to holding law
enforcement agencies accountable for services like crime control and also to the
accountability of individual officers for the treatment they offer to the public in
their use of force and discrimination. Ensuring police accountability involves setting up complex administrative arrangements, some of which have been introduced
under pressure as a result of court proceedings and settlements secured by the
Department of Justice in its mandate to ensure police accountability (p. 11).
According to Walker, there are two elements in the new police accountability:
specific strategies intended to enhance accountability and a framework that brings

strategies and tools together into a program of reform (p. 12). Best practices within policing have focused on a set of strategies relating to the following:

- Reporting the use of force and other critical incidents
- Maintaining an open and accessible citizen complaint procedure
- Establishing an early intervention system that systematically collects and analyzes data on police performance for the early identification of issues needing correction
- External citizen oversight, which may take various forms, including the new concept of the police auditor. (Walker 2005: 12–13)

The conceptual framework within which these strategies operate comprises the following:

- Moving police organizations away from an emphasis on the rotten apple theory and in the direction of actual organizational change that addresses organizational and management issues related to police misconduct
- Controlling street level officer behavior through devices such as use of force reporting systems
- Systematic collection and analysis of data (a process essential to police reform) so as to develop a fact-based depiction of officer activity, including the program known as COMPSTAT that collects and analyzes data on crime patterns
- Convergence of internal and external accountability so that these are seen as interrelated and not as alternatives. (Walker 2005: 14–16)

As well as the typical civilian review board, a new form of oversight in the shape of the police auditor emerged in the 1990s. According to Walker (2005: 135) this office is likely to be more effective as a form of oversight than the civilian review board because of the auditor's focus on organizational change. Unlike civilian review boards, which are concerned with investigating individual complaints against police, the auditor scrutinizes organizational problems that generate such incidents. This opens up examination of systemic issues within the organization that affect training and policy making. For example, if the department provides insufficient training on a policy or procedure, this can lead to inadvertent violations. As of 2005, there were 12 police auditors within the United States, basically clustered in the western half of the country (p. 136). They perform five basic functions (pp. 139–142):

1. Auditing the department's citizen complaint process, including the procedures and records relating to complaints

2. Auditing police operations such as narcotics enforcement, personnel selection for particular policing activities, and specific training

3. Conducting policy review as an outcome of auditing citizen complaints and police operations. Policy is crucial, because recommendations for change in

organizational structures and practices are designed to prevent future misconduct. Thus, the auditor will produce a set of policy recommendations for police chiefs and managers.

4. Community outreach. This includes the auditor meeting with community groups and providing information about the complaints procedure and related activities.

5. Creating transparency. The auditor exposes issues and concerns within the police department to the public gaze, rejecting the historically closed and secretive nature of American policing organizations.

External citizen review takes a number of forms, and Walker and Kreisel (1996) have analyzed 65 citizen review procedures and structures that existed in January 1995. Among the various structures, many lack full independence, because police rather than citizens conduct the initial fact-finding investigations (p. 71). Some have no role in the investigation of individual complaints, while others are empowered to review police policies. A multimember board conducts the vast majority of review procedures, but a small percentage comprise administrative agencies headed by an executive director (p. 75). Boards may range in size from 3 to 24, with an average of 10 members, and some include police representatives. According to the authors, black and Hispanic communities are represented on almost all citizen review boards, reflecting the conception that the review body directly involves all elements of the community, especially minorities, in the review process (p. 77). The authors found that 27% of the 65 review boards include police officer members, and this membership raises questions about the degree of independence of the boards.

The procedures adopted by these citizen review bodies center on four processes: independent investigating power, the power to issue subpoenas, public hearings, and legal representation. Collectively, these elements produce a criminal trial model of complaint investigation. The alternative is an administrative investigation model that is closed to the public and closely resembles an organizational personnel procedure (Walker and Kreisel 1996: 78–79). The authors found that 34% of all citizen review bodies possess independent investigative power, 38% have subpoena power, about half conduct public hearings, and 32% allow legal representation. However, only about 10% possess all these four elements. There are questions about the appropriateness of the criminal trial model, because in practice in the criminal field, few cases actually go to trial (p. 80). As well, in only a handful of cases do the citizen review bodies have the power to impose discipline on police, and most may only make recommendations to the head of the police department. If the criminal trial model is considered inappropriate, other possibilities are the administrative process, which is more inquisitorial in nature, and forms of mediation that are provided by about 19% of review bodies (p. 80).

From a comparative perspective, in many countries police accountability is lacking, because the administrative response to police wrongdoing is deficient. For example, in Argentina, Ecuador, and Paraguay, police fabricate or destroy evidence for disciplinary proceedings (Mendes 1999: 16). In these countries, police forces tend to be militarized, and the police culture reflects an attitude of isolation and animosity toward citizens. Thus, a crime control approach based on the notion of combat has produced torture and extrajudicial violence (p. 17). Chevigny (1999: 74) reports that in Brazil, where criminal prosecution may often be the only viable method of enforcing police accountability, police often resist the prosecution or interfere in investigations. For example, in Sao Paulo it is common for military police to remove forensic evidence by taking already deceased suspects whom they have murdered to a hospital "as though they are still alive" for this purpose. Similarly police will plant a weapon in the hand of a victim they have killed in a shootout (p. 74).

In Canada, a media focus on wrongdoing by provincial police departments has resulted in a number of public enquiries that have generated a demand for effective police accountability. Thus, in 1987 in Manitoba, in 1989 in British Columbia, and in 1990 in Quebec, provinces created structures of civilian oversight, and in 1986, the Royal Canadian Mounted Police Public Complaints Commission was established (Mendes 1999: 25). The Canadian model of civilian oversight leaves it to the police department concerned to make the initial investigation of a complaint and, where appropriate, to conduct any disciplinary proceedings. Civilian oversight arises only if there is a complaint concerning the internal police process (p. 26).

An Australian study on police accountability suggests a number of criteria that need to be satisfied to establish a viable civilian oversight of policing. These include the following:

- Capacity to conduct independent investigations
- Direct access to the legislature in the form of regular reporting
- An independent resource base, so that government cannot thwart efforts to ensure accountability
- Political and moral support to the oversight body and links between government and the oversight body
- Decentralizing the operations of the civilian oversight body, so that it has the capacity to capture all valid complaints rather than being isolated in one or two large cities (Goldsmith 1999: 54–61)

Police anticorruption measures in Australia have been classified in terms of three models: the minimalist, the intermediate, and the advanced (Prenzler and Ronken 2003: 149). Prenzler and Ronken (2003) suggest that the minimalist model gives primary responsibility to the internal police disciplinary mechanisms. Associated with this model is judicial scrutiny of police misconduct and political oversight through reports to the legislature. The authors judge this minimalist model to be inadequate in terms of preventing police misconduct.

The intermediate model adopts the establishment of internal affairs departments as the key to a more aggressive anticorruption approach. This allows police to develop specialist anticorruption skills and provides a stronger focus for anticorruption efforts. This model emphasizes stricter processes of recruitment and increased stress on ethics in training. As well, this model includes the establishment of independent review bodies. The problem with this approach is that it remains essentially passive and relies substantially on recruitment rejecting undesirable potential police officers and on compliance with codes of ethics and conduct.

In the advanced model, there is recognition that police misconduct can take multiple forms. For example, different sections or units of a police department may experience different problems, and systems must be able to cope with a multiplicity of issues (Prenzler and Ronken 2003: 152). In this model there is a much more proactive approach to corruption. Technology and covert methods of investigation are employed; integrated ethics training is considered essential. There may be random integrity testing, and there is a system of external review that is independent and may adjudicate alleged wrongdoing (p. 153). The authors found that within the eight Australian police departments (there are six state police departments, the Northern Territory Police, and the Australian Federal Police), none had adopted the advanced model, and many had hardly advanced beyond the minimalist model.

In Latin America accountability for wrongdoing is said to be exceptionally deficient, with police accountability structures lacking resources and constrained by corruption (Eijkman 2006: 414). Members of the public are reluctant to complain about police because of fear of retribution and because the lack of political will to eradicate corruption tends to generate police impunity in the region. In Costa Rica, police regard accountability as an activity that interferes with the task of policing, and being held accountable is regarded as something hindering police work (p. 415). The majority of police are never involved in charges of misconduct; nevertheless, internal disciplinary mechanisms do impose accountability; for example, in 2002 eight police officers were dismissed for illegal use of force (p. 419).

Whistle-Blowing

Two general types of whistle-blowers have been identified: *internal whistle-blowers*, who report misconduct to another person within the organization who in turn may take corrective action, such as a supervisor or union representative, and *external whistle-blowers*, who expose abuse to outside agents such as police, lawyers, and the media (Miethe 1999: 15). Both external and internal whistle-blowers blow the whistle because they themselves lack the power to directly change organizational practices. Kleinig (1996: 184) suggests that within police departments, whistle-blowing is often defined as involving any reporting outside of an immediate circle of officers. The term *whistle-blowing* is a substitute for derogatory terms such as *snitch*, *fink*, and *sneak* and was developed in response to the recognition that although citizens have become more vulnerable to the acts of large organizations, many of those same organizations demand a loyalty of their employees that can conflict with the public trust they seek to foster.

Whistle-blowers may have to pay a heavy price for blowing the whistle, and some have been dismissed, demoted, ostracized, and even assaulted and their families threatened because they have violated organizational loyalty (see Case Study 2.3). Miethe (1999: 227) reports that for many whistle-blowers, the experience of whistle-blowing is a transformation of their lives, and the process permanently scars many, because the whistle-blowing event overpowers all other aspects of a person's life. Kleinig (1996) argues that whistle-blowers should be offered protection and suggests anonymity and legislation to protect them against harassment or discrimination.

According to Miethe (1999: 212), whistle-blowers are protected by the Constitution, by federal and state statutes, and by common law. However, protection focuses on the disclosure of particular information to particular sources, and so its extent in a particular case may be unclear. For example, under federal and state law, protection is often restricted to *particular* types of workers who disclose *particular* violations of conduct in a *particular* sequence to *particular* agents.

CASE STUDY 2.3   PUNISHED FOR WHISTLE-BLOWING?

In December 2000, two police officers in Wilkinsburg, Pennsylvania, were punished after questioning their chief about his handling of drug money. The police chief, Gerald Brewer, resigned after an investigation resulting from the two officers' complaints.

The officers were punished through the demotion of Sergeant Robert Tuite to patrol officer and the removal of a police vehicle allocated to Lieutenant Thomas Kocon. A lawyer representing the two officers indicated that he would be filing a retaliation charge against the Borough of Wilkinsburg and would also be taking court action to reverse the officers' punishments. Mayor Wilbert Young, who imposed the punishments, denied they were connected to the whistle-blowing acts of the two officers. Their lawyer noted, however, that the action taken against them could have a chilling effect on police officers in that state.

SOURCE: The Pittsburgh Channel 2000.

When is whistle-blowing morally justified? Bowie (in Kleinig 1996: 185) suggests that moral justification exists if the following conditions have been satisfied:

1. It is done in good faith with the intention of exposing wrongdoing that violates human rights, causes harm to third parties, or violates the purpose of the organization. In other words, it should not be motivated by personal revenge, advancement, or other self-interested reasons.

2. Except in special circumstances, the whistle-blower has exhausted all other internal avenues before going public.

3. The whistle-blower has ensured that there is a proper evidential basis for his or her allegation of misconduct.

4. The whistle-blower has carefully analyzed the seriousness of the misconduct, its immediacy, and its definition.

5. The action of the whistle-blower is consistent with the general responsibility of a citizen to avoid or expose moral violations.

6. It has some chance of success, because if it is unlikely to accomplish any significant change, the act of blowing the whistle lacks credibility.

According to Kleinig, these considerations apply equally to police officers who become aware of corruption; however, he warns that any act of whistle-blowing should be regarded as a last resort, because it indicates that a department has failed to look after its own affairs. His view seems to apply primarily to Miethe's (1999) category of external whistle-blowing.

Thus far, corruption has been explained in terms of the receipt of goods and services and the performance of acts that generally involve some kind of financial or other benefit to a particular individual. However, there are other forms of corruption that have their source in discriminatory practices by police.

Discrimination as Corruption

This discussion is concerned with two aspects of discrimination: racial discrimination, in the form of police discrimination against minorities, and discrimination that the police may exercise in the enforcement of the law, either as individuals or as a result of department policy. Police racism and discrimination against minorities refer to the process through which police stigmatize, harass, criminalize, or otherwise discriminate against certain social groups on the basis of cultural markers or national origin (Chan 1997: 17). Police racism can arise in various situations, can take different forms and levels of intensity, and can reveal itself in the form of acts ranging from prejudicial attitudes and discriminatory law enforcement practices to the use of excessive violence against minority groups. Police, like other citizens, may show insensitivity to language and cultural diversity, and while this may not amount to racial discrimination as such, it may well have an influence on police attitudes toward certain minority groups.

Studies have shown evidence of prejudicial attitudes and the regular use of racist language among police officers (Skolnick 1966). The Christopher Commission in Los Angeles, formed after the Rodney King incident, found abusive language by police officers to be prevalent and identified many computer messages between patrol officers that contained racially offensive language such as "I'm back here in the project, pissing off the natives" and "Just got mexercise for the night." White, Cox, and Basehart (in Walker, Spohn, and DeLone 2000: 105) argue that the employment of general profanity by police serves the function of labeling, dominating, and controlling citizens.

In relation to prejudicial attitudes, a study comparing the attitudes of Denver police officers with those of the general public found that police officers were only slightly more prejudiced than the community as a whole. This may suggest that police are essentially ordinary citizens and not significantly different from the general population in their attitudes. However, police have a fundamental desire to be respected, and their inclination when they perceive a community as showing a lack of respect is to react by increasing police activity in that community. It is significant that officers assigned to racial or ethnic minority communities, high-crime areas, and poor neighborhoods in the Denver study believed they received less respect from the public than officers working in other areas.

Skolnick (1994 in Walker et al. 2000) argues that the tendency of police to stereotype people, also called *racial profiling*, is an intrinsic aspect of police work, because officers are trained to be suspicious and to search for criminal activity. Consequently, they develop a "perceptual shorthand" that they believe allows them to pick out suspects among the general population. They identify suspects by relying on visual signs such as dress, demeanor, gender, and age (see Case Studies 2.4 and 2.5). Additionally, Reiner (1985) found that young, low-income, ethnic males were more likely to be stopped and questioned by the police, and minorities were also more likely to be arrested, although there is some discussion that this might be due to factors such as perceived disrespect shown by suspects to police. The same study noted that while police used excessive force against white citizens twice as much as against blacks, the findings were reversed in cases of the use of deadly force.

Racial profiling has become a source of major concern to the African American community, particularly in light of the Rodney King incident and others, where police are alleged to have used excessive force and to have racially profiled African Americans. Studies show that in the 1960s and early 1970s, police fatally shot seven African Americans for every white person (Walker et al. 2000: 95), but following the Supreme Court's decision to declare unconstitutional the *fleeing felon rule* (allowing police to shoot to kill any fleeing suspected felon), the racial disparity between persons shot and killed has narrowed to about 3 to 1 (p. 96). The fact remains that while police continue to profile minority groups in law enforcement activities, there is a greater likelihood that disparity between whites and African Americans in shooting incidents will continue. Case studies 2.4 and 2.5 provide examples of racial profiling.

CASE STUDY 2.4 "LOOKING MEXICAN"

In July, 1997, the city of Chandler, a suburb of Phoenix, Arizona, with a population of 143,000, began Operation Restoration, which was intended to construct a new civic center, including police headquarters, municipal court, and library and revitalize the town. Since its founding in 1912, Chandler had become two cities: one affluent, the other the old impoverished downtown area.

Seeking a cause for the city center's decay, city officials fixed on illegal immigration and focused on alleged criminal activity by illegal immigrants. The city police and the border patrol collaborated on a plan linked to Operation Restoration, and on the first day of the operation, two dozen police officers and five border patrol agents moved through the downtown area, chasing suspected illegal immigrants from worksites and filling up buses with those they captured. In all, police eventually removed 432 illegal immigrants, all but 3 from Mexico.

However, the illegal immigrants in Chandler coexist with a large, well-established Mexican American community, with Latinos making up about 15% of the population. As police questioned those leaving markets favored by Latinos, they encountered U.S. citizens from whom they also demanded identification and immigration papers. The police operations targeted legal residents and U.S. citizens who "looked Mexican."

Four months later, the Arizona attorney general revealed the results of his inquiry into this raid. These included that Chandler police had stopped residents, questioned them, and entered their homes without warrants, relying only on skin color, Mexican appearance, or use of Spanish language to identify them as suspected illegal immigrants. Moreover, the city officials had not requested formal permission from the U.S. attorney general to act against illegal immigrants as is required by federal law.

The city manager officially reprimanded the police chief for the raid, and a group of Latinos launched a $35 million lawsuit against the city. Latinos commented that it would take 10 or 15 years for people to feel comfortable again in the town.

SOURCE: Tobar 1998.

CASE STUDY 2.5 RACIAL PROFILING: WHEN COLOR SIGNALS DANGEROUSNESS

Case One. In Phoenix, Arizona, police questioned a man sitting in his car outside an apartment building. Why was he questioned? Police said he appeared nervous, he moved his car when a marked police car approached, and most of all, as one police officer reported, he was a Mexican male just sitting in his car in a mainly white neighborhood.

Case Two. At the Kansas City airport, a Drug Enforcement Agency agent stopped and questioned a young man. Why was he stopped and questioned? The agent reported that the man was young and not well dressed and had arrived on a direct flight from Los Angeles, known to be a source for drugs. He had no checked luggage, only two carry-on bags, and he walked rapidly to a taxi after his flight. He appeared also to be nervous. The fact that he was black was a factor in the agent's decision to stop him.

Case Three. In California, officers of the Border Patrol questioned the driver of a vehicle at the highway checkpoint some 30 miles north of the U.S.–Mexico border. They also searched his vehicle. Why was he questioned? They were prompted to do so because he was of Mexican ancestry.

Case Four. In Boston, over a period of several weeks, police stopped, questioned, and searched young black men at random following a report that a white man's pregnant wife had been shot and killed in that neighborhood by a black man.

Case Five. In New York City, police stopped and searched a young black man who alighted from a commuter train. He was clean shaven, was carrying a briefcase, and was 6 feet 4 inches tall. Why was he stopped and searched? Police were investigating a report that a black man who regularly rode the train

(Continued)

(Continued)

carried a gun. The report came in the form of an anonymous letter, and the man described in the letter was 5 feet 10 inches tall and had a mustache.

Case Six. After police received a tip that a white man with a bomb was inside an office building, they surrounded the building and entered. They examined white men more closely than nonwhite men.

SOURCE: Kennedy 1991.

Case Seven. Complaints by Arab Americans against racial profiling by airlines have reportedly increased since 9/11, according to the American-Arab Anti-Discrimination Committee. The committee is aware of passengers with a Muslim or Middle Eastern appearance who have been removed from planes. For example, an Iranian-born U.S. citizen who was a software developer living in Dallas was on his way home from Seattle, and, while reading his paper on an American Airlines plane, was approached by an airline employee holding a passenger manifest. He was told to leave the plane because the pilot did not feel comfortable with him aboard. Reportedly, the pilot did not like how he looked. He was questioned by three airport police about where he lived, his marital status, his religion, and where he worked, and he was treated like a suspect. He was allowed to board the next flight to Dallas, and when the plane landed, apologies were offered by an airline official.

SOURCE: CNN.com/Travel 2001.

Analyzing cases of physical assault on minorities by police, Rice (in Walker et al. 2000: 98) found that almost half the victims of excessive police force had either defied the officer's authority or resisted arrest, and that African American suspects were more likely to be disrespectful than whites. He also found that police were more likely to use force against marginalized persons, such as alcoholics and the homeless, and that race in itself was not a determining factor in the use of force. Rather, he concluded, class and not race determined police misconduct, and the typical victim of excessive force was a lower-class male. Whatever may be the true position, it is significant that a 1991 Gallup Poll reported that 45% of African Americans believed there was police brutality in their neighborhood, compared to only 33% of whites (p. 99). Ultimately therefore, it appears, rightly or wrongly, that police are perceived by certain sections of the public to be more likely to brutalize them, and police must address this perception in their interaction with minorities.

The question raised by racial profiling is whether it is morally right to use a person's race as an indication of increased likelihood of criminal conduct. Should police stop African Americans simply because there is official statistical evidence that young African American men are disproportionately involved in drug or gang activity? Kennedy (in Walker et al. 2000: 104) argues that race should be used as the basis for a police action only in extraordinary circumstances. Prohibiting arrest by reference to racial profiling reduces the possibility of police harassment and the perception among minorities that police harbor racial attitudes toward them. Additionally, the hostility created by profiling tends to form barriers in those communities where police find it most difficult to operate, and profiling may also support segregation in the sense that African Americans become reluctant to venture into white neighborhoods for fear of police harassment.

The general public associates racial profiling with traffic stops, and some have argued that the police practice of stopping a disproportionate number of minority citizens for their driving infractions is so pervasive that it should be termed the crime of "driving while black." According to the Bureau of Justice Statistics (Smith and Durose 2006), in 2002 an estimated 8.7% of drivers aged 16 or older were stopped by police, and 11% of young male drivers were physically searched or their vehicle was searched. Among these, blacks (22%) and Hispanics (17%) were searched at higher rates than whites (8%). A number of studies suggest that targeting minority motorists does occur at least in some jurisdictions, and a number of police departments are now recording traffic stop information to establish whether they are racially biased (Warren et al. 2006: 710).

Racial profiling is less likely to be a factor in a routine speeding stop by a highway patrol officer, because it is often difficult to identify the driver's race because of the speed of the vehicle, and also such stops are usually the result of speed detectors rather than sighting the race of the driver (Warren et al. 2006: 714). In one study conducted in 2000 in North Carolina that compared race disparities in highway patrol stops and in local police stops, researchers found only slight evidence of racial disparity in the highway patrol stops but stronger evidence in stops by local police (p. 709).

Police may act on their stereotypical images of suspicious conduct by stopping, questioning, and frisking people on the street, and this practice is a source of tension between police and the community. A study in San Diego found that nearly half of those stopped and questioned were African Americans, despite the fact that African Americans made up only 17.5% and 4.8%, respectively, of the populations of the two precincts covered by the study (Walker et al. 2000). Moreover, all those stopped and questioned were male, and about 60% were juveniles.

The furor concerning racial profiling has spread to Canada, and in 2003 the police in Kingston, Ontario, conducted the first racial profiling survey, in which police officers were asked to record data on pedestrians and drivers they interrogated, suspected, questioned, searched, or detained (Closs and McKenna 2006: 144). The study found that black male residents of the city between the ages of 15 and 24 were three times more likely to be stopped and questioned by police than people from other racial backgrounds (p. 149). Police justify stopping and questioning on the street as an effective crime fighting measure, intended to deter potential offenders through police scrutiny of them and to provide reassurance to the general public that patrol officers are protecting ordinary citizens.

Racial profiling is not confined to the police; other government agencies have also been accused of the same practice. For example, in 2000 the General Accounting Office revealed that even before the War on Terror commencing in 2001, African American women traveling by air into the U.S. were being disproportionately targeted for custom searches (Newsome 2003: 32). The report found that these women were more likely than members of other groups to receive intrusive searches, including X-rays and strip searches.

From the point of view of the public, race and ethnicity play a major part in shaping public attitudes toward police. For example, in a 1998 survey, 61% of white Americans surveyed reported "a great deal" or "quite a lot" of confidence in the police, whereas only 10% had "very little" confidence. However, of the African Americans surveyed, only 34% fell into the first category, and 25% had "very little" confidence in the police (Walker et al. 2000: 91). Police tend to be negatively evaluated by residents in high-crime neighborhoods and by those who fear the incidence of crime in their neighborhoods (Schafer, Huebner, and Bynum 2003: 447), especially when they use aggressive policing techniques designed for zero tolerance policing which have resulted in disproportionate arrest rates for blacks (Eck and Maguire 2005: 228). In the case of Hispanics, attitudes fall somewhere between those of whites and African Americans. As already noted, age can be a factor in police profiling, and age also factors into the views of young people toward the police, because young people, regardless of race, consistently have a more negative view of police than their elders. This can be explained by their more active presence on the street and their greater level of contact with police (Walker et al. 2000: 92).

Police selectivity in enforcing laws may have the effect of discriminating against certain groups in society. For example, police treatment of domestic violence cases has historically involved a pattern of noninterference based on the assumption that such violence was not a proper subject of crime control, unless it involved injury that could be defined as felony assault. Additionally, police gave priority to family solidarity and acted or failed to act in accordance with that goal (Fyfe in Kleinig 1996: 184). Thus, women who were battered by their partners received discriminatory treatment by police, because whether or not action was taken against the batterer depended on whether the crime was considered a felony or a misdemeanor. Similarly, selective enforcement by the police can offer less protection to rape victims, because most rape victims are victimized by known intimates, and police enforcement practice focuses on stranger rapists.

Having discussed various forms of police corruption, this analysis of ethical issues in policing will now consider how ethical issues arise in the detection and investigation of crime. Police regularly interact with suspects and arrested persons, and seek to solve crime through the processes of interrogation and investigation. These interactions can generate important ethical questions and issues.

Ethical Issues in Investigation, Interrogation, and Custody

Ethical issues may arise when police are investigating incidents that suggest a crime has been committed and where persons are suspected of criminal conduct. In investigating crime, police must have regard for the rights of suspects, be sensitive to issues of privacy, and be aware of the moralities associated with attempting to entrap individuals.

Rights of Suspects

A suspect—that is, a person who is only *suspected* of having committed a crime—has certain moral rights as well as specifically defined legal rights. These include a right to life, a right not to suffer ill treatment, and a right to privacy. *Suspects* who become accused persons are entitled to a fair trial, and a trial can be considered fair only if it is based on evidence. It follows that suspects are morally entitled to be convicted based only on evidence that is real and not fabricated and on evidence given by truthful witnesses. Fabricating evidence or committing perjury violates the moral rights of suspects, affects the fairness of trials and ultimately undermines the administration of justice.

Police also have a duty to the *victim* of a crime that extends to the victim's family if there is a need to protect persons who have been terrorized by the crime, although not its direct target. Fundamentally, police are under an obligation to employ the greatest possible effort to apprehend a suspect and to provide evidence for a successful prosecution. In doing this, they satisfy their ethical obligation toward the victim (Miller et al. 1997).

Privacy

This is a constitutional right and a moral right that a person possesses in relation to others, particularly with regard to information possessed by others or in relation to the observation of others. A violation of privacy takes place through acts such as observation and body searches. Similarly, a person's intimate personal relations with others must be regarded as a privacy issue, as is information relating to the ownership of objects or assets where there is a presumption that the person need not disclose assets except in defined circumstances, such as tax collection. Also regarded as private are facts concerned with a person's public roles, such as voting decisions and business plans. Finally, the law grants privacy in respect of certain data collected relating to an individual that may be released only under defined conditions.

The right to privacy is clearly not absolute, and a balance has to be achieved between rights to privacy and confidentiality and rights to protection from crime. In achieving this balance, Miller et al. (1997: 204–205) advocate applying the following principles:

1. Accessing and interception are prima facie an infringement of privacy and are presumed a violation that ought not to be overridden except in exceptional circumstances.

2. The benefits of violating privacy must be greater than the likely costs, especially the cost of reducing public trust in those who seek to violate privacy.

3. Accessing and interception ought to relate to a serious crime; there ought to be probable cause that the person whose privacy is to be violated has committed the crime and that the resulting information is likely to further the investigation of that crime.

4. There must be no practicable alternative method of gathering the information.

5. Law enforcement officials must be accountable for the violation in terms of obtaining any necessary warrant.

6. Persons whose privacy has been violated should be informed of the violation at the earliest possible moment consistent with not compromising the investigation.

Miller et al. (1997) suggest this framework of principles should regulate police action that might violate the right to privacy.

Entrapment

Miller et al. (1997: 206–207) suggest that the practice of entrapment includes operations, such as surveillance, undercover investigations, and entrapment itself, which are of a covert nature and involve deception of one kind or another. Deception seems to be an inevitable part of law enforcement and may not necessarily infringe on moral rights. Entrapment, however, is regarded as morally problematic because of the belief that the offender involved in a case of entrapment has not attained the required degree of criminality to be arrested and must therefore be entrapped. Entrapment may be random or targeted at a particular person or persons, and random entrapment is considered particularly morally problematic. In the case of targeted entrapment, moral objections may cease to apply if certain conditions are met. These are the following:

1. There is sufficient evidence to believe that the target is likely to commit a crime.

2. The person would have committed the crime or a similar crime whether he or she was a victim of the entrapment or not.

3. The entrapment succeeds as a technique of detection where other methods, such as complaints investigation, have failed.

The second condition is the most morally problematic, because it assumes facts that cannot really be clearly ascertained and relies on evidence such as the suspect's disposition to commit crimes, which is a matter of subjective interpretation. It also relies on evidence of opportunity, and this, together with disposition, would lead to the formation of an intention to commit the crime.

In the United States, entrapment is considered a legal limit on the government's use of deception in investigation, and it occurs when a government agent, usually a police officer, initiates action that induces an otherwise innocent person to commit a crime so that he or she may be prosecuted. Entrapment operates as a defense, which, if established, will result in an acquittal. The courts apply a *subjective test* in determining whether the defense of entrapment has been proven. This involves the court looking at the mental predisposition of the offender to commit the crime rather than the objective methods of the police (Marx 1985; Skolnick 1982; Stitt and James 1985). In 1958, a minority of the Supreme Court, in *Sherman v. United States*, proposed an *objective test*, focusing on the nature of the police conduct, as opposed to the predisposition of the offender. Under this test, the court would look at the character of the state's involvement in the commission of the offense; in other words, it would make an assessment of whether the police acted in such a way as would be likely to instigate or create a criminal offense.

Kleinig (1996: 158) suggests an alternative approach based on the nature of the government's involvement in the entrapment, arguing that sometimes this involvement figures so large that it suggests a lack of confidence that the individual would have committed the particular offense. He suggests that if this degree of involvement can be determined, the defense of entrapment should be available (see Box 2.9). He focuses on the power of the government to draw into the entrapment those who might not otherwise engage in that kind of conduct. Barker and Carter (1995) offer the example of the Broward County, Florida, sheriff's department, which began to manufacture $20,000 worth of crack cocaine when it did not have enough crack to provide to undercover officers, to illustrate a situation where the government's involvement could easily be objectively assessed as entrapment. Box 2.10 shows an example of an unsuccessful entrapment defense.

A CLOSER LOOK

BOX 2.9
A Successful Entrapment Defense

On July 31, 2000, Indianapolis police officer Genae Gehring was working an undercover vice detail as a prostitute on the east side of the city along with about 10 other officers, with the objective of arresting those soliciting for prostitution. At about 4 p.m. on that day, James Ferge was driving his truck and was stopped at a two way stop sign. Officer Gehring was walking and made eye contact with Ferge in his stationary truck. She walked over to his vehicle and they spoke. He asked if she needed a ride and invited her to get in. She asked him if he was "looking for a little more," and he replied in the affirmative. She then asked if he was "looking for a little head," and again he replied in the affirmative, and she then suggested a price of $20, to which he agreed.

She told him to meet her in an alley behind a building close to the intersection and walked over to that location. Instead of proceeding to the alley, Ferge drove in another direction for about seven blocks until he was stopped by the police and arrested.

On August 1, 2001, Ferge was charged with patronizing a prostitute, which is a Class A misdemeanor, and at his trial he claimed that he offered the officer a ride because it was raining, that he could not understand everything she said because of the noise of the diesel engine, that he was surprised when she asked him some questions about sex, and that so far as he was concerned, he would give her a ride if she wanted, but if she did not, that was the end of it. He was found guilty, sentenced to serve a year, and given credit for 4 days. The remaining 361 days were suspended, and he was placed on probation for 180 days.

(Continued)

(Continued)

Ferge appealed, arguing that the state had failed to produce enough evidence to negate his defense of entrapment. Under Indiana Code, entrapment is a defense if the conduct charged was the result of a law enforcement officer using persuasion likely to cause the person to engage in the conduct and if the person charged was not predisposed to commit the offense. The court on appeal said that the defense of entrapment turns on the defendant's state of mind, and, in this case, the state had to prove beyond reasonable doubt that Ferge had a predisposition to commit the crime.

The court said that the evidence at trial showed that the police officer initiated the conversation about sex and that the defendant did not meet the officer in the alley but instead drove away until stopped by the police. According to the court, the suggestion of criminal activity, that is, sexual activity, was made by the police officer after Ferge offered her a ride, and his action in driving away from the alley where he had been told to meet her showed that he did not intend to make a deal with her and was therefore evidence that he was not predisposed to commit the crime. Accordingly, the state had not presented enough evidence to prove the crime, and Ferge had successfully established the defense of entrapment.

SOURCE: *Ferge v. State* 2002.

A CLOSER LOOK

BOX 2.10
An Unsuccessful Entrapment Defense

On January 8, 2007, Shahawar Matin Siraj, a Pakistani, was sentenced to 30 years in prison for planning to blow up the Herald Square subway station on 34th Street in New York City. Siraj claimed that he was entrapped by a paid police informant who showed him photographs of inmates being abused at Abu Ghraib prison in Iraq and who recorded on tape his responses in the form of threats against the United States. He was convicted of conspiracy based partly on testimony of police informant Osama Eldawoody, an Egyptian American who was recruited by New York police to monitor radical Muslims following 9/11. Siraj admitted taking preliminary steps to attack the subway station but claimed he had only done so at Eldawoody's prompting. His entrapment defense seemed to have convinced at least half the members of the jury early in the trial, but they later dismissed it. His defense was aided by the fact that the police paid Eldawoody a total of $100,000 for his work as an informer. The defense claimed it was this salary that kept Eldawoody interested in interacting with Siraj and in encouraging Siraj in his plotting.

SOURCE: Hays 2007.

Deception

To what extent, if any, are police entitled to rely on deception in order to promote law enforcement? There are many forms of verbal and nonverbal deception,
and police deception may take forms such as withholding and manipulating information, lying, using ruses, using informants, enacting sting operations, installing
wiretaps and bugging devices, creating false friendships, manufacturing evidence,
and using the good cop/bad cop routine in interrogations (Kleinig 1996: 124).
Many of these forms of deception involve lying in one form or another.

Skolnick (1982), in considering police deception, focuses on three stages of
deception: investigative deception, interrogatory deception, and testimonial deception. He makes the point that the acceptability of deception varies according to the
stage reached in the criminal process. Deception is most acceptable to police and
the courts at the investigation stage, less acceptable during interrogation, and least
acceptable in the courtroom. The reason for this is that each stage implies a greater
number of constraints in the criminal justice process. For example, testimony in
court is given under oath, but in the process of interrogation, it is not.

Investigative Deception

The line between deception and entrapment, and the fact that police justify lying
in the investigative stage as the means justifying the end (noble cause corruption),
has already been discussed. Skolnick (1982) suggests that the courts impose fewer
constraints on lying during this stage, and that judicial acceptance of deception in
the investigation process tends to have the effect of making deception in the other
stages of the process more acceptable morally, and, therefore, likely to increase its
occurrence. In other words, deception in one context is likely to increase its probability in others. For example, Kleinig (1996: 135) points out that both the courts
and society accept the limited use of investigative techniques such as the use of
informants, wiretapping and bugging, unmarked patrol cars, and concealed radar
traps. Marx (2001: 262) contends that there are minimal ethical objections in using
decoys as potential victims to combat a pattern of sexual assault and harassment.
He gives the example of a policewoman used as a decoy after a series of rapes in a
public park. Acceptability here is judged by the fact that crimes have already been
committed, that there has been coercion by an offender, and that the policewoman
acting as decoy is a relatively passive response.

Interrogatory Deception

In the 1966 case *Miranda v. Arizona*, which dealt with the interrogation of a suspect in the custody of the police, the court held that arrested persons must be
informed of their rights to remain silent, that any statement they make may be used
as evidence, that they have the right to the presence of an attorney, and that an attorney will be provided if they cannot afford one. In addition, the court determined
that the state is under a heavy burden in attempting to prove that any waiver of these
rights occurred voluntarily, knowingly, and intelligently. The *Miranda* decision

evolved out of the admission in courts of confessions that were obtained with the use of torture, in the early period, and later, with the use of the third degree, and then using techniques of deception and psychological pressure.

As Kleinig (1996: 138) notes, sometimes interrogations are characterized as "interviews," where the language used is more respectful and the investigating officer constructs himself as a "seeker of truth" rather than "an accuser." Police interviews do not require the police to Mirandize the suspect. However, every custodial situation is inherently coercive, and depending on the circumstances, bears on the issue of whether what a person says can be said to be voluntary. It is clear that in a custodial interrogation, police are able to control the physical conditions of the encounter, the length of the interrogation, the time given to the suspect to respond to questioning, and, generally, the terms under which it takes place. The outcome of the coercive nature of the interrogation, when combined with the police control of it, is that an innocent person or a person easily intimidated may react in ways that imply guilt. Further, a guilty person may be persuaded to confess to a more serious offense than the one he or she has committed. Questions of the mental capacity of the person being interrogated may also arise. In its investigations, the Innocence Project has uncovered many cases in which confessions have been shown to be false, and some of these were given in response to police threats that, absent a confession, the accused person would face the death penalty.

Testimonial Deception

Kleinig (1996) points out that a good deal of police testimonial deception is said to be directed at securing *worthy ends;* that is, the control of crime and the conviction of those responsible (noble cause corruption). However, the police often take the view not only that deception in testifying is done with the aim of furthering the noble cause, but also that they are forced to practice deception in order to correct deficiencies in the criminal justice system. Police might argue that the standards of proof required of the state, the constitutional restraints under which police operate that protect the rights of suspects, and the abilities of cunning defense lawyers and unsympathetic judges mean that the odds are stacked against them, and that evidence therefore ought not to be excluded by technicalities or a case lost because of a clever lawyer. This ignores the fact that *the task of the police is to arrest and apprehend and not convict,* and that police ought to be satisfied at having fulfilled their role within the criminal justice system.

However, like others, police experience dissatisfaction if their work does not produce the desired end. Proposals for reducing police perjury, such as sensitizing police to the dangers of perjury, having laypersons accompany police when executing a search warrant, subjecting police witnesses to lie detection, and requiring that all police action be videotaped, are discussed by Slobogin (1996).

Lying

Barker and Carter (1995) offer a typography of police lying comprising accepted lying, tolerated lying, and deviant lying. In considering *accepted lying,* they note that certain forms of lying are an accepted part of police work, the justification being that they fulfill the objective of controlling crime and arresting the guilty; that is, the noble cause of policing. While lying may be acceptable to the police themselves, this does not answer the question of whether their lies are ethically acceptable. Many deceptive practices involve lying in the broad sense, especially in undercover operations, and in such cases, police must be aware of the possible defense of entrapment. According to Barker and Carter, police believe that it is proper to lie to the media or the public when necessary to protect the innocent, to protect the image of the department, or to bring calm in a crisis. So far as the police are concerned, a lie is acceptable if the following are true:

- The lie is made in pursuit of a legitimate organizational goal.
- There is a clear relationship between deceiving and achieving that organizational goal.
- The lying is such that police and management within the police believe that lying will better serve the public interest than providing the truth.
- The ethical and legal aspect of lying is not considered a concern.

In *tolerated lying,* lies are tolerated as necessary evils, and police will admit a lie when confronted. Again, from the police perspective such lies are seen as necessary to the policing mission. An example is using lies and deception to handle what police regard as "nuisance work" as opposed to "real police work." Given that police are called out to deal with a wide variety of problems, most of which do not involve criminal activity, they sometimes promise to investigate a matter or threaten to take action when they have no intention of doing so, for example, in domestic violence cases, where the officer may have no warrant to arrest, but feels that something needs to be done and may threaten to take action. Similarly, sometimes police lie in a situation where they have no legal authority, for example, telling people on the street to move along when they have no legal basis for giving such a direction.

In the important area of police interrogation, lies are tolerated, and police are even trained to lie. Standard police texts on interrogation techniques advocate and instruct in deceptive and lying practices employed in interrogation. For instance, it is recommended that the officer conducting an interrogation seem sincere to such an extent that he may appear tearful or that an interrogator present a fabricated evidence file to a suspect. A familiar interrogation technique is to separate two suspected offenders and play off one against the other, and here, the interrogation texts suggest that the interrogator may actually inform one suspect that the other has confessed. Again, the justification for these techniques is said to be the noble cause of enforcing the law. Nevertheless, an attitude suggesting that using lies in interrogation is an acceptable practice, because it serves the end of the noble cause, can constitute the beginning of another slippery slope toward what Barker and Carter (1995) call deviant lying.

In *deviant lying,* police use lies that violate police regulations as well as the law. The major example here is police perjuring themselves in giving evidence in court, and at least one well-known defense attorney believes that almost all police lie in court (see Dershowitz 1983). Some police have even developed their own term for police perjury called "testilying" (Commission to Investigate Allegations of Corruption and Anti-Corruption Procedures of the Police Department, City of New York 1994). Barker (1996) has asserted that the public has lost confidence in the police as a result of high-profile cases like the O. J. Simpson trial, and he argues that the effect of this is to create an expectation that police will engage in testilying.

Kleinig (1996: 126) discusses the consequences of police lying and identifies three deleterious consequences:

- *Others Are Harmed.* This occurs in the sense that persons are led to do what they have not chosen to do. They may also be deprived of their possessions or placed at physical risk.
- *Social Trust Is Destroyed.* The argument here is that a person who is lied to and who discovers the lie suffers the consequence of cynicism, and this may in turn affect his or her interactions with others, because suspicion erodes trust.
- *The Liar Is Harmed.* This may occur through the liar becoming more evasive for fear of being found out, developing a suspicion of others, and perhaps developing a reduced ability to resist other forms of corruption.

Finally, having reviewed the major forms of police corruption within the overall framework of noble cause corruption, it is necessary to consider the rationale for police corruption.

Explanations for Police Corruption

How can we explain or understand why police corruption occurs? As we have seen, explanations focus on the individual police officer, on the institutional culture of policing, and on society in general. In the individual approach, corruption is explained as a consequence of a bad moral character, and the principal motive is the pursuit of personal gain. This explanation also accounts for the rotten apple theory, which argues that a handful of corrupt officers can corrupt an entire department. Explanations founded on the institutional culture of policing suggest that the police commitment to good ends, also called the noble cause, can produce a way of thinking about police work that justifies acts of misconduct on the basis that the noble cause of policing justifies bending the rules (Crank and Caldero 2000: 29). The noble cause

> is a profound moral commitment to make the world a safer place to live. Put simply, it is getting bad guys off the street. Police believe that they're on the side of angels and their purpose in life is getting rid of bad guys . . . it's something to which they are morally committed . . . the noble cause is practical and immediate. It's about an officer's conduct in day to day police work. It motivates an officer's behavior with citizens and mobilizes a great deal of police solidarity. (Crank and Caldero 2000: 35)

One aspect of noble cause corruption is the tendency of police to believe that suspects are guilty even where there may be insufficient evidence, or no evidence at all, of guilt. For the police, the following elements justify their thinking (Klockars 1980):

1. *The Operative Assumption of Guilt.* As part of police culture, police assume suspects are guilty, believing that questionable behavior is evidence of some offense.

2. *The Worst of All Possible Guilt.* Not only do police assume guilt, but they also associate danger with that guilt in the belief that someone who has the most to hide will try to hide it by all possible means, including putting the police themselves at risk. It follows that police must discover the truth as quickly as possible, and this justifies the use of severe interrogation techniques.

3. *The Great Guilty Place Assumption.* Given that police are suspicious and tend to operate in selective environments, they see danger where others might see none.

4. *The Not Guilty (This Time) Assumption.* Police do not conclude that a person is innocent when they find no evidence of guilt. They believe that most people have committed crimes but have been fortunate enough not to be caught and that using a little pressure will often show the guilt of the seemingly innocent.

Crank and Caldero (2000) argue that the idea of the noble cause represents a value imported into police work from broader American life. In this sense, the police are no different than others, and they reflect a particular cultural value incorporating a concern for victims and the notion that no one should stand above the law. Other commentators (Delattre 1989; Klockars 1980; Muir 1977) have recognized the existence of noble cause thinking in police work. In addition, Skolnick and Fyfe (1993: 89), in their discussion of police culture, argue that aspects of that culture, such as the police notion of suspicious persons, the *Dirty Harry* problem, the siege mentality (the idea that police emphasize crime control over all police work, this being the police concept of professionalism—a notion that tends to isolate the police from the community), and the code of silence within police departments, together with the police perception of themselves as soldiers engaged in a war on crime, shapes the worldview of the individual police officer on the street. This leads to the conclusion, for example, that "police brutality is inevitable" (Skolnick and Fyfe 1993: 133). It is easy to see that such a worldview can be employed in justifying misconduct in pursuit of the noble cause.

Crank and Caldero (2000: 75) emphasize that when applying the justification of noble cause to corruption, police place personal morality above the law and act as if they are the law. In such an ethical environment, any efforts to control police behavior will be viewed as disloyal, because, in their view, if police are the law, what they do must be right. Consequently, accepting free dinners to look after a restaurant is considered acceptable practice because "society owes it to them," and mistreating suspects means suspects are "getting what they deserve," because police have already decided they are guilty. In contrast to the rotten apple explanation for corruption, when corruption is justified on grounds of noble cause, officers who carry out acts of misconduct themselves are not considered rotten apples but are perceived to be dealing with crime efficiently and effectively. During the O. J. Simpson murder trial, the noble cause explanation came to light when it was revealed that Mark Fuhrman had once stated,

> (If) you find a (needle) mark (on a drug suspect) that looks like three days old, pick the scab. Squeeze it. Looks like serum's coming out, as if it were hours old. . . . That's not falsifying a report. That's putting a criminal in jail. That's being a policeman. (Dershowitz 1996: 55)

Another, more sympathetic explanation for police corruption is offered by Johnston (1995: 301), who suggests that corruption is produced by the pressures society has imposed on police. Citizens place the police in a position of tension, where they are expected to enforce the law but also to obey regulations about how they may obtain information and gather evidence. They are also expected to enforce personal morality while respecting constitutional rights to privacy and due process. Johnston argues that so long as we continue to place these pressures on police, we are fated to endure a certain degree of police corruption and that we should move on to consider the sorts of social behavior we have no choice but to accept and consider questions such as how much police corruption we can tolerate. In essence, therefore, this argument sanctions a level of police corruption and leaves open the question of the extent to that level.

Summary

In the past, effective policing in the United States depended on the police being able to physically dominate the streets. Police were seen as an arm of whichever political party was in power, and there was little or no conception that police needed to observe ethical standards and norms. Police corruption and police abuse of power are inextricably linked to the nature of policing and to police culture. The policing model may be that of the officer as the crime fighter, the emergency operator, or the social peacekeeper, and the type of model chosen by a police department influences relations between the police and community, police culture, and the overall ethical standards employed in policing. Police culture is enormously important in determining the level of police corruption or misconduct, because if the culture adopts the characteristics of cynicism, the use of force in all situations, and the notion that police themselves are victims, ethical standards will take second place to the noble cause of fighting the war against crime.

The police have extensive discretionary powers that can be used for good or ill, and some argue that this discretion is too wide and should be curtailed by the law and by departmental rules and regulations. Others argue that placing limits on discretion is the only feasible option but acknowledge that enforcing these limits can be problematic. Public opinion seems to accept that police should have wide discretion to counter crime, but individual members of the public complain when that wide discretion is directed at them.

Codes of ethics may be one way of limiting police discretion, but there are problems with codes of ethics being rhetorical instruments directed toward a vaguely defined "public." In any event, the evidence seems to show that police mostly depend on their personal notion of ethics.

Police misuse of force is a major area where ethical considerations come up against the practicalities of police work. Although there are rules that stipulate the degree of force to be used in given situations, ultimately the police themselves decide in their discretion what degree of force it is necessary to employ. Their decisions will be influenced by police culture and by the historical fact that force was employed as a matter of course. Often incidents of excessive force will be characterized as aberrations by particular officers rather than as a systemic issue. Questions about appropriate levels of force will continue to be raised, especially where egregious instances of brutality and violence occur.

Police practices in apprehension, investigation, and interrogation may be ethically questionable, because they may violate the rights of suspects, entrap them, and invade their privacy. Methods of deception, especially lying, are an accepted part of police work. Again, these techniques are often justified as the means of supporting the "noble cause," although some argue that it is necessary to accept a degree of police corruption as the price we pay for keeping communities safe.

DISCUSSION QUESTIONS

1. Discuss the ways in which the noble cause argument explains and helps police rationalize police misconduct and involvement in corruption.

2. Are codes of ethics important in guiding police practices and minimizing police misconduct? Explain.

3. How does police culture influence police perceptions about their role and about the means they should use to carry out their duties?

4. Is there any relationship between the style of policing chosen by a department and the ethical practices it feels are legitimate for its officers to use in carrying out their duties?

5. Is it possible or desirable to limit police discretion, and would this step have the effect of minimizing ethical misconduct by police officers?

6. Is it entrapment if the police attempt to catch child molesters on the Internet by pretending to be juveniles?

7. Why do some argue that it is correct to describe racial profiling as a form of police corruption? Explain the effects of this practice.

8. Compare systemic and individualistic explanations of police corruption.

9. What measures can be taken to control the use of excessive force by police?

WEB RESOURCES

Bureau of Justice Statistics, U.S. Department of Justice. http://www.usdoj.gov/bjs

Community Centered Policing: A Force for Change. PolicyLink. http://www.policylink.org/pdfs/ForceForChange.pdf

International Association of Chiefs of Police. http://www.theiacp.org

National Organization of Black Enforcement Executives (NOBLE). http://www.noblenational.org/

Organized for Change: An Activist Guide to Police Reform. http://www.policylink.org/Research/PoliceAdvocacy/

Police Executive Research Forum. http://www.policeforum.org

Racial Profiling Data Collection Resource Center, Northeastern University. http://www.racialprofilinganalysis.neu.edu

Vera Institute of Justice. http://www.vera.org

CHAPTER 3

Racial Discrimination in the Criminal Justice System

Ethical Background

It is generally agreed that discrimination based on racial or ethnic origin is morally wrong and a violation of the principle of equality. The equality principle requires that those who are equal be treated equally based on similarities, and that race not be a relevant consideration in that assessment (May and Sharratt 1994: 317). In other words, it is only possible to justify treating people differently if there exists some factual difference between them that justifies such difference in treatment (Rachels 1999: 94). *Equality* is a nonspecific term that means nothing until applied to a particular context. Thus, in a political context, equality means equal access to public office and equal treatment under the law, and equal treatment extends to equality in terms of job hiring, promotion, and pay.

Race refers to groups of persons who are relatively alike in their biological inheritance and are distinct from other groups (American Anthropological Association 1997: 2). *Ethnicity* is a cultural phenomenon referring to a person's identification with a particular cultural group (Hinman 1998: 403). However, race is socially constructed, and the notion that persons "belong" to a particular race was developed in the last century based on the belief that there was a biological basis for categorizing groups of people. Biologically, however, the term *race* has no meaning, yet society continues to give the notion meaning by using it as a social category. The notion of race gradually took hold in U.S. society when the institution of slavery reinforced the idea that one race could be inferior to another (Banks and Eberhardt 1998: 58). In the United States, the law has had the effect of distributing benefits and burdens based on race, and the assignment of a person to a racial category has often, in the past, determined his or her rights and obligations (for example, in the "Jim Crow" laws passed at the end of the Civil War).

Racism in its most general sense can be defined as "social practices which (explicitly or implicitly) attribute merits or allocate values to members of racially categorized groups solely because of their 'race'" (Zatz and Mann 1998: 3). There are at least three aspects to racism: personal prejudice; ideological racism, where culture and biology are used to rationalize and justify the superior position of a dominant culture; and institutional racism, where the policies and practices of institutions operate to produce systematic and continuing differences between racial groups (p. 4).

One aspect of institutionalized racism has been termed *petit apartheid*. This concept includes daily informal or hidden interactions between police and minorities, such as stop-and-question and stop-and-search law enforcement practices, which may or may not result in an arrest and consequent entry into the criminal justice system (p. 4). The notion of petit apartheid has recently been explored both theoretically and in terms of those activities that might fall within its definitional scope (Milovanovic and Russell 2001). The focus of petit apartheid appears to be attitudinal factors that influence policing and other decisions within the system; that is, "culturally biased beliefs and actions" extending, in the view of Georges-Abeyie (2001: x), to insults, rough treatment, and lack of civility faced by black suspects, the quality and objectivity of judicial instructions to a jury when an African American is on trial, and other discretionary acts within the system.

Petit apartheid contrasts with grand apartheid. The latter encompasses overt racism. Studies on racism within the criminal justice system have been critiqued for giving undue emphasis to overt racism and ignoring petit apartheid (Georges-Abeyie 2001: x). This chapter aims to explore *overt racism* within the criminal justice system. Issues such as racial profiling and racial slurs, which appear to constitute an aspect of petit apartheid as well as being discriminatory practices, have already been discussed in Chapter 2.

Historical Context

African Americans have suffered discrimination on grounds of race, initially through the system of slavery, and then through a pattern of exclusion and segregation, both informal and formal, in the shape of legislation and court decisions that have historically endorsed overt racial discrimination. From the time of the inception of slavery in the early 17th century until 1865, slaves were considered the property of their masters based on a view that they were naturally unequal and inferior people. They were subjected to slave codes, which prohibited the possession of any rights or freedoms enjoyed by whites; experienced brutal and inhumane treatment of an extralegal nature; and were exploited for their labor. Following the Civil War, amendments to the Bill of Rights prohibited slavery and granted all persons, regardless of race, a right to equal protection. However, despite these legal statements of freedom, patterns of discrimination persisted after the war because many states passed Jim Crow laws, which had the effect of maintaining forms of discrimination in legal, social, and economic forums. For example, African Americans were denied the right to vote or to enter into contracts, and the doctrine of *separate but equal* was applied to keep the races separate.

The courts continued to enforce Jim Crow laws until the mid-1900s, and African Americans were also subjected to extralegal treatment in the form of physical assaults and practices such as lynching, where police were often present. About 3,000 African Americans were lynched between the mid-1800s and the early 1900s (B. Smith 2000: 75), and those performing the lynchings were seldom prosecuted. During the 20th century, legal rights were accorded to African Americans and have been protected by the courts. In the landmark case of *Brown v. Board of Education* in 1954, the Supreme Court struck down the "separate but equal" doctrine, and the civil rights acts passed in the mid-20th century attempted to restate and reinforce a policy against segregation.

Today, the black community in the United States is diverse, comprising, for example, Jamaicans, Nigerians, Ethiopians, Somalis, and other African and West Indies nationalities, each with its own culture distinguishable from that of African Americans. Nevertheless, despite this heterogeneity, racist attitudes continue to be manifested based on skin color.

The history of Latinos in the United States has been one of contention with the Anglo American culture. Spanish colonies were established in the United States in the late 16th century, predating the Anglo American presence; however, in 1847, Mexico lost approximately half of its territory to the United States. In recent times, it has been common to associate Latinos with the issue of immigration, and Mexicans in particular are constructed as an illegal immigrant group (De Uriarte in Alvarez 2000: 88). Racist stereotyping of Latinos depicts them as sneaky, lazy, and thieving (Levin in Alvarez 2000: 88), and law enforcement practices and the criminal justice system have been shown to collaborate in discrimination against Latinos in the form of police harassment of Mexican Americans (Turner in Alvarez 2000: 88).

It is important to appreciate the heterogeneity of the Latino population in the United States, because issues affecting Mexican Americans may differ from those impacting Puerto Ricans, Cubans, or immigrants from Central America. For example, Puerto Ricans are the most economically disadvantaged group (Myers et al. in Alvarez 2000: 89), whereas Cuban immigrants to the United States have tended to come from the middle class, be well-educated, and possess significant economic resources. Nevertheless, like African Americans and other black groups, the heterogeneous Latino population tends to be viewed as homogeneous.

American Indians and Alaska Natives are the only indigenous groups in the United States. The history of contact between American Indians and Anglo Americans is replete with acts of violence against American Indians and with the dispossession of their lands. Alaska Natives, as a colonized and marginalized people, have experienced and continue to experience severe trauma generated by social change, with high rates of suicide, alcohol abuse, and a disproportionate representation in the criminal justice system (see, for example, Banks 2002; Brod 1975; Fienup-Riordan 1994; Kraus and Buffler 1979; Travis 1983 in Phillips and Inui 1986; Schafer, Curtis, and Atwell 1997). Similarly, American Indians continue to be disproportionately represented in arrest and incarceration data in those states where they are primarily located (see, for example, Greenfeld and Smith 1999; Grobsmith 1994; Perry 2004; Ross 2000). Both groups suffer economic, educational, and social stereotyping, which is revealed in their treatment by the criminal justice system.

In terms of criminal victimization, blacks disproportionately commit and are victimized by violent crime. They are almost seven times as likely as whites to be murdered and about twice as likely to be robbed, raped or sexually assaulted (Banks *et al.* 2006: 1177). Although they make up less than 13% of the population, in 2004 blacks were arrested for 47.2% of murders, 53.3% of robberies, 31.9% of rapes, and 32.7% of assaults (p. 1178). Blacks represented 45% of the incarcerated population in state and federal prisons in 2002 (Harrison and Beck 2003) and more than 40% in 2004 (Harrison & Beck 2005). In 2001 American Indians represented 2.4% of all offenders entering federal prison and about 16% of all violent offenders in federal prisons (Perry 2004: 21) and they made up 0.9% of the total U.S. population in the 2000 Census (p. 1).

Is There Racial Discrimination in the Criminal Justice System?

One report suggests that racial discrimination does occur at some points in the criminal justice system. Following the Rodney King incident, the report of the Independent Commission on the Los Angeles Police Department (also called the Christopher Commission) (1991) found that there was excessive use of force by LAPD officers and that this was compounded by racism and bias. One quarter of the 960 LAPD officers surveyed by the commission agreed that officers held a racial bias toward minorities, and more than one quarter agreed that this racial bias could lead to the use of excessive force. The commission also reviewed radio transmissions within the LAPD, which revealed disturbing and recurrent racial remarks, often made in the context of discussing vehicle pursuits or beating suspects. Testimony from witnesses depicted the LAPD as an organization whose practices and procedures tolerated discriminatory treatment, and witnesses repeatedly testified about LAPD officers who verbally harassed minorities, detained African American and Latino men who fit generalized descriptions of subjects, and employed invasive and humiliating tactics against minorities in minority neighborhoods. As well as racism in relations with the public, racial bias was also reflected in conduct directed at fellow officers who were members of racial or ethnic minority groups. These officers were subjected to racial slurs and comments in radio messages and to discriminatory treatment within the department.

In another report, that of the New York State Judicial Commission on Minorities (1991), a panel of judges, attorneys, and law professors found that "there are two justice systems at work in the courts of New York State; one for whites, and a very different one for minorities and the poor" (p. 1). The panel found inequality, disparate treatment, and injustice based on race. It reported that many minorities received "basement justice" in that court facilities were infested with rats and cockroaches, family members of minorities were often treated with disrespect and lack of courtesy by court officers, and racist graffiti appeared on the walls of court facilities. The panel also concluded that minority cases often take only 4 or 5 minutes in court, suggesting a form of assembly line justice, and that black defendants outside of New York City frequently have their cases heard by an all-white jury.

In order to determine whether racial discrimination exists within the criminal justice system, criminologists have conducted research studies that have examined the *major decision points* within criminal justice systems in the United States. Most researchers agree with Wilbanks (1987) and Petersilia (1983) that although there is racial discrimination within the criminal justice system, the system itself is not characterized by racial discrimination; that is, that discrimination is not systematic (Blumstein 1993; DiIulio 1996; Russell 1998; Tonry 1995). There are, however, individual cases occurring within the system that appear to demonstrate racial discrimination at certain decision-making points (Wilbanks 1987). According to Petersilia (1983), racial disparities have come about because procedures were adopted within the criminal justice system prior to any real assessment about the effect of those procedures on minorities. For example, she found that

> although the case processing system generally treated offenders similarly . . . we found racial differences at two key points: Minority suspects were more likely than whites to be released after arrest; however, after a felony conviction, minority offenders were more likely than whites to be given longer sentences and to be put in prison instead of jail. (Petersilia 1983: vi)

Petersilia also suggested that "racial differences in plea bargaining and jury trials may explain some of the difference in length and type of sentence" (1983: ix).

The contention that there is no systematic bias in the criminal justice system based on race has been challenged by other researchers who dispute this conclusion on a number of grounds (Russell 1998: 28). These include the fact that prior studies have assessed discrimination at a single stage in the system and have therefore been ineffective in detecting discrimination that might exist at other stages. For example, the finding that there is no racial disparity in sentencing within a system does not exclude the possibility of discrimination in other parts of the system. As already discussed, Georges-Abeyie has drawn attention to how research on racial discrimination in the system focuses on formal, easily observed decision-making points and fails to take account of more informal law enforcement action (Georges-Abeyie in Russell 1998: 32). He argues that this informal decision making determines who will be arrested and who will enter the system and that these encounters should be included in any assessment of whether the system operates in a discriminatory manner. If such informal action were to be included, he suggests that a system of petit apartheid would be revealed that would demonstrate that African Americans are consistently treated in a discriminatory manner as compared to whites.

Another criticism is that official statistics on race and crime do not provide a proper basis for research on discrimination in the justice system, because the data collection procedures make these statistics unreliable and distort analysis derived from them (Knepper 2000: 16). This argument points out that the primary classification scheme employed in crime statistics designates four official races—white, black, American Indian/Alaskan Native, and Asian and Pacific Islander—as well as two official ethnic groups, "Hispanic origin" and "not of Hispanic origin." In contrast, the 1990 census includes 43 racial categories and subcategories. If race is made the focus of inquiry, there is an assumption that races constitute discrete groups, but in fact, the races in America are not monolithic. For example, the designation "black" fails to capture the most significant aspects of what it means to be black in the United States, because the designation "black" includes persons of Caribbean, African, and Central and South American origin, and within each of these groups are populations distinguished by culture, language, and shades of color (Knepper 2000: 19). Knepper argues that no objective statements can be made based on these race categories, which are essentially political rather than social definitions of races derived from a legal ideology of separate races grounded in the institution of slavery (p. 23).

In relation to the juvenile justice system, it has been argued that any discrimination within that system should be considered separately from the adult system for two basic reasons (Pope and Feyerherm 1990). First, a high level of discretion is permitted in the juvenile justice system, and this may tend to produce more discrimination. Second, because most adult offenders begin their contact with the adult system through the juvenile justice system, characteristics acquired in the juvenile system, such as a prior record, may influence their treatment in the adult system.

As to whether racial discrimination exists within the juvenile justice system, after a review of the literature, Pope and Feyerherm (1990) conclude that two thirds of the studies reviewed suggested evidence of direct or indirect discrimination against minorities, or a mixed pattern of bias, especially in the processing of juveniles through the system. Their survey also suggests there is evidence that race differences in outcome may seem to be minor at a certain decision-making stage in the system but that these differences have more serious implications as earlier decisions in the system move toward a final disposition. Third, Pope and Feyerherm state that although the relationship between race and juvenile justice decision making is complex, their analysis suggests that various factors do interact to produce racial differences in juvenile justice dispositions. Certainly race seems to continue as a factor in responses to juvenile crime. Information collected by the organization Building Blocks for Youth (2000) revealed that African Americans represent 15% of the population nationwide, 26% of juvenile arrests, 44% of youth who are detained, 46% of youth who are judicially waived to criminal court, and 58% of youth admitted to state prisons.

In considering racial discrimination within the criminal justice system, researchers have isolated and examined various decision-making points, including arrest, bail, jury selection, conviction, and sentencing. These decision-making points will be considered in the following sections.

Police Encounters With Citizens and Police Arrest

Racial origin may sometimes influence police decisions about making an arrest. In the case of suspected juvenile offenses, research has shown that for minor offenses, police officers may take into account the demeanor of a juvenile in deciding whether to make an arrest (Black and Reiss 1970; Piliavin and Briar 1964). If the police perceive the suspected offender as showing them disrespect, this may increase the likelihood of an arrest. Along with racial origin, D. Smith (1986) found that the context of a particular neighborhood also influenced police decisions about arrest or use of force, because police were more likely to arrest, threaten, or use force against suspects in racially mixed or minority neighborhoods.

Research into how police use their powers against minorities, whatever may be the race of the officer, has been an important issue in policing research, and the approach has been to explore whether white officers treat black citizens differently than nonblack citizens (R. Brown and Frank 2006: 104). In one study of police employed by the Cincinnati Police Division between 1997 and 1998, where about 65% of the population was white and 35% black, researchers examined 614 police–suspect encounters during which 104 citizens were arrested. They discovered that about 18% of the white officer–suspect encounters ended in arrest compared to 15% of the black officer–suspect interactions. Further, male and juvenile suspects were significantly more likely to be arrested than females or adults, and police were significantly more likely to arrest black suspects than white suspects (p. 118). They also found that citizens who show disrespect to the police increase their likelihood of arrest. Interactions involving black officers and black suspects were significantly more likely to result in arrest than interactions involving black officers and white suspects (p. 119). Thus, the authors suggest that black officers are more likely to use coercion with black citizens than white citizens. The authors are unable to offer any explanation for this differential arresting behavior other than that race seems to make a difference and that more research is required (pp. 120–121).

In considering the proportion of blacks involved in police shootings of criminal suspects, Fyfe (1982) demonstrated that in New York City, blacks were more likely than whites to be shot by police, because they were disproportionately involved in armed incidents that involved shooting. In contrast, research in Memphis showed that blacks were no more likely than whites to be involved in armed incidents, but nevertheless, police shot disproportionately more blacks when they were fleeing. Fyfe concludes that police use of deadly force in Memphis is influenced by the race of a suspect.

In Seattle, a study of race and drug delivery arrests revealed that most drugs, including powder cocaine and heroin, are delivered by whites, and that blacks are the majority delivering only one drug, namely, crack cocaine (Beckett, Nyrop, and Pfingst 2006: 129). However, 64% of those arrested for delivering drugs other than crack cocaine are black. The explanation suggested for this disparity is the law enforcement focus on crack cocaine and also the fact that the white drug markets in Seattle receive less attention from law enforcement than the more racially diverse markets in the city (p. 129). Thus, the researchers conclude, "Race shapes perceptions of who and what constitute Seattle's drug problem. . . ." (p. 105).

Why have police in many states prioritized drug enforcement as a police function and engaged in repeated traffic stops to conduct drug searches? Some commentators have argued that the Comprehensive Crime Act of 1984 has been the cause of this high ranking enjoyed by drug enforcement. The reason is that this act permitted local police agencies to retain the proceeds from assets seized in drug enforcement activity where federal and local police cooperated in the investigation

(Mast, Benson, and Rasmussen 2000: 287). As Mast et al. (2000) put it, "Entrepreneurial local police shift[ed] production efforts into drug control in order to expand their revenues" (p. 287). In fact, the Department of Justice went further than the act's provisions, because it decided that local police could arrange for federal authorities to "adopt" local police forces' drug seizures, even when federal agents were not involved in the investigation. Interestingly, drug arrests per 100,000 population in states with limits on the assets that local police could retain averaged 363 during 1989, while the arrest rate in such cases where police were able to keep seized assets averaged 606 per 100,000 (p. 289). Mast et al. (2000: 285), after conducting an empirical study, found that where legislation permits police to keep assets seized in drug investigations raises the drug arrest rate as a proportion of total arrests by about 20% and drug arrest rates themselves by about 18%.

Bail

For most offenses charged, prosecutors and judges have a wide discretion about whether defendants should be released on bail, and the courts may use factors such as dangerousness to the community and the possibility of flight in making bail decisions. Generally, the court looks at the employment, marital status, and length of residence in an area of the accused as an illustration of community ties, which may allow the court to conclude that the accused is unlikely to flee (Albonetti et al. 1989).

Studies tend to show that race is not a factor in bail applications once an accused's dangerousness to the community and prior history of appearance at trial are controlled for. However, race does relate to the decision to grant bail in other ways. For example, in a study of more than 5,000 male defendants, Albonetti et al. (1989) reveal that defendants with lower levels of education and income were less likely to get bail and more likely to receive onerous bail terms. They also found that white defendants with the same education, background, and income as black defendants were more likely to be granted bail, and that in considering bail applications, a prior criminal record counted against blacks more than whites. However, in assessing the criteria for bail, dangerousness and seriousness of the offense were of greater weight for whites than for blacks. Overall, the study shows that under certain conditions, whites are treated more severely on bail applications but that generally, white defendants receive better treatment. Walker, Spohn, and DeLone (2000: 135) note that it is impossible to guarantee that judges will refrain from taking race into account in determining applications for bail and that the simple stereotyping of minorities as less reliable and more prone to violence than whites will likely result in a higher rate of bail denial regardless of any other assessed factors.

Jury Selection

Is there any evidence of racial discrimination in the jury selection process? Historically, laws have tried to entrench racial discrimination into the process of jury selection. In *Strauder v. West Virginia* (1880), the court struck down a statute that limited jury service to white men on the grounds that it violated the Fourteenth Amendment to the Constitution. However, this ruling did not prevent some states from attempting to preserve the lawfulness of an all-white jury by other means. For example, in Delaware, jury selection was drawn from lists of taxpayers, and jury members were required to be "sober and judicious." Although African Americans were eligible for selection under this rule, they were seldom if ever selected, because the state authorities argued that few African Americans in the state were intelligent, experienced, or moral enough to serve as jurors (Walker et al. 2000: 156). The Supreme Court subsequently ruled this practice in Delaware as unconstitutional.

Since the mid-1930s, the Supreme Court has ruled on jury selection issues in a way that has made it difficult for court systems to practice racial discrimination in jury selection. For example, the Court has ruled it unconstitutional to put the names of white potential jurors on white cards and the names of African American potential jurors on yellow cards and then to supposedly make a random draw of cards to determine who would be summoned for jury duty (Walker et al. 2000: 157). Walker et al. (2000) argue that many states still practice discriminatory procedures in selecting jury pools. For example, obtaining the names of potential jurors from registered voters, the Department of Motor Vehicles, or property tax rolls seems to be an objective process, but in some jurisdictions, racial minorities are less likely to be registered voters, own automobiles, or own taxable property (p. 157). The effect, therefore, is to stack the jury pool with middle-class white persons and to marginalize minorities.

Prosecutors and defense lawyers are able to use peremptory challenges to excuse potential jurors without identifying any cause or explanation and without any accountability to the court, so it is therefore possible to employ peremptory challenges in the practice of racial discrimination in jury selection. Initially, the Supreme Court was unwilling to restrict a prosecutor's right to use peremptory challenges to excuse potential jurors on racial grounds, preferring to rely on the presumption that the prosecutor was always acting in good faith in making such challenges. However, the Court determined that it would intervene if a defendant could establish a case of deliberate discrimination by showing that eliminating African Americans from a particular jury was part of a pattern of discrimination in a jurisdiction. Not surprisingly, this stringent test has proved difficult to satisfy, because few defense lawyers possess information proving a pattern of discrimination. In 1986, the Supreme Court rejected this test, ruling that it was not necessary to establish a pattern to show discrimination and that a defendant need only bring evidence showing the prosecutor had exercised his or her peremptory challenges on racial grounds. Once a prima facie case of discrimination has been made out, the state must explain why an African American has been excluded from the jury pool. Even so, Walker et al. (2000: 160) contend that judges have given the benefit of the doubt to prosecutors and have shown themselves willing to accept the prosecutor's explanations rather than make a finding of deliberate discrimination. Case Study 3.1, derived from a *New York Times* newspaper report, illustrates an alleged case of racial discrimination in jury selection.

CASE STUDY 3.1   IN DALLAS, DISMISSAL OF BLACK JURORS LEADS TO APPEAL BY DEATH ROW INMATE

Thomas Miller-El is an African American charged with shooting two white hotel clerks during a robbery in 1985. One of the hotel clerks died, and Miller-El, age 50, is due to be executed by the State of Texas on February 21. He has asked the Texas Board of Pardons to commute his sentence and has appealed his case to the U.S. Supreme Court on the ground that the jury that convicted him was chosen using racial discriminatory standards that have been applied by the Dallas County district attorney's office in many cases. The district attorney's office opposes the appeal, arguing that there is no evidence of any racial discrimination.

The jury in the trial comprised nine whites, one Filipino, one Hispanic, and one African American. Three other African Americans were excluded from the jury by prosecutors, as were seven of eight other African Americans interviewed as prospective jurors.

Racial discrimination in jury selection is prohibited by the Constitution, and until 1986, in order to establish race discrimination, an accused had to meet a heavy burden of proof, because he or she had to show a pattern of discrimination. In 1986, in *Batson v. Kentucky,* the U.S. Supreme Court lowered the standard, determining that if the accused was able to show that the prosecution appeared to be using its peremptory challenges to jurors to exclude minorities, the trial judge could call for an explanation.

Miller-El was convicted and sentenced one month before the Batson ruling, but the decision applies to his case retroactively. To date, both state and federal courts have upheld his death sentence, determining that no racial discrimination occurred during jury selection. Miller-El's argument is that the courts considered only the number of challenges to jurors (10 out of 11 prospective African American jurors) and failed to consider other evidence showing that prosecutors in Dallas County had for years excluded blacks from juries as a matter of routine practice. This argument is supported by four former prosecutors whose terms of office cover the period from 1977 to 1989 and who confirmed that the Dallas County office did apply a policy of excluding blacks from juries. Further supporting this argument is a 1986 article in a local newspaper citing a 1963 internal memo in the district attorney's office advising prosecutors not to include "Jews, negroes, Dagos, Mexicans or a member of any minority race" as a jury member (in Rimer 2002). Further, in the early 1970s the prosecutor's office employed a training manual which contained advice on jury selection to the effect that a prosecutor should not include any member of a minority group because "they almost always empathize with the accused" (in Rimer 2002).

The *Dallas Morning News* has examined 15 capital murder trials from 1980 through 1986 and has revealed that prosecutors excluded 90% of African

Americans qualified for jury selection. Nevertheless, the assistant district attorney in the Miller-El case disclaimed any notion that he had challenged the 10 African American jurors on grounds of race. He claimed that he was trying to assemble the best possible jury and that his office had no policy of racial discrimination. Despite these claims, at least three of the potential African American jurors challenged in the Miller-El case supported capital punishment and wanted to be on the jury.

SOURCE: Rimer 2002.

Conviction and Sentencing

In the aggregate, blacks tend to be convicted less than whites (Petersilia 1983; Wilbanks 1987), and according to Sampson and Lauritsen (1997), no consistent evidence exists of racial discrimination at the point of criminal conviction. Research on sentencing, however, has generated the most interest among those studying racial disparity. A review of a large number of studies conducted for the National Academy of Sciences (Hagan and Bumiller 1983) concluded that it was the prior criminal record rather than race that affected the sentencing disposition and that once this was controlled for, the direct effect of race was basically eliminated. Racial disparities in sentencing arose from the disproportionate representation of minorities in officially processed criminal conduct, and this in turn was reflected in longer or more serious prior criminal records. However, some concerns were raised that race might have a cumulative effect on sentencing by operating indirectly through other factors that disadvantage minorities and that race might interact with other factors, such as initial arrest, to influence decision making.

In studies conducted in the 1970s and 1980s, researchers investigated racial bias by considering the victim's status rather than that of the offender, explored historical changes in sentencing, and included in their research crimes not previously covered, such as drug processing. In drug prosecutions, Peterson and Hagan (1984) found that low-level black drug dealers in New York were treated more leniently than white drug dealers but that major black dealers were treated more harshly than their white counterparts, because they were perceived as inflicting still more harm on the already victimized nonwhite population. Overall, the research conducted during this period seemed to suggest that there was some discrimination, sometimes, in some places.

Research has focused on determinate sentencing, including three-strikes legislation. In one analysis of over 11,000 such cases in California, researchers found some racial disparities in sentencing, but once the results were controlled for prior record and other variables, it was concluded that racial disparity in sentencing was not the result of racial discrimination (Klein, Petersilia, and Turner 1990). The question of whether the exercise of prosecutorial discretion produces discrimination has also been investigated. Where sentences are fixed, charging and plea bargaining become crucial, and attempts have been made to uncover the full dimensions of prosecutorial discretion. Looking at the prosecutor's decision to charge, one analysis of more than 30,000 cases from Los Angeles County showed that cases against blacks and Hispanics were significantly more likely to be prosecuted than cases against whites (Spohn, Gruhl, and Welch 1987). This contrasts with a Supreme Court ruling that the decision to prosecute shall not be "deliberately based upon an unjustifiable standard such as race, religion, or other arbitrary classifications" (Walker et al. 2000: 140). A number of studies have concluded that white defendants are offered plea bargains more frequently and obtain better deals than minorities (Walker et al. 2000: 146), although other studies have found that race has an insignificant effect on plea negotiations (Albonetti 1990; Miethe and Moore 1986).

Researchers have begun to pay attention to macro social and economic contexts, attempting to frame research that could identify the role of poverty, urbanization, and related factors in sentencing. Walker et al. (2000: 62) point out that a large economic gap exists between white Americans and minorities, and that over the past 20 years, there has been considerable growth in the number of the very poor. The first official definition of poverty was developed by the federal government in 1964, and it reflects the minimum income needed for an adequate standard of living. In 1995, the poverty line was $7,763 for a single person and $15,569 for a family of four; in that year, 13.8% of all Americans were below the poverty line (p. 65). In 2005, about 10.6% of all whites were below the poverty line compared with 24.9% of blacks and 21.8% of Hispanics (DeNava-Walt, Proctor, and Lee 2006). Although the African American middle class has grown significantly, the percentage of African Americans among the very poor has also increased. In terms of wealth—that is, the measure of all accumulated assets such as a house, a car, or savings—the 2005 median of white families was $48,554, compared with only $30,858 for African Americans and $35,967 for Hispanics.

As well as investigating decision-making points within the criminal justice system for racial discrimination, the racial disproportion in prison populations and the place of race in seeking and imposing the death penalty have been the subject of research attention.

Imprisonment Disparities

Table 3.1 shows rates of incarceration for different ethnic/racial groups. In 2005, at year end, there were 2,193,798 federal, state and jail prisoners and a rate of incarceration of 737 per 100,000. Black inmates made up an estimated 39.5% of all inmates with sentences of more than 1 year, and white and Hispanic inmates accounted for 34.6% and 20.2%, respectively (Harrison and Beck 2006). Nearly 8.1% of all black males between the ages of 25 and 29 were in prison in the year 2005. This compares with 2.6% of Hispanic males and 1.2% of white males in the same age category. As of February 2008, the latest Pew report announced that 1 in

100 Americans are now behind bars and that for some groups this rate is significantly higher. For example, the report states,

> While one in 30 men between the ages of 20 and 34 is behind bars, for black males in that age group the figure is one in nine. Gender adds another dimension of the picture. Men still are 10 times more likely to be in jail or prison, but the female population is burgeoning at a far brisker pace. For black women in their mid-to-late 30s, the incarceration rate has also hit the one-in-100 mark. Growing older, meanwhile, continues to have a dramatic chilling effect on criminal behavior. While one in every 53 people in their 20s is behind bars, the rate for those over 55 falls to one in 837. (Pew Center of the States 2008: 3)

Table 3.1   Racial and Ethnic Rates of Incarceration

Racial/Ethnic Group	Rate per 100,000
White	412
Black	2,290
Hispanic	742

SOURCE: Harrison and Beck 2006: 11.

How can the racial disproportionality that exists in the U.S. prison population be accounted for? A study conducted by Blumstein (1982, 1993) concluded that between 1979 and 1991, there was an enormous growth in the rate of imprisonment and that the incarceration rate had tripled between 1975 and 1990. While the total number of drug offenders had increased nearly 10 times, there was little change between 1979 and 1991 in the level of racial disproportionality in incarceration rates. Importantly, the War on Drugs had focused on offenses involving high levels of discretion, opening up the possibility of charges of discrimination. In light of the increase in the proportion of those incarcerated that were drug offenders, from 5.7% in 1979 to 21.5% in 1991, Blumstein (1993) suggested that an adequate investigation of racial disproportionality in incarceration should specifically examine the issue of disparity by crime type. In particular, having considered the growth in the number of drug offenders, he concluded that the War on Drugs had contributed to racial disproportionality to a major degree, despite what he saw as the futility of that strategy. The War on Drugs continues to impact African Americans disproportionately; in 1999, black inmates made up 57.6% of all offenders convicted of drug offenses serving time in state prisons (Beck and Harrison 2001). Table 3.2 shows the number of inmates in state and federal prisons and local jails by race, gender, ethnicity, and age; Table 3.3 illustrates the rate of incarceration per 100,000 population through these same categories.

Table 3.2   Number of Sentenced Prisoners Under State or Federal Jurisdiction, by Gender, Race, Hispanic Origin, and Age, Yearend 2005

| | Number of sentenced prisoners | | | | | | | |
| | Males | | | | Females | | | |
Age	Total[a]	White[b]	Black[b]	Hispanic	Total[a]	White[b]	Black[b]	Hispanic
Total	1,362,500	459,700	547,200	279,000	98,600	45,800	29,900	15,900
18–19	26,300	7,200	11,800	5,600	1,200	500	400	200
20–24	218,700	62,700	94,200	50,400	11,900	5,300	3,600	2,300
25–29	244,800	67,000	106,600	59,600	15,300	6,700	4,700	2,900
30–34	224,200	69,800	92,000	51,100	17,400	8,100	5,100	2,900
35–39	207,200	72,300	81,600	41,600	19,400	9,000	6,000	3,000
40–44	185,200	70,900	71,000	31,600	16,500	7,800	5,100	2,400
45–54	189,800	76,300	71,100	29,500	13,800	6,500	4,300	1,800
55 or older	63,500	32,900	17,600	9,000	3,000	1,800	700	300

SOURCE: Harrison and Beck 2006.

NOTE: Based on estimates by gender, race, Hispanic origin, and age from the 2004 Survey of Inmates in State Correctional Facilities and updated from jurisdiction counts by gender at yearend 2005. Estimates were rounded to the nearest 100.

[a]Includes American Indians, Alaska Natives, Asians, Native Hawaiians, other Pacific Islanders, and persons identifying two or more races.
[b]Excludes Hispanics and persons identifying two or more races.

Death Penalty Disparities

Research has shown that when type of homicide is controlled for, race is a factor in the prosecutor's decision to seek the death penalty and in its imposition (Aguirre and Baker 1990; Baldus, Woodward, and Pulaski 1990; Paternoster et al. 2003). It appears that the race of the victim, together with the race of the offender, has a significant influence on the prosecutor's willingness to seek the death penalty and on the willingness of judges and jurors to impose it (see Table 3.4). Black offenders convicted of murdering white victims are at the highest risk for receiving the sentence of capital punishment, and offenders, whether black or white, convicted of murdering black victims are least likely to receive the death penalty. Evidence of discrimination in relation to black offenders is paralleled by similar discrimination in cases involving Hispanic victims according to research that examined all death eligible homicides in one county in California from 1977 to 1986 (Lee 2006: 17).

Table 3.3   Number of Sentenced Prisoners Under State or Federal Jurisdiction per 100,000 Residents, by Gender, Race, Hispanic Origin, and Age, Yearend 2005

| | Number of sentenced prisoners per 100,000 residents | | | | | | | |
| | Males | | | | Females | | | |
Age	Total[a]	White[b]	Black[b]	Hispanic	Total[a]	White[b]	Black[b]	Hispanic
Total	929	471	3,145	1,244	65	45	156	76
18–19	619	274	1,920	791	29	20	61	38
20–24	2,016	948	6,345	2,493	118	85	248	137
25–29	2,342	1,098	8,082	2,618	153	113	339	158
30–34	2,234	1,172	7,726	2,450	177	138	391	165
35–39	1,953	1,067	6,630	2,255	185	134	435	184
40–44	1,641	923	5,472	1,975	145	102	345	164
45–54	899	493	3,136	1,327	63	41	163	85
55 or older	208	135	697	416	8	6	19	13

SOURCE: Harrison and Beck 2006.

NOTE: Based on estimates of the U.S resident population on January 1, 2006, by gender, race, Hispanic origin, and age. Detailed categories exclude persons identifying with two or more races.

[a]Includes American Indians, Alaska Natives, Asians, Native Hawaiians, other Pacific Islanders, and persons identifying two or more races.
[b]Excludes Hispanics and persons identifying two or more races.

Table 3.4   Executions and Other Dispositions of Inmates Sentenced to Death, by Race and Hispanic Origin, 1977–2005

| Race/Hispanic origin | Total under sentence of death 1977–2005[b] | Prisoners executed | | Prisoners who received other dispositions[a] | |
		Number	Percent of total	Number	Percent of total
Total	7,320	1,004	13.7%	3,062	41.8%
White[c]	3,573	584	16.3%	1,517	42.5%
Black[c]	3,005	339	11.3	1,307	43.5
Hispanic	626	67	10.7	197	31.5
All other races[c,d]	116	14	12.1	41	35.3

SOURCE: Snell 2006.

[a]Includes persons removed from a sentence of death because of statutes struck down on appeal, sentences or convictions vacated, commutations, or death by other than execution.
[b]Includes 6 persons sentenced to death prior to 1977 who were still under sentence of death on 12/31/05; 374 persons sentenced to death prior to 1977 whose death sentence was removed between 1977 and 12/31/2005; and 6,940 persons sentenced to death between 1977 and 2005.
[c]Excludes persons of Hispanic origin.
[d]Includes American Indians, Alaska Natives, Asians, Native Hawaiians, and other Pacific Islanders.

There is a substantial difference between white and black views about the death penalty. In the 2002 General Social Survey, 69.8% of whites favored the death penalty as compared with only 42.1% of blacks (Barkan and Cohn 2005: 40). Some argue that racial prejudice plays a significant role in white support for the death penalty, and several studies have found that racial prejudice with a punitive approach among whites (see, for example, Soss, Langbein, and Metelko 2003: 416). Research based on the 1992 American National Election Study (ANES) concluded that "for white people living in an all white county, racial prejudice emerges as the strongest predictor of white death penalty support. . . . In more racially integrated counties this effect is more than doubled" (Barken and Cohn 2005: 41). The results of this study have been confirmed in similar research based on the 1992 ANES and data from the 1990 U.S. Census (Soss et al. 2003). The researchers also found that whites with higher family incomes were more likely to support the death penalty than whites from lower-income-earning groups (p. 407).

Hate Crimes

An act of racial discrimination may take the form of a hate crime. Hate crime statutes fall into two types (Russell 1998: 86), some treating hate crimes as independent offenses and others providing enhanced penalties for crimes that are motivated by bias. Additional penalties may be imposed by the court where it finds that an offense has been committed and was motivated by bias based on race. To successfully convict a person of a hate crime, the prosecution must establish the motive of the accused, which is extremely difficult to do. Sometimes the nature of the crime provides a motive, such as painting a swastika on the side of a house owned by a Jewish family, which common sense would interpret as a hate crime because the family is Jewish. The language used by an offender during the offense may be particularly important, especially if racial slurs are used. Prosecutors also pay attention to the severity of the attack, the absence of any provocation by the victim, any prior history of contact between the victim and suspect, and any history of similar incidents in the same area (Byers and Spillane 2000: 265).

Data collected between 1997 and 1999 under the Hate Crime Statistics Act of 1990 show that 61% of hate crime incidents were motivated by race and 11% by ethnicity and that the majority of such incidents involved a violent offense (see Table 3.5). From July 2000 through December 2003 an annual average of 210,000 hate crime victimizations occurred (Harlow 2005: 1). Most hate crimes were associated with violent crimes such as rape or other sexual assault, and a minority with property crimes. During this period, 55% of hate crimes were motivated by race (Table 3.6). Racially motivated hate crimes most often target African Americans, with 6 in 10 racially based incidents targeting African Americans and 3 in 10 targeting whites (Strom 2001).

Table 3.5   Hate-Bias Incidents, by Type of Bias Motivation, 1997–1999

	Number	*Percent*
Hate crime incidents	*2,976*	*100%*
Race	1,820	61.2%
Anti-black	1,059	35.6%
Anti-white	561	18.9%
Anti-multiracial	92	3.1%
Anti-Asian	60	2.0%
Anti-American Indian	48	1.6%
Religion	431	14.4%
Anti-Jewish	177	5.9%
Anti-other religious group	132	4.4%
Anti-Catholic	29	1.0%
Anti-Protestant	30	1.0%
Anti-Islamic	30	1.0%
Anti-multiracial group	28	0.9%
Anti-atheist	5	0.2%
Ethnicity	329	11.1%
Anti-Hispanic	199	6.7%
Anti-other ethnicity or nationality of origin	130	4.4%
Sexual Orientation	379	12.7%
Anti-male homosexual	167	5.6%
Anti-homosexual	103	3.5%
Anti-female homosexual	65	2.2%
Anti-bisexual	32	1.1%
Anti-heterosexual	12	0.4%
Disability	17	0.6%
Anti-physical disability	12	0.4%
Anti-mental disability	5	0.2%

SOURCE: Strom 2001.

NOTE: Unit of count is incidents (*n* = 2,976).

Table 3.6   Motivation and Evidence in Hate Crime

	Percent of hate crime	
	Incidents	Victimizations
Motivation		
Race	55.4%	56.0%
Association	30.7	30.6
Ethnicity	28.7	27.9
Sexual orientation	18.0	17.9
Perceived characteristic	13.7	13.2
Religion	12.9	12.4
Disability	11.2	10.5
Evidence of motivation		
Negative comments, hurtful words, abusive language	98.5%	98.5%
Confirmation by police investigation	7.9	8.4
Hate symbols	7.6	7.8

SOURCE: BJS, National Crime Victimization Survey, July 2000 through December 2003.

NOTE: Detail adds to more than 100% because some respondents included more than one motivation or evidence of motivation.

Explanations for Racial Discrimination in the Criminal Justice System

How Do We Explain the Existence of Racial Discrimination in the Criminal Justice System?

Most research on racial discrimination draws on consensus and conflict theories to explain discrimination. In the *consensus view,* individuals share their values with the state, which is organized to protect the interests of society and employs criminal law as an instrument of protection. Punishment is based on rational factors such as the seriousness of the offense and prior convictions. On the other hand, *conflict theorists* perceive society as comprising groups with conflicting values, with the state organized to represent the interests of the powerful ruling class. Criminal law is viewed as an instrument of protection for the powerful and elite, and punishment is based on nonrational factors including race and social class. Conflict theorists argue that groups that threaten the power of the rulers are more likely to be the subjects of social control; that is, these groups are more criminalized and suffer greater rates of incarceration. They argue that minorities, the unemployed, and the poor represent these threatening groups (C. Brown and Warner 1995; Chambliss and Seidman 1971).

Laws concerning vagrancy help to illustrate conflict theory. Being a vagrant is defined as simply occupying public space without resources and with no clear purpose for being there. It is argued that only the poor engage in vagrancy, and making vagrancy a criminal act and enforcing laws against it are attempts by the powerful to control the poor (Walker et al. 2000: 18). The era of segregation in the south from the 1890s to the 1960s also demonstrates conflict theory in action. During this period, the criminal justice system enforced laws providing for white supremacy and declared the subordinate status of blacks. Nowadays, street crime is a primary target of law enforcement, and this kind of crime is for the most part committed by the poor and by racial and ethnic minorities. This targeting of street crime contrasts with the relatively sparse enforcement of white-collar crime committed primarily by middle- and upper-class whites. Accordingly, conflict theorists argue that street crime is another demonstration of conflict theory.

Another theoretical explanation for racial discrimination argues that *the symbolic aspect of social conflict drives crime control.* For example, perceptions of threats, rather than actual threats, are influential in the design of crime control policies (Tittle and Curran 1988 in Sampson and Lauritsen 1997). Some studies support this position. For example, one study in Washington State found that nonwhites were sentenced to imprisonment at higher rates in counties with large minority populations, and interviews with justice officials and leaders in the community showed a consistent public concern with "dangerousness" and the "threat from minorities." Accordingly, crime was perceived as a minority problem, and race was used as a code for certain lifestyles and forms of dress thought to signal criminality. According to this view, it follows that the poor and the underclass are seen not as a threat to rulers and elites, but to the middle and working classes who make up the dominant majority of American society.

Sampson and Lauritsen (1997: 362), after reviewing most of the studies on discrimination in the criminal justice system, conclude that discrimination appears on occasion at some stages in the criminal justice system, in some locations. However, there is little evidence of any systematic or overt bias on the part of criminal justice decision makers. They contend that there is a perception of racial discrimination in the administration of justice that is fueled by the regular moral panics and political responses to those panics such as the War on Crime, the War on Drugs, and the concern with sexual predators. These are targeted at particular lifestyles or locations associated with minorities and have the effect of subjecting the behavior of minorities to increased levels of social control (Chambliss 1995; Tonry 1995).

In discussing the relationship between African Americans and the criminal justice system, Mauer seeks to account for the striking increase in the proportion of African Americans incarcerated in the United States, pointing out that blacks represented only 21% of those imprisoned in 1926 compared to one half of all prison admissions today (Mauer and U.S. Sentencing Project 1999: 120). Mauer suggests that to some extent the explanation is rooted in society's response to crime, noting that most crime is intraracial; that is, people fight their neighbors and invade homes in their own communities. Historically, as long as black crime was located within black communities, it was of little concern to law enforcement, but when it was perceived to spill over into white communities, police became proactive. Mauer argues that the influence of race is clearly seen in some parts of the criminal justice system, pointing to death penalty sentences as providing compelling evidence of this.

He suggests that the way in which race plays a role in sentencing decisions is quite subtle and is influenced by a number of factors. These include whether white offenders benefit from greater resources such as a private lawyer, whether whites have access to expert evidence, whether they are able to afford the costs of substance abuse treatment, and whether whites are able to arouse less unease in criminal justice decision makers than minorities. Commenting on these factors, Mauer points out, in relation to the right to counsel guaranteed by the Sixth Amendment, that although minorities are entitled to legal representation at trial and during the process leading up to trial, there is some question about the quality of legal representation provided to indigent defendants by public defenders. Although African Americans are more likely to be defended by public defenders, it does not follow that this is necessarily discriminatory treatment, because some argue that public defenders are underpaid, poorly trained, and lack resources (Weitzer 1996). Others, however, disagree, believing that public defenders have negotiating capital within the criminal justice system that can benefit the indigent defendant, especially through plea bargaining (Wice 1985). In the case of capital offenses, Bright and Keenan (1995) assert that judges often assign inexperienced or incompetent lawyers to represent indigent accused, and the Innocence Project continues to uncover cases in which defendants in capital cases, whether minorities or not, have been poorly advised or represented by court-assigned lawyers (Innocence Project, 2002).

Mauer joins with those who believe that sentencing policies and moral panics target minorities (Mauer and U.S. Sentencing Project 1999). Discussing the history of marijuana policy, he points out that when this drug was first used in the 1900s, it was perceived to be a drug used only by blacks and Mexican Americans. Its use was penalized in the 1950s with a sentence of 2 to 5 years' imprisonment for first time possession. In the 1960s, when marijuana came to be widely used by the white middle class, public attitudes began to change, and marijuana began to be perceived as a relatively harmless drug, nonaddictive, and not likely to lead to other criminal activity. By the 1970s, legislation had separated marijuana out from other narcotics and had lowered the penalties, and some jurisdictions even effectively decriminalized its possession in small quantities.

However, law enforcement practices in relation to marijuana laws vary and may result in acts of discrimination based on race. As an example, Mauer and the U.S. Sentencing Project (1999: 134) cites the city of Milwaukee, where possession was for many years classified as a misdemeanor, whereas the same conduct in the suburbs of Milwaukee was a mere ordinance violation. The outcome of this disparity in classification was that white offenders in the suburbs paid a fine, and in the city, the mostly non-white arrests might result in jail time and a record. In this case, while the policy makers in the city and in the suburbs may not have consciously targeted minorities, their failure to anticipate the impact of their decision making resulted in unconscious targeting.

Some, however, contend that the targeting of drug users is far from unconscious. For example, Tonry (1998: 52) argues that those who launched the drug war knew that "the enemy troops would mostly be young minority males" and that making mass arrests would disproportionately incarcerate those males. He also contends that those promoting these policies were well aware that the laws distinguishing powder from crack cocaine would disproportionately affect blacks. Thus, the War on Drugs exemplifies the effect produced by a deliberate policy choice to focus on the enforcement of drug offenses.

Looking at the situational aspect of drug enforcement, Mauer points out that conducting drug arrests in inner city neighborhoods is easier for law enforcement because of the visibility of street drug dealing as compared to dealing carried out behind closed doors in suburban neighborhoods (Mauer and U.S. Sentencing Project 1999: 148). Furthermore, where dealing takes place openly, residents of black neighborhoods are more likely to complain and ask for police intervention. Lynch and Sabol (cited in Mauer and U.S. Sentencing Project 1999: 149) conclude that the War on Drugs has resulted in increased targeting of black working- and middle-class areas for drug enforcement. While the processes that produce this outcome may not have been racially motivated, they have produced racially disparate outcomes.

The impact of the War on Drugs on women of color is a good example of a racially disparate outcome. This "war" has produced increased conviction rates for low-level drug offenders who have little prospect of negotiating any beneficial plea bargain in exchange for information about other offenders. These low-level offenders are often women, and in 1999, the Sentencing Project revealed that the number of women incarcerated for drug offenses rose by 888% between 1986 and 1996 (Mauer, Potler, and Wolf 1999). Between 1986 and 1995, New York drug offenses accounted for 91% of the increase in the number of women sentenced to imprisonment, and in California, drug offenses accounted for 55% of the increase over the same period (Mauer, Potler, and Wolf 1999).

The most discussed disparity in drug sentencing in recent years has been the issue of sentencing for possession of crack cocaine. The mandatory sentencing laws passed by Congress provided a far harsher punishment for possession of crack cocaine than for powder cocaine in that the sale of 500 grams of powder resulted in a mandatory 5-year prison term whereas possession of only 5 grams of crack cocaine triggered the same mandatory penalty (Mauer and U.S. Sentencing Project 1999: 155). Significantly, crack cocaine is used primarily by urban blacks, and powder cocaine is used by middle- and upper-class whites. These mandatory sentencing laws have had a major impact on blacks, because the vast majority of persons charged with crack trafficking have been black. As a result of the disparity in these offenses, the average prison sentence served by black federal prisoners for possession of crack cocaine is 40% longer than the average sentence for whites convicted of possession of powder cocaine (McDonald and Carson 1993). In December 2007, the Supreme Court ruled that judges could hand down lighter punishments in crack cocaine and ecstasy cases than those specified by federal guidelines in an effort to correct the sentencing disparities created by the crack cocaine laws (see Gall v. United States 2007; Kimbrough v. United States 2007).

Summary

The debate about racial discrimination in the criminal justice system remains unresolved. While most research suggests an absence of systematic racial discrimination, there is agreement among researchers that acts of discrimination occur at specific decision-making points, and some argue that informal and hidden forms of discrimination occur both within and outside the system. It follows that the majority opinion supports arguments that acts of discrimination occur and that they may perhaps be deeply rooted in cultural and social attitudes toward other races. These may express themselves in complex and nuanced ways that are difficult to capture within research strategies. Associated with acts of discrimination is the issue of the public perception of the workings of the criminal justice system. Regardless of the conclusions of research studies, there is a widespread belief amongst minorities that the system discriminates against them and is therefore unjust. To counter this perception, those exercising decision-making powers within the system must act ethically and strive to eradicate any suggestion of racial bias and discrimination from their decisions.

DISCUSSION QUESTIONS

1. Explain why the term *race* is an inadequate category of analysis.

2. What historical events and circumstances influence the possibility of the existence of racial discrimination within the criminal justice system?

3. What are the difficulties involved in focusing on decision-making points in the criminal justice system to determine whether racial discrimination occurs?

4. Explain the concept of petit apartheid and how its existence might generate acts of discrimination in the criminal justice system.

5. How can the study of drug policy and the prosecution of drug offenders assist in establishing the existence of racial discrimination in the criminal system?

6. What theoretical explanations are offered for racial discrimination in the criminal justice system? Explain with examples.

WEB RESOURCES

Brennan Center for Justice at New York University School of Law. http://www.brennancenter.org/dynamic/subpages/download_file_48382.pdf

Bureau of Justice Statistics. Hate Crimes. http://www.fbi.gov/ucr/ucr.htm

Civil Rights Coalition for the 21st Century—Hate Crimes. http://www.civilrights.org/issues/hate/

Drug Reform Coordination Network. http://www.drcnet.org

Drug War Chronicle. http://stopthedrugwar.org/chronicle

Drug Watch International. http://www.drugwatch.org

Families Against Mandatory Sentencing. http://www.famm.org/

The Justice Project. http://www.thejusticeproject.org

Marijuana Policy Project. http://www.mpp.org

The Sentencing Project. http://www.sentencingproject.org

Stop the Drug War. http://stopthedrugwar.org/

CHAPTER 4

Lawyers and Ethics

Legal Ethics: Historical Context

In the early days of colonization in the United States, lawyers working in the colonies were few in number, poorly trained, and not recognized as members of a profession. Although detailed histories of the early legal profession in the United States have yet to be written, researchers such as David Papke (1986) have identified some aspects of the early practice of law in Virginia and Massachusetts.

In Virginia, the planter class conceived the law as functioning to support the existing social structure. The landed gentry supplied judges and legislators. To the Virginia elite, an independent legal profession was problematic; in fact, in 1645, an early piece of legislation ordered all lawyers practicing for a fee to be expelled from office. The leaders in that state felt that lawyers encouraged legal suits and showed more interest in fees than in the good of the community. Well into the 18th century, Virginia sought to limit the practice of law to "gentlemen," and the prescribed form of legal education was study at the English Inns of Court.

In the early days of the colony of Massachusetts, natural law applied in the form of scriptures as well as imported law. (Chapter 1 discusses natural law.) This contributed to the idea that legal education was unnecessary as well as to public skepticism about the usefulness of lawyers at all. By the end of the 17th century, however, the colony had, in effect, accepted the legitimacy of the legal profession, but the courts determined who might take the oath to become a lawyer, what lawyers could charge, and what forms of practice they could engage in. In one case in the late 17th century, the court ordered a lawyer to be whipped for charging excessive fees.

It was not until the mid-18th century in the colonies that the legal profession began to gain general acceptance, but its size remained small; even in cities, lawyers engaged in clerical work, copying, and bookkeeping services, as well as providing legal advice. With greater acceptance and security, lawyers began to develop a professional identity and to become a self-conscious professional group. This, in turn, led the profession to address matters such as professional conduct and ethics, and county bar associations that were generally voluntary in nature began to create ethical rules. The prominence of lawyers such as John Adams, Patrick Henry, and Thomas Jefferson during the Revolutionary War period confirmed the strong growth of the legal profession. In fact, of the 56 delegates who signed the Declaration of Independence, 25 were lawyers.

Between the American Revolution and the Civil War, the practice of law grew rapidly, consistent with the growth of cities and the economy (Papke 1986). During the early 19th century, the public appeared hostile toward lawyers, an attitude fueled partly by their role as postwar debt collectors. During this period, legislators and courts continued to decide issues of legal training and admission to the bar, entrance examinations were often perfunctory, and apprenticeship periods were very short. Legislated codes of professional conduct existed but were short and vague. The legal profession grew from 22,000 lawyers in 1850 to 60,000 in 1880 and to 114,000 by 1900.

The work lawyers performed in the period from 1865 to 1915 varied according to location, but criminal work remained a staple along with debt collection. In rural areas, lawyers began to speculate on land. In the cities, many sole practitioners worked for low rates, and legal specialization existed in the form of the early Wall Street corporate lawyers and criminal law specialists. In 1870, the Bar Association of New York City was founded, and in 1878 the American Bar Association (ABA) was established. With these institutions came comprehensive bar associations that attempted to control the practice of law. During the last decade of the 19th century, some 20 bar associations adopted codes of professional responsibility. In 1908, the ABA accepted a draft of Canons of Professional Ethics inspired by *An Essay on Professional Ethics* written by George Shars Wood in 1854 (Papke 1986). Wood insisted that lawyers' primary responsibility was to their clients and argued that social utility was not a factor that should concern lawyers in any cause they argued. He advocated prudence, restraint, and a taste for fine literature as the best qualities for lawyers. His proposals concerning contingency fees provoked some argument; however, many lawyers agreed with him that such fees corrupted and degraded the profession. Nevertheless, with urbanization and industrialization, work- and transport-related accidents had made such fees common, and the Supreme Court ruled them valid in 1877.

By 1914, three quarters of all state bar associations had adopted the Canons, and in most states complaints about lawyer misconduct were heard by bar association committees followed by a possible appeal to the court. By this time, the profession was virtually self-directed in ethical matters. With the 20th century came bureaucratization as private law firms, sometimes with hundreds of lawyers, spread throughout the cities, and nearly every corporation had in-house legal staff. In the public arena, the number of prosecutors and defense lawyers expanded, raising questions about the relevance of the Canons as well as issues relating to admission standards.

After World War II, law school enrollments grew rapidly, and in the 1960s, with the civil rights movement and professional self-criticism, some lawyers began to argue in favor of public interest law and against too great a concern with making money. In 1969, the ABA replaced the Canons with a new Code of Professional Responsibility specifying ethical considerations for all lawyers. Since that time there has been a continuing debate about legal professional ethics, and the dialogue has centered on the ABA's Commission on Evaluation of Professional Standards, which was formed in 1977. In 1980, the commission provided the ABA with new draft Model Rules of Professional Conduct that were approved in a revised version in 1983. The Model Rules also proved controversial, and the American Trial Lawyers Association offered an alternative code.

The ABA has been active in reviewing law school courses on legal ethics and professional responsibility with the aim of strengthening ethical standards. Despite this, a high percentage of law students in an ABA survey of seven law schools indicated that they were "not very" or "not at all" concerned with the subject of professional responsibility or ethics (Papke 1986: 45).

The Nature of Professional Ethics

"Professional ethics" is an expression that has a multitude of possible meanings, and it is frequently used to signify rules governing professionals and professions. The standards of conduct for professions are organized around the way in which a profession carries out its work. The development of canons and codes of ethics within professions has given professional ethics the status of law within those professions. Setting ethical standards is one way in which professions seek to persuade the public to entrust their affairs and confidence to members of the profession. *Trust* is an aspect of professionalism, and the encouragement of trust has become a fundamental characteristic in professional relationships, because clients depend on the superior knowledge of the professional. In the legal profession, trust is a core value, because trust between a lawyer and client is crucial if the lawyer is to gain full knowledge of the client's concerns. From the client's viewpoint, trust is an expression of faith or confidence in an expectation of honesty, competence, and diligence on the part of the lawyer. Breaching a client's trust undermines faith in the legal profession.

Discussions about the role of the lawyer often stress the lawyer's commitment to the pursuit of justice as a central purpose. Lawyers tend to see their role in securing justice as an important contribution toward establishing an efficient legal system, as supporting law as an institution, and as promoting procedural justice. These objectives are derived from the *adversarial system* that equates justice with the protection of rights. In the adversarial system, the decision maker or judge adopts a passive role, listening to the arguments from both sides and making a decision based on the evidence and arguments presented. This contrasts with the *inquisitorial system* in which the judge takes an active role and controls the progress of the case. The adversarial system gives lawyers a great deal of control over the court process, and an underlying assumption of the system is that if lawyers do their job well, the court will reach a wise decision.

The Principle of Partisanship

The adversarial system reflects an individualistic ethic, and this emphasis on the individual in society means that in some cases lawyers will do things for clients about which they may have moral qualms, such as misleading others or engaging in bullying tactics. In other words, lawyers may on the one hand exercise virtue in their relationships with clients but in pursuing their clients' interests may engage in practices that could be considered unfair, uncooperative, or selfish, acts that would not be considered virtuous. Once it is accepted that lawyers see justice in terms of defending the rights of individuals, the lawyer's role in society becomes one of giving citizens access to vigorous representation, and this commitment is embodied in codes of conduct and ethics. In terms of ethics, therefore, the Anglo American criminal adversarial system has the effect of putting the interests of the client above all other considerations, including the general social good. The ethical standards of conduct promulgated in codes and canons reflect this emphasis.

The Principle of Neutrality

The principle of neutrality requires that lawyers adopt a neutral stance in relation to their clients or their causes and that they defend causes that they may personally find morally repugnant. The lawyer must, therefore, put aside questions of personal morality when deciding to represent a client and determining how best to represent that client. The exercise of this principle enables the lawyer to abdicate responsibility for assisting a client in achieving a purpose that the lawyer might otherwise consider morally questionable.

The principles of neutrality and partisanship are seen as supporting the notion of equality before the law, which is itself considered a social good. Arguably, the effect of these two principles is to narrow the number of moral choices that lawyers may face, because lawyers will make moral choices based on the duty owed to their clients and on their need to maintain neutrality in relation to clients' causes.

Wasserstrom (1986: 122) argues that the lawyer's concentration on the interests of the client above all other considerations, including moral considerations, is especially justified in the case of the criminal defense lawyer. Specifically, he argues that factors such as the potential deprivation of liberty, the vast prosecutorial resources of the state, and a concern about punishment and its nature and extent justify what might be considered the "amoral" behavior of a defense lawyer.

In contrast to this argument that lawyers are entitled to disregard any issues of morality in the interests of their clients, Simon (1994) has suggested that such a position is an affront to the dignity of the legal profession and the legal system, because it turns lawyers into mere instruments of their clients and the trial into an irrational battle. He argues that the purpose of judicial proceedings is to produce wise and informed decision making and that within this context the lawyer's task is to assist the decision maker in achieving such decisions. Therefore, according to Simon, the lawyer's obligation to protect and advance his client's interests ought to be subordinated to the process of truth seeking, and the lawyer ought not to mislead the decision maker by discrediting accurate testimony. The lawyer's basic job is, therefore, to introduce accurate evidence, and any attempt by lawyers to influence decision makers based on their own judgment of the evidence would usurp the function of the decision maker. Simon (1994: 196) contends that lawyers have a "professional duty of reflective judgment" and should therefore assess the client's instructions to establish if they are "likely to promote justice." In other words, he suggests that lawyers should not assist clients who wish to employ procedural rules or technicalities to defeat, rather than promote, the interests of justice. This, he argues, applies even in an adversarial context.

Fried (1994) attempts to resolve the issue of lawyers' morality or amorality by equating the lawyer and client relationship with one of friendship. He argues that friends typically do things for each other that they would not do for a stranger and that this behavior is widely accepted in society. However, this argument has been subjected to considerable criticism, because it appears to license a pure form of legal advocacy, such as would justify a lawyer remaining silent when a client lies under oath or lawyers attempting to influence the evidence of potential witnesses.

Pepper (1994) reasons that the autonomy of the client gives moral justification to the lawyer's role, contending that law in itself is a public good, and through the courts and legislature, society has created the means enabling individuals to achieve goals and resolve conflicts. The system of freedom under the law is founded upon individual autonomy as a social and moral good, so all persons should be entitled to make their own choices, and our legal system accommodates such individual autonomy and choice. The exercise of autonomy may require access to the law, and this is usually available only through a lawyer. Pepper suggests that it would be wrong for lawyers to impose their moral judgment in such a way as to interfere with the exercise of their clients' autonomy and that to do so would put the lawyer's morality above client autonomy. According to this argument, therefore, the lawyer should not merely participate in a client's immoral objective but is *obliged* to do so. However, Pepper does recognize that there may be circumstances that are so offensive to the lawyer's sense of morality that the lawyer may decline to represent the client; he calls this "conscientious objection."

The Lawyer–Client Relationship

The most fundamental expression of legal ethics is that the client's interests should take precedence over those of the lawyer. Clients are dependent upon lawyers to accomplish the particular tasks they assign their lawyers but are unable to assess the adequacy of the work that lawyers carry out. Thus, the lawyer's relationship with the client is such that incompetence or wrongdoing on the lawyer's part is considered a betrayal of the client's trust. The lawyer–client relationship requires that the lawyer hear a client's individual story before deciding what is to be done. This is part of a continual dialogue between lawyer and client. The progress of the lawyer's work should be evaluated at regular intervals in the context of the lawyer's aims and interests, and the relationship should be client centered, involving shared decision-making responsibility and the mutual participation of both lawyer and client. Neither the lawyer nor the client should dominate the relationship. In effect, the client controls decision making while the lawyer takes the role of a technical advisor and counselor.

This modern view of the lawyer–client relationship can be contrasted with the older paternalistic view that held that once engaged by the client and broadly instructed about the client's objectives, the lawyer was left to make decisions in the best interests of the client. The paternalistic view contends that lawyers have superior knowledge, skills, and experience and therefore must know what is best; the issues being considered too complex for clients to understand and hence the need for a lawyer in the first place. The code of the American Bar Association does not mention the best interest of the client, but it does stress that the role of the lawyer is to do whatever the client requires, even if this is unwise. Thus, lawyers must "abide by a client's decisions concerning the objectives of the representation" (American Bar Association and Center for Professional Responsibility 1998: Model Rule 1.2). As Luban (1984: 262) concludes, "The American model is loyalty to the client's wishes and not his interests."

Is a lawyer required to accept any client who approaches him for assistance? In the United States, there is an obligation to accept particular types of clients based on the ABA Model Rule 1.2, which requires that legal representation should not be denied to those who are unable to afford legal services, whose cause is controversial, or who are the subject of popular disapproval. However, the comment to Model Rule 6.2 adopts a flexible approach by stating that a lawyer is not ordinarily obliged to accept a client whose character or cause the lawyer regards as repugnant. However, a lawyer has pro bono responsibilities under Model Rule 6.1 that can be met by accepting a fair share of unpopular matters or indigent or unpopular clients.

When does the lawyer–client relationship end? ABA Model Rule 1.16 allows lawyers to withdraw their representation if "a client insists upon pursuing an objective that the lawyer considers repugnant or imprudent." Sometimes it may be difficult to determine when the lawyer–client relationship has ended, and in some situations duties toward clients, such as confidentiality and avoiding conflicts of interest, will continue even when there is no active relationship.

Can a defendant be required to accept a lawyer in a criminal case? The Supreme Court in *Faretta v. California* (1975) held that even in a serious criminal case, a defendant cannot be forced to be represented by counsel. The Court argued that the right to defend is personal, and the defendant will bear the personal consequences of a conviction; the lawyer or the state will not. The minority opinion in that case thought that the integrity of the system and public confidence in the system are undermined when the defendant's waiver of counsel results in an easy conviction.

Confidentiality

Keeping the affairs of the client confidential is a fundamental ethical duty imposed on lawyers. Confidentiality represents a respect for privacy, and in practical terms, clients will be reluctant to consult lawyers who are known to gossip about their affairs. Further, breaching the duty of confidentiality would run afoul of other principles such as acting in the client's best interests and not personally profiting from information given by the client. It is important to note that this confidentiality belongs to the client and not to the lawyer, and thus only the client can waive it. Where the client is accused of a crime, confidentiality is particularly important, because without confidentiality, the client is likely to be less than frank, which will affect the lawyer's ability to represent a client and give a zealous defense. The concept of confidentiality between lawyer and client has been doubted by some who argue that ethical rules relating to the practice of law should not protect the guilty client over an innocent third party (Simon 1988; Wasserstrom 1975). For example, as long ago as 1827, Bentham strongly attacked the notion of confidentiality that protected a lawyer from testifying when a client had admitted guilt (in Kipnis 1986: 75). Similarly, Goldman (in Kipnis 1986: 75) argues that there ought to be limits to confidentiality and disclaimers warning clients of those limits. However, as Kipnis (1986: 75) points out, the arguments favoring limiting confidentiality necessarily lead to the conclusion that clients will not disclose information for fear of it being revealed, and this might prevent a zealous defense.

The general duty of confidentiality to the client should not be confused with lawyer–client privilege. The latter is a principle of evidence relating to revealing information during trial, and it provides that client confidences that are revealed by an attorney may not be used as evidence (Luban 1988: 187). The duty of confidentiality is broader, because it requires the lawyer to keep the client's confidences generally, whereas the privilege relates only to confidences being used as evidence.

Client Perjury

What should a lawyer do when a client commits perjury or makes it clear that he or she intends to commit perjury? Freedman (1966) argues that the first duty of the lawyer is to try to persuade the client not to commit perjury, but if the lawyer cannot persuade the client, the lawyer should present the testimony as if it were true. He contends that imposing a duty on the lawyer to divulge perjury would involve the lawyer in a situation of inconsistent obligations. Thus, the lawyer must find out all the facts of the case in order to offer the best defense and must keep the client's confidences but must also divulge that the client's testimony is false, a fact that has been learned through the client's confidences. It is clear that if any two of these are to be honored, the third cannot be honored. Attempting to withdraw from the case is not a solution, because doing so would merely provide defendants with an excuse for a delay or a mistrial, and in any event, the next lawyer would be faced with the same situation as the withdrawing lawyer.

Until the mid-1980s, the law on this ethical issue was unclear, but courts generally held that in a civil case, a lawyer who is aware that a client has committed perjury must disclose it to the court if the client refuses to do so. However, in criminal cases, there is an added constitutional dimension that produces more complexity, the argument being that informing on one's own client is such a grave violation of the confidentiality rule as to be unconstitutional. Model Rule 3.3 now requires that lawyers "take reasonable remedial measures" when they come to know that evidence is false, and this duty applies even if it involves the disclosure of confidential information (Luban 1988: 198–199).

Client Crime

Lawyer–client confidentiality is completely negated if the client consults the lawyer in furtherance of a crime or fraud. This applies even if the lawyer was unaware of the true nature of the client's purpose. Where this exception applies, information that would otherwise have been privileged must be disclosed when a proper demand is made (Hazard and Hodes 2002: 9–34). In addition, Model Rule 1.6 (b) (1) allows a lawyer, in certain narrowly defined circumstances, to disclose confidential client information to prevent future harm. For example, disclosure is permitted to the extent necessary to prevent a client from committing a criminal act that the lawyer reasonably believes is likely to result in imminent death or substantial bodily harm. It is important to note that this exception applies to crimes that have *yet to be committed,* and it should be contrasted with completed *past* crimes for which disclosing client information is *not permitted*. A good example of the completed crimes rule is the "Buried Bodies" case, discussed in Case Study 4.1.

CASE STUDY 4.1 BURIED BODIES CASE

Lawyers represented a defendant charged with murder, and during the period before trial the defendant told his lawyers about two other murders he had committed and described where the bodies were buried. The lawyers located the bodies, which were those of two young women who had been missing for some time. It happened that the authorities came to suspect the defendant of murdering the missing women and the father of one of the victims asked one of the lawyers if he knew anything about her fate. The lawyers did not disclose the location of the bodies to the authorities or the father but attempted to use their knowledge to the advantage of their client in plea bargaining. It was only when those negotiations failed and the case went to trial that the location of the bodies was revealed together with the lawyers' knowledge of that fact. The lawyers had information about a completed crime given to them in confidence by a defendant in a criminal case and acted properly within the bounds of the ABA Code of Ethics in withholding that information.

In moral terms, it can be argued that even without a rule of nondisclosure, nondisclosure would not have been morally required, because the victims were already dead and could not be helped. Of course, the victim's father suffered, and withholding the truth increased his period of uncertainty, but if such suffering were to outweigh confidentiality, a client's disclosure of a past crime would never be protected. If, in this case, the lawyers had discovered the two victims wounded but still alive, then they would have been faced with a scenario falling under the rule concerned with preventing future harm. Morally, however, it is hard to imagine any lawyer leaving the victims to die, and in practice, rules of ethics would play little part in such a scenario.

SOURCE: Hazard and Hodes 2002: 9–79.

If, in Case Study 4.1, the lawyers had taken physical possession of the bodies or had in some other way impeded the police discovery of that evidence, the confidentiality situation would be different, because despite the existence of lawyer–client confidentiality, courts commonly require lawyers to make voluntary disclosure of the benefits and means of their client's crimes. Court decisions concerning this duty begin with the principle that a lawyer may not actively participate in hiding an item or take possession of it in such a way as to impede its discovery by the authorities (Hazard and Hodes 2002: 9–103). For example, in one case a lawyer removed a sawed-off shotgun and the proceeds of a robbery from a client's safety deposit box and put them in his own box in the same bank. The court held the lawyer's conduct to be improper. The court cases also indicate that lawyers must comply with statutes that prohibit destroying, altering, or concealing evidence or that require lawyers to voluntarily turn over physical evidence that has come into their possession. For example, the Alaska Supreme Court has ruled that a lawyer had a duty to turn over a client's written kidnap plan to prosecutors even without having been asked for it, and in a California case, after the defendant was arrested on charges of strangling his girlfriend, his family found incriminating writings in his room, which they gave to the defendant's lawyer, who passed them to the judge, who in turn gave them to the prosecutor (*Morrell v. State* 1978). The court held that the defendant's lawyer was fulfilling his legal obligation when delivering the documents to the judge (Hansen 2005: 3).

Defense Lawyers

The two main systems under which lawyers represent clients in the West are adversarial and inquisitorial. In *adversarial* systems of law, the parties and their lawyers play the principal role of gathering evidence and examining witnesses in court, and the court plays a less active role. In the *inquisitorial* system, the court plays the main role in gathering evidence and questioning witnesses. It is sometimes argued that the judge in the inquisitorial system is more concerned with *discovering "the truth"* whereas in the adversarial system, lawyers dominate, and judges, acting as referees, are mainly concerned about *due process and procedures being followed* and not so much the search for "the truth." Frankel (1975) contends that the legal profession in the United States is held in low regard because establishing "truth" has a low priority as an overall objective of the process. This raises the issue of the adversarial system privileging procedural fairness over "truth," and Frankel suggests that too much emphasis is placed on the advancement of the client's interests and not enough on public interest in discovering "the truth." Freedman (1975a) refutes Frankel's position by arguing that the notion of "truth" has been an elusive concept throughout history, and that those who devised the adversarial system took account of the complexities of determining "truth."

Luban (1988: 67–93) outlines six reasons commonly argued in favor of the adversarial system:

1. It is the best system for discovering "the truth."

2. It is the best way of defending the rights of clients.

3. The nature of the lawyer–client relationship is intrinsically good.

4. It prevents abuse through checks and balances.

5. It honors human dignity.

6. It is so embedded in the social fabric that adopting another system would be too disruptive.

After examining each justification, Luban concludes that only the last has any validity, because in his view, the adversarial system has merit in the sense that it is not shown to be worse than any other system. In terms of criminal defense, Luban (1990: 1019) suggests that adversarial advocacy is crucial for protecting the rights of individuals "against a powerful and potentially dangerous bureaucratic institution."

The defense lawyer carries out the function of representing an accused within an adversarial system that emphasizes *due process.* According to Model Rule 1.3, a lawyer is to act with reasonable diligence and promptness in representing a client. The comment to this Model Rule makes it clear that the lawyer is expected to use *zeal, commitment, and dedication* and that zeal is an appropriate method in litigation (Hazard and Hodes 2002: 6–4). Lawyers operate as agents of their clients and must serve their clients' interests loyally and effectively. There is no absolute standard against which a lawyer's performance may be measured, and every case in which an issue of diligence or promptness arises is dependant on its own context (Hazard and Hodes 2002: 6–8).

It has been suggested that criminal defense lawyers may run into conflict with the commitment that a lawyer must use the utmost zeal and dedication in representing clients. In particular, because criminal defense lawyers may have aims and motivations that extend beyond the interest of their client, they can be regarded as "cause lawyers" (Etienne 2005: 1200), that is, "activist lawyers who use the law as a means of creating social change" (p. 1196) including public interest and poverty lawyers. Thus, for the cause lawyer, the client's defense is not necessarily an end in itself, because the cause lawyer has a broader set of objectives such as using the law as a vehicle to build a better society. An example of a potential conflict comes from the field of so-called "impact litigation" where lawyers select certain cases to raise certain issues. In this sense, the criminal defendant and the case are a means for effecting social change; this departs somewhat from a client-centered approach to the conduct of the law (p. 1251). An impact litigation lawyer might forego an argument in one case that could possibly benefit the client in order to employ that argument in another case where there is a greater chance of its success. Ethically, this is a questionable practice in view of the lawyer's duty to devote herself to the client's interest with the utmost zeal.

The ethical questions that commonly arise in the minds of nonlawyers about the role of a defense lawyer include the following three questions:

1. Is it ethically proper to represent a client accused of a criminal offense when the lawyer knows the client is guilty?

Some commentators have stated that lawyers will seldom be in a position to conclude from the available facts that their client is definitely guilty. However, there will still be times when lawyers will be quite confident of their client's guilt. When lawyers know their client is guilty, can they still conduct a defense leading to their acquittal? Model Rules 3.1, 3.3, and 6.2 set the ethical standard in such situations. Under these rules, a lawyer is not permitted to defend a proceeding unless there is a basis for doing so that is not considered frivolous. Further, a defendant's lawyer in criminal proceedings may defend the proceedings in order to require that every element of the case be established.

The comment to these rules requires that if a defendant has admitted to defense counsel the facts that establish guilt, and defense counsel's independent investigation has also established that the defendant's admissions are true, yet the defendant insists on standing trial, defense counsel must strongly discourage the defendant from perjury in testifying. Further, if in advance of the trial the defendant insists that he or she will take the stand and perjure him- or herself when testifying, the lawyer may withdraw from the case and seek leave of the court to do so if necessary, but the court must not be advised of the lawyer's reason for seeking to withdraw.

The problem with lawyers determining that their client is guilty is that a lawyer will not really know that the client is factually guilty unless the client admits all the facts that constitute the offense. This is the case even in circumstances when the client may be lying, or mentally ill, or mistaken. Also, a client who confesses to his or her lawyer may not understand the existence of certain legal defenses such as provocation or self-defense, and admitting guilt might result in the lawyer failing to explore these possibilities. In addition, the prosecution is required to prove to a jury that the client is guilty beyond a reasonable doubt, and it is argued, therefore, that a client cannot be legally guilty so far as the lawyer is concerned without undergoing the full scrutiny of a trial.

There are significant differences between a client who may be *factually guilty* and a client who is *legally guilty* (Pool 1979). Usually, the standard required for a lawyer to be satisfied that a client is guilty is that the lawyer has proof of the client's guilt through credible evidence that meets the standard of "beyond reasonable doubt." However, some commentators go further, arguing that lawyers need to be certain, not merely of guilt, but that a conviction will be obtained (Subin 1987). One lawyer suggested that the fleeting and temporary nature of the truth was rationale enough for this argument when he expressed his view of this issue in the following statement: "Truth cannot be known. Facts are indeterminate, contingent, and in criminal cases, often evanescent" (Babcock 1983: 177).

Lawyers offer a number of reasons for defending those who are "guilty." They might argue that by providing defendants with competent counsel, whether or not they have committed a serious offense or are innocent, they uphold the human dignity of that person. Freedman (1975a) endorses this view, arguing that the right to counsel is a significant demonstration of our regard for the dignity of the individual. Further, he makes the case that lawyers have an obligation to protect their clients and not to sit in judgment over them, because the determination of a client's guilt or innocence is not a lawyer's function.

Another reason put forward for lawyers not to decide their clients' guilt is that it is their function to ensure that those operating the criminal justice system do so in a proper manner. In this context, criminal defense lawyers not only induce prosecutors to prove their case but also ensure that they do so ethically and legally. The adversarial system requires lawyers to present a fearless defense of their clients, and lawyers may therefore argue that they are simply fulfilling the aims of that system. From this perspective, the lawyer is a functionary in the system.

Others justify the representation of the "guilty" by reasoning that lawyers have an obligation as agents in the legal system to provide their services to those in need. Shaffer (1981), for example, contends that by serving the guilty, lawyers fulfill their Christian role to those in need. Thus, defending criminals is considered by Shaffer as an act of Christian charity by helping and not judging one's neighbors. Finally, some defense lawyers argue that by providing a defense, they may prevent people who are guilty, but who do not deserve to be put in prison, from going to prison. As Mitchell (1980: 334) states,

> Those guilty of serious crime merit the wrath of our society. But almost no one deserves the hellholes we call jails and prisons. There is almost no case I would not defend if that meant keeping a human, as condemnable as he or she may be, from suffering the total, brutal inhumanity of our jails and prisons.

2. Is it ethically proper to cross-examine a witness with the aim of discrediting the witness's credibility or reliability when the lawyer knows the witness is telling the truth?

Assume a lawyer represents a criminal defendant charged with robbery who admits to his lawyer that he committed the crime but does not testify at his trial. The lawyer then attempts to attack the credibility of a truthful prosecution witness who observed the crime. The lawyer does this by establishing through cross-examining the witness that she had been drinking heavily before the crime, had a violent argument with the defendant immediately before the crime, and had convictions for shoplifting. Essentially, the lawyer intends to mislead the jury and challenge the credibility of this truthful witness.

It might be argued here that the lawyer's conduct, even though legally permissible, is immoral because it is an effort to obscure the truth and frustrate justice and because it inflicts harm on the innocent witness. There seems to be no social good in this case, because the only purpose of the deception is to obtain an undeserved acquittal for the client (Haskell 1998: 66). However, Freedman (1966) argues that in light of the importance of the lawyer's adversarial role as protection against the power of the state, a lawyer is obliged to act zealously, and it therefore follows that the lawyer in this example is entitled, and in fact obliged, to do everything he or she can on the client's behalf to discredit a witness known to be telling the truth.

Noonan (1966) protests that Freedman (1975a), in conceiving trials as battles in which lawyers are bound do everything in zealous defense of their clients, misrepresents the nature of the justice system. He contends that a lawyer's duty is to assist the judge in making an impartial, wise, and informed decision in seeking to establish "the truth." In other words, a lawyer's level of zeal should be defined by the promotion of a wise and informed decision in the case. Fundamentally, therefore, the argument is that unrestrained zeal undermines the system of justice. In addition to the zeal argument, it can also be said that the lawyer may have no absolute knowledge of the witness's truthfulness. How does the lawyer know the witness is truthful? From this point of view, the level of honesty may often be discovered only through a rigorous cross-examination that tests the witness's credibility.

Additional arguments against Freedman's view include the nature of the lawyer's duty to the court, particularly in not misleading the court, given that it can be argued that lawyers ought not to attack the credibility of a truthful witness when they have no basis to do so (Noonan 1966). Such an attack conflicts with a lawyer's duty to the court and with his or her overriding obligation to promote justice. Ultimately, the resolution of this difficult question seeks to define the limits of a zealous defense and calls into question conflicts between the lawyers' duty to clients and duty to the court, to the administration of justice, and to the promotion of truth seeking in criminal proceedings. It should be noted that Freedman does not advocate the lawyer's unlimited zealousness in noncriminal proceedings. However, in the final analysis, many would argue that in criminal proceedings, the lawyer's duty to protect the client against the state justifies the lawyer's conduct.

3. Is it ethically proper to have a witness give testimony when the lawyer knows that the witness will commit perjury?

Freedman (1966) proposes that the most common method of avoiding this problem is for the lawyer to withdraw from the case in circumstances where the witness is the accused. However, he suggests that the accused would simply find another lawyer and withhold the facts of his or her guilt from that new lawyer. Accordingly, on ethical grounds, the first lawyer ought not to withdraw, because perjured testimony will ultimately be presented. Freedman concludes that the obligation of confidentiality in the context of the adversarial system gives the lawyer no alternative but to put the perjuring witness on the stand without disclosing his or her knowledge of the perjury to the court or jury. Noonan (1966) disagrees, arguing again that the presentation of such evidence must be unethical, because it will lead to injustice. Two cases contradict Freedman's position. In one, the court decided that the lawyer was entitled to withdraw from a case in which the client admitted perjury and would be subject to disciplinary action only if he continued the case without reporting the matter to the court (*McKissick v. United States* 1967). In the other case, the conduct of a lawyer who advised several persons, including the client, to perjure themselves was considered bad enough to warrant disbarment (*Dodd v. Florida Bar* 1960). In other countries, Freedman's position is considered untenable, because lawyers may not knowingly lend themselves to any false story being put before the court and, if asked to do so, must immediately cease to act for the client.

Will disclosure of future perjury violate the Sixth Amendment to the Constitution? In *Nix v. Whiteside* (1986), the U.S. Supreme Court held that a criminal defendant has no right to the assistance of counsel in giving false testimony and that lawyers who refused to give such assistance or who threatened to disclose the future perjury of the client have not denied the client effective legal assistance under the Sixth Amendment to the Constitution. The ABA has endorsed the view put forward in this case but also points out that the case may not overcome the constitutional provisions of some states that may still prohibit the lawyer's disclosure of the client's perjury. It should be noted that under Model Rule 3.3 lawyers may not assist a client in committing perjury. Lawyers have attempted to avoid a violation of this rule by adopting what is called a "narrative approach" in which they do not question the client but simply allow the narration of evidence without asking questions. However, this narrative approach can also be criticized, because when the lawyer does not question the client and does not refer to the narrative in closing arguments, it may seem obvious to the jury that the defendant has given flawed testimony.

The Prosecutor

Freedman (1975b: 79) explains that ethical difficulties and their solutions differ between prosecution and defense lawyers because of the significantly different roles and functions they each play. In essence, the contest between prosecution and defense counterbalances the rights of the individual to the power of the state. The prosecutor has extraordinary discretion in directing investigations, deciding upon the crime to be charged, and influencing the punishment to be imposed. In contrast, the defense lawyer has particular responsibilities that link with the adversarial system and to issues of lawyer–client confidentiality as well as the assertion of constitutional rights to due process and to freedom from self-incrimination.

In their role as protectors of the state and the public, prosecutors act in an adversarial capacity, which requires zealous advocacy. Prosecutors are supposed to represent the public interest, but they may also see themselves as accountable to the police and to victims. Unlike other lawyers, prosecutors, in their representation of the public, in effect make their decisions without the assistance of a client. Prosecutors ought to place themselves in the shoes of the public, who is the client, before deciding upon the best course of action. It follows that, in practice, prosecutors have an important role in the creation of public policy within criminal proceedings.

Many district attorneys are required to maintain a high conviction rate and to win big public cases that arouse strong passions. Failure to do so might lead to the loss of their office in the next election (Fisher 1988). Thus, prosecutors are subject to a number of stresses and tensions including their public constituency; their need to adhere to professional codes and standards; and pressure from academics, the judiciary, and the media to act fairly. As Gershman (2001: 6–2) notes, a prosecutor who is under a duty to keep the public informed about pending cases has a corresponding duty not to make statements out of court that might prejudice the right to a fair trial, and prosecutors must also not use the media in a way intended to benefit themselves personally.

Gershman argues that many prosecutors have violated these duties and that experienced news reporters are able to draw improper statements out of prosecutors by using trickery and persuasion. With respect to statements to the media, Gershman explains that prosecutors have come under criticism for calling press conferences to celebrate indictments and for using such occasions to "improperly characterize charges, disparage defendants, disclose evidence, and otherwise employ inflammatory rhetoric that often presumes guilt" (2001: 6–4). Among the prohibitions on prosecutorial conduct, Gershman lists the release of grand jury material, making references to a defendant's bad character, commenting on the nature of the crime with which a defendant is charged, and revealing a defendant's confession to the media.

The Duty to Ensure Justice Is Done

At least since 1935, when the Supreme Court decided *Berger v. United States,* it has been the law that for prosecutors, winning is not everything. According to the Supreme Court, the primary duty of a prosecutor is to see that justice is done. In other words, the prosecutor must "seek justice, not merely to convict" (American Bar Association 1993: Standard 3–1.2 (c)):

> While (a prosecutor) may strike hard blows, he is not at liberty to strike foul ones. It is as much his duty to refrain from improper methods calculated to produce a wrongful conviction as it is to use every legitimate means to bring about a just one. (*Berger v. United States* 1935)

In performing the function of achieving justice, the prosecutor must assist the court in arriving at "the truth" fairly. Thus, if an accused has incompetent counsel who neglects to present all the material facts that might assist the defendant, the prosecutor has an ethical duty to make sure these facts are presented consistent with the responsibility to achieve a just result (Fisher 1988). Gershman (2001) specifies that prosecutors have a duty to the truth based on a number of sources, such as their role as a "minister of justice," their constitutional obligation not to use false evidence or suppress evidence favorable to the defendant, the ethical rules that apply to the prosecutor, their domination of the criminal justice system, and their role as a representative of the state. Gershman sets out instances in which prosecutors may violate their duty to "the truth." These include situations in which the prosecutor engages in misleading conduct by confusing the jury's view of the evidence; inflammatory conduct, such as appeals to racial or class biases, in the practice of attacking the defendant's character; and subverting and suppressing "the truth." Fisher (1988: 218) seeks to further define the prosecutor's quest for justice and concludes that its definition is problematic. He argues that the prosecutor's role in seeking justice suggests that "justice" has some independent meaning of special relevance to prosecutors. However, he suggests that its meaning may shift according to the context. Thus, where effective adversarial system safeguards exist, the role most consistent with "justice" is to be a zealous advocate; however, where those safeguards are lacking, the prosecutor's quasi-judicial function should be emphasized (p. 226). Further, he suggests that where safeguards do function properly, the prosecutor's primary duty is to promote crime control values (p. 254).

Model Rule 3.8 sets out the general duties for a prosecutor in a criminal case, which are designed to ensure that an accused receives a fair trial. Specifically, a prosecutor

- must not prosecute a charge unless it is supported by probable cause;
- must make reasonable efforts to ensure that an accused has been advised of the right to obtain counsel and has been given a reasonable opportunity to do so;

- must not seek to secure from an unrepresented defendant any waiver of important pretrial rights such as the right to a preliminary hearing;
- must make timely disclosure to the defense of all evidence or information that the prosecutor is aware of that tend to negate the guilt of the accused or that mitigate the offense; and
- with respect to sentencing, must disclose to the defense and to the court all mitigating information known to the prosecutor unless the court directs otherwise.

In terms of the administration of criminal justice, ABA standards state that prosecutors are administrators of justice and advocates and officers of the court and must exercise sound discretion in the performance of their functions. Prosecutors are subject to the same standards of professional conduct as other lawyers. However, additionally, the prosecutor has a general obligation to improve the administration of criminal justice and to seek remedial action if defects are discovered in the system.

Discretion to Bring Charges

The prosecutor has broad discretion over bringing charges; this charging decision is protected by almost absolute immunity. It is arguable that the probable cause standard adopted in Rule 3.8 is an insufficient deterrent against prosecutorial abuse, because a violation of that rule can generally be found only in instances in which prosecutors must have known that they lacked probable cause (Hazard and Hodes 2002: 34–6). Hazard and Hodes argue that rather than knowledge, a better basis is "reasonable belief" in the presence of probable cause, that is, whether prosecutors can show that they carefully considered the issue and formed a reasonable belief that a conviction would be secured. Freedman (1975b) argues that merely being charged with a crime results in a damaged reputation, regardless of a failure to convict. The anguish, anxiety, and emotional strain of a criminal trial as well as the financial burden are all set in motion when an indictment is sought. In view of the grave consequence of an indictment, Freedman (p. 85) suggests that this test (that charges be supported by probable cause) is inadequate, because probable cause may be based on hearsay and satisfied by less than a substantial likelihood of guilt.

Gottfredson and Gottfredson (1988: 114) point out that the breadth of the discretion granted to the prosecutor in making the decision to charge is not accompanied by any controls over its exercise and that the decision of whether or not to charge is "the single most unreviewed exercise of the power of the criminal law available to an individual in the American system of justice." They argue that there is no guidance available about the exercise of this discretion in statutes and that charging decisions are not judicially supervised. For example, in a study of felony processing in Washington, DC, in half of the felony arrests referred by police, the prosecutor decided not to charge, but the decision not to prosecute was not justified publicly or reviewed by any authority (p. 115).

Sometimes prosecutors elect not to enforce a particular statute and follow a policy of nonprosecution. Abrams (1975, cited in Gottfredson and Gottfredson 1988: 118) suggests some criteria that might influence a prosecutor to adopt such a policy, including community opposition, difficulties in legally enforcing a statute, the existence of an alternative, and the ability to prosecute for another offense. The ABA (cited in Gottfredson and Gottfredson 1988: 119) suggests that in deciding whether to bring charges, the criteria to be considered should include

- the prosecutor's assessment of guilt,
- the harm caused by the offense,
- the disproportion of the punishment to the offense,
- the possibility of improper motives for a complaint,
- any extended nonenforcement of a statute where the community accepts that nonenforcement,
- the reluctance of the victim to testify,
- the cooperation of the accused in the arrest or conviction of others, and
- the possibility of prosecution by another jurisdiction.

Although welcoming any criteria that would circumscribe the prosecutorial discretion, Gottfredson and Gottfredson note that criteria of this kind do not go far enough and that the criteria need to be ranked in priority and given weighting and better definition. Fisher (1988: 232) has suggested that in deciding to bring charges,

> the prosecutor's usual orientation should be one of special alertness to the existence of facts supporting guilt and a corresponding eagerness to seek them out. In "borderline" cases she should rely on rebuttable presumptions of guilt to resolve factual conflicts and certainties against the defendant.

Forst (1983 in Gottfredson and Gottfredson 1988: 132) summarizes the results of an empirical study of prosecution decisions, noting that for many, if not most cases, the decision to prosecute is virtually automatic regardless of whether the evidence is weak or strong, or the offense serious or minor. Most recently, a study in Maryland has found that prosecutors there are far more likely to seek the death penalty for accused African Americans charged with killing white victims (Levine and Montgomery 2003). The research suggests that offenders who kill white victims are significantly more likely to be charged with a capital crime and that the probability of such a charge is twice as high as when an African American kills another African American. As well, geography has proved a significant factor in prosecutorial decision making in capital cases. The study found, for example, that in Baltimore County a death sentence was 26 times more likely than in the city of Baltimore and 14 times more likely than in Montgomery County.

Prosecution Disclosure of Evidence to the Defense

Rule 3.8 requiring disclosure of evidence to the defense is broader than the Brady rule upon which it is based (Hazard and Hodes 2002: 34–8). The prosecutor's constitutional duty to make voluntary disclosure of evidence to the defense is set out in *Brady v. Maryland* (1963) and subsequent cases. In considering this constitutional duty, the courts determined that a conviction can be overturned based on the prosecutor's failure to provide evidence. However, this constitutional rule takes account of other factors such as the significance of the evidence and whether the defense made a proper request for it. Where a prosecutor fails to disclose evidence to the defense and suppresses that evidence, the Supreme Court in *United States v. Agurs* (1976) held that exculpatory evidence not made available to the accused could result in denial of the constitutional right to a fair trial, with the outcome that a new trial will be ordered. This duty to disclose exculpatory evidence applies even if it has not been requested by the defense.

Plea Bargaining

After charging but before trial, the prosecutor may begin negotiating with the defense to arrive at a plea bargain. The aim is to achieve a compromise by reducing the charges against the defendant or securing a reduced sentence in exchange for a guilty plea (McDonough, McDonough, and Keenan 2000: 58). Plea bargaining is not supported by the public even though it disposes of 95% of all criminal cases (Bureau of Justice Statistics 2002: 416, tbl. 5.17). For example, in a survey of public attitudes in Washington State, while most expressed positive views toward courts, 82% of respondents rejected plea bargaining as a means of processing criminal cases (Herzog 2004: 590–591). Similarly, in a survey in Chicago, 64% rejected the practice. Some have suggested that this negative public attitude reflects its punitive views on criminality and that the secretiveness of plea negotiating practices increases public suspicion (p. 591). Thus the more lenient the sentence handed down the less support for plea bargaining.

In relation to plea discussions, ABA Standard 3–4.1 states that it is "unprofessional conduct for a prosecutor knowingly to make false statements or representations in the course of plea discussions." The ABA Standards Relating to Administration of Criminal Justice were adopted in 1971 and have strong moral force (Hazard and Hodes 2002: 34–35). In spite of the moral force of these standards, a prosecutor may deliberately overcharge a defendant as a plea-bargaining tactic. Hazard and Hodes (2002: 34–36) give the example of a prosecutor charging an accused with three offenses arising out of the same incident, intending to accept a guilty plea to the least serious charge in exchange for dismissal of the others, assuming that such a plea bargain is advised by the defense. In such a situation, the prosecutor is aware that he or she lacks probable cause for the first and most serious of the charges and has deliberately included it purely as a bargaining chip. The second charge could be sustained, but the prosecutor doubts whether he or she could gain a conviction, and in any event, is not inclined to put in the effort required to prove it. In this sense, therefore, this second charge is also a bargaining chip. The inclusion of the first charge is clearly improper and a violation of Rule 3.8, and the prosecutor must not present it. Presenting the second charge is not considered improper and is normal procedure in plea bargaining. The second charge is proper, because it could legitimately be prosecuted to a conclusion, and if the prosecutor gives up this charge in a plea bargaining, he gives up something of legal significance.

Freedman (1975b: 88) points to the device of overcharging as a means of obtaining a sufficient number of plea bargains, arguing that cases are commonly drawn up as felonies with prosecutors ready to accept a plea for a misdemeanor and thereby coercing defendants into foregoing their right to trial by jury. He argues that the justification for this practice, seen to be the need to transact a great volume of business through the criminal justice system, is insufficient to justify the infringement of a constitutional right by "duress and trickery." He refers also to instances in which prosecutors have failed to advise the court of ineffective assistance provided to an accused by counsel and to situations in which prosecutors have placed their prosecution of a case in a forum where the defense lawyer is likely to overlook defects in the prosecution's case.

McDonough et al. (2000) point out that although some may see a plea bargain as beneficial to the defendant, in fact, a plea bargain benefits the prosecutor, because a guilty plea saves many hours of the prosecutor's time, and, in eliminating the expense and time of a trial, prevents the criminal justice system from becoming overloaded. They note that plea bargains may also assist the prosecutor if an essential element of the prosecution case is weak (p. 59). For example, Pepinsky (2000: 67) reports that in his home county in Indiana, prosecutors bring only 25 to 30 criminal cases a year to jury trial and that these together compose less than 1% of all prosecuted cases. He points out that this number is all that can be accommodated on the local court calendar each year. In 1974 in New York City, 80% of all felony cases were settled as misdemeanors through plea bargains, and only 2% of all felony arrests resulted in a trial (Kipnis 2001: 362). As long ago as the 1920s and 1930s, crime surveys documented the dependence of the criminal justice system on plea bargaining. Researchers found that plea bargaining had largely displaced trial by jury so that, for example, in Chicago, 85% of all felony convictions resulted from guilty pleas. Similar rates applied in Detroit (78%) and Los Angeles (81%) (Remington 1993: 80).

In discussing the negotiated plea, Kipnis (2001: 362) points out that both sides have bargaining power. The prosecutor may be burdened with conducting many cases, and perhaps in some there is insufficient evidence to secure a conviction. At the same time, the prosecutor is under administrative and political pressure to complete cases and secure convictions. On the defense side, a number of factors may influence a defendant to plead guilty. These include feelings of guilt, which may or may not be relevant to the crime charged; the stresses of being locked up before trial; the costs of going to trial; and the delays that always occur in awaiting trial (p. 363). Kipnis points out that the practice of negotiating pleas has never been discussed by any deliberative body or legislature, but rather, it has evolved within the criminal justice system in an unregulated, ad hoc manner (p. 364).

Plea bargains are required to be voluntary; however, the question of whether duress has been applied can be problematic. The Federal Rules of Criminal Procedure require the court to be satisfied that a plea of guilty is voluntary through "addressing the defendant personally in open court, determining that the plea is voluntary and not the result of force or promises apart from a plea agreement" (in Kipnis 2001: 365). Kipnis notes two cases in which defendants agreed to plead guilty in order to avoid probable death sentences and where the court decided that the pleas were voluntary even though in one case the defendant testified at the time of the entry of his plea that he was innocent of the crime charged and had pleaded guilty because he said he had been told that if he did not "they would gas me for it" (p. 365). The essence of plea bargaining in such situations is that a defendant must make a hard choice between something certain and something uncertain, and even when the defendant is innocent and the prosecution's case weak, the defendant may accept the plea bargain for its certainty rather than take the chance on what may happen at trial.

Kipnis points out that hard choices of this kind contain an element of duress where "the state forces a choice between adverse consequences that it imposes" (2001: 367). He concludes that plea bargaining "falls short of the justice we expect of our legal system" (p. 371). He identifies plea bargaining's adverse effects in its coercion of criminal defendants, its acceptance of a measure of punishment less than that consistent with a guilty plea, and its relaxation of the standards for conviction.

Gerber (1999: 31) agrees that the issue of duress harms innocent defendants and that "the accused enjoy few truly realistic strategic choices." He suggests that innocent defendants may plead guilty because of their lack of expertise in plea bargaining and their inability to demonstrate their innocence (p. 32). Gottfredson and Gottfredson (1988: 130) summarize the criticisms of plea bargaining as follows:

- Some innocent persons may be induced to plead guilty by promises of leniency.
- Plea bargaining results in excessive leniency.
- It is impossible to control.
- It shifts sentencing policy from the judge and legislature to the prosecutor and in so doing blurs the distinction between guilt and proper punishment.

What would be the effects of a ban on plea bargaining? White (1980, cited in Gottfredson and Gottfredson 1988: 130) studied the effects of a ban on plea bargaining in Alaska and concluded that the court processes did not become overloaded, that defendants seemed to plead guilty at the same rate, and that there was little change in conviction rates.

Giving a judicial view of plea bargaining, Gerber, a judge of the Arizona Court of Appeals, maintains that the complexity of the criminal trial is a major cause of plea bargaining, because detailed trial procedures have meant that the trial has "ceased to be an efficient routine disposition of a criminal charge" (Gerber 1999: 25). He argues that the strongest justification for plea bargaining is expediency and that there are no principled arguments to justify the practice. In his view, the practice is unfair, because it determines a defendant's guilt without investigation, evidence, or fact finding by an impartial body and may adversely affect the poor and unsophisticated (p. 26). Gerber suggests that lawyers' caseloads are a major reason for the practice and that neither prosecutors nor defense lawyers want to try criminal cases. The prosecutors' aversion arises because they cannot progress with their cases without guilty pleas, and the defense lawyers entertain plea bargains because they are less able to secure new clients if they are tied up with a multitude of trials. Gerber stresses that victims often find plea bargaining to be an offensive practice because they believe that the sentence imposed in a plea is more lenient than would have been imposed for the original charge. He agrees with other commentators that prosecutors often overcharge to gain a negotiating advantage (p. 28).

Gerber (1999) explains the political aspect of plea bargaining by suggesting that an elected district attorney is concerned with securing a high conviction rate, maintaining his or her good relationships with private lawyers of influence in the community, and avoiding losing high profile trials. Ensuring a conviction through plea negotiation keeps the conviction rate high and supports the likelihood of re-election at the end of the prosecutor's term (p. 29).

One consequence of plea bargaining is the absence of a public trial showing accountability and condemnation. Gerber (1999: 35) suggests that a criminal justice system that displaces guilt out of the public space of the courtroom and avoids the public display of due process, guilt, and punishment, abandons the public role of criminal law.

Prosecutorial Misconduct

Freedman (1975b: 79) argues that the ABA ethical standards are inadequate in ensuring the ethical duty of a prosecutor. Specifically, he suggests that the prosecutor's decision about whether to investigate a suspected crime is not the subject of any code of professional responsibility, even though the prosecution's motive in conducting an investigation might be open to question. He reasons that selective prosecution based on improper motives is an abuse of official power and a violation of fundamental rights, and as such, it constitutes unethical conduct.

There have been a number of reported cases of prosecutorial misconduct, some of which result from overzealousness in seeking a conviction, but most of which involve issues such as conflict of interest, failure to enforce the law, and filing charges vindictively (Wolfram 1986: 764). Gershman (1986: 132) provides examples of what he terms "outrageous conduct," such as *Miller v. Pate* (1967), where the prosecutor in a murder case concealed from the jury a crucial piece of evidence, namely, the fact that a pair of undershorts with red stains were stained not by blood but by paint. Another example was in the case of *United States v. Perry* (1981), where the prosecutor in his summation said that the "defendants and their counsel are completely unable to explain away their guilt." The Center for Public Integrity in Texas identified almost 600 appeals in Texas between 1970 and 2003 in which defendants raised allegations of prosecutorial misconduct. In 152 of those cases, a court held that the prosecutor's conduct prejudiced the defendant and that 118 of those cases involved improper trial behavior including making improper statements during arguments, improperly cross-examining witnesses, discrimination in jury selection, withholding evidence from the defense, and failing to correct false testimony (Gier 2006: 193). Prosecutorial misconduct was a factor in 45% of recent cases overturned because of DNA evidence and in 24% of recently overturned death penalty cases (Scheck, Neufeld, and Dwyer 2000).

In considering the issue of why misconduct occurs, Gershman (1986: 133) suggests that the reason lies in its success, pointing out that if prosecutors are prepared to take ethical risks in argument, they do so because they believe that approach to be effective. The opening statement by the prosecutor is crucial in the process, according to Gershman, because juries are most affected by the first strong presentation they observe and hear. As well as using an action-packed opening statement, a prosecutor who uses the same strategy for the closing argument is more likely to be effective.

Gershman (1986: 136) concludes that when prosecutors are faced with a difficult case, they might be tempted to influence the jury to decide in favor of a conviction by referring to a matter that might be highly prejudicial. Referring to inadmissible and stricken testimony, Gershman (2001) argues that such testimony does have an impact on the individual juror, and this is known to the prosecutor, who is aware of jury psychology. He suggests that prosecutors have a general duty to the truth, which includes refraining from misleading conduct that distorts the search for truth. Although he argues that the prosecutor has the capacity to mislead at many stages during the trial process, he identifies the prosecutor's relationship with the jury as one area where misleading conduct occurs. Arguing that the jury is likely to place great confidence and trust in the prosecutor, he notes that familiar types of misleading conduct include

- attempts to place in the jurors' minds innuendo that is damaging and prejudicial to the defendant,
- allusions to expert testimony casting doubt on a defense witness's credibility,
- attempts to enhance a witness's credibility by referring to the witness's willingness to take a polygraph test, and
- comments and questions that suggest that a defendant's reliance upon constitutional rights establishes evidence of guilt.

For example, a defendant who offers an innocent explanation for his conduct at trial may have that explanation impeached by the prosecutor, who insinuates that the defendant's failure to give an account of his conduct following a Miranda warning suggests that his account is fabricated. Similarly, Gershman asserts that it is misleading for a prosecutor to ask a jury to conclude that the defendant's failure to testify is evidence of guilt. Distortion of the process can occur when prosecutors appeal to a jury's fears and prejudices, and Gershman also points out that presenting gruesome physical evidence and engaging in impassioned oratory can have the effect of manipulating the jury's prejudices.

Gershman (1986: 141) suggests that prosecutorial misconduct continues to exist because of the absence or inadequacy of penalties imposed on the prosecutor for such misconduct. Even where an appellate court does sanction a prosecutor by cautioning him or her or by reversing the case, this may not be enough to dissuade prosecutors from further impropriety. Fisher (1988: 213) argues that for prosecutors, the endorsement of "conviction affirmed" in appellate opinions is more important than any condemnation of prosecutorial misconduct. He notes that such opinions often refrain from identifying the prosecutors whose conduct has been condemned and that the courts rarely make references to disciplinary bodies in such incidents. Furthermore, prosecutors are not personally liable for their misconduct and enjoy absolute immunity, so that during the course of a trial, the prosecutor is free from any civil liability arising from any misconduct, even if it was performed with malice (Gershman 1986: 142).

Explanations for prosecutorial misconduct include the notion that prosecutors aim to secure justice and, believing most defendants to be guilty, feel compelled to avoid problems that might render a not guilty verdict. Such conduct would include allowing a witness to lie in the interests of serving the prosecutor's "truth" (Schoenfeld 2005: 252). Thus it is the prosecutor's firm belief in the defendant's guilt that allows him or her to use means that justify the end. In this sense prosecutorial misconduct appears to mirror the police noble cause corruption discussed in Chapter 2. Other explanations blame misconduct on the mentality that compels prosecutors to win at all costs (p. 252). A district attorney may, for example, be under some pressure to secure convictions to ensure reelection, because voters commonly look at conviction records to assess the competence of a prosecutor.

Some commentators also suggest that the Supreme Court has been reluctant to control prosecutorial misconduct (Fisher 1988). For example, Gershman (1987: 218) contends that the court has refused to specify ethical standards for prosecutors and has encouraged "prosecutorial overreaching." In one case, the Illinois Supreme Court said that a prosecutor had acted improperly but refused to discipline him, because he was motivated by "a sincere, if misguided, desire to bring corrupt attorneys to justice" (*In re Friedman* 1979). Generally, in cases of prosecutorial misbehavior, the courts excuse mis behavior by applying arguments of fundamental fairness and harmless error. Allen (1985: 335) has concluded that the problem of controlling prosecutorial excess "is one of . . . [the] great unsolved problems in criminal law administration." Allen (p. 334) cites the position taken by a court in Texas on an apparently deliberate attempt by a prosecutor to mislead a jury when the court decided that even though there had been a deliberate attempt to mislead, it would only consider the effect of the prosecutor's comment and not the intent of the speaker. In that case, the court found that the error had been ameliorated by the court's instruction to the jury.

State bar associations and disciplinary bodies are empowered to sanction prosecutorial misconduct but do so infrequently. For example, a 1999 investigation by the *Chicago Tribune* found that not one single prosecutor was sanctioned by a professional body in relation to 381 convictions reversed on appeal because of misconduct (Schoenfeld 2005: 261). The possibility of criminal prosecution for misconduct is equally remote, and according to Schoenfeld, "Criminal sanctions for misconduct are practically nonexistent" (p. 261). She gives one example, however, of a prosecutor who fabricated and withheld evidence and knowingly introduced perjured testimony who received a $500 fine and an official censure from the court (p. 261).

Model Rule 3.6 forbids prosecutors from making specific kinds of statements out of court that might prejudice a criminal trial. However, the rule includes an exception for necessary statements directed toward public information and for legitimate law enforcement purposes. Hazard and Hodes (2002: 34–13) give the example of an accused escaping from prison after murdering a guard and the prosecutor being permitted to issue a warning that the accused was armed and dangerous as a legitimate exception.

The practice of deferred sentencing, in which the prosecutor delays the sentencing of a witness who has pleaded guilty but will not be sentenced until after giving testimony against another defendant in a way satisfactory to the prosecution, is also condemned (Freedman 1975b: 89). Freedman points to another common form of witness coercion involving the use of prior convictions to impeach a defendant or defense witness as an instance where the prejudicial effect on the jury outweighs the attempt to cast doubt on credibility. He suggests that a prosecutor's actual motive in using prior convictions should be considered, noting that in one case the prosecutor argued before the jury that it should consider the "kind of person the defendant was" in view of the criminal records of the defense witnesses with whom the defendant had associated. Freedman (p. 91) also notes that prosecutors must maintain strong relationships with the police, and this may influence the prosecutor's conduct, because it could lead to covering up police abuses such as brutality, perjury, and unlawful interrogation.

Case Study 4.2 is an example of a determined prosecutor who resisted DNA evidence that would have exonerated a convicted rapist who asserted that he had given a false confession because of threats from the police who interrogated him.

**CASE STUDY 4.2 CONVICT'S DNA
SWAYS LABS, NOT A DETERMINED PROSECUTOR**

In May 1987 Bruce Godschalk, 26, was convicted of raping two women who lived in the same housing complex in a suburb of Philadelphia. He was sentenced to 10 to 20 years in prison, and his conviction was based largely on a confession that he retracted long before his trial. Following his conviction, tests by two laboratories engaged by the prosecution and the defense produced the same outcome, namely, that both rapes were committed by the same man, but that Mr. Godschalk was not the perpetrator.

The Montgomery County District Attorney, Bruce L. Castor Jr., has rejected cause to release Mr. Godschalk, claiming that the DNA testing is flawed and that he has confidence in the tape-recorded confession. Mr. Castor wanted more time to review the DNA testing results in Godschalk's case, orders for which Godschalk obtained after seven years of battling with prosecutors. Over the last decade, DNA testing has freed more than 100 wrongfully convicted persons, with about 20% of those convictions resulting from false confessions. Mr. Godschalk's only previous arrests were for possession of marijuana and driving while impaired.

During the investigation, Mr. Godschalk's picture was shown to one of the rape victims by police six months after the rape incident, and after considering his and other photographs for more than an hour, the victim identified Godschalk as the rapist. Godschalk was then interrogated by a police detective and admitted the crime, but the detective did not record the hours of interrogation leading up to the confession. According to Mr. Godschalk, his confession was false as a result of threats made by the detective, but his motion to suppress the confession was denied during the trial. Mr. Castor refused to let Mr. Godschalk out of prison and stated, after being asked what scientific basis he had for deciding the testing was flawed, "I have no scientific basis. I know because I trust my prosecutors and my tape-recorded confession. Therefore the results must be flawed until someone proves to me otherwise" (in Rimer 2002).

At the request of the *New York Times,* the DNA test results from the prosecution and the defense were reviewed by a third expert, who concluded that Mr. Godschalk was not the rapist.

SOURCE: Rimer 2002.

Case studies 4.3 and 4.4 reveal prosecutors who withheld information in the interests of securing a conviction.

CASE STUDY 4.3 PROSECUTOR WITHHOLDS EVIDENCE

In 2004 Ernest Ray Willis was released from death row, after spending 17 years there for a crime he did not commit. He was convicted in 1987 of setting a house on fire and killing two women. During his trial the prosecutor referred to him as a "rat," "an animal," "a mean vicious dog," and "a satanic demon." Jurors had to decide during the sentencing procedure whether Willis posed a future danger to society, and they answered in the affirmative and sentenced him to death.

It was discovered during a post-conviction investigation that a state psychologist had examined Willis before trial and reported that he would not present much of a future danger to society, but this information, which could have helped him avoid a death sentence, was never given to this lawyer. However, the prosecutor did know of this report, because a federal express record showed that it had been delivered to his office, and additionally the psychologist remembered personally meeting with the prosecutor and advising him that Willis would not make a convincing death penalty case. The prosecutor has denied lying about the psychologist or the report.

A federal judge ordered the state to retry Willis or set him free, determining that suppressing the report plus other factors violated his rights. Following the investigation, the new district attorney requested Willis's immediate release from jail. The original prosecutor maintains that Willis was guilty and has no second thoughts about his prosecution of the case (Gier 2006: 192).

CASE STUDY 4.4 RELEASE AFTER 14 YEARS

On December 28, 2000, Michael Ray Graham Jr., 37, was freed from death row at Louisiana State Penitentiary at Angola after 14 years of incarceration. The state had dismissed all charges against him, because it did not have any credible evidence linking him to the crime for which he had been incarcerated. As compensation he received only a check for $10 from the prison to cover his transportation out of Angola.

In another trial, Albert Ronnie Burrell, 45, had been convicted of the same crime as Mr. Graham, the murder of an elderly couple in Louisiana, and he, too, had spent almost 14 years at Angola on death row. He, too, had all charges against him dismissed by the state. Mr. Burrell, who is mentally challenged and illiterate, came very close to being executed, missing by only 17 days.

The release of the men brought to eight the number of wrongfully imprisoned death row inmates exonerated in the year 2000; altogether over 100 such inmates on death row have been cleared of all crimes and released since the reintroduction of the death penalty in 1973.

According to their lawyers, prosecutorial misconduct was the cause of the incarceration of these two men. No physical evidence linked them to the crime, and their convictions rested largely on the evidence of a jailhouse snitch, who, according to law enforcement officials, was known to them as a habitual liar. The snitch claimed that both men had confessed to the murders while in jail, but he admitted at his own trial that he had spent time in several mental hospitals and had written countless bad checks. The fact that the prosecution had made a plea agreement with the snitch had not been revealed at Mr. Graham's trial nor had the fact that the snitch had previously been found to be mentally incompetent. As well, demonstrating the weak case against Mr. Graham and Mr. Burrell, even the prosecutor had admitted to the court that the case should never have been taken to the grand jury.

SOURCE: Truth in Justice 2001.

Judicial Ethics

The judicial function is a core part of our society. Judges must be competent and ethical, and their actions must always promote respect for their decisions. Judges have considerable power and authority over individuals, and they exercise substantial discretion when acting judicially. They are expected to conduct themselves according to high standards of professional conduct and are held to higher standards of law than lawyers or other persons not invested with the public trust. A judge's duty extends beyond the limits of his or her court and into the judge's personal life, where standards of propriety are far higher than those set for others

(Shaman, Lubet, and Alfini 2000: 1). These strictures concerning judges and judicial conduct are reflected in the Code of Judicial Conduct of the American Bar Association (American Bar Association 1999).

A Model Code of Judicial Conduct was adopted by the ABA in 1990 and establishes standards for ethical conduct by judges. The ABA warns that the code is not intended as an exhaustive guide for the conduct of judges but is intended to state basic standards governing judicial conduct and provide guidance to assist judges in maintaining high standards of personal and judicial behavior. Some of the most important canons of the code relate to impartiality and bias. Under Canon 3, judges are to perform their duties without bias or prejudice and are not to exhibit bias or prejudice, including that based on race, sex, religion, national origin, disability, age, sexual orientation, or socioeconomic status. Further, judges are not to allow staff and court officials to show bias or prejudice.

Judges must also be faithful to the law; must not be swayed by partisan interests, public clamor, or fear of criticism; and must be patient, dignified, and courteous to those with whom they deal. Judges are not to make public comments about proceedings that are pending in court that might reasonably be expected to affect the outcome of such proceedings, impair their fairness, or substantially interfere with a fair trial. However, judges are allowed to make public statements explaining the procedures of the court for public information.

One significant aspect of the U.S. judicial system is the election of judges, sometimes through partisan elections. This raises questions about the influences that elected judges may be subject to in performing their judicial duties. In many states, judges are elected through partisan or nonpartisan elections. Where an election is nonpartisan, the candidate's political party affiliations do not appear on the ballot (Comisky, Patterson, and Taylor 1987: 9). In states that use partisan elections, judicial candidates are usually nominated in primaries or conventions or through nominating petitions. The proponents of partisan elections for judges argue that judges are policy makers and should therefore be directly chosen by, and be accountable to, the people who are affected by those policies; that a partisan election is an open method of selection; and that identifying a potential judge's political affiliation gives voters an indication of his or her political ideology (p. 8).

Those who argue against partisan judicial elections contend that

- voters generally have no knowledge of the candidates' qualifications and in any event are not competent to assess qualifications;
- that nominees are selected by political leaders based on political grounds rather than merit;
- that successful candidates are likely to feel obligated to the political leaders who selected them and to those who contributed to their campaign funds;
- that many otherwise qualified candidates are deterred from seeking office because they are required to conduct political campaigns;
- that voters have a tendency to be influenced by nonjudicial qualifications such as political affiliation; and
- that having to periodically seek re-election discourages many potentially worthwhile candidates. (Comisky et al. 1987: 8)

To what extent do judges take ideological approaches in their judging? Even though judges in Arizona are no longer elected but are appointed, Philips (1998: 22) found that the judges with whom she worked generally agreed that the judicial selection process remains a political one. In one study of judges in a superior court in Arizona, Philips (p. 14) found that judges presented themselves as mere implementers of law, divorced from their political and social backgrounds, despite the fact that they were required to be significantly involved in local political processes in order to become judges. Her research indicates that judges who take a procedure-oriented stance on due process represented a politically liberal approach to the role of the state in relation to the individual. By contrast, judges who take a record-oriented stance followed a politically conservative notion of the role of the state in relation to the individual (p. 79).

Philips's study revealed that the conservative view sees the state as attempting to minimize interference in the lives of individuals, whereas the liberal view considers the state as the protector of human liberties (p. 79). In looking at judicial approaches to guilty pleas, she observed that record-oriented judges did not regard it as their responsibility to ensure that a defendant knowingly and voluntarily pleads guilty. These judges often referred to their assumption that defendants are aware of what they are doing and that they are capable of comprehending judicial instructions. In the case of procedure-oriented judges, however, the responsibility for protecting the defendant's due process rights is taken on by the judge, who also recognizes that some persons need more help than others in comprehending court procedures. Philips's study, along with the systems of political appointment and partisan election of judges, raises the issue of the linkages between political ideology and judicial performance, especially in relation to the ethical duty of a judge to make nonpolitical, unbiased decisions (see Box 4.1).

A CLOSER LOOK

BOX 4.1
Election of Judges Proposed
for Maricopa County, Mesa, Arizona

In Maricopa County, judges have not been elected since 1974, when a system was installed under which judges are chosen by a panel of legal experts and the state governor. However, in a recent move to change the system, Representative Russell Pearce (R-Mesa) wants to change the law and have judges elected, as they are in other states. Critics of the move say that the proposal will result in the election of judges who will make decisions based on political popularity.

Chief Justice Ruth McGregor of the Arizona Supreme Court is firmly against the proposal, pointing out that the present system has meant that judges have not had to campaign to secure office and that they have been able to remain independent of political influence in their decision making. The chief justice believes that changing the system to a ballot of judges will conflict courtrooms because of the influence of lawyers and lobbyists who provide campaign funds. Also, she points out that judges are not representative officials and are responsible for upholding the laws and the constitution.

Chief Justice McGregor thinks that if passed the measure will vastly increase the number of Republican judges, disturbing the existing balance where the courts have an even number of Democrats and Republicans. McGregor favors every judge in Arizona to be appointed and says she will oppose the proposal, which is expected to appear on the November ballot, where voters would decide whether Maricopa County judges should again be elected.

SOURCE: "Judges Might Go" 2008.

Ethical Rules Governing Judges

As well as acting without prejudice or bias, judges are expected to disqualify themselves in any proceeding in which their impartiality might be questioned. This includes instances in which a judge has a personal bias or prejudice concerning a party or lawyer, has personal knowledge of disputed evidence, or has previously served as a lawyer in the matter in dispute.

In terms of a judge's personal life, under Canon 4, personal activities are categorized as "extra-judicial activities," and judges are required to minimize the risk of conflict between those activities and their obligations as judges. Accordingly, judges are not to act in extrajudicial activities in a way that will cast doubt on their impartiality, demean the judicial office, or interfere with the proper performance of judicial duties. The commentary to this canon gives as examples of expressions of extrajudicial bias or prejudice racial slurs and jokes that may cast doubt on the judge's capacity to act impartially.

In financial activities, judges are not to engage in financial and business dealings that may be seen as exploiting their positions as judges or to become involved in transactions or business relationships with lawyers or other persons likely to come before the court. Judges are not to accept, and are to urge members of their families not to accept, gifts, loans, or favors, except those permitted as listed in the code. Permitted activities include accepting public testimonials or gifts, ordinary social hospitality, scholarships and fellowships, and loans, provided they are not from lawyers or their firms if they have come or are likely to come before the judge.

Canon 3 prohibits judges from commending or criticizing jurors for their verdict. In Utah, which has a code of judicial conduct almost identical to the ABA Code, a judge was criticized for violating this prohibition. He reportedly told the jury "this was a pretty clear case. . . . I don't know how you came out with this result, and this is one of the very few times I've criticized the jury" (Averett 2004: 698).

Case studies 4.5–4.9 show examples of breaches of judicial ethics.

CASE STUDY 4.5 PROSECUTOR SAYS TAPE SHOWS BROOKLYN JUDGE TOOK A BRIBE

On February 8, 2002, the *New York Times* reported that a Brooklyn judge had been arraigned on a charge of accepting a bribe. Prosecutors had obtained a covert tape recording showing the judge laughing as he persuaded a lawyer to give him what both men seemed to understand was a payoff in a civil case that would net the lawyer a $1.6 million fee. The lawyer had been wired by the prosecutors and had delivered $18,000 to the judge's robing room at the state supreme court in Brooklyn. Prosecutors claim the judge wanted the payment in exchange for his approval for the settlement of a civil case. Justice Barron was charged with one count of bribe receiving and could face a prison term of 15 years. The prosecutor explained that his investigators were expanding their inquiry into judicial wrongdoing in Brooklyn, including examining hundreds of Justice Barron's cases.

SOURCE: Glaberson 2002.

Judicial Misfeasance

The following case studies provide examples of judicial misfeasance.

CASE STUDY 4.6 FEDERAL JUDGES AND FINANCIAL INTEREST CONFLICTS

Responding to criticism from Congress about lapses in judicial ethics, the Chief Justice decided in 2006 that all federal judges would be required to install software on their computers to avoid unknowingly participating in cases in which they have a financial interest. Also judges were prohibited from being reimbursed for attending a private seminar, unless the seminar sponsor filed a public disclosure statement on the program content and financing sources. About 700 complaints a year are received about federal judges.

SOURCE: Greenhouse 2006.

CASE STUDY 4.7 APPEARANCE OF PARTIALITY

In October 2006 a panel of the Washington Supreme Court reprimanded a judge of the court who visited a facility holding sexually violent predators who had completed their sentences but had been determined by the court to be likely to engage in predatory acts of sexual violence. The judge was sanctioned with admonishment, the mildest punishment, for creating an appearance of partiality when he questioned inmates and accepted documents from them at the facility. The complaint had been made by prosecutors, and the judge had been invited by several inmates.

SOURCE: Liptak 2006

CASE STUDY 4.8 JUDICIAL BRIBERY

In August 2004 it was reported that surveillance tapes recorded in a Brooklyn matrimonial judge's office showed the judge offering a lawyer detailed instructions on how to argue a case before him and informing the lawyer that he would award his client the rights to a house in a divorce case. The judge has been charged with accepting cash, cigars, and dozens of meals from the lawyer in exchange for giving him an advantage in divorce cases and referring clients to him. The tapes also show the judge accepting $1,000 cash and a $250 box of cigars from the lawyer.

SOURCE: Newman 2004: 1

CASE STUDY 4.9 GROSS ABUSE OF POWER

In December 2004 it was reported that an upstate New York judge had been censured for sending people to jail for minor misbehavior at his courthouse. In one case, a college student at Skidmore College was told by the judge that he was "an obnoxious young man," to which the student responded that the judge was "an obnoxious old man." In retaliation the judge ruled the student in contempt and sent him to jail, where he was held in solitary confinement for 4 days. In a second case, the judge ordered the parents of a young man to attend before him after their son had pleaded guilty on some traffic tickets. Reportedly the judge told the parents he had overheard them exchange curse words in the parking lot before the court case began. The judge ordered the father to be handcuffed and taken to a jail cell and despite her objections told the wife that she needed an order of protection from her husband. The state's Commission on Judicial Conduct censured the judge, calling the two acts a gross abuse of power.

SOURCE: Baker 2004: 5

Summary

Like members of most professions, lawyers enjoy the benefit of detailed rules concerning ethical conduct, and judges are in a similar position. Ethical dilemmas for lawyers can usually be resolved by applying the relevant ethical standard. This mechanism has the effect of simplifying moral issues that arise in legal practice. There are notable tensions within the criminal justice system affecting lawyers, and the adversarial system itself underpins and promotes these tensions. Questions about a defense lawyer's proper role are answered by ethical standards, but the morality of keeping silent about a client's criminal conduct continues to provoke debate among the general public. However, once an understanding is gained about the connection between the protection of individual rights in the criminal process and the task of the defense lawyer in ensuring those protections are enforced, these moral issues can be seen within context, particularly within the framework of the adversarial system.

Prosecutors are in a special position because of the tensions and conflicts to which they may be subjected. To a great extent, these arise as a result of the existence of wide prosecutorial discretion. Whether the primary concern is for the victim, the community, reelection, or discovering "the truth," prosecutors must make choices and decide their constituency, either generally or in a particular case.

Generally, there exists considerable potential for judges and prosecutors to become corrupted because they enjoy such wide discretions and powers. Although judges perform in public and are subject to a high level of accountability, prosecutors' positions are much more problematic due to the lack of transparency surrounding their prosecutorial decision making.

DISCUSSION QUESTIONS

1. Explain the importance of lawyer–client confidentiality, and discuss any exceptions to the confidentiality rule.

2. The existence of the adversarial system and the need for lawyers to act zealously explains why lawyers are not troubled by what some see as their "immoral" actions in defending those they know to be guilty. Discuss.

3. In what circumstances must lawyers disclose crimes committed by their clients?

4. What are lawyers' responsibilities if their clients insist on perjuring themselves in testimony to the court?

5. Consider the advantages and disadvantages of plea bargaining from the prosecutor's point of view.

6. Prosecutors have too much discretion and are accountable to no one for the exercise of their discretion. Discuss.

7. If accused individuals have incompetent counsel who neglect to present all the material facts that might assist them, prosecutors have an ethical duty to make sure these facts are presented consistent with their responsibility to achieve just results. Discuss.

8. Explain how public opinion about crime might influence the decisions of prosecutors and judges in light of the fact that both are often elected officials.

9. Discuss the ethical requirement for prosecutors to "seek justice, not merely to convict" and how this expectation might be enhanced in the justice system.

10. The practice of overcharging as a means of obtaining a sufficient number of plea bargains, where cases are commonly drawn up as felonies with the prosecutor ready to accept a plea for a misdemeanor, coerces the defendant into foregoing the right to trial by jury. Discuss and explain the consequences.

11. The exercise of discretion granted to the prosecutor in making the decision to charge is not accompanied by any controls, and the decision of whether or not to charge is "the single most unreviewed exercise of the power of the criminal law available to an individual in the American system of justice" (Gottfredson and Gottfredson 1988: 114). The ABA has made recommendations for criteria that a prosecutor should consider when deciding to charge, including the disproportion of the punishment to the offense. Discuss the prosecutor's decision to overcharge in drug offenses in light of the mass incarceration outcome of the War on Drugs, mandatory sentencing, three-strikes-and-you're-out legislation (see chapters 3 and 7) and the conspiracy laws that punish small drug users and dealers the same as kingpins.

CHAPTER 5

The Purpose of Criminal Punishment

Does society have the right to punish? Is the infliction of punishment morally justifiable? These complex questions will be addressed in the following discussion of the rationale, justification, and nature of punishment. Rules about punishment, such as how much punishment can be inflicted and for what kinds of behavior, are of course contained in laws and regulations, so in this sense law justifies punishment. However, the moral justification for punishment is a separate issue from the legal justification, because although the law may provide for the infliction of punishment, society's moral justification for punishment still has to be established.

In order to better understand the nature of punishment, it is first necessary to examine its conceptual basis and then to consider the various theories that have been developed to morally justify society's infliction of punishment. These theories are deterrence, retribution, just deserts, rehabilitation, incapacitation, and more recently, restorative justice. As well, it is important to appreciate that there are three perspectives about the issue of punishment: the philosophical, the sociological, and the criminological. Each perspective represents a different and distinct way of looking at the issue of punishment, and each will be addressed in this chapter.

What Is Punishment?

We use the word *punishment* to describe anything we think is painful; for example, we refer to a "punishing work schedule" or a "punishing exercise program." We also talk of punishment in the context of parents or teachers disciplining children. However, in this discussion we will consider punishment in a particular sense. Flew (1954, in Bean 1981: 5) argues that punishment, in the sense of a sanction imposed for a criminal offense, consists of five elements:

1. It must involve an unpleasantness to the victim.

2. It must be for an offense, actual or supposed.

3. It must be of an offender, actual or supposed.

4. It must be the work of personal agencies; in other words, it must not be the natural consequence of an action.

5. It must be imposed by an authority or an institution against whose rules the offense has been committed. If this is not the case, then the act is not one of punishment but is simply a hostile act. Similarly, direct action by a person who has no special authority is not properly called punishment and is more likely to be revenge or an act of hostility.

In addition to these five elements, Benn and Peters (1959, in Bean 1981: 6) add that the unpleasantness should be an essential part of punishment.

The value of this definition of punishment resides in its presentation of punishment in terms of a system of rules and in its differentiation of punishment from other kinds of unpleasantness. Another definition of punishment, proposed by Garland, is "the legal process whereby violators of criminal law are condemned and sanctioned in accordance with specified legal categories and procedures" (Garland 1990: 17). This chapter will not be concerned with punishment that takes place in schools, within families, or in other institutions but instead will discuss forms of punishment that take place as the result of legal processes defined above. It will examine the major arguments relating to punishment, illustrate the ways in which those arguments relate to justice and the justice system, and examine how that system would be affected should one argument prevail over another.

Theoretical Approaches to Punishment

Thinking about the issue of punishment gives rise to a number of questions, the most fundamental of which is, why should offenders be punished? This question might produce the following responses:

- They deserve to be punished.
- Punishment will stop them from committing further crimes.
- Punishment tells victims that society disapproves of the harm that they have suffered.
- Punishment discourages others from doing the same thing.
- Punishment protects society from dangerous or dishonest people.
- Punishment allows offenders to make amends for the harm they have caused.
- Punishment ensures that people understand that laws are there to be obeyed.

Some of the possible answers to the question of why offenders should be punished may conflict with each other. This is because some answers are based on reasons having to do with preventing crime, whereas others are concerned with punishment being deserved by an offender (Hudson 1996: 3). When a court imposes a punishment on an offender, it often tries to balance the sorts of reasons for punishment noted earlier, but sometimes certain purposes of punishment dominate other purposes (p. 4). Over time there have been shifts in penal theory, and therefore in the purpose of punishment, due to a complex set of reasons including politics, public policy, and social movements. Consequently, in a cyclical process, an early focus on deterrence as the rationale for punishment gave way to a focus on reform and rehabilitation. This, in turn, has led to a return to punishment based on the notion of retribution and just deserts

The concept of punishment has been theorized by moral philosophers, social theorists, and criminologists, and these various approaches will be considered in this chapter in order to provide a better basis for understanding the place of punishment within the criminal justice system and society in general. As Garland (1990) argues, punishment is a complex concept, and an approach to punishment that is limited to a reading of moral philosophy fails to represent the full dimension and complexity of the subject. For moral philosophers, the "ought" of punishment is of great importance and leads to a set of questions, including the following:

- What should be the goals of punishment?
- What should be the values contained in and promoted by the criminal law?
- What is the purpose of punishment?

In contrast to the philosophical view of punishment, the sociological perspective is concerned with the "is" of punishment; that is, what punishment is actually intended for, and the nature of penal systems (see Hudson 1996: 10). Criminologists and policy makers, who focus on penalties for offenses and policy concerns relevant to the punishment of offenders, offer the third perspective on punishment. Some critics, such as Bean (1981: 9), argue that criminology has tended to ignore the moral and sociological implications of punishment in favor of the social and personal characteristics of offenders as well as the nature of penal institutions and methods of social control. In the same vein, Nigel Walker (1991) points out that the practical ends of penal action, particularly with the aims of sentencing and the administration of prisons and probation, are concerns that pay little attention to the philosophy or sociology of punishment. The criminological perspective will be discussed in Chapter 6 in the context of corrections; this chapter will explore the philosophical and sociological perspectives.

Why Punish? The Philosophical Approach

In the philosophical debate about punishment, two main types of theories of punishment dominate: utilitarian theory and retributive theory. (Utilitarian theory is discussed more fully in Chapter 10.) These philosophical theories have in turn generated further theoretical discussions about punishment concerned with deterrence, retribution, incapacitation, rehabilitation, and more recently, restorative justice.

Theories that set the goal of punishment as the prevention of future crime (deterrence) are usually referred to as *utilitarian*, because they are derived from utilitarian philosophy. Past-oriented theories (theories that focus on the past actions of the offender) are referred to as *retributivist*, because they seek retribution from offenders for their crimes. The retributivist conception of punishment includes the notion that the purpose of punishment is to allocate moral blame to offenders for the crimes and that their future conduct is not a proper concern for deciding punishment (Hudson 1996: 3). Theories of deterrence, retribution, just deserts, rehabilitation, and incapacitation as well as the idea of restorative justice will be considered in this chapter. Each of these theories tries to establish a basis for punishment as a response to the question, "Why punish?" Box 5.1 gives a short history of the concept of punishment in Western cultures, while Case Study 5.1 provides a contemporary example of corporal punishment.

A CLOSER LOOK

BOX 5.1
Punishment and History

Before the installation of constitutional governments in most of Western Europe in the 18th and 19th centuries, penalties were arbitrary, dependent on the whims of monarchs or the local nobles to whom they delegated authority to punish. There was very little proportionate graduation of penalties, with capital punishment available for everything from murder and high treason to fairly minor theft (as reflected in the old saying "one might just as well be hanged for a sheep as a lamb") (Hudson 1996: 19).

Draconian Punishments

The notion of "draconian punishments" derives from the laws promulgated for Athens in 621 B.C. by Draco (see, for example, Carawan 1998). It appears from later accounts of the Draco code that the punishment of death was prescribed for even the most trivial offenses. Draconian punishments are essentially deterrent in nature, being so severe as to dissuade most people from committing crimes. Draconian-type notions of punishment are often advocated by those in the "get tough on crime" lobby.

CASE STUDY 5.1 THE NATURE OF THE PUNISHMENT: CORPORAL PUNISHMENT

On May 4, 1994, Michael Fay, a U.S. teenager who had pleaded guilty to several acts of vandalism in Singapore, was caned by Singapore's authorities (in Nygaard 2000: 1). He was stripped, bent at the hip over a padded trestle, tied down at his ankles and wrists, and his buttocks were lashed by a martial arts specialist four times with a 4-foot long, half-inch wide stick of rattan soaked in antiseptic. Fay, 18, had lived in Singapore since 1992. He was sentenced to 4 months in prison, a fine of $2,230, and the caning after his guilty plea.

The sentence of corporal punishment secured great media attention in the United States, with many people expressing their views. President Clinton, in a personal letter to the Singapore president, urged him to spare the rod and revoke the punishment, which Clinton described as "extreme." Also, 24 U.S. senators appealed to the president of Singapore that clemency would be "an enlightened decision." However, U.S. public opinion expressed support for the punishment, some even writing to the Singapore embassy in Washington expressing their approval. In Dayton, Ohio, where Fay's father lived, citizens supported the punishment by a 2 to 1 margin.

The Singaporean courts and government rejected the various appeals for clemency, except for reducing the number of lashes. A Home Affairs Ministry official stated that Singapore was able to keep its society orderly and crime free because of its tough laws against antisocial crimes and that Singapore did not have a situation like that in New York, where acts of vandalism were commonplace and where even police cars were vandalized.

Deterrence

People are deterred from actions when they refrain from carrying them out because they experience an aversion to the possible consequences of those actions. Walker (1991: 15) suggests that although penologists believe that penalties do, in fact, deter, it is hard to determine whether the kind of penalty or its severity has any effect on whether a particular penalty is successful. Some question whether deterrence is morally acceptable. They argue that it is unacceptable because it is impossible to achieve, and if deterrent sentences are not successful, inflicting suffering in the name of deterrence is morally wrong (p. 13).

To utilitarian philosophers like Bentham, punishment can be justified only if the harm that it prevents is greater than the harm inflicted on the offender through punishing him or her (Hudson 1996: 18). In this view, therefore, unless punishment deters further crime, it simply adds to the totality of human suffering. In other words, utilitarians justify punishment by referring to its beneficial effects or consequences. In this sense, utilitarian theory is a consequentialist theory that considers only the good and bad consequences produced by an act as morally significant (Ten 1987: 3). Bentham is considered the main proponent of punishment as deterrence, and he expressed his early conception of the notion as follows:

> Pain and pleasure are the great springs of human action. When a man perceives or supposes pain to be the consequence of an act he is acted on in such manner as tends with a certain force to withdraw him as it were from the

commission of that act. If the apparent magnitude be greater than the magnitude of the pleasure expected he will be absolutely prevented from performing it. (in Bean 1981: 30)

Becarria took a position similar to Bentham's, arguing that "the aim of punishment can only be to prevent the criminal committing new crimes against his countrymen and to keep others from doing likewise" (in Bean 1981: 30). Utilitarians understand punishment only as a means to an end and not as an end in itself. They perceive punishment in terms of its ability to reduce crime and do not focus on the punishment that "ought" to be imposed on offenders. To utilitarians, a "right" punishment (or one with the greatest utility) is one that is beneficial to the general welfare of all those affected by the criminal act (Bean 1981: 4). Critics of utilitarianism argue that because utilitarians see the aim of punishment as promoting public welfare and maximizing the happiness of all, this means that utilitarians are willing to punish the innocent in order to achieve that objective (p. 4).

Those supporting the theory of punishment as deterrence distinguish between *individual deterrence* and *general deterrence*. Individual deterrence involves deterring someone who has already offended from reoffending; general deterrence involves dissuading *potential* offenders from offending at all by way of the punishment administered for a particular offense (Hudson 1996). Individual deterrence relies on offenders receiving a taste of the punishment they will receive if they reoffend, and it can be seen operationally in "short, sharp, shock punishments," such as boot camps, which are used as an alternative to imprisonment and are clearly aimed at subjecting offenders to a regime that will shock them out of any further criminal conduct. General deterrence takes the form of legislation imposing penalties for specific offenses in the belief that those penalties will deter or prevent persons from committing those offenses. An example of an attempt at general deterrence would be significantly increasing the penalties for driving under the influence (DUI) in an effort to deter citizens from drunk driving.

Does Deterrence Work?

Beyleveld (1979, cited in Hudson 1996: 23), after carrying out a comprehensive review of studies that have considered the deterrent effects of punishment, concluded that

there exists no scientific basis for expecting that a general deterrence policy, which does not involve an unacceptable interference with human rights, will do anything to control the crime rate. The sort of information needed to base a morally acceptable general policy is lacking. There is some convincing evidence in some areas that some legal sanctions have exerted deterrent effects. These findings are not, however, generalizable beyond the conditions that were investigated. Given the present state of knowledge, implementing an official deterrence policy can be no more than a shot in the dark, or a political decision to pacify "public sentiment."

The empirical evidence suggests that, generally, punishment has no individual deterrent effect (Ten 1987: 9). Walker (1991: 16) argues that evidence from research studies has established that capital punishment has no greater effect than life imprisonment. Nagin (cited in Ten 1987: 9) comments on the difficulty in distinguishing between individual deterrence and rehabilitation. In another overview of research on deterrence, Nagin (1998: 345) identifies three sets of studies, which he refers to as interrupted time-series studies, ecological studies, and perceptual studies.

The first set, time-series studies, explores the effect of specific policy initiatives such as police crackdowns on open-air drug markets. Nagin finds that such policy targeting has only a temporary effect and is therefore not a successful deterrent.

Ecological studies look for a negative association between crime rates and punishment levels that can be interpreted as having a deterrent effect. Nagin points out that a number of such studies have been able to isolate a deterrent effect.

In perceptual studies, the data come from surveys. Such surveys have found that self-reported criminality is lower among those who see sanctions, risks, and costs as higher. Nagin therefore concludes that, collectively, the operations of the criminal justice system exert a substantial deterrent effect.

In discussing whether the threat of punishment has a deterrent effect, Andenaes (1972: 345) explains that two positions are usually debated. Bentham's position is that man is a rational being who chooses between courses of action having first calculated the risks of pain and pleasure. If, therefore, we regard the risk of punishment as sufficient to outweigh a likely gain, a potential criminal applying a rational approach will choose not to break the law. The alternative position considers this model unrealistic, arguing that people remain law-abiding, not because they fear the criminal law, but as a result of moral inhibitions and norms of conduct. Criminals, they argue, do not make rational choices but act out of emotional instability, through lack of self-control, or as a result of having acquired the values of a criminal subculture (p. 345). Andenaes points out the dangers of generalization; that is, he suggests it is necessary to distinguish between various offenses such as murder and drunk driving. Offenses vary immensely in terms of an offender's motivation, and any realistic discussion of general deterrence ought to take into account the particular norms and circumstances of each particular type of offense.

He also notes that the threat of punishment, although directed to all persons, affects individuals in different ways (Andenaes 1972: 346). For example, in his view, the law-abiding citizen does not need the threat of the law to remain law-abiding. On the other hand, the criminal group may well fear the law but still break it, and the potential criminal might have broken the law if it had not been for the threat of punishment. It follows that the threat of punishment seems relevant only to the potential criminal. In some cases, however, there is evidence that punishment has a deterrent effect on individuals. Andenaes refers to a study of department store shoplifting where amateur shoplifters were treated as thieves by the store management and reacted by changing their attitudes and experiencing great emotional disturbance (1972: 343). This contrasts with the professional shoplifter who does not register any shock at getting caught and accepts jail as a normal hazard of the trade.

Tullock (1974: 109), after surveying the economic and sociological models of deterrence, concludes that multiple regression studies show empirically that increasing the frequency or severity of punishment does reduce the likelihood of a given crime being committed. However, Blumstein, Cohen, and Nagin (1978: 66) contend that although the evidence does establish a negative association between crime rates and sanctions, this does not necessarily establish the general deterrent effect of sanctions. This is because, in their view, the negative association can be explained by lower sanctions being the effect, and not the cause, of higher crime rates. Overall there seems to be little agreement among researchers that punishment has a general deterrent effect.

How Much Punishment Must Be Imposed to Deter?

For the utilitarian who regards punishment as bad in itself, a particular punishment will be justified only if the suffering it inflicts is less than the harm caused by the criminal act that would have taken place had there been no punishment. If various forms of punishment would achieve the same result, a utilitarian will opt for the most lenient punishment that minimizes the potential suffering. It follows that if a sentence of capital punishment and the lesser punishment of a term of imprisonment are both equally effective in deterring murder, the utilitarian will choose the lesser punishment and regard capital punishment as unjustified. However, utilitarian approaches can result in the infliction of excessive punishment. Ten (1987: 143) gives the example of petty thefts being widespread in society with hundreds of cases occurring, frequently perpetrated by efficient thieves who are difficult to catch. The harm caused by each individual theft is minor, but the total harm, according to utilitarian approaches, is great and may, therefore, be greater than the harm caused by severely punishing one minor criminal. If a newly enacted law were to impose a punishment of 10 years imprisonment on a petty thief, and no less a penalty would have a deterrent effect, it is arguable that a utilitarian would have to accept what would be considered an excessive sentence for the one petty thief unlucky enough to be arrested and convicted (Ten 1987: 143–144).

Retribution

Retribution is the theory that punishment is justified because it is deserved. Systems of retribution for crime have long existed, with the best known being the *lex talionis* of Biblical times, calling for "an eye for an eye, a tooth for a tooth, and a life for a life" (Hudson 1996: 38). Retributionists claim a moral link between punishment and guilt and see punishment as a question of responsibility or accountability (Bean 1981: 14–15). Once society has decided upon a set of legal rules, the retributivist sees those rules as representing and reflecting the moral order. Society's acceptance of legal rules means that the retributivist accepts the rules, whatever they may be; accepts that the rule makers are justified in their rule making; and claims that those who make the rules provide the moral climate under which others must live. Accordingly, retributivists cannot question the legitimacy of rules. They argue that retribution operates on a consensus model of society where the community, acting through a legal system of rules, acts "rightly," and the criminal acts "wrongly" (Bean 1981: 17). It follows that the retributivist position makes no allowance for social change or social conditions, looking instead only to crime. Raising the issue of the social causes of crime and questioning the effectiveness of punishment are irrelevant considerations to a retributivist.

Van den Haag (1975) and Kleinig (1973) have suggested that in historical terms, the *lex talionis* did not operate as a demand for retribution. Instead, it set a limit on the nature of that retribution and therefore prevented the imposition of excessive penalties in the course of acts of vengeance. Capital punishment may be the only form of punishment still supported by appeals to the *lex talionis*. The basic principle of *lex talionis* is that punishment should inflict the same on offenders as offenders have inflicted on their victims. It can, therefore, be seen as a crude formula, because there are many crimes to which it cannot be applied. For instance, what punishment ought to be inflicted on a rapist under *lex talionis*? Should the state arrange for the rape of the offender as his due punishment? In addition, the *lex talionis* can be objected to because its formula to determine the correct punishment considers solely the harm caused by the crime and makes no allowance for the mental state of the offender or for any mitigating or aggravating circumstances associated with the crime. Thus, even though a person's death may have been brought about accidentally or negligently, the *lex talionis*, strictly applied, would still call for the imposition of the death penalty (Ten 1987: 152). A further objection is found in the view that in a civilized society, certain forms of punishment are considered too cruel to be defended as valid and appropriate. For example, a sadistic murderer may horribly torture his or her victim, but society would condemn the imposition of that same form of punishment on the offender. It can also be said that although the death penalty may constitute a just punishment according to the rule of *lex talionis*, it should nevertheless be abolished as part of "the civilizing mission of modern states" (Reiman 1985: 115).

Retributivists believe that wrongdoers deserve to be punished and that the punishment imposed should be in proportion to the wrongdoing the offender committed. In contrast to utilitarians, retributivists focus their line of reasoning on the offender's just desert (a proportionate punishment) and not on the beneficial consequences of punishment. Retributivists ask questions such as "Why do offenders deserve to be punished?" and "How are their just deserts to be calculated and translated into actual sentences?"

A number of explanations have been suggested to justify retribution, including the notion that retribution is a payment of what is owed; that is, offenders who are punished are "paying their debt to society" (Walker 1991: 73). Walker notes that this seems to confuse "the victim" with "society," because we generally do not perceive offenders as liable to pay compensation or make restitution to their victims; furthermore, if society is compensated for anything at all, it is for a breach of its peace (p. 73).

Censure is also an important component in retributivist thinking. For example, Andrew von Hirsch, the leading theorist on just deserts sentencing, writes,

> Desert and punishment can rest on a much simpler idea, used in everyday discourse: the idea of censure. . . . . Punishment connotes censure. Penalties should comport with the seriousness of crimes so that the reprobation on the offender through his penalty fairly reflects the blameworthiness of his conduct. (in Walker 1991: 78)

For von Hirsch (1994: 120–121), censure is simply holding individuals accountable for their conduct and involves conveying the message to perpetrators that they have willfully injured someone and must face the disapproval of society for that reason. On the part of the offender, an expression of concern or remorse is expected. As well, the censure expressed through criminal law has the role of providing third parties with reasons for not committing acts defined as criminal. In other words, censure can have a deterrent effect. Some theorists of desert argue that notions of censure cannot be adequately expressed verbally or symbolically and that hard treatment is needed to properly express societal disapproval. The notion of the *expressive* or *communicative* character of punishment is closely associated with the idea of "punishment as censure." This conception recognizes punishment as comprising not merely harsh treatment but also elements of condemnation, denunciation, and censure. Thus, for example, punishment in the form of a fine is quite different from the payment of a tax, although both involve payment to the state. In the same vein, imprisonment contrasts with other forms of detention such as quarantine or detention for psychiatric disorders (Duff and Garland 1994: 13–14). Imprisonment, it is argued, carries with it an expressive function of censure, whereas detention for reasons of quarantine or for mental disorder does not. Feinberg (1994: 74) explains the expressive function of punishment in the following terms:

> Punishment is a conventional device for the expression of attitudes of resentment and indignation, and of judgments of disapproval and reprobation, on the part either of the punishing authority himself or of those "in whose name" the punishment is inflicted. Punishment, in short, has a symbolic significance largely missing from other kinds of penalties.

Feinberg (1994: 76) further argues that punishment expresses more than disapproval; it amounts to a symbolic method of hitting back at the criminal and of expressing "vindictive resentment." In similar fashion, H. Morris (1994: 92) contends that punishment serves to teach offenders a moral lesson so that in the process of being punished and being made aware that a crime violated communal values, they will come to see what is good and choose it in the future. According to this account, the aim of punishment is to persuade and not to manipulate or coerce. However, as Morris himself points out, this approach does not account for the punishment of those who are already repentant, nor is it able to cope with those who understand the values of society but are indifferent or opposed to them (p. 106).

Over the last few decades, the notion of punishment as a *communicative practice* has developed (Duff 1999: 48). This notion asserts that punishment communicates to the criminal a response appropriate to the crime committed. Communication requires that the person to whom the communication is directed must be an active participant in the process and must receive and respond to the communication. Additionally, the communication should appeal to the person's rational understanding. The communication must be focused primarily on the offender being punished as a response to him or her and must be justified by his or her offenses (Duff 1999: 50). The message communicated by punishment must focus on and be justified by the offender's past offense and must be appropriate to that offense. Duff (1999: 50) argues that the message communicated should be the degree of censure or condemnation the crime deserves. In the context of criminal law, censure might be communicated in a formal conviction of guilt or through a system of harsh punishments such as imprisonment, fines, or community service. Duff (p. 51) argues that the aim of hard treatment is ideally to cause offenders to understand and repent crimes committed. It should attempt to direct their attention to the crime and give them an understanding of crime as a "wrong." It should also cause offenders to accept the censure that punishment communicates as deserved. By undergoing hard punishment, offenders can become reconciled with the community and restored back into the community from which the offense caused them to be excluded.

Philosophers such as Duff (in Walker 1991: 79) see the main benefit of punishment as *the effect on the offender.* They argue that punishment has the effect of restoring the offender to the community in the same way that penance restores a penitent to the communion of the church. Nozick sees retributive punishment as a *message* from those whose values are assumed to be correct and normative to someone whose act or omission has displayed incorrect and non-normative values (in Walker 1991: 81). Walker (1991: 81) explains that "man is a rulemaking animal," and that rules and notions of rules are acquired during childhood. *Rules,* in the form of transactions involving promises, establish codes of normative conduct including "penalizing rules" that specify action to be taken against those who infringe the rules (Garfinkel in Walker 1991: 84–85). It follows that failing to penalize an offender for infringing the rules would itself be an infringement of those rules; thus, an unpunished infringement would create two infringements.

Another theory that attempts to justify punishment as a retributive act is that an offender should be viewed as a person who has taken an *unfair advantage* of others in society by committing a crime and that imposing punishment restores fairness (Ten 1987: 5). Philosophers such as Herbert Morris, John Finnis, and Jeffrie Murphy subscribe to the *unfair advantage* theory. For example, Morris argues that the effect of criminal law is to confer benefits on society, because others are not permitted to interfere with areas of an individual's life, given that certain acts are proscribed and prohibited. In order to gain the benefits of noninterference, individuals must exercise self-restraint and not engage in acts that infringe the protected areas of the lives of others (in Ten 1987: 53). It follows that when people violate the law but continue to enjoy its benefits, they take an unfair advantage of others who follow the law. Punishment, it is argued, is therefore justified, because it removes this unfair advantage and restores the balance of benefits and burdens disturbed by the criminal activity.

The unfair advantage argument has been challenged by those who argue that it distorts the nature of crime itself. For example, the wrongfulness of rape does not merely consist of taking an unfair advantage of those who obey the law. Also, it is difficult to show that offenders have in any real sense "willed" their own punishment (Murphy 1994: 44). Additionally, although unfair advantage might constitute an ideal theory for the justification of punishment, the question arises about whether it can be applied to an actual society. In other words, do those who commit criminal acts actually take an unfair advantage for themselves?

Finally, some retributivists argue that punishment is morally justified, because it gives *satisfaction*. James Fitzjames Stephen, an English Victorian judge, is often cited as an advocate of this theory. He expressed his view of punishment as follows:

> I think it highly desirable that criminals should be hated, and that punishments inflicted upon them should be so contrived as to give expression to that hatred, and to justify it so far as the public provisions of means for expressing and gratifying a healthy, natural sentiment can justify and encourage it. (in Bean 1981: 21)

In 1972 and 1976, the U.S. Supreme Court stated that it considers retribution "a legitimate justification for capital punishment" (*Furman v. Georgia* 1972; *Gregg v. Georgia* 1976).

Is Retribution in Fact Revenge?

Retributive theories of punishment argue that punishment should be imposed for past crimes and that it should be appropriate to the nature of the crime committed; that is, the severity of the punishment should be commensurate with the seriousness of the crime. Sometimes, retributive punishment is confused with notions of revenge. Critics of retributionist theories of punishment argue that retribution is basically nothing more than vengeance. However, Nozick argues that there is a clear distinction between the two, because "retribution is done for a wrong, while revenge may be done for an injury or harm or slight and need not be a wrong" (1981: 366). He also points out that whereas retribution sets a limit for the amount of punishment according to the seriousness of the wrong, no limit need be set for revenge. In this sense, therefore, revenge is personal, whereas the person dispensing retributive punishment may well have no personal tie to the victim. As Nozick points out, "Revenge involves a particular emotional tone, pleasure in the suffering of another" (1981: 367). A further distinction between the two is that retribution in the form of punishment is inflicted only on the offender, but revenge may be carried out on an innocent person, perhaps a relative of the perpetrator.

Just Deserts

Up until about 1970, criminologists generally thought of retribution as vengeance. During the 1970s, criminologists reconsidered the idea of retribution and advanced new formulations. By the 1980s, the new retributionist theory of just deserts had become influential (Hudson 1996: 39). Importantly, the new thinking indicated that although there should continue to be treatment programs, a defendant would not ordinarily be incarcerated in order to receive treatment (N. Morris 1974). Influential writings such as *Struggle for Justice* (American Friends Service Committee 1971) and *Doing Justice* (von Hirsch and Committee for the Study of Incarceration 1976), the latter written in the aftermath of the riot at Attica Prison in 1971, elaborated on the new retributivism in philosophical and civil libertarian terms.

This theory gained support as a reaction against the perceived unfairness of systems that favored treatment, which had developed over the first half of the 20th century, especially the use of the indeterminate sentence. This form of sentence vested the power of determining the date of release to a parole board and signifies the practice of individualized sentencing. The intent was to sentence according to the treatment needs of the offender rather than the seriousness of the offense (Duff and Garland 1994: 12). One of the criticisms of indeterminate sentencing was the fact that the sentencing courts had a wide discretion in choosing a sentence, and although they tended to adopt tariffs for classes of crime, individual judges could depart from them without providing reasons. Along with the just deserts movement, many states and federal sentencing authorities repealed indeterminate sentencing laws with the aim of reducing judicial discretion in sentencing and promoting consistency and certainty as well as a set of standards that would help in the process of deciding the sentence.

Among the retributivists, Kant argued that the aim of penalties must be to inflict desert and that this was a "categorical imperative." (Kant's categorical imperative is discussed as an aspect of deontology in Chapter 9.) By this he meant that inflicting what was deserved rendered all other considerations irrelevant (Walker 1991: 53). Just deserts proponents emphasize the notion that punishment should be proportionate; that is, there should be a scale of punishments with the most serious being reserved for the most serious offenses, and penalties should be assessed according to the seriousness of the offense (Hudson 1996: 40). This is often called *tariff sentencing*. In this method of punishing, the offender's potential to commit future offenses does not come into consideration, but his or her previous convictions are taken into account, because most proponents of just deserts support reductions in sentences for first offenders. Desert theorists contend that punishment should convey blame for wrongdoing and that blame is attached to offenders because they have done wrong. Consequently, the blameworthiness of the offender is reflected in the punishment imposed.

Thus, advocates of desert focus on two dimensions only—the harm involved in the offense and the offender's culpability. Von Hirsch (1998: 669) enlarges on these two main elements, stating that, in looking at the degree of harm, a broad notion of the quality of life is useful, because "invasions of different interests can be compared according to the extent to which they typically affect a person's standard of living" (p. 670). As to culpability, he suggests that the substantive criminal law, which already distinguishes intentional from reckless or negligent conduct, would be useful in sentencing law.

Von Hirsch (1998: 667) argues that a focus on the censuring aspect of punishment has coincided with a change in criminological thinking. Criminologists had previously regarded the blaming aspects of punishment as a stigmatizing label that might create obstacles to the reintegration of the offender into the community and might also cause offenders to reinforce their own deviance, making them more likely to continue offending. Desert theorists now emphasize that responding to criminal acts with a process of blaming encourages the individual to recognize the wrongfulness of the action, to feel remorse, and to make efforts to refrain from such conduct in the future. In contrast, a deterrent punishment requires the individual to simply comply or face the consequences. The difference between the two approaches is that a moral judgment is required from the offender under just deserts that is not required under a purely deterrent punishment. During the 1980s, many states, as well as the Federal Sentencing Commission, introduced desert-based sentencing schemes (Hudson 1996: 43).

In considering questions of proportionality and seriousness, the issue arises as to how offenses are to be ranked in terms of their seriousness. Who is to determine the degrees of seriousness? In some jurisdictions, the judge's views determine the issue; other approaches include the use of sentencing commissions and legislating sentencing schedules. In California, the Determinant Sentencing Laws allow politicians and others to raise the tariffs for offenses in response to public or media pressure in order to give effect to "get tough on crime" policies (Zimring 1976, 1994).

Some critics argue that just deserts theory leads to harsher penalties, but von Hirsch (1998: 672) contends that the theory itself does not call for harsher penalties and that sentencing schemes relying specifically on just deserts theory tend not to be severe. He draws attention to sentencing guidelines in Minnesota and Oregon that provide for modest penalties by U.S. standards. The Minnesota Sentencing Guidelines provide a grid with a horizontal axis showing previous convictions and a vertical axis showing offense type (Hudson 1996: 44). The sentencing judge is required to locate the appropriate cell on the grid for the offender being sentenced, where the severity of the offense and the number of previous convictions intersect. Each cell stipulates a presumptive prison term that represents the normal period of incarceration for a standard case of that offense. In addition to the presumptive sentence, there is a band indicating the range that should apply in the actual case. For example, in the case of an aggravated burglary, where the offender has three previous convictions, there is a presumptive term of 49 months and a range of 45 to 53 months. The actual sentence depends on aggravating and mitigating factors. According to Hudson (1996: 45), sentencing guidelines have had the effect of reinforcing relatively lenient punishments in states with that tradition, although states with a history of imposing severe punishments, such as New Mexico and Indiana, have produced severe schedules and guidelines.

The fundamental difficulty with deserts theory is that it lacks any principle that determines a properly commensurate sentence (Hudson 1996: 46). Deserts are determined by a scale of punishment that fixes the most severe penalty. This might be imprisonment or death. It then determines ordinally proportionate penalties for lesser offenses. It follows that if imprisonment is the most severe penalty, then proportionality will provide shorter terms of imprisonment and noncustodial penalties for lesser offenses. If the term of imprisonment for severe offenses is moderate, then short sentences and penalties such as probation will soon be reached when considering proportionate sentencing options on the scale of seriousness. If the penalty for the most serious offenses is death, it follows that long terms of imprisonment will be considered proportionate penalties for less serious offenses. This is the situation that prevails in many states.

Many argue that retribution based on just deserts fails to account for the problem of just deserts in an unjust world. Just deserts theory ignores social factors like poverty, disadvantage, and discrimination and presumes equal opportunity for all. Tonry (1994: 153) notes that most sentencing commissions in the United States will not allow judges to bring personal circumstances into account in their sentencing decisions, despite the fact that the average offender has a background that is likely to be either deeply disadvantaged or deprived. Zimring (1994: 165) suggests that desert sentencing fails to take account of the fact that there are multiple discretions involved in the sentencing power. He points to the legislature that sets the range of sentences, the prosecutor who has the legal authority to select a charge, the judge as the sentencing authority, and the correctional authority, which is able to modify sentences after incarceration, as constituting a multiplicity of decisions and discretions that make the task of achieving just and proportionate sentences extremely problematic. Since prosecutors and legislators act under political influence and attempt to implement policies that reflect public opinion, the sentencing process is not the monopoly of the trial judge but is all too often an expression of varying perspectives based on periodic concerns about whether current philosophies reflect notions of being "tough on crime."

Reconciling Utilitarian and Retributive Theories

Is it possible to reconcile utilitarian and retributive theories of punishment? For utilitarians, desert is not seen as necessary to justify punishment nor as a reason for punishment, because desert does not look to the consequences of punishment—it simply punishes. For the utilitarian, the only good reasons for punishment relate to the consequences of that punishment. The contrast between the two theories lies in the fact that for utilitarians, the aim of punishment is to control future action, whereas the retributivists see the aim in terms of desert (Bean 1981: 32). The strength of the utilitarian argument is that rules can be changed according to changes in society but that no such change is built into theories of retribution.

Can a retributivist ever be forgiving or merciful? During the sentencing process, offenders often say they are remorseful for their actions, and in this sense remorse represents regret and self-blame. Those charged with the task of determining the sentence are urged to accept statements of remorse as mitigating factors. The issue, therefore, is whether genuine remorse should lead a sentencer toward leniency. If the sentencer is a utilitarian, he or she will be concerned only about whether a remorseful offender will be less likely to reoffend. However, for the retributivist, the question is whether remorse should mitigate culpability (Walker 1991: 112). According to Walker, forgiveness has no degrees but may take the form of "interested" or "disinterested" forgiveness, with the victim being interested and the sentencing authority disinterested. He suggests that the sentencing authority, whether working from a utilitarian or retributivist viewpoint, must choose the sentence that is most appropriate and that a retributivist may take extenuating circumstances into account. He considers, however, that forgiveness, being an act of absolution, should not be considered an extenuating circumstance (p. 113). Thus, according to Bean, "Forgiveness is a moral sentiment where ill-will is no longer retained. It may occur before or after punishment but does not affect it" (1981: 99).

Mercy must be distinguished from forgiveness, because granting mercy is an act, but forgiveness is an attitude of mind (Walker 1991: 115). Mercy may be prompted by expressions of remorse or by a statement that the victim has forgiven the offender. Walker argues that mercy is not equivalent to "reasoned leniency" and that mercy, in effect, suggests other considerations such as proportionality, any suffering experienced by the offender, and mitigation generally (p. 116). Fundamentally, therefore, mercy is a synonym for various kinds of leniency and has no force or effect of its own.

Rehabilitation

Retribution and deterrence involve a process of thinking that proceeds from the crime to the punishment. However, rehabilitation is a more complex notion involving an examination of the offense and the criminal and a concern for the criminal's social background and punishment. Further, those in favor of rehabilitation theories acknowledge the possibility of additional problems developing during the offender's sentence or treatment that may be unconnected with the offense and that may require an offender to spend additional periods in treatment or confinement (Bean 1981: 54).

Utilitarian theory argues that punishment should have reformative or rehabilitative effects on the offender (Ten 1987: 7–8). The offender is considered reformed, because the result of punishment is a change in the offender's values so that he or she will refrain from committing further offenses, now believing such conduct to be wrong. This change can be distinguished from simply abstaining from criminal acts due to the fear of being caught and punished again; this amounts to deterrence, not reformation or rehabilitation by punishment. Proponents of rehabilitation in punishment argue that punishment should be tailored to fit the offender and his or her needs, rather than fitting the offense. Underpinning this notion is the view that offenders ought to be rehabilitated or reformed so they will not reoffend and that society ought to provide treatment to an offender. Rehabilitationist theory regards crime as the symptom of a social disease and sees the aim of rehabilitation as curing that disease through treatment (Bean 1981: 54). In essence, the rehabilitative philosophy denies any connection between guilt and punishment (p. 58).

Bean (1981: 64) outlines the strengths of the rehabilitation position as being its emphasis on the personal lives of offenders, its treatment of people as individuals, and its capacity to produce new thinking in an otherwise rigid penal system. He suggests its weaknesses include an unwarranted assumption that crime is related to disease and that social experts can diagnose that condition; that treatment programs are open-ended and do not relate to the offense or to other defined criteria; and the fact that the offender, not being seen as fully responsible for his or her actions, is capable of manipulating the treatment to serve his or her own interests. In addition, rehabilitation theory tends to see crime as predetermined by social circumstances rather than as a matter of choice by the offender. This, it is said, denies the agency of the offender and arguably treats an offender in a patronizing, infantilizing way (Hudson 1996: 29).

Indeterminate sentences gave effect to the rehabilitative perspective because terms of imprisonment were not fixed at trial, but rather the release decision was given to institutions and persons operating within the criminal justice system, including parole boards, probation officers, and social workers. The notion of rehabilitation enjoyed considerable political and public support in the first half of the 20th century, but modern rehabilitationists now argue that fixed rather than determinant sentences should be the context for rehabilitation (Hudson 1996: 64). They argue that with indeterminate sentences, offenders become preoccupied with their likely release date, and this leads to their pretending to have made more progress in treatment than is really the case.

The demise of rehabilitation as a theory of punishment began in the 1970s and was the result of a complex set of factors, one of which was a much quoted article by Martinson (1974), who was perceived to have argued that "nothing works," that is, that no treatment program works very successfully in preventing reoffending and that no program works better than any other. Martinson later attempted to rectify this pessimistic view of rehabilitation and treatment by acknowledging that some programs work, sometimes, for some types of offenders.[1] Nevertheless, from that point on, policy makers and legislators abandoned rehabilitation as an objective of punishment. On the issue of indeterminate sentencing, the publication of *Criminal Sentences: Law Without Order* by Marvin Frankel, then a federal judge, which argued that judges exercised "almost wholly unchecked and sweeping authority" in sentencing (1972: 5), provided substantial support to the proponents of determinate sentencing. By the 1980s, the retributionist theory of just deserts had become the most influential theory of punishment.

Nowadays, rehabilitationists contend that their rationale for punishment is the only one that combines crime reduction with respect for an offender's rights. According to this view, although capital punishment and long terms of imprisonment may deter and will certainly incapacitate, rehabilitation can be accomplished only if criminals reenter society; consequently extreme punishments should be ruled out. Rotman (1994: 286), for example, argues in favor of a "rights oriented rehabilitation," which accepts the offender's liability to receive punishment but claims a corresponding right on his or her part to "return to society with a better chance of being a useful citizen and staying out of prison." This perspective is often termed "state-obligated rehabilitation" and contends that if the state assumes the right to punish, it should ensure that no more harm is inflicted than was intended when the sentence was pronounced. That is, the intent of the prison sentence is deprivation of liberty and not loss of family ties or employability (Gallo and Ruggiero 1991). Rotman (1994), for one, argues that a failure to provide rehabilitation amounts to cruel and unusual punishment. Carlen (1994) and Matthews (1989) argue that states are entitled to punish offenders because offenders act out of choice. However, they suggest that the offenders' choices are often limited because of circumstances and social conditions like poverty and inequality, which

---

1. A recent meta-analysis found that adult correctional treatment is effective in reducing recidivism; that behavioral cognitive treatments are more effective than others; and that intensive in-prison drug treatment is effective, especially when it operates in conjunction with community aftercare (Gaes et al. 1999: 361). In assessing the effectiveness of interventions, Duff and Garland (1994: 24) point out that we need to ask not just "what works" but "what should be counted as working?"

might lead people into crime. Therefore, Hudson (1996: 66) claims, the state should recognize that it plays a part in causing crime and should recognize its role in crime prevention by providing rehabilitation to assist offenders in not committing further crime. Offenders, on their part, have a corresponding obligation to take part in rehabilitation programs offered by the state. Nevertheless, even for those offenders who are unwilling to enter rehabilitation programs, rehabilitation may be coerced or pressured in the sense that their decision about whether or not to undertake the program will be influenced by the existence of adverse consequences for nonparticipation, for example, the denial of parole if the program is not completed (Day, Tucker, and Howells 2004: 259). In this view, rehabilitation may be seen as an alternative to punishment rather than as something to be achieved through the means of punishment. As Carlen (1994: 329) contends, a purely punitive approach to sentencing does little to decrease crime and serves only to increase the prison population.

Incapacitation

Penal practice has always tried to estimate the risk that individual offenders might commit crimes in the future and has tried to shape penal controls to prevent such crimes from happening. Through the incapacitative approach, offenders are placed in custody, usually for long periods of time, to protect the public from the chance of future offending (H. Morris 1994: 238). In utilitarian theory, incapacitation is seen as a good consequence of punishment, because when serving their sentences, offenders are removed from society and are therefore unable to commit further offenses. This applies regardless of whether offenders are deterred, reformed, or rehabilitated through the punishment they are given. Incapacity may also be present in other forms of punishment such as parole, in the sense that although offenders are free from incarceration, they are placed under supervision, which may restrict their opportunity to commit crime (Ten 1987: 8).

Some criminologists claim that certain offenders commit crimes at very high rates and that applying a policy of selective incapacitation aimed at these "career criminals" will assist with the aims of crime prevention. There are two basic objections to following a policy of incapacitation based on selecting offenders for this kind of punishment. The first is that predicting criminal dangerousness is problematic and will inevitably mean that a number of persons will suffer incapacitation who would not have committed further crimes if left free, because, given the inaccuracies of prediction, it is necessary to lock up or incapacitate large numbers of nondangerous offenders so we can ensure we incapacitate dangerous offenders. Second, there is the moral objection that it is wrong in principle to punish offenders based on a prediction of their future conduct; that is, they ought to be punished for what they have done and not for what they *might* do in the future. H. Morris (1994: 241) argues that sentences intended to incapacitate an offender ought to be permitted only where there exists reliable information showing a high probability of future offending. Morris suggests that taking account of dangerousness in the future should be considered as statements about an offender's present condition and not as a prediction of future conduct.

Some of the problems inherent in incapacitative sentencing include that it works only if

- we lock up those who would have committed further offenses if they had been left free;
- those we lock up are not immediately replaced by new recruits; or
- the crimes committed after release are not so frequent or serious so as to negate the effects of the crimes prevented through incapacitative sentencing.

Ethical questions that arise from the sentencing rationale of incapacitation include (also see Travis 2002):

- Is it ethical to punish persons for crimes not yet committed?
- Is it ethical to base punishment on inaccurate predictions?
- Is it ethical to punish repeat offenders for past crimes they committed and have already been punished for?

The notion of incapacitation is reflected in such punishment policies as three-strikes legislation, mandatory minimum sentences, and truth in sentencing. These polices will be discussed as penal policies in Chapter 7.

Restorative Justice

Braithwaite (1998: 323) argues that restorative justice has been "the dominant model of criminal justice throughout most of human history for all the world's peoples," and that it is grounded in traditions from ancient Greek, Arab, and Roman civilizations and in Hindu, Buddhist, and Confucian traditions. Braithwaite emphasizes that restorative justice means restoring victims as well as offenders and the community. In addition to restoring lost property or personal injury, restoration means bringing back a sense of security. He points to the shame and disempowerment suffered by victims of crime. He observes that Western legal systems generally fail to incorporate victims' voices because the justice system often excludes their participation. Restoring harmony based on an acceptance that justice has been done is, in his view, inadequate. Essentially, restorative justice proponents emphasize the need to support both victims and offenders and see social relationships as a rehabilitative vehicle aimed at providing formal and informal social support and control for offenders (Bazemore and Schiff 2001: 117). Rather than separating out the offender as a subject for rehabilitation, restorative justice sees social support and social control of offenders as the means to rehabilitation.

The origins of restorative justice in the United States lie in part in court orders for reparation taking the form of restitution and community service. Since the 1970s, restitution and community service have been employed as sentencing tools in criminal and juvenile courts, and during the 1980s an expansion occurred in victim–offender mediation programs resulting partly from interest in restitution and community service programs (Bazemore and Schiff 2001: 25). Along with the increased interest in these alternative sanctions, attention to the interests of victims increased during the 1990s, focusing on repair and healing influenced by the "faith community" and feminists (p. 26). Today, numerous programs can be brought under the rubric of restorative justice, but they often remain small-scale experiments and tend to be associated with community approaches to crime control.

In considering the nature of a restorative justice approach to offenders, it is useful to note the three core principles suggested by Van Ness and Strong (1997: 8–9).

1. Justice requires the healing of victims, offenders, and communities injured by crime.

2. Victims, offenders, and communities should be permitted to actively involve themselves in the justice process in a timely and substantial manner.

3. Roles and responsibilities of the government should be rethought, and in its promotion of justice, government should be responsible for preserving a just order, and the community should be responsible for establishing peace.

Restorative justice may be considered unique in its emphasis on not just one component of the criminal justice system such as punishment, but as incorporating victims, offenders, and the community in its strategies and designs. It is considered important that all three parties actively participate in the restorative justice process so that relations among them can be restored. Programs that do not include all three parties are not considered true restorative justice programs, because at least one important component of the triangle is absent. Thus, mediation programs that focus on achieving a resolution only between the offender and victim and leave out the community are normally not considered true restorative processes. Probation is a sentence of the formal system and, although a sentence carried out in the community, involves the official system through the supervision of the offender by the probation officer, but does not involve the community in resolving the harm caused by the offense. It leaves out victims in terms of their participation in the process. Even though some probation sentences include an order to pay the victim restitution or compensation for the offense committed, the participation of victims is passive in that their role is only to receive that payment.

In relation to offenders, Bazemore and Dooley (2001: 108) state that there is a normative focus on harm and repair. Repair, in the context of restorative justice, implies a particular form of rehabilitation. However, Bazemore and Dooley concede that there is an absence of theory to explain how the operation of restorative justice is supposed to bring about a change in the offender. Some restorative justice proponents argue that repair in relation to offenders involves a focus on *restoring, strengthening, and building relationships between offenders, victims, and communities* (p. 111), and therefore intervention intended to prevent future crime must focus not only on the offender's obligation to repair harm done to victims and the community but also on the need to repair broken relationships between the offender and the community, the victim and the community, and the victim and the offender.

Critics of restorative justice point to its too ready assumption that it will be possible to secure agreement between offenders, victims, and communities. Garland (1990) notes that one of the functions of punishment is to relieve the feelings of victims and communities where crimes are committed and that restorative justice avoids the ceremonies and rituals of criminal law that recognize these emotions (in Hudson 1996: 150). In addition, it can be argued that a greater reliance on restorative justice and a consequent restriction on the operation and expression of criminal law might lead to a situation in which those victims processed through restorative justice might come to believe or feel that the harm they have suffered is of less importance than "real crime." Feminists, who have argued for severe sentencing for domestic violence as well as for sexual offenses, have adopted this argument (Daly and Stubbs 2007). Criminalization and punishment show the limits of tolerance, and depenalizing through restorative justice processes tends to suggest that society has a different attitude toward certain kinds of behavior (Daly and Stubbs 2007: 158–159; Hudson 1996: 151). Von Hirsch, in his investigation into the basis for restorative justice, contends that no clear principles have been formulated for restoring the harm done by offenders to community standards, and unlike victim restitution, which involves a task of mediation between the victim and the offender, there are no disputed claims involved in crime because, for example, a robber appropriates something that is clearly the property of the victim (1998: 674–675). Volpe (1991) has warned of the propensity of restorative justice to widen the net of social control.

Why Punish? The Sociological Approach

In sociological terms, punishment raises questions such as why particular punishments were used and why they are no longer used, why a punishment like capital punishment has been abandoned to a great extent in the West, and why imprisonment has become the major form of punishment for criminal activity.

In social terms, research has concluded that punishments depend less on philosophical arguments and more on the currents and movements in social thinking and in climates of tolerance and intolerance. A focus on history and changes in social conditions has illuminated the relationship between punishment and society, which in turn has broadened the investigation of the notion of punishment into questions concerned with how order and authority are maintained in society. Garland (1990: 10) summarizes social theory about punishment as "that body of thought which explores the relations between punishment and society, its purpose being to understand punishment as a social phenomenon and thus trace its role in social life."

Garland (1990) has argued that punishment is the product of social structure and cultural values. Thus, whom we choose to punish, how we punish, and when we punish are determined by the role we give to punishment in society. If we construe criminal punishment as a wrong for a wrong, then we must conclude that society is, in a sense, wronging the offender. We must therefore ask, "Can the infliction of pain or a wrong upon an offender be justified ethically?" To answer this question, one must first look at the purpose of criminal punishment and question the various rationales put forward for punishment, such as deterrence, incapacitation, rehabilitation, just deserts, retribution, and restorative justice.

Sociological perspectives on punishment include the thinking of Durkheim, Weber, the Marxist tradition, and post-Marxist sociologies of punishment, particularly that propounded by Foucault. Sociologists expand the notion of punishment to "penality," which they explore in various societies at various times. Hudson defines penality as

> the complex of ideas (about proper punishment, about effective punishment), institutions (laws, policies and practices, agencies and buildings) and relationships (who has the power to say who is punished, whose ideas count, what is the relationship of those who punish and are punished to the rest of society) involved in the punishment of offenders. (1996: 6)

Only a broad outline of the various perspectives on penality will be provided here.

According to Durkheim, society has an objective reality apart from the individuals who compose it, and he argues that people behave according to social rules that, together with customs and traditions, form a culture for a particular society (in Hudson 1996: 81–86). Durkheim took a functionalist approach; that is, he examined aspects of social life in terms of the functions they performed in society. He applied this approach to punishment by looking at the functions that punishment fulfills in maintaining social order. Durkheim identified beliefs and sentiments held by members of society, which he called the "conscience collective," and argued that crimes are those acts that violate that conscience collective and produce a punitive reaction (in Garland 1990: 29).

He developed two laws of penal evolution. The first is that punishment is more intense the less developed a society is and the more the central power within that society is of an absolute nature. Thus, in industrial societies, collective sentiments are embodied in law rather than in religion, so crimes are seen as wrongs against individuals. He tried to demonstrate that penalties changed from ancient societies to his time, from aggravated penalties such as death with torture and mutilation to reduced forms of punishment. In his second law, he developed the notion of punishments having lesser intensity, arguing that imprisonment will become the main punishment replacing death and torture.

Overall, Durkheim saw the function of punishment as promoting social solidarity through the affirmation of values, and he argued that punishment's importance lies in its expression of outrage upon the commission of an offense. He believed punishment to be a "passionate reaction" to crime, and this expressive view of punishment can be seen in modern-day notions of censure in retributivism. His focus was not, therefore, on whether punishment was effective in controlling crime but in its function as a means of maintaining social solidarity through expressions of outrage and through the affirmation of societal values. Among critics of Durkheim, Garland (1990) suggests that Durkheim's analysis of punishment is focused too strongly on punishment's expressive function, causing all other explanations to be discarded. Nevertheless, Garland (1990: 252) points out that Durkheim's insight into the role of punishment—as one of expressing community outrage against criminal acts—does single out one aspect of punishment that seems to resonate in the context of today's debates about "getting tough on crime." In similar fashion, Mead in *The Psychology of Punitive Justice* contends that the indignation that members of society feel toward the criminal amounts to a cultural sublimation of the instincts and hostilities that the individual has tamed in the interest of social cooperation with others (in Garland 1990: 64).

Weber's ideas on punishment are implied rather than made explicit in his notions about authority and power in modern society. Having identified three types of authority, the traditional, the charismatic, and the legal, Weber promoted legal authority—the process of making rules by those given the right to rule—as being the most appropriate form of rule for modern societies. For Weber, legal authority carries with it a duty to obey laws. He argued that systems of laws might be rational or irrational; in a rational system of criminal law, crimes would be defined and rules put forward for adjudicating those crimes. He favored formal rationality, which he termed "bureaucratic rationality," and saw this as an essential feature of a modern state. His notion of bureaucratic rationality appears in certain features of modern society, such as our processes for making judgments according to rules and the way in which officeholders exercise authority. Developments such as a professional police force and a judiciary as well as due process can be traced to the bureaucratization of society.

Marxist perspectives on punishment evolve out of Marx's concern for the place of capitalism and the relations between production and society. In his view, institutions like law are shaped to parallel the relations of production and the maintenance of the capitalist system. Marxist penologists have argued that punishment regulates the supply of labor; this view was put forward in 1939 by Rusche and Kirchheimer in *Punishment and Social Structure* (in Howe 1994: 12). In discussing the history of punishment in Europe from the 13th century until the development of capitalism, the authors perceive the severity of punishment as being tied directly to the value of labor. Thus, the severity of punishment, they argue, is relatively lenient when labor is scarce and its value high, whereas when labor is abundant, punishments become more intense.

Another key aspect of their view is the principle of *less eligibility* (Howe 1994: 12). The argument is that the conditions offenders will experience in prison must be worse than anything they are likely to endure outside the prison in order to restrain the "reserve army of labor" from crime, that is, to serve as a deterrent to the lowest social classes. The idea of less eligibility encompasses matters like discipline, diet, accommodation, and general living conditions in prisons. Rusche argued that this principle limited penal reform, because punishments and prison conditions could not be improved beyond a point that would bring the offender into line with the standard of life of the least advantaged nonoffender (in Howe 1994: 20). This analysis has been criticized for its economic reductionism. (It offers only an economic argument to explain changes in punishment.) (Howe 1994: 20). Nevertheless, it has led to a series of studies that have tested the basic framework and found some correlation between punishment and the labor market in the

United States over time. The important point is that the authors, together with other Marxists, have provided the insight that all punishment cannot be understood simply as a response to crime. In other words, when changes in the use of imprisonment and other punishments are examined in historical contexts, other factors appear to have influenced their development.

Other Marxist theorists like Melossi and Pashuknis have asked why imprisonment persists as opposed to other forms of punishment. One answer from Pashuknis is that there is a correspondence between the development of wage labor, which puts a price on time, and paying for crime by "doing time." In this sense, Marxist theory concerning the relations of production is found mirrored in the punishment of imprisonment, and Marxists therefore argue that a crucial principle in society is the exchange of equivalence. Punishment, therefore, becomes an exchange transaction in which the offender pays his debt, an expression commonly used today both in that form and in the notion of "paying a debt to society" (Garland 1990: 113). Feminists have heavily criticized Marxist analysis of society generally for ignoring gender and for outmoded interpretative frameworks (Howe 1994: 41).

In 1977, Michel Foucault published *Discipline and Punish: The Birth of the Prison*, revolutionizing the study of penality and punishment by presenting the notion of penality and highlighting *discipline* as the key element in modern forms of punishment. In his complex exploration of penality, Foucault follows an approach that examines the issue from the ground up through a detailed examination of penal practices. His central focus is the *exercise of power* in modern society and its linkages with knowledge to exercise power of and over the body. Describing first the effect and content of the public execution, Foucault shows how the infliction of pain on the body gave way to an exercise of power through the new practice of disciplining the individual through institutions such as the factory and the modern prison and how this led to the development of a class of "delinquents." Foucault claims that disciplinary regulation is the fundamental principle of social control in modern society and is most fully realized in the form of the prison.

Foucault (1977) emphasizes the role of punishment in producing the "right-thinking citizen," that is, the trained and disciplined individual (Hudson 1996: 7). He draws on both Weber (in his emphasis on bureaucratization) and Durkheim (in his description of punishment as an expressive force) in his account of penality. However, he adopts a much broader analytic framework that links punishment and penality and connects them directly to changes in society and to the exercise of power over the individual. Foucault's ideas have inspired many followers, including David Garland who, in *Punishment and Modern Society* (1990), argues that a full understanding of punishment and penality should incorporate the theoretical insights of all the writers discussed in this section, together with those of Norbert Elias and his notion that the West has undergone a "civilizing process" that has sensitized society against harsh punishment. Importantly, Garland has drawn attention to the need to consider punishment not simply as the consequence of a criminal act but as a "complex social institution" requiring us to think beyond simply crime control. Punishment, he argues, should be viewed as a social institution, and its social role and significance can be properly understood only through developing the insights of social theorists.

Summary

The morality of punishment rests upon theories of deterrence, retribution, just deserts, rehabilitation, incapacitation, and most recently, restorative justice. These theories attempt to justify society's imposition of punishment on offenders and try to provide an adequate ethical rationale for inflicting harm. Deterrence maintains that people are deterred from crime because they are concerned about the possible consequences of their actions. Utilitarian philosophers first put forward this justification for punishment. A number of studies have considered the effectiveness of deterrence as a theory, but there is no clear conclusion about whether deterrence works.

Retribution theorists argue that punishment is justified because it is deserved, and punishment therefore becomes a question of responsibility and accountability for acts that harm society. In retribution theory, the punishment imposed should be proportionate to the wrongdoing. Retribution is justified in a number of ways, including the notion that offenders are paying their debt to society, that they are being censured by society, and that punishment has an expressive character that ought to be communicated to an offender.

The emergence of just deserts theory in the 1980s put an end to indeterminate sentencing and introduced sentencing guidelines and sentencing commissions as attempts were made to fix proportionate sentences. Just deserts theory lacks any principle that determines how to constitute a properly commensurate sentence, and it ignores social factors as well as the multiple decisions and discretions that go into the sentencing decision.

Rehabilitation shows a concern for an offender's social background and regards crime as the outcome of a social disease that should be cured through treatment. In the past, indeterminate sentences supported rehabilitation programs, because the release decision was given over to boards and not determined by the court. The idea that "nothing works" brought about the demise of rehabilitation, which had been the dominant rationale for punishment until the 1970s. It has now been displaced by just deserts and incapacitation.

According to incapacitation theorists, placing offenders in custody for lengthy periods of time protects the public from the chance of future offending, but this means that offenders are being punished based on a prediction of what they might do in the future. It raises the question of whether it is ethical to punish persons for crimes they have yet to commit.

Restorative justice is a newcomer to the field of penal theory, and some suggest that it lacks theoretical support. However, its emphasis on community involvement in solutions to crime and on the victim have attracted a body of support, at least at the local level, where it has been employed to deal with delinquency and relatively minor offenses.

The philosophical approach to punishment is concerned with the "ought" of punishment, whereas the sociological approach raises questions about the use and severity of particular punishments and the relationship among punishment, society, and social change. The criminological approach focuses on the fact of imprisonment and on penal policy making and crime control. Some suggest that no single approach adequately provides justification and rationale for punishment and that a full explanation can be gained only by combining these various perspectives.

DISCUSSION QUESTIONS

1. Offenders are punished because we hold them accountable and responsible for their actions. Explain by reference to the various theories of punishment.

2. Does deterrence work? Explain with examples.

3. How can just deserts theory be criticized, and why has just deserts become the predominant view in penal policy?

4. Contrast rehabilitation and incapacitation as theories of punishment, explaining their justification, their operation, and the criticisms that have been made of them.

5. What advantage would society gain if restorative justice were the only method of punishment? In your answer consider all the advantages and disadvantages offered by a restorative justice approach to punishment.

6. Contrast the philosophical and sociological perspectives on punishment.

7. What is the *lex talionis,* and what are its drawbacks as a form of punishment?

CHAPTER 6

Ethics in Corrections

The preceding chapter explored philosophies of punishment and the rationales for punishment generally and set the context for the discussion in this chapter concerning ethics in corrections. Here, we are concerned with the prison system, inmates, and guards and with ethical dilemmas that may arise within the prison system. A further concern is the treatment afforded to those who are incarcerated. For example, is it ethically correct to impose severe restrictions on amenities and comforts for prisoners? Is an offender sent to prison *for* punishment or *as* punishment for an offense? Should offenders, in effect, be warehoused in prison and left to languish under strict supervision, or should they be provided with treatment programs, psychological services, and educational opportunities? First, however, it is necessary to set the context by looking at the state of the prison system in this country.

The Prison Explosion

The number of state and federal prison inmates increased from 400,000 in 1982 to almost 1.3 million in 1999; as of December 31, 2002, the number of male prisoners in state and federal prisons had reached 1,440,655, and the number of female prisoners had reached 97,491 (Harrison and Beck 2003). During the period from 1982 to 1999, over 600 state and at least 51 federal correctional facilities were opened. In the same period, the number of jail inmates tripled from approximately 200,000 in 1982 to 600,000 in 1999, and the number of adults on probation increased from more than 1.3 million to almost 3.8 million persons (Gifford 2002). Moreover, the number of correctional staff more than doubled from nearly 300,000 to over 700,000 in same period.

The cost of corrections has also increased by a staggering amount. For example, in 1982, federal expenditure on corrections was $541 million; by 1999 this had increased to $4 billion, an increase of 650%. In the states during this same period, there was a 476% increase in corrections expenditure (Gifford

2002). In fiscal year 2001, correctional authorities spent $38.2 billion to maintain correctional systems, and day-to-day operating expenses amounted to 28.4 billion (Stephan 2004: 1) and by 2007 it had risen to $44.06 billion (Pew Charitable Trusts 2008: 12). State spending on corrections for the period 1986 through 2001 increased from $65 per resident to $134, and between 1982 and 2003, corrections expenditure increase 423% from $40 to $209 per U.S. resident (Hughes 2006: 1). The federal government increased its expenditure on corrections between 1982 and 2003 by 925% (p. 2).

Projections for the future are even greater. According to the Public Safety Performance Project (2007), the U.S. prison population is likely to increase by 13%, or more than 192,000 inmates, between 2007 and 2011 (p. ii). The cost of this increase could be as much as $27.5 billion. This will mean more than 1.7 million people are incarcerated in prison (not including jails), a rate of 562 per 100,000 or 1 in 178 Americans. The number of women prisoners is expected to grow by 16% by 2011 (p. ii). The current average annual operational cost per prisoner for the states is $23,876 (p. 20), and construction costs range from $25,000 for a minimum security bed to more than $100,000 for a maximum security cell (p. 22). Prisons currently constitute the fourth highest state budget item after health, education, and transportation (p. 25). According to Steen and Bandy (2007: 5), because so many state governments have focused on retribution and incarceration and have seen correctional expenses outpace state revenue, there is a growing realization that punitive punishment policies originating in the 1980s and 1990s are now unsustainable. States are therefore now focusing on changing their laws and reducing their fiscal expenditures.

This vast expansion of the corrections system in the United States has meant that at yearend 2005, 737 per 100,000 U.S. residents were incarcerated in a state or federal prison or local jail (Harrison and Beck 2006). About 1 in 108 men and 1 in 1,538 women were sentenced and placed in state or federal institutions. Overall, at the end of 2005, 1 in every 136 U.S. residents was in prison or jail. Of the more than 1.46 million sentenced inmates in 2005, an estimated 547,200 were African American males, composing 39.5% of all inmates with a sentence of more than one year. Incarcerated white males numbered 459,700 and 34.5% of all male inmates, while Hispanic males were 279,000 and 20.2% of all male inmates. In 2005, an estimated 8% of black males between the ages of 25 and 29 years were in prison; this compared to 2.6% of Hispanic males and 1.1% of white males in that age group (Harrison and Beck 2006).

By the beginning of 2008, 1,596,127 adults were locked up in state or federal prisons and an additional 723,131 in local jails with a total of 2,319, 258, making the rate of incarceration 1 in every 99.1 adults (Pew Charitable Trusts 2008: 5) or 750 per 100,000 population (p. 35). Of all men 18 or older, 1 in 54 was in prison. When this group is broken down by race, 1 in 106 white men, 1 in 36 Hispanic men, and 1 in 15 black men were in prison. Of black men ages 20–34, 1 in 9 was in prison (p. 6). These figures are even more astounding when you compare the total prison population in the United States (which has a total population of almost 300 million) to the total prison figures for 36 of the largest European nations (which together have a total population of more than 800 million).

Table 6.1   The U.S Inmate Population Compared to the 36 Largest European Inmate Populations (Years Yary)

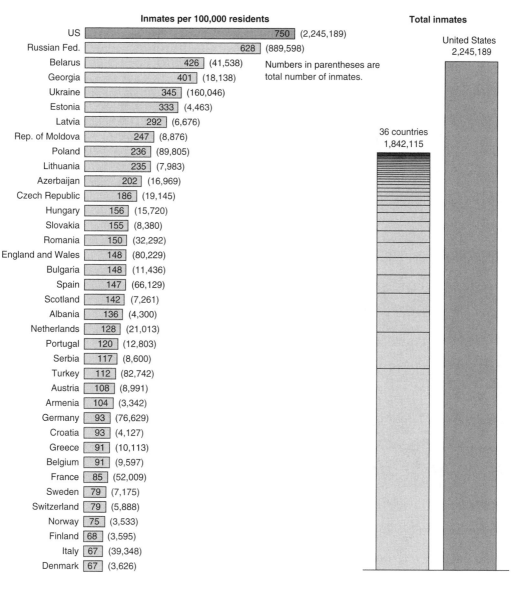

Total resident populations
United States 299.4 million
36 countries 802.4 million

SOURCE: Pew Charitable Trusts 2008: 35.

Combined the total prison population of the 36 European countries is about 400,000 less than the U.S. inmate population on its own, as Table 6.1 shows. (Pew Charitable Trusts 2008: 35).

The female prison population has more than doubled since 1990, with an annual growth rate since that year of 7.6%, which was higher than the 5.9% average increase in the number of male inmates. Between 1990 and 2001, the total number of male prisoners increased 77%, but the number of female prisoners increased 108% (Gifford 2002). By the end of 2007, the incarceration rate for females between the ages of 35 and 39 was 1 in 355 for white women, 1 in 297 for Hispanic women, 1 in 100 for black women, and 1 in 265 for all women ages 35–39 (Pew Charitable Trusts 2008: 6). The number of male prisoners grew 34% between 1995 and 2005, and the number of females grew 57% (Harrison and Beck 2006: 4). During the same period the annual rate of increase for female prisoners was an average of 4.6%, compared to 3.0% for male prisoners (p. 4). In 2005, females made up 7.0% of all prisoners, up from 5.7% in 1990 and 6.1% in 1995. The rate of imprisonment for females was 65 per 100,000 population, and it was 929 per 100,000 males in the general population (p. 4).

In order to better understand the ethical issues that may arise in correctional practice, it is helpful to have a general knowledge of prison regimes and conditions. A knowledge of the daily routine within some kinds of prisons and the nature of the restrictions that both prisoners and staff experience in their daily interactions helps reveal how the management and administration of a captive population generates ethical issues and dilemmas. In particular, contextualizing ethical issues in this way highlights questions of control and coercive power and reveals how a rationally organized bureaucracy (see discussion of Weber in previous chapter) administers a "total institution" (Goffman 1959, 1961) as well as how it formulates and operates policies and procedures within a professional and ethical framework. Representations of the daily experience of imprisonment under maximum security and incarceration in a women's prison are discussed in the following sections, followed by general descriptions of medium and minimum security prisons.

Maximum Security

In his classic work on a maximum security prison, Sykes (1958, reprinted 1999) singles out as central to maximum security the fact that "the maximum security prison represents a social system in which an attempt is made to create and maintain total or almost total social control" (1999: xiv).

In his exploration of conditions at the New Jersey State Maximum Security Prison in 1958, Sykes noted that the prison did not inflict acute "physical discomforts" or impose hard living conditions. Instead, for Sykes, it appeared to possess "a grinding dullness, an existence lacking the amenities of life we take for granted, but an existence which is still tolerable" (1999: 8). Sykes identified the task of keeping persons in custody as the main task of the custodians at New Jersey State Prison, with the maintenance of internal order as the next priority. Rules and regulations were designed both for custody purposes and for maintaining order. The inmates viewed the regulation of their conduct to the minutest degree as a form of punishment, whereas administrators justified prison codes of conduct in the name of custody and internal order.

Conditions in maximum security prisons have changed since Sykes conducted his research in 1958. For example, the conditions at Wisconsin's Supermax Correctional Institution are depicted by the district court in the class action *Jones 'El and others v. Berge and Litscher* (2001) as follows:

- This supermax prison has 500 beds and is designed to incarcerate the worst of the worst offenders.
- There are a number of levels of achievement within the prison as part of an incentive program, with Level 1 being the lowest level with the most restrictive conditions of confinement.
- New prisoners are assigned to Level 1 on arrival and remain there until they have been evaluated in terms of behavior and medical and program needs. They are housed in single-person cells and have little face-to-face contact with staff. The cell doors are constructed of solid metal and are boxcar doors, which are constantly slammed as inmates move in and out of their cells. Light accesses the cell through a five-inch strip of opaque glass running along the top edge of one wall, and if he stands on his bed and cranes his neck, an inmate may see the sky through a small sealed skylight. Inmates are not permitted to wear watches or have clocks.
- Cells are illuminated 24 hours a day. Lighting cannot be turned off, but it can be adjusted from high to low. At night inmates must sleep in a way that allows guards to see their faces, and they will be awakened if they have covered their faces.
- Inmates are not able to regulate cell temperature, there is no air conditioning, and the solid cell doors and lack of windows inhibits air circulation. A report that monitored the temperature and humidity showed an inside cell temperature of 91 degrees when the outdoor temperature was also 91 degrees, producing a heat index in excess of 100 degrees.
- Although cells contain showers that might provide relief from the heat, inmates may only shower three times a week.
- Inmates are allowed 4 hours of exercise a week in an exercise cell, which is a slightly larger version of a regular one-person cell with no windows and no exercise equipment. The room will permit only pacing or stationary exercises; inmates are transported to the exercise cell wearing restraints and are patsearched before entering the cell and after leaving it. There is no regular exercise schedule, and exercise is permitted at the discretion of correctional officers.
- There is a small law library set up in a cell, but inmates using the library must be shackled and cuffed with their cuffs attached to a belly chain while out of their cells. Inmates are not allowed face-to-face visits except with their lawyers and must rely on video visitation, where inmates remain in their cell block and see their visitors on small video screens with poor audio quality. During video visits, inmates remain handcuffed, shackled, and belly chained.
- Level 1 inmates are permitted one 6-minute telephone call each month. They are not allowed library books in their cells, but they may keep a Bible, Quran, or equivalent and up to 25 letters.

- Inmates who start at Level 1 spend a minimum of 30 days in that level and, if they advance to a higher level, may be demoted back to Level 1 if staff determine they have behaved improperly.
- Confinement in a supermax security prison is known to cause severe psychiatric morbidity, disability, suffering, and mortality.
- The isolating conditions in supermax confinement mean that many prisoners are unable to maintain their sanity and a high number attempt suicide.

The class action also alleges that prisoners are obsessed with suicidal thinking, smear feces, swallow metal objects, cut their flesh, and attempt to hang themselves and that excessive use of force is a daily occurrence at the prison.

Another example of maximum security is Pelican Bay, a supermax prison in California located in a very remote area. The prison is entirely automated and is constructed so that inmates have almost no face-to-face contact with guards or other inmates (Austin and Irwin 2001: 127–128). Inmates are confined in their windowless cells constructed of concrete and stainless steel for 22½ hours a day. They are not permitted to work in prison industries, have no access to recreation or to other inmates, and are not permitted cigarettes. All meals are eaten in their cells, which they leave only for brief showers and the daily 90-minute exercise, which is taken in miniature yards enclosed by 20-foot-high walls. The doors of their cells contain slots for food trays, and meal delivery is almost the only time guards approach cells, because unlike the usual prison arrangement, guards do not walk tiers but are locked away in glass-enclosed booths, communicating with the inmates through a speaker system. The majority of Pelican Bay's inmate population comes from the Los Angeles area, located 900 miles away with no access by air, making family visits extremely difficult.

Women's Incarceration

The Central California Women's Facility (CCWF) is the largest women's prison in the world. New inmates are assigned a classification signifying their level of security risk derived from the offense for which they were imprisoned and their history of prior commitments (Owen 1998: 64). Over 75% of the inmates are classified as low risk. The prison is divided into four separate units including administrative segregation (AD SEG), security housing, and a death row. Women are received into the prison in the receiving and release building, which is located within A-Facility, the most closely controlled section of the prison. Women may not walk around unescorted in A-Yard, which contains the most secure housing unit, unless they wear state-issued clothing. The inmates occupy two-person cells. The daily schedule begins at 6:30 a.m. when the inmates are required to get up, clean their rooms, and make their beds by 7 a.m. Morning and afternoon activities take the form of job or school assignments, and the women return to their housing units after dinner to socialize before returning to their cells for the evening (Owen 1998: 88).

The administrative segregation unit functions like a jail, and women are moved to this facility if they are under investigation for rule infractions or for other offenses, and following such investigations, they may be housed in this facility for short periods of time as punishment for minor offenses. Typically, inmates are confined to AD SEG for fighting, drug-related offenses, and assaults on staff. It is common for terms of less than 1 month to be served in AD SEG. The security housing unit (SHU) houses the small number of women whose behavior constitutes a danger to themselves or others in the institution, and it is best conceived of as a prison within the prison (Owen 1998: 113). The SHU is used for women found guilty of a serious offense, and programs in SHU may last for more than 6 months and perhaps even years. The length of term served in SHU is determined by the nature of the offense committed within the prison; offenses include assaults on staff or inmates, weapons possession, and serious drug misconduct. The daily life within these units takes the form of a lock-down, and women can only conduct loud conversations with their "vent-partners" or shout across the unit in a group discussion (Owen 1998: 115). In death row, the few women sentenced to death are confined within a 6-cell-wide area.

Medium Security

Approximately one third of all inmates are incarcerated in medium security prisons, which generally secure inmates with double fences topped with barbed wire. Most medium security prisons have been built since 1925. Although the term *medium security* suggests a diminished focus on security, in fact, medium security prisons adopt many of the practices found in maximum security, such as head counts and a high level of supervision and guarding. One difference between maximum and medium security prisons is that inmates work without constant supervision in medium security facilities.

Minimum Security

Minimum security prisons hold only about 10% of all prisoners; most were constructed after 1950. The emphasis in this form of incarceration is on vocational training and treatment. Minimum security inmates are generally nonviolent, first time offenders and white collar criminals who are not considered dangerous. Generally, minimum security prisons emphasize a more normal lifestyle, the gates are open, and inmates even have a degree of privacy. These prisons provide a range of programs, and some supply family visiting facilities where prisoners are able to stay with their families for up to 3 days at a time.

These partial descriptions of prison and prison life provide some sense of the order and regimentation of incarcerated male and female inmates. Later discussion will explore relations between prisoners and guards, especially in terms of the power and authority that guards exercise over inmates and the corresponding "power" of inmates. The nature and employment of this coercive correctional power has been a focus of correctional studies, because it often generates ethical issues and ethical dilemmas for staff.

This chapter does not provide an exhaustive history of the development of the penitentiary or of incarceration generally in the United States. The emphasis in this discussion is on ethical conduct within the prison environment. Instead, the following discussion explores the history of Stateville Prison in Illinois, as explained by James Jacobs (1977) in his classic study. The aim is to show through Jacobs's study how prison administration moved from being ad hoc to being bureaucratized and professionalized and how ethical standards and norms within the prison changed over time to parallel social change. This examination also reveals how changes in the bureaucratic structure reflected changes in agency as correctional administrators introduced new policies and practices.

Stateville Prison: The Changing State of Corrections

In his study of Stateville Prison in Illinois, James Jacobs (1977) showed how patterns of authority in prison changed over time. In the early days of the Stateville penitentiary, rules about conduct were made on an ad hoc basis, and discipline was exercised in an arbitrary and capricious way. Subsequently, as the prison administration became bureaucratized, the early authoritarian regime was replaced with one that depended on rules and regulations and emphasized a professional approach to corrections. Jacobs (1977: 9) traces the introduction of the rule of law into Stateville to the judicial activism of the 1960s and to legislation concerned with civil rights, the poor, and the criminal defendant.

Stateville opened in 1925, and during its first decade of operations it was free from any form of outside oversight. Early wardens were political appointees, usually former sheriffs, and political patronage even decided the appointment of guards, who lost their jobs with each change in the governorship of the state (Jacobs 1977: 21). In the 1930s, guards worked up to 16 hours a day and regularly worked 12-hour shifts. They were untrained, underpaid, and physically unfit. Disciplinary measures included locking up an inmate in solitary confinement and "stringing up," a process in which the inmate stood handcuffed to the bars of his cell 8 hours a day for up to 15 days, and perhaps longer (p. 22). Violence between staff and inmates was common, the prison was overcrowded, and most inmates were left idle.

During the period from 1936 to 1961, Stateville was "ruled" by Warden Joe Ragen, who sought to make Stateville the world's most orderly prison. He exercised control over every detail and established an authoritarian regime that transformed Stateville into a venue internationally known among penologists. Ragen demanded absolute loyalty from his guards; in exchange, he often ignored their physical assaults on inmates (Jacobs 1977: 30). Guards exercised intense supervision over inmates and applied countless rules covering every aspect of prison life. In place of the earlier system where the untrained and politically appointed guards relied on inmate bosses and gang leaders to maintain order, Ragen established a patriarchy rule based on what Jacobs calls "charismatic authority" (p. 31). The warden distrusted all outsiders and declined to share authority with any subordinates. The backbone of the Ragen administration was its informers, who contributed to an atmosphere of insecurity and distrust that was exemplified in Ragen's concern with the behavior of his guards on and off the job (p. 38).

As for the inmates, although he stressed their entitlement to good food, clothing, and housing, Ragen maintained that they had no other entitlements beyond this and that all other benefits were considered privileges. Order was maintained within the institution through a system of internal security that ensured complete enforcement of a set of comprehensive rules and regulations. For example, an inmate's failure to button a shirt or salute a captain was reason enough for disciplinary action. Although Ragen reformed the practice of "stringing up," inmates in isolation were nevertheless required to stand at attention in silence inside their cells for 8 hours a day (Jacobs 1977: 42). In spite of the severity of the disciplinary regime, exceptions had to be made to the code of discipline if the organization were to function, and this resulted in a reciprocal relationship in which guards overlooked infractions in exchange for inmate compliance, especially in supplying information.

In the Ragen era, rewards were a much more effective tool of prison management than is the case today because of the great disparities in the living conditions of inmates, who, in the 1940s and 1950s, faced very long prison terms. Whereas the average prisoner was confined with two other men in a tiny cell from 3 p.m. to 7 a.m., inmates who held administrative positions could work at night and remain in their offices as well as enjoy mobility within the prison. The warden offered top jobs to inmate leaders and tough prisoners as a form of reward. In 1955, the disciplinary system was described as "absolute" with a silent system enforced in the dining room and while marching in lines. Even when the ideology of rehabilitation came into vogue in the 1950s, Ragen was able to cast himself as a humanitarian, claiming to place the underprivileged and those from the slums on the path of morality (Jacobs 1977: 44–45). The movement for prison reform resulted in Ragen increasing the size of his academic and vocational schools, but the vocational school reportedly was devoted to performing personal services for staff by repairing cars and electrical equipment—staff would bring in run-down cars and appliances, pay for the parts and supplies, and have the labor provided free by the inmates.

The relationship between guards and inmates during Ragen's regime was one of great social distance. The rule was that fraternization was to occur no more than was necessary and that relations between guards and inmates were to remain impersonal (Jacobs 1977: 49). Those who attempted to challenge the warden's authority by complaining to outsiders, by trying to escape, or by defying an officer could expect to be beaten by the guards or their selected inmate helpers (p. 50). When Ragen left Stateville in 1961, the institution underwent a transition from a charismatic to a traditional system of authority and then emerged as a professional bureaucratic institution in the style that is now prevalent in all correctional systems.

In the 1960s, under a traditional authority administration, the system of informers died out, and relationships between guards and inmates became more complex and problematic with a greater number of African American guards. Privileges for inmates became less valued, and the civil rights movement contributed to inmate politicization when black Muslims made demands for the recognition of their religion and linked the prison to racism and repression (Jacobs 1977: 59).

As Crouch (1980b: 12) explains, during the 1960s the courts reoriented their view of inmate petitions and claims, defining four general categories of prisoners' rights:

1. Prisoner access to the court to challenge convictions and treatment during confinement

2. The Eighth Amendment prohibition on cruel and unusual punishment, extending it to include conditions such as overcrowding and isolation

3. Procedural protections applying to decisions on issues like discipline, transfer, and eligibility for parole

4. The First Amendment freedoms of religion, assembly, and speech as well as the prohibition on discrimination on grounds of race

As a result of judicial activism and the social activism of the late 1960s, many inmates, especially minorities, were provided with a political rhetoric and ideology that radicalized prisons (Crouch 1980b: 22).

During the period from 1960 to 1980, there was a marked change in the inmate population, because prisons increasingly housed African Americans and young men who had access to radical ideas. Traditional solidarity among inmates gave way to sectional arrangements based on race, and the fundamentals of the old inmate code, like doing your own time and avoiding confrontations with staff, were displaced in the face of new attitudes by young, tough, and often gang-affiliated inmates (p. 23). As Crouch notes, such inmates did not adhere to the familiar pattern of interactions between guards and inmates, resulting in a much greater level of uncertainty for the guards in these interactions. In the case of women inmates, Owen (1998: 176) similarly noted in her research in a California women's prison that the old convict codes had changed now that gangs had entered the prisons, with the older inmates stressing the rude, disrespectful, and inconsiderate attitudes of the new young gangbangers.

At Stateville Prison, professional administration emerged during the period from 1970 to 1975, based on what Jacobs calls a rational-legal bureaucracy comprising the state Department of Corrections, an educated elite occupying the highest administrative positions, and civilians filling specialized treatment roles in the prison. The state Department of Corrections now took a much greater role in governing Stateville, and a new code of corrections introduced a more legalistic relationship between guards and prisoners, with a complex of administrative regulations covering matters that had previously been within the authority and discretion of guards. However, the gap between rules and working procedures was evident, because rules were simply not followed (Jacobs 1977: 79).

The new administration viewed the inmates as men who were redeemable, in contrast to the view under Ragen that the inmates were a separate species who needed to be kept away from society (Jacobs 1977: 82). The principal reason for ignoring rules was disorganization amongst the staff, because job responsibilities were not clearly defined, and staff operated according to tradition and not procedure. The introduction of counselors for the inmates complicated the guards' task, because this change had the effect of taking away the guards' role as the "givers of favors" for inmates, leaving them only with the "dirty work." Consequently, the guards' ability to offer rewards in exchange for adherence to the rules was much diminished (p. 97).

Finally, concluding his historical account of Stateville in 1975, Jacobs (1977) explains how the new relationship between guards and inmates became formalistic and bureaucratic. This is best exemplified by a grievance procedure under which inmates might lodge complaints about any aspect of prison life and have those complaints investigated and answered in writing within 10 days. Holding the staff accountable in this way had the effect of setting norms against which the legitimacy of decisions could be measured. This clearly affected the authority and power of the guards and created a new level of uncertainty. Nevertheless, Stateville could no longer cope with the demands of prisoners, interest groups, and the courts and still maintain control without the governance of a rational, legal bureaucracy (p. 103).

Guenther and Guenther (1980: 162) agree that this uncertainty is a factor in correctional work, in contrast to other occupations, due to the artificial nature of the relationship between the captives and the captors, their need to physically coexist, and the intensified emotions within the prison environment. They see these factors as producing a "unique organizational climate" (p. 166). As one lieutenant close to retirement at a prison in Atlanta told them,

> The toughest part of this job is the anticipation that goes with each watch. You're constantly under stress because you don't know what will happen, much less what you can do about it until it breaks. No one can remain alert month after month, year after year to all the things that can go wrong in this old place. (in Guenther and Guenther 1980: 169)

For the staff at this prison, a normal day would be made up of a number of inmates becoming ill, inmates refusing to work and violating regulations, and others whose conduct was influenced by personal problems; in each case, a guard would be involved in an incident, the terms of which would be unpredictable. Kauffman (1988: 214) recalls one officer who drew a parallel between the anxieties generated by working at Walpole Maximum Security Prison in Massachusetts to the months he had spent patrolling a military base perimeter in Vietnam. Kauffman (p. 234) found that many guards were unable to divorce themselves from prison work when at home and tended to adopt the same commanding, aggressive attitude toward their family members as they did toward inmates. Many would become apathetic and withdrawn and refrain from discussing their work at all, believing that no one could understand the prison environment unless he or she actually worked there. These circumstances would cause them to turn more and more to their fellow guards for companionship and less to their families.

What does the history of Stateville Prison tell us about ethics and ethical norms in the prison environment? Insofar as the history of Stateville can be considered a representative history of correctional change, it shows how the discretion given to prison guards over their captives changed over time, as an authoritarian regime relying on inmate informers and favors, such as awarding administrative jobs to selected inmates, and a regime of intense supervision and an extreme level of discipline was replaced with an administration accountable to the courts and an environment where radicalized prisoners practiced social activism, political rhetoric, and ideology. As the nature of the prison population changed, so did interactions between guards and inmates, and in terms of ethical standards, a level of uncertainty in relations between guards and prisoners was generated as traditional prison attitudes were radicalized. With the coming of professional administration after 1970, a new managerial approach introduced different levels of governance and a much more legalistic relationship between guards and prisoners. Now, administrative regulations replaced guard discretion, but rules were nevertheless broken because of an absence of clearly defined job responsibilities. Over time, guards became subject to oversight through grievance procedures, and an atmosphere in which ethical conduct could be monitored by prison administrators and by the prisoners themselves replaced the certainties and absolutism of the early period.

Guarding Ethically

The modern era of corrections brought with it a set of written ethical standards for correctional officers and management. The Code of Ethics shown in Box 6.1 balances the welfare and legal rights of prisoners with obligations toward colleagues and the public. There are specific rules prohibiting corruption in the form of gifts, personal privileges, and conflicts of interest. There is also an obligation for staff to report corrupt or unethical behaviors as well as a declaration of commitment to professional and compassionate service.

A CLOSER LOOK

BOX 6.1
American Correctional Association
Code of Ethics Preamble

The American Correctional Association expects of its members unfailing honesty, respect for the dignity and individuality of human beings, and a commitment to professional and compassionate service. To this end, we subscribe to the following principles.

Members shall respect and protect the civil and legal rights of all individuals.

Members shall treat every professional situation with concern for the welfare of the individuals involved and with no intent to personal gain.

Members shall maintain relationships with colleagues to promote mutual respect within the profession and improve the quality of service.

Members shall make public criticism of their colleagues or their agencies only when warranted, verifiable, and constructive.

Members shall respect the importance of all disciplines within the criminal justice system and work to improve cooperation with each segment.

Members shall honor the public's right to information and share information with the public to the extent permitted by law subject to an individual's right to privacy.

Members shall respect and protect the right of the public to be safeguarded from criminal activity.

Members shall refrain from using their positions to secure personal privileges or advantages.

Members shall refrain from allowing personal interest to impair objectivity in the performance of duty while acting in an official capacity.

Members shall refrain from entering into any formal or informal activity or agreement which presents a conflict of interest or is inconsistent with the conscientious performance of duties.

Members shall refrain from accepting any gifts, service, or favor that is or appears to be improper or implies an obligation inconsistent with the free and objective exercise of professional duties.

Members shall clearly differentiate between personal views/statements and views/statements/positions made on behalf of the agency or Association.

Members shall report to appropriate authorities any corrupt or unethical behaviors in which there is sufficient evidence to justify review.

Members shall refrain from discriminating against any individual because of race, gender, creed, national origin, religious affiliation, age, disability, or any other type of prohibited discrimination.

Members shall preserve the integrity of private information; they shall refrain from seeking information on individuals beyond that which is necessary to implement responsibilities and perform their duties; members shall refrain from revealing nonpublic information unless expressly authorized to do so.

Members shall make all appointments, promotions, and dismissals in accordance with established civil service rules, applicable contract agreements, and individual merit, rather than furtherance of personal interests.

Members shall respect, promote, and contribute to a work place that is safe, healthy, and free of harassment in any form.

SOURCE: American Correctional Association, 1990. Adopted August 1975 at the 105th Congress of Correction; revised August 1990 at the 120th Congress of Correction; revised August 1994 at the 124th Congress of Correction. Reprinted with permission from The American Correctional Association.

Commentators and correctional administrators have offered their own views about correctional ethics. The former commissioner of corrections in Massachusetts, George A. Vose Jr., articulated a philosophy of corrections around the concept of "good citizenship." He saw offenders mainly as individuals who had failed in their obligations as citizens (in Carroll 1998). This failure was often the result of their having received fewer benefits from that citizenship than others. He argued that if offenders are to become responsible citizens, it was essential that they were treated in a civil manner by correctional authorities, whose task was to model good citizenship by protecting certain fundamental rights. According to Vose, prisoner rights include "the right to safety, adequate care, personal dignity, meaningful activity, [and] ample opportunity for self improvement and hope for the future" (in Carroll 1998: 262). Inmates upon whom these rights are conferred must in turn act responsibly and respect the rights of others, and those inmates who do not act accordingly should be called to account through the firm, consistent, and lawful enforcement of correctional rules and regulations.

In his discussion of ethics in corrections, John Kleinig (2001: 7) singles out the issue of punishment as central. He emphasizes that it is incarceration itself that is the punishment, and that the purpose of incarceration is not to administer additional punishment over and above the inmate's deprivation of liberty. It is true that confinement and deprivation of liberty carry with them other deprivations, but he argues that these need to be related to the deprivation of liberty and must not be constructed so as to impose additional penalties. For example, control over visits may be justified as part of prison security but ought not to invalidate other practices concerning visitation and conjugal relations. Similarly, searching prisoners can also be justified on grounds of security, but the predominant practice of strip searching[1] may be considered as carrying an element of humiliation outside the bounds of proper security considerations. As Kleinig specifies, inmates "do not forfeit their essential humanity" (2001: 7). Treatment that is intended to degrade or dehumanize inmates is not authorized by the sanctions society has imposed on them. Ultimately, most inmates will reenter society, hopefully having learned during incarceration more about their social responsibilities.

Agreeing with Kleinig, Richard Lippke (2007: 2), in suggesting the need for a normative theory of imprisonment, argues that many countries imprison offenders under conditions that cannot be morally justified. As he puts it, "Harsh and restrictive prison conditions, combined with disrespectful or abusive treatment of inmates, sends the message that offenders are contemptible, little more than dangerous wild animals to be severely chastised and restrained" (p. 3). In relation to conditions of confinement, Lippke makes a case for "minimally restrictive and reasonably humane prison conditions" in contrast to "extreme conditions of confinement" (p. 104). The latter category equates to supermaximum security prisons, and Lippke argues that as a matter of morality we ought to prefer minimum conditions that are more consistent with the aims of punishment. Lippke's view is that basic prisoner welfare demands that prisoners receive adequate food and nutrition, are protected from violence, are not exploited or preyed upon by others, receive physical and mental health

---

1. As Margaret Leland Smith (2001: 34) notes, the process of a strip search involves a presentation of nakedness and an inspection of body openings, during which mouths and ears are pulled open and the inmate is required to bend over and pull open the vagina or anus using the fingers and to cough energetically.

care, live in clean and properly ventilated accommodation with adequate heat or air conditioning, wear appropriate clothing, and are provided with the means to maintain personal hygiene and enjoy some degree of privacy (p. 112).

Kleinig suggests that a correctional ethic should also take account of the roles played by guards, especially of how they interact with their co-workers, the way in which their work is coordinated with others employed in the prison system, and the connections they make with the correctional administrative structure (2001: 9). There will also be ethical considerations in relation to the larger society and to institutions like legislatures. Relations where strong power differences exist, where conflicts of interest are likely, or where decisions are made in uncertain situations are all areas where particular attention to ethics is needed. As Kleinig (2001: 10) notes, Kauffman's description of the prison system in Massachusetts portrays a culture where guards are corrupted and inmates are denied their humanity; these concerns are repeated in Conover's work (2001), where he portrays the correctional training process as a course in "emotional detachment" and "degrading treatment." It is significant that, as Conover reveals, there was no ethical content in his correctional training, and, as Kleinig points out, "An academy training that fails to focus explicitly and pervasively on the ethical dimensions of correctional work undermines any claim it may have to professionalism" (2001: 11). Margaret Leland Smith argues that the "intractable brutalities that inhere in the practice of imprisonment" (2001: 30) make it extremely difficult to establish any moral basis for the role of a prison guard. She calls attention to the failures that have occurred within the prison system as a whole, causing the federal courts in the 1970s and 1980s to impose oversight on prison practices to ensure compliance with constitutional norms of conduct.

More recently, human rights activists have shown how brutalizing and degrading practices continue to exist in the prison system. Similarly, Derek Brookes (2001: 40) claims that "anything posing as a correctional ethics is a nonsense." Henriques (2001: 194) agrees that the operation of a humane correctional system is rendered almost impossible, because correctional practice has retribution as its dominant ideology, and in institutions where inmates' rights are easily violated, it is easy to ignore ethical and professional standards of conduct. In the case shown in Case Study 6.1, the U.S. Supreme Court decided that the guard's failure to respond to the threat of violence against Dee Farmer amounted to "deliberate indifference."

CASE STUDY 6.1 MALE PRISON RAPE AND "DELIBERATE INDIFFERENCE"

Dee Farmer, a young African American man, was brutally raped while serving a 20-year prison sentence (Wyatt 2006: 585). As a preoperative transsexual, Farmer "projected female characteristics" when he entered the prison and was consequently viewed as a problem case for the Federal Bureau of Prisons. Despite his protests, prison staff classified Farmer as male and placed him in

(Continued)

(Continued)

general population with other male prisoners, which left him a target for sexual assault (Vaughn 1996: 141). Farmer was sometimes housed in general population but more often in protective custody and was therefore kept away from other prisoners. After being transferred to a federal penitentiary for disciplinary reasons, he was placed in general population with more "troublesome prisoners" and again found himself the victim of physical and sexual assault.

In a lawsuit against the prison administration, Farmer claimed that prison officials were "deliberately indifferent to his constitutional rights to be free from inmate-against-inmate assault" (Vaughn: 1996: 141). In its decision in *Farmer v. Brennan* (1994), the U.S. Supreme Court held that "deliberate indifference resides on a continuum between mere negligence . . . [and] something less than acts or omissions for the very purpose of causing harm or with knowledge that harm will result" (p. 141). The Court also held that prison officials violate the Eighth Amendment when they "deliberately disregard the occurrence of male rape" (Wyatt 2006: 585). The Court noted that "prison officials have a duty under the Eighth Amendment to provide humane conditions of confinement. They must ensure that inmates receive adequate food, clothing, shelter, and medical care, and must protect prisoners from violence at the hands of other prisoners. . . . A constitutional violation occurs only where the deprivation alleged is . . . 'sufficiently serious' . . . and the official has acted with 'deliberate indifference' to inmate health and safety" (*Farmer v. Brennan* 1994).

The Experience of Guarding

In order to understand how ethical issues arise in the practice of corrections, it is necessary to contextualize the experience of guarding. This contextualization can expose the anxieties and pressures faced by guards within the prison environment. A number of authors (Conover 2001; Crouch 1980b; Lombardo 1989) have pointed to common characteristics in those choosing a career in corrections. In particular, they note that people do not typically aspire to become prison guards; rather, seeking this work is often a reaction to the need for employment or is a result of unexpected job changes. For most seeking positions as guards, job security and a regular salary are paramount. In many rural areas, working in the prison system represents the only form of employment, and the prison offers the opportunity to remain in the local environment rather than having to travel to the city for work.

Lombardo (1989: 140) explains that about one third of the officers he interviewed at Auburn Prison considered danger and mental tension as the most dissatisfying parts of their job. From their point of view, "danger" referred not to the likelihood of violent events, but to the unpredictability of a violent occurrence. Conover (2001: 82) reports one incident in Sing Sing involving an inmate porter who had been sweeping the flats outside the cells with a push broom. When another inmate appeared, the porter attacked him, broke the broom handle over his head, and then tried to spear his face with the splintered ends. Most guards consider prison violence a constant possibility that might result from seemingly arbitrary events, and they believe in their ability to sense the likelihood of violence through their awareness of behavior patterns within the prison.

Guards frequently experience personal challenges from inmates. It follows that security and control are fundamental tenets of guard work, because inmate misconduct not only threatens the prison order but also may impact the guards' personal safety (Crouch and Marquart 1980: 89). This concern for security and order tends to cause guards to view suspiciously any events that interrupt prison routines. For instance, the entry of "free world" treatment personnel into the prison is a particular cause of concern for most guards, who believe that outsiders know very little about inmates and fail to appreciate the need for constant security. Nonetheless, as was explained to May (1980: 111) by one prison commissioner, guard attacks on inmates have been greatly reduced because prisons are now far more open to outsiders. However, according to the same prison commissioner, when there is a physical conflict between a guard and an inmate and force is used to bring the inmate under control, inmates commonly claim that the guard "gets in a few extra licks" (p. 128). According to Crouch and Marquart (1980: 90), additional tenets of guard work taught to new recruits include the need to maintain social distance from the inmates and the dictum that guards must be "tough, knowledgeable, and able to handle inmates." "Knowledgeability" relates to the need for guards to understand the informal rules and processes that shape daily prison interactions and how to avoid being manipulated by inmates.

Guards are concerned about the lack of inmate understanding of their situation, especially in view of the fact that the inmates want the guards to understand their position. Some guards pointed to the sarcasm and perpetual insults they receive from inmates on a daily basis, which they say creates a hostile environment for them (Lombardo 1989: 143). Similarly, guards felt that they lacked the support of their supervisors and administrators, saw themselves as working against everyone, and felt isolated from both inmates and supervisors. Webb and Morris (1980: 150) found that guards perceived prison administrators as outsiders with political connections whose main focus was "looking good" and who did not possess the guards' knowledge of the institution and the inmate population.

The guards in Lombardo's study showed a particular concern for what they regarded as benefits conferred on inmates by the state Department of Corrections (1989: 155). For these officers, programs like work release, education release, and the ability for an inmate to receive a college education were considered improper benefits for inmates, because in their view, inmates were obtaining work while law-abiding citizens were unemployed.

Corruption of Authority

The notion that a guard's authority over inmates can become corrupted is well established in correctional studies and is frequently referred to as a category of ethical misconduct. In essence, "corruption of authority" refers to a practice by guards of deliberately refraining from enforcing prison rules and regulations.

Contrasting police and prison guards' use of discretion, Lombardo (1989: 201) notes that when a policeman decides whether and how to enforce the law, this decision is considered an exercise of his or her discretion; however, when a guard decides when and how to enforce rules, his or her decision is constructed as an exercise in corruption of authority. This is because deciding not to enforce the rules is perceived by guards as necessary to gain inmate cooperation and is a reflection of the guards' relative powerlessness. Both decisions are exercised with discretion, but the police action is cast in positive terms and the guard's decision in negative terms, thus reflecting the general perception that guard work is distasteful, unrewarding, and of low, nonprofessional status.

Sykes (1999) describes the corruption of authority, and Crouch and Marquart (1980: 77–78) summarize two other forms of potential corruption. The first is the loss of authority that may arise when guards become too friendly with inmates and fail to maintain the required social distance. This may be particularly prevalent with new recruits when the new guard feels herself or himself to be closer to the inmates than to superiors. The second form of potential corruption involves handing over guard tasks to inmates. When inmates carry out duties like mail delivery and housekeeping, the guards may become dependent on their labor, and to that extent, their authority may be undermined or dissipated. Webb and Morris (1980: 150), in their interviews with guards, found that although guards frequently commented on the need for discipline and thought that strict discipline was good for inmates, they were also quick to point out the need not to go strictly by the book, that rules were made to be broken, that rules were not absolutes, and that a commonsense approach had to be taken in applying discipline.

Hepburn (1989: 191) discusses how guards operate as agents of social control and draws attention to the "role ambiguity" that guards experience as a result of having to perform both treatment and custodial roles. The *treatment* role requires that guards demonstrate helping behaviors, enforce the rules with discretion, and establish a degree of personal relations with inmates. In contrast, the *custody* role calls for impersonal relationships, a controlling demeanor, and complete enforcement of prison rules. As well, role ambiguity is created when vague or contradictory instructions determine how the role is to be exercised. While guards are expected to show flexibility and discretion, they are still liable to be disciplined themselves if they violate or allow inmates to violate prison rules. Guards are also dependent on prisoners for their own physical safety, and they depend on inmates for the successful fulfillment of their own duties (1989: 193). For example, inmates may resist guard control through work slowdowns or an increase in disciplinary problems, and this tends to focus the prison administration on a guard's inability to maintain control. Guards may, therefore, have to depend on prisoner cooperation to demonstrate their ability to manage prisoners and to obtain recognition and promotion. At the same time, guards may not be provided with adequate or clear rules for managing a potentially hostile inmate population.

Power and Authority in Prison: Controlling the Inmates

The most obvious fact about the prison environment is that guards are vested with power and authority over the prisoners and exercise that power to control them in accordance with prison rules and regulations. A number of studies have attempted to explain the basis and nature of this coercive power and authority. It is the exercise of this power that creates ethical issues and dilemmas.

In his conceptualization of power in prisons, Hepburn (1985: 146) catalogs five forms of power: legitimate power, coercive power, reward power, expert power, and referent power. With *legitimate power,* guards are invested with authority to command as a result of their position as a guard of prisoners. It is the position of guard itself within the institutional structure that confers the right to give instructions and to be obeyed. In other words, a guard's orders are obeyed because they are the orders of a guard, and prisoners comply by virtue of their status as prisoners. In a 1981 survey of prison guards at New York's Auburn Prison, Lombardo (1981, in Hepburn 1985: 46) found that nearly half of the 50 guards surveyed believed the source of their power over prisoners derived from their position as enforcers of prison rules.

Coercive power is based on inmate perceptions that guards have the capacity to punish prisoner disobedience. As was discussed earlier, Sykes notes that guards who rely on this kind of power run the risk of prisoner retaliation as well as the risk that their superiors will question their ability to exercise control over inmates.

Reward power describes situations where prisoners perceive that guards are able to issue rewards, for example, through making recommendations to committees dealing with matters such as work assignments, participation in programs, and release on furlough. The fact that guards may confer rewards is itself a basis of power. However, as a result of bureaucratic and judicial action, guards nowadays are less able to influence internal decisions than they have been in the past. Nevertheless, although the ability to make these formal rewards may have lapsed, a system of informal rewards has been sustained under which guards will compromise with prisoners on the basis of reciprocity. This form of reward making encompasses such things as the toleration of minor rule violations, petty stealing, and making concessions to inmate leaders.

Expert power derives from the prisoners' perception that guards have some special skill or expertise. Such power is especially likely to arise in prisons where treatment is emphasized and where guards are seen as part of the overall therapeutic environment. This power may be undermined by the unwillingness of prisoners to acknowledge the competence of guards as well as through bureaucratic administrative procedures that reduce guard autonomy and consequently provide them with fewer opportunities to demonstrate expertise.

Finally, *referent power* is the power a guard exercises as a result of gaining the respect and admiration of prisoners. Here, the guard's personal qualities, including in particular leadership skills and success in the art of persuasion, give some guards what Lombardo calls "personal authority" (1989: 149). Guards with this power are considered fair in their relations with prisoners, as showing a degree of respect for them, and as not acting out of malice or in an arbitrary manner.

In his survey of how these kinds of power operated in one prison, Hepburn discovered that prison guards thought that their powers of control derived largely from their position as guards—that is, from their legitimate authority—and from their reputation for competence and good judgment (that is, Lombardo's "personal authority") (1985: 155). Of the five bases of power, guards considered legitimate and expert power to be instrumental in ensuring prisoner compliance, followed by referent power, coercive, and finally, reward power. Also, the greater the guard's experience, the greater the importance he or she attached to expert power and the less importance was placed on coercive and legitimate power (Hepburn 1985: 160).

Lombardo (1989: 93) developed a typography of guard authority comprising *personal authority* and *legalistic authority*. In his survey of guard attitudes toward inmates, over 60% of the guards perceived that their authority derived from their personal style of presentation—that is, from the way they handled and dealt with inmates—and from their interactions with inmates. These officers did not feel that rules or the fact that they were wearing a uniform endowed them with authority, and they thought it was necessary to develop and, in effect, *earn,* the necessary authority, the key to which was the ability of the guard to get an inmate to recognize the legitimacy of his authority. Most agreed that consistency was key in gaining legitimacy. However, earning legitimacy was seen to be a long-term process, and some officers suggested that a period of 5 to 10 years was required. These guards saw reliance on rules as unnecessary once a guard had developed a realistic appreciation of his own abilities and of inmates' expectations. At this point, rules no longer constituted a major source of authority and were deemed necessary only in extreme cases. The more experienced officers thought that the younger guards, who were unsure of themselves, would experience more difficulty in gaining compliance from inmates. They considered that interactions with inmates about rules could erupt into major confrontations, principally because the younger guards would be anxious not to "lose face" and have what they considered their weak authority diminished further (Lombardo 1989: 94).

In the case of legalistic authority, a group of guards thought their authority derived from legal foundations, and they saw no need to earn the right to it. They saw themselves as a part of the criminal justice system having lawful authority over those who had broken the law. Some thought this legally based view of authority derived from their job description as a correctional officer, whereas others considered its origin to be the rules and regulations of the institution, backed up with support from the prison administration (Lombardo 1989: 97).

Those professing a belief in personal authority as well as those favoring legalistic authority agreed that full enforcement of institutional regulations would effectively cause the institution to cease operating, because all inmates would be forever locked down for rule violations. As a whole, guards were always cognizant of the actual or potential impact of any inmate's conduct on the guards themselves, on other inmates, and on the overall climate within the institution. As well, most agreed that it was not the rules per se that created problems but inconsistencies in rule enforcement, a matter of great concern to the inmates (Lombardo 1989: 99).

The Battle for Compliance

According to Sykes's 1958 study, prison officials saw themselves engaged with the prisoners in a "battle for compliance" that superceded any task of reform or rehabilitation (1999: 38). To support this observation, he points to the existence of violence, sexual violence, and theft as commonplace events within prisons. One might think that the prison bureaucracy would be able to impose its will on the inmates in an unchallenged fashion and would be able to act in an arbitrary or capricious manner if it thought fit. However, Sykes insightfully observed that the prison guards were in fact "engaged in a continuous struggle to maintain order" and that their dominant position did not reflect the prison reality (p. 42). He concluded that the reason the guards needed to negotiate their power rather than simply enforce their authority arose in part from constraints imposed on guards' use of force by the prison society. Physical coercion, while it might seem an obvious way of enforcing an authoritarian rule, was simply ineffective, and guards had to fall back on a system of awards and punishments in negotiating order with the inmates. Physical violence was always affected by the low guard/inmate ratio and by the danger that using violence might touch off further violence.

Evaluating Guards

The close, intimate relationship and association between guards and prisoners in the New Jersey State Maximum Security Prison in Sykes's study (1999) gave rise to a relationship of reciprocity, because guards could not remain distant from inmates or completely withdraw from them. Guards would be evaluated by their supervisors on their ability to control inmates; they would want to demonstrate that they were able to perform their tours of duty with the minimum amount of trouble; and they would always be aware that riots and hostage taking are possible causes of ruptures in the negotiation of power. This view of evaluating a guard's capability to handle inmates is supported by Poole and Regoli (1980: 221), who found in a survey of guards that a high rate of disciplinary action was perceived by superiors as evidence of poor work performance and of an inability to handle inmates. This is an inevitable consequence of evaluating guards in terms of the inmates they control. Similarly, in a study in three California prisons, Glaser and Fry (1987: 34) found that a clear majority of staff at all three institutions agreed with the statement that officers reporting all rule violations coming to their notice would be seen by supervisors as individuals who could not control the inmates on their units.

Rewards and Punishments

Sykes (1999: 50) does not think that the use of rewards and punishments offers an adequate basis for guards to enforce control. He considers that punishments are insufficiently different to the regular routine of prison life to count for anything and notes that rewards are already offered at the start of a prison term, principally in the form of "good time."[2] Thus, privileges and rewards are not specifically tied to everyday conduct and compliance but are already granted, and this means there is an absence of any ongoing positive incentives for either guards or inmates (p. 52). Sykes argues that ultimately the authority of the guards is corrupted by their having to continually compromise with their captives so that, paradoxically, their dominant position can only be enforced through accommodations with inmates (p. 58).

In her study of the prison system in Massachusetts, with a central focus on Walpole, the maximum security prison, Kauffman (1988: 54) discusses inducements and rewards and finds that at Walpole in particular, systematic rewards for inmates were essential to ensure their sustained cooperation. For example, inmate workers in the institution were allowed to obtain food from the kitchen, and even small tasks performed by inmates prompted award giving. According to Kauffman (pp. 54–55), although rewards might be limited to a packet of cigarettes or buying an inmate a soda, guards might offer more significant rewards in the form of contraband (especially drugs), information, and refraining from prosecuting inmate offenses. Nevertheless, award giving was not without its dangers, including these possibilities:

- Inmates might try to corrupt guards and make allegations about officer corruption (such allegations were regularly made).
- Rewards might be used by inmates to blackmail guards to ensure the continuation of those rewards.
- The rewards themselves might cause disputes or even violence among inmates unless they were evenly distributed.
- Valuable rewards such as drugs would engender more conflict.
- Officers engaging in the reward process ran the risk of endangering their own fellow guards—for example, through bringing drugs into the prison.
- Rewards might not be adequate to induce compliance.

Enforcing Rule Violations

Based on his study, Lombardo (1989: 105) maintains that the process of corruption is far more complex than Sykes describes it and that although inmate cooperation with guards is a factor, the relationship between guards and inmates with respect to rules also plays a part in handling minor rule violations. Guards who write violation reports for minor offenses are seen by the inmates as lacking the ability to handle things on a man-to-man basis and as having a strategy designed to avoid losing the cooperation of the inmates

---

2. The term *good time* refers to the proportion of the inmate's sentence that is deducted for "good behavior." In indeterminate sentences, this time is automatically deducted from the sentence imposed by the court, unless the inmate commits a new offense while in prison or violates disciplinary rules that result in a reduction of the reduced period of the sentence. Although the deducted period in indeterminate sentences is automatically applied if there are no violations within the prison environment, it is considered "earned" on the basis of the inmate's good behavior. Indeterminate sentences were developed under the rehabilitative model of punishment. However, the fact that good time is automatic except when violations of prison rules occur can reduce its value as an incentive. In cases where the court sentence specifies a determinate sentence, the possibility of good time does not apply. Determinate sentences without good time are the result of "truth in sentencing" policies.

by creating tensions over minor rule violations. Minor violations included failing to shave or have a haircut and violating rules concerned with cell neatness, a common occurrence (p. 106). The guards' focus was very much on the use of rule violations within an ongoing testing process with the inmates. Informing the inmate of a rule violation rather than writing a citation for it was not considered an exercise of leniency. Instead, it was regarded as an act of strength, because the guard was asserting his control over the situation, and by not writing a citation, the guard was demanding the inmate's acknowledgment of the guard's control (p. 109). Like police officers dealing with the public, the inmate's attitude or perceived attitude becomes crucial in determining a guard's response to a minor rule violation; many guards in the Lombardo study perceived inmate attitude as more important than actual conduct. Clearly, guards are alert for challenges to their authority and person, and are prepared to interpret conduct as a personal challenge, sometimes pursuing questions of attitude and ignoring the behavior that prompted the interaction with the inmate. One guard summed up his view of inmates' behavior as follows:

> Seventy to seventy-five percent there's no problem with. Tell them to do things and they do it. They look at the CO as doing a job. But fifteen to thirty percent you have problems with regardless. They hate the world and the CO's because they deal with the CO's most frequently and the CO's represent the state. Those guys give you lots of problems with drugs, extortion and verbal abuse. They're constantly into something. (in Lombardo 1989: 115)

Guards pointed out that inmates are better educated and more organized than before and move in groups that are involved in drugs and extortion (Lombardo 1989). They stressed that control within the prison is now in the hands of younger inmates and gangs rather than with the "old timers," as was previously the case.

Noting the changes at Auburn Prison between 1976 and 1986, guards affirmed that violence and drugs were now factors that were not present in 1976, that individual discretion had been replaced during that period by formal procedures requiring staff to give explanations to inmates, and that this change had rendered them more accountable (Lombardo 1989: 121). One outcome of this reduced discretion is that guards no longer perceive themselves as participants in the functioning of the institution and that they sense a lack of support from administrators. These perceptions have created a greater sense of isolation, because guards feel alienated both from the workplace and from the administration.

Informal Controls

In addition to formal controls over inmates through the formal disciplinary process, it is common within the prison environment to find that guards exercise various informal controls. Again, the operation of these controls can produce ethical issues and dilemmas.

An example of these informal controls operated within the Massachusetts state prison system. Writing disciplinary reports was not seen as an appropriate means of maintaining control, because writing reports for rule breaches resulted in inmate threats of reprisals, derision from fellow guards, and a general loss of respect for the ticket writer (Kauffman 1988: 62). Kauffman found that most guards rarely wrote disciplinary reports except for major infractions. The actual disciplinary sanctions that might be imposed were limited and did not substantially affect a prisoner's status, because they were restricted to loss of "good time," being placed in isolation, or being relocated to a more secure block within the prison. The limited sanctions meant that guards considered writing disciplinary tickets a waste of their time, and they therefore resorted to informal punishments. As one guard put it, "If you give them your own type of punishment they'll think more" (1988: 64). At Walpole, a guard might resort to locking inmates in their cells instead of issuing a disciplinary report for an infraction such as an inmate refusing to get back into line. This informal punishment would be implemented when the guard simply refrained from unlocking that inmate's cell during the daily prison routine. This practice of locking down the guilty inmate would be especially effective on Friday nights, because the inmate usually had to wait in his cell until Monday morning before he could see the deputy superintendent.

Similarly, Lombardo (1989) found that at Auburn guards sometimes resorted to unofficial action if they believed that established procedures would be ineffective. For example, an officer might submit a violation report on Friday knowing that no action would be taken on that violation until Monday. However, issuing the violation would have the effect of placing the inmate in "keep lock" for two days, whereas the actual penalty would probably have been less severe.

Other informal methods of control included guards flushing toilets back into particular cells, shutting off the electricity for an entire tier of cells, turning off the hot water, withholding toilet paper or matches, or even keeping back food (Kauffman 1988: 65). Sometimes, more indirect and secretive methods were employed, such as making inmates wait substantial periods of time before allowing them to make phone calls, denying access to writing paper, destroying an inmate's plants that he had carefully cultivated in his cell, or scratching a piece of furniture manufactured by an inmate in the prison factory. As one guard explained, "There's so many ways you can get these guys" (1988: 66). These methods would often be employed as an alternative to physical reprisals that might provoke administrative action against the guards themselves.

Lombardo (1989) noted forms of informal control at Auburn. For example, one device included locking a man out of his cell for some time while others were locked in, isolating the inmate and causing a sense of anxiety. Guards also resorted to disconnecting an inmate's water supply or electricity supply and leaving a "keep lock" tag on a cell door, which would result in an inmate being locked up for a number of days until it was discovered that the tag was an error. Methods of getting back at inmates in an unofficial way included not informing an inmate of a scheduled appointment. In these extralegal approaches, it is important that the inmate is aware of the deliberate nature of the guard's action and appreciates that a message is being given that the guard can make the inmate's life uncomfortable (Lombardo 1989: 101).

Guarding With Discretion

As already noted, although guards' discretionary powers have been curtailed over time, they nevertheless continue to exercise significant discretion in carrying out their day-to-day tasks. Discretionary power can easily involve questions of ethical conduct, and some argue that it is preferable to limit discretion even more by expanding the written rules and regulations of the prison. Gilbert (1999: 275) argues that administrators ought to allow correctional officers to exercise discretion whenever there is an absence of policy or where that policy is vague or inconsistent, on the basis that full enforcement of prison rules, policies, and procedures is an impossibility. The discretionary power of guards is shaped less by formal rules than by "an explicit understanding of the shared operational values and ethical principles that govern correctional practice" (Pollock 1994 in Gilbert 1999: 275). Gilbert calls for formal training in order to develop an ethical framework within which officers may exercise their discretion. He sees a need for managers to assist guards to understand the limits of their discretion but also to recognize that guards will make exceptions to rules that are "ethically defensible." He argues that if guard decisions are reasonable and in line with legal and ethical parameters, guards should not be disciplined for making reasonable exceptions to rules when they face complex situations. In situations when following the rules would make little sense or would constitute a danger to security, this approach, he suggests, should be supported even more. Conover (2001: 249) also recognizes the discretionary powers of guards, writing,

> After five months at Sing Sing, I understood. Experience mattered. More precisely, it took time (and confrontations) to decide (or to discover) what kind of person was going to be wearing your uniform. A hardass or a softy? Inmates' friend or inmates' enemy? Straight or crooked? A user of force or a writer of tickets? A strict overseer or a lender of hands? The job was full of discretionary power and the decisions about how to use it were often moral.

Crouch (1980a: 33) agrees that the quality of prison life for inmates has been affected by the increase in political and racial awareness and by judicial activism to the extent that inmates now have the ability to look outside the prison for the norms of prison life. As Crouch puts it, inmates became

> increasingly able to compete with their keepers in the daily process of defining prison situations. That is, what was once an unambiguous case of rule violation may now be interpreted by inmates as a case of racial disrespect or legal deprivation. (1980a: 33–34)

Guenther and Guenther (1980: 162), in their research at an Atlanta prison, identified strategies that guards employed to minimize loss of control. These included the shakedown (locating and confiscating contraband), either routinely or on an ad hoc basis; using informers to locate contraband or gain information about potential violence or escape attempts; "the count" (counting prisoners at regular intervals becomes a core activity causing all other activities to be suspended); and the "siphon," screening inmates to eliminate troublemakers and simplify the process of maintaining order, based on the belief that only a very small proportion of the inmate population causes trouble. In Atlanta, this latter method takes the form of maintaining a list of records of inmates with potential for trouble that guards consult from time to time.

Up to this point, we have discussed the experience of being a prison guard and how a guard's authority can become corrupted in different contexts. The power and authority of a prison guard seems absolute, but in fact is constantly being negotiated as guards make concessions to prisoners to gain their cooperation and to keep the prison routine running smoothly. Informal controls and rewards and privileges allow guards to circumvent the rules or to ignore the rules either as a strategy to reward prisoners for their cooperation or to punish them informally, but effectively. A major component of prison life for both guards and inmates is the prison guard subculture, which plays as important a role in the prison environment as it does in law enforcement (see Chapter 2).

The Gray Wall of Silence: Prison Guard Subculture

The notion that an inmate subculture exists in prison was first proposed by Donald Clemmer (1940) in *The Prison Community,* where he argued that inmates take on the customs and culture of the penitentiary. Later studies, however, have proposed that features of the inmate subculture are imported into institutions by the inmates themselves and are not derived from the culture developed through prisonization.[3] *Is there a guard subculture that parallels that of the inmates?* If so, is it imported, or is it generated by prison work itself? How does the guard culture impact ethical practice and standards?

In light of the popular image of prisons and guards suggesting that guards are brutal and uncaring and that inmates and guards maintain relations that are hostile and even violent, it is easy to argue that men and women become prison guards because the occupation of guarding captives appeals most to those who are sadistic and who enjoy exercising arbitrary power over the powerless. Kauffman (1988: 166), drawing on her experience as a prison guard and as a researcher in prisons, contends, however, that the importation model is inappropriate, and that the prison subculture as it relates to guards is fostered and maintained by the prison work itself. She explains that initially she entered the prison with sympathetic attitudes toward inmates and skeptical attitudes toward guards, but within a short period her sympathies had reversed. She observed that other new guards also appeared to be substantially influenced by their prison experience and underwent a similar transformation. Her own study of the issue suggests that neither importation nor prisonization by itself shapes guard recruits and the guard culture but that the culture appears to be the product "of a complex interaction of importation, socialization, deportation, and cultural evolution" (1988: 167).

Kauffman argues that prison officers possess a distinct subculture, setting them apart from other professions. The central norms of this subculture inform their daily performance of duty. She distinguishes the norms shown in Table 6.2, which she says amount to a code for prison guards (1988: 86–117).

---

3. The term *prisonization* was coined and defined by Donald Clemmer (1959 in Wheeler 1961: 697) as "the taking on in greater or lesser degree, of the folkways, mores, customs and general culture of the penitentiary." The outcome, according to Clemmer, was that inmates internalized a "criminal outlook" that made them impervious to conventional values systems (p. 697).

Table 6.2   The Prison Guard Code

Norm	Comment
Always go to the aid of an officer in distress.	This is the foundation for guard solidarity, applying to any officer in distress. It permits conduct that might otherwise violate bureaucratic norms. The norm applies whatever may be the standing of a particular guard, regardless of race or the guard's own record in responding to calls of distress. This norm is fundamental. Ignoring this norm is likely to result in a guard being ostracized by his or her coworkers.
Don't lug drugs.	This again is regarded as fundamental because of its potential for causing danger to coworkers, such as the possibility of violence by inmates acting under the influence of drugs or alcohol. Sanctions for breach of this norm include removal from the job and physical reprisal. Many guards are prepared to rat on an officer who violates this norm, and such ratting is supported by coworkers.
Don't rat.	This takes the form of not "ratting" on an officer to an inmate and never cooperating with authorities in an investigation or, worse, testifying against a fellow guard about a guard's treatment of inmates. Betraying a fellow officer to inmates is regarded as a great sin likely to jeopardize the other guard's safety and is associated with the taboo against giving inmates information about the identity and background of guards. As for testifying against other guards, Kauffman (1988) found that the norm was not absolute. Where an inmate was killed, at least some guards would take into account the circumstances of the death and the identity of those involved and would consider testifying against the responsible guard(s). Guards who opposed violence but felt the need to show loyalty to their coworkers found this norm very troubling, and those who violated it would never work again at that prison.
Never make a fellow officer look bad in front of inmates.	Violations of this norm are perceived to undercut guard solidarity and enhance the vulnerability of guards as a group. This injunction extends to an unwillingness to stop fellow guards taking part in a beating at least while it is in progress.
Always support an officer in a dispute with an inmate.	This is the counterpart of the above norm and reflects the belief that a guard ought to supply unquestioning support to his or her coworkers, especially in the face of inmate resistance and unreliable support from prison administrators. Unlike behavioral norms, the sanction for the violation of this norm was less severe. For example, a guard might refuse to sign a disciplinary

(Continued)

Table 6.2 (Continued)

Norm	Comment
	report for a violation that he or she had not personally observed but would not be sanctioned because someone else would be found to sign that report.
Always support officer sanctions against inmates.	This goes beyond general support for coworkers and extends into active participation in applying informal sanctions such as physical force and coercion in response to inmate violence. Among the guards, Kauffman found some differing perceptions about the adherence to this norm. For example, whereas many new guards felt they had to participate in a situation involving beating up an inmate or be judged an outcast, others consistently refused to take part, or would deal with situations without using violence. In such instances, fellow guards might frown upon not becoming the aggressor. Kauffman found that a few guards, well regarded by their coworkers, sometimes intervened to stop beatings and did not incur any sanctions for doing so other than a short period of rejection by their coworkers.
Don't be a white hat.	This prohibits any conduct indicating sympathy or identification with inmates, and this is the norm most easily and regularly violated. Breach of this norm is perceived as likely to jeopardize fellow guards who did not themselves show leniency or sympathy to inmates. Although it is considered appropriate to be respectful of inmates and engage in small talk, deep conversations with inmates are disapproved, and guards who cross that line are likely to be termed "Joe nice-guy." Nevertheless, senior guards who do not violate any other norms concerning guard/inmate relations enjoy considerable discretion in adhering to this norm.
Maintain officer solidarity against all outside groups.	This relates to outsiders such as the administration, the media, and even a guard's own family. It reflects the general feeling found by prison researchers among guards that the prison administration does not care for them, neglects them, and has no confidence in their abilities. Relations between guards and those outside the prison, as regulated by this norm, require that guards never talk about the institution to outsiders, especially the news media, because journalists are seen as allied with inmates and not capable of adopting the guard perspective. Speaking to journalists is considered so serious that a violation would invoke a sanction similar to that applied to those testifying against their coworkers in court. Although many guards refrain from talking about their work to their families to avoid

| | creating concern and worry about the dangers of their job, others adopt the view that no one could possibly understand the job and this includes members of a guard's family. |
| Show positive concern for fellow guards. | Although this covers a range of conduct, Kauffman identifies two situations: Never leave another guard a problem, and help your fellow guard with problems outside the institution. Leaving problems for other guards to address can include causing problems in a fellow guard's block or leaving at the end of a shift with an outstanding problem that must be faced by the incoming guard. Kauffman notes that in practice, this norm is widely violated, largely because there are few sanctions that can be imposed from one shift to another. In relation to problems outside the institution, the ideal guard helps out fellow guards by offering assistance to the family if a guard is injured or by taking up collections to meet debts. |

SOURCE: Kauffman 1988: 86–117.

Kauffman's prison guard code highlights a number of situations where guards, in supporting a particular norm, would likely be acting unethically. For example, helping other guards beat an inmate would usually be regarded as unethical conduct but from the guard's point of view would conform to the norm that a guard must always support another guard against inmates. Clearly, there is considerable scope for conflicts to occur between ethical standards and the norms of the prison subculture.

Subculture and Socialization

Guard recruits are socialized to the guard subculture during their training, and their individual motivation for joining corrections may contribute to their socialization. Looking at the motivation of guard recruits, Kauffman (1988: 170) found that the guard occupation appealed to those who were unemployed or were from communities in which any state job was considered a significant benefit. More than half of the 40 recruits in her study gave financial considerations as their only or primary reason for becoming prison officers, and recruits were typically drawn from locations with high unemployment rates where any state job was welcomed, not only by the individual, but also by his or her family members. Some recruits gave social work motivations for seeking employment as guards, seeing the prison guard career as a stepping-stone to other careers in criminal justice. Some 20% of those interviewed gave their main motivation as a desire to become law enforcement officers, and this group would seem to be the one most attracted by the power and authority enjoyed by guards (p. 175). This group exemplified the stereotype of the prison guard (the "frustrated cop") for whom corrections is a second choice but at least gives them the opportunity to sanction criminals in the prison if not on the street. This group focused mainly on family tradition and their wish to achieve status within the community. In terms of tradition, a number of groups were the sons or relatives of police or prison officers, and others saw themselves as having grown up with the law.

When the recruits as a whole were asked to respond to hypothetical dilemmas involving inmates, most approved of a guard acting in a sympathetic manner toward inmates. For example, 95% responded that an officer who broke up a fight between inmates should investigate the cause but do nothing if the fight was not serious, instead of giving the inmates an automatic disciplinary charge (Kaufmann 1988: 179). In terms of ethical standards of conduct, 45% approved of an officer not intervening if he or she observed fellow guards assaulting an inmate (p. 180). This question evoked the least sympathetic response toward inmates.

In discussing the socialization of prison guards, Kauffman (1988: 186) found that guards tended to appropriate the values of the prison over their own established behavioral norms. There was a considerable dichotomy between the formal training program the guards had undergone and their on-the-job training at Walpole, because the new recruits were left on their own to handle difficult and dangerous positions within the institution without, as they perceived it, receiving any substantial support from the administration. To add to their burden, new officers received little or no support from their fellow guards, who tended to show indifference to their plight, even ignoring them altogether beyond the minimum communications necessary to change shifts. Conover (2001) reports a similar experience at Sing Sing (see Chapter 4).

Kauffman discusses how the new recruits found themselves in a state of depression about the institution and the inmates, seeing themselves faced with the reality of violence and the pervasive atmosphere of fear. Therefore, in contrast to typical guards, recruits entered the prison tasked, as a result of their training, with the aim of being sympathetic to inmates. Once there, they were thrown into a hazardous and difficult job, suffering isolation from colleagues and feeling the same degree of alienation from the administration and inmates. In order to survive, guards had to give up old values and norms of behavior and adopt those of the officer subculture (Kauffman 1988: 198). Kauffman (p. 206) explains that some guard recruits were unable to vary their behavior toward inmates, and as a result of making their sympathy toward inmates widely known, became casualties and were expelled by their fellow guards, who would respond angrily and with resentment to their liberal views about inmates. These recruits suffered complete isolation (one was assigned to the guard towers on the midnight shift), and many guards refused to talk to these recruits. Finally, as one recruit put it, "You're either going to have to fit in and be like these people or you're going to get hurt" (p. 207).

Accordingly, those recruits who were unable to adapt to prison values and complete the process of socialization were subjected to ostracism, harassment, or assignment to the outermost bounds of the prison as forms of expulsion from the prison culture. In some cases, where expulsion was neither practical nor desirable, but where socialization had also failed, the prison culture was obliged to accommodate differing values. This was particularly true during the early 1970s, when prison riots occurred at Attica and in New Mexico, and values had to change. In this respect, Kauffman reports that Walpole was quite a different institution in the late 1970s than it had been at the beginning of that decade (1988: 209).

Guard Types

Noting that guards varied in their attitudes toward inmates and other guards, Kauffman (1988: 250–251) identified five types of guards: pollyannas, white hats, hard asses, functionaries, and burnouts. *Pollyannas* were guards who cared about their colleagues but were critical of the manner in which they dealt with inmates. These guards adopted a helping strategy as a means of coping with the prison environment, and they expressed their sympathy for inmates, helped them if they had needs, talked to them, and found rewards in doing these things. *White hats* were guards holding positive attitudes toward inmates but negative attitudes toward their fellow guards. They were invested in working with people, showed compassion and understanding for inmates, and pointed out the absence of such compassion in their fellow guards. *Hard asses* were the antithesis of white hats, showing hostility toward inmates but identifying closely with fellow guards. This group was typically young and inexperienced, regarded Walpole as an adventure, and found its violence stimulating. They tended to see the prison world as guards in conflict with inmates—a conflict of good against evil. Nevertheless, Kauffman found hard asses few in number at Walpole, mainly because the attitudes displayed by the hard asses were likely to provoke payback from inmates. *Burnouts* displayed negative attitudes toward both their fellow guards and inmates and were able to cope with the prison experience only barely, if at all. For these guards, prison had become such a dominating factor in their lives that they were unable to cope with the outside world. For example, one burnout always kept his back to the wall, another would jump if a door slammed, and another was unable to cope with the crowds in the city or in stores. *Functionaries* coped with prison by closing their minds to it, including both inmates and guards. They saw prison work as a dead end, as nonproductive, and as "maintaining that human warehouse" (Kauffman 1988: 257). They expressed no enjoyment in their work, simply needing the job and finding no reward in it.

Crouch and Marquart (1980) argue that the guard subculture is crucial to the process of socializing the newly recruited guard, because for all intents and purposes, recruits imitate the more experienced guards and learn from them how to perceive inmates, how to manage them, and how to anticipate trouble. According to their study, new recruits are taught to perceive inmates as lazy, averse to work, and having "turned to crime" as the easy way out. New recruits are continuously reminded to dominate inmates, to keep a social distance from them, and to keep the upper hand in dealing with inmates through using profanity freely and routinely.

Some researchers argue that there is no guard subculture. For example, Klofas (1984: 174) makes the case that while prison work has unique aspects, there is no set of norms adverse to inmates, something that underpins popular conceptions of a prison guard subculture. He suggests that existing studies indicate that the notion of a guard subculture serves only to reinforce guard stereotypes. In his view, a more accurate account of the practice of guarding reveals important processes in the guard group that merely provide the illusion that certain guard norms favor harsh attitudes toward inmates.

Use of Force

Many situations in the prison environment might provoke the use of force by guards to control inmates. Each instance of the use of force may give rise to an ethical question about whether the force ought to have been used at all, whether excessive force was used, or whether the force was justified, perhaps for the purpose of self-defense against inmate attack.

Kauffman's research (1988: 222) found that most guards were horrified at the extent and nature of violence within prison. Guards tended to characterize the issues they faced within the prison as "moral dilemmas" involving a clash between their own personal ethical standards and the expectations of them as guards. In coping with these dilemmas, many attempted to avoid actions that would injure inmates by refusing, explicitly or implicitly, to carry out certain duties. However, as they spent more time within the prison and absorbed its culture, as well as the guard subculture, their ability to abstain from morally questionable acts weakened, and they began to construct the prison as a separate moral realm and to perceive their dealings with prisoners as outside common ethical norms.

Alternatively, some would shut their minds to the implications of the actions of others as well as to their own actions. Kauffman makes a case that guard recruits who come to prison work with no prior exposure to violence are initially shocked at the events they witness, including the stabbings and murders. Veterans, however, had seen such violence before and seemed unaffected by it (1988: 223).

Over a period, the less experienced guards gradually became inured to the violence, got used to it, and said they were no longer bothered by it. As this process of socialization continued, many officers became dismayed by the changes they saw in themselves, especially in relation to their acceptance of the use of violence. Some rationalized their changes by stressing the difference between prison and the outside world: "This is a prison and it's not society. When you step in here, you step into a different world. . . . It's brutality anyway you look at it. . . . But you got no other choice" (Kauffman 1988: 229).

As Kauffman points out, constructing a separate moral world within the prison and living in that world as well as in the "normal world" can provoke behavioral conflicts. For instance, one officer acknowledged that signing disciplinary reports about events that he had not witnessed was morally wrong outside the prison context (1988: 230). Another guard, heavily involved in violence, judged his conduct to be wrong and then spoke of co-workers who behaved in a similar way as being persons he would not wish to associate with out on the streets. As already mentioned, it was possible for some guards to rationalize morally suspect behavior by judging inmates as beyond morality and as having relinquished their claims to morally correct treatment when they committed their crimes. As one guard put it, "They're just programmed. These guys have nothing in their brains or nothing in their lives other than violence and danger. . . . Those aren't really like people. Most of them are animals" (Kauffman 1988: 230). Overall, such rationalizations operated to lower barriers to violence.

The American Correctional Association Code of Ethics (1990) stipulates that members of the ACA must respect the "dignity and individuality of human beings" and must be committed to "professional and compassionate service." The ACA subscribes to a number of principles in its Code of Ethics, including respect and protection of the civil and legal rights of all individuals, and it requires that members report any corrupt or unethical behavior "where there is sufficient cause to initiate a review."

In considering his training experience in New York State, Conover (2001: 32) explains the position on use of force under various directives, laws, and employee manuals in that state. He reports that in New York it is permissible to "lay hands on or strike an inmate for self-defense, to prevent injury to a person or to property, to quell a disturbance, to enforce compliance with a lawful direction, or to prevent an escape." Deadly physical force can be used in three situations: to prevent an escape, in self-defense, or to prevent arson. Conover remarks that although the trainees spent a significant time learning about firearms, including the range of different types of buckshot as well as actually firing weapons, there was no discussion about "what shooting someone meant, in an ethical sense—how officers might be not only legally but morally justified in doing it" (p. 43).

Generally, guards' use of force in prison takes place within the formal structure and framework of prison rules and regulations designed to control prisoner conduct. However, sometimes force may be used informally, that is, outside the boundaries circumscribed by rules. For example, in a study of a Texas penitentiary, Marquart (1986) investigated the unofficial use of physical force and concluded that the exercise of force outside the terms prescribed was a strategy for the control of prisoners and that this strategy ran parallel to the formal control process and was entrenched within guard subculture. He himself was employed as a guard at the prison and was able to observe guard violence first hand. The guard culture at this prison defined "good officers" as those who were able not only to perform routine prison actions like counts but also to break up fights and maintain discipline without citing inmates for disciplinary infractions. Marquart found that a willingness and initiative to break up fights, a readiness to engage in confrontations with inmates, and an inclination to fight inmates were essential attributes for promotion. While most prisoners were controlled through the structure of sanctions and privileges embodied in the prison rules, there were some inmates who were controlled through verbal intimidation and the use of punitive physical force (see Box 6.2). Verbal assaults were intended to bring about an inmate's humiliation and to destroy his standing in the eyes of other prisoners. Such assaults commonly included name calling, the use of racial terms of abuse, and threats. For example, one officer was recorded as saying to an inmate, "You stupid nigger, if you ever lie to me or any other officer about what you're doing, I'll knock your teeth in" (in Marquart 1986: 351). Sometimes the threats included a promise of physical injury or even death, and those who failed to vary their conduct after verbal assaults "were roughed up as a matter of course" (p. 351).

A CLOSER LOOK

BOX 6.2
Forms of Coercion

Marquart identified a number of forms of coercion. He referred to the first type as *counseling* or *a tune-up* (1986: 352). This kind of force was used for minor offenses such as refusing to obey an order, and such incidents rarely involved serious physical injury, being limited to verbal abuse, kicks, and slaps to the head and body. He documents an instance in which a guard was experiencing difficulties with an inmate who had pushed his way into the food line. The inmate was ordered to get to the back of the line, and the guard reported him to his supervisor. The inmate resisted by yelling at the guard, and as a result he was taken to the major's office (the location for the enactment of discipline) by the guard and his supervisor. There he was slapped across the face and tackled by the guard and supervisor. A third officer joined the original two in punching and kicking the inmate, and one officer threatened to cut his head off with a knife.

The second form of physical force was termed *ass whippings,* and was employed in more serious rule breaches such as threatening an officer or fighting back during a tune-up. For ass whippings, weapons such as blackjacks and riot batons were used by the guards, although the amount of force applied was limited in order to avoid hospitalization. In one case, a guard stood on an inmate's head while another hit him on the buttocks and thighs with a riot baton and several others kicked him.

The third form of coercion involved *severe beatings* and was reserved for inmates who violated rules considered sacred, such as those concerned with escaping or attacking guards (p. 353). In this coercive form, the intent was to cause physical injury, even to the extent of requiring hospitalization. Marquart observed one situation in which an inmate who had earlier struck a guard was dragged from the hall into the major's office, beaten, and then beaten again while confined in a solitary cell. Sometimes beatings were staged in public to set an example, but most took place out of sight of witnesses.

Marquart (1986: 355) concludes that these instances of violence were illegal in both civil and criminal terms and certainly violated prison rules and policy. However, he points out that the use of this kind of unofficial coercion was so common in the institution in which he worked that it had become a norm for the guards, and it was not employed in an arbitrary fashion but in a structured and systematic process intended to maintain control, enforce inmate deference behaviors to guards, and build guard solidarity. Guards who used this informal system were regarded as good promotion prospects.

In terms of the guard subculture, fighting an inmate was seen as an expression of guard masculinity and machismo. As one guard put it, "You have to make a convict fear you or respect you or you won't make it here" (Marquart 1986: 359). Further, because the unofficial use of force had become a parallel system for social control within the prison, it built a culture of secrecy in which guards at the higher levels refrained from talking about coercive displays of force with lower-ranking guards. Although lower-ranking guards often asked their superiors about instances of use of force, their questions were never met with a substantive response but rather with a simple denial of any knowledge of an incident (p. 361). Despite the fact that the prison was managed as a large bureaucracy, Marquart found that its informal structure seemed to be the predominant method used for managing the prison. Unlike other researchers, he found that this prison, like others in Texas, had a high degree of autonomy from the central administration, which rarely interfered in prison administration. As a result, guards had wide discretion, which was exercised in the form of the extensive use of physical force, and this became the underpinning of the guard subculture there.

Kauffman (1988: 59), based on her study of the Massachusetts prison system, observes that the use of force varies from prison to prison according to the level of security applied. She points out that the use of force is itself limited in that it cannot be relied upon to ensure that routine tasks are accomplished. Nor can it be employed in daily tasks such as moving inmates through the prison. She notes that serious inmate offenses are supposedly within the jurisdiction of prosecutors and the courts but that prosecutions for such offenses committed inside prisons are rare, and internal systems of punishment are usually relied upon.

As for guard violence against inmates at Walpole, while a few guards claimed never to have witnessed or participated in such events, the majority confirmed their participation or the fact that they had witnessed violence and their assumption that such events were common knowledge within the prison (Kauffman 1988: 130). However, the term *inmate assault* itself was questioned in terms of its definition, and some guards framed their discussions about guard violence by concentrating on the "deserved" nature of a beating. This nuanced approach toward violence extended to the distinction made between force used in restraining a violent inmate and force that went beyond what was necessary to restrain. The latter category included beatings inflicted by groups of guards on a single inmate in situations, for example, where inmates were moved to segregation (p. 132). One guard recalled a beating in which he was involved:

> There was a black guy who threw some urine in [the supervisor's] face. . . . Here there were nine beating the shit out of one guy. Then they'd back off and they'd taunt him and say "had enough, had enough?" And the guy would stand there and start swinging. . . . That particular guy didn't deserve what he got. But there are guys who deserve what they get. (in Kauffman 1988: 132)

In another incident, described in Case Study 6.2, a guard described five or six guards beating an inmate's head with chains and punching him using prison keys.

CASE STUDY 6.2 SEX OFFENDERS AND USE OF FORCE

Kauffman confirms general knowledge that within the prison world, sex offenders are considered the "lowest of the low" and are most likely to suffer violence at the hands of guards or inmates. In Massachusetts, at the treatment center for sexually dangerous persons, where inmates were treated more as patients than inmates, guards refused to accept the notion that their captives were sick, believing themselves to be dealing with "the scum of the earth." Guard attitudes were based on the inmates' crimes and on the experiences of the victims rather than on inmate conduct within the institution. In this sense, guards raged about just deserts for sex offenders, holding the position that many of the inmates deserved the death penalty but instead were housed in relative comfort. In fact, the inmates' crimes so repelled the guards that one fantasized about machine gunning them, another of gassing them, and another of bombing the institution.

SOURCE: Kauffman 1988: 147–149.

When discussing their *justifications for using violence,* guards focused on the inmate himself, on relationships among guards, and on the individual guard who engaged in the violence (Kauffman 1988: 141). Guard violence was commonly justified as a means of controlling inmates, and many guards felt unable to maintain control without at least referring to violence. Another justification offered was the belief that guard violence deterred inmate violence against guards. The systematic use of violent reprisals was seen as a means of preventing future assaults as well as punishing past ones. Guards defined self-defense very broadly so as to *anticipate the need to defend themselves,* and many guards and inmates believed they needed to establish and uphold a reputation for meeting aggression with aggression. If an inmate assaulted a guard, reprisals were considered not only appropriate, but essential. As one guard put it, an inmate who assaulted a guard

> should be beaten until he can't stand up anymore. And if he does stand up, beat him some more. Beat him until it gets through his head what will happen and then he'll think twice about what he is doing. (in Kauffman 1988: 142)

Fundamentally, the exercise of violence by guards was not intended as a symbol of their power, but was rather a reflection of their sense of vulnerability. Guards were often dissatisfied about official punishments and therefore sought their own form of justice (p. 145). In particular, although inmates involved in violent acts against guards would be sanctioned when it came to furloughs or parole, there was little by way of sanctions in the short term that would protect and reinforce the guard's position of having to be present in the prison every day.

As expressed in the following guard norms, regardless of their personal views, guards at Walpole experienced considerable pressure not only to acquiesce to violent means of handling the prisoners but also to engage in violence consistent with norms requiring guards to support their colleagues in disputes with inmates and to support guard sanctions against inmates. These pressures to conform (Kauffman 1988: 153) were reinforced by the guards' genuine fear for their survival. Guards seemed to take the attitude that while they might not personally participate in violence, they would not object if it occurred, and they would gradually acquire the belief that this was the way things happened in a prison environment. However, some guards reported that their co-workers enjoyed the violence, thrived on it, seemed to get "high" on it, and even instigated it to cause excitement and a break in the monotonous prison routine (p. 153). Comments ranged from "I like having action" to "It really peps up my day." Some guards, however, believed that co-workers who initiated violence had a need to prove themselves, to show that they were not scared, and that their persistent acts of violence were attempts to constantly prove themselves.

Some guards saw no need for explicit justification, seeing violence as natural, as a way of life, and even as a game and part of the prison culture. These guards perceived violence as a routine method of resolving differences and effectively screened out any other courses of action. In one situation, inmates confronted one guard after he had beaten another inmate, and he rationalized the beating as a response to the inmate, calling his mother a "punk." The guard saw no need to justify his actions, reporting that anyone would respond in the same way (Kauffman 1988: 158). In ethical terms, many guards at Walpole honestly believed that the use of violence was an appropriate course of action, especially in cases when an inmate had assaulted a guard. These guards had an honest belief in the correctness of their approach and were convinced that the institutional environment demanded such violent reprisals. Guards who accepted this view suggested that those outside the prison, including local and political leaders, had no interest in events inside prisons, accepted no responsibility, and demonstrated no real concern for what occurred inside prison walls (p. 163). Nevertheless, some guards categorically rejected the use of violence, considering it counterproductive given their assumption that violence begets more violence. Some opposed it on humanitarian grounds and were appalled at the severe beatings they had witnessed or even participated in. One guard expressed the view that beating an inmate into submission was the worst thing he could do, "because it's not the right thing to do" (p. 164).

Kauffman (1988: 67) remarks that during the 1970s, the Massachusetts prison system relied on brutality and physical coercion, despite the fact that its use had declined considerably within the United States as a whole over the first half of the 20th century. During that period, guards routinely used violence to enforce control. In discussing the advantages and disadvantages of extralegal force, Kauffman points out that many of the inmates in maximum security institutions have committed violent crimes and may be serving multiple life sentences. In effect, they have nothing more to lose, and some guards consequently conclude that they need to meet violence with violence. Other guards attributed inmate violence to the fact that many inmates have spent their entire lives in situations where force has determined the course of events, and accordingly, they will only respond to like treatment when guards attempt to establish control. For that reason, some guards took the position that maintaining order often required the "cracking of a few heads," at least initially, to establish control (p. 68).

Kauffman concludes, however, that the use of physical coercion failed at Walpole and other Massachusetts prisons because guards were unable and generally unwilling to use the extreme measures that were perceived as necessary to ensure absolute control. She contrasts Walpole with the Texas penal system, which she believes has its roots more in southern slavery than in the emergence of the prison system (1988: 69). In addition, she argues that the use of coercion as a technique was a failure because it could not be applied to the inmates generally but had to be enforced inmate by inmate, and also because coercion tended to fuel inmates' anger and hatred rather than suppressing their resistance and rebellion. Another difficulty was that the use of coercion required staff to constantly increase the severity of sanctions if they were to be useful over the long term. Ultimately, in her view, coercion failed because it was unable to resolve the inherent conflict between inmates and guards. At some point, inmates would take the position that only so much could be taken away from them and, with this conclusion, they would have effectively won the battle even if beaten time and time again (p. 71).

The Court's View of Correctional Officer Use of Force

Walker (1996: 144) examines the attitude of the courts toward correctional use of force, noting that over the past few decades the courts have limited such force but that correctional officers are still given more latitude than police officers in the use of deadly force. In *U.S. v. Nix* (1974) the U.S. Supreme Court articulated its rationale for the use of deadly force against escaping prisoners, arguing that a determined escapee may kidnap a hostage or kill a guard or commit other unlawful acts to ease his escape. This aspect of dangerousness was sufficient to convince the Court in favor of the use of deadly force against escaping prisoners. In *Whitley v. Albers* (1986), a prison guard shot an inmate during a disturbance, and the Supreme Court ruled that cases of excessive force in corrections are governed by the Eighth Amendment, which prohibits cruel and unusual punishment. The legal standard for brutality is whether the force is "applied in a good faith effort to maintain or restore discipline, or whether it was applied maliciously and sadistically for the very purpose of causing harm" (*Hudson v. McMillian* 1992; *Whitley v. Albers* 1986). Following the case of *Clark v. Evans* (1988), where a correctional officer shot and killed an inmate trying to escape, arguments were made concerning whether the guard could have used a different means to prevent the escape or whether he should have only used force sufficient to disable the escaping inmate rather than using deadly force. The court decided in favor of the guard on both issues, holding that there was no duty to use disabling force rather than lethal force.

There have been some decisions that have gone against correctional officers, such as *McCullough v. Cady* (1986), in which a guard shot a prisoner during a disturbance while attempting to break up a fight among the prisoners. He initially fired a warning shot and then shot a prisoner who, it was later determined, was not involved in the fight. Here the court found that even though the guard shot with the intention of wounding the inmate, the use of force was not a decision of last resort made after all other means of restoring order had failed, and therefore, the guard's actions amounted to deliberate infliction of pain on the prisoner.

In *Kenny v. Indiana Youth Center* (1991), a guard shot an 18-year-old inmate in the process of escaping from a juvenile institution. Before shooting, the guard gave a verbal warning that she intended to shoot. The court noted that it was relevant to look at various factors in deciding whether the guard had inflicted unnecessary and wanton pain and suffering. Such factors included whether force needed to be used, the relationship between that need and the amount of force used, the actual injury inflicted, the nature of the threat to the safety of staff and inmates, and any efforts made to adopt a less severe course of action. The court concluded again that "dangerousness" was the predominant consideration, and repeated its view from the *Nix* case that any inmate who is attempting to escape is dangerous enough to justify using deadly force, provided the force is applied in good faith to maintain or restore discipline. Taken together the above rulings illustrate that prison guards are basically free to use deadly force to prevent escapes.

Correctional Policy on the Use of Force

Walker (1996: 149) presents an analysis of the policies in four states on the acceptable use of deadly force. All policies explicitly authorize the use of deadly force to prevent escapes, and in two states the policies suggest that disciplinary action will be taken against guards if they fail to use deadly force. The American Correctional Association suggests that a policy on deadly force should be more specifically related to the institution the inmate is escaping from, and ACA guidelines propose, for example, that a halfway house denotes offenders in its custody who do not represent a threat to public safety and in respect of whom deadly force might be prohibited. The Federal Bureau of Prisons explicitly limits deadly force by prohibiting the use of firearms in minimum security institutions in ordinary circumstances. It does permit deadly force to prevent an escape but only when authorized by the warden or when based upon a guard's judgment that the use of firearms is necessary to prevent the loss of life or grievous bodily harm. There is, however, a specific prohibition on using firearms if a guard sees that the potential escapee is a juvenile. A similar prohibition applies in ACA policy statements and in the state of Nebraska, but the Nebraska Department of Corrections explicitly declares that all persons housed in its correctional system are deemed to be adults.

Each of the states' policy statements deals with the use of warning shots, but policies vary widely. Nevertheless, a common feature is that warning shots should not be fired if it is likely that innocent persons might be injured. One state absolutely prohibits the use of warning shots, and another confines warning shots to within the grounds of a facility unless there is an immediate threat to life. These policies reflect the possibility that warning shots will harm innocent bystanders, and it is significant that almost all police departments in the United States prohibit the use of warning shots.

Prisoner "Power"

The notion that prisoners have any "power" within a prison seems to contradict the very nature of the prison environment. However, some activities on the part of inmates can be viewed as attempts to gain power or to resist guard power; these actions include using the court process to enforce rights, manufacturing weapons, employing unprovoked violence against guards, and coercing other inmates.

Kauffman (1988: 71) points to the upsurge in prison litigation during the 1960s and 1970s as instances of inmate "power" that counterbalanced administration power over inmates. During this period, jailhouse lawyers began to gain status within the prison as sources of authority who could contest prisoners' rights with guards and with the administration. Similarly, some inmates attempted to influence the course of events within the prison through their positions as trustees. For example, in some prisons trustees unofficially break in new officers and provide them with assistance in maintaining control. Most important, some inmates seek to control guards through coercion, either through direct violence or threats. A more nuanced approach to gaining power takes the form of inmates competing with officers for control over the inmate population, such as through the formation of gangs or through persuasion, inducement, and manipulation. This kind of control can include victimizing other inmates, itself a major problem in U.S. prisons (p. 73). For example, at Walpole, inmate coercion of other inmates included stabbings over card games or a carton of cigarettes, rapes, robbery, and murder (p. 74).

In the contest between inmates and guards, inmates may manufacture weapons. In contrast, guards do not carry guns, which are consigned to the prison perimeter and never brought inside. Guards are limited to the use of batons or, in larger scale conflicts, tear gas and perhaps dogs. The exercise of guard power also relies on the flow of information, and in this respect, Kauffman reports that in Massachusetts prisons, guards were often ill informed about occurrences amongst inmates (p. 79). Guards were few in number, were socially distant from their captives, and were present in the prison only while on duty, as compared to inmates, who occupied the prisons continuously. Generally, while the use of coercion and force might have some attraction in offering an immediate solution to a power struggle, its use may cost officers dearly over time by decreasing their authority and undermining their legitimacy (1988: 79).

Kauffman (1988: 125–126) distinguishes spontaneous and unprovoked violence against guards from spontaneous provoked violence. Spontaneous and unprovoked violence was feared the most by guards, and they considered drugs to be the main cause of such unprovoked acts. In the case of provoked violence, guards would sometimes precipitate spontaneous violence against themselves through miscalculation or ineptness by forcing inmates into situations where they felt compelled to resist with violence. The most common occasion for such provoked violence was within an inmate's cell block at a time when he was about to be removed to segregation. In such situations, some inmates would resist; however, they were usually handled. Others would fight after provocation or because of their belief that they would receive a beating no matter what they did. Sometimes inmate violence would be calculated as an act of retaliation for the guard's conduct. A guard who wrote too many tickets or beat too many heads would eventually set himself up for payback, usually within a year or even two years.

Unethical Situations

Prison researchers have examined the nature of imprisonment, its changing structure over time, the exercise of power by both guards and inmates, the guard subculture, and the use of force within prisons. Other specific forms of unethical conduct are illustrated in the following sections, including violent attacks through acts of rape on inmates, the importation of contraband into prisons, and other forms of corruption that occur in prisons.

Rape in Prison

Prisoner rape has been defined by the organization Stop Prison Rape in a report, "Stories from Inside: Prisoner Rape and the War on Drugs" (2007: 4) as "all forms of sexual violence inflicted on anyone in custody, including someone awaiting trial in a county jail." The first study measuring rates of sexual assault among male inmates was conducted in 1966 in Philadelphia, and the researcher found that 4.7% of inmates reported sexual assaults while incarcerated or being transported to and from court (Hensley, Koscheski, and Tewksbury 2003: 18). A 1980 study of New York State male prisons revealed that 28% of inmates reported being targets of sexual aggression but only one inmate reported being raped. In 1977, a study of 400 male inmates in six North Carolina state prisons showed an average report rate of sexual assaults of 2.4% (p. 18). Other studies have similarly shown a wide variation in sexual assaults and coercion. For example, a 1982 study in a California prison produced a rate of 14%, and a study of 17 federal prisons in 1984 revealed a 2% rate of "sexual targets" and a 0.3% rape rate (p. 19). The highest rate of sexual victimization was found in a study conducted in 1994 in the Nebraska prison system, where 22% of male inmates reported being pressured or forced to have sex against their will (p. 19). In the most recent study, conducted in 2003 in three Oklahoma prisons, about 14% reported being sexual targets and 1.1% victims of completed sexual assaults (p. 20). A study of sexual coercion in a female southern prison found about 4.5% had been victims of attempted or completed rapes (p. 20). It appears that prisons with higher numbers of inmates are more likely to have official reports of sexual attacks or threats of attacks filed, while this is less likely at minimum-security prisons (p. 23). Thus, reducing the size of the inmate population may result in a reduction of sexual assaults (Stop Prisoner Rape 2006: 11).

A 2001 study by Human Rights Watch on male rape in U.S. prisons argues that acts of rape are far more pervasive than is acknowledged by prison authorities (see Case Studies 6.3 and 6.4). In another 2001 study of 378 state male prisons in the United States, wardens were asked about their knowledge of forced and consensual sex in their institutions. Generally speaking, the wardens responded indicating that sexual activity was "relatively rare" in their institutions (Hensley and Tewksbury

2005: 186). There is a wide disparity between reported rapes as noted by prison authorities and as shown by inmate victimization surveys. The latter show far higher rates than the official statistics. This underreporting is exemplified in a 1996 Nebraska study, which found that only 29% of victimized inmates reported abuses (Human Rights Watch 2001: 132), and a 1968 study of prisons in Philadelphia, which found an estimated 2,000 rapes, only 96 of which had been officially reported. Human Rights Watch suggests that prisoner failure to report rapes is a response to prison administrators' indifference toward such reports. If, it is argued, prisoners could be certain of protection, they would be more likely to report rapes (2001: 132). The study contends that many inmates point out that guards fail to take protective measures on their behalf when they seek help and instead advise them to fight their attacker. In this sense, the prison system condones forced rape as, for example, was found in Florida, where physical sexual attacks were revealed as commonplace in Florida prisons (p. 142). The response of correctional authorities to rape is often the imposition of minor disciplinary sanctions, such as 30 days in segregation or moving rapists to another facility. In contrast, the victims of the rape may have to be located in protective custody with all the restrictions that such confinement imposes (p. 143). It is a reflection of the lack of seriousness with which authorities regard this issue that almost half of all state jurisdictions do not even collect statistics regarding incidents of rape and that those that do report claim it to be a very rare event (p. 145). This, however, will change significantly given the Supreme Court decision in *Farmer v. Brennan* (1994) and the subsequent passing of the Prison Rape Elimination Act 2003 (see below), which requires a zero tolerance policy for sexual assault in prison.

CASE STUDY 6.3 RAPE IN PRISON

In 1993, Eddie Dillard was serving time in a California prison. He was a young first timer, a slight man, and was transferred to share a cell with Wayne Robertson, a huge muscular man, nearly twice the weight of Dillard, serving a life sentence for murder. Robertson was known by all as "the booty bandit," having earned this nickname through his practice of violently raping prisoners. Before the end of the first day in the cell they shared, the inevitable had occurred: Robertson had beaten Dillard and sodomized him, and he continued to do this for the next two days until finally, Dillard ran out of the cell, refusing to return. A correctional officer working on the unit informed the *Los Angeles Times*, "Everyone knew about Robertson. He had raped inmates before and he's raped inmates since." Documentation submitted to a California legislative hearing supported this report, showing Robertson had committed more than a dozen rapes inside that and other prisons.

SOURCE: Human Rights Watch 2001: 148–149.

**CASE STUDY 6.4 TRANSGENDERED
EXPERIENCES OF PRISON RAPE**

Jackie Tates told Stop Prisoner Rape (2007: 11) that when she was incarcerated in Sacramento, "the deputies were letting inmates into my cell to have sex with me against my will. The first time it happened, I tried to the tell the inmate no. He showed me some autopsy photos. He said, 'This is what happens to people who fuck with me.' I ended up submitting. I did what he told me to do. I orally copulated him, and he sodomized me. Thirty or forty minutes later, the deputy came onto the speaker and asked him if he was done. He said, 'I'm done.' The door clicked and let him out.

"They must have let 12 to 14 inmates into my cell to have sex. One day, I said to a deputy, 'If you're going to make me do this, could I at least have some condoms so I don't get AIDS?' He told me to shut the fuck up. The next day, he came in and threw 15 condoms at me.

"Where I am now, it's just as bad. They have me in general population. I've asked over and over to be put on the unit with the gay and transgender inmates, but I always get denied.

"In September 2004, it was so crowded here that they had us sleeping on pads on the floor of the day room. The inmate on the next pad over told me to come to the shower with him, or he was going to slice me. I was afraid, so I went with him. He was fucking me in the shower when a deputy walked by. He just started laughing.

"Later, they moved me to a cell, and I was so happy, because I thought I had escaped this inmate. Then they moved him into the cell with me. When I finally got out of there, I had two black eyes that were completely closed up. I didn't deserve this.

"In September 2005, I was put into a 'protective custody' tank with five or six other inmates. Two of them jumped me right away. They both made me suck them off. The deputy walked by and saw me fighting and struggling with them, but he didn't do anything.

"The next day, the deputy made jokes about it. He asked me how much I charge for that.

"Gay people, transgender people in this jail—they put us in compromising positions. They chain us to 12 inmates and throw us in the back of a van with no supervision. People get dragged into bathrooms. One of my friends got dragged into a bathroom—she walks with a walker now.

"The deputies call me names–they call me 'it,' and 'he/she,' and 'punk,' and 'faggot.' They whistle at me in the shower. They come to my cell door asking to see my breasts.

"Sometimes I want to die. I'm scared to close my eyes at night."

SOURCE: Stop Prisoner Rape. 2007: 11. Reprinted by permission of Jackie Tates and Stop Prison Rape.

According to Human Rights Watch (2001), the response of guards to complaints of rape is often inadequate and even callous, and gay inmates in particular, unless able to show clear physical injury, tend to have their complaints ignored, because prison officials tend to assume consent in sexual acts involving gay inmates. Many guards respond to such charges and complaints with the advice that the inmate should defend himself against attack. This is tantamount to guards abdicating their responsibility to protect prisoners from violence (p. 153) and amounts to guards urging inmates to commit disciplinary infractions, because the use of force by inmates, even in self-defense, is usually a punishable act.

In September 2003 the president signed the Prison Rape Elimination Act, the first U.S. law addressing the issue of male prison rape. The purposes of the act include

- setting a zero tolerance standard for prison rape;
- prioritizing the prevention of rape in each prison system;
- devising and implementing national standards to detect, prevent, reduce and punish rape;
- collect data and information on the incidence of rape;
- increase prison staff accountability for failing to detect, prevent, reduce or punish rape. (Mair, Frattaroli, and Teret 2003: 602; also see National Institute of Justice 2006)

The act establishes a Review Panel on Prison Rape within the Department of Justice; the panel is required to hold public hearings each year on operations in three prisons in the country with the highest and the two prisons with the lowest incidents of rape. The attorney general is required to submit annual reports to Congress on the review panel's activities. The act also establishes a National Prison Rape Reduction Commission made up of nine members with expertise on the subject. This body is principally a research commission with a comprehensive mandate including examining the extent to which prison rape contributes to the transmission of HIV (Mair et al. 2003: 604). In 2004 the Bureau of Justice Statistics of the Justice Department conducted the first survey of administrative records of sexual violence in adult and juvenile facilities, which revealed 8,210 allegations of sexual violence; 42% of these allegations were against prison and jail staff and 37% against other inmates (Melby 2006: 4).

Corruption

McCarthy (1995), in examining the official records of an internal affairs unit of a state department of corrections, distinguished patterns of corruption and the level of staff involved in that corruption, as shown in Table 6.3. Defining corruption as "the intentional violation of organizational norms (i.e., rules and regulations) by public employees for personal material gain," McCarthy (1995: 281) examined 122 cases of alleged corrupt practices in the department, which revealed four major offense categories and a miscellaneous category comprising theft, embezzlement, trafficking, and misuse of authority. Theft made up one quarter of all cases.

Petty theft was alleged by inmates in complaints of loss of both personal valuables and contraband claimed to have been stolen during cell searches or following their handing it over to staff for safekeeping. Complaints were also made by visitors that their possessions had been stolen during searches in the visiting room. Also, goods and materials were alleged to have been stolen from the state, including articles such as a walkie-talkie, tools, and a calculator. Generally, acts of theft appeared to be opportunistic individualistic acts with an absence of evidence indicating any conspiracy.

Trafficking with inmates relates to *smuggling contraband* (see Case Studies 6.5 and 6.6) into prisons for money, drugs, or services, usually of a sexual nature. McCarthy identified a number of contraband items including drugs, alcohol, money, and weapons, as well as items such as food and reading materials. He found that the more individuals involved in smuggling contraband, the more organized was the operation with a greater scope of items being made available. Sophisticated smuggling rings had inmates as ring leaders. These operations ranged from a guard bringing in alcohol for a single inmate to large-scale conspiracies involving drug smuggling. Generally, those involved in smuggling were guards, but sometimes counselors and job placement officers were implicated. Guard involvement varied from simply collecting drugs from prearranged locations and transporting them into the prison to actually controlling smuggling operations by directly selling items to inmates and by using inmates as pushers and salesmen within the prisons.

Worley, Marquart, and Mullings (2003: 185) point out that trafficking with inmates also involves inmates who exploit relationships with guards to make illicit profits in the underground prison economy. Reported cases include a male inmate who befriended a female staff and persuaded her to bring in contraband cigarettes by the carton; a female prisoner who deliberately developed a relationship with a male guard to the extent that he began bringing into the prison eye liner, perfume, and cigarettes, which the female sold in the prison economy; and inmates who entrap guards by offering them a candy bar or soda to establish an inappropriate continuing relationship (pp. 186–187). In Texas, where it is difficult to hire sufficient staff to run the many correctional facilities, guards' salaries are low, and according to one inmate account, prison staff earn extra money to the extent of $1,000 a week by bringing in cocaine (p. 188).

Conover (2001: 104) explains how *contraband* comprising weapons, drugs, and alcohol entered Sing Sing Prison. All these items could easily be obtained inside the prison. According to Conover (p. 104), some drugs came in during prison visits, but he noted that most drugs entered the prisons through officers who were paid off to allow their entry.

Embezzlement relates to the conversion of state property or goods to one's own use. Acts involved guards, shopkeepers, and clerks embezzling money from administrative units within the prison system such as canteens, commissaries, and prison warehouses. Staff audits commonly reveal that these acts involve both staff and inmates working alone or together; for example, colluding with each other through working together in commissaries.

The *misuse of authority* concerns a willful misuse of one's discretion for personal material gain; this conduct accounted for almost one half of complaints received by the internal affairs unit (see Case Studies 6.5 and 6.6). The kinds of discretion involved were transfers, assignment to jobs and housing blocks, and overlooking minor infractions or rules. McCarthy (1995) distinguished a number of forms of misuse of authority, including accepting gratuities for favorable consideration of inmate requests. For example, a guard in charge of a work release program was alleged to have solicited a $20 fee from an inmate for finding him a job. Other examples of misuse of authority include accepting gratuities to protect illicit activities, such as allowing gambling, drugs, or prostitution in a facility or protecting illicit activities from discovery or competition from other inmates; extortion through mistreatment or harassment involving shaking down inmates and personally sanctioning inmates for refusal to obey instructions; mismanagement, including allegations concerning the operation of prison industries for personal gain; and a miscellaneous group, including suspicious deaths of employees, concealment of prior criminal backgrounds by prospective employees, and charges of sexual coercion against a supervisor by a female employee.

Table 6.3   Pattern of Corruption by Type of Decision

Corrupt Acts by Type of Decision	Officials Involved
Misfeasance	
Provide preferential treatment and special privileges	Line staff
Selective application of rewards and punishments	Line staff
Forms of legitimate release	Administrators
Misappropriation of resources	Administrators
Malfeasance	
Trafficking	Line staff
Extortion/exploitation	Line staff
Protection rackets	Line staff
Embezzlement/theft	Line staff and administration
Criminal conspiracies	Line staff
Nonfeasance	
Failure to enforce regulations	Line staff
Cover-ups	Line staff and administration

SOURCE: "Keeping an Eye on the Keepers: Prison Corruption and its Control," by Bernard McCarthy in *The Prison Journal, 64*(2): 113–125. Reprinted by permission of Sage Publications, Inc.

CASE STUDY 6.5 JAIL GUARDS CHARGED WITH SMUGGLING

In 1994, 10 guards at Westchester County Jail were charged with smuggling con-traband to prisoners in the form of food, vodka, cash, and cocaine. In exchange for bringing in the contraband, the guards were paid bribes of up to $1,000 and given trips to Atlantic City. The guards even facilitated escape attempts; in one case it was alleged that a guard had provided a prisoner with a key to unlock his shackles and handcuffs. The acts of the guards came to light through a sting oper-ation involving federal agents who posed as the relatives of some cooperating inmates. These inmates provided guards with contact numbers for their relatives. When the guards met with the relatives, they discussed various deals to bring in contraband. One guard reportedly bragged to the federal agents that he had been engaged in this kind of conduct for the last 15 years.

SOURCE: Berger 1994.

CASE STUDY 6.6 FIXING A DRINK IN PRISON

Webb and Morris recount an event that occurred at the penitentiary where Webb conducted research while training to be a guard. He was escorting about 40 inmates to the commissary, where all transactions are conducted by ledger and where currency is not permitted. As a result, he was unable to purchase a soft drink at the commissary. He asked an experienced guard how to acquire a drink and noted that the guard simply walked to the counter, spoke to the inmate employee, and returned with two drinks. He explained that it was impos-sible to pay for the drinks, but the guard would someday do a favor for the inmate, for example, fix a disciplinary charge for him in the same way a traffic policeman might fix a traffic ticket. Webb and Morris also discovered that guards did not perceive inmate gambling to be a serious disciplinary matter. They regarded the most serious inmate offenses to be physically assaulting or threat-ening a guard, showing disrespect to a guard, and refusing to work or comply with an order.

SOURCE: Webb and Morris 1980: 150.

During his first five years as director of corrections in Massachusetts, George Vose, Jr. fired or permitted to resign between 80 and 100 staff as a result of forms of misconduct (Carroll 1998: 282). In one case, an affair between an officer and an inmate was discovered when the inmate was found using the officer's phone card to call her while she was on vacation. In another case, an officer assaulted a co-worker on duty over a gambling debt, and it transpired that the officer who was subjected to the assault was a bookie employed by a major organized crime figure. In the first two months of 1996, two officers were arrested for smuggling heroin into the prison, another was arrested for bookmaking and possession of a needle and syringe, and another for possession of marijuana (Carroll 1998: 283).

In the case of *Dreyer v. Jalet* (1972), inmates testified that "building tenders" (the term used to describe inmate guards who were used to supplement the power of employed guards) were given access to pipes, bats, and clubs to administer discipline on behalf of the regular guards. In one case involving building tenders, 10 of these inmates, armed with axe handles, clubs, and iron pipes, assaulted a group of prisoners while accompanied by an assistant warden and several officers.

CASE STUDY 6.7   "EX–S.C. CORRECTIONAL OFFICER SENTENCED"

A former correctional officer was sentenced recently to 3 months in jail for having sex in prison with Susan Smith, who is serving a life sentence for drowning her two sons in a lake in 1994. South Carolina Circuit Court Judge Lee Casey Manning also sentenced Houston Cagle to 5 years' probation and 250 hours of community service.

Cagle pleaded guilty in August to having sex with Smith and another inmate at the Women's Correctional Institution in Columbia last year. Investigators found out about the relationship between Cagle and Smith last summer when they were looking into a tabloid report alleging that Smith had been beaten in prison.

While reviewing medical records, officers found Smith had been treated for a venereal disease. She then admitted she had sex with Cagle. He was fired shortly after his arrest.

The revelations led to a broad investigation into prison misconduct. More than a dozen Corrections Department officers and employees have been charged with having sex with inmates or smuggling drugs since a state investigation began last year.

Two prison officers, including Cagle, and three other corrections workers have pleaded guilty to having sex with inmates.

SOURCE: "Ex–S.C. Correctional Officer Sentenced" 2001.

Whistle-Blowing in Corrections

Hamm (1995: 202) provides several case studies of whistle-blowing that had a positive effect on a correctional organization (see Case Study 6.7). In one case, a warden used institutional funds to purchase equipment he later used to operate a section of his cattle ranch. Further, the warden insisted that guards supervise inmate labor at his ranch while they operated this equipment. Two guards complained, claiming that the warden had abused his authority, and their complaint was upheld by the state personnel board, which ruled that the guards had been required to act in ways that were undefined and not relevant to their job descriptions.

In 1997, the television news program *60 Minutes* reported cases of whistle-blowing by two guards at a California prison concerning what they considered unethical conduct by their fellow guards. They claimed that inmates from different ethnic groups in the prison had been set up to fight each other in a small prison exercise yard and that it was not unusual for guards to place bets on the outcome of such fights. They further claimed that when the fights got out of control, guards would sometimes shoot at the inmates and that since the prison had opened in 1988, eight inmates had been shot dead by guards and many others wounded in this way. On the program, video footage was shown of two inmates of the same ethnic origin fighting two other inmates of a different ethnic origin. One of the inmates, not considered the aggressor, was shot and killed during the fight, and the claim was made that guards had told this inmate after he had assaulted a guard that he would never leave the prison alive (Jones and Carlson 2001: 76).

In the mid-1980s, a female guard at a medium security prison reported her fellow guards for sleeping on night shift, claiming she had approached them and advised them that she felt unsafe and vulnerable while they slept. She warned them that if their conduct did not change she would have to report them to the superintendent. They continued to sleep, she reported them, and the consequences were severe for her in that she was later the subject of graffiti on the prison walls and received abusive phone calls and letters, and her car was deliberately damaged in the parking lot (Jones and Carlson 2001: 77).

Ethical Considerations in Probation and Parole

Probation and parole functions are commonly considered a component of corrections, because both functions are concerned with the management and control of former inmates. Like corrections, probation and parole officers must concern themselves with ethical issues, and their association has developed a code of ethics (see Box 6.3).

Ethical issues in probation and parole center around tensions between the role of parole or probation as treatment or as punishment, the supposed ineffectiveness of probation and parole as a form of punishment, and concerns relating to the duty of these officers toward their clients. Traditionally, probation and parole have involved supervising offenders in the community, and this supervision suggests there will be regular contact between the officer and those who make up his or her caseload. Yet, these contacts vary from full counseling sessions to brief, perfunctory contacts once a month. The supervisory role brings to the fore the conflict between treatment and control functions, or as some describe it, between surveillance and service (Studt 1973). Studt argues that parole is more surveillance than service-oriented, because, for example, officers are instructed to make surprise visits to parolees. Some argue that this tension can be eliminated by giving the surveillance function to the police, leaving probation officers to provide services (Conrad 1973, 1982), whereas Rosecrance (1986) holds that probation officers provide neither service nor surveillance but in effect, function primarily as report writers for the courts.

There has been a trend over the past decade toward making probation tougher, emphasizing risk control, and stressing the enforcement of sanctions for breaches of probation. Parole has always had a greater law enforcement emphasis than probation, even though it has come to be regarded as the agency responsible for "letting inmates out of prison early" (Petersilia 1999: 480).

Abadinsky (1982) has proposed a typography of probation officer styles of probation work comprising the *law enforcement model,* the *therapeutic model,* and the *synthetic model.* The law enforcement model involves a primary role of public protection, the therapeutic model sees rehabilitation and aiding the offender as central, and the synthetic model is a combination of both law enforcement and rehabilitation.

Like corrections officers, probation and parole officers are faced with decisions about whether to emphasize the protection of society or to aid the offender, and they are also accountable to demands from administrators and politicians about how their duties should be carried out. Domurad (2000: 43) suggests that as administrators try to organize the implementation of new concepts and programs, such as restorative and community justice, this has the effect of placing additional roles and responsibilities onto line officers and creates more confusion for them about the purpose of their work.

In many states, probation agencies are located in the executive branch of government, where they operate as rational bureaucratic agencies far removed from the probation officer in the field. This separation has the potential to create conflicts for the officers. For example, conflict can occur in cases where state-level policy makers make demands about how probation officers should interact with their clients, while at the same time the local community may have different requirements and demands of these interactions (Silverman 1993: 89). When probation is located within the judicial branch of government, there is less likely to be administrative pressure on probation work, because the supervision and treatment functions may be considered subordinate to sentencing and punishment. Nevertheless, it is possible that a probation officer may have to make decisions about treatment that can conflict with the intentions of the adjudicated punishment. This becomes even more complicated due to the fact that local-level judicial officers are often subject to local pressures in their punishment decisions (Silverman 1993: 90).

A CLOSER LOOK

BOX 6.3
Probation and Parole Officer's Code of Ethics

- I will render professional service to the justice system and the community at large in effecting the social adjustment of the offender.
- I will uphold the law with dignity, displaying an awareness of my responsibility to offenders while recognizing the right of the public to be safeguarded from criminal activity.
- I will strive to be objective in the performance of my duties, recognizing the inalienable right of all persons, appreciating the inherent worth of the individual, and respecting those confidences which can be reposed in me.
- I will conduct my personal life with decorum, neither accepting nor granting favors in connection with my office.
- I will cooperate with my coworkers and related agencies and will continually strive to improve my professional competence through the seeking and sharing of knowledge and understanding.
- I will distinguish clearly, in public, between my statements and actions as an individual and as a representative of my profession.
- I will encourage policy, procedures and personnel practices, which will enable others to conduct themselves in accordance with the values, goals and objectives of the American Probation and Parole Association.
- I recognize my office as a symbol of public faith and I accept it as a public trust to be held as long as I am true to the ethics of the American Probation and Parole Association.
- I will constantly strive to achieve these objectives and ideals, dedicating myself to my chosen profession.

SOURCE: American Probation and Parole Association, n.d. Reprinted with permission of the American Probation and Parole Association.

Today, in most states, the role of the probation officer has gained a new law enforcement emphasis, and the probation officer is identified more closely with law enforcement agencies. It is now common for probation officers to be proactive in enforcing probation conditions through measures such as monitoring, surveillance, search and seizure, drug testing, and even by accompanying police on enforcement actions (Small and Torres 2001: 24). It is now a regular practice for such officers to take part in vehicle surveillance, the execution of search and arrest warrants, gang task forces, and even sting operations (p. 26). Legally, a probation or parole officer may ask law enforcement personnel for assistance in searching probationers, but the primary purpose of that search must be related to probation or parole and must not be a cover for other police purposes (del Carmon et al. 2001: 115). If police attempt to induce a probation officer to exercise his or her powers to search and if the officer agrees to the search, he or she must be satisfied that it is necessary for the proper functioning of the probation system.

A common condition of probation is that a probationer agrees to waive Fourth Amendment rights and allow searches to be conducted on his or her person, residence, and automobile. The California Supreme Court has held that as a general rule, probationers have "a reduced expectation of privacy," and this leaves them open to intrusions by governmental authorities, which "are necessitated by legitimate governmental demands" (del Carmon et al. 2001: 116). In one case, police searched a juvenile who was associating with suspected gang members at a football game and discovered marijuana on his person. Police did not know that the juvenile was on probation, a condition of which allowed a search of his person, and no probation officer was present when the search was conducted. In this case, the California Supreme Court ruled that the probation condition allowing searches was sufficient to authorize the police search of the juvenile (*In re Tyrell* 1998).

Today, police rely on probation officers for information about probationers including their place of residence, living situation, and behavior, and in return, probation looks to law enforcement for protection when brought into contact with high-risk offenders (Small and Torres 2001: 26). Increasingly, probation officers supervise offenders convicted of violent crimes, because probation is being granted to those with serious criminal backgrounds and substantial drug abuse histories, especially in metropolitan areas. As well, the workload of probation and parole officers has dramatically increased with the rise in intensive probation supervision. According to the Department of Justice, there were some 2.6 million adults on probation in 1990; by 2001 this number had increased by 33% to 3.9 million (Glaze 2002; U.S. Department of Justice 2000). By yearend 2005 there were 4,162,536 persons under probation supervision (Glaze 2006: 1). Of the 4.1 million, 50% had committed felonies and 49% misdemeanors. The largest percentage were convicted of drug violations (28%) followed by DWI (15%) and larceny/theft (12%). Women composed almost 1 in 4 probationers, representing 23% of adults on probation, up from 21% in 1995 (Glaze 2006: 6). The Department of Justice statistics show that California has the largest probation population, amounting to 388,260 adults.

Arming Probation Officers

A major ethical debate within the probation field concerns the issue of arming probation officers. (Parole officers carry weapons in two thirds of the states.) Some argue that probation officers cannot carry out the traditional role of a probation officer effectively while armed, because bearing arms contributes to an atmosphere of distrust between the officer and the client. On the other hand, officers who are more enforcement-oriented typically view carrying firearms as a means of protection from risk, especially as they have come to associate with more violent or high-risk offenders. Some contend that officers should not be required to carry firearms if they are personally opposed to carrying weapons, but rather, they should be given the option to carry them on certain assignments where risks would warrant such protection (Small and Torres 2001: 27). One possible result of increased arming, however, is that probation officers will be regarded more as police officers than probation officers, and this will further diminish any treatment role they may still have. This debate has now entered the juvenile justice arena, and in some states, for example, in most jurisdictions in Arizona, juvenile probation officers now carry firearms (Banks, Rector, and Jackson: 2005).

The American Correctional Association's view on this issue is that there should be a demonstrated need for firearms, and once this need is clear, adequate and ongoing training in their use must be provided. In many ways the issue of carrying arms strikes directly at the difference between probation and police work, and it is significant that those entering the profession of probation do not receive the training and awareness in the use of firearms that is provided to law enforcement personnel. Psychologically, probation officers have not traditionally been sensitized to the use of weapons, and probation officers have not been recruited with a role involving weapons in mind.

Treatment or Control?

As already noted, the traditional tensions between treatment and control have been affected by an increased focus on dangerousness, risk, and criminality. As a result, treatment is de-emphasized, and security tends to be stressed. Nevertheless, the notion that probation is granted for the purpose of treatment persists, and a goal of probation remains one of matching the probationer with treatment and rehabilitation services in the community. The increased numbers of probationers have put an end to the commonly accepted notion that individual officers' caseloads should be set at between 30 and 50 cases (Champion 1996: 437). Consequently, probation officers are challenged ethically in terms of having to choose who among their clients will receive adequate treatment services, especially as the caseloads continue to rise (Silverman 1993: 91). Associated with the problems in supervising large caseloads and the decisions about treatment responsibilities are the increased demands for, and time constraints in, the preparation of presentence reports. With very large caseloads, officers may well lack the time to prepare detailed presentence reports or may have to trade off one offender against another in the interests of performance (p. 91).

Parole

According to Petersilia (1999: 479), 14 states have now abolished discretionary parole release for all offenders, and 21 have severely limited its use. Nevertheless, the Department of Justice reports that at yearend 2005, 784,408 adults were being supervised on parole out of an estimated correctional population of 7,056,000 representing a rate of 350 per 100,000 U.S. general population (Glaze 2006). Although parole systems remain, treatment programs are scarce, and parole officers focus their efforts on surveillance rather than on rehabilitation. Safety and security are now major issues in parole services (Petersilia 1999: 482), and in large urban areas parole agents are commonly occupied in drug testing, electronic monitoring, and verifying curfews. Greater numbers of parolees are not completing their parole supervision and are being returned to prison, which contributes to the explosion in the prison population (p. 483). For example, parolees were 11% of the correctional population in 2005 and accounted for a 9.1% increase in correctional population growth (Glaze 2006). In California, parolees represent a rate of 421 per 100,000 population (p. 7). Partly due to zero tolerance policies, a greater number of parole violations are being detected, and revocation to prison is becoming a routine affair, because the process of being sent to prison, later released on parole, and then sent back again to prison sets up a revolving door for parolees.

Over the past several years, at least for parole officers, the tensions between treatment and control roles appear to have been resolved in favor of control, and consequently ethical considerations in relation to this issue would seem to be much less of a concern than for probation officers. Nowadays, the parole officer's task is to all intents and purposes a policing role, because parole officers have legal authority to carry and use firearms, to search without Fourth Amendment constraints, to order arrests without probable cause, and to confine without bail (Rudovsky et al. 1988). Some argue that these powers make the parole officer a "walking court system." According to Petersilia (1999: 505), over 80% of parolees are supervised on caseloads that average 69 parolees, and parolees are seen face to face less than twice a month. Parole officers complain about lack of time and resources, increased paperwork, and higher caseloads. Moreover, newly recruited parole officers now tend to adopt the surveillance rather than the rehabilitation model of parole and perform a "quasi-policing role" in some areas (p. 508). For the future, in light of the convergence of the roles of parole officer and police officer, parole officers are likely to find themselves having to respond to ethical issues similar to those that confront police officers.

Summary

Crime control policies over the last two decades have produced an explosion in the prison population, and it is in the context of a policy of mass imprisonment and the consequent concerns about security and safety that ethical concerns in the prison environment now arise. When considering ethical issues it is crucial to have an understanding of how prisons operate, their disciplinary regimes, and the experience of being both a prisoner and a guard. Contextualizing the prison environment and the experience of imprisonment provides a basis for analyzing and assessing ethical issues and dilemmas. This chapter has therefore provided this contextualization.

The organizational framework of guarding inmates has changed over time as early ad hoc individualistic approaches gave way to managerial and bureaucratic regimes that formulated detailed standards and rules about prisoner conduct. The composition of both the prison and the guard population has also changed over time, as prisoners have become radicalized and have claimed their rights through the courts.

What should be the basis for an ethical system of guarding prisoners? Some researchers emphasize the issue of punishment, pointing out that it is deprivation of liberty that is sanctioned by the courts and not additional penalties such as controlling visits, strip searching, or depriving prisoners of normal amenities. An ethical standard, therefore, that recognizes the essential humanity of prisoners would reflect the purpose of incarceration and protect prisoners from additional abuse. The role of guards and their interactions with co-workers and administrators are factors that should play a part in a correctional ethic. Strong power differences exist between guards and inmates, and decisions are constantly being made in uncertain situations. This creates a need to incorporate an ethical dimension into guard work. One extreme position, however, suggests that such is the nature of imprisonment that establishing any moral basis for the role of a guard is problematic. The brutality and degradation engendered by incarceration, it is argued, make it almost impossible for ethical and professional standards of conduct to be applied.

The detailed contextualization of prison work provided in this chapter shows how guards choose correctional employment, how they consider danger and mental tension as the core of their work, and how security and control are fundamental in their interactions with inmates. From this framework comes a guard's sense of suspicion about events that are different or which interrupt prison routines. A number of studies have shown how guards have no absolute power over inmates but are required to negotiate their dominance and how this can lead to what is called "corruption of authority." Tensions within the role of guard include those between their treatment role and custodial role, each calling for different skills and perspectives. Ultimately, guards are dependent on the prisoners for their own safety, and at the same time have to show to their superiors an ability to manage prisoners competently. This means that rule books are often ignored in the interests of flexibility and negotiation.

Studies have examined the nature of power in prisons, how guard authority is made up of a guard's personal authority and his or her legalistic authority, and how informal controls are employed to get back at inmates and to convey messages that reinforce guard authority. As with law enforcement, discretion is an important part of correctional work even though the correctional discretion is considerably constrained by written rules and regulations that determine conduct for both guards and inmates. Closely linked to the issue of discretion is the prison guard subculture, which has been extensively studied, revealing how new guard recruits are socialized to follow the prison guard code, especially those aspects that promote solidarity between guards against all outside groups, including inmates. Typographies of guards have been produced showing types ranging from those who adopt a helping strategy to others who display negative attitudes toward both guards and inmates and are barely able to cope with the prison environment.

Guard use of force is a major ethical issue in the prison environment, and it is clear that in the early period, guard violence was endemic. Despite detailed rules and regulations about the use of force, including deadly force, it is clear that some prison systems allow extralegal physical force to be used against inmates and that this represents a part of the guard subculture, because fighting an inmate is regarded as an expression of guard masculinity and machismo. Justifications for using violence include the guard perspective of being unable to maintain control without violence or the threat of violence and the belief that violence deters inmate violence against guards. Self-defense tends to be defined very broadly, and reprisals for inmate assaults are considered not only appropriate but also essential. Ultimately, however, unrestricted violence against inmates can only threaten the security of guards themselves, because it tends to fuel inmates' anger and hatred rather than repress their resistance. As well as rule books regulating the use of violence, the courts and state and federal governments have issued their own standards and directives, especially in relation to the use of deadly force.

Studies have identified a number of other forms of unethical conduct, including how guards react to rapes in prison and how corruption can be maintained through smuggling, drug trafficking, embezzlement, and theft. Sometimes whistle-blowing reveals acts of corruption, but at other times, whistle-blowers themselves are penalized for revealing misconduct.

Probation and parole raise some similar ethical concerns to those in corrections, especially in relation to the tension between treatment and punishment. Increasingly, probation is less directed toward treatment and more focused on enforcement and punishment, and probation officers appear to have moved closer to a policing role, which has included carrying weapons and collaborating with law enforcement officers in various activities. Parole officers have always been regarded as enforcement agents, and they have become even more law enforcement–oriented, resulting in a situation where the ethical issues that affect parole may in fact be similar to those relevant to the policing function.

DISCUSSION QUESTIONS

1. There have been dramatic increases in the number of persons imprisoned in the U.S. over the last 20 years and a trend toward constructing supermax prisons. Discuss at least three ethical concerns that these two developments have given rise to in relation to inmates.

2. Explain the relationship between the different styles of prison management and how ethical issues might differ under each style of management.

3. In an ethical correctional system, all prisoners would be treated with humanity. Explain how prisoner humanity would be respected in the use of force and in the conditions of confinement.

4. What are some of the issues faced by prison guards in their interactions with inmates, and how do they cope with these issues?

5. What models explain guards' power? How can guard authority be corrupted?

6. We know that guards often overlook minor rule violations because they need inmate cooperation. Is this ethical?

7. Does the guard subculture provide answers to ethical issues and dilemmas? If so, evaluate those solutions in terms of ethical standards.

8. How do guards justify the use of force against inmates? Are there any ethical implications in their justifications?

9. Explain why guards are ethically responsible for protecting the safety of prisoners. What situations might arise where this responsibility should be exercised?

10. What ethical issues do probation and parole officers face in carrying out their duties? Given the recent emphasis on law enforcement in probation and parole practice as well as on policies of zero tolerance, explain how this change from treatment to enforcement affects ethical issues and standards for the professions.

WEB RESOURCES

American Civil Liberties Union National Prison Project. http://www.aclu.org/issues/prisons

Amnesty International Women in Prison. http://www.amnestyusa.org/women/womeninprison.html

Amnesty International Women's Human Rights. http://www.amnesty-usa.org

Correctional Association of New York. http://www.corrassoc.org

Corrections Officers Codes of Ethics. http://www.advocateweb.org/HOPE/correctionsethics.asp

Family and Corrections Network. http://www.fcnetwork.org

Human Rights Watch: Prisons. http://hrw.org/doc/?t=global_prisons

International Center for Prison Studies. http://www.kcl.ac.uk/depsta/rel/icps

National Institute of Corrections (NIC). http://www.nicic.org

National Prison Rape Elimination Commission. http://www.nprec.us/resources.htm

Penal Reform International. http://www.penalreform.org

Prison Reform Advocacy Center. http://www.prisonreform.com

Rightsforall-usa.org. http://www.rightsforall-usa.org/info/action/index.html#prisons

Stop Prisoner Rape. http://www.spr.org

The Corrections Connection. http://www.corrections.com

United Nations Asia and Far East Institute for the Prevention of Crime and the Treatment of Offenders (UNAFEI). http://www.unafei.or.jp

Vera Justice Institute. http://www.vera.org

Women Coping in Prison. http://curry.edschool.virginia.edu/prisonstudy/

CHAPTER 7

The Ethics of Criminal Justice Policy Making

The Ethics of Policy Making

Policy making on criminal justice issues including crime control takes place at many different levels in society, ranging from the local community that introduces a neighborhood watch program to the formulation of strategies at the national level after debate in Congress. Policy makers at these different levels must make choices and analyze options, and in determining the approach to follow they should take into account any ethical aspects involved in their plans and proposals. The policy-making process involves predicting certain future conditions assuming an uninterrupted flow of events, projecting the future implications of a particular course of action, identifying a preferred outcome from a set of available choices, generating a program or policy that will result in the preferred outcome, and creating an adequate monitoring system (Meehan 1990: 41).

In considering how particular policies are justified, Reamer (1986: 224) identifies three grounds, which he calls "ideological," "empirical," and "ethical." Policy made on *ideological* grounds argues that certain policies are desirable because they fit a set of assumptions that may be based on religious beliefs, practice, or even basic intuition. For example, an argument that spending on social services should be decreased may be founded on the ideological assumption that historically, America has stressed minimum government intervention in the lives of citizens. *Empirical* grounds relate to science and research and to what is known from that research about the likely outcome of a particular policy. For example, a policy concerned with subsidizing childcare might draw on research evidence that shows that mothers who are able to take advantage of childcare are more likely to seek work, and therefore less likely to want assistance for their dependent children. In contrast to these grounds, those based on *ethical* grounds rely on conclusions drawn from an analysis of what is "right and wrong" or "good or bad" in a moral sense. For example, empirical or research evidence may show that paying subsidies to ailing corporations is less costly than allowing them to fail. Some would argue, however, that it would be ethically wrong for the government to intervene in the workings of a private enterprise in such a fashion. The critical difference between ethical and ideological grounds is that policy making on ethical grounds requires a calculated, philosophical analysis of the morality upon which the policy is based. This is not true for ideological grounds.

This chapter will examine some specific criminal justice policies, focus on the ethical issues that are implicated in those policies, and explore the way those ethical implications have been addressed and debated. Of course, criminal justice strategies are not formulated in a vacuum. They take account of ideologies and politics current at the time and, in many cases, are presumed to be giving effect to social movements and public concerns. Policy makers are subjected to many influences in their analysis of policy issues and in their decision making. For example, elected politicians react to the media, to their constituents, and to the many lobby groups that operate on both sides of all policy issues. Ethical issues, therefore, arise within a pattern of influences, and sometimes the ethical correctness of a particular course of action is used to support an argument that a particular policy action should be followed.

There are at least two ways of thinking about the ethics of criminal justice policy making:

- First, there is the general issue, applicable to all policy making, that those designing policies should *act ethically* in formulating their plans and projects (Fischer and Forester 1987: 24; Heineman et al. 1997: 67).
- Second, specifically in relation to policy making on punishment, it is arguable that punishment itself is a *morality policy* (certainly capital punishment is such a policy) and that making policy about punishment therefore involves ethics (Studlar 2001: 39).

This is not the place for an extended discussion of ethical policy making, but Anderson notes that policy analysis "involves a clarification and ordering of values and any policy analysis inevitably rests on some conception of desirable public purpose," and that "policy analysis that ignores the moral dimensions of public choice and public service is an inadequate pedagogy" (1987: 23).

The reasons advanced for the absence of ethical policy making include a reliance on cost-benefit analysis, which tends to be the primary method of policy analysis (Amy 1987: 46). As Tong (1986: 14) explains, cost–benefit analysis comprises several stages, including defining goals, determining the various methods of achieving those goals, determining costs and benefits of the various methods, comparing and ranking the costs and benefits of the various alternatives, and taking account of major uncertainties. In government, some argue that policy makers are prevented from making ethical decisions by a kind of machismo that sees any concern for ethical issues as a sign of political weakness, that is, as an unwillingness to make "tough" policy decisions (Amy 1987: 58). Others argue that "unethical" policy making includes reacting to events and issues that create "moral panics" by making ad hoc, capricious, and arbitrary policies that are not reasoned and not rational. In contrast to unethical policy making of this kind, an ethical piece of policy would involve a reasoned and considered analysis of a particular issue and a rational and informed approach. Where moral panics arise, such as occurred in the War on Drugs or the threat of "superpredators," there is a tendency for politicians and others to react viscerally, instinctively, and instantly rather than follow a reasoned and informed policy approach. In fact, many people would think that if politicians did not react instinctively to moral panics, they would be failing to "get tough" on crime and criminals.

The term *moral panic* was coined by Stanley Cohen (1972) in his work *Folk Devils and Moral Panics*. Cohen described moral panics in terms of the emergence of a condition, event, or group of persons that becomes defined as a threat to the values and interests of society. It is presented in a stylized and stereotypical fashion by the mass media, and groups of experts and "right-thinking people" take moral positions, make judgments, and suggest how the threat should be coped with. Cohen noted that the condition that produced the moral panic then either disappears or becomes more visible. Cohen's argument was that moral panics are generated by the media or special interest groups that use the media to publicize their concerns.

A second theory of moral panic was developed by Goode and Ben-Yehuda (1994) who proposed an "elite-engineered model." This theory is further developed by Hall and others (1978) in their well-known work *Policing the Crisis: Mugging, the State, and Law and Order*. Hall agreed that the media were a powerful force for shaping public consciousness about controversial issues. However, he also argued that typically, moral panics about law and order had their origin in statements by the police and judges that were then taken up and elaborated on by the media. (Hall was writing about the situation in England.) Also, Hall went further by arguing that the definition of a moral panic included the notion of an irrational response to that panic that was out of all proportion to the actual threat offered. This is in contrast to Cohen's view that moral panics are a product of "cultural strain and ambiguity."

A third theory advanced by Goode and Ben-Yehuda (1994) stresses the level of popular participation in moral panics; this is termed the "grass roots model." According to this theory, moral panics are founded on genuine public concern, which is picked up and promoted by the media. In this theory there is a shift of attention away from politicians and toward the opinions of the general public. It treats moral panic as a cultural phenomenon, as does Stuart Scheingold who, in *The Politics of Law and Order* (1984), argued that moral panics about street crime had little to do with actual crime, being more concerned about the pervasive presence of violence in contemporary American society.

Theories about moral panic show that the term is problematic, but it has come to represent a situation where, generally speaking, public reaction to an event is disproportionate to the actual problem faced. In other words, there may be a problem, such as street crime, but there is an overreaction about how it should be addressed in terms of crime control.

There is a link between moral panics and "morality policy making." Moral panics are often responded to in the form of policy changes and, ultimately, legislation that contains and reflects those policy changes. Clearly, there is a decision-making process by legislators and others that involves policy assessment and analysis and a consideration of policy options to deal with the moral panic. It is during this policy process that irrational, arbitrary, and therefore unethical policy making can occur. Moral panics and morality policy making together form the organizing framework for this discussion on ethics in criminal justice policy making.

Consider the War on Drugs, which resulted from public, media, and political concern about drug dealing and drug consumption. Responding to this concern, Congress passed legislation that launched a "War on Drugs." Was this legislation the result of rational, thorough, and informed debate, or did it originate as an instinctive, nonrational response to public fears and concerns? If the latter, then arguably, legislators in this case promoted and enacted legislation that reflected an unethical decision-making process (see Case Study 7.1).

CASE STUDY 7.1 AN EXAMPLE OF UNETHICAL POLICY MAKING?

Legislation enacted in 1986 shaped the War on Drugs by prescribing mandatory minimum penalties for drug trafficking based on the amount of drugs involved and by making a distinction between possession of cocaine and possession of crack cocaine. A penalty was imposed of a minimum of 25 years imprisonment for possession of 5 or more grams of *crack cocaine* (the form of cocaine for which African Americans are disproportionately arrested). In contrast, an offender found guilty of possession of *powder cocaine* (the type commonly used by middle- and upper-class whites) would only be liable for a mandatory minimum sentence of 5 years if the amount of cocaine exceeded or equaled 500 grams. The legislation was firmly aimed at social control and included provisions that eliminated probation and parole for certain drug offenders and allowed for the forfeiture of assets. Fundamentally, drug abuse had been perceived and defined as a national security issue for the United States, and the War on Drugs was portrayed as a matter of national survival. After 1986, however, media and public attention drifted away from the issue of drug abuse.

By the mid-1990s, three out of four persons doing time for drug offenses were African American, and in the federal courts, 94% of persons tried for drug offenses were African American. In 1995, the U.S. Sentencing Commission urged that there be parity in penalties for the different forms of cocaine, explaining that there was no rational basis for this differentiation in sentencing (Glassner 1999: 136). The commission's recommendations had never before been refused, but the White House and Congress aggressively opposed these recommendations, which were struck down in the House of Representatives by a vote of 332 to 83. Rather than give equity to African Americans charged with drug offenses, the White House and Congress preferred to avoid being labeled as "soft on drugs."

Morality Policy

Morality policies are policies that are viewed and constructed by the media, politicians, and sections of the public as involving moral and ethical issues. For example, what should be the policy on capital punishment? What should be the policy on abortion? In formulating criminal justice policy on issues of morality (morality policy making), policy makers should act ethically, undertake formal policy analysis, and avoid promoting ad hoc, arbitrary, and irrational policy solutions.

Morality policies share common features that include the fact that they are driven by public opinion, media coverage, lobbying by interest groups, the political concerns of elected officials, and sometimes by ideology. As well, unlike other policy issues, morality policies are considered easy to understand and require no special expertise for opinions and views to be expressed (Glick and Hutchinson 2001: 56). As Meier puts it, everyone is an "expert" on morality (1994 in Mooney 2001: 116). In designing and legislating policy on morality issues,

> Members of Congress and their staff use more information about constituents' personal experiences and other emotive information than technical policy analysis, they seek out less information, and they use the information they receive more selectively than when they are designing nonmorality policy. (Goggin and Mooney 2001: 131)

As Mooney (2001: 3–5) points out, morality policy involves a debate in which one party portrays the issue as one of morality and uses moral arguments in support of its view. It is the perceptions of the parties that make a particular policy a morality policy, and in such policies, moral judgment relies more on feelings than on reason. The death penalty is a classic instance of a morality policy, because prohibiting the death penalty has the effect of validating a particular value about the sanctity of human life. Issues like the death penalty inevitably invite a higher degree of public participation, because democratic theory argues that such policies must incorporate the views of the people (p. 10). It is common for advocacy groups to contest morality policies. Generally, they claim to be supporting some public interest rather than promoting any personal gain. Policy making on issues that call for morality policy usually involves less formal policy analysis than policy making for nonmorality policy (p. 13).

Mooney argues that the United States has a preoccupation with morality policy and suggests that the reasons for this relate to

1. the high adherence to religions in American society, promoting the likelihood of clashes on fundamental values, which are often based in religion;

2. the heterogeneity of society that encourages a clash of values; and

3. the fact that, in contrast to other democratic states, in the United States "there is a seemingly endless array of alternative venues in which morality policy advocates can pursue political satisfaction" (2001: 16).

Those who rely on their intuition to guide their thinking on a particular issue usually take a moral position. However, the danger in following only our intuition is discussed by Baron (1998: 18), who points out that while most people take stands on public issues on the basis of intuition about what they consider is "right," this approach usually results in only a partial understanding of the issue. Moral panics can sometimes be generated by specific events and lead to instant legislation or policy making. Examples of moral panics include movements to condemn pedophiles, the enactment of mandatory minimum legislation, the War on Drugs, and what to do about "juvenile predators." Another way of understanding policy emanating from moral panics is to see them as the expressive side of policy making in the sense that, as well as doing things, such policies transmit values and intentions. For example, advertisements urging people not to drink and drive reinforce values of sobriety, and capital punishment expresses toughness on criminals (Maynard-Moody and Stull 1987: 249–250). These policies are, in fact, designed to send a message and are intentionally expressive. Of course, not all policy making in criminal justice is expressive, but punishment policy often involves employing the rhetoric engendered by moral panics. This serves to shift policy away from rational, calculating models of policy making toward the expressive forms of policy.

Penal policies over the past two decades have resulted in mass imprisonment. For example, by the beginning of 2008, a total of 2,319, 258 people were locked up in federal or state prisons and jails, making the rate of incarceration 1 in every 99.1 adults (Pew 2008: 5). The rush to incarcerate has increased the rate of imprisonment from 230 per 100,000 in 1979 to 601 in 1995 (Harrison and Beck 2006: 2) and to 750 per 100,000 by the end of 2007 (Pew 2008: 35). Disaggregated by race, 1 in 106 white men 18 years or older were in prison; of all men 18 or older, 1 in 54; of Hispanic men aged 18 or older, 1 in 36; of black men 18 years or older, 1 in 15; and of black men aged 20–34; 1 in 9 (Pew 2008: 6). To these figures must be added 4,162,536 persons on probation and 784,408 on parole giving a total for jail, prison, probation, and parole of 7,056,000 (Glaze and Bonczar 2006: 1). David Garland (2001: 2) points out that "mass imprisonment was not a policy that was proposed, researched, costed, debated and democratically agreed [to]." As he notes, in contrast to the rational and informed policy making of the past in, for example, the New Deal and the Great Society, "mass imprisonment emerged as the overdetermined outcome of a converging series of policies and decisions" (p. 2). Pointing to the war against drugs, mandatory sentencing, truth in sentencing, and the development of private prisons, Garland emphasizes that these measures did not form a rational and coherent program. Rather, America has drifted into a situation where mass imprisonment has been accepted as the sole method of crime control. He asks the question, "What does it mean for the United States to be a mass imprisonment society and what are the implications?" For example, "What limits are there to this process and can they be reversed?" and "What is the social impact on communities and neighborhoods?"

Public Opinion About Punishment

Should public opinion be the determinant of sentencing and correctional policies? Is it ethical for morality policies, in particular, to be formulated solely on the basis of what is perceived to be public opinion on a particular issue? Some argue that public opinion on crime control and punishment fluctuates in response to certain events, such as urban turmoil and escalating crime rates. The alternative view expressed by others, including Scheingold (1984) and Beckett (1997), is that public opinion does not become shaped by the events of the day but is fashioned and manipulated by politicians and the media. Beckett, for example, investigated how the timing of shifts in public opinion converged with politicians undertaking initiatives such as calling for a "war" on a problem or introducing legislation and with media attention focused on an issue. She concludes that changes in public opinion about crime control and drugs most often follow increases in political initiatives and media coverage that emphasizes these issues rather than changes in events in the wider environment (in Cullen, Fisher, and Applegate 2000: 63). In other words, she suggests that political initiatives and media coverage create moral panics that result in morality policy making.

Since the mid-1970s, there has been a fundamental shift in the ideology of punishment, because punitive approaches and the new penology have supplanted the rehabilitative model. Many believe the reasons for this transformation are complex, but some offer the simple explanation that these new punitive policies merely represent the wishes of the public. For example, DiIulio (1997 in Cullen et al. 2000: 2) argues that citizens have become fed up with crime rates and with offenders victimizing them, and have concluded rationally that more offenders should be locked up for longer periods of time. In this style of thinking, getting "tough on crime" is a manifestation of democracy at work. The discussion of prison and amenities in Box 7.1 addresses one aspect of this issue, amenities in prison.

A CLOSER LOOK

BOX 7.1
Prison and Amenities

What standards and conditions should be applied to imprisonment? The topic of what level of amenities should be supplied to prisoners resurfaces in the media periodically. Those politicians who wish to demonstrate a "tough on crime" approach protest that prisoners are provided access to weight-lifting equipment, televisions, radios and "good" food (Banks 2005: 137). In Maricopa County, Arizona, Sheriff Joe Arpia's policies of housing inmates in tents without air conditioning in the more than 110 °F summer weather, clothing inmates in pink underwear and striped uniforms, chain gangs for both men and women, and providing basic and unappealing food such as bologna on dry bread exemplify this attitude. Such politicians argue that if prisoners have standards of incarceration that are superior to the standard of living of the man on the street, then they cannot be said to be suffering punishment. The media fuel this debate by reporting that prisons are "holiday resorts" where prisoners enjoy extravagant amenities and conditions (see Lenz 2002). In response to this political discourse,

(Continued)

(Continued)

the No Frills Prison Act was passed in 1996; it bans televisions, coffeepots, and hot plates in the cells of federal prisoners. It also prohibits computers, electronic instruments, certain movies rated above PG, and unmonitored phone calls (Lenz 2002).

The underpinning assumption to this legislation is that a deterrent effect will be achieved "by making a sentence more punitive, that is, making the inmate suffer more" (Banks 2005: 138). Thus, it is assumed that an inmate will be "less inclined to reoffend knowing the harsh conditions in prison" (p. 138). The problem is that there is no existing research that can support this assumption. Some have argued that state costs are saved to the prison system and to the taxpayers through this approach, but again this is not supported given that the 31 states which allow inmates televisions in their cells do not pay for them (prisoners or their relatives pay for them), and cablevision is paid for out of profits from the prison commissary, vending machines, and long distance telephone charges (Finn 1996: 6–7).

Interestingly, prison administrators are often in favor of permitting amenities in the prisons, because staff rely heavily on a system of rewards and punishments to maintain control in their institutions (Lenz 2002: 506). They recognize that keeping inmates busy provides important benefits to inmate order and inmate activities. In other words, bored and unhappy prisoners are more likely to cause security problems that staff who are in short supply will have to respond to.

As Cullen et al. (2000: 3) point out, policy making based on what citizens want is unfortunately constrained by the ignorance of the public on many aspects of crime and crime control. Researchers have discovered that in most areas of crime control, there is a widespread lack of knowledge, and this is particularly true for sentencing, where, for example, it is unclear whether citizens are aware of the existence of sanctions other than imprisonment and of the content of community-based sanctions. Research has established that public punitive attitudes about crime do not fluctuate as might be expected as crime rates rise and fall but instead that punitiveness and favoring harsher penalties remain constant.

The views of the public on crime are often investigated through telephone surveys that ask only a limited number of questions about a major policy issue such as capital punishment. However, it is clear that the opinions of the public on crime control often change if multiple questions rather than a single question are used (see Table 7.1). For example, respondents tend to express a less punitive attitude when they are given detailed information about the nature of the offender and his or her criminal offenses. This is also the case if they are given a list of potential sentencing options, including noncustodial sentencing options, to apply to actual offenders. This contrasts with answering broadly worded questions about unspecified criminals (Cullen et al. 2000: 7). In a review of surveys concerning public opinion on crime control and sentencing, Cullen et al. (2000: 8–9) developed seven main conclusions:

1. Generally the public is punitive toward crime.

2. However, their punitiveness is "mushy"; that is, even when they express a punitive opinion, people tend to be flexible enough to consider a range of sentencing options if provided with adequate information.

3. Members of the public must be given a good reason not to be punitive and are prepared to moderate their punitive attitudes.

4. Violent crime divides the punitive from the nonpunitive, because citizens are reluctant not to incarcerate dangerous offenders. However, they are prepared to consider a wide range of sentencing options for nonviolent offenders.

5. Despite attacks on rehabilitation and the treatment of offenders, the public continues to believe in rehabilitation as a goal of corrections.

6. There is strong support for child saving; that is, for the rehabilitation of youthful offenders and for interventions that attempt to divert children at risk away from criminality.

7. The central tendency of the public is to be punitive and progressive—to desire a response to offenders that is balanced and which includes the objectives of achieving justice, protecting society, and reforming offenders.

Research demonstrates widespread support amongst the public for locking up offenders. As Warr (in Cullen et al. 2000: 28) writes,

Americans overwhelmingly regard imprisonment as the most appropriate form of punishment for most crimes. Although the proportion who prefer prison increases with the seriousness of the crime, imprisonment is by far the most commonly chosen penalty across crimes.

In one survey in 1994, researchers assessed the extent to which public opinion about sentencing was consistent with the punishments specified in the Federal Sentencing Guidelines. They found that respondents favored imprisonment, although rarely for more than several years, with the median sentence being 3 years and the mean sentence 7.2 years (Cullen et al. 2000: 30). These results broadly mirrored the sentencing guidelines overall, but there were wide variations in individual opinions about sentences. Warr asked respondents to indicate their goals of punishment and concluded from the results that there was no single dominant determinant of punishment among the public; that persons commonly invoked more than one theory of punishment, such as just deserts, rehabilitation, or deterrence; and that no one theory dominated public thinking on this issue (p. 34).

This discussion has shown that ethical decision making is often sacrificed in the interests of expediency and under pressure from cost–benefit analysis. In the case of morality policy making, such as that regarding punishment, moral panics and ideological stances prevail over rational, reasoned, and ethical decision making. The lack of an ethical focus in criminal justice policy making will be illustrated through an analysis of several criminal justice policy issues. These are mandatory minimum sentencing, the War on Drugs, truth in sentencing, predators and superpredators, capital punishment, and privatizing prisons.

Table 7.1   Public Preferences for the Main Goal of Imprisonment, 1968–1996 (percentage agreeing with each goal reported).

Main Emphasis of Prison Should Be	Harris 1968	Harris 1982	Gallup 1982	Cincinnati 1986	Cincinnati 1995	Ohio 1996	National 1995	National 1996
Rehabilitation	73.0	44.0	59.0	54.7	32.6	41.1	26.1	48.4
Punishment	7.0	19.0	30.0	5.7	27.2	20.3	—	14.6
Protect Society	12.0	32.0	—	35.3	36.8	31.9	—	—
Punish and Put Away	—	—	—	—	—	—	58.2	—
Crime Prevention/ Deterrence	—	—	—	—	—	—	—	33.1
Not Sure/Don't Know/Other	9.0	5.0	11.0	4.3	2.5	6.7	13.4	3.9

SOURCE: From "Public Opinion About Punishment and Corrections," by F. Cullen, B. Fisher and B. Applegate in Crime and Justice: A Review of Research, edited by Michael Tonry. Copyright © 2000. Reprinted by permission of the University of Chicago Press.

NOTE: 1968 and 1982 Harris polls reported in Flanagan and Caulfield (1984, p. 42); 1982 Gallup poll reported in "Public Backs Wholesale Prison Reform" (1982, p. 16); 1986 and 1995 Cincinnati polls reported in Cullen et al. (1990, p. 9) and in Sundt et al. (1998, p. 435); 1996 Ohio poll reported in Applegate, Cullen, and Fisher (1997); 1995 and 1996 national polls reported in Maguire and Pastore (1997, pp. 154–155). All are cited in Cullen et al. 2000: 49.

The Harris, Cincinnati, and Ohio polls asked: "What do you think should be the main emphasis in most prisons—punishing the individual convicted of a crime, trying to rehabilitate the individual so that he might become a productive citizen, or protecting society from future crimes he might commit?" The Gallup poll asked whether it was "more important to punish [men in prison] for their crimes, or more important to get them started on the right road" (which was categorized as "rehabilitation"). The 1995 national poll asked whether the government needs to "make a greater effort" to "rehabilitate" or "punish and put away criminals who commit violent crimes." The 1996 national poll asked what should be the main goal "once people who commit crimes are in prison."

Mandatory Minimum Sentencing

The development of policies fixing minimum terms of imprisonment for certain offenses or types of offenders exemplifies the expansion of punitive policies in the criminal justice system. In the 1970s and 1980s, a movement developed away from rehabilitative philosophies that had previously guided criminal justice policy makers toward a more punitive approach involving the creation of a set of policies intended to punish offenders, enhance the status of victims, and placate public fears about crime and criminals. Before this period, crime had not registered in the public mind as a significant issue, and most attribute the emergence of crime as a serious political issue to charges made by Republican Senator Barry Goldwater, who ran for president in 1964 against Lyndon Johnson. Goldwater criticized Johnson for rising crime rates and accused the president of being "soft on crime" (Robinson 2002: 34). Legislation enacted as part of the War on Drugs, as well as habitual felony laws made initially in Washington and California to punish violent felony offenders, are high-profile instances of this new punitive approach toward criminals and crime.

Habitual felony laws, commonly known as "three-strikes" legislation, began in 1993 when an initiative was placed on the ballot in Washington State mandating the punishment of life imprisonment without parole for offenders convicted for a third time of specified violent or serious felonies (Austin and Irwin 2001: 184). This initiative was promoted by those concerned about the death of a woman murdered by a convicted rapist who had recently been released from prison. Additional impetus was provided by the kidnapping and murder of Polly Klaas in California by a former inmate with an extensive record of violence. Both Washington and California voters, and later those in other states, passed three-strikes ballot proposals, and by 1997, 24 other states and the federal government had enacted mandatory minimum sentencing legislation.

In California, the three strikes legislation was drafted independently of government and became law with no significant influence from either the executive or legislative branches (Zimring, Hawkins, and Kamin 2001: 3). In the view of Zimring et al. (p. 3) the legislation "was an extreme example of a populist preemption of criminal justice policy-making." According to these authors, the legislation was heavily promoted by victim's associations, the Prison Guard Union, and the National Rifle Association (p. 11). In relation to victims, they suggest that issues of penal policy, at least in California, have become a contest in which the voter decides a penal issue by choosing between offenders and their victims. There is an assumption that anything bad for offenders must benefit victims; thus, "no punishment seems too extreme if anything that hurts offenders benefits victims" (p. 224). This simplification of policy making on criminal punishment renders expert advice, analysis, and assessment unnecessary and irrelevant in the eyes of the public. In policy terms, the proponents of this type of legislation argue that deterrence will be achieved if severe and certain punishment is imposed on habitual offenders; that is, the offender, aware that the next conviction will result in life imprisonment, will carefully consider the consequences of committing a further offense.

Many argue that this is an unrealistic expectation and bad policy making, because it relies not only on offenders being informed of the consequences of further offenses but also on a high probability of their arrest and conviction. It assumes, too, that all offenders make rational, calculating decisions about their future actions, carefully weighing risks and making choices in an informed and measured manner (Austin and Irwin 2001: 185). Proponents of three-strikes legislation also argue that its outcome, incapacitation, has the effect of targeting habitual criminals who must, in their view, be permanently isolated from society. In other words, it is argued that habitual offenders can be identified, and the assumption is made that a habitual offender will continue to offend over time. In fact, studies have shown the difficulty of accurately identifying the so-called habitual offender. Also, the argument ignores the fact that most criminal careers do not continue beyond a certain age. These major policy considerations were, however, ignored, and the initiative proceeded as a morality policy based on a moral panic about habitual violent offenders.

Most legislation imposing three strikes includes the definition of offenses for which a mandatory minimum can be imposed, the number of strikes needed to qualify for the ultimate sanction, and definitions of the ultimate sanction. For example, in California, any felony qualifies as "a strike" if the offender has one prior felony conviction appearing on a list of strikeable offenses, or if the offender has two prior felony convictions from that list. In the first case, two strikes will result in a mandatory sentence—that is, twice that for the offense involved—and in the second case, the sanction is a mandatory life sentence with no parole for 25 years (Austin and Irwin 2001: 187). The California law is one of the most severe in the country, first, because it provides for a wide number of felonies constituting strikes, and second, because in California, the third strike can be any felony whatsoever, as opposed to a violent felony, a provision found in no other state's law.

In California, this legislation was predicted to more than double the prison population within 5 years; however, those estimates were later adjusted downwards. Nevertheless, between the years 1994 and 1998, the total number of cases sentenced to California prisons under the three-strikes law was 45,207 (Austin and Irwin 2001: 197). The types of crimes committed by those subject to three strikes range from an offender who attempted to steal a parked truck, held the owner at bay with a knife, fled on the freeway, and was finally placed under arrest and sentenced to 27 years to life with a minimum of 22.95 years to an offender who received a sentence of 27 years to life for attempting to sell stolen batteries to a retailer, where the value of the batteries was $90 (p. 208).

The disproportionate punishments imposed in these sample cases highlight the unethical nature of the legislation. According to Austin and Irwin (2001: 207), the research data show that in California, most inmates who receive second- and third-strike sentences are not violent or habitual offenders. The courts and prosecutors have generally attempted to find ways to avoid imposing these lengthy sentences, and this has assisted in ameliorating the effect of the legislation (p. 213). As a result, the impact has not been nearly as severe as projected. In effect, bad policy making has been countered by administrative action by the courts and prosecutors.

Shichor (2000: 1) argues that three-strikes laws have a number of adverse implications. For example, he points to the situation under the California law that gives prosecutors the right to decide whether the third-strike offense should be charged as a felony or a misdemeanor. Also noted is that despite its claims to establish a higher level of uniformity in sentencing, the legislation has actually increased punishment disparities both in individual cases and within jurisdictions, because punishment policies are shaped by the local district attorneys. For example, by May 1997, Los Angeles County, which contained 29% of the state's population, accounted for 41% of three-strikes prison admissions, whereas San Francisco County with 5.3% of the population made up only 0.5% of such admissions (P. 2000: 15). Shichor (p. 16) notes that the effect of the legislation was to shift power relationships in sentencing away from the courts and in favor of politically motivated prosecutors. This effect was apparently never considered in the policy making that led to the legislation.

Another criticism leveled at the legislation is its reinforcement of the race bias in punishment by its concentration on street crimes and drug offenses. Geis complains that three-strikes laws fail to meet standards of equal justice for like kinds of criminal wrongdoing, because these laws omit white-collar crimes and demonstrate "the strong and ugly strains of race, class, and ethnic bias that have produced these laws" (1996: 261). In an important article on penal ideology, Feeley and Simon (1992) contrast this new trend in penology, a component of which is three-strikes legislation, with the old penology that focused on individuals and individual-based theories of punishment. They emphasize that the new penology is concerned with aspects like "dangerousness" rather than with the question of how to treat and punish an individual offender. Certain groups within society are identified as "career criminals" or "habitual offenders" and are selected for special surveillance, management, and incapacitation. As Henry and Milovanovic (1996: 114) put it, this new penology operates on utilitarian considerations rather than moral ones. Shichor (1999: 424) argues that these changes in punishment ideology have flowed from the pessimism experienced since the 1970s about the ability of the criminal justice system to turn offenders into law-abiding citizens. Feeley and Simon (1992) argue that penology is now directed toward managing a population of criminals considered to be permanently dangerous and incapable of reform or of being rehabilitated. In this sense, therefore, the labeling of a criminal class through this criminal justice policy parallels the depiction of an underclass, that is, a marginal, unemployable population lacking education and skills.

Shichor (1999: 425) explains that in theory, three-strikes legislation is meant to target violent and dangerous offenders for selective incapacitation. He relates the concept of controlling dangerous offenders to a sociocultural position that encourages the emergence of moral panics. That is, a public perception develops, is reinforced, and is perhaps even engendered by the mass media that dangerous offenders pose a threat to society and the moral order (see Cohen and Young 1973). Where such expressive arguments are advanced, moral considerations about punishment and retribution may tend to overshadow any empirical evidence as to the likely effects of implementing a particular criminal justice policy (Vergari 2001: 202). Mass values may, therefore, override reasoned policy analysis (Heineman et al. 1997: 54).

Does the public support three-strikes laws? In referenda in Washington and California in 1993, the first three-strikes statute was approved in Washington by a 3-to-1 margin and in California by a margin of 72% for and 28% against (in Cullen et al. 2000: 38). Similarly, a *Time*/CNN poll conducted in 1994 reported that 81% of adults favored mandatory life imprisonment for persons convicted of a third serious crime. Nevertheless, it is arguable that citizens do not always wish to apply three strikes to every offender who would be eligible for life without parole, because in studies where concrete cases are rated, there is some variation in the impact of prior record on sentencing preferences (Cullen et al. 2000: 39). For example, in a study in 1995 in Cincinnati, where specific offenses were included as three-strikes offenses, the respondents were asked to select a sentence from a range of no punishment and probation to life in prison with and without parole. Only 16.9% chose a life sentence. The results overall suggest that the public can hold views that appear to be incompatible, because while they favor three strikes, they do not believe that the principle should be applied indiscriminately to specific offenders under specific circumstances.

The War on Drugs

There are four distinct periods in the history of the so-called War on Drugs. In 1972, President Nixon declared the initial war on crime and drugs, and in 1973 created the Drug Enforcement Agency (Robinson 2002: 163). In 1982, President Reagan also declared a "War on Drugs." Both "wars" aimed to reduce individual drug use, stop the flow of drugs into the United States, and reduce drug-related crime. However, it was not until 1986 and 1988 that actual drug abuse legislation was enacted at the federal level. This moved the focus away from major drug dealers and treatment to users and street-level dealers, with an emphasis on those using and dealing crack cocaine (Bush-Baskette 1999: 212). The legislation enacted in 1986 and 1988 came about through an intense media focus on drugs, beginning in 1984 with media accounts about cocaine in California. By the 1986 congressional elections, at least 1,000 newspaper stories had appeared nationally on the issue of crack cocaine, and documentary-style programs representing cocaine use and sales as a national epidemic appeared on television as cocaine, and especially crack cocaine, became campaign issues in the election (p. 213).

The Anti–Drug Abuse Act of 1986 provided mandatory minimum penalties for drug trafficking based on the quantity of drugs involved, and it differentiated between possession of cocaine and possession of crack cocaine. A mandatory minimum of 5 years with a maximum of 20 years was prescribed for those convicted of possessing 5 or more grams of crack cocaine, whereas an offender found guilty of possessing powder cocaine would be liable only to a 5-year mandatory minimum if the amount equaled or exceeded 500 grams. In this legislation, drug abuse was presented as a national security issue, and the War on Drugs was depicted as necessary for the survival of the United States. In contrast to 1986, the issue of drug control waned in 1987 as the media and public turned their attention to other issues; in fact, one poll in 1987 reported only 3–5% of the public considered drugs to be the most pressing social problem (Bush-Baskette 1999: 214). In 1988, another presidential election brought drugs back as a high-profile issue, and about 1½ weeks before the election, another antidrug abuse act was passed. This 1988 act included more funding for treatment and prevention, although most of it was still directed toward law enforcement, punishment, and increased penalties for certain crack cocaine offenses. By 1990, media attention to the issue had normalized, and the National Drug Control Strategy of 1991 lacked the intense focus on crack and cocaine of previous years.

The increased and more punitive response to drug abuse over this period has enormously impacted the extent of drug prosecutions and incarceration rates for drug offenses. Prosecution efforts were stepped up, and between 1982 and 1988 there was a 52.17% increase in the number of convictions for drug offenses and an increase of 48.48% of those incarcerated for drug offenses (Bush-Baskette 1999: 215). Federal spending on the "drug war" amounted to $13.2 billion in 1995, two thirds of which was used for law enforcement. If all the costs of incarcerating drug offenders are brought into account, the total expenditure on the War on Drugs would amount to approximately $100 billion every year (p. 215). In 2004 an estimated 333,000 prisoners were held for drug law violations, 21% of whom were held in state facilities, making up 21% of state inmates and 55% of federal inmates (Mumola and Karberg 2006: 4).

The figures for female offenders are even more startling. In 1986, 26% of federal female prisoners were incarcerated for drug offenses; by 1991 this figure had risen to 63.9%. In addition, there were significant increases in the mean sentence length for drug offenders. Whereas the mean sentence in 1982 was 54.6 months, by 1991, it had increased to 85.7 months (Bush-Baskette 1999: 220). By 2004 the figures were 82,800 for women incarcerated in state prisons for drug offenses and 9,100 in federal prisons (Mumola and Karberg 2006: 11).

Copying the federal government, most states enacted similar drug legislation; New York, in particular, became well-known for its legislation, enacting the severe "Rockefeller drug laws" in 1973. These imposed mandatory sentences requiring that a convicted offender in possession of 4 ounces of heroin or cocaine, or attempting to sell 2 ounces of heroin or cocaine, receive a mandatory 15 years to life in prison. Some major components of the Rockefeller laws have been repealed following the determination that they had little or no effect on drug use or crime in New York (Bush-Baskette 1999: 221).

As well as increasing the size of the inmate population generally, the War on Drugs has had the effect of disproportionately incarcerating African American men and women. At the state level there was an 828% increase in the number of African American women incarcerated for drug offenses between 1986 and 1991, whereas the rate for white women was 241% (Bush-Baskette 1999: 222). For the same period, there was an increase of 429% for African American men.

In a reaction to the overwhelming focus of the War on Drugs on incarcerating drug offenders and in a move toward a more treatment-oriented approach, in November 2000 the voters of California approved by a large majority a proposition that would provide drug treatment instead of prison for first and second time drug offenders who were not charged with other crimes. This law was expected to divert 36,000 offenders each year away from prison and into treatment programs (Spohn 2002: 250). In a similar shift toward treatment for drug offenders, in June 2000, the chief judge of New York State ordered the commencement of a program that would require nearly all nonviolent criminals who were drug addicts to be offered a treatment option instead of jail time. The objective was to radically reduce the number of repeat drug offenders coming before the courts and the inmate population in the state (Finkelstein 2000).

In February 2001, legislation was introduced into the U.S. Senate calling for $2.7 billion in spending over 3 years to increase the extent of drug treatment programs in prisons. However, the legislation also proposed more severe sentencing guidelines for those committing drug offenses in the presence of minors or who used children in drug trafficking (p. 250).

Gaines and Kraska (1997: 4) in their critique of the War on Drugs, claim that

> waging war on drugs—as if the drugs themselves constitute our "drug problem"—allows us to overlook the underlying reasons why people abuse these substances. . . . The language of ideology fools us into thinking that we're waging war against drugs themselves, not real people.

In an attempt to correct the sentencing disparities created by the crack cocaine laws, in December 2007, the Supreme Court ruled that judges could hand down lighter punishments in crack cocaine and ecstasy cases than those specified by federal guidelines and that they could depart from sentencing guidelines in cases involving ecstasy distribution (*Gall v. United States* 2007; *Kimbrough v. United States* 2007). (See Box 7.2.)

A CLOSER LOOK

BOX 7.2
Lighter Sentences Possible for Crack Cocaine Cases

Under a 1986 law, first-time offenders convicted of selling 5 grams of crack cocaine receive the same 5-year mandatory prison sentence as dealers of 500 grams of powder cocaine. African Americans account for about 80% of federal crack cocaine convictions, and sentencing guidelines set lighter sentences for selling powder cocaine, a substance popular with whites and Hispanics. This divergence in sentencing has provoked criticism that the judicial system is explicitly racially biased in such cases. There has been consistent pressure in Congress to revise the law, but lawmakers have seemed reluctant to take action for fear of appearing to be "soft on crime," especially on drug offenses.

On April 7, 2008, the Supreme Court addressed this long-standing issue and ruled that judges can impose lighter sentences for crack cocaine and ecstasy cases than are specified in the federal guidelines. The ruling was made by a decisive 7-to-2 margin and comes a day before the U.S. Sentencing Commission is to determine whether or not to make retroactive a reduction in recommended crack-cocaine penalties.

The Supreme Court had already decided in 2005 that federal sentencing guidelines were not mandatory and that sentencing judges could therefore apply their discretion in sentencing drug offenders. This most recent ruling involved an African American who received a 15-year prison term for selling crack and powder cocaine, as well as for possessing a firearm, in Virginia. The trial judge rejected as excessive the prison term of 19 to 22 years called for under the guidelines. The Supreme Court did not agree with the appeal court that reducing the sentence to 15 years amounted to "an abuse of discretion."

SOURCE: Mikkelsen 2007

The War on Drugs is a prime example of morality policy making. The media framed the drug issue as a moral panic, and this was followed by a series of political actions that resulted in the production of an unethical, discriminatory policy that has made a huge contribution to the development of mass imprisonment in the United States. The War on Drugs demonstrates the perils that can be caused by singling out one subject of criminal activity for special punitive treatment.

Truth in Sentencing

The new, more punitive penology, together with widespread public concerns about "lies in sentencing," resulted in the enactment of so-called truth-in-sentencing laws. The concern with truth in sentencing relates to offenders being sentenced to prison for substantial periods but being released on parole, in some cases after serving less than one half of their sentences. For example, an article in Alabama's *Birmingham News* from July 2000 referred to two cases—the first involving brothers sentenced to 40 years for kidnapping and rape who were released on parole after serving less than half their sentences, and the second involving a woman sentenced to 25 years for murder and eligible for parole after only 8 years imprisonment (in Spohn 2002: 252).

The policy intent of truth in sentencing was to ensure that a substantial period of a prison sentence was actually served. Through legislation, the federal government set the standard at 85% of the sentence imposed. It is significant that these laws were enacted following the passage of the 1994 Crime Act, which authorized and appropriated grants of nearly $10 billion to the states to build and expand correctional facilities. In order to be eligible for federal funding, states must require those convicted of violent crimes to serve at least 85% of the court-imposed sentence. By 1999, 27 states and the District of Columbia had adopted laws that met the federal standard, and 13 other states required offenders to serve from 50% to 75% of the sentence imposed (Spohn 2002: 253). Data from states that followed the federal model showed that the average time served by violent offenders increased between 1993 and 1997, as would be expected because of the minimum period of custody required.

Truth-in-sentencing policy and legislation follow the model of mandatory minimum sentencing by basing themselves on the belief that habitual offenders are responsible for a disproportionate amount of crime committed and that incarcerating them for lengthy periods will reduce the crime rate. Petersilia (1999: 497) notes that in order to satisfy the 85% test, states have limited the powers of parole boards to fix release dates and of prison administrators to award "good time." The effect of truth in sentencing policy has therefore been not only to effectively eliminate parole but also to eliminate most "good time." In ethical terms, the conjunction between this policy and the availability of federal funds to construct more prisons is significant. Even if the states had misgivings in policy terms about truth in sentencing, they seemed unable to resist the offer of federal funding. Perhaps this is a good example of the maxim, "If you build it, they will come."

Predators and Superpredators

Sexual Predators

During the 1990s, sex offenders emerged as a distinct and dangerous criminal class, associated with a belief that children are more vulnerable to sexual abuse and molestation. There now exists in this country a set of assumptions that sexual abuse is pervasive, that it constitutes an issue of immense scope, that child molesters are compulsive individuals, and that their pathologies are resistant to rehabilitation or cure. In addition, it is assumed that sexual molestation generates a cycle of abuse, because the original molestation so affects the victim that he or she will ultimately commit the same act against children of the next generation (Jenkins 1998: 1–2).

Philip Jenkins (1998) has explored the history of child abuse and the moral panics connected with child abuse for the period from 1890 until the emergence of the "sexual predator" in the 1990s. He has shown how, over that period, concern about the sexual offender has fluctuated with a series of peaks and dips in the social construction of this issue. The first so-called sexual pervert was identified as deviant and dangerous in the early 1900s, but at the end of the 19th century, sexual perversion was considered akin to defectiveness and degeneracy, and those viewed as perverts could be sterilized to prevent their defective genes being passed on. Policies of that nature for perverts were applied in the 1930s. Later, conceptions about deviancy changed away from biological explanations toward the psychiatric model, and laws were passed requiring indefinite confinement of those considered to be sexual psychopaths. These offenders were evaluated and treated by psychiatrists in mental institutions. Commencing in the late 1950s and continuing until the 1970s, the restrictive measures previously adopted were eased. Formal legal intervention was now seen as counterproductive, because it was inconsistent with greater sensitivity in the courts about racial issues in sex crime prosecutions and procedural rights. During this liberal period, questions were asked about the appropriateness of even criminalizing deviant sexual acts.

The ebb and flow of the social response to sex crimes continued. By the 1980s, there was a surge in concern about sex offenses, because feminist activism brought the issue of rape and pornography to the forefront and emphasized the subjugation of women and children. Concern expressed by feminists about women and children as victims of violence fed into a conservative atmosphere that advocated getting "tough on crime." Sex offenders became a group highlighted for policy making. As well, Christian fundamentalists linked homosexuality, nontraditional sexual relationships, and the sexual violation of children. By the 1990s, the general public, politicians, and the media had begun to express a sense of crisis about sex offenders and sexual predators. This concern was translated into legislation in some states. For example, in 1994, California enacted a law imposing a 25-year sentence with 15 years minimum before eligibility for parole for those convicted of specified sex crimes. In 1996, California enacted a nonvoluntary chemical castration punishment for child molesters that was mandatory following a second conviction and applicable to a first offense if it met certain criteria (Lynch 2002: 532). In 2003 Congress passed the PROTECT Bill (known as Amber Alert) that created a national system of notification of child kidnappings. By an amendment to this bill, Congress also changed the sentencing guidelines for crimes involving pornography, sexual abuse, child sex, and child kidnapping and trafficking by eliminating downward sentencing departures that would serve to reduce sentences, including family ties, diminished capacity, and educational or vocational skills (Bibas 2004: 295–296).

Apart from incarceration for their offenses, convicted sex offenders are now subject to a range of identification and surveillance strategies in most states; these laws are often referred to as "Megan's Laws." Although there are variations in different states, the basic format is that specified sex offenders are required to register certain information with local law enforcement, either for several years or even for the rest of their lives. Specific offenders may also be required to have their particulars, such as information about their address, provided to certain community groups and members of the public, such as schools and child care facilities (Lynch 2002: 533). Much of this information, as well as the criminal histories of sexual offenders, is now available on the Internet.

There is another group known as "sexually violent predators" who are subject to even more restriction after release from prison. They may be detained in locked facilities for indefinite periods subject only to a periodic review (see Box 7.3). Even though this gives the appearance of continuing a term of imprisonment that has supposedly terminated, this form of detention is labeled "civil commitment" rather than criminal punishment. A further step is that some states have authorized capital punishment as a sentence for specified child molesters (Lynch 2002: 533). For example, in Louisiana, the aggravated rape of a person under 12 is a capital offense. The federal government has increasingly involved itself in the punishment of sexual predators, and in 1994, included in a crime bill the requirement that funds made available for federal crime fighting be withheld from those states that did not have sex offender registration systems. Naturally, this legislation spawned registration programs, and by 1996, 49 states had registration systems in place (p. 533). Moreover, in 1996, further legislation was enacted providing for the nationwide tracking of convicted sexual predators in a database maintained by the FBI (p. 535). In at least a dozen states, policy makers are now linking intense supervision of sex offenders with constant GPS monitoring of their location (Lyons 2006). For example, in Florida, a 2005 law called the Jessica Lunsford Act after the abduction and murder of 9-year-old Jessica Lunsford requires the lifetime GPS monitoring of sex offenders.

A CLOSER LOOK

BOX 7.3
States Detain Sex Offenders After Prison

New York State considers itself at the forefront of a growing national movement to confine sex offenders after their prison terms have expired using a civil commitment law. These programs have been criticized for not meeting their stated goal of "treating the worst criminals until they no longer pose a

(Continued)

(Continued)

threat" (Davey and Goodnough 2007: 1). The number of pedophiles, rapists, and other sexual offenders who are being held indefinitely in special treatment centers in 19 states is estimated at 2,700 with a cost to taxpayers at 4 times the cost of keeping them in prison. Slightly less than 3,000 sex offenders have been committed since the law was passed in 1990 (p. 1). Of those only 81 have been fully discharged from commitment because they are considered ready. Another 115 have been released due to "legal technicalities, court ruling, terminal illness or old age" (p. 1). Texas and Arizona have released an additional 189 and 68, respectively, under supervision or conditions.

Such laws have been upheld by the U.S. Supreme Court on the understanding that offenders will receive treatment in confinement and that it is not a second punishment. However, only a fraction of sexual offenders committed under this legislation "have ever completed the treatment to the point where they could be released free and clear" (Davey and Goodnough 2007: 1). The programs are expensive and unproven, and although they are resident in the programs, patients often accept their lawyers' advice and fail to show up for sessions that require them to confess all their crimes, even those unknown by police (p. 1). Instead they spend their time gardening, watching TV, or playing video games.

President Bush has signed a law that offers money to states that commit sex offenders to such facilities following their prison sentences. The sex offenders selected for such commitment have, according to a *New York Times* investigation of existing programs, not been the most violent. They discovered that committed offenders included exhibitionists, while some rapists were not included, and some were beyond the age where they are considered dangerous. They found, for example, that one confined person was a 102-year-old man in Wisconsin who had memory losses and poor hearing. The average annual cost per person is $41,845.

SOURCE: Davey and Goodnough 2007.

In her analysis of the debates in Congress during the formulation of sex offender legislation, Lynch (2002: 543) highlights the language of the legislators on sex offenders that has tended to stress the gender of these offenders (always described as male) and their characterization as "stranger" and "outsider." This characterization was made despite the fact that only about 3% of sexual abuse offenses against children and about 6% of child murders are committed by strangers. In fact, most children who are sexually abused, neglected, or killed suffer that abuse at the hands of someone in the family (p. 546). When the legislators discussed the Internet and child pornography, they constructed the child sexual predator as a "cyber-predator" "stalking children on the Internet" (p. 547). This enabled some to characterize all material appearing on the Internet as contaminating to children and even to adults, perhaps fulfilling a different agenda than that promoted during debate.

Another aspect of the moral panic engendered by this crime, which is actually very broadly defined, was the legislators' insistence on constructing the sexual predator as uniquely threatening, as compared to an ordinary felon. Speakers referred to unspecified scientific studies showing that those who commit sexual violence against children have the highest rate of recidivism and are unable to exercise any self-control (Lynch 2002: 546). As Lynch puts it, the debates revealed a sense of apprehension by speakers who considered that "the very fiber of traditional family units is under siege by sex offenders" (p. 549). Speakers used language suggesting that families were doing all they could to keep their children safe from pedophiles cruising the Internet and that children had to be protected from inherently vicious child predators.

It is clear that there is a strong current of emotion rather than rationality in the discourse on child predators which emphasizes risk, danger, and the need to impose punitive measures to manage such monsters. A more rational approach would be for legislators to pursue the predominant group of child abusers—those who offend within families—and develop relevant and rational sentencing policy rather than merely focusing on the stranger pedophiles, who constitute a much smaller group of offenders. Lynch (2002: 558) argues that these emotional reactions reflect issues surrounding sexuality, the family, and gender roles, and they appear to be manifestations of a theme that calls for protecting the "idealized version" of the family from harm.

Jonathan Simon (2000: 15) points out in a discussion of Megan's Law that the use of the terms *predatory* and *prey* connotes forms of danger that are nonhuman. He observes also that this language links with terms such as *monster* to define sexual predators as nonhuman and therefore unworthy of any treatment consistent with human dignity. He notes that Megan's Law contains no provision for the treatment of sexual offenders, its aim being one of surveillance, control, and a long-term continuation of punishment. This process of dehumanizing sex offenders and emphasizing the needs and situation of the victim to the exclusion of everything else has the effect of rendering sexual predators "beyond humanity." They become a species apart from the rest of us, and this legitimizes the kind of legislation embodied in Megan's Law. Jenkins (1998: 225) suggests that moral panics on issues such as sexual predators are a cover for a different agenda. In the case of campaigns to protect children, the agenda often involves attempting to reestablish control over those children and the weakened family, perhaps through political or social change. In other words, as he puts it, "preventing sexual acts against the young can be a way of regulating sexual acts by that population" (p. 225).

Superpredators

Tonry (2001: 168) argues that repressive crime policies reflect cyclical patterns of increased intolerance for crime and criminals and that a series of moral panics amplified and expounded by the mass media has interacted with each cyclical period. The moral panics and patterns exacerbate the effects of each other and together establish an environment that welcomes symbolic and expressive crime control policies that pay little attention to their direct or collateral effects. During the 1990s, another moral panic emerged, this time in the form of grave public concern about violence, youth, and so-called superpredators. The campaign against superpredators is well illustrated in the following passage from *Body Count* by William Bennett, John DiIulio, and John Walters (1999):

> America is now home to thickening ranks of juvenile "super-predators"— radically impulsive, brutally remorseless youngsters, including ever more pre-teenage boys, who murder, assault, rape, rob, burglarize, deal deadly drugs, join gun-toting gangs and create communal disorders. They do not fear the stigma of arrest, the pains of imprisonment or the pangs of conscience.

This rhetoric was based on an increase in violence committed by and against youth during the late 1980s and early 1990s. Those predicting the coming wave of superpredators projected this increase in juvenile violence as continuing in a straight line into the future. Although it was correct to say that all forms of youth violence had increased significantly in this period, research indicates that this violence remained located in the group most victimized over time, namely, young African American men (Moore and Tonry 1998: 7). Among the explanations advanced for this increase in violence was the notion that youth violence was associated with the epidemic of crack cocaine use and an increased supply of lethal weapons to youth. Cook and Laub (1998: 27) in their study of youth violence dismissed notions of superpredators; they found that there was a clear indication of increased gun availability during the so-called epidemic and that every category of homicide and other violent crimes showed an increase in gun use.

The supposed epidemic never eventuated, and statistical data showed that arrests for juveniles for violent crimes, especially juveniles aged 10–14, actually declined in 1995 (Brownstein 2000: 122), and that the number of arrests of juveniles for violent crimes had declined by 23% between 1973 and 1995 (p. 128). Significantly, on January 31, 1998, DiIulio published a letter in the *Washington Post* newspaper retracting his earlier statements:

> I have written a number of articles in major newspapers and journals and have testified in Congress, to correct the misperception that a large fraction of juvenile offenders are "super-predators." Also, I have been on record for more than two years now in opposition to efforts to incarcerate violent juveniles in adult facilities. (in Brownstein 2000: 128)

Among the consequences of this particular moral panic has been the movement to have juveniles tried as adults, the call for juveniles older than 16 to be made subject to the death penalty, the call for more punitive punishments for juvenile crime, and moves to ensure that juveniles who "commit the crime, do the time."

Capital Punishment

I have already suggested that the subject of punishment generally is a morality issue. Capital punishment, as a form of punishment, is clearly the preeminent morality issue within the category of punishment. The following discussion will concentrate on the moral arguments advanced about capital punishment, including arguments that are often deployed as part of a policy debate on the subject.

In terms of legal authorization for this particular form of punishment, according to Ernest van den Haag (1985), one of the foremost advocates of capital punishment, the Constitution authorizes the death penalty in the Fifth Amendment when it states that "no person shall be deprived of life, liberty, or property, without due process of law." He argues that the Constitution authorizes deprivation of life provided that due process of law is made available. A contrary view is, however, expressed by one of the leading proponents of the abolition of capital punishment, Hugo Bedau (1997), who does not see the Constitution as authorizing the death penalty but as presenting the government with a choice to either repeal the death penalty or carry it out in accordance with the requirements of due process. Whatever may be the correct position on legal authorization, the fact is that in policy terms the decision about whether capital punishment is on the statute books rests with each state. It follows that states that have no capital punishment provision have made a conscious policy decision, perhaps on moral grounds, to prohibit this particular punishment. Equally, those states that retain or have reintroduced capital punishment have made a similar decision in favor of this punishment.

In 1972, the Supreme Court in *Furman v. Georgia* struck down the death penalty in the 35 states that then imposed capital punishment. Some 4 years later, as a result of three other cases, the Supreme Court authorized capital punishment so long as certain procedural guidelines protecting the accused were adhered to. In response to that ruling, by 1975, 27 states had revised their capital punishment statutes, and by the end of 1997, 29 states in all parts of the country had executed inmates by various means (Culver 1999: 287). Five states accounted for 65% of all executions between 1977 and 1997, and one third of all executions have occurred in the State of Texas. In contrast to the attachment that Texas obviously has to the death penalty, the history of Oregon shows how policy on this issue can change. The death penalty was abolished in Oregon in 1913, restored in 1930, rejected in 1964, and then readopted in 1978 and 1984.

In policy terms, following the Supreme Court's rulings, states have a degree of flexibility in deciding which homicide offenses can be charged as capital offenses. Most states set out a number of special circumstances or aggravating factors that operate to define a murder as capital. For example, there are 18 aggravating circumstances in Alabama, Delaware has 22 special circumstances, and Kansas has 7 "homicide situations" (Culver 1999: 294). This considerable variation in factors and circumstances reflects the policy debate in some states about capital punishment, a debate that, in the view of Simon and Spaulding (1999: 96) can be characterized by "populist punitiveness" and as reflecting the extent to which punishment has been democratized at the political level. In a climate where politicians must beware of being accused of being "soft on crime," few elected officials within or outside the criminal justice system are prepared to argue against the death penalty (Culver 1999: 289). As Bedau (1996: 50) puts it,

> It is now widely assumed that no political candidate in the United States can
> hope to run for President, governor, or other high elected office if he or she

can successfully be targeted as "soft on crime"; the candidate's position on the death penalty has become the litmus test. . . . The death penalty has become part of partisan political campaigning in a manner impossible to have predicted a generation ago.

Culver notes that concerns may arise when the capital punishment debate involves the judiciary because of the likelihood that judicial independence will be compromised by weighing its views to accord with public opinion on the death penalty. In Tennessee, a justice of the Tennessee Supreme Court became the first appellate judge in that state to be defeated in an election for a continuation of her term due largely to her support for the majority opinion in a rape/murder conviction where the death sentence was overturned (Culver 1999: 289). Being "tough on crime" and supporting capital punishment until recently included being "tough on juveniles," because the Supreme Court held in *Stanford v. Kentucky* (1989) that the execution of offenders aged 16 and 17 years is sanctioned by the Constitution. James (2001: 184) argues that executing juvenile offenders not only is contrary to fundamental principles of American justice but also violates customary international law. It should be noted that since 1990 only seven countries have reportedly executed juveniles. In 2005 the Supreme Court revisited the issue of the death penalty for juvenile offenders and decided in *Roper v. Simmons* that the Eighth and Fourteenth amendments of the Constitution forbid the execution of offenders who were under the age of 18 years when their crimes were committed.

During the last 35 years, the number of countries that have abolished the death penalty (abolitionists) has grown more than threefold, numbering at yearend 2001 75 totally abolitionist countries, 14 abolitionist for ordinary crimes, while 105 states have retained the death penalty (Hood 2002: 13). Moreover, as of December 2001, some 34 countries had abolished the death penalty de facto by not implementing it, despite it being a punishment option. There are now only 71 countries that have executed anyone in the last ten years, and apart from the United States, Cuba, Guyana, and some island states of the Caribbean, these countries are all located in the Middle East, Asia, or Africa.

Public Opinion on Capital Punishment

In a comprehensive review of public support for capital punishment, Cullen et al. (2000: 10) note that Americans are most often polled on their attitude to this form of punishment, and that when asked if they support it for convicted murderers, about 7 in 10 respondents reply in the affirmative. This level has remained constant since the early 1970s. However, if respondents are asked not only if they support the death penalty but also whether they would choose the death penalty or life imprisonment without parole, support for capital punishment declines markedly (Cullen et al. 2000: 10). Polling data also reveal that citizens may advocate capital punishment even when the innocent are executed. For example, a Gallup Poll found that 57% of respondents continued to support capital punishment even when asked to take into account that 1 out of 100 people sentenced to death was actually innocent (pp. 11–12). It is interesting to note that in the two decades preceding the 1970s, support for capital punishment was much lower, amounting to 61% in 1936 and 68% in 1953 and declining to 45% in 1965. In 1966, more Americans opposed the death penalty (47%) than favored it (42%) (p. 13). Explanations for this change in the public view include the rising crime rate of the 1960s and fear of crime generated by the politicization of crime, the emergence of racial conflicts, the introduction of tough policies on crime appealing to underlying racist attitudes, a general lack of confidence in the criminal justice system, and a general move away from social causes of offending toward individualistic explanations of crime that emphasize free choice (p. 13).

As to people's motives for supporting the death penalty, research indicates that deterrence and retribution figure highly as justification, along with the notion that it is unfair for taxpayers to keep convicted murderers in prison for life. However, the largest percentage of supporters (74% in one poll) justified the death penalty on the basis that "it removes all possibility that the convicted person can kill again" (Cullen et al. 2000: 19).

Some polls have analyzed how views on the death penalty would be affected if the option of life without parole were available. They have reported that the percentage favoring capital punishment would significantly decline from 71% to 52% (Cullen et al. 2000: 19). Thus, the regular polling showing continued support on this issue gives rise to the possibility that the public may not prefer it to other sentencing options and that people should be asked if they support the death penalty or "other alternative sentences." It is noteworthy that support for an alternative to capital punishment becomes especially strong when respondents are offered the choice of a sentence of life without parole with restitution to the victim. This option was favored by 60.7%, compared to 31.6% favoring the death penalty (p. 20). As for those who design the laws, a 1991 survey of New York legislators found that even with the option of life imprisonment without parole and restitution, 58% still preferred the death penalty. In the same survey, it was noted that legislators misconceived the views of the public, reporting that among their constituents they believed 73% would support the death penalty over the alternative of life imprisonment (p. 21). The obvious conclusion is that legislators appear to be a significant barrier to substituting alternatives for capital punishment. It is worth noting that although many Americans continue to support the death penalty, the ability to use DNA to ascertain with certainty the identity of perpetrators and the growing number of persons found to be innocent after years on death row based on DNA evidence has begun to influence the public discourse about the legitimacy of this form of penalty.

What impact does religion have on support for the death penalty? Polls show that 61% of Americans believe that religion is a "very important" part of their lives (Cullen et al. 2000: 24) and that 96% of Americans say they believe in God. One study found that white fundamentalists (those with fundamentalist religious membership or beliefs) are most supportive of capital punishment, whereas African American fundamentalists are less supportive. Research suggests that religious fundamentalism and biblical literalism are positively related to punitive attitudes, including retribution for crime, support for tough criminal legislation and harsh sentencing, and favoring more severe treatment of juvenile offenders (p. 25).

What are the moral arguments usually advanced against capital punishment in policy debates? The core moral arguments against capital punishment are usually formulated as follows (Bedau 1997; van den Haag 1985):

1. The death penalty has been distributed in a discriminatory manner because African American or poorer defendants are more likely to be executed than equally guilty others, especially when the victim is white (Russell 1998: 134).

2. Miscarriages of justice occur and the innocent are executed.

3. The death penalty expresses a desire for vengeance—a motive too volatile and indifferent to the concept of justice to be maintained in a civilized society.

4. Capital punishment is considered to be degrading to human dignity and inconsistent with the principle of the sanctity of life.

5. It is morally wrong to authorize the killing of some criminals when there is an adequate alternative punishment of imprisonment.

Each of these arguments will now be considered:

1. The death penalty has been distributed in a discriminatory manner because African American or poorer defendants are more likely to be executed than equally guilty others, especially when the victim is white (Russell 1998: 134).

Walker, Spohn, and DeLone (2000: 231) make a case for the existence of racial disparity in the application of the death penalty, pointing to the fact that although African Americans make up only 10–12% of the population, they are disproportionately represented among those sentenced to death and executed. In addition, they suggest there is compelling evidence that those who murder whites—and particularly African Americans who murder whites—are disproportionately sentenced to death.

2. Miscarriages of justice occur and the innocent are executed.

The American Bar Association (ABA) has urged the appointment of experienced, competent, and adequately compensated trial counsel for death penalty cases and has lobbied for the adoption of its *Guidelines for the Appointment and Performance of Counsel in Death Penalty Cases.* These guidelines call for the appointment of two experienced attorneys at each stage of a capital case, such appointment to be made by an authority capable of identifying lawyers who possess the necessary professional skills. Clearly, the ABA believes that standard professional qualifications are insufficient for capital cases. No state has fully embraced the ABA recommended system, and it is a notorious fact that unqualified and undercompensated lawyers continue to represent capital clients. In spite of these deficiencies, in 1996 the federal Antiterrorism and Effective Death Penalty Act undermined the ability of death row inmates to use federal habeas corpus procedures to have their cases reviewed in federal courts. It also removed federal funding for postconviction defender organizations that provided legal representation for many prisoners contesting their sentences (Sarat 1999: 9).

The process involved in appealing capital cases varies from state to state, but according to Haines (1996: 56–57), the process is typically as follows: Death sentences are automatically appealed to the highest state court, with appeals in this first round being limited to the trial record and to procedural errors. If the state court affirms the conviction, the prisoner can appeal to the U.S. Supreme Court for review, but the Supreme Court generally agrees to hear only 2–3% of these appeals. If a request for a review is denied, a second cycle of appeals can be brought, in this case not limited to the trial record. These appeals are filed in the lower court; then the higher state courts, and finally again in the U.S. Supreme Court. During this round of appeals, an inmate is able to argue that he or she was provided with an incompetent defense or, for example, that there is newly discovered evidence showing innocence. If, after these two rounds of appeals, the prisoner is still under sentence of death, he or she can file for a federal habeas corpus review, during which alleged violations of constitutional rights can be raised. Habeas corpus proceedings work their way through the federal system from the district court to the circuit court of appeals and finally again to the U.S. Supreme Court.

There has been concern about miscarriages of justice in capital cases since at least the 1820s, and in 1987 Bedau and Radelet argued that some 350 persons had been wrongly convicted of potentially capital offenses between 1900 and 1985 (in Haines 1996: 88). There is further evidence in the form of a congressional subcommittee report that at least 45 death sentences were in error in the period 1976–1993, and numerous incidents of wrongful convictions have come to the attention of the courts and the media in the last decade since the advent of DNA testing. In one case in 1989, a prisoner spent 12 years in a Texas prison and came within 3 days of lethal injection before his conviction was overturned. The court ruled that the prosecutors had used perjured testimony and had knowingly suppressed evidence in order to obtain a conviction for killing a police officer. In another case, an African American school custodian was wrongly convicted of the rape and murder of a 16-year-old white girl. The errors comprised forensic evidence suggesting the crime was committed by a white man, which was never mentioned to the jury and was "misplaced," and evidence pointing to a different suspect, which the police ignored (Haines 1996: 88).

Those in favor of capital punishment characterize these cases as indicating how well the criminal justice system's procedural safeguards work, but this tends to ignore the fact that not only is the convicted person deprived of years of freedom while waiting on death row, but he or she must also deal with the mental consequences of waiting to be put to death. The activities of the Innocence Project, particularly in DNA testing, have continued to reveal errors and cases of innocence. In *United States v. Quinones* (2002), Judge Rakoff argued that the use of capital punishment is unconstitutional, because there is no longer any certainty of a person's guilt in a capital offense. He contended that advances in DNA testing render capital punishment problematic, because DNA testing is able to prove absolutely that some condemned persons are actually innocent. In 2004, Congress passed the Justice for All Act establishing federal prisoners' access to DNA evidence for a minimum of five years following their conviction. The act allocates funds to deal with a reported backlog of 350,000 untested DNA samples in rape cases (Sarat 2005: 45).

After many years of hearing death penalty cases, in February 1984, Justice Harry Blackmun of the Supreme Court announced, "From this day forward I no longer shall tinker with the machinery of death." He did not reject the death penalty because of its violence, but rather focused on the procedures applying to death sentences, explaining that

> despite the efforts of the states and the courts to devise legal formulas and procedural rules . . . the death penalty remains fraught with arbitrariness, discrimination, caprice, and mistake. . . . Experience has taught us that the Constitutional goal of eliminating arbitrariness and discrimination from the administration of death . . . can never be achieved without compromising an equally essential component of fundamental fairness—individualized sentencing. (in Sarat 1999: 7–8)

For all intents and purposes, therefore, Justice Blackmun concluded that the death penalty cannot be administered in accordance with the Constitution and that no procedural rules or regulations can save it from its deficiencies.

3. The death penalty expresses a desire for vengeance—a motive too volatile and indifferent to the concept of justice to be maintained in a civilized society.

The notion that revenge can stand as a motive for official policy on punishment is entirely inconsistent with a rational system of justice conducted by the state on behalf of society (Bedau 1999: 50). Proponents of the death penalty tend to suggest that they favor its application, not for revenge but for retribution. Those against the death penalty respond that if we are to support capital punishment for murder under this retributive principle, we should equally require rapists to be raped and torturers to be tortured, forms of punishment any civilized society would be reluctant to carry out. In addition, they argue that the extreme punishment of life in prison without parole can be imposed for murder, and this in itself is retributive. As explained in Chapter 3, in 1972 and 1976, the U.S. Supreme Court stated that it considers retribution "a legitimate justification for capital punishment" (*Gregg v. Georgia* 1976; *Furman v. Georgia* 1972).

4. Capital punishment is considered to be degrading to human dignity and inconsistent with the principle of the sanctity of life.

The argument is that human life, having infinite value, should be respected and protected and that even murderers' lives should be valued in the same way. Advocates of this position are absolutists and would be against capital punishment no matter which arguments are put forward about the conduct of a particular murderer. Bedau (1999: 42) suggests that abolitionists who rely on this argument should insist that the burden of argument lies on those who favor the death sentence. In other words, for the purposes of assessing punishment, society ought to assume that everyone's life is valuable and that all our lives have equal value.

Associated with the value of life argument is the view that we are morally forbidden to take the life of a murderer, because he or she has an inalienable right to life which is violated by sentencing a person to death and executing that person. This argument is normative, and again Bedau (1999) suggests that the burden of argument should be on those who would kill through capital punishment to justify that killing. The notion that this form of punishment violates the fundamental right to life has been endorsed by the Council of Europe and the European Union, which have declared that "the death penalty has no legitimate place in the penal systems of modern civilized societies, and that its application may well be compared with torture and be seen as inhuman and degrading punishment" (Hood 2001: 331).

In relation to human dignity, Bedau (1997) has extended Justice Brennan's concurring opinion in *Furman v. Georgia,* in which the justice identified four principles explaining why the death penalty was an affront to human dignity. The principles expounded in that dissenting decision are that a punishment must not by its severity be degrading to human dignity, that a punishment must never be inflicted in a wholly arbitrary fashion, that a severe punishment must not be unacceptable to contemporary society, and that the unnecessary infliction of suffering is also offensive to human dignity. Bedau supplements these principles by suggesting that it is also an affront to the dignity of a person to be forced to undergo harm at the hands of another when entirely at his or her mercy, as is always the case with legal punishment. He further suggests that it offends a person's dignity when the person imposing punishment is free to arbitrarily choose which offenders are to be punished very severely, when all deserve the same severe punishment if any do. Finally, he proposes that it is offensive to the dignity of a person to be subjected to such a punishment.

5. It is morally wrong to authorize the killing of some criminals when there is an adequate alternative punishment of imprisonment.

Bedau (1997) argues that to do so would be an affront to human dignity. Associated with this argument is that which insists there is no convincing evidence that the rate of murder is consistently lower when the death penalty can be invoked and enforced. The death penalty has not proved to be a more effective deterrent than the alternative sanction of life in prison without parole, and it therefore constitutes an irrational burden within a rational system of criminal justice (Hood 2001: 332). Finally, as Beccaria noted as early as 1764, the death penalty is counterproductive in terms of its moral message, because it legitimizes the very behavior—killing—that the law seeks to repress. Its effect, therefore, is to undermine the legitimacy and moral authority of the entire criminal justice system (in Hood 2001: 332).

In policy terms, as we have seen, retribution, as opposed to rehabilitation, is now cited as the appropriate justification for punishment, and the intuitive anger felt toward criminals, often now labeled as monsters and predators, can be seen expressed in the notion of capital punishment as an abstract policy. Showing one's support for the death penalty is a symbolic act announcing that one is a supporter of a "tough on crime" policy approach and favors holding criminals morally responsible for their actions. In the political arena, it seems highly unlikely that there will be any widespread movement toward abolition, but abolitionists have recently been comforted by the Supreme Court's decision prohibiting the death penalty when the prisoner can be shown to be mentally challenged or under 18 years of age. Abolitionists must rely on the Supreme Court to continue this approach of eroding the death penalty by stages as has happened in the case of executing juvenile offenders.

Private Prisons

For many years, certain institutions concerned with offenders have been de facto privatized, because juvenile institutional facilities and adult community facilities were contracted out early on to the private sector. For example, in Massachusetts, juvenile institutions changed from being a network of state-run institutions in 1969 to a series of community-based programs and facilities by 1974. The Massachusetts Division of Youth Services operates all community-based facilities through private contractors (Logan 1990: 15).

Logan (1990: 13) defines private prisons as "those that are privately owned, operated, or managed, under contract to government" and Shichor (1995: 2) regards private prisons as "prisons or other institutions of confinement (jails, immigration and nationalization service facilities, detention centers, and secured juvenile justice facilities) operated and managed by private corporations for profit." Adult community facilities managed and operated by private contractors include shelters and halfway houses, while institutional facilities include detention and diagnostic centers and training schools (p. 14). In addition, the Immigration and Naturalization Service has for many years contracted facilities to detain illegal aliens awaiting deportation. The most recent form of privatization has been the contracting of adult confinement facilities. By mid-1989, about a dozen private companies were running almost two dozen adult confinement institutions in about one dozen states (p. 20). Prison privatization has spread to other countries, including the United Kingdom, Australia, and Canada, and is being actively promoted in South Africa.

The proponents of prison privatization tend to justify their support by advancing pragmatic, rational arguments that emphasize the supposed economic benefit of contracting. Those against privatization stress the ethical and moral implications. This discussion will confine itself to the ethical implications, which fall broadly into four categories of questions:

1. Is it appropriate for imprisonment to be administered by anyone other than the state and its employees?

2. Is the profit motive compatible with the task of imprisoning offenders?

3. Does the existence of private prisons, in effect, create a demand for imprisonment that needs to be satisfied by greater levels of imprisonment than would otherwise be the case?

4. How do private prisons cope with the issue of use of deadly force?

These questions will now be considered:

1. Is it appropriate for imprisonment to be administered by anyone other than the state and its employees?

A core issue in the ethical debate about private prisons is the role of the state in administering punishment. As Lippke puts it,

> Punishment has been seen as a state function in order to limit if not eliminate the influence of private interests over the detection, trial, and sanctioning of law breakers—in short, to ensure that all individuals are treated equally before the law. (1997: 26)

As already explained in Chapter 5, a legal punishment is defined as that which is imposed and administered by an authority established by the legal system against which the offense has been committed. Punishment involves the state, because the legal rules that constitute offenses are created by a legislature that operates in the name of the state. Theories concerning the relationship between the individual and the state involve the notion of the social contract. Hobbes argued that individuals freely transfer their rights to a powerful authority, the head of the state, who is thereby enabled to ensure that those individuals keep their promises and contracts. In exchange for this surrender of rights, the head of the state provides security and protection for citizens. John Locke argued along somewhat similar lines that individuals give up their political power to secure order, but he maintained that this power remains with those individuals who collectively constitute society. The task of the state is to protect individuals, but if the state fails in this task, individuals have the right to dissolve the state. In other words, Locke argued that the transfer of powers to the state operates conditionally on the state maintaining the life and liberty of its citizens (Shichor 1995: 47).

Classical liberal thinking argues that in spite of this social contract, political power remains with the individuals who have delegated their powers to the state and that therefore ultimate power remains in the hands of the people. Consistent with this approach is the ideal of the "minimal state," which sees the state using a restricted coercive power. Nozick (1974: ix) argues that this coercive power is limited, for example, for the purpose of citizens giving aid to others or for the purpose of prohibiting activities for the good or protection of people. The notion of privatization stresses the role of the state as minimal, and in fact questions the very principle of a state monopoly on crime control and punishment.

Opposed to classical liberal philosophy is the view that the state has the sole right to use legal coercive power (Weber 1964). Weber argues that offenders violate laws, and those laws are created by representatives of the state, and in fact in themselves constitute the state. Therefore, it is the state that possesses sole authority to use coercive force for punishment, because its sovereignty, based on the supremacy of the rule of law, has been violated by the criminal act (Reisig and Pratt 2000: 214). Rawls supports this view, arguing that in a liberal society, coercive agencies must be under the control of the state, because rational individuals would not endorse a political system that allows coercive force to be used privately. However, he sees the state as having the right to delegate lower-level functions of the state to private contractors if it serves the interests of society (in Reisig and Pratt 2000: 214).

Related to this debate is the constitutional question of whether, and to what extent, the state may delegate to private entities the power of punishing law breakers. On this issue, in 1986 the American Bar Association criticized private prisons, expressing the view that "incarceration is an inherent function of the government and that the government should not abdicate this responsibility by turning over prison operation to private industry" (in Shichor 1995: 52). The ABA therefore takes the position that there is a principle that prevents the state from delegating the administration and control of punishment to private contractors and that the scale of delegation of state authority is irrelevant.

Those who argue in favor of privatization point to the fact that the state has the power to delegate its functions and has done so for many years in the field of punishment through juvenile programs and institutions and adult correctional programs. However, it can also be argued that the prison, as a total institution with almost complete control over inmates' lives, is in a special position in the field of punishment. In other words, the high level of coercion exercised by the state militates against any extensive delegation of its power to punish.

Associated with this issue of state delegation is the specific issue of the quasi-judicial functions exercised by prison administrations. There are a number of stages and issues in the process of imprisonment that give rise to quasi-judicial duties. For example, the term of imprisonment may depend on parole decisions, and the computation of good time and of release dates relies on administration reports about the conduct of inmates. Also, disciplinary action may have to be taken against inmates, and generally reports about inmate behavior are significant in the decision-making process. Those who favor privatization argue that proper government oversight and monitoring can ensure that these substantive and due process issues can be properly addressed. However, this tends to ignore the fact that the administration and staff of private prisons owe a duty to the company that employs them and may give loyalty and allegiance to the company rather than to a set of rules imposed by the state responsible for a particular private prison.

Opponents of privatization raise the issue of the symbolism surrounding punishment in the form of the uniform and insignia of correctional staff and the judiciary that express the public nature of punishment. Supporters of privatization argue, on the other hand, that symbolism is less important than substance and that those working in corrections are not elected by the people or politically appointed and are seen as symbols of the state's role in punishment only by virtue of their jobs (Shichor 1995: 55).

2. Is the profit motive compatible with the task of imprisoning offenders?

Those against the privatization of prisons find it a cause of concern that private corporations are attempting to make a profit on the punishment of people by running prisons. Shichor (1995: 259) argues that the government ought not to create such opportunities for private profit, but DiIulio (1990) does not think the profit motive amounts to a moral issue in the debate. The American Civil Liberties Union has argued that "the profit motive is incompatible with doing justice" (in Logan 1990: 72). This position essentially questions whether a private corporation is likely to put its own interests and welfare ahead of the interests of justice when it views the profit motive as crucial and therefore argues its incompatibility with the interests of justice. Historically, the prison system has, however, profited from the use of prison labor employed by private contractors and, particularly in the Southern states, leasing out prisoners to corporations was a standard feature of the prison system. In this sense, therefore, profit and incarceration have a long tradition of association, and it makes little sense to suggest that the entire task of managing prisoners is somehow more morally objectionable than profiteering from the labor of inmates.

3. Does the existence of private prisons in effect create a demand for imprisonment that needs to be satisfied by greater levels of imprisonment than would otherwise be the case?

The argument here is that the corporations running private prisons may seek to influence policy makers and administrators through lobbying and associated activities to ensure that private prisons continue to be built and that they continue to profit from a high rate of incarceration. Originally, privatization was seen as a solution to the immense overcrowding caused by a deliberate policy of incapacitation and was intended to be a supplement to the existing prison system. The argument against privatization is that expanding the state's resources to punish will increase state control and that large numbers of people who would otherwise not be incarcerated will come under state control. In other words, an expansion of the prison system will be self-perpetuating; if prisons are built, they will be filled (Shichor 1995: 61).

Some now see corporate involvement in crime control, that is, the involvement of private industry in crime control generally, and in particular, the continuation of high incarceration rates, as part of an evolving criminal justice industrial complex. In states like New York where prisons have been constructed in rural areas, they provide in some cases almost the only form of local employment and have replaced dying local industries (Christie 2000: 137). There is a powerful political and economic argument (often made by correctional unions) that these prisons must be supported as a source of employment and local economic activity. While unions may make this argument, it is easy to see how private corporations running prisons can ally themselves with such views and advocate them themselves. As Christie (2000: 140–141) points out, the prison industry absorbs a large part of the workforce, and he estimates that the crime control industry employed 4% of the entire labor force in 1999. As of January 1998, 60 prisons were being constructed, and in 1997, 31 new institutions were opened in 15 different jurisdictions. Between 1988 and 1995, Texas added 90,000 state beds in prisons at a cost of $2.3 billion (Merlo and Benekos 2000: 97). In June 1993, some 20,000 adult prisoners were confined in private correctional facilities, making up a 1.5% market share of the prison population; by the end of 1997, the number of prisoners in private facilities had grown to almost 80,000, with a market share of 5.9% (p. 98). By yearend 2005 there were 107,447 federal and state prisoners in private facilities across the nation, up 7% from 2004 (Harrison and Beck 2006: 6). Almost half of those inmates (51,823) were held in private prisons in southern states, and of those, more than 17,500 were held in Texas.

Lilly and Knepper (1992: 175) have analyzed the characteristics of this criminal justice industrial complex and have shown that participants in the field of corrections have a close working relationship; that there is an overlap between the interests of corporations, unions, and agencies, for example, in terms of influence and the transfer of personnel (many employed in private prisons as guards and administrators were formerly public employees in the same field); that this complex operates with little public scrutiny; and that the participants define themselves as acting in the public interest by referring to their role in the punishment of law breakers.

4. How do private prisons cope with the issue of use of deadly force?

Chapter 6 discussed the legal position on the use of force by prison guards, pointing out that there are severe restrictions on its use. Those opposed to private prisons argue that, as a sensitive and complex issue, the use of force by employees of private companies against inmates raises questions about the legitimacy of any exercise of force by those employees. Some believe that private companies will try to cut costs through inadequate staffing and training of private prison staff and that this will result in a greater willingness to use force to maintain order (Shichor 1995: 102). It is unrealistic to argue that private prison staff should be prohibited from using any force, because this might endanger their own safety and is not a realistic option. If it were to be prohibited, this would presumably mean that state employees would have to be located in the prison and called upon for the use of force when needed. This, however, would defeat the purpose of privatization and add significantly to the organizational problems within the prison. Another suggestion is that private staff should be able to use nondeadly force under a set of rules reserving the use of deadly force for government employees. Again, however, common sense suggests that this would be unworkable in practice. This issue has only recently become significant, because private companies have only lately become involved in managing maximum security prisons and housing offenders considered violent (Harding 1998: 635). The private sector was able to compete for the management of a maximum security prison for the first time in 1990 when bids were requested for a federal detention center in Kansas, and as of December 1996, private contractors were operating seven maximum security prisons (see Case Study 7.2).

CASE STUDY 7.2 PRIVATE PRISONS— A GOOD POLICY CHOICE?

Report to the Attorney General: Inspection and Review of the Northeast Ohio Correctional Center

On November 25, 1998, the Department of Justice concluded a report to the U.S. Attorney General reviewing the management and operations of the Northeast Ohio Correctional Center in Youngstown, Ohio, owned and operated by the Corrections Corporation of America (CCA).

The report cited "fundamental breakdowns attributable to the institution and corporate management in meeting their most basic security missions" (p. 19). Among the major events that occurred at Youngstown prison were the following:

- The escape of six inmates
- Two homicides, including one that took place between known enemies in the high-security unit

- The stabbing of approximately 17 inmates as well as many other serious assaults on staff and inmates
- The discovery of numerous homemade weapons—30 were discovered in the first 2 months of operation
- The facility being forced to operate under full or partial lockdown to prevent further incidents

Among the particular issues of concern noted in the report was the absence of experienced midlevel managers and uniformed supervisors. Many persons placed in supervisory and senior positions lacked the experience and training required. For example, among the 30 sergeants, 16 had no prior correctional experience, and among the 9 lieutenants, 2 had no prior correctional experience.

The practical arrangements for monitoring CCA performance at Youngstown involved the Department of Corrections hiring a consultant firm to monitor the contract to CCA on a less than full time basis. No contract monitors were placed on site. However, finally, an experienced deputy warden was placed at the facility for monitoring purposes.

The report indicates that within 2 weeks of the arrival of the first inmates at the facility, serious disturbances occurred due in some cases to missing personal property of inmates, causing inmates to make threats to staff. One incident involved a supervisor ordering three canisters of gas to be dropped in each housing unit, causing the inmates to pour water on them, place garbage cans over them, and throw them into the showers. Inmates began making weapons, and two inmates were stabbed within a month.

SOURCE: Department of Justice 1998

Disenfranchising Inmates of Their Voting Rights

According to The Sentencing Project (2008: 1), all states other than Maine and Vermont prohibit inmates from casting a vote while incarcerated for a felony. The Sentencing Project estimates that "5.3 million Americans, or 1 in 41 adults, have currently or permanently lost their voting rights as a result of a felony conviction." The organization points out that 13% or 1.4 million African American men are disenfranchised at a rate 7 times the national average and that 676,730 women are ineligible to vote based on a felony conviction. Two million white Americans (Hispanic and non-Hispanic) are disenfranchised and 1 in 4 African American men are permanently disenfranchised in five states that deny the vote to ex-offenders. Felons on parole may not vote in 33 states, and in 29 of these felony probationers are also excluded. Seven states disenfranchise categories of ex-offenders or disqualify them for specified periods of time after which they may seek restoration of their right, and six states permanently disqualify ex-offenders (Kleinig and Murtagh 2005: 217–218). It is estimated that on the basis of present incarceration rates, some 40% of African American males will come to be permanently disenfranchised in the states that exercise that option. Significantly, in the 2000 presidential elections, Florida contained an estimated 600,000 ex-offenders who could not vote. Disenfranchisement has an ancient history and in modern times reflects the Common Law notion of attainder, under which offenders could lose all their civil rights (p. 218). Under the U.S. Constitution, the Fourteenth Amendment provided for disenfranchisement for "participation in rebellion, or other crime" (p. 219). The Supreme Court in 1974 interpreted the reference to other crime to allow disenfranchisement for any crime (p. 219).

What justifies the notion of disenfranchising felons? For example, although many would consider the right to vote a crucial activity in a democracy, only 51.3% of those eligible to vote actually voted in the 2000 presidential elections (Kleinig and Murtagh 2005: 219). Arguments that are used to support disenfranchisement include these:

- *The social contract argument.* The idea here is that the felon rejects established authority and has rejected the constraints of the social contract. Given that attitude, such a person ought not to be allowed to participate in the electoral process (p. 220). Even if this argument is accepted, it does not necessarily justify a perpetual prohibition extending beyond imprisonment.
- *So-called electoral purity.* The Alabama Supreme Court in a case in 1884 cited the importance of the "purity of the ballot box" (p. 222). The idea here is that only worthy persons are fit to cast a vote, that allowing convicted felons or ex-felons to participate would undermine the electoral process, and that adverse consequences could flow from allowing felons to participate. For example, it might call into question the legitimacy of the outcome (p. 224).

Kleinig and Murtagh (2005: 227) argue that there may be some offenses that justify disenfranchisement, such as electoral offenses and offenses representing a rejection of the state's authority, that is, offenses committed by those on death row or sentenced to life imprisonment. They suggest, however, that there should be no automatic presumption of forfeiture during a period of imprisonment. They offer three arguments in favor of prisoners having the right to vote:

- Voting would encourage prisoners to take a more active role in society as they reintegrate back into it.
- Ethically, it can be argued that those affected by decisions ought to have some say in the making of those decisions. For example, the concerns of prisoners and their interest in events affecting the prison system are not currently considered.
- If prisoners were able to vote, politicians would need to take account of their concerns, and they might reveal the serious deficiencies that exist in penal policy and practice. (Kleinig and Murtagh 2005: 229–230)

Several questions are raised by this issue. For example, is disenfranchisement part of the punishment for the crime or is it a civil sanction that is a consequence of the crime? Is it morally justifiable as a policy and practice, especially when the contemporary effect is to disenfranchise significant numbers of African Americans?

Conversely, can we really argue that the franchise is such a crucial attribute of democracy when only slightly more than half of those eligible to vote actually voted in the year 2000? Can there be any justification for disenfranchising anyone permanently and if so under what circumstances?

Box 7.4 gives an example of an additional ethical consideration for the treatment of prisoners.

A CLOSER LOOK

BOX 7.4
Cutting Prison Time for Organ Donors: Is This Ethical?

South Carolina legislators are considering a law that would allow prisoners to donate organs or bone marrow in exchange for a reduced sentence. Questions about the ethics of this proposal include a comment from the executive director of Donate Life South Carolina who is reported to have said, "It really muddies the water about motive. We want to keep it a truly altruistic act." Given the coercive environment of the prison and the reward for donating organs is this not akin to selling body parts?

SOURCE: Adcox 2007.

Summary

Policy making in criminal justice usually takes the form of policies and legislation relating to crime control. Justifications for particular policies might be ideological, empirical, or ethical. Those based on ethical grounds result from an analysis of what is "right and wrong" or "good or bad" in a moral sense for a particular issue. Ethics fits into criminal justice policy making in two forms. Firstly, there is a general issue in policy making that those who formulate policies should act ethically; second, there is an ethical responsibility in making policies about subjects like punishment. As Tonry (2006: 53) notes, a "legislator or governor who proposes or enacts policy changes he knows will not achieve their purported aims and will, if enacted, cause new injustices, because he hopes it will help him get reelected, is behaving unethically." This kind of policy making can be termed "morality policy making." Most policy making results from a cost–benefit analysis that does not include ethical models. A policy that is considered unethical would include reacting to events by formulating irrational, capricious, and arbitrary policies. In the criminal justice policy field, it is possible to link the existence of moral panics and morality policy making. A moral panic occurs when an event arises that is defined as a threat to the values of society—for example, the sale and consumption of drugs or the existence of sexual predators. These events are promoted by the media and engender public concern and political action, usually in the form of legislation. It is here that morality policy and moral panics produce unethical legislation. For example, the present situation of mass imprisonment is not the result of a democratically agreed upon and analytically constructed policy but has emerged from a set of converging policies and decisions that do not form a rational and coherent response.

The views of the public about crime and crime control are also linked to moral panics. Surveys show that the public has a general tendency toward punitive measures, and that Americans regard imprisonment as the most appropriate form of punishment for most crimes. There has been steady support for capital punishment since the 1970s, and those seeking public elective office are expected by the public to support the continuation of this form of punishment. Political and media attention to certain categories of crime has resulted in mandatory minimum sentencing, the War on Drugs, truth in sentencing laws, and legislation designed to combat sexual predators and superpredators. Capital punishment is a major issue of morality policy, and the ethical arguments for and against capital punishment are discussed in this chapter.

A significant criminal justice policy issue is the development of private prisons. This raises a set of questions involving ethical issues, such as should imprisonment be administered by anyone other than the state, is the profit motive compatible with the state's right to punish through imprisonment, does the existence of private prisons fuel a demand for further and greater levels of imprisonment, and how do private prisons resolve ethical issues concerned with the use of force? These issues are also considered in this chapter.

DISCUSSION QUESTIONS

1. Why is ethics important in criminal justice policy making? How do unethical and ethical policy-making decisions differ?

2. Explain the consequences that have resulted from one policy choice in the field of criminal justice, choosing from the following: the War on Drugs, truth in sentencing, sexual predators.

3. Discuss the ethics of the California law that gives prosecutors the right to decide whether the third-strike offense should be charged as a felony or a misdemeanor while providing no oversight of prosecutor charging decisions.

4. Outline the moral arguments against capital punishment.

5. How important is public opinion in criminal justice policy making? Explain by referencing two examples.

6. Why is it considered unethical by some for the state to abdicate its responsibility for the administration of prisons to private companies?

7. Comment on the ethics of prisoner disenfranchisement in light of the fact, for example, that if such disenfranchisement is permanent, more than 40% of the African American male population will have no say in the policies and laws that have a significant effect on them.

WEB RESOURCES

Center for Criminal Justice Policy Research. http://www.cj.neu.edu/center_for_criminal_justice_policy_research/index.php

Common Sense for Drug Policy. http://www.csdp.org

Criminal Justice Policy Coalition (also includes information on internships). http://www.cjpc.org

Criminal Justice Policy Foundation. http://www.cjpf.org

Department of Defense Task Force on Domestic Violence: www.dtic.mil/domestic violence/

Families Against Mandatory Sentencing: http://www.famm.org

Federal Prison Policy Project: http://www.fppp.org

Justice Policy Institute. http://www.justicepolicy.org/article.php?list=type&type=109

The Justice Project. http://www.thejusticeproject.org

PolicyLink (Leadership for Policy). http://www.policylink.org/Research/Leadership/

Stanford Criminal Justice Center. http://www.law.stanford.edu/program/centers/scjc/

The Sentencing Project: http://www.sentencingproject.org

Violence Against Women Online Resources. http://www.vaw.umn.edu; http://www.ojp.usdoj.gov/vawo/

CHAPTER 8

Ethics and the "War on Terrorism"

The purpose of this chapter is to explore some of the ethical issues associated with the "War on Terrorism" that was declared following the events of 9/11. Establishing a normative and ethical approach toward countering terrorism may not seem to be salient to some in the face of the overwhelming events of 9/11. Nevertheless, as indicated in the first chapter of this volume, ethics is about how we "ought" to live, and "ethical considerations are central to decisions involving discretion, force and due process that require people to make enlightened moral judgments" (Banks 2004: 4). Just as there are normative standards about how to conduct wars (the so-called just war) and rules about what actions may be taken in time of war against combatants and civilians caught up in the conflict (the Geneva Conventions), so there are normative considerations applicable to the War on Terrorism.

This chapter will examine a number of the ethical issues arising out of the War on Terrorism that began on September 11, 2001. It will not address the issue of whether terrorism can ever be morally justified, an issue that has been the subject of scholarly comment elsewhere (see, for example, Corlett 2003; Frey and Morris 1991; Held 1991; Narveson 1991; Steinhoff 2005). Rather, the chapter will explore the following issues:

- The meaning of "terrorism"
- Why the United States responded to the events of 9/11 by declaring a War on Terrorism instead of treating the terrorist attack as a criminal justice or law enforcement issue
- The ethical boundaries of counterterrorist operations
- The issue of the morally justifiable constraints and restrictions that a government should be permitted to impose on its citizens in order to succeed in the War on Terrorism
- In the context of events post-9/11, the ethics of applying torture to suspected terrorists

Defining Terrorism

Fundamental to any discussion of terrorism is an understanding of the meaning and scope of the term. Unfortunately, the definition of terrorism is problematic, and there exist a number of "official" and legal definitions as well as those suggested by researchers and commentators. Some explanations of the meaning of terrorism focus only on terrorism carried out by individuals and groups and ignore state terrorism altogether, others emphasize the political objective of terrorist acts, and still others frame terrorist acts as criminal events and downplay the political motivations. One clearly understood factor amongst all of these approaches is that terrorism is a method or means of achieving an objective. It is not an aim or objective in itself.

One definition proposed by academic commentator Paul Wilkinson (2001: 12–13) is that

> terrorism is the systematic use of coercive intimidation, usually to service political ends. It is used to create and exploit a climate of fear among a wider target group than the immediate victims of the violence, and to publicize a cause, as well as to coerce a target to acceding to the terrorists' claims.

Here, there seems to be a clear focus on the political nature of terrorism. By contrast, the United Nations Security Council in Resolution 1566 of October 2004, condemning terrorist acts, adopts more of a criminal perspective with no explicit mention of political objectives and also co-opts definitions in international agreements on terrorism:

> Criminal acts, including those against civilians, committed with the intent to cause death or serious bodily injury, or taking of hostages, with the purpose to provoke a state of terror in the general public or in a group of persons or particular persons, intimidate a population or compel a government or an international organization to do or to abstain from doing any act, which constitutes offenses within the scope of and as defined in the international conventions and protocols relating to terrorism. (Wilkinson 2006: 2)

Terrorists are motivated by political objectives, and while criminals employ violence (often similar to that of terrorists like kidnapping, murder, arson) to achieve their ends, their motivation is quite different from that of terrorists, because criminals commonly act solely to secure a material gain. As discussed later, the United States regards terrorism not as criminal activity but as a "form of war" and "as a threat to national security" (Whittaker 2003: 262).

In the United Kingdom, terrorism is defined by the Terrorism Act of 2000 as meaning the use or threat of action designed to influence the government or intimidate the public where the use or threat is intended to advance a political, religious, or ideological cause (Wilkinson 2006: 3). Action constitutes terrorism if it involves serious violence against a person or serious damage to property, endangers a life, creates a serious risk to the health or safety of the public, or is designed to interfere or disrupt an electronic system.

The U.S. Code Title 22, Section 2656, avoids any reference to state terrorism, limits itself to violence, and introduces a separate notion of international terrorism:

> The term terrorism means premeditated politically motivated violence perpetrated against noncombatant targets by sub-national groups or clandestine agents, usually intended to influence an audience. The term international terrorism means terrorism involving citizens or the territory of more than one country. The term terrorist group means any group practicing, or that has significant subgroups that practice, international terrorism. (Wilkinson 2006: 3)

The FBI relies on a definition in the U.S. Code of Federal Regulations that focuses on coercion, unlawfulness, and offenses against property and includes social as well as political objectives:

> Terrorism is the unlawful use of force and violence against person or property to intimidate or coerce a government, the civilian population, or any segment thereof, in further of political or social objectives. (Kapitan 2005: 21)

The U.S. Defense Department defines terrorism as

> the unlawful use or threatened use of force or violence against individuals or property to coerce or intimidate governments or societies, often to achieve political, religious, or ideological objectives. (Kapitan 2005: 21)

This definition includes a wider range of objectives than that used by the FBI and also encompasses threats as well as actual use of violence.

These multiple definitions demonstrate Freeman's (2005: 44) point that there is no "correct" definition of terrorism and that the term bundles together a multiplicity of acts and motivations. According to Paul Hoffman (2004: 938), the chair of the International Executive Committee of Amnesty International, the tendency to give a broad and expansive definition to "terrorism" has caused nonterrorist activity to be caught up within the prohibition and has provided a basis for repressive regimes to conduct so-called antiterrorist campaigns.

As an organizing concept, the term *terrorism* conveys a moral judgment about the illicit activity of a group of persons and the act of labeling a group "terrorist" transmits moral condemnation. Irrationality and fanaticism are also associated with terrorism, and these connotations tend to enhance the security threat and promote citizen solidarity in response to that threat. Both the media and government have deployed a new rhetoric of terror constructed from the events of 9/11. They represent and define terrorism as any activity that offends against the rules of legitimate political violence by ignoring the distinction between combatants and civilians and that employs methods that are unsanctioned, such as highjacking commercial airliners and murdering hostages (Kapitan 2005: 23). Acts of terrorism committed by states are excluded from this discourse even though, as Kapitan (2005: 27) notes, terrorism by states is a more prevalent and deadly form of terrorism than terrorism by groups. As Laqueur (1987: 146) observes, "Acts of terror carried out by police states and tyrannical governments, in general, have been responsible for a thousand times more victims and more misery than all actions of individual terrorism taken together."

A discourse that demonizes all terrorists, whatever their motivation or strategy, denies an understanding of the terrorist point of view and means that government policies that might have contributed to the grievances of those who have adopted terrorism are not scrutinized. As well, it minimizes the likelihood of negotiating with any terrorists, even the more "traditional" terrorist groups, encourages the use of force and violence to counterterrorists, and enables governments to exploit the fears of the public and overrule any objections to the means employed to respond to and counter terrorists (Kapitan 2005: 27).

Thus, the intricacies of the legal definition of terrorism, the rhetoric associated with terrorism, and the contemporary discourse that shapes and represents terrorism so inadequately illustrate the complexity of explaining terrorism and therefore of developing strategies to counter it.

Warfare or Crime Control?

The United States has designated its counterterrorist strategy a War on Terrorism, and its plans and operations have been characterized as warfare rather than law enforcement. Unlike the "wars" against drugs, poverty, and crime proclaimed by various U.S. administrations, the War on Terrorism is a real war that incorporates elements of a conventional war but with significant differences. For example, traditional or conventional conflicts characterized as "wars" are fought against other states, have a definite duration, and conclude when one of the parties is acknowledged as the victor. In contrast, the War on Terrorism is directed not at states but at individuals and groups of persons who practice terrorism as a method of achieving their political and other goals. Also, the U.S. administration has indicated that the War on Terrorism will continue until terrorism is ultimately defeated. Given that the War on Terrorism is neither a metaphorical war like those concerning crime, poverty, and drugs, nor a conventional war, it generates a set of moral questions about how it should be conducted.

The War on Terrorism has adopted both warlike and law enforcement measures in its overall strategy. For example, while measures have been taken under the Patriot Act to strengthen crime control in the United States with the aim of preventing terrorist acts in the homeland, the administration has also conducted wars in Iraq and Afghanistan that employ conventional military forces and military strategies.

How should the War on Terrorism be viewed and conceptualized from the criminal justice perspective? Crank and Gregor (2005: 9) argue that "issues in counterterrorism in the U.S. are framed by the conflict between the competing justice perspectives of crime control and due process" and that the administration has opted for the crime control model. This is said to be evidenced by the enactment of the Patriot Act and its predecessor, the 1996 Antiterrorism and Effective Death Penalty Act. Collectively, these laws have weakened a variety of controls that previously ensured due process and privacy rights (p. 78) and have instead reinforced the kind of punitive crime control strategies outlined in chapters 6 and 7 of this book.

However, it can be argued that Crank and Gregor's (2005) perspective on the policy response to 9/11 is too narrow, because they locate counterterrorism only within the field of criminal justice and fail to recognize that issues in counterterrorism in the United States are framed by the notion of protecting national security and not by ordinary policies and programs of crime control at all.

For example, in response to the events of 9/11, the Bush administration enacted the USA Patriot Act of 2001. The act sought to enhance national security through what had previously been regarded as generic crime control measures. It introduced more than 1,000 provisions concerning surveillance on financial transactions and border control, as well as new criminal offenses and penalties against terrorism. The act is targeted at non–U.S. citizen terrorists (Mertens 2005: 285), was formulated to augment national security, and both conceptually and in policy terms is outside the conventional parameters of crime control legislation.

Crime control measures of the conventional kind such as increased penalties for offenses are integrated into the criminal justice system. In the War on Terrorism however, the criminal justice system has been judged inadequate or inappropriate. Thus, while the United States considers itself "at war," it does not regard many of those taken prisoner in that war as prisoners of war who are to be treated in accordance with the rules laid down in the Geneva Conventions (ICRC 2006), especially the Third and Fourth Conventions, which are concerned with the protection and treatment of combatants captured during an international armed conflict and with civilians who are involved in the armed conflict. Article Five of the Third Convention says that if there is a doubt about the status of persons, the issue has to be determined by a competent tribunal, and in the meantime the persons must enjoy the protection of the convention. Proponents of the convention approach to the war argue, contrary to the U.S. strategy, that prisoners arrested following 9/11 are to be considered prisoners of war (POWs) until a competent tribunal determines otherwise (Kanstroom 2007). The United States, however, has categorized prisoners as unlawful combatants with no Geneva Convention rights.

Thus, in the War on Terrorism prisoners captured in Afghanistan or in other countries have been labeled "unlawful combatants"[1] and interned without trial in a prison at Guantanamo Bay, Cuba, or in a selected number of U.S. bases overseas. According to a military order issued on November 13, 2001, prisoners who are not U.S. citizens and who are alleged to be terrorists are not to be tried in the U.S. federal courts but by a system of military commissions composed of military officers (Wilkinson 2006: 62). Military commissions are rooted in U.S. history and were employed during the American Revolution, the Mexican-American War, and especially during the Civil War. Guantanamo Bay itself, and the special procedures and processes that are being employed to bring suspected terrorists to justice, clearly stand apart from the U.S. criminal justice system.

---

1. Emcke (2005: 237) suggests that terming the prisoners unlawful combatants was a device to "avoid all the existing rules, laws, and conventions regarding prisoners of war or other prisoners" and that creating this new category meant that the U.S. administration need not concern itself with rights issues that would have restricted its ability to incarcerate, interrogate, prosecute, or torture those arrested.

Why has the U.S. administration elected to wage a war in response to the events of 9/11 rather than pursue a law enforcement approach? Paul Hoffman (2004: 939) believes that the question of whether the War on Terrorism is a war, and if so, what is the nature of that war, are crucial questions in examining counterterrorist activity that challenges the international regime protecting human rights. As he puts it, "One of the characteristics of the War on Terrorism is a refusal to accept that any body of law applies to the way this 'war' is waged" (p. 939). He argues that the U.S. response to 9/11 has led to the attrition of rights, because by defining the War on Terrorism as a "war," the United States eliminates many of the protections of international human rights law and international humanitarian law (p. 940). Hoffman further suggests that the war "exists in a parallel legal universe in which compliance with legal norms is a matter of executive grace or is taken out of diplomatic or public relations necessity" (p. 940). He therefore calls into question the morality of the U.S. counterterrorist strategy.

How then should a democratic government respond to terrorism if it is inappropriate to wage a war against it? Wilkinson (2001: 94–95) elaborates a "hard-line approach" that nonetheless remains within the boundaries of the criminal justice system. His model includes the following elements:

1. The government must avoid over-reaction and repression that could have the effect of eroding or even negating democracy.
2. The government must avoid under-reaction, as this would permit terrorists to control territory or otherwise determine the course of events
3. Both the government and its security forces must adhere to the rule of law, because failure to do so will undermine their legitimacy and diminish public confidence in the criminal justice system.
4. The government must conduct a successful intelligence war.
5. Intelligence agencies must be responsible to civilian authorities and fully accountable.
6. Special legislation needed to counter terrorism must be temporary or contain "sunset clauses" that make it subject to renewal by the legislative body.
7. Terrorists should be treated as criminals and not afforded any special status such as that of a political prisoner.
8. Terrorist propaganda must always be countered to avoid terrorists achieving their aims through political advocacy.
9. The government should avoid granting major concessions to terrorists, because this encourages a perception that government is weak in the face of pressure.

The U.S. president has explicitly abandoned a criminal justice strategy in countering terrorism. In his State of the Union speech given on January 20, 2004, the president stated,

I know that some people question if America is really in a war at all. They view terrorism more as a crime, a problem to be solved mainly with law enforcement and indictments. After the World Trade Center was attacked in 1993, some of the guilty were indicted and tried and convicted and sent to prison. But the matter was not settled. The terrorists were still training and plotting in other nations and drawing up more ambitious plans. After the chaos and carnage of September 11th, it is not enough to serve our enemies with legal papers. The terrorists and their supporters declared war on the United States, and war is what they got. (in Ackerman 2004: 1871)

Clearly, the "war they got" bears no resemblance to the metaphorical wars declared by previous administrations, namely, the wars on drugs, on organized crime and drug racketeers, and on poverty, all of which were preceded by the cold war.[2] The U.S. administration simply took the position that the events of 9/11 were so horrendous that the appropriate response should be nothing less than a declaration of war, and it viewed the justice system as lacking the capacity to prosecute terrorism.

In considering the strategy of a U.S. War on Terrorism, it is appropriate to look at the experience of other states faced with similar threats to national security. In the case of the terror campaign mounted by the Irish Republican Army against the United Kingdom government in Northern Ireland, the role of the military was to support the police and civil authorities in countering the terrorist threat.[3] As McEldowney notes, as in the United States, the effect of tough new antiterrorist laws in the United Kingdom has been to accrete power to the executive (2005: 773).

Ackerman (2004) argues that the U.S. response to terrorism is not a war but a "state of emergency," a concept located in the constitutions of many states in time of war or national emergency that permits derogations from guaranteed human rights provisions, usually for limited periods, to deal with the emergency. In Ackerman's view, public acceptance of a war against "something as amorphous as terrorism" lowers the bar for engaging in more conventional wars against actual states and avoids having to justify each engagement in the "war" as a separate and distinct war of its own. For example, Ackerman (2004) argues that the actions taken against Afghanistan and Iraq have been packaged as "battles" subsumed within the entirety of the amorphous War on Terrorism. As he points out, it is far easier in constitutional terms for the president to conduct mere battles without congressional authorization, because he can argue that he is simply exercising his powers as commander in chief.

In discussing a War on Terrorism that includes offensive operations and military reprisals against terrorists overseas, as well as their sponsor states, and that does not adopt the criminal justice approach, Wilkinson (2001: 128–129) points out several risks. For example, there is the danger that a military response could provoke a wider conflict involving a diminished focus on the relevant terrorist group in favor of a broader multistate strategy, the danger that the death of innocent civilians will diminish international sympathy for the victim state and shift the moral high ground away

---

2. Writing about the War on Crime, Alison Young notes that employing "'a militaristic metaphor' shuts down debate, draws boundaries about which side is morally in the right and incorporates the belief in an ultimate outright winner" (Young 1996: 7).

3. In the United Kingdom, the events of 9/11 resulted in the enactment of the Anti-Terrorism, Crime and Security Act of 2001, granting powers to arrest and detain suspected terrorists without giving reasons and for indefinite periods (McEldowney 2005: 771).

from that state, the difficulties associated with gaining and ensuring the continuing support of allies when military actions are taken unilaterally, and the danger that military action will give rise to false expectations of a total defeat of terrorism.

Using military forces to counter terrorism carries several specific risks including the probability of deaths or injury of members of the civilian population given the lethality of modern weaponry and firepower (Wilkinson 2001: 104). Morally, causing death or injury to civilians in countering terrorism seems to mirror the acts of the terrorists themselves, and thus targeting only terrorists and not civilians would be the most ethical approach. Of course, this raises the issue of the degree of certainty that a suspected person is in fact a terrorist. Wilkinson contends that war constitutes a greater evil than terrorism because of its potential to cause a far greater number of deaths and far greater destruction. This implies that a war against terrorism pursued internationally could potentially generate multiple wars not only against terrorist groups but also against states alleged to be sponsoring terrorism. Nevertheless, he acknowledges that the military warfare model does carry with it some advantages, including responding to public demands for tough action.

Overall, Wilkinson (2001: 125) favors employing a criminal justice model in countering terrorism and using law enforcement agencies as the spearhead. He notes that these agencies enjoy advantages over the military in handling terrorism particularly because of their legitimacy in the eyes of the public but also in relation to local knowledge, of their familiarity with the law and with techniques of criminal investigation, and of their access to international sources of assistance and cooperation through agencies such as Interpol.

In support of the warfare approach some commentators suggest that the kind of terrorism practiced by Al Qaeda is of an entirely different nature than that conducted by more "traditional" terrorist groups such as the ETA in Spain or FARC in Colombia or the IRA in Northern Ireland. Unlike those groups, Al Qaeda has explicitly embraced a strategy of mass killing, or as Brian Jenkins has written (in Wilkinson 2006: 5), terrorists in the 1970s and 1980s wanted "a lot of people watching, not a lot of people dead."

The aims and objectives of Al Qaeda were announced on February 23, 1998, when Osama bin Laden issued a *fatwa* setting up a World Islamic Front for *Jihad*, announcing, "It is the duty of all Muslims to kill U.S. citizens—civilian or military, and their allies—everywhere" (in Wilkinson 2006: 5). Al Qaeda's objectives are to expel U.S. citizens and other infidels from the Middle East, to topple Muslim governments that they believe fail to practice true Islam, and ultimately, to set up an Islamist caliphate comprising all Muslims everywhere. These may seem unrealistic goals, but Al Qaeda does not necessarily expect to achieve these aims within a short time span and is firmly convinced that these events will come to pass, because they have the support of Allah. Organizationally, the Al Qaeda network differs from other terrorist groups precisely because it is a network of other networks that provide the capacity to operate in some 60 countries. As Wilkinson (2006: 5) acknowledges, "It is the most widely dispersed non-State terrorist network ever seen, and this is what gives the movement 'global reach.'" It is obvious that there is no basis for negotiating or compromising with a terrorist group that advocates mass killing to achieve its goals.

Wilson (2005: 30) proposes that under a criminal justice model, terrorist crimes ought to be categorized, not as acts of war, but as crimes against humanity sanctioned through national and international justice institutions. He suggests that a justice strategy would involve less abuse of detainees' human rights, because law enforcement agencies are trained in respecting suspect's rights.

What Are the Morally Justifiable Constraints and Restrictions That a Government Should Be Permitted to Impose on Its Citizens in a War on Terrorism?

Since 9/11, philosophers and terrorism theorists have been debating the extent of the permissible restrictions on rights and freedoms perceived "necessary" to prosecute the War on Terrorism. Essentially, the debate has centered on whether any restrictions at all should be imposed, and, if they are, the correct balance between rights and restrictions in a counterterrorist situation. Experience since 9/11 has shown that the U.S. public has become more willing to accept restrictions on rights and freedoms, and Messelken (2005: 58) explains that "the first aim of terrorist violence is the production of fear, horror etc. among a broad group of persons" and that the "terrorist calculation" relies on unpredictable random violence and the creation of insecurity and fear. Terrorist strategies can include rural and urban guerilla warfare and even full scale conventional war. These effects and the emotions generated by acts of terrorism can promote great public insecurity.

Wilkinson points out the belief that in the War on Terrorism, terrorists must be suppressed "with crushing military force" on the assumption that "the only good terrorist is a dead terrorist" (2006: 63). Thus, some advocate that the ends justifies the means, that terrorists through their actions have forfeited constitutional and human rights, that the criminal courts are inappropriate for these prisoners, and that even torture can be justified in some circumstances. Others argue that the ends do not justify the means and that abandoning due process protection under U.S. law conflicts with the values and principles that are the foundation of the democracy being defended against terrorist attack (p. 63). Wilkinson argues that abridging rights corrupts public officials and the military and promotes major injustices in the name of national security (p. 63).

In support of the notion that it is possible to defeat terrorism without seriously restricting rights, Wilkinson cites the example of measures taken in Italy during the 1970s when that country experienced significant terrorist activity by the Red Brigades. In 1975, the Italian minister for justice introduced legislation giving the police increased powers of arrest and search on suspicion of an offense and expanded the permitted use of firearms (Wilkinson 2006: 65). Additionally, the Italians promoted and established effective coordination between police and intelligence services under a newly created coordination office. This produced high-quality intelligence that enabled the justice system to disrupt and ultimately terminate the activities of the Red Brigades (p. 66). In the early 1980s judges were empowered to reduce sentences imposed on convicted terrorists who agreed to give testimony for the state under a so-called *pentiti* (repentant) law. This enabled the government to break open the Red Brigades' cells. Whether the events of 9/11 and subsequent events are congruent with the activities of the Red Brigades is perhaps open to question.

As noted above, the U.S. response to terrorism has included the enactment of the Patriot Act, which introduced restrictions on some democratic rights, including giving the FBI wide and unprecedented access to information previously kept private (a power that the FBI employed, using a so-called national security letter, to illegally accumulate intimate information about some 52,000 persons and store it in a database accessible to about 12,000 federal, state, and local law enforcement agencies) (Smith 2007). This voluminous law was passed only 6 weeks after 9/11.

As well, a package of measures forming part of the overall counterterrorist strategy impacted rights and freedoms. The measures are noted by Peter Manning (2006: 458) as follows:

- New visa and immigration procedures (which included detaining more than 1,200 immigrants of Middle Eastern descent following 9/11 based on no other factors than their origin)
- New screening procedures for passengers boarding aircraft
- Designing and integrating extensive databases covering visitors to the United States and U.S. citizens
- Consolidating data gathered at immigration and customs locations
- Establishing the Department of Homeland Security with some 170,000 employees
- Establishing the Transport Security Administration (TSA) within the Department of Homeland Security and thereby federalizing the business of airport security
- Establishing a federal directorate of intelligence

These measures were of course supplemented by the use of the U.S. facility at Guantanamo Bay, Cuba, to hold alleged terrorists; the use of extraordinary rendition to move terrorists from country to country for purposes believed to relate to their interrogation (allegedly through torture); and the invasions of Afghanistan and Iraq.

Some commentators believe it is misconceived to represent the issue of rights and restrictions or security and liberties in terms of achieving a balance. Ronald Dworkin (2005: 286) maintains that the appropriate response is to ask what justice requires. He contends that the government must treat everyone as having equal status and with equal concern, because every human life has an equal value. Thus, a system of criminal law should treat all equally in equal cases, and if it denies one category of suspects rights considered essential for others, it acts unfairly. If a system unfairly targets non–U.S. citizens, as does the Patriot Act, Dworkin judges that it must satisfy two requirements. First, it must acknowledge that it is differentiating suspects unjustly for security reasons, and second, it must diminish that injustice by permitting only the minimum curtailment of rights possible. Dworkin argues that the Patriot Act does not satisfy these conditions (in Mertens 2005: 286).

Where a terrorist event causes a government to take emergency action such as suspending habeas corpus, it runs the risk of alienating its citizens and playing into the hands of terrorist tactics (Wilkinson 2001: 23). More fundamentally, Wilkinson contends that it must be a cardinal principle of a liberal democracy in dealing with the problems of terrorism, however serious these may be, never to be tempted into using methods which are incompatible with the liberal values of humanity, liberty, and justice. (2001: 115)

Thus, he argues, a liberal democracy faced with terrorism must follow a path between, on the one hand, the dangers of repression, and on the other hand, inaction. It is crucial that counterterrorist measures are limited to just that, countering terrorism, and that a government should not take advantage of a terrorist situation to abuse exceptional powers by using them for extraneous purposes. Thus, both politically and morally, a government facing a terrorist threat must avoid repressive overreaction (Wilkinson 2001: 115). As an example of overreaction, Wilkinson cites the use of emergency powers by the British government in Northern Ireland that authorized internment without trial. This measure is now widely regarded as having been counterproductive, because although it was originally introduced to protect witnesses, juries, and magistrates from intimidation, it was in practice used by the security forces to arrest large numbers of people who had no connection with terrorist operations (p. 116). According to Wilkinson (p. 116), internment without trial "should only be contemplated in the eventuality of a full-scale civil war, when all other means of curbing the escalation of violence on a massive scale have failed." In Northern Ireland, using internment promoted recruitment into the Irish Republican Army, motivated many Catholics to give support to the terrorist cause, and greatly increased the level of violence as well as funding support for the IRA from the United States.

Writing post 9/11, Wilkinson contends that those who claim that the world can no longer afford to ensure that measures to prevent and combat terrorism accord with the rule of law and principles of human rights are themselves "guilty of being soft on terrorism" (2006: xvi). He argues that supporting or condoning violations of human rights and liberal democratic principles undermines respect for international and national laws and places those who advocate or support such violations on the same moral level as the terrorists. As he puts it, "By suppressing human rights in the name of protecting national security they play into the hands of terrorists" (p. xvi). Simpson (2005: 204) agrees with Wilkinson that the justifications offered by the U.S. government for invading personal privacy are self-contradictory and counterproductive. He articulates his concern by asking, "How can the U.S. proclaim its goal in the War on Terrorism to be defense of the free and civilized world if its own domestic acts are denials of freedom and civilization?" (p. 204).

Wilson (2005: 6) sees a distinct policy dichotomy between security and rights, contending that following 9/11 "the Bush Administration advanced a formulation of international security that detached rights from security concerns." He claims that the U.S. government's hostility to the International Criminal Court is an example of this gulf between human rights and national security as is the emphasis in Afghanistan and Iraq on fighting terrorism rather than re-establishing the rule of law and human rights.

Luban (in Wilson 2005: 26) suggests it is wrong to focus on whether democratic freedoms should be sacrificed in the interests of national security. This approach assumes that the rights of others are being sacrificed for "our security," that favoring additional security demonstrates a tough-minded response to terrorism, that issues of guilt or innocence have to be decided by the president, and that exceptional measures to counter terrorism are necessary but will only be short term.

Freeman (2005: 53) observes that striking a balance between human rights and security in an age of terrorism is a complex matter and that we need to "analyze clearly which human rights are at stake under the threat of terrorism, and which risks we ought to take." Since we, the general public, do not know the risks of terrorism, we rely on government for advice, and our government controls the information. Freeman (2005: 53) explains that while we should give the government considerable discretion, "democratic politicians should not be trusted too much." Freeman points out that legislative and judicial oversight may not be sufficient to protect rights and advocates an active civil society as a counterbalance to the power of the state.

In his contribution to the debate on balancing rights and restrictions, Teson (2005: 64) argues that the balancing test should be that "a security measure is justified if, and only if, the amount of freedom it restricts is necessary to preserve the total system of freedom threatened by internal or external enemies." He contends that threats to security almost never justify restricting personal liberties, because human rights are deontological concepts (see Chapter 9) and are conceived as trumping the pursuit of utility or the general welfare (2005: 64). Teson illustrates his argument with the following example (2005: 65–66):

A villain who asks me to shoot an innocent person says if I refuse he will shoot two innocent persons. If I refuse, I can justify my decision not to kill even with the certain consequence of the death of two others in two ways. Firstly, I may say the right to life is absolute and my duty not to kill an innocent person cannot be overridden by the consequences of complying with that duty even if the consequences are the murder of more innocent persons. Secondly, I can say that I am prohibited from violating the innocent person's right to life by shooting her regardless of what others may do.

Applying this example to restrictions in the interests of national security, Teson (2005: 65–66) notes that a liberal would argue that violating individual rights is a graver issue than the government allowing deaths to occur by terrorist attacks. A second argument is that rights can be categorized in terms of their fundamental importance, so for example, the freedom against torture or against indefinite detention rank as being more vital than other rights. Thus, in the interests of national security, while other rights might be restricted, those ought not to be sacrificed to the general welfare (p. 67).

In a major contribution to this debate, Michael Ignatieff (2004: viii) explores the issue of how a democracy can respond to terrorism without destroying the values for which it stands. He takes a position between those who argue in absolutist terms that no restrictions on rights ought to be imposed or justified and those advocating a consequentialist approach who judge counterterrorist measures purely by their effectiveness. Ignatieff would prohibit certain torture, illegal detention, and unlawful assassination on the basis that they violate "foundational commitments to justice and dignity" (p. viii). He notes that democracies commonly permit derogations from guaranteed rights and freedoms in emergencies, so rights do not always trump other considerations like national security, but ultimately, in his view, it is the task of the courts, the media, and the legislators to scrutinize such measures for justifiability. Ignatieff points out that in an emergency, like a terrorist attack, we have to trust our leaders to respond rapidly in our interests but that over the longer term, in determining the balance between security and liberty, we must rely on our democratic institutions to conduct oversight and scrutiny. Ignatieff's overall approach is a "lesser evil position" (2004: 8) under which, in a terrorist emergency, rights do not trump necessary measures, but neither do such measures trump rights. Instead, Ignatieff sets a series of tests for leaders as follows:

1. Do the proposed national security measures violate individual dignity? Within the concept of individual dignity, he includes rights against cruel and unusual punishment, torture, penal servitude, extrajudicial execution, and the rendition[4] of prisoners to states that practice torture.

2. The national security measures must pass "the conservative test" (Ignatieff 2004: 24) that questions the necessity for the proposed measures. Ignatieff argues this test would bar measures such as suspension of habeas corpus, would require all detention to be subject to review by the courts, and would ensure that prisoners have access to counsel.

3. Applying a consequentialist approach (see Chapter 10) to counterterrorist measures means asking whether they will render citizens more secure in the long term. Necessary measures must function as a last resort in the sense that less coercive means must be judged as inadequate, and all measures should be capable of being sanctioned by the courts at some point in time.

4. Finally, the measures should be congruent with international obligations relating to rights and freedoms.

Ignatieff's view is that if the proposed countermeasures fail the above tests, the War on Terrorism will have to be waged without them, because, as he puts it, "It is the very nature of a democracy that it not only does, but should, fight with one hand tied behind its back" (2004: 24).

In his critique of Ignatieff's views, Wilson (2005: 19) notes that "Michael Ignatieff's 'lesser evil' ethics and over reliance on a consequentialist ethics places him much closer to the antirights philosophical tradition of utilitarianism than the liberal tradition of human rights." Philosophically and politically, "utilitarian

---

4. International rendition is illustrated by the case of Maher Arar, who was detained at JFK Airport in September 2002 while in transit to Canada, who is a dual Canadian/Syrian citizen, and was traveling on a Canadian passport. He was held in U.S. custody for 13 days, interrogated about his supposed links to Al Qaeda, and then transported on to Jordan and then Syria without notice to his family or to the Canadian consulate. In Syria he was held without charge for a year and was tortured and treated in a cruel and inhumane way (Hoffman 2004: 947–948). He was finally released by Syria.

consequentialism is about as far from an ethics of human rights as one can travel"
(p. 19). As Wilson explains,

> Lesser evil reasoning makes a virtue out of lowering accepted standards and
> surrendering safeguards on individual liberties. In the hands of government
> officials, it enables unrestrained presidential authority and a disregard for long
> standing restraints on the conduct of war. (2005: 19)

In the debate on restrictions on rights and freedoms in the interests of national security and countering terrorism, the differing perspectives all seek the normative framework for government action. While some advocate no restrictions, arguing that
governments will abuse special powers and that restrictions on liberty mirror the tactics of the terrorists themselves, others believe that we must place confidence in government and rely on oversight through the legislature and the judiciary. When
governments impose restrictions, they can usually rely on public support, at least in
the short term, but they must guard against overreacting and becoming too repressive.
Thus, striking a balance is seen by many ethicists as a key issue, and many advocate no
restrictions on rights they believe to be basic and inviolable such as the prohibition
against torture. However these complexities are resolved, it is imperative that a government faced with a terrorist threat or campaign actually address the morality of
measures that will restrict liberty instead of reacting with no real moral compass.

What Moral Restrictions Apply to the Conduct of Counterterrorist Operations?

Ethically, it is necessary that those combating terrorism refrain from indiscriminately killing, maiming, or imprisoning persons who are unrelated to the terrorist
activities. Additionally, there are moral restrictions on means as well as ends. For
example, the conduct of antiterrorist operations must take account of the risk to lives
of innocent civilians (Bauhn 2005: 131). According to Bauhn (p. 132) antiterrorist
activities that lead to operational excesses may nevertheless be morally justified under
the principle of "double effect." This states that an unintended but foreseen morally
bad effect of an action can be excused if both the action and the intended effect are
morally permissible. Take the case of an act of self-defense where a person resists an
assault on her life and at the same time accomplishes the morally bad effect of killing
the aggressor. Here, the victim attacked only with the intention of warding off the
assault. The attacker's death can be morally excused even if the victim may have been
aware that the attacker's death would be a probable outcome of self-defense. Adopting
this principle, however, could result in counterterrorist agencies classifying all innocent victims as unintended casualties in the war against terrorism.

Walzer (in Bauhn 2005: 132) has suggested that the principle of double effect
should be modified so that members of the armed forces should not only refrain from
intending to kill civilians who are noncombatants but should also intend to protect
them from being killed, even if this means risking their own lives. Of course if this
approach is adopted, it will require that counterterrorist agencies increase the risks for
their own personnel in conducting terrorist operations in order to diminish the risks

for innocent bystanders. Bauhn (p. 132) suggests that this implies more ground and face-to-face encounters with the terrorists and less use of strategic and tactical bombing where "collateral damage" often occurs. He further suggests that antiterrorist operations are not only morally justified but also morally necessary in the same way that it is morally necessary for law enforcement to catch criminals. Thus, counterterrorist agencies are morally justified and indeed morally obliged to employ force to the extent necessary to terminate terrorist activity. Nevertheless, as indicated above, it is also necessary, he suggests, that the double effect principle be modified so that the risk of injuring innocent civilians is taken on by the counterterrorist forces (p. 133).

Coady (2005: 145) notes that responding to terrorism involves morality issues, because it "cannot permit morally unconstrained reactions." He views responses to terrorism that in themselves involve terrorism as immoral. For example, a casual or indifferent attitude toward collateral damage, in Coady's view, is immoral and "can exhibit a spirit close to that of terrorism" (p. 145). He advocates the use of means other than military might to deal with a terrorist threat, because that level of force is likely to engender widespread death and destruction. Therefore, in his opinion, the option of warfare should be the last resort.

Elements of a counterterrorism strategy can include the assassination of actual or suspected terrorists and their torture in order to obtain intelligence information. Is the counterterrorist technique of assassination morally justified? Khatchadourian (2005: 178) argues that assassination in the context of counterterrorism is never morally justified where the victim's life is taken, and no process of law is adhered to that enables him or her to bring a defense against alleged charges. As well, the outcome of an assassination is the termination of the victim's life by the assassin, who takes the law into his own hands to dispense punishment that is capital in nature and who in doing so becomes the judge of the victim's deeds. An assassination also violates the victim's right to life.

Rachels (in Khatchadourian 2005: 179) disagrees with this standpoint, arguing that the right to life can be forfeited to "eliminate great suffering" but not "merely to increase the happiness of already minimally contented population." Rachels gives the hypothetical example of Hitler suffering assassination for having violated the rights of so many others. According to Rachels, this consequentialist rationale is only justified if the following conditions are met:

1. The outcome of the assassination must be such in terms of the good achieved as to outweigh the act of destroying a human life.

2. The assassination must be the only or the least objectionable method of achieving the good results.

3. Out of all the possible actions available, it should represent "the best overall balance of maximizing good and minimizing evil" (p. 179).

Rachel's consequential theory is a form of rule utilitarianism (see Chapter 10). Khatchadourian argues, however, applying deontological theory (see Chapter 9), that while some nonabsolute rights can be overridden by stronger moral claims, the only absolute human right not susceptible to being overridden is the right to be treated as a moral being: "to be treated with respect and consideration as a person, not to be treated as a thing or an object" (p. 180). Khatchadourian points out that a rule utilitarian approach to assassination would cause the public to lose faith in the justice system and that this approach would never be adopted as a public policy or practice by a state (p. 184), because to do so would mean that the state was undermining the rule of law. It is more likely, then, that the state would adopt a policy prohibiting all assassinations in principle. Adopting a covert policy in those terms, he suggests, would not resolve the issue, because it is always possible that the covert would be made overt by domestic or foreign media. Another objection to this approach is the possibility of reciprocal action by another state, which might target the home state.

Simpson (2005: 202) asks how we are to "resist the evil of terrorism with good." His response is that we should counter terrorism with all the good we can command, but he points out that we also need to be aware of the nature of the force and any associated conditions and limits that may be used in resisting terrorism. He asserts that force will only be good if it has the promotion of the human good as its goal and that it may only be used as a last resort and for as long as is necessary (p. 202). Thus, a decision to use armed force in counterterrorism must be based on sufficient and compelling reasons in the sense that no other options are plausible or available. As well, the force used should be proportionate to the goal sought to be achieved. In particular, the force should not target the innocent and should aim to reduce collateral damage to the very minimum (p. 204).

Corlett (2003: 158) contends that the government response to an act of terrorism is typically a violent reaction seeking punishment for the terrorists as exemplified by the declaration of the War on Terrorism. While recognizing that such a response is the predictable outcome, Corlett argues that it is unreasonable and lacking in reflection. Instead, he urges a reaction based on reason, all available evidence, and the application of moral principles, including due process and the presumption of innocence, which, he argues, are so fundamental that not even a state of war should negate them. Corlett goes so far as to suggest that a society that ignores due process in responding to a terrorist attack "ends up being a rogue society bent on meting out what it thinks is justice when in fact it is simply reacting out of self-interested egoistic, self-serving emotion" (p. 159). He scorns the broad-brush approach to counterterrorism strategy, pointing to the many forms that terrorism takes and its motivations, which he believes call for a proper and rational assessment of each individual act of terrorism (p. 160).

As appears from the above discussion, the broad ethical framework for the conduct of terrorist operations is problematic, and specific measures all have their advocates. Assassination and torture have been sanctioned in the War on Terrorism, and a public debate on the use of torture has shown that many in the United States believe it is justified.

Is Torture Morally Permissible as a Counterterrorist Strategy?

In the war against terrorism, as well as in allegations of torture in the U.S. detainee facility at Guantanamo Bay, prisoner mistreatment has been identified in reports written after the disclosure of abuses at Abu Ghraib prison, Baghdad. Instances of acts that could amount to torture included raping a female detainee, raping a 15–18 year old male detainee, beating a detainee with a broom and breaking and pouring a chemical light over his body followed by sodomizing him with the broom, and being assaulted by two female military police (Hooks and Mosher 2005: 1629).

In his written advice to the president, White House Counsel and later Attorney General Gonzales advised that "the War on Terrorism is a new kind of war . . . [that] renders obsolete the Geneva's strict limitations on questioning of enemy prisoners and renders quaint some of its provisions" (in Hooks and Mosher 2005: 1634). In August 2002, the Justice Department advised that the Congress had no power to regulate the president's ability to detain and interrogate enemy combatants. In his opinion on the meaning of torture, the assistant attorney general, Jay S. Bybee, advised that the term meant "extreme acts . . . where the pain is physical it must be of an intensity akin to that which accompanies serious physical injury such as death or organ failure . . . because the acts inflicting torture are extreme, there is [a] significant range of acts that, though they might constitute cruel, inhuman, or degrading treatment or punishment, fail to rise to the level of torture" (in Hooks and Mosher 2005: 1634). According to Hooks and Mosher then, this sets a threshold for torture far higher than that established under any international human rights conventions (p. 1634).

Title 18, Section 2340 of the U.S. Code defines torture as "an act committed by a person acting under the color of law specifically intended to inflict severe physical or mental pain or suffering (other than pain or suffering incidental to lawful sanctions) upon another person within his custody or physical control" (Massimino 2004: 75). Torture is a federal crime punishable by up to 20 years in prison and even death if the victim dies following the torture. This law applies to torture committed outside the United States but includes acts by U.S. citizens (Massimino 2004: 74–75).

Khatchadourian (2005: 192) argues that even an act utilitarian (see Chapter 10) would be unable to justify torture in practice and that a rule utilitarian approach would expressly prohibit torture in principle on the same basis that would cause a state to prohibit the practice of assassination. To torture a human being is to treat him or her not as a moral person but as an object, and according to Ronald Dworkin, a "core list of human rights" would include the right not to be tortured. In his view, torture constitutes "the most profound insult to (its victim's) humanity, the most profound outrage of his human rights" (2006: 38–39)

Khatchadourian (2005: 192) observes that the double effect principle cannot justify torture even by arguing that the pain and suffering inflicted is intended to produce a greater good and with the torturer claiming he intended only the good and not the bad consequences of the torture. The reason is that in the practice of torture it is impossible to isolate the intention from the act itself.

Michael Ignatieff argues that the prohibition against torture underpins the liberal democratic project and points out that eliminating torture as an affront to human dignity is the aim of a number of international instruments as well as being the domestic law of most states (2004: 137).

Nevertheless, the events of 9/11 have prompted some to argue that torture is justified as a national security counterterrorist measure in the interests of defending democracy. For example, Alan Dershowitz has suggested that torture might be applied and regulated by the judiciary through a "torture warrant" that would prescribe the kinds of torture to be inflicted and its limits, and federal Judge Richard Posner has written that anyone who doubts that torture "is permissible when the stakes are high enough should not be in a position of responsibility" (in Massimino 2004: 74). Ignatieff rejects this approach on the basis that legalizing torture would effectively render it a routine matter. John Kleinig (2005: 626) also opposes issuing warrants to torture, asking if there is any reason to suppose that judges will be discriminating in torture cases brought before them in light of their wholehearted support for issuing warrants under the Foreign Intelligence Surveillance Act.[5] For Kleinig, as a matter of morality, authorizing torture by judicial warrant would be "pasting a veneer of moral respectability over practices that do not deserve it" (p. 627), and he argues for an absolute ban on torture as a matter of policy.

Some argue that torture is justified under the "ticking bomb argument." They envisage a situation where, for example, terrorists have planted a nuclear device that will explode and devastate a huge city area within the hour. There is no possibility of saving many lives in the time available, but one of the terrorists has been captured. The argument goes as follows: Are we not morally justified in using whatever means are appropriate, even torture, to get our captive terrorist to reveal the location of the bomb, so it can be deactivated and save countless lives? Certainly many would agree that they would personally resort to whatever means are necessary in such a situation, but Kleinig (2005), among others, points to some of the issues raised by the ticking bomb argument:

- It suggests there is a known threat—not just a possibility or probability—but in practice such a high degree of certainty is unlikely to occur (p. 616).
- There is a need for immediate action, because it is certain that the bomb will explode—again, is this degree of certainty likely to be common in practice?
- The magnitude of the danger is enormous, and so it is said to be permissible to apply torture, but Kleinig argues that the moral status of any alternative decision is unclear. Similarly, there is no moral clarity about whether or not torture is justified, excusable, or regrettable in these circumstances.
- It is claimed that only the application of torture will secure the necessary information, but we cannot really be sure there are no other alternatives. Also torture ought not to be regarded as a kind of shortcut that is convenient in such circumstances (p. 617).
- It would seem essential that the person we intend torturing be the maker of the threat. This is so because, as Kleinig points out, the moral justification for torture seems much weaker if we encourage him to talk by, for example, torturing his child or his aging mother in front of him.
- It is said that the outcome of the torture will be the removal of the threat. It is assumed, then, that information gained from the torture will almost certainly dispel the danger, but can this be claimed with absolute certainty?

---

5. In 2002, 1,228 warrants were applied for, and all were approved; in 2003, 1,724 out of 1,727 were granted; in 2004, 1,754 out of 1,758 were approved, and none were denied (Kleinig 2005: 626).

As Kleinig points out, these assumptions can be given some weight but are unlikely to be found in the real world, and if they cannot be replicated, the case for torture is that much weaker. Even assuming that the ticking bomb scenario is accepted as a basis for torture, Kleinig and others would nevertheless maintain, contrary to Dershowitz and others, that the ticking bomb situation could never sanction a *policy* authorizing torture. Instead, each case where torture was contemplated would have to be justified by reference to the specific facts and circumstances (2005: 623).

Like Ignatieff, Kleinig fears the routinization of torture. As he points out, we are on a slippery slope once torture is accepted as a possible course of action, because the ticking bomb argument will inevitably lead to an expansion of the situations where torture is acceptable (2005: 619). For Kleinig, then, torture "threatens and undermines the very characteristics that constitute our human distinctiveness, and attacks them in a way that does not merely extinguish them—as killing does—but in a way that humiliates, degrades and perverts" (p. 619).

Significantly, the High Court in Israel has struck down practices that amounted to torture on the grounds that they offended human dignity. Torture, it held, could not be permitted even in a state preoccupied with national security, and no regulation of practices amounting to torture is permissible. While those prosecuted for torture may plead necessity in mitigation of any penalty, necessity may not be pleaded as a defense or as justification.

Is torture permissible in this "new kind of war"? Ignatieff (2004: 143) proposes that the practice of torture cannot be condoned in a war on terror; "for torture, when committed by a state, expresses the state's ultimate view that human beings are expendable."

Summary

This chapter has explored definitions of terrorism and the normative ethics of counterterrorism and has questioned why, following the events of 9/11, the U.S. administration declared a War on Terrorism instead of allowing the criminal justice system to respond to that act of terrorism. The discussion has revealed the complexity of the moral arguments and debates surrounding the application of torture, the ethical aspects of counterterrorist measures, and the extent to which citizens' rights ought to be restricted in the interests of national security.

A number of major themes have emerged from this discussion. They include, first, that there exists no single "correct" definition of terrorism and that the current terrorism discourse, which includes connotations of irrationality and fanaticism, has obscured the fact that most varieties of terror are conducted or sponsored by states that practice far more deadly forms of terrorism than groups or individuals. Second, the War on Terrorism is not a conventional war but is shaped almost entirely by the events of 9/11 and is a reaction to those events. Third, post 9/11, terrorism is perceived by U.S. strategists and policy makers as an issue of national security, not crime control, and therefore as calling for a response that is warlike but falls short of a conventional war. As well, protecting U.S. citizens against further terrorist attacks necessitates the creation of special courts and procedures, the abandonment of the U.S. criminal justice system, and probable violations of national and international law. Defending citizens also means that their rights and freedoms can legitimately be restricted, presumably for as long as it takes to "win" the War on Terrorism. Fourth, exceptional measures, including violently assaulting the integrity of the human person through torture, are regarded by many as justified and even imperative in conducting the war.

Antiterrorist strategies have been challenged on moral grounds. Charges have been made of abuse of government powers. It is said that the administration has acted unethically by rejecting customary legal rules and procedures in the pursuit of victory. Devices such as categorizing suspected terrorist prisoners as "unlawful combatants" have been employed, allegedly to avoid legal rules and enable incarceration and torture.

The morality of the War on Terrorism itself has been called into question on the basis that representing a counterterrorist strategy as warfare lowers the bar for engaging in more conventional wars against actual states. It also enables the United States to conduct events called "battles" subsumed within the entirety of an amorphous and unending War on Terrorism. As well, commentators have pointed out that ethically, causing death or injury to civilians in countering terrorism seems to mirror the acts of the terrorists themselves.

Thus, the War on Terrorism can be seen as constituting a greater evil than terrorism itself. In the face of such charges, is it sufficient to maintain that citizens must rely on judicial and legislative oversight to ensure that the administration's excesses are corrected? Ultimately, the question may be whether condoning breaches of human rights and liberal principles in conducting a War on Terrorism also risks undermining respect for national and international laws that destroys foundational commitments to justice and human dignity.

DISCUSSION QUESTIONS

1. The definition of *terrorism* is problematic. How does this affect our view of terrorism?

2. Which is the better approach—to treat terrorism as a criminal activity or to fight terrorists as if they were enemies in a war? Explain.

3. Does the Patriot Act give the executive branch of government too much power in pursuing terrorism? What effect does the exercise of that power have on civil rights in the United States?

4. What measures should a democratic government take to respond to terrorism that are consistent with its ethical responsibilities?

5. Is it ever ethically acceptable to torture a person in the War on Terrorism? Explain.

6. What, if any, human rights should be suppressed in the interests of winning the War on Terrorism, and how would suppressing these rights contribute toward "victory"?

PART II

The Application of Ethical Theories to the Criminal Justice System

In Part I of this book, concrete ethical issues within the criminal justice system are presented and contextualized. The role of moral philosophy in answering the questions "What is right behavior?" and "How ought I to live?" has been explored and the meaning of these questions addressed. We saw in chapters 2 through 8 that professionals working in the criminal justice system may have to confront ethical issues and ethical dilemmas. Part of the process of responding to ethical issues and dilemmas involves reflecting upon ethical theories and applying them.

Part II presents various ethical theories that can be applied to the resolution of ethical dilemmas. The leading ethical theories are deontology and consequentialism (utilitarianism), although virtue ethics has found increasing acceptance among moral philosophers, sufficient even to raise its prominence to the level enjoyed by deontology and consequentialism. This theoretical discussion extends beyond these principal theories to include the classical Greek theories of hedonism and Stoicism as well as the theory of ethical egoism. The theories of social justice and feminist ethics are represented in the works of John Rawls and Carol Gilligan, respectively. As explained in the Introduction, the format of the book is an inversion of the usual presentation and is deliberate. The aim is to ensure a grounding in the practical issues before grappling with ethical theory and applying those theories to ethical issues found within the system. Those who prefer to focus on philosophical theory before examining the ethical issues that can arise in the criminal justice system are encouraged to reverse the order of the book to accomplish their purposes.

In Part II of this book, each ethical theory will be examined in some detail, and the leading theories of utilitarianism, deontology, virtue, social justice, and the ethic of care will be incorporated into specific case studies as part of an analysis of criminal justice ethical issues. These analyses will help illustrate the concrete application of these ethical theories in the resolution of ethical issues. Neither the classical Greek theories nor ethical egoism are generally considered viable ethical theories today.

In this introduction to Part II, an attempt will also be made to demonstrate how philosophical notions about ethics have developed and changed over time. This brief discussion of present-day thinking about ethics includes the postmodern perspective. As explained in Chapter 1, humans employ concepts of morality as an approach to trying to make their lives better. The aim is to create a social framework that guarantees the conditions required by human beings to live good lives. Morality formulates the principles that guide our evaluations of individual lives, of human action, and of social institutions as "right or wrong," or "good or bad," as they bear on the goodness of human lives. It involves our attempt to shape a world that is not particularly hospitable to our endeavors, to adjust our endeavors to what is unchangeable in this world, and to harmonize our often conflicting individual endeavors so that we can pursue them with minimal interference from one another (Kekes 2000: 18). Morality is a collection of different ways of performing in different situations; these ways develop as we struggle with the many problems we meet in daily life (Wallace 1996: 14). Morality should not be seen as something separate from specific ways of acting, because our knowledge of morality is caught up with our decisions about how to act in our everyday lives. We do not learn how to be a good family member or friend and then learn about the virtues of honesty and loyalty, because the two go together.

Consequentialism (utilitarianism) and deontology are contrasting ethical theories. Consequentialist theories contend that the right thing to do always depends on the goodness of consequences. Utilitarianism is a consequentialist moral doctrine, because, for the utilitarian, morality is solely a matter of consequences (Hinman 1998: 163). In contrast, deontological theories focus on considerations other than good and bad effects. The term *deontology* is widely used in moral philosophy, yet there is no standard definition of the term. It is more straightforward to simply say that deontologists are those who reject consequentialism. Generally deontology connotes a constraint, and deontologists, in contrast to consequentialists, believe in constraints or rules that cause moral barriers in the promotion of the good (Kagan 1998: 73). Those who favor a deontological approach tend to believe that acting ethically or morally involves accepting constraints or rules that place limits on how we pursue our own interests as well as on the pursuit of the general good. Deontologists argue that the consequentialists' pursuit of furthering their own interests or pursuing the general good fails to provide morally sufficient reasons for taking action (Davis 1991: 205). They believe that certain acts are wrong in themselves and morally unsupportable and that such acts are an unacceptable way to pursue any ends, even those that are morally good.

Deontologists take the view that to act rightly, persons must first of all refrain from doing things that can be said to be wrong before the fact; these wrong acts are defined by what are variously called rules, laws, and constraints. For a deontologist, it is not the wrongness of the consequences of a particular lie or of lying in general that makes it wrong to lie. For them, lies are wrong because of what they are, and they are therefore wrong even when they produce good consequences (Davis 1991: 207).

Deontological theorists claim that the rightness or wrongness of an act depends entirely upon the kind of act that has occurred and not upon its consequences. Accordingly, for example, it is right to keep one's promises because, by its very nature, a promise must be carried out regardless of a person's inclinations or the effects that carrying it out will have. Deontological theories are sometimes called duty ethics, because they stress ideas of obligation and duty.

As Scarre (1996: 13) points out, often consequentialist and deontological approaches will, in practice, lead to similar moral conclusions. For example, a deontologist would argue that the act of breaking promises or stealing goods is wrong because such acts break the moral law or because they infringe on people's right to be told the truth or the right of persons to keep their private property. A consequentialist would agree that promise breaking and theft are morally wrong, but his or her judgment would rely on the negative impact of these practices on human welfare, not on the intrinsic wrongness of these acts. A conflict will arise, however, in those exceptional cases where performing an act normally considered to be wrong is likely to increase the utility or benefit achieved in the outcome.

Julia Annas points out that

> there has been a growing sense that there is something deeply inadequate about the view that when we systemize theories about our ethical view we are faced with the traditional option, a simple choice between consequentialist and deontological ways of thinking. If this is our option, then we must choose between calculating consequences to discover the right way to act, or rely on moral rules to guide us. (in Kopperi 1999: 1)

In response to this constraint, philosophers have returned to the classical forms of moral thought and especially to the virtue ethics of Aristotle. Virtue theories aim to provide a person with a clear picture of the good life and a means of ordering one's priorities in a way that enables the good life to be realized. In contrast, modern ethics, relying on consequentialist and deontological approaches, does not engage with questions such as, "What aims should I pursue?" "What books should I read?" or "What friends should I have?" As Annas puts it, "A great deal of modern literature and psychology arises and revolves around the way people reflect about their lives, but thought about one's life is no longer seen as central to ethical philosophy, at least to ethical theory" (in Kopperi 1999: 9–10). More recently, a number of philosophers have argued for an approach to ethics that would include all aspects of human life. For example, Nussbaum seeks to replace the distinction between the moral and nonmoral aspects of life with a notion that would include all aspects of that life (in Kopperi 1999: 10). Solomon promotes a virtue ethics approach to business ethics, relating business practice and ethics to individual responsibility and character and not to abstract principles or moral rules (p. 11).

In his philosophy, Kant criticizes virtue ethics for confusing happiness and morality. He argues that concerns about one's own happiness and broader concerns about morality are entirely different issues, each with their own objectives, and that they should be kept separate (Kopperi 1999: 12):

> Whereas virtues in ancient theories enable a human being to live a good life and to achieve her final goal, in modern ethics they enable her to follow the moral law that is, in turn, independent of the notion of the good life. (Kopperi 1999: 15)

Ancient ethics stands in contrast to modern ethics, because each advises persons to seek guidance about moral actions from a different direction. Whereas ancient theories call upon the notion of the good life when determining the moral worth of particular acts, modern moral theories see morality and the good life as two quite distinct issues. The modern view is that a particular action is not morally right simply because it contributes to the good life or to happiness (Kopperi 1999: 22). The classical moral theorists believed that persons have a specific end given to them by nature and that realizing or achieving this end would constitute their good life and happiness (pp. 26–27). They considered that ethics ought to tell us how to realize our true natures and reach these specific ends. In this way of thinking, a good life is one in which one's potentialities as a human being are fulfilled. Once it is assumed that there is a clearly defined end for a person, it is then possible to work out what kinds of behavior ought to be encouraged and what character traits should be developed in order to lead a good life. This ancient notion of human nature having a specific end was jettisoned by the modern moral philosophers as modern science developed in the 16th and 17th centuries. According to the new interpretation, there are no final ends or purposes and no conception of the good life.

For Plato, Aristotle, the hedonists, and the Stoics, the questions are "What sort of life is best?" and "What sort of life constitutes 'happiness'?" (Sharples 1996: 84). The Greek conception of the world was of an orderly system where everything had a proper place and where everything in nature existed for a purpose (Rachels 1997). In this ordered system, for example, rain existed for the sake of growing plants, which in turn existed to benefit animals, which in turn existed to benefit people, whose well-being was the prime consideration. After the Greeks came Christian thinkers, who, while accepting this rational orderly system, believed that God was needed to complete the picture. According to their way of thinking, rain helps growing plants because that is what God intended, and animals benefit humans because that is what God made them for (p. 34). This Greek and Christian view of the world generated a number of ethical notions including those of the importance of human life and the preeminence of humans over animals as well as over nature. The rational and orderly world gave rise to laws of nature and notions of natural and unnatural acts. In the 16th century, with the advance of science and the knowledge of the earth's position in the universe, humankind's central place in the divine scheme of things was displaced, and Galileo, Newton, and others explored natural phenomena using empirical methods. Now it was found that the rain did not fall to help plants grow but because of physical causes (p. 35).

Like many disciplines, philosophy has been impacted by postmodernism. In a detailed exploration of postmodern ethics, Bauman (1993: 4) argues that postmodernism has brought about a change in the way we address moral problems. Instead of responding to those problems through a philosophical search for universal principles and universal theories, postmodernism claims that absolute obligations and principles are oppressive, and that in the postmodern age the individual need not seek to attain moral ideals and guard moral values (p. 2). Bauman's contention is that rather than rejecting moral concerns altogether, what is required is a new way of approaching ethics. He identifies a number of aspects associated with the postmodern perspective on ethics, including the following (pp. 10–14):

- The notion that humans are essentially good and are merely in need of moral guidance has been discredited and replaced by the notion that humans are in fact morally ambivalent, and therefore no coherent ethical code can satisfy all needs. The absence of a moral code means we need to learn how to live without those sorts of guarantees.
- The assumption that morality and ethics function like law in trying to define what is proper or improper in given situations substitutes a body of rules for the individual moral self. This notion, says Bauman,

  leave[s] no "grey area" of ambivalence and multiple interpretations. In other words, it acts on the assumption that in each life-situation one choice can and should be decreed to be good in opposition to numerous bad ones, and so acting in all situations can be rational while the actors are, as they should be, rational as well. But this assumption leaves out what is properly moral in morality. It shifts moral phenomena from the realm of personal autonomy into that of power-assisted heteronomy. It substitutes the learnable knowledge of rules for the moral self constituted by responsibility. (p. 11)

- Postmodernism holds that few ethical choices can be considered unambiguously good and that the majority of such choices are made on the basis of impulses, which are often contradictory. As Bauman (1993: 11) writes, "The moral self moves, feels and acts in the context of ambivalence and is shot through with uncertainty." There is, therefore, a stress on moral acts seldom providing complete satisfaction and on the uncertainty that accompanies any ethical decision making.
- Morality is not universalizable.
- Morality is irrational in the sense that attempts to erect a body of rules for ethical conduct meet resistance in the form of the autonomy of the moral self.
- Power plays a role in shaping moral codes, because such codes purport to be the final authority on morality. In contrast, the postmodern perspective holds ethical codes to be relative and sees the moral practices they recommend as being the outcome of political exercises of power that claim the status of "universal" for ethical codes. Codes of ethics that deny relativism as well as the local and the particular substitute rule-bound ethics for personal morality.

The postmodern trend in ethics is exemplified in the work of Richard Rorty, who has argued that philosophy in its traditional form is dead and that the privileged position of philosophers as guardians of the truth has ended. Rorty sees a need for philosophy to help individuals and society break free from philosophical vocabularies and attitudes that he regards as outdated and worn out. As Rumana (2000: 4) explains, Rorty does not accept the notion that "truth is something waiting to be discovered; that only Universal claims are to be accepted; or that there are clear boundaries that separate academic disciplines into neat departments." Rorty's statement appears to be correct, because an association has developed between ethics and literary and cultural theory that has generated collaboration between these various disciplines (see, for example, Rainsford and Woods 1999). Like Bauman and Rorty, Emmanuel Levinas rejects universal laws and favors a postmodern approach to ethics that emphasizes goodness and responsibility. He sees ethics as shaped by relationships rather than by ethical codes (in Atterton 2002: 231).

The exploration of ethical theories begins with the principal theories of deontology (Chapter 9: Duty and Principle), consequentialism (Chapter 10: Considering the Consequences), and virtue (Chapter 11: The Importance of Character); and it continues with Stoicism, hedonism, and ethical egoism (Chapter 12: Egoism, Pleasure, and Indifference), social justice (Chapter 13: A Sense of Justice), and finally the ethic of care and peacemaking (Chapter 14: Caring for Others).

CHAPTER 9

Duty and Principle

Immanuel Kant (1724–1804) is considered one of the greatest of the modern philosophers. He argued that morality depends upon following absolute rules. For example, he believed that lying is never right, no matter what the circumstances. The central issue for Kant is "What ought I to do?" and he attempts to determine the rules, maxims, or fundamental principles of action that we should adopt (O'Neill 1991: 176). For Kant, motive is essential, and actions possess moral worth only if they are performed in accordance with what he termed the "categorical imperative" and out of the motive of duty (Benn 1998: 172).

Kant's focus was on the morality of the act and not on its outcome. He relied on rational arguments for his evaluation of morality, arguing, for example, that reason requires that we never lie. He contends that it is important not only to do what is right, but also to do it for the right reason or motive, and that the only motive that provides us with moral worth is the motive of what he calls duty (Holmes 1998: 113). That is, *we do what is right because it is right, and it is right because it is our duty.* Persons who act from the motive of duty are said to "have a good will." Kant's approach is therefore to focus on an internal orientation. He takes no account of the consequences of a particular act, of preferences, or of any theological framework (O'Neill 1991: 184).

Kant's philosophy does not mean that morality should be based on feelings or emotions but rather on the concepts of duty, obligation, and rationality. Morality requires that we act as fully rational beings would act, and therefore moral conduct is rational conduct (Holmes 1998: 114). In answering the question, "What is a moral action as opposed to an unethical action?" Kant would reply that a moral action is one done from a respect for duty, and therefore a moral person is one who acts from a motive of duty and not from inclination or simply in accord with duty. He offers the example of a person who refuses the temptation to commit suicide even though his life is miserable and wretched (Hinman 1998: 212). If the refusal to commit suicide is motivated by duty, it has moral worth according to Kant. However, if the refusal were motivated by other factors, such as one's fears about the act of killing oneself or from a desire to live, it would not have moral worth. In another example, Kant contrasts two types of people who help others. One type helps others without motives of vanity or self-interest, but simply because he receives inner pleasure from helping others. Kant argues that such actions have no moral worth, because they are not done for the sake of duty but out of a desire for "good feelings." The second type of person helps others for the sake of duty alone, even though she has problems of her own, has no inclination to become involved in aiding others, and has no feelings of care or sympathy (Hinman 1998: 214). Kant argues that this person's actions have moral worth for the reason that it is morally valuable for a person to help others because it is the right thing to do even though she is overwhelmed with her own problems. In Kant's vision of morality, there are some actions we must perform. We impose a moral law on ourselves that creates an obligation to act in certain ways. Kant does not see morality as arising from acts that make us want to help others but instead sees it as a struggle, as the moral strength of our will to overcome the temptations that might lead us to go against the moral law (Schneewind 1992: 310).

Hypothetical and Categorical Imperatives

Kant distinguished hypothetical or conditional imperatives from categorical imperatives. *Hypothetical imperatives* are courses of conduct governed by the word *ought* that establish a pattern that we have a certain wish and recognize that a particular course of action will help us to achieve that wish, and, as a consequence, we decide that we should follow that course of action (Rachels 1999). An example of a hypothetical imperative might be, "If you want to achieve good grades, you will have to study hard."

In contrast, moral obligations do not depend upon particular desires but are categorical, taking the form, "You ought to do such and such." A *categorical imperative* commands and lays down a law (Scruton 2001: 85). Such acts are unconditional. For example, the categorical rule is that you should be helpful to people regardless of your particular wants and desires. In contrast, the hypothetical imperative would state that you ought to help people *if* you care for them or *if* you have some other purpose that might be served by helping them. Kant developed two versions of the categorical imperative: the principle of universality and respect for all persons. These two versions of the categorical imperative are discussed in the following sections.

The Principle of Universality

Kant expounded the principle of the categorical imperative (first version) in 1785 in his work *Groundwork of the Metaphysics of Morals.* He expressed this form of the categorical imperative as follows: "Act only according to the maxim by which you can at the same time will that it should become a universal law" (in Rachels 1999: 124).

Kant suggests that this version of the categorical imperative can determine what one's duty will be in a particular set of circumstances. He contends that because human beings are rational creatures, they ought to behave rationally, and, for Kant, this means that one ought always to behave as if one's course of conduct were to become a universal law. That is to say, every action must be evaluated according to how it would be regarded if it were to be a code of behavior that applied to everyone universally. This principle suggests a procedure that can be used to determine whether an act is morally permissible.

What is a maxim? According to Schneewind (1992: 318) a maxim "is a personal or subjective plan of action, incorporating the agent's reasons for acting as well as a sufficient indication of what act the reasons call for." The term *maxim* includes both principle and motive (Scruton 2001: 85). A maxim is a subjective rule, and there are many commonly known rules that can be described as maxims. Some examples include the following:

- Always be loyal to your friends.
- Always watch out for number one.
- Never act in a way that would make your parents ashamed of you. (Hinman 1998: 222)

A rational person tests his or her maxims before acting upon them. The "maxim of the act" means the rule you would be following if you were to do that act. You must then ask whether you would be willing for that rule (maxim) to be followed by everyone all the time so that it would be a "universal law." If this criterion is satisfied, the rule or maxim may be followed, and the act is permissible. If, however, you would not be willing for everyone to follow the rule, you ought not to follow it, and the act would be considered morally impermissible. Hill (2000: 39) suggests that the universal law formula is concerned with our "willingness to reciprocate, to avoid being a free-rider, and to check one's personal policies by reflecting about what would be reasonable from a broader perspective." However, he also acknowledges the difficulty of working out the details through which this simple formula can operate as a test for determining right and wrong in particular cases. He notes that a significant literature has developed as followers of Kant have constructed devices to make the formula work as an "action guide."

Holmes (1998: 119) calls our attention to the fact that the categorical imperative makes no reference to goodness and does not advocate promoting the good of anyone. In this sense, the imperative is not concerned with consequences or with goodness, and if we follow the categorical imperative, we will be cultivating goodwill purely for the reason that we will be trying to do what is right because it is right. Kant believes people have goodwill in the sense that they act in accordance with the motive of duty; that is, they show respect for the moral law.

Kant provides a number of examples of this maxim in operation, one of which concerns borrowing money. Suppose a man needs to borrow money and is aware that no one will make a loan to him unless he promises to repay (Rachels 1999: 124). He is aware of this, but he also knows that he will not be able to repay the loan. He therefore faces the following issue: Should he promise to repay knowing he cannot do so, in order to get someone to make him the loan? If this is what he decides to do, the maxim or rule he would be following can be stated as follows: Whenever you need a loan, promise to repay it even though you know you will not be able to do so. Applying the principle of the categorical imperative, we would ask ourselves, "Could this rule become a universal law?" The answer is clearly no, because it would be self-defeating—no one would believe promises to repay any longer, and no one would make loans.

Kant argues that the categorical imperative binds rational agents because they are rational (Rachels 1999: 130). Therefore, he insists that a person who did not accept the categorical imperative would be not only immoral but also irrational. This means that a moral judgment must be backed by good reasons (it must be rationally arrived at). You may not say that you accept reasons some of the time but not all of the time, and moral reasons must be binding on everyone all the time. The basic idea here is that individuals cannot regard themselves as special from a moral point of view, and they must accept that moral reasons require a consistent approach.

Kant proposed that the rule against lying is a categorical imperative, and he wrote that lying in any circumstances is "the obliteration of one's dignity as a human being" (in Rachels 1999: 125). He argued that the prohibition against lying flowed from the categorical imperative. We cannot will that it be a universal law to lie, because such a law would be self-defeating. People would quickly realize they could not rely on what other people said, and lies would not be believed. Thus, one should never lie, because if lying became a universal law, all relations based on trust and honoring promises would become unworkable.

Respect for All Persons

As well as the formulation of the first version of the categorical imperative noted above, Kant provided a second formulation and stated that the ultimate moral principle can also be expressed as follows: "Act so that you treat humanity, whether in your own person or that of another, always as an end and never as a means only" (in Rachels 1999: 133).

Kant apparently believed that this version of the categorical imperative expressed the same basic idea as the earlier version and was intended to be its equivalent in that it would yield the same moral judgments for particular situations (Holmes 1998: 123). It is a command requiring us to respect other people because they are rational human beings just like us. This respect should not be based on social rank, individual talents, or even moral goodness but is grounded in the dignity of humanity, a value possessed by everyone who has the capacity to be a moral agent (Hill 2000: 64). If we do not treat others as ends in themselves but only as a means of achieving what we want, we disregard their humanity and treat them as things. Kant proposed a perspective based on the idea that human beings are ultimately the source of all our values, moral and personal (Hill 2000: 68). As Hill puts it, "The common framework Kant proposes . . . is a basic requirement across cultures and individual differences, to respect every human being as a source of value" (p. 77).

In Kant's view, human beings have an intrinsic worth or dignity that is not enjoyed by other animals. He saw animals merely as a means to an end, with man as the end. In Kant's perspective, therefore, animals could be used any way we liked, but humans could never be used as a means to an end. He thought that humans had intrinsic worth and dignity because they are rational agents. That is, humans are free agents able to make their own decisions, set their own goals, and guide their conduct by reason. He argued that the moral law is an expression of the law of reason, and therefore rational beings embody the moral law itself. Since rational beings have a value beyond all price, they ought always to be treated as an end and never as a means. This means, for example, that we have a strict duty to strive to promote the welfare of others; we must respect their rights and avoid causing them harm. We must also respect their rationality, which means we must never manipulate or use people to achieve our own purposes (Holmes 1998; Rachels 1999).

Kant provides an example of this version of the categorical imperative similar to the borrowing example used to illustrate the first version (Rachels 1999: 134–135). He says, suppose you need money and want a loan but know you cannot repay it. You are desperate and consider giving a false promise to repay to induce a friend to give you the money. You might need the money for a good purpose and be able to convince yourself that lying to a friend would be justified. Nevertheless, Kant argued, if you lied to your friend, you would be manipulating her and using her as a means to an end. Suppose on the other hand you told the truth, explaining that you needed the money for a particular purpose and could not repay it. In this case, your friend could make up her own mind about whether to give you the loan, and she could exercise her own powers of reason and make a free choice. If she did decide to give you the money, she would be choosing to make your purpose for the money her own. So in this case, you would not be using her to achieve your goal. This principle has been important in theories of democracy, because it supports the notion that all people are created equal (where this notion signifies that no one should be discriminated against before the law).

In another example, Hinman (1998: 229) describes research done in the 1930s in the United States on the long-term effects of syphilis. The researchers decided to take a group of black men who had already been diagnosed with syphilis, not tell them they had syphilis nor treat them with penicillin, and simply observe the development of the disease in the group until they died. These men therefore became the unknowing subjects of a medical research project that continued until 1972 and cost them their lives and their well-being. There are a number of objectionable factors in this case, such as the obvious fact that these men were allowed to die when they could easily have been treated to prevent their death from syphilis. We therefore object to the pain and suffering that resulted from this decision. It is also objectionable that they were deceived about their condition, and we recognize that because they were not told about the research, they had no choice about participating in it.

Hill (2000: 114) argues that treating others with basic human respect applies even to the perpetrators of serious crimes, who should not be seen as having forfeited that respect based on the criminal acts they committed. He also argues that the use of force to protect oneself against an opposing force is both a right and a responsibility, but that proportional responses to threats against us should not show contempt for the attacker. Even where self-protection warrants the use of lethal force, Hill suggests that a readiness to kill when absolutely necessary need not include a contemptuous attitude toward the attacker, because such an attitude would be indicative of our judgment that the aggressor has forfeited all respect as a human being. Thus, he argues that a self-defender showing respect for human dignity would prefer that aggressors retreat peacefully, that they not suffer permanent pain or humiliation, and that ultimately they would be able to rejoin the law-abiding community.

Basic respect for human dignity is also signified by providing fair trials and access to legal advice, ensuring processes of appeal, taking into account mitigating circumstances, and creating prison conditions that do not degrade the individual who has received the just punishment of society already in the form of deprivation of liberty (Hill 2000: 116). Fundamentally, Hill suggests that punishment and moral censure ought to be just and respectful, consistent with the presumption that all human beings have dignity, a status "that need not be earned and cannot be forfeited" (p. 117).

Kingdom of Ends

A third formulation of the categorical imperative commands that we

act only so that the will through its maxims could regard itself at the same time as universally law giving. (Holmes 1998: 124)

The emphasis in this form of the categorical imperative is that when we act morally, we fully choose our own moral decisions as autonomous moral agents. When we act on rules or maxims that can be universally accepted by all rational beings, it is as if we are legislating for all rational beings as though we were each of us universal law givers. We should not, therefore, allow our choices to be made for us by anyone else, because we would be compromising our autonomy. Consequently, we cannot rely on society, government, or religious leaders to tell us what our moral decision should be. Also, we must not allow our choices to be determined by our own desires, preferences, or wishes, as this would ultimately reduce all decisions about choices to acts of self-love. On the contrary, we must act from the motive of duty to achieve a goodwill (p. 124).

This notion that every adult is an autonomous agent broke radically from the views prevailing at the time, because the theorists who were influential in the 17th and 18th centuries did not believe that most people had the ability to know what was right without being told what morality required of them (Schneewind 1992: 311–312). The theorists of the time accepted that God had given everyone the ability to know basic principles of morality, but they did not believe that persons were capable of grasping by themselves what moral action was required in particular cases. During that time, most theorists thought of morality as centering on obligations imposed by law and backed by threats of punishment for violations.

Conflicting Duties

The notion that there are absolute moral rules—such as a rule against lying—that do not allow any exceptions gives rise to a problem in conflict cases (Rachels 1999: 129). These are instances when one is faced with two alternative courses of action, both of which are held to be absolutely wrong. What does a person do when faced with two absolutely wrong choices when she must act and no other alternatives are available? An example occurred during World War II when Dutch fishermen often smuggled Jewish refugees in their boats. These boats would sometimes be stopped by Nazi patrol boats when they had refugees in the hold. The Nazi captain would ask the Dutch captain questions about the boat's route and who was on board, and the Dutch fishermen would lie and bring their refugees to safety. It is clear that in this case, the fishermen had only two alternatives: to lie, or to allow themselves and their passengers to be taken and shot. There was no third alternative, because they had to answer the questions and they could not outrun a fast patrol boat. If the two rules, "It is wrong to lie" and "It is wrong to allow innocent people to be murdered" are both taken to be absolutes, the Dutch fishermen would have to do one or the other, and so a moral argument that prohibits both absolutely makes no sense. The way out is to argue that in certain circumstances only one of these rules is absolute, although this alternative may not work in every case and there is always the possibility that two absolute rules will come into conflict.

One way of dealing with this problem of conflict of duties is to argue that moral rules should be treated as generalizations and not as categorical rules without exceptions. Thus, in general, we should tell the truth, but there may be circumstances where we would feel morally obliged to tell lies. *In other words, telling the truth is an obligation that should be kept provided there are no other overriding factors present.* Another deontological philosopher, W. D. Ross (in Dancy 1991: 219), has referred to those obligations that a person is obliged to perform in the absence of any other overriding factors as "prima facie duties." His view is that all sorts of things matter, and it is not possible to maintain a neat list of morally significant features. He argues that we have a prima facie duty to help others, to keep promises, to repay past acts of kindness, and not to let down people who rely on us. For Ross, these things matter morally and have to be taken into account in considering what we should do and in assessing whether we have acted rightly in what we choose to do. However, these duties are only prima facie, and other things matter too (Dancy 1991: 221). In other words, we have other prima facie duties as well, for example, to increase the welfare of others. In a particular case, we cannot tell in advance which prima facie duty will turn out to matter most, and all we can do is consider the circumstances and try to decide which course of action is more important. In doing this, no set of rules can answer the question for us.

Nevertheless, as Hill (2000: 52) points out, in Kantian moral theory, strict moral dilemmas are conceptually impossible. Therefore, if it seems a duty forbids action A and action B, but we cannot avoid doing one or the other, then the solution is to go back and rethink the issue. This includes, if necessary, reviewing the reasoning that initially led us to think of A and B as strict duties in the first place.

Applying Deontological Theory

Case Study 9.1 illustrates how deontological theory can be applied to an ethical dilemma within the criminal justice system.

**CASE STUDY 9.1 ROUGH JUSTICE
IN A JUVENILE INSTITUTION**

Joe is a corrections officer in a juvenile detention center and works on a unit housing 15 young offenders, many of whom suffer mental health problems. Joe has worked at the institution for about two months, he feels comfortable with the job, and he has been accepted by the other staff and he admires them for the skills they show. He has not had any significant problems with the juveniles and is generally enjoying the work and is learning skills on the job.

It is lunch time on Monday, and Joe is in the dining room supervising the juveniles as they eat their lunch. At one table sit six juveniles, one of whom is a 17-year-old named Brian who Joe thinks has a developmental disability. Brian displays offensive table manners, which on this day put Joe off his own meal. Brian keeps adding ketchup in vast quantities to every dish and slurping it from the plate. He also uses his hands instead of his fork, keeps talking while he is eating, and spits food across the table. Joe can see that the other juveniles are repulsed by this behavior in the same way that he is.

Joe is surprised to see his co-worker, Daren, suddenly get up from the table, go over to Brian, grab him by the shirt collar, and move him away from the table. Daren takes Brian off to the kitchen and returns with a large mixing bowl. He then tells Brian to scrape out what is left of his meal into the bowl and, taking Brian to the center of the dining room, he puts the bowl on the floor and tells Brian to eat. He tells him he has disgusting manners and if he is going to eat like a dog at the table, he might as well get down on the floor like a real dog. He tells him to stay down there until he has licked his bowl clean.

Joe does not react to these events. Later Daren explains to Joe and other staff members who were present that the reason he acted in that way with Brian was to shock him into understanding that his table manners were highly offensive. He thought that if he used "tough love" on Brian in that way, Brian would be less likely to alienate his co-detainees, and this might help him get through the experience of being in the institution.

SOURCE: Jones and Carlson 2001: 165–166.

In resolving what may be an ethical dilemma, Joe will follow the process of resolving an ethical dilemma set out in Chapter 1:

1. *Is Joe faced with an ethical dilemma?*

   Joe is faced with the dilemma of whether to report Daren's treatment of Brian. He might also consider whether he ought to have intervened to prevent Brian's mistreatment.

2. *What are the facts and circumstances of the incident?*
Joe needs to review in his mind the facts and circumstances and perhaps write them down in the form of a report so that his memory of the events is quite clear.

3. *What are the facts relevant to the decision he has to make? What are his own values about the issue and what are the values of his workplace about such an issue?*
The relevant facts are the following:

- Joe has worked at the institution for only a short time.
- He has confidence and trust in the experience and skills of other staff.
- Brian may be mentally challenged or have a developmental disability.
- Daren's conduct toward Brian was certainly offensive and unpleasant to watch.
- Daren's conduct in relation to Brian was surprising to Joe.
- Joe takes note of Daren's explanation for his conduct.
- Joe agrees with Daren that it is important for the juvenile detainees to get along with each other during their time in the institution.

Joe is in sympathy with the juveniles detained at the institution and does not have a punitive attitude toward them. He believes his job is worthwhile, and he believes in professionalism in the workplace. In relation to the values of the workplace, he is aware because of his training that there is a code of ethics that regulates his conduct as a correctional officer; he is also aware of various departmental rules and regulations about how he is to conduct himself that make him responsible for the safety and well-being of those in his custody. Informally, he is aware of an institutional culture that he shares with his co-workers. This culture is complex but it does stress loyalty and support for co-workers generally.

4. *What ethical theories does he call to mind to assist him in resolving the dilemma?*
In this case, Joe will apply deontological ethical theory to the dilemma.

5. *What are Joe's available courses of action?*
Joe made no move to intervene at the time of the incident, so the time has passed for decision making in relation to the actual incident. This leaves him with two alternatives: He can take no further action, or he can prepare a written report of the incident and give it to his supervisor.

6. *Joe will make his decision after applying, in this case, the deontological approach to each alternative course of action, and he will choose the course of action that is the most ethically appropriate for him under deontology.*

A process for assessing an ethical dilemma from a deontological perspective is set out in Box 9.1. Applications of the criteria listed are shown in Box 9.2.

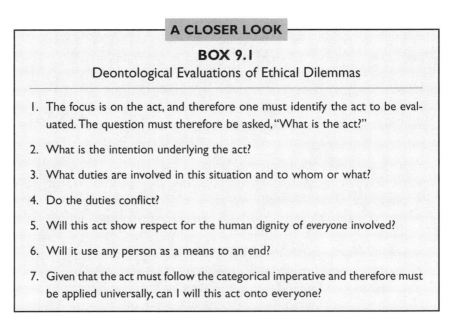

A CLOSER LOOK

BOX 9.1
Deontological Evaluations of Ethical Dilemmas

1. The focus is on the act, and therefore one must identify the act to be evaluated. The question must therefore be asked, "What is the act?"

2. What is the intention underlying the act?

3. What duties are involved in this situation and to whom or what?

4. Do the duties conflict?

5. Will this act show respect for the human dignity of *everyone* involved?

6. Will it use any person as a means to an end?

7. Given that the act must follow the categorical imperative and therefore must be applied universally, can I will this act onto everyone?

A CLOSER LOOK

BOX 9.2
Applying Deontology

1. The focus is on the act, and therefore one must identify the act to be evaluated. The question must therefore be asked "What is the act?"

   There are two possible options: to report the incident or to do nothing.

2. What is the intention underlying the act?

   In reporting the incident, the underlying motive is to protect Brian from any further injury, to protect other juveniles from the same kind of treatment, and to deter Daren and possibly other staff from taking such action again.

   In doing nothing, the underlying motive is to support co-workers through a demonstration of loyalty and to agree with Daren that, on balance, Brian's interests are better served by tough love treatment like this, so that he can reform his behavior and have good relations with his codetainees.

3. What duties are involved in this situation and to whom or what?

   Joe and all juvenile workers have a duty to protect those in their custody from mistreatment. At the same time, Joe and his co-workers have a duty to support each other in carrying out their duties within the bounds set by ethical standards and departmental rules and regulations.

4. Do the duties conflict?

   Yes, the duties conflict with each other, and this creates a problem under the deontological approach, because Kant offered no way of resolving such conflicts other than to go back and rethink the ethical dilemma and the relevant duties.

5. Will this act show respect for the human dignity of everyone involved?

    Reporting the matter will show respect for the dignity of Brian. Not reporting fails to show respect for the dignity of Brian, because it condones a humiliating act and raises the possibility that Daren or others might do the same or similar acts in the future.

6. Will it use any person as a means to an end?

    If Joe reports the incident, he is not using anyone as a means to an end, and in particular, he will not be using Brian or his colleague, Daren, in making that report, because in the process he will be respecting their humanity and dignity.

    If Joe does not report the incident, he will be using Brian as a means to an end, because his end will be to cover up the incident and protect Daren; in doing this he will be sacrificing the interests of Brian and his duties toward him.

7. Given that the act must follow the categorical imperative and therefore must be applied universally, can I will this act onto everyone?

    If he reports the incident, the maxim would be that "I ought to protect juveniles in my custody from harm and mistreatment," and he can will this maxim as a universal law.

    If he does not report the incident, he cannot formulate any universal maxim. The reason for not reporting is either because Joe believes he has a duty to be absolutely loyal to his co-workers or because he accepts Daren's explanation that this particular act was one of "tough love" and therefore was for the good of the juvenile. It is not possible to have a universal law of absolute loyalty to co-workers, because this would allow any act, however harsh or barbaric, to be condoned. Tough love is often used as justification for conduct that is seen by the perpetrator as appropriate in the particular circumstances. Such conduct may vary from case to case. Since it lacks precise definition and because others may not agree with the perpetrator that it is appropriate conduct, it cannot stand as a universal law.

    In all the circumstances, it is clear that the appropriate course of action for Joe, applying the deontological perspective, is to report the incident to his supervisor.

Summary

Kant's answer to the question "What ought I to do?" is that one should act in accordance with duty and obligation and in a rational manner. For Kant, the consequences of an act are irrelevant, and duty and the formulation of absolute rules for behavior ought to supercede all other considerations. For deontologists, moral obligations are seen as categorical, and the categorical imperative, as formulated by Kant, lays down the law that must be followed regardless of one's individual wants and desires. It is our duty to follow a categorical imperative.

Kant believed that humans are rational creatures and that every act should be evaluated as if one's behavior were to become a universal law. In other words, this evaluation would determine whether everyone should act this way and therefore whether an act was morally permissible. The test for the categorical imperative is whether an individual is willing for a particular rule to be followed by *all* persons at all times, and if it is, this gives it the status of a universal law. This seems simple on the surface but can give rise to specific problems. For example, Kant proposed that the rule against lying was a categorical imperative and argued that it was wrong to lie under any circumstances. However, in practice, people will sometimes lie when faced with moral choices about how to act. For example, it is both wrong to lie and wrong to allow innocent people to be murdered, and in some situations these two rules can conflict. A number of solutions have been suggested to resolve this conflict, including treating moral rules not as absolute categorical rules but as generalizations. In other words, we should always tell the truth provided there is no other overriding factor that would morally justify telling a lie.

Another important principle developed by Kant is that we should respect other people because they are rational human beings with dignity, and we should not treat them as a means to an end but as an end in themselves. This means that we should not use people to satisfy our own ends, and we should always respect others' rights, promote their welfare, and avoid causing them harm. In doing so, we promote the worth and dignity of individuals. This concept appears in practice in the criminal justice system in the form of ensuring fair trials, giving access to justice, and treating prisoners with dignity, compassion, and humanity.

DISCUSSION CASE

Consider the following circumstances and the individual ethical duty of Officer Ricardo Colon by applying the deontological criteria.

No Special Treatment?

In the early evening hours of February 12, 1998, Captain James Brady of the Homicide Division of the Philadelphia Police Department, a 27-year veteran, finished his shift at police headquarters and headed for a popular bar just a few blocks away, where he partied with co-workers, New York police, and some justice professionals. He drank 64–80 ounces of alcohol. At about 11 p.m., Brady departed the bar, leaving behind a brief case containing his pistol, his cell phone, and some case files. He drove off to his home.

That evening an eyewitness filed a report with police. She had heard a loud noise outside her apartment shortly after 11 p.m. A police report recounted that a 1992 blue Honda Civic sedan had been struck at that location not far from the bar where Brady had been drinking. Brady had hit this vehicle and then left the scene of the accident. The front grill of his car was badly crushed, the left side of the hood jutted straight up, and the air bag had inflated from the force of impact. Brady was driving an unmarked police vehicle, a 1989 Plymouth Grand Fury. Officer Ricardo Colon, who noted the unmarked police car riding slowly by with heavy damage, observed Brady driving away from the scene of the accident. Colon sounded two blasts on his air horn signaling the driver to stop, but Brady continued driving until Colon switched on his lights and siren. Colon then notified police radio that he had the car stopped and the dispatcher requested, as was customary, that an officer back-up Colon in his investigation.

Without waiting for the backup to arrive, Colon approached the vehicle, and Brady identified himself as a police captain. At this point, Officer Gregory Yatcilla arrived. He, like Colon, had less than a year on the job. By this time Brady had exited the vehicle and was wobbling as he stood and was slurring his speech. Also the inseam of Brady's pants was soaked, indicating that he had wet his pants. Colon understood the seriousness of the situation and, as he had been trained to do, radioed for a supervisor who arrived shortly in the person of Lieutenant Joseph DiLacqua, a 25-year veteran.

DiLacqua had been disciplined on numerous occasions. He conducted a private conversation with Brady and then ordered Yatcilla to move the damaged car onto the sidewalk. DiLacqua then radioed in an auto accident report that gave the impression that no injuries had occurred and that an oncoming vehicle had invaded Brady's route. When the Department's Accident Investigation Division (AID) arrived (called because a city vehicle was involved), they were told the same story by DiLacqua. Brady said nothing. After AID gave their release, DiLacqua drove Brady back to the bar to pick up his briefcase, but it had already been transported back to police headquarters, the return having been organized by a bartender. Brady was then driven home by Yatcilla. No blood alcohol test was administered.

That night, accident investigators photographed the scene, and the photographs revealed a different story than that told to AID. There was no debris underneath the car, and a trail of engine coolant from the radiator stretched for 14 blocks back to the original point of impact. There were no skid marks showing that Brady had swerved or braked when he was allegedly run off the road.

What is Colon's ethical dilemma? What should Colon do according to a deontological perspective?

SOURCE: From "Policing the Brass: A Case Study in Command Malfeasance," by William Giannetti in *Criminal Justice Ethics*, Volume 22, Number 2 (Summer/Fall 2003), pp. 32–50. Reprinted by permission of The Institute for Criminal Justice Ethics, 222 West 57th Street, Suite 607, New York, NY 10019-1029.

DISCUSSION QUESTIONS

1. Do you agree that formulating absolute rules for behavior helps us to live a moral life? Explain with reference to Kant's principles.

2. Explain how acting according to absolute moral rules might present moral conflicts in practice. Provide examples for your explanations.

3. What is the place of emotion and intuition in Kant's thinking? Explain with examples.

4. Respect for other people is a crucial aspect of deontological theories. Discuss with reference to policing and correctional practice.

CHAPTER 10

Considering the Consequences

When we think about the right ethical action to take in a particular situation, we might ask ourselves whether we should always act in order to bring about the best possible consequences. Consequentialism is an important and widely discussed theory of ethical action, and according to this approach, what makes an act morally right or wrong is its consequences and nothing more (Benn 1998: 60). The motives for the act or the nature of the act itself are not important considerations in consequentialism. The classical utilitarian (consequentialist) theorists were Jeremy Bentham (1748–1832) and John Stuart Mill (1806–1873). Bentham is considered to have originated the doctrine of consequentialism and Mill to have provided a more refined version of it. Bentham led a group of radicals who sought to reform the laws and institutions of England using utilitarian approaches. Mill was the son of James Mill, a distinguished Scottish philosopher and historian, and a follower of Bentham (Rachels 1999a: 97).

The utilitarians attempted to lay down an objective principle that would determine if a particular action was ethically right or wrong; they called this principle the *principle of utility*. Mill referred to the principle of utility as the Greatest Happiness Principle (Rachels 1999a: 97). It states that an action is right in so far as it tends to produce the greatest happiness for everyone affected. In other words, this principle states that if we have a choice about which action or social policy to follow, we ought to choose the one that will give the best overall consequences for all concerned (p. 97). Therefore, utilitarians reject the idea that actions are right because God says they are or because they are inherently moral in their own right (Benn 1998: 62). Bentham and Mill rejected appeals to intuitive commonsense judgments that justified established practices that were philosophically suspect (Darwall 1998: 110). Mill, for example, who also wrote against the subjugation of women, believed that subjecting women to men's domination and control could not be justified by arguing that such social practices seemed natural and appropriate.

Utilitarians argue that morality is simply an attempt to bring about as much happiness as possible (Rachels 1999a: 97).

At the time this idea was first promoted, it was considered revolutionary (Rachels 1999a: 98). Bentham and Mill associated happiness with pleasure, and Bentham believed that mankind was governed by pain and pleasure. He argued that some things give us pleasure, whereas others cause us pain, and this basic fact explains why we behave as we do—we look for pleasure and attempt to avoid pain. It also explains why we determine some things to be good and others evil. Bentham therefore followed the reasoning that morality consists of trying to bring about as much pleasure as possible, for as many people as possible, while at the same time attempting to minimize the amount of pain in the world (Rachels 1999b: 65).

Also connected with the idea of pleasure is the theory of hedonism, which contends that the only ultimate intrinsic good is pleasure. This notion will be discussed more fully as a separate doctrine in Chapter 12. It is considered an attractive theory, because it is simple and expresses a notion that we find intuitively right—that things are good or bad because of the way they make us feel (Rachels 1999a: 108).

After publication of his work *Utilitarianism* in 1863, Mill was criticized for the hedonistic aspect of his doctrine, which was categorized by many as being "worthy of swine" (Benn 1998: 62). Applying the idea that happiness equates with pleasure, the principle can be said to state that an action is right if it produces the greatest amount of pleasure for the greatest number affected. If it does not achieve this goal, the action is considered morally wrong. However, many modern philosophers who are utilitarians do not interpret utilitarianism in this hedonistic manner; instead, they take "preference satisfaction" (Hinman 1998: 164) and not happiness as the final goal (Benn 1998: 61). Preference satisfaction refers to satisfying human preferences, interests, or desires (Scarre 1996: 3). The idea is that what should be maximized is not the balance of pleasures over pain, but the satisfaction of preferences more generally (Goodin 1991: 243).

Utilitarianism emphasizes the effects of an action, and if an action produces more beneficial effects than harmful effects, it is considered an ethical action; otherwise, it is not. It is crucial to understand that the consequences of an action determine whether it is right or wrong, and not the motive which prompts it to be done. For example, even Hitler may have believed that he was acting from a genuine desire to improve the German State, but his acts generated pain, genocide, and ultimately caused the collapse of the German State. A utilitarian would therefore say that Hitler's behavior produced more pain than pleasure, and so his acts were wrong for that reason.

In determining whether an action was right or wrong, consequentialists argue that it is possible to measure action. For example, it is possible to find out whether a particular action caused more pleasure than pain for all affected by the situation. We can calculate the amount of pleasure and the amount of pain and then determine whether the act was right or wrong by calculating which is greater. Bentham, in fact, developed a method for this calculation which he called the "hedonistic calculus." This hedonistic calculus has seven elements, including the intensity of the pleasure and its duration, which allow the amount of pleasure or pain of an act to be measured. He thought that numerical values could in principle be attached to these elements and then an arithmetical operation performed to determine the relative merits of varying courses of action (Scarre 1996: 75). Nevertheless, he did not believe that this process needed to be strictly pursued in the case of every moral judgment but rather that the notion of a calculus should be kept in mind as an ideal model of moral deliberation to which actual decision making should conform as closely as possible. It follows from this belief that the main outcome of utilitarianism is to separate the rightness or wrongness of an action from the motivation of the agent performing it, in other words, to distinguish the worth of the action from the worth of the agent. Obvious problems with Bentham's hedonistic calculus are the difficulties in accurately predicting consequences and its time-consuming nature.

It is important to appreciate that utilitarianism does not require us to ignore what may be good for ourselves. It does, however, require that we extend our concern to encompass the good effects on all those people affected by our actions (Holmes 1998: 131). In other words, we should try to bring about the greatest balance of good over bad that we can for *all* people. Rachels (1999a: 107–108) summarizes utilitarian theories in the following three propositions:

1. Actions are to be determined right or wrong by virtue of their consequences, and right actions are those that produce the best consequences. Nothing else is relevant.

2. In assessing consequences, everything is irrelevant except the amount of happiness or unhappiness that is produced. Accordingly, right actions are those that produce the greatest balance of happiness over unhappiness.

3. In calculating happiness or unhappiness, each person's welfare is equally important, and right actions are those that produce the greatest possible balance of happiness over unhappiness, taking into account each person affected.

According to Hinman (1998: 201), utilitarians conduct their lives according to two basic principles. The first is that utilitarians will always be concerned about the actual effects of their choices. They will be continually concerned about the basic facts of moral life such as who will suffer pain or hurt and who will gain pleasure resulting from a particular decision. They will try to predict outcomes accurately but will also accept, if they are not able to make accurate predictions, that there is an element of luck in leading a moral life. Accepting that luck will play a part may be problematic but does not mean abandoning utilitarianism as an adequate moral theory. Second, because utilitarianism is a "benevolent moral doctrine" (p. 201), utilitarians want to make the world a better place for all and increase the extent of well-being throughout the world. Utilitarians believe that their theory produces a happier world, reducing pain and suffering, and that morality should operate to make the world a better place for all.

Pleasure and Happiness

Mill argued hedonistically that the only ultimate value is pleasure or happiness, and he appears to equate the two. Yet, pleasure and happiness are not interchangeable, because it is possible to experience pleasure without being happy, and vice versa. Also, pleasure is generally linked to a particular activity or feeling in contrast to happiness, which is more a state of mind. Hinman argues that we think of pleasure in terms of the body and of sensuality, and that happiness is less directly related to the body (1998: 165). In response to criticisms of his emphasis on pleasure, Mill expressed the view that some pleasures were higher or more elevated than others; in other words, pleasures can be compared in terms of their quality (Benn 1998: 64; Scarre 1996: 90–92). He thought that a satisfying human life must contain "pleasures of the intellect, of the feelings and imagination, and of the moral sentiments," which he regarded as having a higher value as pleasures "than those of mere sensation" (Scarre 1996: 92). According to Hinman (1998: 167), there is no one choice for the standard of utility, and there may well be advantages in having utility signify a number of different factors and for consequences therefore to be measured according to various standards.

Act Consequentialism

Utilitarians who are considered act consequentialists argue that we should ask ourselves, in relation to each separate act, whether or not it promotes the greatest good. This means that individual decisions would be made on a case-by-case basis. Act consequentialists equate good with pleasure and believe that we should determine the rightness of individual acts according to whether each act would produce more pleasure than pain (Holmes 1998: 137). If more pleasure is produced, the act will be considered morally right; if less pleasure is produced, the act will be considered morally wrong. These theorists do not consider themselves bound by rules about, for example, stealing or lying, but they might believe that these acts should be avoided, because they usually produce bad consequences. Nevertheless, they do not believe that there is a rule that forbids them.

Hinman (1998: 180) notes a number of objections to act consequentialism, including the fact that it is extremely time-consuming to calculate the consequences of every individual action; that it is too difficult to predict the consequences of individual actions, especially in the long term; and that it generally neglects moral rules. In relation to the time-consuming argument, act utilitarians respond that they follow basic rules of thumb which incorporate the past experience of many situations and argue that what society generally considers a good outcome will usually produce the best consequences for everyone. Yet they insist that such rules are not absolute moral rules and are only summaries of what has occurred previously in relation to individual acts. Concerning the criticism that it is difficult to predict consequences, act utilitarians agree there are limits to prediction, but they see this as a difficulty with life in general and not their theoretical position. As such, the proper response according to them is not to reject their theory but to attempt to increase our ability to foresee consequences (p. 181).

Rule Consequentialism

In contrast to act consequentialists, this group of utilitarians argues that it is possible to link the consequentialist view of what makes acts right or wrong with moral rules (Holmes 1998). In other words, they believe that keeping to certain rules produces better consequences than trying to determine what consequences will follow from every individual action. For example, most people believe it to be their duty to speak the truth, even when doing so would cause more pain than pleasure. They do not advocate obedience to rules just because they are rules, but because they see following rules as the best way to achieve the general good or the best outcome for all affected (Holmes 1998: 137). In other words, an act is right only if it is in agreement with a rule that would maximize overall net happiness for all people affected as any alternative rule (Darwall 1998: 135; Holmes 1998: 137). Rule consequentialists are subject to criticism for the argument that if they take rules to be absolute and without exception, then they will have abandoned consequentialism (Hinman 1998: 183). If they acknowledge exceptions to rules, then they could really be described as act consequentialists.

Public Policy and Utilitarianism

Since it is consequentialist in nature, a utilitarian strategy and approach to public policy making would require that government officials base their actions and programs on the most accurate and detailed information of particular circumstances and of the likely results of the alternatives and options available to them. Mill maintained that ethical questions could be settled only by empirical investigation. As Shaw puts it, "Realism and empiricism are the hallmarks of a utilitarian orientation, not customary practice, unverified abstractions, or wishful thinking" (1999: 171). For example, in considering public policy about punishment, a utilitarian would argue that punishment is justified if

- the pain and suffering to those who are punished is outweighed by the benefits of punishment, and
- those benefits cannot be achieved with less suffering or at a lower cost to those who are being punished. (Shaw 1999: 174)

The utilitarian perspective on punishment is more fully considered in Chapter 5.

Arguments Criticizing Utilitarianism

We have seen that utilitarian theory urges us to accept the notion that only consequences matter. Significant arguments against the utilitarian approach propose that there are other considerations, in addition to utility, that are important in determining whether actions are right. Critics argue that utilitarianism is incompatible with the ideal of justice, according to which we should treat people fairly, taking account of their individual needs and merits. Critics say this is not a priority of the utilitarian perspective. The following example is offered by McCloskey (1965 in Rachels 1999a: 110–111):

> Imagine a utilitarian visiting an area where there is racial strife. During his visit, an African American man rapes a white woman, and this causes race riots with white mobs and the police attacking and killing African Americans. Imagine the utilitarian is in the area when the rape is committed and his evidence could convict a particular African American man who was innocent.

As a utilitarian, if he knows that an early arrest will stop the race riots, he must surely conclude that he has a duty to give false evidence in order to bring about the punishment of an innocent person. This might have some bad consequences—for example, the innocent African American man might be executed—but a utilitarian would consider that this would be outweighed by the good consequences that the riots would be stopped. Accordingly, applying utilitarianism, the best consequences would be achieved by lying, and lying would be the most ethical act. However, it could be argued that it would be wrong to be the cause of the execution of an innocent man; therefore, in implying that it would be right to bring about that execution, utilitarianism must be an incorrect theory.

Critics of utilitarianism state that the theory is inconsistent with the notion that people have rights that may not be infringed simply because good results are anticipated:

> In a 1963 case in the U.S. Court of Appeals Ninth Circuit (in Rachels 1999a: 112–113), an appellant, Ms. York, approached the police department in Chino, California, to file charges for an assault committed on her. Officer Story of the police department told her that photographs would have to be taken of her, took her to a room in the police station, and told her to undress. She was also told to adopt various indecent positions, and he photographed her in those positions. Ms. York objected to the undressing, pointing out there was no need to take photographs because the bruises would not show up. Later Officer Story told her that the photographs had not come out and that he had destroyed them, but contrary to what he told her, the officer in fact circulated her photographs amongst police officers at Chino. Later, two other officers made further prints of the original photographs and circulated these amongst police. Ms. York brought proceedings against all three officers for violating her legal rights and won.

Considering the morality of the conduct of the officers, act utilitarianism would argue that their actions can be defended if they produce a greater balance of happiness over unhappiness. In other words, we should consider the unhappiness caused to Ms. York and compare it with the amount of pleasure created for the officers by viewing the photographs. It is certainly arguable that more happiness than unhappiness was caused, in which case, a utilitarian would have to conclude that the police officers' actions were morally correct. In this case, Ms. York's right to privacy has been violated and most people do not think that our rights should be set aside so easily. The idea of rights includes the notion that there are limits on how others may treat us regardless of the good purposes that might be accomplished and the happiness that breaching those limits might bring.

Another criticism offered is that utilitarianism is mistaken in claiming that only consequences matter, and this can be illustrated by reference to "backward-looking reasons" (Darwall 1998: 131; Rachels 1999a: 113–114). Imagine you have promised to meet someone this afternoon, but when the time comes to carry out that promise, you don't want to do it, because you have judged that your time would be better spent working. What should you do? Imagine you decide that the utility of accomplishing your work slightly outweighs any inconvenience caused by standing up your friend. As a utilitarian, you would then conclude that working is the right course of action, but intuitively this does not seem correct. This is due to the fact that making a promise imposed an obligation on you that you cannot escape so easily. In other words, a small gain in utility does not overcome the obligation imposed by the promise you gave. This example illustrates the fact that utilitarianism emphasizes that the rightness of an act has to do with the future; that is, it has to do with what will happen as the result of our actions. However, as this case demonstrates, we also think that past considerations are important, and our promise to meet someone is a fact about the past and not the future. Here, therefore, utilitarianism seems inadequate, because it takes no account of backward-looking considerations.

Utilitarianism, it is argued, eliminates the distinction between obligatory actions that are morally required and *supererogatory actions,* which, although not strictly required, are still praiseworthy (Goodin 1991: 234; Rachels 1999a: 115). Absolute adherence to the utilitarian standard would require us to give away our resources to the point where economic equality is reached. While we might admire people who are prepared to give away their goods or give up their pleasures to help others, we do not see them as simply doing their duty but as going beyond what is required by duty. In other words, a moral ethic that requires us to subordinate everything to promoting the general welfare would have the effect of causing us to give no priority to our own interests and to abandon most of the acts that we do for ourselves that give our life character and meaning. Peter Singer argues that

> because giving money is regarded as an act of charity, it is not thought that there is anything wrong without giving and . . . people do not feel in any way ashamed or guilty about spending money on new clothes or a new car instead of giving it to famine relief. (1979: 269–270)

Singer contends that we ought to give money away and that it is morally wrong not to do so, rejecting the notion of supererogatory actions and taking the position that if we have the chance to make the world a better place, we are morally obliged to take it.

An important element of utilitarian theory is the notion that every person's life and interests rank equally with everyone else's (Rachels 1999a: 115). While this sounds appealing, in practice it would require that we give up our special relationships with family and friends where we show partiality and preference (Goodin 1991: 234). Family and friends are not just members of humanity, they are special to us, and the argument that we should show no more concern for their welfare than for anyone else's is quite counterintuitive. Take the example of a parent who allows his child to burn in a building on the basis that others are in the building who should be saved because their future contribution to the general welfare seems likely to be greater than the child's. That parent would not be considered a hero but rather regarded with horror and contempt and would be considered to have acted immorally.

Rachels (1999a: 116) explains that utilitarians rebut these criticisms by pointing out that the arguments are unrealistic because they do not describe real-world situations but are imaginary. It is argued that utilitarianism is a guide for making decisions in the real world and for situations we actually face. Rachels suggests that utilitarianism counters these criticisms by modifying the theory to introduce rule utilitarianism and act utilitarianism. In the case of the race riot example, rule utilitarianism would ask which general rules of conduct would promote the greatest happiness. A society that contained a rule against false testimony or one that did not? Would people be better off in the former or the latter society? Clearly, in terms of utility, the former society is to be preferred, and therefore the rule against giving false evidence would be accepted and the person should not testify against the innocent man. In contrast, an act utilitarian faced with the same situation would likely give false evidence because the consequences of that particular act would be good.

A final defense against criticisms of utilitarianism is more radical—it essentially asks, so what? It reverses the presumption that utilitarianism is irrational and does not accord with our moral and intuitive common sense by asking "Why should we assume that our feelings are always correct?" and "Why should we reject a rational theory of right conduct just because it conflicts with those feelings?" This defense argues that it is the feelings and not the theory that should be discounted (Rachels 1999a: 119). This defense therefore implies that many of our commonly held moral feelings may be mistaken, and it challenges us to rethink those views and feelings (p. 120).

It is sometimes suggested that consequentialism is a less than efficient way of living and deliberating on issues, because it requires long and complicated calculations of utility that tend to make a person overly hesitant and ineffectual (Scarre 1996: 13). Far better for human welfare, it is argued, if people are able to act on simple moral rules such as keep your promises, pay your debts, and help the needy.

Two examples of the application of utilitarian theory to moral issues are shown in boxes 10.1 and 10.2.

A CLOSER LOOK

BOX 10.1
A Case of Euthanasia

Matthew Donnelly, a physicist, worked with X-rays, and perhaps through too much exposure contracted cancer and became blind. He was told that he had about one year to live and was in constant pain. He decided he did not want to carry on living in that condition and begged his three brothers to kill him. Two refused, but the youngest brother, Harold, brought a pistol into the hospital and shot Matthew to death.

Was Harold's Act Immoral?

We can assume that he was motivated by compassion and love for his brother and wished only to relieve his pain. Also, Matthew had asked each of his brothers to help him die. We therefore feel sympathy toward Harold and feel that we should be lenient toward his acts. However, according to the dominant moral tradition, the Christian tradition, what Harold did was morally wrong. Christianity teaches that intentionally killing innocent people is always wrong.

What Would a Utilitarian Approach Be to This Issue?

A utilitarian would ask, considering the choices available to Harold, what course of action would produce the best overall consequences—the greatest balance of happiness over unhappiness for all concerned? If Harold did not kill Matthew, Matthew would continue to live in pain for a while longer, and this would cause significant unhappiness. How much unhappiness is difficult to calculate, but we do know that Matthew himself preferred death to continuing in that unhappy state. We also know that killing him would allow him to escape his pain and misery. A utilitarian would therefore argue that euthanasia in this case might be morally correct, contending as follows:

- The right action is that which will bring about the greatest balance of happiness over unhappiness.
- Sometimes the greatest balance of happiness over unhappiness can be occasioned by mercy killings.
- Therefore, at least sometimes, mercy killing may be morally correct.

SOURCE: Rachels 1999a: 99–100.

A CLOSER LOOK

BOX 10.2
The Treatment of Animals

The Christian tradition holds that only man is made in the image of God, and animals do not possess souls. This means that, according to the natural order, humans may use animals for whatever purpose they wish. As Saint Thomas Aquinas wrote, "It is no wrong for man to make use of them, either by killing them or in any other way whatever." However, Aquinas agrees that it is wrong to be cruel to animals, not because of the welfare of the animals, but because being cruel to animals impacts human welfare, because it has a tendency to encourage men to be cruel to other men. This might seem a rather extreme statement about animals, but in fact we do eat animals, use their skins for various purposes, confine them in zoos, and use them for experiments in science. As well, we hunt and kill them.

Utilitarians do not support the above view because they believe that what matters is whether an individual is able to experience happiness and unhappiness, pleasure and pain. If an individual is able to experience suffering, then a

(Continued)

(Continued)

utilitarian would say we have a duty to take that into account in our acts even if the individual is an animal and not human. Since both humans and animals can suffer, we ought not to mistreat either and therefore both are entitled to moral concern.

The philosopher Peter Singer first wrote about animal liberation in 1975, arguing in accordance with utilitarian principles that the way we treat animals is cruel and objectionable. He cites the example of research on the behavior of dogs that involved giving intense electric shocks to dogs, causing them considerable suffering. The question he argued was whether there was any compensating gain in happiness for this suffering because if there was not, the experiment was not morally acceptable. The pain caused to the animals requires justification, and we cannot apply Christian doctrine that because they are not humans we may act as we wish. Utilitarianism therefore claims that we must expand the moral community to include all those whose interests are affected by what we do, and we should not consider that human beings alone are worthy of moral consideration.

SOURCE: Rachels 1999a: 102–104

Applying Utilitarian Theory

Case Study 10.1 illustrates how utilitarian theory can be applied to an ethical dilemma within the criminal justice system.

CASE STUDY 10.1 GOOD FRIENDS ARE HARD TO FIND

When Ben first joined the police department, a long-standing friend in the same department told him that he would only have cop friends and that no one else understood police except other police. Ben felt uncomfortable about this, and, together with his wife, made a conscious effort to find friends outside of the police force. They succeeded in part because Ben's wife, who was a teacher, was able to make friends from that profession. Nevertheless, Ben found that many people treated him differently than an ordinary citizen when they found out he was a policeman. They tended to blame him for all the troubles they encountered and especially for any citations they received from other police officers.

In order to deal with this problem, Ben and his wife decided not to tell any new acquaintances about his job. He would just say that he worked in public relations in the city, and after they became friends, then he would tell them what he really did. This seemed to work quite well and after a while Ben and his wife began to develop a circle of good friends. He found that these friends would alter their schedules to accommodate his shift work. For example, if a party was planned, Ben and his wife were contacted first to make sure that he would be available and could get the night off. Ben thought that some of these friends might be recreational drug users but they always respected his position as a police officer and he never observed them taking drugs in his presence.

Two friends, Jim and Sandy, invited Ben and his wife to dinner one Friday night, and when they arrived, Jim immediately gave Ben his favorite drink, which was scotch on the rocks. Jim put on some music and Ben's wife went to help Sandy in the kitchen while Ben and Jim sat in the living room. Ben needed something to put under his drink so that it would not leave rings on the coffee table, and he saw a wooden box on the coffee table that looked the right size and shape to hold coasters. He reached out and opened the box. It did not contain coasters but several joints of marijuana. He put the lid back on the box, looked up and saw fear in Jim's eyes.

SOURCE: Close and Meier 1995: 171.

In resolving what may be an ethical dilemma, Ben will follow the process of resolving an ethical dilemma set out in Chapter 1:

1. *Is Ben faced with an ethical dilemma?*
   Ben is faced with the dilemma of whether or not to arrest Jim for possession of an illegal substance.

2. *What are the facts and circumstances of the incident?*
   Ben needs to review in his mind the facts and circumstances so that he is clear about the issue with which he is faced.

3. *What are the facts relevant to the decision he has to make? What are his own values about the issue and what are the values of his workplace about such an issue?*
   The relevant fact is that Ben has found evidence of an offense, and as a police officer he has discretion as to whether or not to arrest the alleged offender. His own values are as follows: As a police officer he believes in upholding the law; he understands that the police culture tends to compel police to have only coworkers as friends, but he values friendships outside law enforcement and does not want to be completely enveloped by the police subculture. In terms of workplace values, he is well aware of police codes of ethics and of standing rules that relate to the exercise of his discretion in making arrests. He is also aware of the informal police subculture, which is more complex than the written rules and regulations and which is ambivalent about incidents like this. Some of his co-workers would not hesitate to arrest in such circumstances, but others would be prepared to overlook the minor infractions of their good friends.

4. *What ethical theories does he call to mind to assist him in resolving the dilemma?*
   In this case, Ben will apply utilitarian ethical theory to the dilemma.

5. *What are Ben's available courses of action?*
   Ben has the choice of arresting Jim or deciding not to arrest him and therefore ignoring the incident. As a police officer with the discretion as to whether or not to arrest, he could always tell himself that it was a minor offense and not worth processing all that paperwork anyway and therefore decide not to arrest. He could also give Jim a warning not to repeat the offense.

6. *Ben will make his decision after applying, in this case, the utilitarian approach to each alternative course of action, and he will choose the course of action that is the most ethically appropriate for him under utilitarianism.*

A process for assessing an ethical dilemma from a utilitarian perspective is set out in Box 10.3. Applications of these criteria are shown in Box 10.4.

A CLOSER LOOK

BOX 10.3
Utilitarian Evaluation of Ethical Dilemmas

The focus is on the outcome of the decision in each option; if it is good for all, then it is ethical. Utilitarianism considers the greatest good for *all* those affected by the decision and often uses persons as a means to an end. Whatever means are used to achieve the best outcome are acceptable as long as the outcome is good for all those affected. This approach to ethics often fails to protect individual rights—the individual experience is sacrificed to the interests of all. Thus, for utilitarians, consequences count—utilitarians always want to know what actual effects their choices will have on real people. Utilitarians want the world to be a better place for everyone affected (including organizations and the community) and therefore seek to increase the amount of well-being in the world and to reduce the amount of pain and suffering.

1. Identify all the options.

2. Identify all those affected by the decision. Consider individuals and organizations as well as the community.

3. Describe the harms and benefits for all those affected under Option 1, then Option 2, and so on.

4. Choose the option that produces the most benefits for all those affected by the decision after calculating the difference between the good and bad effects.

A CLOSER LOOK

BOX 10.4
Applying Utilitarianism

---

1. Identify all the options.
   Ben has the options of arresting Jim or of taking no further action.

2. Identify all those affected by the decision.
   Those likely to be affected by the decision are Jim and Sandy, Ben and his wife, other friends of Ben and his wife who are also friends of Jim and his wife, the police department, and the local community.

3. Describe the harms and benefits for all those affected under Option 1, then Option 2, and so on.

   Under **Option 1,** to arrest, the harms and benefits will be as follows:

   Jim and Sandy—They will suffer harm because they will cease to be friends with Ben and his wife, Jim may be convicted of a criminal offense, they will suffer shame in the community, and Jim's job may be affected by a conviction. They will receive no benefits.

   Ben and his wife—They will suffer harm because they will lose Jim and Sandy's friendship, they may lose other friendships with those who hear about the arrest, they may end up with no friends other than policemen, and Ben's wife's teaching job may be affected when her co-workers hear about the arrest. In terms of benefits, if he arrests, Ben will be following formal ethical codes and departmental rules, and he will be showing that he is an impartial police officer interested in performing his duty with integrity.

   Other friends of Jim and Sandy—They may be harmed because they may cease their friendship with Ben and his wife and perhaps also with Jim and Sandy.

   Police department—The department will benefit because it will be aware that Ben is prepared to arrest his friends who commit criminal offenses and therefore that he upholds ethical codes and departmental rules.

   Community—The community will benefit because it will be aware that at least one police officer is not prepared to turn a blind eye to evidence of criminal offenses, even by his friends, and is prepared to apply the law with impartiality.

   Under **Option 2**, which is to do nothing or to give Jim a warning not to repeat the offense, the harms and benefits will be as follows:

   Jim and Sandy—The benefit is that they will continue to be friends with Ben and his wife. The harm is that they will know that Ben is prepared to condone criminal conduct by his friends.

   Ben and his wife—They will continue to benefit from Jim and Sandy's friendship and Ben will have demonstrated his loyalty to his friends in that he is prepared to

(Continued)

(Continued)

overlook acts of criminal conduct. The harm is that Ben may be placed in the same situation again with either Jim or other friends. Another harm is that Jim and Sandy may tell their other friends about Ben's willingness to compromise his position as a police officer. If this gets back to the department it might lead to disciplinary action against Ben by the department and will constitute a harm for Ben.

Other friends of Jim and Sandy—They will not be affected except that they may benefit by learning about Ben's willingness to overlook his friend's indiscretions.

Police department—The department will be harmed by not being aware that Ben is prepared to overlook his friends' criminal offenses. It is possible that the department might learn from the community about Ben overlooking the offense. This might harm the department's reputation in the community.

Community—The community might hear about Ben's inaction in not arresting Jim and may think that this action is typical of police in the community. This would be harmful for the community because it would affect their view of the integrity of the police force. It is also possible that some members of the community may tell the police department about Ben's willingness to overlook the offense. This would be a benefit to the community because hopefully the police would take disciplinary action against Ben and restore the police reputation in the community.

4. Choose the option that produces the most benefits for most of those affected by the decision after calculating the difference.

   According to the utilitarian perspective, it would be necessary to assign values to the harms and benefits and then calculate which option benefited all parties affected by the decision. Assuming a greater value would be given to benefits to the community and to the police department, the option producing the most benefits would be to arrest Jim.

Summary

Consequentialists, also known as utilitarians, believe that what makes an act morally right or wrong is its consequences, and that all other considerations are irrelevant. Therefore, when we are considering the correct moral approach to an issue, we should always ask which action would bring about the best possible consequences. This principle, known as the principle of utility, requires that we act so as to produce the greatest happiness for everyone affected. Utilitarians therefore reject the idea that duty should determine how we choose to act.

The classical utilitarians, Bentham and Mill, saw happiness as equivalent to pleasure, and they argued that humans look for pleasure and try to avoid pain and that this explains how we make choices about how to act. Nowadays, a more modern approach is to aim for preference satisfaction and not for happiness. The idea is that we should not aim for pleasure over pain but instead should determine how we can best satisfy human preferences, interests, or desires.

Act utilitarians argue that the motive behind an act is irrelevant and that it is possible to measure whether an act causes more pleasure than pain and therefore has more "utility." This would seem a very difficult and time-consuming exercise and, therefore, act utilitarians adjust this basic principle by following rules of thumb that draw on past experience. In contrast, rule utilitarians link consequentialism with moral rules and argue that if we follow certain rules, better consequences are likely to result. In this sense, rule consequentialism may be said to blend with deontology to a limited extent. For example, most of us believe that as a rule we should speak the truth, even when doing so in a specific instance would cause more pain than pleasure, and that in the long term telling the truth produces greater benefits overall.

One main criticism of consequentialism is that it puts the outcome of an action above the ideals of justice, such as treating people fairly. It can also be argued that utilitarianism requires us to give away all our resources to others because that would promote the general welfare and pleasure of others. In choosing between duty and consequences, we have to weigh absolute rules about how we should act against the need to calculate which act will provide the most pleasure for the greatest number of people.

Consequentialism is considered an important theory in punishment policy and practice, because a major focus of policy making for the punishment of offenders is deterrence, that is, attempting to deter crime by drawing attention to the penalties that will be imposed for criminal acts. This approach assumes that giving certain individuals or groups of offenders more severe punishments in order to deter others from committing similar crimes is for the benefit of everyone.

DISCUSSION CASE

Punishing a Police Officer for False Testimony

New York police officer James Sullivan, 34, had a distinguished record, having made nearly 100 arrests and earned nearly two dozen commendations during his 9-year career. A man he had arrested in 1998, who was subsequently convicted and jailed and then released on parole, was appearing before the U.S. District court in Brooklyn on a parole revocation hearing. Sullivan had received a subpoena to testify at this hearing.

The background to the case was that Sullivan and his partner had arrested Mr. Francis on charges of attempted murder and firearms possession following a shooting. Francis, who had three prior convictions, including one for conspiracy to distribute cocaine, was tried in state court and acquitted on all charges arising from the Sullivan arrest. However, following his acquittal, Francis was indicted by federal prosecutors for firearms possession and convicted and jailed. As a convicted felon he could not legally possess a firearm.

(Continued)

(Continued)

Sullivan and his partner Melin had both testified in the state trial that they had taken the weapon from Francis, placed it in the trunk of their vehicle, and then driven straight to the police station. The officers also testified that Sullivan had picked the weapon up from the place where Francis had dropped it. However, Sullivan later told federal prosecutor Tirschwell that in fact Melin had picked up the gun, had handed it to him (Sullivan), and that Sullivan had put it on the front seat of the patrol car. During the federal trial of Francis, prosecutor Tirschwell revealed that Sullivan had given this false testimony in the state trial.

In 1996, New York City Police Commissioner Howard Safir had announced a policy that he would fire any officer for lying to a superior or in an official proceeding. Because of this policy and his false testimony, Sullivan had been told to bring a lawyer to the parole revocation hearing in case any action was taken against him. When asked their intentions regarding Sullivan and his false testimony, the state prosecutors indicated that they had not decided whether or not to pursue perjury charges against Sullivan. The main deciding factor would be that the false testimony he had given was not material to the case and would not have affected the verdict. However, despite no decision having been made about Sullivan, some action had already been taken against Officer Melin, who had been placed on modified duty.

It was uncertain whether further action would be taken against Melin and Sullivan.

SOURCE: Adapted from Rashbaum 2000.

After applying the criteria for a utilitarian analysis, should the state prosecutor's office charge the officers with perjury?

DISCUSSION QUESTIONS

1. What are the main principles advocated by consequentialists?

2. How does consequentialism help us to make the right moral choices?

3. What criticisms can be made of a consequentialist approach toward resolving ethical dilemmas?

4. How does consequentialism deal with the rights of individuals in ethical decision making?

5. Explain how consequentialist theories are applied to policy making on crime control and punishment.

CHAPTER 11

The Importance
of Character

I n Chapters 9 and 10, we examined ethical theories based on duty and on consequences. According to deontologists such as Kant, the answer to the question of "How should we act?" is that we should always act for the sake of duty, because it is the right thing to do. According to consequentialists, the rightness or wrongness of acts does not depend on intentions but on consequences, and the right action is that which produces the greatest amount of happiness or pleasure. Kantians and consequentialists hold in common the notion that ethics is an answer to the question "What ought I to do?" (Hinman 1998: 323). These modern philosophers ask a different question than did the classical or ancient philosophers, and because of this, their thinking moved in a different direction, developing theories concerned with rightness or obligation rather than virtue. This chapter is concerned with the ethics of virtue, an approach that emphasizes our virtues or moral character as opposed to a theory that emphasizes duties or rules or one stressing the consequences of actions.

Contemporary virtue theory has been inspired by the Greek philosopher Aristotle (384–322 BC), in particular by his work *Nicomachean Ethics* (see Box 11.1). In contrast to Kantian and consequentialist approaches, Aristotle does not seek to uncover a fundamental principle telling us what to do and how to act in an ethical way. Rather, he is concerned about the sort of people we must become if we are to live the good life, in other words, an ethical life. For example, take a case where it is obvious that I ought to help someone who is in need (Hursthouse 1999: 1). A utilitarian or consequentialist will stress the fact that the consequences of helping will maximize well-being. A deontologist will emphasize the fact that in helping that person I will be following a moral rule such as "do unto others as you would have done unto you." A virtue ethicist, however, would emphasize the fact that offering help would demonstrate my charitable or benevolent character. Most recently, virtue ethics has been promoted by a number of philosophers as a third way of approaching ethical questions and dilemmas. In 1958, the distinguished British philosopher G. E. M. Anscombe published an article suggesting that modern moral philosophy was misguided and that philosophers should stop thinking about obligation, duty, and rightness and place virtue center stage (Rachels 1999: 177).

According to Darwall (1998: 191), many philosophers have realized that Aristotle presents a more subtle, rich, and realistic picture of the ethical life, and they have found theories such as Mill's and Kant's to be unrealistically abstract. The proponents of virtue theory join with Aristotle in believing that ethical knowledge involves a degree of wisdom or judgment that cannot be expressed in the form of an absolute rule. Others criticize nonvirtue theories as being too individualistic, arguing that the prominence that Aristotle gave to the social dimension of human life and to community should prevail over individualistic notions of conflict.

For Aristotle, rather than asking the question, "What ought I to do?" ethics should be concerned with answering the question "What kind of person should I be?" or to put it another way, "What character traits should I acquire?" In Aristotle's view, once we have answered this question, we may be in a position to answer the question "What ought I to do?" Virtue ethics is primarily concerned with persons and character rather than with duties or with the consequences of actions (Holmes 1998: 32). Aristotle is mainly interested in virtues and vices; in other words, the strengths and weaknesses of character that operate to promote or hinder the flourishing of the human personality.

A CLOSER LOOK

BOX 11.1
Aristotle

Aristotle, one of history's greatest philosophers, was born in 384 BC in the north of Greece. His father was a medical doctor and a court physician. Due to his father's position at court, Aristotle formed an early association with the ruling elite. In 367 BC, Aristotle entered Plato's Academy as a student, and he remained there until Plato's death in 347 BC. While it seems clear that Aristotle respected and admired Plato, he was not a rigid follower of Plato's teachings, and he often used Plato's philosophy as a springboard from which to develop his own views. In 347 BC, he left Athens for about 12 years, traveling and conducting research. During this time he married and was also a tutor to the young Alexander the Great. In 335 BC, he returned to Athens and founded his own school, the Lyceum. Most of the works of Aristotle that we still possess were written during this period.

When Alexander the Great died in 323 BC, the people of Athens, who were anti-Macedonia, charged Aristotle with impiety because of his friendly relations with Alexander. In response, Aristotle left Athens rather than having to face a trial. He died the following year.

Most of the works of Aristotle that we possess are treatises, which may have been his own notes for lectures given in the Lyceum. Historically, the

Nicomachean Ethics has been the subject of more study and has become more influential than his other works, and it contains his definitive statement on ethics.

Book 1 of the *Ethics* is an investigation of happiness or the good life; he defines this life in terms of virtue. The notion of virtue is discussed in depth in Book 2. Book 3 examines the concepts of choice or preference, and Books 4 and 5 consider particular moral virtues. He argues that moral virtues require the virtue of practical wisdom for their proper exercise, and he examines this concept in Book 6. Moral weakness, which is a failure of practical wisdom, is examined in Book 7. Books 8 and 9 concern friendship, and Book 10, the concluding book, is concerned with pleasure and a reconsideration of the good life.

SOURCE: Prior 1991: 144–146.

Virtues

In considering the nature of virtue, several questions arise: *What is a virtue? What character traits (a disposition to act in a certain way, e.g., to tell the truth, to help those in need) constitute virtues? What do these virtues consist of? Why are these qualities good for a person to have?* Virtues are personal qualities or traits of character, shown through habitual action, that make us persons of excellent character. They can include natural qualities such as intelligence or strength, learned or acquired qualities, qualities relating to temperament, religious qualities, and qualities of character (Holmes 1998: 32). The repetition of virtuous actions causes a person to develop a virtuous character, and once that character is formed, it becomes the source of that person's virtuous actions. As Aristotle wrote,

> By abstaining from pleasures we become self-controlled, and once we are self-controlled we are best able to abstain from pleasures. So also with courage: by becoming habituated to despise and endure terrors we become courageous, and once we have become courageous we will be able to endure terror. (Book 2, in Prior 1991: 158)

For example, in relation to the virtue of honesty, it is not enough for someone to tell the truth sometimes or only when it is to his or her advantage. An honest person, in the sense of a virtuous person, is a person who is truthful as a matter of course regardless of the outcome. It is important that virtuous action be habitual, because when practices become habitual they make up the fixed character that determines the identity of an individual (Tessitore 1996: 25). In the best case, a person may have a natural inclination to the virtuous, but the additional training of habitually virtuous action must complement this natural disposition. This guidance is usually provided by parents and teachers and through laws.

A virtuous person will ask him- or herself: How will I be good in this situation? What would be the normal course of action? In this way he or she encourages moral persons to demand of themselves the highest degree of excellence of which they are capable (Tessitore 1996: 46). According to virtue ethics, what is wrong with lying is not that it is unjust because it violates others' right to the truth or their right to be treated with respect but that it is dishonest, and dishonesty is a vice (Hursthouse 1999: 6). Similarly, what is wrong with wrongful killing is not so much that it is unjust and violates the right to life but that it is callous and contrary to the virtue of charity.

Which character traits should be cultivated as virtues? Aristotle proposes a much larger list of virtues than did Plato and Socrates, who identified only four or five primary virtues (wisdom, courage, temperance, justice, and piety) (Prior 1991: 163). Aristotle discusses a dozen virtues that do not include justice or wisdom. Rachels (1999: 178) provides the following as his list:

Benevolence	Industriousness
Civility	Justice
Compassion	Loyalty
Conscientiousness	Moderation
Cooperativeness	Reasonableness
Courage	Self-confidence
Courteousness	Self-control
Dependability	Self-discipline
Fairness	Self-reliance
Friendliness	Tactfulness
Generosity	Thoughtfulness
Honesty	Tolerance

Each virtue has its own special features, and some raise distinctive issues. For example, the virtue of *courage* can present troublesome cases. Consider the case of a terrorist who gives his life for a cause, such as the destruction of Israeli society, by blowing himself up with explosives and causing the death of innocent people. Is he courageous? It can be argued that the terrorist does not really possess the virtue of courage, because courage in an unworthy cause is not a virtue (Rachels 1999: 179). If his motive was not to destroy another society but to fight for the right of existence of a Palestinian nation, the analysis about whether he is acting out of courage might be altered. Another example is the Nazi soldier who fights bravely but in an evil cause. It does not seem right to say that he is not courageous. An alternative explanation is that he is displaying two qualities, one that is admirable (being brave in the face of danger) and one that is not (being willing to fight for an evil regime that aims to destroy Jews). His courage is deployed in the promotion of an evil cause and on the whole is not virtuous (p. 180).

In considering the virtue of *generosity*, how much is enough to give? Utilitarians would argue that it is your duty to do what will produce the best overall consequences for everyone affected, and this means being generous with our wealth until we reach the point where giving more would be more harmful to us than it would be helpful to others. However, adopting this approach would provide a severe constraint on our normal living, and we would have to abandon our everyday lives, give up our projects and plans, and live in a very different way. Rachels (1999: 181) suggests that a reasonable mean in relation to the virtue of generosity is that "we should be as generous with our resources as is consistent with conducting our ordinary lives in a minimally satisfying way."

In deontological ethics, the imperative is to do what is right, whereas in virtue ethics, the imperative is to be a good person. Usually when we refer to a "good person," we mean a person who is morally good, because even though someone may possess many of the qualities referred to earlier, this does not mean that he or she possesses moral integrity. It is important to appreciate that a person can possess good qualities but still not be a good person overall. The critical point is that virtues are necessary for conducting our lives *well* (Rachels 1999: 185).

As already stated, moral virtues are represented by habits, traits, or dispositions of character and, according to Aristotle, must be acquired through practice. For example, in order to become a generous person, one must carry out generous acts with regularity. Similarly, a person who always acts courageously over a period of time will find that the character trait of courageousness will become habitual.

Aristotle and Happiness

Aristotle adopted an empirical approach to ethical problems so that instead of simply reflecting on ways to discover the nature of the good life, he examined the behavior and ways of people in everyday life. He noticed that some people were regarded as leading good lives and others as leading bad lives. He considered that the so-called good life contained the characteristic of happiness, and in contrast, the life regarded as a bad life contained unhappiness. In answer to the question of what is a good life for man, he therefore concluded that it is a life of happiness. However, what exactly is meant by the word *happiness?* The word Aristotle uses can also be translated into notions of "flourishing" or "well-being," and virtues and vices should be understood in that context. Aristotle regards happiness as the good to which all human action aims, and he seeks to encourage his students to develop a more satisfying understanding of happiness (Tessitore 1996: 20). According to Aristotle, when we develop as we "ought," we live well, thrive, and flourish, and when we do not, we suffer and decay (Darwall 1998: 195). Therefore, virtues are strengths of character that promote human flourishing and well-being, and vices are weaknesses of character that hinder human flourishing or well-being (Hinman 1998: 326).

Aristotle tries to explain the meaning of the term *happiness.* In a famous definition in his book *Nicomachean Ethics,* he defines happiness as "an activity of the soul in accord with perfect virtue." It is not immediately clear just what this means, and various interpretations of this definition have been offered. One commonly accepted interpretation is that Aristotle is emphasizing that happiness is not static but is rather an activity, something that accompanies activities rather than being a goal of them. Happiness, therefore, becomes a way of doing things—for example, of not being defeated by circumstances. It is a way of engaging in life's various activities in a certain way. When we make choices during our lives, promoting our own happiness ought not to motivate the moral choices we make (Kopperi 1999: 16). Instead, what is a morally right or wrong act is ultimately to be judged in contrast to our final goal of happiness. In this sense, therefore, moral norms should be seen as rules that tell us how to live and direct us toward realizing our own good. Failing to follow these rules or norms will separate us from our own happiness.

Aristotle argues that "flourishing" arises out of virtuous activity. He writes that all things have a function or activity, and he offers the example of playing a musical instrument (Darwall 1998: 199). He contends that not just anything counts as playing that instrument, and that the activity of playing has certain standards built into it. If one plays well, one flourishes as a player of that instrument. Similarly, an object like a knife is designed for a certain purpose, and its function determines what it is that makes it perform well. Aristotle concludes from this that human beings also have a function, as does every natural thing. For example, for plants, the function is a life of nutrition and growth. What is distinctive about human beings is the way in which ethical conceptions are located in our thoughts, feelings, or actions, and the ways in which we can affect our choices by performing our functions well. Therefore, a flourishing life becomes one of excellent, distinctively human activity; that is, a life of virtuous activity. Aristotle does not think that man's function is simply biological living or perception, because plants and animals also live biologically and some animals perceive (Benn 1998: 162). He concludes, therefore, that man's function is that which is unique to us as human beings: "an activity of soul exhibiting excellence."

The Golden Mean

Having determined that the good life is a life of happiness, Aristotle went further by proposing that people should behave in ways that will achieve happiness. From this notion developed the idea of the mean or the *golden mean* (Holmes 1998: 42). In situations where we have to make practical decisions, we can see that there are two extremes and a mean or average between them. Our aim should be to find that mean, and this will enable us to act rightly. How do we find the mean in particular cases? Aristotle advises that "such things depend on particular facts, and the decision rests with perception" (Holmes 1998: 43). This suggests that you should look at all the relevant facts of the situation, including the kind of person you are, your strengths and weaknesses, and your tendencies and dispositions. The mean lies between an excess and a deficiency so that, for example, eating too much is an extreme or excess and eating too little is going to the other extreme and is a deficiency. Eating just the right amount is the mean. However, the mean is often relative and varies according to the individual, so for example, an act of generosity for a millionaire may be quite different from that of a beggar on the street. This leads to the consequence that ethically there are different correct ways of living for different people. What may be good for one person may not be good for another, and it is impossible to tell, using reason alone, which is the correct way of living for a particular person. The correct way can be discovered only by experimentation and trial and error. Aristotle's ethics is therefore relativistic, because the right thing to do in a situation may not be the same for different people (Prior 1991: 160). This explains why his ethics may not be reduced to a set of rules to be applied universally.

Therefore, Aristotle argues that the proper way to behave in an ethical or moral sense is in accordance with the mean (Hinman 1998: 333). For example, courage is the mean between cowardice and rashness; pride is the mean between vanity and humility; and generosity is the mean between extravagance and stinginess. Aristotle concludes, therefore, that in order to achieve happiness, a person ought to act moderately and attempt to find the mean between the two extremes (see Figure 11.1).

Practical Wisdom

Aristotle emphasizes the way in which well-being and flourishing relate to "practical wisdom," and he argues that people of practical wisdom are those able to effectively deliberate about what is good for their life as a whole as opposed to what may just be expedient. Practical wisdom equates to prudence and forethought as well as intelligence, and this notion is at the very heart of Aristotle's conception of the moral life (Hinman 1998: 355). Essentially, practical wisdom involves applying excellent character to a situation in light of an overall conception of what amounts to a good life. Aristotle makes a distinction between a wise person and a person who is simply clever. He contends that the clever person knows the best means to a particular end but does not have the wisdom to understand which ends are worth pursuing. In contrast, the wise person knows how to achieve a particular end and also understands which ends are worth achieving (Hinman 1998: 356). Applying practical wisdom is therefore a thinking process in which we reflect on circumstances and apply our wisdom to a specific case.

An individual of practical wisdom is a person able to reason correctly about ethical matters and is someone who has the vision to see which is the correct course of action (Prior 1991: 161). A person who exercises practical wisdom is able to make choices about how to act, that is, to see which specific act would satisfy the goal of acting nobly in a particular situation (Darwall 1998: 211–212). Such a person is able to deliberate well in the sense that she is able to understand what action justice, temperance, and courage calls for. Aristotle proposed that practical wisdom should

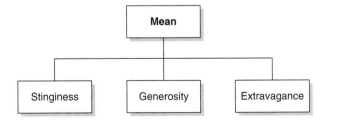

Figure 11.1   The Golden Mean

be seen as a kind of insight or perception, and he contended that it was impossible for individuals to know what to aim for when considering courses of action unless they were already virtuous. Persons who practice ethical wisdom deliberate well and reflect ethically, not just about what is good in a particular sense, but also about the good life in general. Such persons stand apart from their activities to see what makes sense as they reflect; in this process of reflecting, they perform ethical philosophy (Darwall 1998: 213).

What's Wrong With Virtue

It is important to keep in mind that Aristotle was writing at a particular time in history in a flourishing Greek civilization where the community (the *polis*) was an essential component of the social life in the city-state of Athens (Hinman 1998: 328–329). His notion of what amounted to a community differs significantly from that used today, and there is a political as well as a social component to community in Aristotle's teachings. For the Greeks, the political realm was an essential part of well-being and flourishing. It is therefore important to locate Aristotle's teachings historically and not to abstract his ideas from the cultural and social environment in which he lived and thought (MacIntyre 1984: 11). Aristotle spoke as an educated Athenian man addressing the best citizens of the best city-state in the belief that the city-state was the unique political form in which the virtues of human life could be genuinely and fully realized (p. 148). Aristotle regarded the Athenian gentleman as the epitome of human excellence, and he considered that virtues were not available to all, because some virtues, such as magnanimity and generosity, were confined to people of great wealth and high social status (p. 182).

Both Aristotle and MacIntyre (1984) have linked virtue to particular forms of social life. Lawrence Blum (1996) carries on that approach in the modern day in his exploration of possible linkages between virtue and the community. He identifies a number of possible links that are located in the literature on virtue, including notions that virtues can be learned only within forms of social life like families; that virtues can be sustained only in communities, because members of the community are able to support moral strengths and identify weaknesses; that since the communities in which we live shape the way we apply our moral principles, without communities, we would not know how to act ethically in our social lives; and that some virtues such as trust and tolerance are particularly appropriately exercised in communities (Blum 1996: 232–233).

The notion of the golden mean has been criticized, because, although the idea of finding a mean seems reasonable and plausible initially, there will be situations where this notion does not work. For example, what is the middle course between keeping a promise and not keeping one? It is obvious that there is no middle course, because one either keeps a promise or does not, and we tend to feel that those who keep promises are moral and those who do not lack morality. The same argument can be applied to truth telling, because one either does or does not tell the truth.

Thus, it seems that certain virtues like promise keeping and truth telling are absolute and not relative to various people and situations. It might, however, be argued that keeping promises and truth telling are actions rather than virtues. The virtues of loyalty, dependability, and honesty could collectively equate to promise keeping and truth telling, and these virtues do have a middle course.

A further criticism of the teachings of Aristotle is that he is, for all intents and purposes, proposing the notion that happiness will result from moderate behavior. While this may be true in some cases, there are other cases in which behavior in excess of the mean is proper for an individual. For example, a man who is by temperament passionate and zealous may find that moderate behavior does not suit him, and that person cannot be happy if forced to exercise control by acting in a moderate way. Therefore, for those who have this temperament, Aristotle has little to offer.

Aristotle has been criticized for his account of virtue ethics, because it is said that his is an ethics for the ruling class, that is, for the privileged, free, adult, Greek males whose main concerns were politics, war, and leisure. At the time Aristotle was writing, women, foreigners, and slaves were excluded from many of the activities of life in Athens despite the fact that the privileged class enjoyed benefits that were largely generated by these excluded groups. Certainly, the audience for his ethics was composed fundamentally of those who had benefited from a noble upbringing, had some experience of life, and had reached a certain level of maturity (Tessitore 1996: 17). Aristotle considered that the good life and the happiness of an adult, male citizen of noble birth differed from that of a woman or a slave (Kopperi 1999: 28). Women's natures as well as slaves' were seen as different from those of men of noble birth, and, therefore, the form of human life appropriate for them also differed. Significantly, what was best for a woman or a slave was not for them to decide for themselves; the appropriate conception of the good life for women and slaves was based on what was thought to be their human nature, and they were expected simply to accept this conception.

It is a common criticism of Aristotle that his list of virtues is arbitrary, and it is certainly constructed by reference to Aristotle's cultural boundaries and shaped by the values prevailing in ancient Athens. However, Hinman (1998: 334–335) argues that there are some universal elements in his list of virtues. He suggests that we all need to develop certain attitudes to cope with our lives, such as the way we react to the suffering of others. Here, Hinman suggests that the excess is pity or bleeding heart, the deficiency is acting callously, and the mean compassionately. Similarly, he proposes that we all need to develop an attitude toward our friends where the mean would be loyalty, the excess flattery, and the deficiency, indifference. Hinman offers the table shown in Table 11.1 to illustrate the mean (the most virtuous response) to various attitudes or spheres of existence. He draws our attention to the fact that when we attempt to develop virtuous responses to these attitudes, we must focus on the patterns in our behavior, because these, rather than specific acts, reveal our character (2003: 279).

A central criticism of Aristotle's approach to ethics is that it fails to tell us how to act (Hinman 1998: 359). Notwithstanding what he tells us about good character,

Aristotle does not provide us with answers to moral questions like those of the death penalty and euthanasia. Proponents of deontological and consequentialist theories argue that virtue ethics has no ethics of action and is therefore incomplete. In answer to this charge, it can be argued that an ethics of action needs an ethics of character such as that provided by virtue ethics. For one reason, a person with a morally sensitive character is more likely to apply a moral rule of action with insight, and without good character there may be a temptation to act insensitively. Rachels (1999: 189) agrees that developing a theory combining the best features of right action theory with aspects of the virtue approach, supplementing a theory of right action, would give a better account of moral character.

Pincoffs (1998: 442–449), in a general discussion of what he terms "quandary ethics" (ethical dilemmas), suggests that when faced with an ethical dilemma, the approach is to ask what is the right thing to do, emphasizing action rather than character. His contention is that the question of "whether an act is right" is difficult to separate from the question of "whether the agent is praiseworthy" and that seeing dilemmas only in terms of the elements of the situation that a person is faced with is an inadequate strategy, because reference to individual standards and ideals is an essential feature of moral deliberation. Although not specifically addressing virtue ethics as an aspect of resolving ethical dilemmas, Pincoffs does seem to suggest that the development of a notion of the moral self is a necessary prerequisite, because the absence of a developed moral self means that moral dilemmas will simply not arise for an individual. He specifically mentions the qualities of "loyalty, generosity (and) courage" as other features of moral character, bringing his argument closer to that of virtue ethics (p. 447).

However, other philosophers argue that virtue ethics can stand alone as an alternative to other ethical theories, and at least one philosopher, Hursthouse (1999: 26), argues that virtue ethics can provide action guidance. She proposes that an action is right if it is what a virtuous agent, acting in character, would do in the circumstances and that a virtuous agent is one who has, and exercises, certain character traits, namely, the virtues (pp. 28–29). Benn (1998: 168) offers an example. When confronted with the choice between keeping quiet and divulging a friend's confidence in order to be entertaining, the question is, "What would the person with the relevant virtue do?" In this case, loyalty is an integral part of friendship, because it is the virtue that makes friendship possible. Therefore, here the question would be, "What would a loyal person do?" Rachels (1999: 190) suggests that one approach is to assess an action as being right or wrong by reference to the reasons that can be given in favor of or against it, but the reasons given must be reasons connected with the virtues. In other words, the reasons in favor of doing an act will relate to whether the act is honest, generous, fair, and so on, and the reasons against doing it will relate to it being dishonest, unfair, and so on.

Hursthouse (1999: 43) argues that the requirements of different virtues can lead us in different directions that conflict with each other. For example, the virtue of charity may prompt me to kill a person who would truly be better off dead, but the virtue of justice forbids it. It follows that virtue ethics gives no guidance over the

Table 11.1 Virtues and Spheres of Existence

	Deficiency	Mean	Excess
Attitude Toward Self	Servility Self-deprivation	Proper self-love Proper pride Self-respect	Arrogance Conceit Egoism Narcissism Vanity
Attitude Toward Offenses of Others	Ignoring them Being a doormat	Anger Forgiveness Understanding	Revenge Grudge Resentment
Attitude Toward Good Deeds of Others	Suspicion Envy Ignoring them	Gratitude Admiration	Over-Indebtedness
Attitude Toward Our Own Offenses	Indifference Remorselessness Downplaying	Agent regret Remorse Making amends Learning from them Self-forgiveness	Toxic guilt Scrupulosity Shame
Attitude Toward Our Own Good Deeds	Belittling Disappointment	Sense of accomplishment Humility	Self-righteousness
Attitude Toward the Suffering of Others	Callousness	Compassion	Pity "Bleeding heart"
Attitude Toward the Achievements of Others	Self-satisfaction Complacency Competition	Admiration Emulation	Envy
Attitude Toward Death And Danger	Cowardice	Courage	Foolhardiness
Attitude Toward Our Own Desires	Anhedonia	Temperance Moderation	Lust Gluttony
Attitude Toward Our Friends	Indifference	Loyalty	Obsequiousness
Attitude Toward Other People	Exploitation	Respect	Deference

SOURCE: From *Ethics: A Pluralistic Approach to Moral Theory,* 3rd ed., by Hinman, 2003. Reprinted with permission of Wadsworth, a division of Thomson Learning: www.thomsonrights.com. Fax: 800-730-2215.

rightness or wrongness of euthanasia. Another example is the question of whether a doctor should lie to a patient who has a limited time left to live. The virtue of honesty tells doctors that they should tell the truth even though it may be devastating, but kindness and compassion suggest a course of remaining silent or even of lying. Hursthouse makes the point that deontologists are also faced with this conflict problem (p. 43). However, it might be argued that one does not do a person any kindness by concealing this sort of truth from him or her, even though the truth may also be devastating.

Okin (1996: 211) offers a critique of virtue ethics from a feminist viewpoint. She contends that the notion of virtue has been constructed as a quality regarded as admirable in free men with high social standing and that Aristotle's account of the virtues is written from the perspective of the "free, educated, and leisured male members of society" (p. 212). Accordingly, his arguments are predicated on the exclusion of women. In fact, Aristotle's views on women assume their inferiority, and he concludes that women—whom he calls "a deformity of nature"—exist only to perform their role of sexually reproducing men (p. 213). Similarly, Okin attacks Aristotle's notion of growth and nurturing, because he conceives that process as something each person achieves alone, when in fact it was women and slaves who provided the food and services that made such growth possible (p. 214). Okin points out that Aristotle's discussion of virtues is constructed in terms of men only and is bounded by the social hierarchy and domination present in the society in which he lived. She concludes by arguing that there has been little advance in formulating a specifically feminist account of virtue ethics (p. 229).

For Aristotle, gaining access to ethical ideas and thought is dependent on an upbringing that teaches and fosters maturity and growth and brings about the right habits and character (Darwall 1998: 214). An upbringing and education of this kind is necessary for a person to develop emotional and cognitive knowledge that may lead to the acquisition of ethical knowledge. It follows, then, that ethical knowledge may not be available to everyone and that ultimately judgment and wisdom result from maturity, growth, nurturing, and applying the wisdom of earlier generations. This view of ethics stands in complete contrast to the views argued by Mill and Kant, which are law-based. Aristotle's conception of ethics differs in that it is based on a set of ideals. As we practice the virtues, we make choices that demand judgment. It follows that the exercise of virtues requires a capacity to judge and "do the right thing in the right place at the right time in the right way," and the exercise of this judgment does not constitute an application of rules in a routine way (MacIntyre 1984: 150).

Applying Virtue Theory

Case Study 11.1 illustrates how virtue theory can be applied to an ethical dilemma within the criminal justice system.

CASE STUDY 11.1
PROFILING IN THE NEIGHBORHOOD

Rodney is a rookie police officer assigned to a mainly white middle-class neighborhood. On the evening shift, Rodney and his partner Max, a more senior officer, are patrolling the neighborhood when Max says, "Hey, look at that kid. He doesn't belong here. Let's question him." Rodney stops the patrol car, and he and Max get out and approach the boy, asking him for his identification. The boy produces his identification, and asks the two officers "Why have you stopped me? Is it because I'm black?" They do not respond, and Max just searches him and then arrests him. Later that night Max tells Rodney that the boy "pissed him off" with his attitude. He tells Rodney to write a report of the incident and charge the boy with "loitering."

SOURCE: Adapted from Goodman 1998: 59.

In resolving what may be an ethical dilemma, Rodney will follow the process of resolving an ethical dilemma set out in Chapter 1:

1. *Is Rodney faced with an ethical dilemma?*
   Rodney is faced with the dilemma of whether or not to write a report about the incident, when he knows that he is being asked to write a false report and to bring a false charge based on a false arrest.

2. *What are the facts and circumstances of the incident?*
   Rodney needs to review in his mind the facts and circumstances of the stop and arrest and perhaps write them down in the form of a report so that his memory of the events is quite clear.

3. *What are the facts relevant to the decision he has to make? What are his own values about the issue, and what are the values of his workplace about such an issue?*
   Rodney and his partner stopped the boy because he was an African American moving around at night on foot in a white middle-class neighborhood; he was questioned and provided his identification but protested being stopped, suggesting that the sole reason was that he was black; Rodney and Max had no basis for stopping or making an arrest; Max admitted to Rodney that the boy had "pissed him off" with his attitude; and Max has instructed Rodney to write a false report of the incident to justify the stop and arrest.
   Rodney's personal values relate to his position as a rookie cop; that is, he wants to do well in the job and make arrests, and he looks to his more experienced coworkers for guidance. His workplace values comprise the formal police code of ethics and police rules and regulations about stopping and searching and arresting as well as the police subculture on these issues. In many police departments,

racial profiling is a routine event, and police are expected to show loyalty toward each other and to support their partners.

4. *What ethical theories does he call to mind to assist him in resolving the dilemma?*
   In this case, Rodney will apply virtue ethical theory to the dilemma.

5. *What are Rodney's available courses of action?*
   Rodney may comply with his partner's request and complete the false report; he may refuse to fill out the report and tell Max, who instigated the incident, to make the report himself; or he may simply report the whole incident as well as Max's request to his supervisor.

6. *Rodney will make his decision after applying, in this case, the virtue approach to each alternative course of action, and he will choose the course of action that is the most ethically appropriate for him under virtue theory.*

A process for assessing an ethical dilemma from a virtue perspective is set out in Box 11.2. Applications of these criteria are shown in Box 11.3.

A CLOSER LOOK

BOX 11.2
Virtue Ethics Evaluation of Ethical Dilemmas

The focus is on the character of the decision maker. As a person with moral character, I must assess the knowledge I have or will need to reach my full potential and become a virtuous person.

1. Regardless of the dilemma, I must first ask what kind of person (police officer, prosecutor, correctional officer, judge, etc.) I should become to be the best person I can be in that role.

2. I must then ask which virtues will allow me to become the best person (officer, prosecutor, correctional officer, judge, etc.) I can become. I will identify which virtues I must practice in this situation and explain to myself why they are relevant to my goals of becoming virtuous and developing good moral character, including integrity, honesty, compassion, courage, duty, and so on.

3. Once I have decided what kind of person I will need to become to be a virtuous person and which virtues I will need to practice to achieve that goal, I must ask myself which option in the dilemma allows me to practice these virtues and explain to myself how this option allows me to practice these virtues and why the other options would not.

4. I will then practice these virtues until they become habit and part of my character so that when ethical dilemmas present themselves to me in the future, I will know what to do and will no longer face a dilemma of this kind.

A CLOSER LOOK

BOX 11.3
Applying Virtue Ethics

1. Regardless of the dilemma, I must first ask what kind of person (police officer, prosecutor, correctional officer, etc.) should I become in order to be the most virtuous person I can be in that role.

   I might say, for example, that a virtuous police officer is one who is honest, has integrity, has respect for the individual and for the dignity of the individual, and is fair, civil, courageous, and self-disciplined.

2. I must then identify which of the above virtues will allow me to become the best person (officer, prosecutor, correctional officer, judge, etc.) I can become in this situation. I need to explain why these virtues are relevant to my goal of becoming a virtuous person.

   I might say that in the given situation, the best person would have the virtues of courage (because as a rookie officer I need to be able to say no to my more experienced partner), honesty (because I am being asked to make a false report), fairness (because I am being asked to treat a person unfairly), and respect for the dignity of the individual (because racial profiling forms the basis of my dilemma, and this practice is inconsistent with the dignity of the individual).

3. Once I have decided what kind of person I will need to become to be a virtuous person and which virtues I will need to practice to achieve that goal, I must ask myself which option in the dilemma allows me to practice these virtues, and explain to myself how this option allows me to practice these virtues and why the other options do not.

   Rodney has the options of writing the report, refusing to write the report, telling Max to write it himself, or reporting the whole incident to his supervisor. Rodney has identified the virtues of courage, honesty, fairness, and respect for human dignity as relevant virtues in this situation.

   The option of writing the report does not satisfy the virtues of courage, honesty, fairness, or respect for human dignity.

   The option of telling Max to write his own report satisfies the virtue of courage only in the sense that Rodney is refusing to write a false report himself. It does not satisfy the virtues of honesty, fairness, or respect for human dignity, because the report will be false even though Rodney does not write it, and it is based on a false arrest that is in turn based on racial profiling and nothing more.

   The option of reporting the incident to his supervisor satisfies all of the above virtues, because it will expose the incident as being an act of racial profiling, it will show that the stop and arrest were based on nothing more than racial profiling, and it will show that the arrest was false and that the

   (Continued)

(Continued)

officer was merely trying to penalize the African American boy for question-ing his authority. It will also show that the charge brought was a false one.

The most virtuous option for Rodney is to report the entire matter to his supervisor, because that action allows him to practice the most virtues in this particular incident.

4. I will then practice these virtues until they become habit and part of my char-acter so that when ethical dilemmas present themselves to me in the future, I will know what to do and will no longer face a dilemma of this kind.

Rodney will now practice the virtues of honesty, courage, fairness, and respect for human dignity until they are part of his character, and in a simi-lar situation he will know how to react instinctively.

Summary

Whereas deontology focuses on duty and utilitarianism on consequences, virtue ethics is concerned with virtue and moral character. Virtue ethics began with the Greek philosopher Aristotle, who was interested in the kind of person we must become in order to lead the good life. Instead of posing the question "What ought I to do?" virtue ethics poses the question, "What kind of person should I become?" and contends that it is only when we have answered this question that we can deter-mine what is the right thing to do.

Virtues are personal qualities or character traits that are developed through habitual action and that help us to become, over our lifetime, persons of excellent character. The virtues include both natural and acquired qualities like intelligence, honesty, generosity, loyalty, and self-control. Whereas deontology absolutely pro-hibits lying and consequentialism may permit it if the consequences are beneficial, virtue ethics argues that lying is dishonest and that dishonesty is a vice, not a virtue. Sometimes virtues can raise problems. For example, is the terrorist who gives his life for a cause he believes in by committing suicide acting courageously? If gen-erosity is a virtue, how generous is one required to be?

An important aspect of Aristotle's notion of virtue is the concept of happiness, because Aristotle believed that a good life was one that included happiness. By hap-piness he meant well-being or flourishing, and Aristotle therefore argued that virtues promote flourishing and well-being. Aristotle's concept of happiness is dif-ficult to define with any precision, but it is generally thought of as an activity rather than a state of mind, and for that reason it can be thought of as a way of doing things that is positive and as demonstrating an active engagement with life. He argued that we should act in ways that will bring about happiness, and he proposed the idea of the mean or the golden mean. According to the golden mean, when we have to make decisions, we should look for a mean or average between two extremes. For example, we should not eat to excess or insufficiently but consume just the right amount, that is, the mean. It is easy to see how this idea can be applied to everyday ethical behavior.

Another idea promoted by Aristotle is that of practical wisdom, which involves the notion of applying one's excellent character to a situation in the overall context of establishing a good life. Applying practical wisdom means thinking about the circumstances, reasoning correctly, and making the right choices. Individuals who practice practical wisdom have a kind of insight or perception that guides them in making the right decisions.

Virtue ethics as explained by Aristotle has been criticized for being historically specific, because it was formulated in the context of Athenian society at a particular point in history, and this society assumed that virtues were confined to those who possessed great wealth and high social status. Nevertheless, modern philosophers have linked virtue ethics to modern social life and the community, emphasizing the virtues that can be learned within the family as well as within communities. Some see Aristotle's list of virtues as arbitrary, but others think that there is a universality about the notion of virtue and that we all need to develop balance and positive attitudes in our lives.

A major criticism is that virtue ethics does not tell us how to act. For example, it gives us no basis for looking at issues like the death penalty. One answer to this charge is that virtue ethics, as an ethics of character, is essential because it supplements and complements approaches that take an ethics of action. Others argue that developing a moral self means first developing a virtuous nature and that it is only possible to resolve ethical dilemmas if one possesses the necessary individual qualities and character. Some modern philosophers take the view that virtue ethics can stand on its own and that a right action is one taken by a virtuous person acting in character in particular circumstances. In thinking about virtue ethics and the criminal justice system, it is easy to see how character is important in law enforcement and in avoiding abuse of authority and corruption.

DISCUSSION CASE

A Virtuous Prosecutor?

U.S. Attorney Thomas Marks is to prosecute three persons charged with distributing 5 kilograms of cocaine and with conspiracy. They were arrested in a sting operation when an undercover police officer sold them the cocaine for $75,000. They were arrested after one of the defendants had given the undercover officer the money and had taken possession of the cocaine.

According to the Federal Sentencing Guidelines, each of the three defendants faces a mandatory minimum jail sentence of 10 years. Each defendant had a different role in the transaction that led to their arrest as follows:

(Continued)

(Continued)

Defendant One—This person appeared to be the primary ring leader, used his business premises for meetings to discuss the drug conspiracy, and had the largest role in negotiating price and terms of sale. According to police, he is the leader of a drug organization that markets about 20 kilograms of cocaine each month and launders the proceeds through his business.

Defendant Two—This person appeared to act as Defendant One's lieutenant; he made several incriminating statements recorded on tape during the sale negotiation revealing a knowledge of the cocaine business and his plans to resell the drugs. He has no prior criminal record.

Defendant Three—This person basically acted as a lookout during the transaction; he can be convicted as an accomplice but was not a substantial player. He drove the other defendants to meetings and searched the police undercover officer on the date of the sale.

Defendants One and Two have no criminal records, but Defendant Three has a significant record of violent crime that includes assault convictions, domestic violence, firearms possession and use, and stalking.

The lawyer for Defendant Two informs the prosecutor, Marks, that his client will testify against Defendants One and Three if the distribution charges against him are dismissed and if the court is given a recommendation for a short jail term on the conspiracy charge.

Question: After applying the criteria for a virtue approach, should Marks accept the plea bargain offered?

SOURCE: Cassidy 2006.

DISCUSSION QUESTIONS

1. How does one become a virtuous person? Consider with reference to Aristotle's ideas and theories.

2. Why do modern philosophers regard virtue ethics as an alternative to deontological and consequentialist ethical decision-making approaches?

3. What are the main criticisms leveled against virtue ethics?

4. How do professional codes of ethics relate to virtue ethics, and why are they important in ethical decision making in criminal justice?

CHAPTER 12

Egoism, Pleasure, and Indifference

T his chapter will present three ethical theories, namely, ethical egoism, hedonism, and Stoicism. Of the three, only Stoicism has any present-day following in the field of moral philosophy (see, for example, Becker 1998).

Stoicism

In its time, particularly after the death of Alexander the Great, Stoicism was a very influential ethical philosophy. It dominated Roman thinking about moral philosophy until Christianity replaced it. Stoicism, as a philosophy, has been refined and developed over time from its initiation by Zeno (3rd century BC), who is supposed to have lectured from a porch called a *stoa,* from which Stoicism derives its name.

It is important to appreciate Greek history in order to understand how Stoicism developed. In summary, Phillip, the father of Alexander the Great, placed Greece under Macedonian rule, ending the regime of the Greek city-states (Prior 1991: 194–197). During his life, Alexander the Great extended the Macedonian empire and began the process that dispersed Greek language and civilization throughout the Mediterranean. The period of transition from Greek city-states to an empire is known as the Hellenistic period. These changes to Greek civilization were influential, because Greek philosophy became widely available throughout the region. The city-states were replaced by imperial rule. This change seemed to make much of the work of Plato and Aristotle on ethics and politics obsolete, because now philosophers began to see themselves as part of a single enterprise rather than as representing the individual city-states.

The classical Greek philosophers shaped their view of virtue and the good life from the community of small city-states, but this form of social organization no longer existed. Questions were now asked about how virtue would apply in this new age. It was thought that the new social structure required a new philosophy. In addition, much of the daily activity of a citizen in classical Athens had changed with the onset of imperial rule. The political and social life of the city continued, but the close relationships between individuals as well as the social life of the city had changed. In response to these dislocations, new religions arose in an attempt to give individuals a new sense of citizenship. As well, some turned to philosophy instead of religion, and this led to the development of the schools of Epicureanism and Stoicism.

The Stoics reacted to the collapse of the closed social system of the city-states by offering advice to individuals in what for them was a crumbling world. Although Stoicism is a complex moral theory, the basic principle advocated by Stoics is that *one should learn to be indifferent to external differences.* Many of the writings of the early and later Stoics have disappeared, but among those remaining are the writings of Epictetus, who began life as a Roman slave. He advocated a philosophy of *indifference,* believing that this practice would constitute progress for the individual. In the early period, Zeno was succeeded as head of the Stoic school by Cleanthes and later by Chrysippus (Prior 1991: 208). The best known Stoic philosophers today are the Roman emperor Marcus Aurelius and Epictetus, both of whom focused on the presentation of Stoicism in a popular form.

The Stoics assumed that good or evil depends upon the self and that although others have power over events that may affect you, if you can nevertheless be indifferent to those events, others will not be able to exercise power over you (Prior 1991: 209). Epictetus writes,

> All existing things are either in our power or not in our power. In our power are thought, impulse, will to get and will to avoid, and, in a word, everything which is our own doing. Things not in our power include the body, property, reputation, office, and, in a word, everything which is not our own doing. (in Prior 1991: 209)

Epictetus explains, "Virtue resides in the will—only the will is good or bad." Therefore, if one has a good will, achieved by remaining indifferent to external events, external events will not destroy one's character, and a person will be a free person, independent of the world. In other words, for Stoics, virtue consists of learning to accept whatever happens. Epictetus urged a person to compel or force his or her will to conform to events and to try not to force events to conform to his or her will. This reflects the Stoic teaching about living life in accordance with nature (Prior 1991: 211); that is, we should live in accordance with our own human nature, and we should live consistently with the nature of the universe of which we are a part. Since our knowledge is inherently limited, we ought to follow the guidance of our own nature, but if things turn out other than we expect, we should accept them as if they turned out for the best (Sharples 1996: 101).

The ethics of the Stoics should be understood in the context of their belief in predestination; that is, *all that happens in the world is fixed according to some preconceived divine plan, and nothing happens by chance* (Prior 1991: 209). Stoics believed that whatever happened had a rational explanation and was for the best.

For them, virtue is achieved through a will that operates in accordance with the happenings of nature. Appreciating and accepting that events have been fated allows one to avoid frustration and despair in trying to alter those events and, conversely, it is the person who struggles to change events who is not free. Similarly, death should not be considered a bad thing, because it has been predestined by God and therefore must be considered good. *The aim is to achieve a state of being where one is not susceptible to passion or emotion* (p. 212). One of the main effects of Stoicism is that it places the onus for becoming good or bad directly upon the individual, in the sense that cultivating the appropriate frame of mind will lead to virtue. Virtue alone is good. According to Stoics, our health and wealth are not to be taken into account, and we ought to be indifferent to them (Sharples 1996: 102).

The Stoics believed in a commitment to serving the public. This distinguishes Stoicism from hedonism, because the latter advocates a withdrawal from public life and living with a circle of like-minded friends (Sharples 1996: 87). The Romans, with their tradition of public service, admired this aspect of the Stoic philosophy (Prior 1991: 214). The goal of the Stoic philosophy is, therefore, a life of complete rationality and of developing oneself so one remains invulnerable to passion and emotion. The Stoics depicted the person who lived such a life as a "sage," and believed that philosophy was the means of achieving this life. Stoicism is a philosophy that advocates acceptance of life and events and is pessimistic in tone. A good example of this detached attitude appears in the following passage from Epictetus:

> When you go to visit some great man, prepare your mind by thinking that you will not find him in, that you will be shut out, that the doors will be slammed in your face, and that he will pay no heed to you. And if in spite of all this you find it fitting for you to go, go and bear what happens and never say to yourself "it was not worth all this"; for that shows a vulgar mind and one at odds with outward things. (in Prior 1991: 219)

In contrasting Stoicism and hedonism, Prior (1991) points out that both assist in providing a means for dealing with events beyond our control. The Stoics explain that certain things may not be within our power, and the strength of both philosophies is that they teach us "how to bear with dignity those events which truly are beyond our control" (1991: 223). In addition, both Stoics and hedonists would agree that one cannot become just or courageous if one behaves in an unjust or cowardly manner (Sharples 1996: 82). In other words, character cannot be separated from action.

Hedonism

Traditionally, hedonism has been expressed as the view that "pleasure alone is intrinsically good," "pleasure is the only thing worth seeking for its own sake," and "pleasure is the good" (Feldman 1997: 80). Hedonism is the doctrine that pleasure is the sole good. The foremost exponent of hedonism was the Greek philosopher

Epicurus (see Box 12.1). His name appears in the form of the English words *epicure* and *epicurean,* meaning a person whose main enjoyment is derived from exotic and carefully prepared food and wine. In fact, this connotation is far removed from the philosophy expounded by Epicurus himself. He advocated living moderately yet pleasurably and considered pleasure to be the good for which humans aim. Nevertheless, he also appreciated that pursuit of pleasure might itself result in pain (Prior 1991: 200). For example, if, in seeking pleasure, individuals drink to excess, they will suffer headaches and stomachaches. Therefore, in Epicurus's view, the proper way to live is to live "pleasantly" and at the same time not suffer any of the undesirable effects of that pleasant living. Epicurus stated that the aim of human existence was "health of the body and tranquility of mind" (in Prior 1991: 201). He did not endorse a life of endless pleasure or sensuality because by "pleasure" he meant "the absence of pain in the body and of trouble in the soul" (p. 201). Tranquility is attained by philosophical understanding and through practical wisdom. The former teaches that death should not be feared and the latter advocates living virtuously (p. 203).

There are two forms of hedonism, *psychological hedonism* and *ethical hedonism.* The psychological form suggests that people pursue pleasure and only pleasure in their lives and that all their activities are directed toward *achieving pleasure and avoiding pain* (Feldman 1997: 109). Ethical hedonism is the view that not only do people seek pleasure, but they also *ought to seek pleasure* because pleasure alone is good. According to psychological hedonism, every action is motivated by a search for pleasure, whereas ethical hedonism goes one step further, seeing the pursuit of pleasure as normative. Hedonism in both its forms can be criticized for attempting to provide a single explanation for every human act. In other words, in psychological hedonism every act is supposedly motivated by a desire for pleasure.

According to proponents of ethical hedonism, the question of how one ought to live is answered by the contention *that the good life consists of a life of pleasure and that a person ought to act in such a way as to acquire pleasure.* As already noted, Epicurus attempted to find pleasures that did not produce painful consequences, having recognized that some pleasures might be accompanied by pain or might produce pain. For example, some find that smoking cocaine gives pleasure, but it will also produce severe adverse physical and mental effects if continued beyond a certain point.

In practice it seems difficult to separate pleasure from pain in the way Epicurus advocated. For example, friendship, a pleasure, can be accompanied by depression and sadness at the death of a close friend. It is difficult, therefore, to see how ethical hedonism can function as a guide for behavior in our daily lives, because advising a person to seek pleasure is often also advice to seek pain. In addition, although the notion that people ought to conduct themselves in such ways as to acquire pleasure seems reasonable and plausible, it also seems to violate our commonsense views about how we ought to act. Generally, people feel that sometimes it is acceptable to act in order to gain pleasure, but few would regard this as the sole objective in life. For example, we frequently have to fulfill obligations even if we receive little or no pleasure in the process.

A CLOSER LOOK

BOX 12.1
Epicurus

Epicurus was born in 341 BC on the Greek island of Somas, but his father was an Athenian. He moved to Athens and established a school there in 307 BC called "The Garden" because it met in the garden of his home. Unusually, women and slaves were permitted to become members of the school. Epicurus lived and taught at The Garden until his death in 271 BC. He is said to have written over 300 scrolls, but only a tiny number have survived. It is thought that many of his works were destroyed, because they were considered adverse to Christianity. Epicurus's main aim was to establish a philosophy concerned with the attainment of happiness. He thought that the main constraint to happiness was the fear and unease caused by religion.

SOURCE: Prior 1991: 198.

Ethical Egoism

Typically, an egoist is self-centered, inconsiderate, unfeeling, and a pursuer of the good things in life, whatever may be the cost to others. Egoists think only of themselves, and if they think about others at all, it is merely as a means to their own ends. Essentially, egoism involves putting one's own well-being above that of others (Baier 1991: 197). It argues that the right actions are those that promote self-interest, and the wrong actions are those that detract from self-interest (Hinman 1998: 138). This stands in contrast to most other systems of morality, which recommend that we ought to act unselfishly, that we ought to take other people's interests into account, and that we should care for, rather than harm, other people (Rachels 1999: 70). Hinman (1998) argues that, in fact, egoism does not amount to a moral theory at all.

Psychological Egoism

There are two theories of egoism, *psychological egoism* and *ethical egoism.* The former theorizes that all persons are egoists in the sense that our actions are *always* motivated by our own best interests. Proponents of psychological egoism suspect that altruistic explanations of behavior are superficial and without substance (Rachels 1999: 71). In other words, they contend that when a person's motives are properly analyzed, although it may seem that he or she is acting unselfishly—for example, by doing volunteer work in a hospital or church or by saving a child from a burning house—his or her actual motives would tell a different story. For example, the hospital volunteer may be making amends for some misdeed in his or her past or may be trying to build a good résumé, and the person saving the child may be motivated by a desire to be recognized as a hero. This approach can be criticized as being based on the assumption that we will never find the real explanation for someone's behavior until we have discovered an appropriate egotistical motivation (Baier 1991: 199). In other words, a way can always be found to set aside acts of altruism and self-sacrifice and see in them a self-centered motive. However, if one is to interpret all acts in terms of their lack of altruism, one must surely distinguish between acts that are done solely out of selfish motives and those done out of a motive to help others but which also produce feelings of satisfaction and enhance our self-perceptions as "good persons." Surely one has more moral worth than the other.

Thomas Hobbes (1588–1679) was a believer in psychological egoism, and he tried to give a more general account of it by listing motives and showing how each could be read as egoistical acts or intentions (Rachels 1999: 72). For example, in relation to the motive of charity, Hobbes concluded that it constituted the pleasure one takes in demonstrating one's powers; that is, charitable persons confirm to themselves and others that they are more capable than others. Not only can these individuals take care of themselves, but they also have a surplus available for those who are not as accomplished. In demonstrating charity, they are really emphasizing their own superiority.

Another example is pity. Here Hobbes concluded that the real reason we feel pity for others' misfortunes is that we are reminded that the same thing might happen to us. As Rachels (1999: 73) notes, psychological egoism appeals to a "certain cynicism in us, a suspicion that people are not nearly as noble as they seem." As he points out, it is not possible to prove psychological egoism, because the theory shows only that it is possible to interpret all motives in an egotistical manner.

Ethical Egoism

Ethical egoism claims that *promoting one's own greatest good is always to act in accordance with reason and morality* (Baier 1991: 201); that is, everyone ought to pursue his or her own self-interest exclusively (Rachels 1999: 83). Whereas psychological egoism is a theory about *how people actually behave,* ethical egoism is a theory about *how we ought to behave.* It says that we have no duty other than to do what is best for ourselves (p. 84). It is important to understand that ethical egoism does not advocate promoting one's own interests in addition to the interests of others. Rather it stresses that the *only duty* we have is to promote our own interest. However, at the same time, ethical egoism does not require us to avoid actions that might help others. Therefore, if a particular act would benefit our own self-interest as well as the interests of others, that act will not be considered contrary to the goals of ethical egoism.

Those who support ethical egoism argue that if we all look after our own interests, it is more likely that we will all be better off. In other words, if we want to do the best for others, we should not act altruistically, because, for example, while we are fully aware of our own individual wants and needs, we are not completely aware of others' needs. This line of reasoning suggests that we should not set out to act altruistically, because we are not in a good position to do so. Some also insist that looking out for others intrudes into their privacy and that giving charity degrades others and robs them of dignity (Rachels 1999: 85). Ayn Rand, for example, proposes that ethical egoism is the only philosophy that respects the integrity of human life. Rand argues that altruism is a destructive idea devaluing the individual

(Hinman 1998: 149; Rachels 1999: 86), because it claims that one's own interests ought to be sacrificed for another's interests. It is in this sense that altruism does not value the individual. In contrast, Rand suggests that ethical egoism does affirm the value of the individual and is the only moral position to do so.

Rachels (1999) explains that although philosophers have rejected ethical egoism, it is nevertheless a theory that has been returned to again and again. He gives three typical arguments that reject this doctrine. The first is that ethical egoism does not assist in resolving conflicts of interest but rather exacerbates them (p. 91). The second is that it is logically inconsistent, and the third is that ethical egoism is unacceptably arbitrary in the same way that racism is arbitrary (p. 94). Like racism, it advocates dividing people into groups where the interests of one group are considered to count more than the interests of others. This is contrary to the general principle that we can only justify treating people differently where there is a factual difference between them that is relevant and justifies a difference in treatment.

In the same way, ethical egoism contends that we should each divide the world into two categories of people, our self and the rest, and that we should regard the interests of the first group as more important than those of the second group. However, this division, and therefore ethical egoism itself, is quite arbitrary, because there is no general difference between one's self and others. An additional difficulty for ethical egoism is suggested by Hinman (1998: 152)—that while ethical egoists can have acquaintances, it is not clear that they are able to have deep friendships with others, because such friendships are usually founded on the basis of a mutual concern for each other's welfare, and ethical egoism seems to preclude that concern. Hinman also suggests that ethical egoists suffer from moral insensitivity and an unwillingness to help others (p. 154). Compassion and concern for others is completely opposed to self-interest, and therefore these values are prohibited by this philosophy. This means that ethical egoists would respond to issues such as world hunger by claiming that starving people should be helped only when it is in their own self-interest to do so. This seems rather implausible and callous.

Applying the Theory of Ethical Egoism

Case Study 12.1 illustrates how ethical egoism can be applied to an ethical dilemma within the criminal justice system.

CASE STUDY 12.1 GIVING YOUR OWN PUNISHMENT

Harry is a corrections officer at the Grim Correctional Center. He has a reputation among his co-workers for being very strict with inmates and always being ready to issue violations for the slightest breach of prison rules. One of

(Continued)

(Continued)

the inmates he has charge over on his wing is George, a career criminal and experienced prisoner. George and Harry do not like each other, and George often tries to challenge Harry's authority by breaking prison rules or threatening to break them. In the past, Harry has reacted to this resistance by issuing many citations for rule violations and having George dealt with through the inmate disciplinary process. Harry has now reached the stage where he is tired of having his authority questioned by George and has decided to show him who is really the boss. He decides that he will use informal methods to punish George and reinforce his own authority over him. One Friday Harry inspects George's cell and finds that George has two more pictures in his cell than is permitted by the rules according to his inmate classification. Harry considers whether or not he should seize upon this violation to use informal means to impose his will on George or whether he should follow proper prison procedures for dealing with rule violations. He knows that prison officers can use various informal ways of controlling prisoners even though the rules do not allow these methods to be used. Examples would include not telling an inmate about a scheduled visitor appointment, withholding toilet paper, or shutting off the hot water to an inmate's cell. He decides to think about a possible informal way to deal with George. In his mind he formulates the following plan. Instead of issuing a disciplinary report for the extra pictures, Harry will not unlock George's cell the next morning during the daily prison routine and will secretly place a "keep lock" tag on George's cell door. This tag will indicate to other correctional officers that George is to remain locked in his cell and will suggest that a formal order has been given to this effect. This also means that George will remain locked in the cell until he can get someone's attention and complain to the deputy superintendent, who will not be on duty until Monday morning. Harry now has to decide whether to act formally or informally.

In resolving what may be an ethical dilemma, Harry will follow the process of resolving an ethical dilemma set out in Chapter 1:

1. *Is Harry faced with an ethical dilemma?*
   Harry is faced with the dilemma of whether to use informal means to reinforce his authority over George or to use the formal inmate disciplinary process.

2. *What are the facts and circumstances of the incident?*
   Harry needs to review in his mind the facts and circumstances.

3. *What are the facts relevant to the decision he has to make? What are his own values about the issue, and what are the values of his workplace about such an issue?*
The relevant facts are as follows:

- Harry and George have a history of clashes over Harry's exercise of his authority.
- Harry feels he needs to demonstrate to both inmates and other staff that he is always in control, and he sees this as essential for his work as a correctional officer. In his view, those who demonstrate the most power in the prison environment will prevail.
- Harry has always used formal methods to control George before, but it seems to him that this approach has not changed George's attitude toward him.
- Harry wants his co-workers to see that he can control George, because this is expected by the correctional guard culture, which requires that officers never show leniency toward inmates and that they provide unquestioning support to co-workers, especially in the face of inmate resistance.
- Harry knows that informal methods are sometimes more effective with inmates than formal processes.

4. *What ethical theories does he call to mind to assist him in resolving the dilemma?*
In this case, Harry will apply ethical egoism to the dilemma.

5. *What are Harry's available courses of action?*
Harry can either follow the formal disciplinary process, or he may use informal methods to punish George.

6. *Harry will make his decision after applying, in this case, the ethical egoism approach to each alternative course of action, and he will choose the course of action that is the most ethically appropriate for him under ethical egoism.*

A process for assessing an ethical dilemma from an ethical egoism perspective is set out in Box 12.2. Applications of these criteria are shown in Box 12.3.

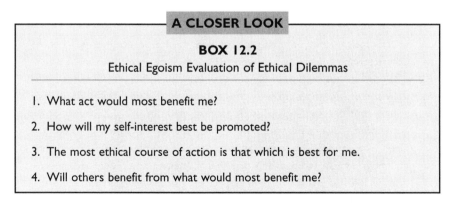

A CLOSER LOOK

BOX 12.2
Ethical Egoism Evaluation of Ethical Dilemmas

1. What act would most benefit me?

2. How will my self-interest best be promoted?

3. The most ethical course of action is that which is best for me.

4. Will others benefit from what would most benefit me?

A CLOSER LOOK

BOX 12.3
Applying Ethical Egoism

1. What act would most benefit me?

   In considering whether to use formal or informal methods to punish George, Harry must consider which action will give him the most benefit. If he takes a formal approach, he knows from past experience that George will continue to resist his efforts to bring George under his control. He feels this will make him look bad in the eyes of other inmates as well as his co-workers. If he takes an informal approach toward controlling George, something he has never done before, he thinks it might be more effective in establishing his control over George. He also thinks he would look better in the eyes of his colleagues if the informal approach works.

2. How will my self-interest best be promoted?

   Harry believes his self-interest will be best served by gaining control over George, and therefore the question is which method, informal or formal, will give him that control over the inmate. He is aware that formal methods have not worked so far, and his inclination is that informal methods will best serve his self-interest.

3. The most ethical action is that which is best for me.

   Harry thinks that what is best for him is to adopt the best method to finally get control over George. Again he has to decide based on his past experience whether formal or informal methods of disciplining George will be best for him. He also has to consider whether the act of breaking prison rules by applying informal disciplinary methods will have a negative affect on him or on his career if his actions are discovered. In this case, he believes that his actions will not be discovered by the administration, because the guard subculture will ensure that his informal methods of punishment are not revealed to his supervisors. Even if they are discovered, he believes he can claim he just made a mistake

4. Will others benefit from the action that would most benefit me?

   Ethical egoism does not require that one choose an act that will benefit others. It only requires that an act benefit oneself. However, if an act also benefits others in the process of benefiting oneself, that act is still considered ethically correct under an ethical egoist approach. In this case, Harry thinks that gaining control over George using informal methods will also benefit other correctional officers, because, if he is successful, they will be able to control George more effectively as well and will not have to resort to informal means of controlling him. He also feels that after his demonstration of guard superiority, all inmates will show more respect for guards generally in the future.

   In all the circumstances, it is clear that the appropriate course of action for Harry, applying the ethical egoist perspective, is to take informal action against George, because that will best serve his own self-interest.

Recalling that egoists are self-centered, inconsiderate, unfeeling pursuers of the good things in life, whatever may be the cost to others, and that egoists also put themselves above the well-being of others, it is hard to advocate this approach to ethical decision making as an ethical approach at all. It contrasts with almost all other systems of morality, which take the view that we ought to act unselfishly, that we ought to take other people's interests into account, and that we should care for, rather than harm, other people (Rachels 1999: 70).

Summary

Stoicism, ethical egoism, and hedonism have very little following among moral philosophers even though egoism and hedonism celebrate self-gratification in ways that seem to accord with the values of modern consumer society. However, in ethical terms they appear to have little to offer.

Stoicism is a complex ethical theory founded, like virtue ethics, during a particular period in history when one civilization was being replaced with another and when philosophical issues were generated by societal change. Stoics argue that a person should learn to become indifferent to external differences and should cultivate a life of indifference. Essentially, it asks that we accept that some things are within our power to change and influence, and others are not. Stoicism tries to persuade us that we can achieve a good will by remaining indifferent to external events and by learning to accept things we cannot change. This is consistent with the Stoic belief in predestination, which emphasizes that nothing happens by chance, that whatever happens has a rational explanation, and that whatever happens is always for the best. Stoics argue that if we try to resist events that have been predetermined, we simply generate frustration and despair within ourselves. In some respects, Stoicism shares the concern of virtue ethics with individual character, because it argues that developing the appropriate stoic frame of mind will lead us to virtue.

Hedonism advocates the pursuit of pleasure as the sole good. There are two types of hedonism: psychological hedonism and ethical hedonism. Psychological hedonism assumes that we all look for pleasure in our lives and that all our actions are aimed at achieving pleasure and avoiding pain. Ethical hedonism is the moral version of hedonism, asserting that people not only seek pleasure, but also ought to seek pleasure, because pleasure alone is good. Quite simply, the answer to the question, "How ought I to act?" is answered by hedonists through their contention that the good life is a life of pleasure and that a person ought to act in ways that will achieve pleasure. However, it is difficult to accept that this notion can form the sole basis for deciding how to act ethically in our lives.

Ethical egoists try to persuade us that the right action is one that promotes our own self-interest, and typically, egoists advocate the pursuit of the good things in life regardless of the feelings or concerns of others. Like hedonism, egoism is divided into two forms, namely, psychological egoism and ethical egoism. Psychological egoism suggests that all humans are motivated and act according to egoist concerns and denies all altruistic explanations of behavior, instead contending that apparently unselfish acts are always carried out for egotistical reasons.

Ethical egoists claim that morality and reason are served only by promoting one's own greatest good and self-interest and that we ought to behave in a way that is best for ourselves. This does not mean that we must avoid actions that might help others but rather that we are duty bound to stress the promotion of our own interests.

Among the many criticisms of ethical egoism is the fact that it is quite arbitrary and resembles racism in its regard for the interests of one group as being more important than the interests of others. That is, it divides the world into others and ourselves, and subordinates all other interests to our own interests. Additionally, it would seem that ethical egoists are unable to develop deep friendships or compassion for others, because they are so much focused on their own interests. This would mean, for example, that ethical egoists would deny any assistance or compassion to starving people, unless they could see such assistance as serving their own self-interest. In the criminal justice system, ethical egoism can be used to justify acts that most would consider lacking in compassion or that are corrupt, abusive, or inhumane.

DISCUSSION QUESTIONS

1. Why is ethical egoism not considered a legitimate ethical theory?

2. How can ethical egoism be applied to the criminal justice system, and what are the implications of using this approach in ethical decision making?

3. Contrast virtue ethics and Stoicism, and explain why you prefer one approach to the other.

4. What parallels do you see between hedonism and ethical egoism?

CHAPTER 13

A Sense of Justice

J ohn Rawls was a prominent philosopher and theorist who wrote about the concept of justice. In *A Theory of Justice,* Rawls aims to "work out a theory of justice that represents an alternative to utilitarian thought" (1973: 22). He asserts it is the business of moral theory to establish fundamental principles that would govern a morally good society. Rawls favors an emphasis on the rights of individuals rather than the means–end technique of thinking used by utilitarians, and in this respect, he follows a Kantian approach to ethics (Blocker and Smith 1980: xv). For Rawls, a theory of justice is a theory of morality that sets out the principles governing our sense of justice (1973: 50–51). He argues that moral persons have two distinguishing features (p. 505). First, they have an understanding and conception of "the good," and second, they are capable of possessing a sense of justice; that is, a desire to apply and act upon principles of justice. Rawls defines principles of justice in his work and sees these principles as playing a crucial part in our moral thought and action (p. 121).

Rawls's conception of justice has an ancient and classical origin (Holmes 1998: 147). For example, Plato emphasized the importance of justice for social living and believed that we all possess a sense of justice. While observing young children at play, the psychologist Piaget noted the presence of a sense of justice in their activities. When justice is thought of in moral terms, rather than in terms of rules and procedures contained in legal systems, it is often perceived of as a virtue or as a moral principle by which we can guide our behavior. Aristotle maintained that justice could be thought of as an aspect of morality, and it is in this sense that the contribution of John Rawls toward embedding justice in our daily lives will be explored.

Rawls's argument is complex and detailed and has given rise to a vast secondary literature. In this chapter, the outline of his argument will be presented and some of its implications explored. As noted, Rawls argues that moral persons possess a sense of justice as well as the capacity to pursue a conception of "the good" in a rational manner. In order for moral persons to develop these moral capabilities, it is necessary for them to create a society and agree on the principles that will govern it; this agreement should be the result of a fair procedure designed with fair conditions (Alejandro 1998: 20–21). In his model, the persons who must decide and conclude this agreement from what is called the *original position* are men and women of ordinary talents and tastes. They do not know their place in society or their class or social position and are unaware of their natural assets and abilities or of their level of intelligence (Rawls 1973: 12). Rawls contends that we can discover the nature of a just society by ascertaining the kind of society that would be chosen by those in the original position. The persons choose the principles of justice behind a *veil of ignorance.* This ensures that no one will gain an advantage or suffer a disadvantage because of his or her particular circumstances in society (Holmes 1998: 189). For example, a wealthy person might support a principle that favored those with wealth, but under the veil of ignorance one could not be influenced in this way, because the person would not know whether he or she was wealthy in the actual society where the principles apply. Similarly, a poor person would most likely choose principles favoring the poor, but because of the veil of ignorance, that person would not have knowledge of the economic or class conditions in which he or she would be living. After concluding the agreement, these men and women would return to their position in society and make moral judgments based on the principles they have chosen.

Rawls attempts to demonstrate that if the parties are rational and act only in their own self-interest, they will choose the two principles of justice that Rawls puts forward. These principles are the following (Rawls 1973: 60):

- Each person is to have an equal right to the most extensive basic liberty compatible with a similar liberty for others.
- Social and economic inequalities are to be arranged so that they are both (a) reasonably expected to be to everyone's advantage and (b) attached to positions and offices open to all.

Rawls describes these principles as principles of social justice that provide a means of assigning rights and duties in the institutions of society and that define an appropriate distribution of benefits and burdens (Rawls 1973: 4). Rawls maintains that a well-ordered society ought to be regulated by a public conception of justice where everyone accepts and knows that everyone else agrees to the same principles of justice and where basic social institutions follow these principles. For Rawls, a public conception of justice is "the fundamental charter of a well-ordered human association" (p. 5).

Social justice is the crux of Rawls's discussion, and he sees *justice* as the basic structure of society and as the basis for describing how major social institutions distribute fundamental rights and duties. He does not pretend to identify the totality of principles that would satisfy the demands of the basic structure of society. He regards such a conception as a social ideal, and for Rawls, the principles of justice make up only a part, although they are perhaps the most important part, of the complete set of principles needed to define this ideal (1973: 9). Nevertheless, he advocates the notion that a just society would conform to the above two principles by incorporating them into its basic structure. He sees the inclusion of a Bill of

Rights within the U.S. Constitution as one significant way in which the first principle of justice could be institutionalized in a given society (Martin 1985: 24).

Application of the Principles

Rawls intends to formulate a set of principles that would help us to make judgments about institutions and actions. Rawls's notion is that if we apply his principles to our beliefs as well as to the facts and circumstances, we will make judgments that will give effect to the principles (Rawls 1973: 46). If we make judgments in accordance with those principles, we will be acting morally. The principles apply to the basic structure of society. They govern the assignment of rights and duties and regulate the distribution of social and economic benefits (p. 61).

Part (a) of the second principle stated earlier is also known as the *difference principle* (Rawls 1973: 75). The difference principle would seem to apply naturally to inequalities arising from the creation of new jobs, to offices and positions that carry special monetary rewards, or to an increase in income from an existing job. However, the principle's application is much broader, because it is to apply to all inequalities in primary social goods. It is not limited to jobs, positions, or offices, but rather, the principle is to include all of the general features within a society and its structures that create unequal shares of primary social goods (Scanlon 1989: 192).

The *difference principle* says that although primary goods and services are to be equally distributed, there is nevertheless a way in which certain inequalities can be considered just. Rawls contends that any inequality must benefit everyone but in particular it must benefit the least advantaged (Jones 1980: 284). If the least advantaged are better off within an unequal situation than they would be with equality, then the principle argues that there is no injustice. Therefore, equality is a mark of social justice, and any acts promoting equality are justified provided they do not worsen the situation of the least advantaged.

Conversely, actions that move away from equality are justified only if they benefit the least advantaged. A corollary is that if society wishes to treat all persons equally, it must give greater attention to those victimized by injustice and to those who, because of unfair treatment, have ended up in the less favorable social positions. The *difference principle* reflects the Kantian principle that people are never to be treated as means to an end but always as ends in themselves (Darwall 1980: 317). In proposing the difference principle, Rawls is promoting the idea that a good society is a society that operates to counteract those natural inequalities that come from birth, ambition, talent, and circumstances, all of which are features that tend to contribute toward the unfair distribution of wealth. For Rawls, the common good is to be assessed by reference to basic benefits to individuals who would otherwise be economically disadvantaged. Overall, the *difference principle* is egalitarian in nature in the sense that it places a restriction on the amount of inequality that is permitted, and it therefore has a strong appeal to those who favor a close connection between fairness and equality (Benn 1998: 122). Rawls generally defines the basic liberties of citizens as comprising political liberty (meaning the right to vote and stand for public office), freedom of speech and assembly, liberty of conscience and freedom of thought, liberty of the person and the right to hold property, and freedom from arbitrary arrest and seizure.

As to the distribution of wealth and income under the second principle, while the distribution of these need not be equal, it must be to the advantage of all, and positions of authority and offices of command must be accessible to everyone. The first principle must be satisfied before the second, and therefore any departure from equal liberty may not be justified by greater social and economic advantages. Rawls sees the two principles as part of a more general conception of justice, which he expresses in the following terms:

> All social values—liberty and opportunity, income and wealth, and the basis of self respect—are to be distributed equally unless an unequal distribution of any, or all, of these values is to everyone's advantage. (1973: 62)

Rawls emphasizes that the principles are for institutions to follow and stresses the need to avoid confusing principles of justice that apply to institutions with those that apply to individuals and their actions (1973: 54). He clarifies the term *institution* as meaning a "public system of rules which defines offices and positions with their rights and duties, powers and immunities," mentioning specifically parliamentary institutions (p. 55). Jones (1980: 275), in seeking to apply Rawls's theory to a discussion of discrimination, argues that it is possible to extend the principles to individuals, suggesting that the way an individual should act ought at the very least be consistent with the requirements of justice for institutions. He also points out that Rawls makes an explicit statement that individuals should follow the principle of supporting and furthering just institutions.

It is important to keep in mind that the principles and the *original position* concern hypothetical people in a hypothetical situation, and therefore, what is revealed is simply that if there were such people who went through that process, then the principles they agreed on *would be* justified (Holmes 1998: 191). This is not to say that those principles are *actually* justified. In other words, it is not clear what application those hypothetical arguments have in the real world. It can, however, be argued that Rawls's model ensures that at least the principles are impartial and that this is a desirable feature of moral principles. At the very least, this might demonstrate that we should give serious consideration to applying these principles to the real world. However, Benn (1998: 125–126) suggests that it is unrealistic to discount talents and abilities, as Rawls proposes in the *original position*. He argues that any credible theory would have to make reference to the abilities of the parties, but nevertheless he accepts that it is hard to deny that a society would be unfair if it took account of race or parental occupation in deciding life chances.

Justice as Fairness

Rawls explains that his intention is to present a model of justice that is abstract in nature. There is no intention on his part to establish principles for a particular society or for a particular form of government. Rather, on a hypothetical basis, the principles previously discussed are those which free and rational persons would accept. They specify the kinds of social cooperation that can take place and the forms of government that can be established. Rawls describes this way of looking at the principles of justice as "justice as fairness" (1973: 11). He explains that it transmits the idea that the principles of justice are agreed to in an initial situation that is considered fair (p. 12).

Moral Development

Rawls discusses moral development particularly in the context of the family (1973: 462). He sees a sense of justice as being gradually acquired by children as they grow and contends that the necessity to teach moral attitudes to children is one of the conditions of human life. He assumes that the well-ordered society includes the family unit and, on the assumption that children are first subject to their parents' authority, sees this first stage of moral development as the *morality of authority* (pp. 462–463). He envisages that parents will love their children, and in so doing, will become the objects of their children's admiration. This, he argues, will influence their children to develop a sense of their own value as well as a desire to emulate the parents. Parents will explain rules of conduct and the reasons justifying them in clear terms and as exemplifying the morality they teach their children.

In the second stage of moral development, which Rawls calls the *morality of association,* the family itself is seen as a small association, with each member having rights and duties and with the child being taught standards of behavior as he or she develops (1973: 467). Similar associations arise through the school and the neighborhood, and through these institutions, the child learns morality. At the same time as the process of attaining morality through association with these institutions develops, an understanding of the principles of justice is acquired, (p. 472) and therefore, there is a progression from mere association to actual knowledge of the standards of justice, which Rawls calls the *morality of principles* (p. 473). The idea is that the child, having developed an attachment to certain individuals and communities, is likely to follow the moral standards that are reinforced by social approval and disapproval. The child complies with moral positions largely because of bonds of friendship and feeling for others and because he or she wishes to gain the approval of the wider society. Rawls sees the well-ordered society as containing citizens who take an interest in political affairs and hold public offices and who therefore are required to apply and interpret the standards of justice.

Okin (2003: 247) notes that alone among modern theorists of justice, Rawls "treats the family seriously as the earliest school of moral development." However, she contends that Rawls makes an assumption that family institutions are "just" institutions and that he ignores the operation of gender in the family. She explains that in her view, a just society would give women the same opportunities as men to exercise political power, develop their talents, and be economically secure within families. In reality, the sexual division of labor has been a fundamental part of the marriage contract. Notions of public and private have penalized women, and this has resulted in neglect of the family by those who theorize about justice.

Rawls suggests that his two principles of social justice will create harmony and cooperation among citizens and will regulate the likelihood that human beings will perform unjust acts. His model places considerable emphasis on the state, and people show solidarity toward each other through the state. At the same time, while the state does not seek to abolish inequalities, it does aim to regulate them through fair bargaining power. This does not mean that employees will always be successful in negotiations with their employers. What is implied, however, is that although employers may be able to cap salaries according to Rawlsian fairness, employees would have opportunities to argue their cases, challenge employers in court, or lobby their congressional representatives; that is, to apply to public institutions that have the capacity to restrain the power of employers. As Alejandro (1998: 25) puts it, "Rawlsian fairness is constrained power." In other words, in the Rawlsian scheme of things, power, especially that derived from private wealth, can be a danger to a stable, well-ordered society and therefore ought to be regulated, not through individuals, but through public institutions that are themselves representative of the regularity and stability essential to the maintenance of a harmonious society (Alejandro 1998: 25). Alejandro (p. 28) sums up the Rawlsian vision of a good society:

> Rawls wants a society where wealth is distributed widely, people engage in meaningful work, citizens have the opportunity to participate in the political process and political parties advance a vision of the public good. He wants a society where inequalities are not explained away as natural but are justified to least-favored members.

Applying Rawlsian Theory

It is clear from this outline of Rawls's complex theory of social justice that Rawlsian conceptions of social justice cannot be applied to individual ethical dilemmas. Rather, his theory is directed at social institutions, at achieving social justice, and at the question of how to construct a well-ordered society. In addition, Rawls emphasizes that his conceptions are abstract and hypothetical and are not intended to be applied in the real world. However, some have applied his conceptions to concrete issues (see, for example, Jones 1980), and it would seem possible to apply some of his broadly formulated principles to aspects of the criminal justice system. Rawls's discussion of inequality might, for example, be linked to the analysis in Chapter 3 of discrimination in the criminal justice system. This might be achieved by posing the questions shown in Box 13.1 concerning discrimination drawn from the Rawlsian discussion of social justice. Applications of these criteria are shown in Box 13.2

─── **A CLOSER LOOK** ───

BOX 13.1
Social Justice Evaluation of Ethical Dilemmas

1. Is there fair, equal, and just application of the laws, or are laws applied unfairly, unequally, or unjustly to certain groups by the criminal justice system?

2. Is there discrimination based on race, gender, or socioeconomic status within the criminal justice system?

3. Is there equal and fair access to justice regardless of race, gender, or socioeconomic status in the criminal justice system?

─── **A CLOSER LOOK** ───

BOX 13.2
Applying Social Justice

1. Is there fair, equal, and just application of the laws or are laws applied unfairly, unequally, or unjustly to certain groups by the criminal justice system?

   Any examination of questions of inequality, unfairness, and the just application of laws would have to consider the position of marginalized groups such as the poor, minorities, and those without power in society. Are such groups treated unjustly by the criminal justice system? For example, are they subject to higher rates of arrest than other groups? Are they policed more intensively? Are they subjected to greater levels of surveillance and control by law enforcement or public institutions generally? Does legislation impose social controls that have the effect of penalizing some groups over others? For example, consider the position of legislation penalizing panhandling, soliciting money from the public, and sex work.

2. Is there discrimination based on race, gender, or socioeconomic status within the criminal justice system?

   The discussion in Chapter 3 reveals that criminologists dispute the existence of any systematic discrimination within the criminal justice system but agree that discrimination does occur at specific points in the system. For example, racial origin may influence decisions about who to arrest, social background may adversely affect an application for bail, and stereotyping certain groups as being more dangerous to society than others may have the effect of denying bail to members of those groups. Jury selection has been a prominent issue historically where explicit discrimination was practiced, and in sentencing decisions, poverty, urbanization, and related factors seem to play a part in determining the length of a prison sentence. Does the criminal justice system treat women differently than men, and has increased policing of drug use affected women disproportionately?

(Continued)

(Continued)

3. Is there equal and fair access to justice regardless of race, gender, or socioe-conomic status in the criminal justice system?

An examination of this issue would have to consider the racial disproportionality of the U.S. prison population and in particular the effects of the War on Drugs and three-strikes legislation. Questions about the death penalty would also be raised, because research has shown that race is a factor in a prosecutor's decision to seek the death penalty and in its actual imposition. In a society where money buys the best legal representation, is it fair for some to have more than competent legal advice and representation when others must rely on often overburdened and inexperienced lawyers in public institutions? How wealth is distributed within U.S. society affects the level of legal representation available to a person who is arrested. If minorities have less wealth, does this mean they are disadvantaged if they come into contact with the criminal justice system? Can access to justice be improved for those without wealth, or must we simply accept the fact that inequalities will continue and that society will not follow Rawls's hypothetical model of surrendering equality in favor of advantaging the disadvantaged?

Summary

Unlike the other ethical approaches discussed in earlier chapters, the work of John Rawls is concerned with establishing fundamental principles that would govern a morally good society rather than with individual ethical choices and acts. His approach is Kantian in nature because his theoretical position favors establishing principles to govern our sense of justice. That is, he sees us acting on principles rather than looking at consequences or at our individual character. Rawls's conception of justice is concerned with justice as a form of morality in the sense of fairness and not with legal rules and procedures found in legal systems. Justice is seen as a principle that can guide the way we behave as a society.

Rawls believes that moral persons possess a sense of justice and the potential to pursue a conception of the good. In order to realize this potential, we must create a just society and agree on the principles that will govern it. He imagines or hypothesizes an agreement between a group of persons who decide on the nature of this society and who do so from a classless social position and without regard to any natural assets or abilities. Rawls argues that this group of persons would choose two principles of justice, one of which is concerned with the equal right to basic liberties and the other with social and economic inequalities. Under the first principle, persons would enjoy personal liberty such as the right to vote and stand for public office and freedom of speech and assembly. Under the second principle, part of which is known as the *difference principle*, there is to be an equal distribution of primary goods and services. However, certain inequalities will be considered just if they benefit everyone, especially the least advantaged. Thus, if the least advantaged are better off in an unequal situation than they would be with equality, there would be no injustice. This means that if it wishes to treat everyone equally, a just society must give more attention to those who are victimized by injustice or to those who, because of unfair treatment, are placed in a less favorable position. This argument parallels Kant's principle that people should be treated as ends in themselves and not as means to an end.

In his general conception of justice, Rawls emphasizes that the principles he expounds should be followed and applied by social institutions, and that the principles are hypothetical and no attempt should be made to apply them to the real world. Nevertheless, Rawls does maintain that his principles would be accepted by free and rational persons and would give effect to the idea of "justice as fairness."

Like Kohlberg (discussed in Chapter 14), Rawls sets out three stages of moral development in a person's life, beginning with the *morality of authority* developed by parents, moving to the *morality of association* arising through contact with the school and the neighborhood, and then to the *morality of principles* where individuals follow moral positions as a result of earlier moral development and because they wish to secure the approval of the wider society.

In terms of creating a society that values social justice, Rawls believes his principles will create harmony and cooperation and reduce injustice. The state should regulate inequalities for the good of all and manage its power to create a stable, well-ordered society. As applied to the criminal justice system and its institutions, it can be argued that Rawlsian notions of social justice can assist in overcoming inequalities in access to justice as well as forms of discrimination within the system.

DISCUSSION QUESTIONS

1. What are the merits of Rawls's approach to ethical decision making within public institutions?

2. Explain Rawls's conception of social justice.

3. How do you think Rawls's approach to social justice can be linked with other ethical theories to produce a just society?

4. How could Rawls's theories be applied to the issue of the racial disproportionality of the U.S. prison population?

5. After applying the criteria for a social justice approach to the War on Drugs and the applicable laws, decide whether or not the relevant social and criminal justice institutions (the political process, law enforcement, courts, jails and prisons) can be said to be achieving the principles of social justice. Make sure to provide detailed support for your answer.

CHAPTER 14

Caring for Others

A number of philosophers have already been considered in this book. It is apparent from this examination that men have historically dominated the study of moral philosophy. While this has changed in recent years, it is nevertheless true that moral philosophy is concerned almost exclusively with men's moral experiences (Hinman 1998: 365). The absence of women's voices has caused contemporary feminist ethical theorists to argue that classical and traditional moral philosophy is distorted. Hinman (1998: 367–369) summarizes feminist criticisms of classical and traditional moral philosophies as follows:

- They assume the notion of the isolated individual, independent and separated from everyone else, and, as a consequence,
- they envisage the objective of moral philosophy as theorizing and explaining how *individuals* ought to treat each other;
- they rely on theories concerning the development of a social contract as a way for the person to enter into moral relationships; and
- they emphasize impartiality and universality in their ethical theories.

In contrast, feminist ethical philosophers have drawn attention to the connectedness that exists between human beings, and they argue that basing ethical theory on the isolated individual and relying on social contract approaches does not reflect the reality and centrality of relationships or the notion of trust, which is grounded in relationships. As to impartiality and universality, feminists argue that traditional ethical theory ought to concern itself with the reality of everyday moral experience and detach itself from supposed notions of impartiality and universality, focusing instead on the conditions of life and the particularity of the human experience.

Kohlberg and Gilligan

The starting point for a dramatic review of the place of women in moral philosophy was the publication in 1982 by Carol Gilligan of *In a Different Voice: Psychological Theory and Women's Development.* Prior to the publication of this book, Gilligan had become interested in psychology and moral development and in Lawrence Kohlberg's work on the psychology of moral development (Hinman 1998: 370).

A Theory of Moral Development

Kohlberg wanted to understand why people would break a written law for a purpose they held to be a higher good. In particular, this question arose for him from the time when Israel was struggling for statehood and was subject to a strict embargo prohibiting the import of food, medicine, weapons, and people. Some defied this embargo and broke the law in order to involve themselves in the formation of the State of Israel.

Kohlberg posed a number of questions to the participants in his study, including a problem known as "*Heinz's dilemma*" (Rachels 1999: 163). He interviewed children of different ages, and after presenting them with various dilemmas, invited their responses with the aim of establishing the nature and content of their moral judgments (Darwall 1998: 219). In the case of Heinz's dilemma, the scenario was presented as follows:

> Heinz's wife was near death, and her only hope for living was a drug being sold by a pharmacist at an excessive price. The drug had cost $200 to make but was being sold for $2,000, and Heinz was only able to pay $1,000. He offered this sum to the pharmacist but his offer was rejected. Heinz said he would pay the rest later but still the druggist would not accept his offer. Now desperate, Heinz considered stealing the drug. Would it be right for him to do that? (Darwall 1998: 219)

Kohlberg discussed the reasoning offered in individual cases. For example, the dilemma had been given to an 11-year-old boy named Jake who considered it obvious that Heinz should steal the drug, explaining that a human life was worth more than money. However, when the dilemma was put to a girl, Amy, also 11 years old, her response was much less emphatic and she appeared hesitant and evasive. She did not agree that stealing was right, thinking there might be other ways such as borrowing the money. Rachels (1999: 165) quotes from the girl:

> He really shouldn't steal the drug—but his wife shouldn't die either. . . . If he stole the drug, he might save his wife then, but if he did, he might have to go to jail, and then his wife might get sicker again, and he couldn't get more of the drug, and it might not be good. So, they should really just talk it out and find some other way to make the money.

Despite attempts by the interviewer to elicit a more positive response from Amy, she would not change her perspective, essentially refusing to accept the terms of the problem itself. She reformulated the issue as a conflict between Heinz and the pharmacist that should be talked out between them. Amy's response tends to focus on personal relationships, whereas Jake appeals to rules and principles, namely, that a human life is worth more than money. Kohlberg concluded that people pass through stages of moral development (see Table 14.1), most achieving the fourth of six stages (Hinman 1998: 371). He assumed these stages are universal, that they operate in sequence, and that they are irreversible.

Table 14.1   Kohlberg's Theory of Moral Development

Level One *Preconventional Morality*	The emphasis is on the self and on self-interest. Morality is based on a hedonistic approach which maximizes pleasure and minimizes pain. The main criteria of morality is seeking reward and avoiding punishment. The rightness and wrongness of an act is assessed by its consequences.
Stage One: **Punishment and Obedience**	This is dominated by the desire to avoid punishment. The criterion for morality is avoiding punishment through obedience.
Stage Two: Reciprocity	This stage embodies an attitude of reciprocity; that is, you do a favor for me and I'll do one for you. We obey to obtain rewards for the favors that can be returned. It is an attitude of "I'll scratch your back if you scratch mine."
Level Two *Conventional Morality*	The emphasis is on society and conformity to social rules. At this level a person tries to do what is expected by others in order to get the social approval of others and to show respect for legitimate authorities. One is moral if one considers the consequences for others. Morality is defined as conforming to the rules of authorities (including parents and law makers).
Stage Three:	This stage is termed the "good boy/nice girl orientation," where the child aims to be a good person in his or her own eyes and in the eyes of others where personal relationships are paramount.
Stage Four:	This stage shows a law and order mentality where the child/adult follows authority rules. Morality means rigid adherence to social rules and the laws of society for the sake of conformity—guilt is associated with this stage and we are concerned with what others think of us.
Level Three *Postconventional Morality*	We exercise internalized principles of ethics and develop personal conscience. Moral judgments are made on the basis of universal moral principles and impartiality and go beyond social convention. Most don't achieve this level, and if achieved it is rarely sustained consistently all throughout life.
	This level involves a concern for a universal principle such as respect for all humans as individuals and considers that all humans have inherent dignity.
Stage Five:	In this stage, individual rights are accepted and reviewed in response to critical discussion. Respect for the rights of others takes precedence over rigidly following social rules.

(Continued)

Table 14.1 (Continued)

Stage Six:	In this stage, there is an orientation towards the acceptance of universal ethical principles of justice, reciprocity, equality, and respect. Only a few persons of high moral repute, like Gandhi and Martin Luther King Jr., reach this stage. At this stage we use our conscience to guide moral behavior that values mutual respect and trust. The focus is on universal principles of justice such as equality, respect, and reciprocity. The key to morality is to respect the rights of others by following our internalized ethical principles. This stage corresponds with Kant's themes of universality and rationality. The test of a just act is whether it can still be considered just after reversing the roles of the actor and the recipient. An act is considered just if it can still be regarded as just when everyone in society acts that way, and this results in its development as a universal principle.

SOURCE: Hinman 1998: 371.

"In a Different Voice": Carol Gilligan

Carol Gilligan studied women's moral development and noted that women's responses did not coincide with Kohlberg's moral stages (Rachels 1999: 166). According to Kohlberg's model, women can achieve only the *second level*, because they are focused on caring for others. Gilligan (1993) suggests that his model is incorrect in explaining women's moral development, because women have different moral stages than men. She interviewed both boys and girls using Kohlberg's theory. Following her study, she specifically attacked Kohlberg's conclusions about Jake and Amy.

Kohlberg argued that Jake had advanced one or two full stages beyond Amy and that he was operating at stage four or five, while Amy had only achieved stage three. Gilligan argued that the two children thought differently, but this did not mean that Amy's way of thinking was inferior. She contended that Jake's response could be located at a higher moral level only on the assumption that an ethic of abstract principle was superior to an ethic that stressed caring and personal relationships. She asked why such an assumption should be made, noting that it seemed to have been made on the basis that most moral philosophers (mostly male) had favored a form of ethics based on rules and principles.

Gilligan concluded that women, as opposed to men, tend to see moral life in terms of care rather than justice and in terms of responsibility rather than rights. Whereas men see treating everyone fairly and impartially as a moral standard, women view caring as a moral imperative and "moral requirements as emerging from the particular needs of others in the context of particular relationships" (Flanagan and Jackson 1993: 70). Therefore, women are more likely to try to resolve issues by seeking solutions that maintain relationships. In contrast, men apply rules fairly, impartially, and equally. Gilligan argues that men's moral decisions are concerned with individual rights and autonomy and that noninterference is highly valued, as is the application of rights and rules to abstract hypothetical dilemmas (Nicholson 1993: 90). They ask, "Have the rules been properly followed and applied?"

In contrast, Gilligan argues that in their moral decision making, women focus on relationships and interdependence and on feelings of empathy and compassion, and women are situationally oriented. In Gilligan's view, women's moral decision making is contextual rather than categorical, often responding to ethical situations with, "It depends" (Nicholson 1993: 90). Women judge moral issues after considering the suffering of other people. In assessing morality, women ask, "Have relationships been maintained or were people hurt?" and focus on the quality of relationships rather than on impartiality. Gilligan also sees women as developing moral appreciation through stages and has identified three full levels or stages and two transitional stages, which are outlined in Table 14.2.

The conclusion Gilligan reached was that the caring approach is an equally valid moral perspective that has generally been ignored in both moral theory and psychological research because of male bias (Sterba 2001: 52). In 1984, Kohlberg acknowledged, "An orientation of care and response usefully enlarges the moral domain" (in Benhabib 1987: 156). However, Kohlberg still did not consider notions of "care and responsibility" to be a separate track of moral development but rather regarded them as a moral orientation in conjunction with "justice and rights." It was Gilligan's conclusion that there seemed to be two quite different ways of thinking about ethics that led her to depict that difference in terms of voices. She termed this different voice, which did not fit into Kohlberg's categories and was evidenced more among females, the *ethic of care*.

Table 14.2   Gilligan's Theory

Level One Orientation to Individual Survival	*Individual survival* is paramount, and moral considerations are relevant only when one's own needs are in conflict. Morality consists of imposed sanctions on the self.
First Transition	*From selfishness to responsibility* in which women begin to become aware of their responsibility for others' well-being. They are aware that morality requires that they become responsible for the well-being of others.
Level Two Goodness as Self-Sacrifice	*Goodness becomes identified with self-sacrifice*; that is, to be a good person involves taking care of other people (family) at the expense of oneself. Social norms and consensus are the basis for moral judgments and concern for others, especially others' feelings, and the possibility of hurting others is of major concern. Goodness in the form of selfsacrifice is joined with the desire to care for others.
Second Transition	*From goodness to truth.* Women now understand that care includes caring for themselves as well as others. Women begin to struggle when they learn they need to care for themselves as well as for others and may initially see this as a regression to the first stage.
Level Three Morality of Nonviolence	*Moral goodness is seen as caring both for oneself and for others.* The previous issue between being selfish and showing responsibility to oneself is resolved in a principle of nonviolence, and an injunction against hurting others is established. At this point, care becomes "a universal obligation." This level takes on the ideals of inclusiveness and nonviolence and condemns exploitation and hurt. Morality is primarily about caring.

SOURCE: Gilligan 1993: see Chapter 3.

Gender and the Ethic of Care

Gilligan's research was conducted with female participants, but she emphasized in her work that the *ethic of care* was not differentiated according to gender. It follows, therefore, that the caring approach is not exclusively female, and there may be women who make decisions based on principles and men who make them on the basis of care and relationships. It might also be argued that women might be more attracted to an approach that emphasizes caring because of the social role that they have traditionally performed (Rachels 1999: 168). Thus, women have traditionally been given responsibility for caring for children and for the domestic aspects of life, and, therefore, the ethic of care is simply an outcome of women's socialization and lived experience.

An alternative view might be offered that women demonstrate a caring perspective because it is an innate characteristic of their sex. For example, Noddings claims that "an ethic built on caring is . . . characteristically and essentially feminine . . . [arising] . . . out of our experience as women, just as the traditional logical approach to ethical problems arises more obviously from masculine experience" (Noddings 1984: 8). This view has been derided by feminists who argue that it is social conditioning that constructs and creates gender boundaries rather than sex roles (Grimshaw 1991: 493). They contend that if this argument were accepted, women would be forever consigned to the domestic sphere and that this would render them permanently oppressed.

Grimshaw (1991: 493) outlines two responses to this question of differential male and female thinking. The first is that there are typical differences in male and female thinking on moral issues but that this difference must not be expressed in terms of a deficiency on the part of women. In other words, the stereotypes of women being incapable of reason, as emotional, and unable to act on principle must not be reinforced. Grimshaw argues that difference can be recognized without that difference connoting deficiency. The second is that social practices such as caring for others and particularly mothering, which have traditionally been regarded as within the female domain, can be seen as generating forms of virtue that can stand as corrective influences to those domains commonly dominated by men.

An Ethic of Care

Gilligan's conclusions have been adopted by moral philosophers, both male and female, and a number have theorized about the nature and extent of an ethic of care. This form of ethics conceives moral life as a network of relationships with particular persons, and it sees living well as caring for those people within those relationships (Rachels 1999: 170). It affirms the priority we give as a matter of course to our family and close friends and goes beyond the notion that being a loving parent is simply a duty. We are all aware that a loving parent acts from motives beyond that of duty and that a caring relationship with one's children that merely satisfies duty is likely to be construed as a nonloving relationship by one's children. Both Gilligan (1993) and Noddings (1984) argue that women resort less to rules and principles than men and are more likely to want concrete rather than abstract reasoning. As well, they argue that women seek a detailed knowledge of a particular situation and to resolve dilemmas by reference to the relationships involved (Grimshaw 1991: 495).

How does the notion of caring for others constitute an ethic? It is first necessary to consider how the ethic of caring differs from traditional ethics. As noted earlier, the ethic of care rejects the idea of relying on rules to assess morality, regarding them as guidelines and not as determinants of right or wrong. It argues that we should respond caringly to those with whom we interact in life. One difficulty is that "acting caringly toward others" gives the appearance of a principle, stating, as it does, that a person ought to enhance notions of caring in oneself and in others (Blum 1994: 208; Holmes 1998: 204). If this is true, and the admonishment to care for others is in fact a principle, then the ethic of care does not dispense with principles, as its proponents claim. Blum (p. 208) argues, however, that the ethic of care does not establish a principle but rather expresses certain sensitivities and attitudes toward others that can be promoted as good ways to act and live in particular situations. Holmes (1998: 205) seems to agree with this position, arguing that if it is read as a principle, the ethic is derived from judgments about particular cases. The rightness of particular cases is not resolved by appealing to the principle but rather by referring to particular cases in order to arrive at the principle.

Another question raised by the ethic of care is "*How do we recognize what is the right or caring thing to do in particular situations?*" While it may be easy to determine how we should care when dealing with our family members and friends, it may be more difficult to recognize a caring act when considering world problems and international relations. Holmes (1998: 205) considers that the challenge to the ethic of caring is to decide what is morally correct in cases outside the scope of family and friends. Slote (1998: 171) questions whether the morality of caring can "really provide a total framework for moral thought and action." He points to the fact that in order to deal with our obligations to those with whom we are not acquainted, as well as to address wider issues in society, a morality of caring seems to need supplementation from notions of rights and justice. He nevertheless argues that the ethic of caring can be sustained in the form of a specifically "virtue-ethical manner" as a form of virtue ethics, where it can be plausibly articulated and defended. In other words, he sees it primarily tied up with virtue ethics. Slote suggests that even if the ethic of caring calls for a show of greater concern for those who are nearer and dearer to us, it might still condemn indifference to strangers, and he draws a distinction between the depth and breadth of concern or of caring. His suggestion is that the morally most attractive or virtuous individual "is one who has *deep* concern for particular others . . . but who is also *broadly* concerned with the well being . . . of other human beings" (Slote 1998: 181).

Developing the Ethic of Care

An ethic of care, according to Rachels (1999: 171), focuses on close personal relationships, and caring cannot occur in the absence of those relationships.

Noddings (1984), in *Caring: A Feminine Approach to Ethics and Moral Education*, agrees with Rachels that there can be a caring relationship only if there is a personal one-to-one encounter and that there is no obligation to help "the needy in the far regions of the earth," because it is impossible to do so (in Rachels 1999: 171). She perceives caring for starving children in Africa as being an impossible task, because it would require that she abandon the caring she is obligated to perform here (Noddings 1984: 86). She therefore defines the extent of the caring obligation by looking at the possibility of completing a particular act of caring. Noddings sees two classes of persons eligible for caring by virtue of their relationship with the caregiver. The first class is composed of those related to the caregiver or who will potentially be related, therefore creating an absolute obligation to care. The second class is composed of those with whom there is a "dynamic potential for growth in relation" (1984: 86).

In contrast, Held (1987: 118) argues that particular others with whom a person has relationships can include children starving in Africa and even future children in that situation. Rachels (1999) suggests that a response that ignores starving children in other parts of the world feels uncomfortable and wrong. He proposes that an alternative approach is to state that the ethical life "includes both caring personal relationships and a benevolent concern for people generally" (p. 171). In other words, the ethic of care can be seen as supplementing traditional theories of obligation rather than replacing them. Rachels ultimately concludes that there is a clear nexus between virtue theory, with its emphasis on a moral person possessing certain character traits, and the ethic of care, and he sees the ethic of care as one part of virtue ethics. He goes so far as to contend that most feminist philosophers view virtue ethics in this light (p. 174).

Grimshaw (1991: 495), pointing to the difficulty in describing the differences between male and female thinking about moral issues, emphasizes the need to avoid any suggestion that because it may be different, women's thinking is somehow deficient. She suggests that the answer may be not so much that men and women reason differently about moral issues but that they have different ethical priorities and, therefore, what women see as important in terms of principle, such as maintaining relationships, is viewed by men as a failure of principle. She suggests that if women's life experiences are different from those of men, it is reasonable to assume that ethical priorities will be gendered. She points to the experience of women in pregnancy, in childbirth, and in child rearing as illustrative of this.

Ruddick (1980, in Grimshaw 1991: 496) contends that the act of mothering itself generates a conception of virtue and that this experience is central to women's ethical life (also see Held 1987: 114). Whitbeck (in Grimshaw 1991: 496) has similarly suggested that motherhood is at the very center of the female practice of caring for others and that this caring can provide an ethical model that contrasts with competitive and individualistic norms that inform life experience. Grimshaw cautions, however, that there are dangers in suggesting that female practices are able to generate an alternative form of ethics, because such practices are always located in the social sphere and are impacted by issues such as class, race, culture, and well-being (1991: 496). Nevertheless, she sees these practices and life experiences as constituting a source from which to mount a critique on the male-dominated public sphere

(p. 498). In agreeing that there is a need for an ethic of care, Held (1987: 120–121), in contrast, calls for a more pluralistic view of ethics, arguing that appealing to one or several simple principles cannot solve all ethical problems. She stresses the experiences open only to women and suggests it is necessary to consider their significance for moral experience and theory. She understands mothering as central and fundamental to social relationships and argues that morality ought to make room for the social bond between the mothering person and the child (p. 115).

Blum (1994: 108) takes the view that although Gilligan and other writers recognize a notion of care, they do not develop the implications of this theoretically in a way that would sustain a morality of care, and they do not sufficiently articulate the different virtues and sensitivities which make up that notion. He contends that it is necessary to explore whether care may take different forms in different contexts and draw on different virtues and sensitivities. He offers the example that being able to appreciate that someone is depressed and having the ability to lift that person's depression is a different quality than being constantly available to others to perform caring functions. Both may be expressions of caring in a general sense, but they contain components of distinct sensitivities. He argues that an analysis that promotes the contextual nature of caring will ultimately give the ethic of care a greater theoretical power and scope, and he is inclined to extend the boundaries of the ethic of care beyond personal relations and into more public domains such as professional life (p. 111). Even within personal relations there is differentiation—for example, caring for children is not the same as caring for friends—and appreciating the existence of care in less intimate relationships can have the effect of broadening the scope of the ethic.

Whereas Gilligan understands relationships and caring in terms of concrete persons with whom one stands in specific relationships, such as father, teacher, brother, or friend, Michael Sandel (in Blum 1994: 219) sees a person as "encumbered," and extends encumbrances to forms of communal identity such as being a member of a particular nation, religious or ethnic group, class, or neighborhood. He therefore suggests that any ethic of care could draw wide boundaries in terms of relationships. Responding to Sandel's point, Blum (1994: 249) imagines a situation in which someone utters a racial slur about Kevin, a member of my racial group. To illustrate the differences between individual and group approaches, two possibilities are identified. The first is that in responding to the racial slur, I might be concerned about Kevin as an individual and how the slur has affected him. I therefore am attentive to his needs, and I help him talk through how he feels about the abuse he has suffered and what we might do together to formulate an appropriate response to what has happened. This represents the individual caring mode.

The second response to this event is that I perceive it from the perspective that a member of my race has been targeted with a racial slur. Here, my moral concern is not on the basis of friend to friend but as a member of a group toward another member. Therefore, my focus will be not only on how Kevin is injured by the racial attack but also on how all members of the group have been harmed. This represents the group and not the individual response to relationships.

Finally, in his presentation of views about the development of the ethic of care and its relationship to traditional moral philosophy, Darwall (1998: 228) suggests that the ethic of care may not stand in opposition to traditional moral theory but instead can operate as an important supplement and a different path, bringing issues of relationship to the fore that have been relatively neglected in the past. As he puts it, "The ethics of care provides a way of seeing equal concern and respect as themselves rooted in ways of relating to others as particular individuals" (p. 228).

The Ethic of Care and Justice

How might the ethic of care be applied to the criminal justice system? In a provocative essay, Robin West argues that caring should be at the center of an understanding of public and legal virtues as well as private and personal virtues, and that specifically it should be central to the meaning of legal justice (1997: 9). West agrees with those who have suggested that caregiving should be thought of as an ethical activity and goes beyond this to ask whether judges ought to act in accordance with an ethic of care when deciding cases coming before them in the same way that they perform in accordance with an ethic of justice. Noting that care is associated with context, relationships, and the private sphere, she explains that although judicial work has plenty of evidence showing judicial respect for the ethic of justice, there are few signs of an ethic of care. She contends that instead of being oppositional, the ethic of justice and the ethic of care are interdependent and interrelated and are each necessary conditions of the other (p. 24).

West contrasts the virtue of legal justice with that of compassion or care in a number of cases, using images of legal justice to highlight the differences (p. 30). She explains that legal justice demands that judges operate according to the rule of law and with respect for precedent, that they demonstrate personal integrity, and that they show impartial universality in the form of an unbiased approach to issues brought before them. The images of care she identifies include the mother's nurturance of the newborn, images of compassion, and the protection and care that a woman shows for her child. She concludes that care images appear to be oppositional to images of justice (p. 32). West underscores the feminist belief, developed since the late 1970s, that care, no less than justice, is a moral activity and not a purely emotional response, and she argues that this should result in a broad-based reexamination of virtually every field of inquiry. She does not see caregiving as confined to family life, arguing that if a caring response is a moral response, then public life and public decision making should also include this virtue (p. 34). West contends that if the ethic of care were applied in the exercise of justice, injustice would be avoided, for example, through a "more compassionate reading of the applicable law" (p. 48). She provides, as an example of justice and care combined, the decision in DeShaney (in West 1997: 49) that ruled it is the task of a juror in death penalty cases to give a decision that does not take into account the life circumstances of the defendant. She considers this ruling as a demonstration of an imbalance between justice and compassion.

Generally, West sees the ethic of care as a morality that should be followed in the judicial system so that justice, compassion, and care go hand in hand. To this extent she expands the boundaries set by Gilligan and others beyond the personal and into the field of public administration, law, and dispute settlement. For West, doing justice ought to include showing care and compassion as a matter of moral rightness.

Noddings (1984: 36) also raises the issue of justice. She rejects abstract notions and argues that when women are faced with moral dilemmas, they will follow a process that allows them to envisage and examine a concrete situation. She offers the example of determining the appropriate punishment for a particular crime. She contends that the traditional approach, which she considers a masculine approach, is to identify the principle that applies to the particular case. In contrast, Noddings argues that a feminine approach would require more information about the offender and the victim(s). She suggests that a woman might even begin to analyze a dilemma by thinking "what if this were my child." She contrasts the process of legal abstraction, isolated from the complicating factors such as persons, places, and events, with a process that is concrete and based on facts, others' feelings, and life histories. As she puts it, "The father might sacrifice his own child in fulfilling a principle; the mother might sacrifice any principle to preserve her child" (p. 37). She concedes that this approach is too simplistic to be definitive, but she does consider it instructive.

Peacemaking

Some criminal justice practitioners advocate an approach that is variously termed *peacemaking criminology* or *peacemaking*. Braswell and Gold (1998: 26) suggest that there are three aspects of peacemaking: *connectiveness,* meaning that we are not simply isolated individuals but rather are connected to all other human beings, animals, and the environment; *caring,* which, as we have seen already, is an element considered critical in ethical decision making with a focus on "caring for" and "relationships with" others; and *mindfulness,* an aspect that advocates thinking about our actions and the needs of others in the long term and acting in ways that demonstrate our knowledge of the correct thing to do in the long term.

Peacemaking criminologists argue that the ethic of care has linkages with peacemaking, because it includes the notions of caring, connectiveness, and mindfulness in its formulation of ethics. For example, the authors of *Corrections, Peacemaking, and Restorative Justice* view peacemaking as a "broad, encompassing process" that draws on ancient philosophical traditions and on spiritual sources as well as "from Nel Noddings' feminist concept of caring" (Braswell, Fuller, and Lozoff 2001: 1). Since these authors describe peacemaking as a process, they may not be claiming that it provides the basis for explaining how we ought to live. As well, the fact that it is linked to the ethic of care may suggest that, if it is a philosophical approach, it is agent-based rather than action-based.

Fuller (1998: 55) has designed a pyramid of concepts that he believes constitutes peacemaking criminology (see Figure 14.1). The foundation of the pyramid is *nonviolence,* which he includes due to the status of nonviolence as a fundamental peacemaking principle. The intent here is that violence and coercion, including capital punishment and excessive force, ought to be outlawed from the criminal justice system. The next level is *social justice,* and Fuller argues that criminal justice solutions must take account of social justice so that they do not reflect practices involving racism, sexism, or ageism. The next level, *inclusion,* means that there must be participation by all concerned parties in solutions. Solutions must be arrived at through the next level of *correct means;* these entail nonviolent means, social justice, and inclusion, as well as due process rights. Solutions must be sought that incorporate values of cooperation, nonviolence, and compassion. The next level is referred to as *ascertainable criteria,* and these criteria must be understood, be considered valid, and be trustworthy to all concerned parties so that one party does not hold all the power to define and decide the factors to be considered in the solution (p. 56). The apex is formed by the *categorical imperative* developed by Immanuel Kant. For Fuller, the categorical imperative must be applied, because we must act in a way that we can "will" that act onto all others in similar circumstances and so that the action can become a "universal law." Fuller argues for the inclusion of the categorical imperative on the basis that solutions to problems in criminal justice should have as their foundation "underlying moral reasoning" (1998: 57).

Fuller's multifaceted approach seems to be programmatic rather than theoretical or philosophical, because, in his view, the peacemaking model emphasizes "social justice, conflict resolution, rehabilitation, and a belief that people need to cooperate in democratic institutions to develop meaningful communities" (p. 41).

Fuller stresses that peacemaking ought not to be confused with peacekeeping, but Pepinsky's (1999: 52) notion of "peacemaking criminology" seems to adopt an

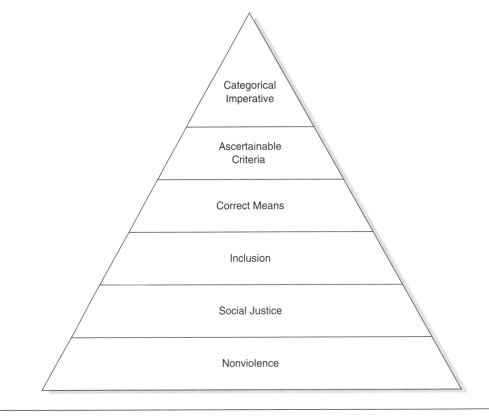

Figure 14.1   Peacemaking Solutions to Criminal Justice Problems: Peacemaking Pyramid

SOURCE: Fuller 1998: 55. Reprinted with permission.

approach grounded in peacekeeping. Pepinsky is rather more precise about the principles included in his version of peacemaking and conceives peacemaking as being linked to social control. He sees two contrary approaches toward social control in the forms of *war making* and *peacemaking* (p. 56). The four principles he advocates in social control solutions are, first, taking time to review one's own feelings and impulses in order to generate choices for oneself; second, "introducing oneself to the apparently weakest, or quietest victim" (p. 62); third, making a deliberate attempt to draw out victims and hear their stories, especially their fears and pain; and fourth, to join with those who have no voice in confronting those who hold the most power in given situations and who threaten or discount the needs and interests of weaker groups (p. 56). Pepinsky sees these peacemaking steps as being incorporated into social interactions, and he advocates using the four principles as an alternative to blaming and attacking one's enemies (p. 57). Pepinsky's approach seems to stress a kind of nonviolence when confronted with exhibitions of power that threaten one's security. As he puts it, "Peacemaking is the art and science of weaving and reweaving oneself with others into a social fabric of mutual love, respect, and concern" (p. 59).

Currently, writers advocating peacemaking write from many perspectives, ranging from nonviolence to Christian ethics as well as from a Buddhist position. Certainly the notion of peacemaking is attractive in a general sense, although it seems to be in need of greater definition and specificity.

Applying the Ethic of Care

Case Study 14.1 illustrates how the ethic of care can be applied to an ethical dilemma within the criminal justice system.

CASE STUDY 14.1 TOUGH LOVE

Jay Barros was a delinquent. He would even admit it freely. He'd done just about everything and had been on probation and in and out of institutions for years. The psychologists had long ago classified him as a typical sociopath: no conscience, never learning from the past, impulsive, and manipulative.

Harold "Red" Chapman was a probation officer. He was also an ex-cop. He didn't counsel his charges; he supervised them with an iron hand. He had one rule: Any misconduct and you get violated. No questions, no excuses. It was odd, though; he didn't violate that many kids. Most of his probationers led pretty straight lives when they were on Red's caseload.

Jay knew he had messed up. He had been cutting classes, had been caught drinking, and didn't come home for three straight days. Jay's mother had called Red to report on Jay's behavior, and Red had called Jay into his office for a conference. Jay figured that it was back to the state's boys' school again, as he walked into Red's office.

(Continued)

(Continued)

"Sit down and shut up," Red said in a stern voice. "We're gonna talk. As I see it, you've got two choices. Your first choice is a quick trip to the detention center and an even quicker trip out to the boys' school. But that's a lot of paperwork on my end."

"Yeah, and what's my second choice?" Jay asked, beginning to think if he played his cards right he might just get out of this. Red reached into his lower drawer and brought out a piece of leather two and one-half inches wide and three feet long.

"This is a strop. Barbers use them to sharpen razors. I use this one to adjust attitudes. That's your second choice. Ten with the strop and you walk out of here. It's your choice." Jay stood up and grabbed his ankles.

While this was happening, Mary, another probation officer, walked past Red's door, overheard the whole incident, and saw Jay bend over to receive his punishment while Red was holding the strop.

SOURCE: Adapted from Close and Meier 1995.

In resolving what may be an ethical dilemma, Mary will follow the process of resolving an ethical dilemma set out in Chapter 1:

1. Is Mary faced with an ethical dilemma?
Mary is faced with the dilemma of whether to intervene and stop the corporal punishment and do nothing further, or to allow the incident to occur but report it immediately to her supervisor. The option of doing nothing is *not* an ethical option, because it would conflict with Mary's duty as a probation officer to protect juvenile probationers from harm and abuse.

2. What are the facts and circumstances of the incident?
Mary needs to review in her mind the facts and circumstances.

3. What are the facts relevant to the decision she has to make? What are her own values about the issue and what are the values of her workplace about such an issue?
The relevant facts are as follows:

- Red has an unprofessional attitude toward his work as a probation officer.
- He believes in tough love in the form of corporal punishment rather than following the rules relating to violations of probation.
- He adopts a tough love stance because it saves him work, not because of any genuine belief in its efficacy.
- Jay, the probationer, is prepared to accept corporal punishment to avoid being reincarcerated, but this will inevitably affect his relationship with Red, because he will know that Red is prepared to bend the rules to suit his own convenience.

- Mary is a professional probation officer who believes in upholding the rules and standards of probation, including the protection of juveniles.
- The values and culture within probation generally support the notion that a probation officer should back up his or her co-workers. However, where juvenile probation officers are concerned, workplace values do not support actions that harm the probationer and flout the rules.

4. What ethical theories does she call to mind to assist her in resolving the dilemma?
In this case, Mary will apply the ethic of care to the dilemma.

5. What are Mary's available courses of action?
Mary may intervene and stop the assault on Jay and do nothing further, or she may allow the assault to take place and immediately report it to her supervisor. She does not have the option of doing nothing at all about the assault, because it would not be considered ethical for her to do nothing about the incident in light of her duty to protect the well-being of juvenile probationers.

6. Mary will make her decision after applying, in this case, the ethic of care approach to each option. She will choose the option that is the most ethically appropriate for her under the ethic of care.

A process for assessing an ethical dilemma from an ethic of care perspective is set out in Box 14.1. Applications of the listed criteria are shown in Box 14.2.

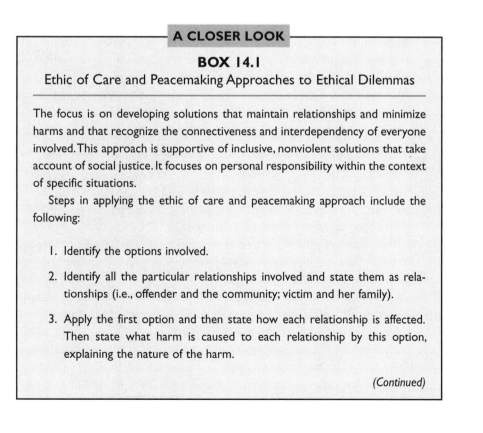

A CLOSER LOOK

BOX 14.1
Ethic of Care and Peacemaking Approaches to Ethical Dilemmas

The focus is on developing solutions that maintain relationships and minimize harms and that recognize the connectiveness and interdependency of everyone involved. This approach is supportive of inclusive, nonviolent solutions that take account of social justice. It focuses on personal responsibility within the context of specific situations.

Steps in applying the ethic of care and peacemaking approach include the following:

1. Identify the options involved.

2. Identify all the particular relationships involved and state them as relationships (i.e., offender and the community; victim and her family).

3. Apply the first option and then state how each relationship is affected. Then state what harm is caused to each relationship by this option, explaining the nature of the harm.

(Continued)

(Continued)

4. Apply the second option and then state how each relationship is affected. Then state what harm is caused to each relationship by this option, explaining the nature of the harm.

The most ethical option will be that which, while it affects relationships, minimizes the harm caused by the impact of the dilemma on those relationships. Accordingly, if most relationships are affected but the harm caused by a particular option is minimized, then this is the most ethical option under an ethic of care.

A CLOSER LOOK

BOX 14.2
Applying the Ethic of Care

1. Identify the options involved.

   Mary may intervene to stop the corporal punishment and do nothing further. She may let the incident occur without intervention but immediately report it to her supervisor.

2. Identify the particular relationships involved and state them as relationships (i.e., offender and the community; victim and her family). There are the following relationships:

   Between Red and Jay
   Between Red and Mary
   Between Mary and the probation department
   Between Red and the probation department
   Between the probation department and the community

3. Apply the first option and then state how each relationship is affected. Then state what harm is caused to each relationship, explaining the nature of the harm.

   Red and Jay—This relationship will continue and Red will continue to be Jay's probation officer. The relationship will be harmed because Red will be able to repeat his unprofessional abusive behavior toward Jay and to others unless Mary or someone else intervenes again.

   Red and Mary—Their relationship will continue but harm will be caused because Mary has become aware of Red's abuse and she will have no confidence or trust in him as a co-worker.

   Mary and the probation department—The relationship will continue as before. It will not be harmed because the department will not have been informed of Red's conduct or Mary's intervention.

   Red and the probation department—The relationship will continue and will not be affected, but harm will result because the department will not be aware of Red's abusive practices and he will likely continue using them.

The probation department and the community—The relationship will continue and remain unaffected, but harm will be caused because Red may abuse Jay and other children again, and this will reduce the Department's standing in the community due to the fact that no action is taken to stop Red.

4. Apply the second option and then state how each relationship is affected. Then state what harm is caused to each relationship, explaining the nature of the harm.

   Red and Jay—This relationship will end because Red will be fired. No harm will result in ending this relationship because Red will not be permitted to act unprofessionally again.

   Red and Mary—Their working relationship will end, but no harm will be caused because Mary will no longer have to work with an unprofessional and abusive co-worker.

   Mary and the probation department—The relationship will be strengthened and no harm will be caused. In fact, this relationship will be enhanced because Mary will be seen to be taking action against abusive probation officers and protecting children, as is her duty under the law.

   Red and the probation department—The relationship will end but no harm will be caused because the department will now be rid of an abusive probation officer.

   The probation department and the community—The relationship will continue and will be enhanced. No harm will result because the community will know that the department is prepared to fire abusive and unprofessional probation officers in order to protect children, as is its duty.

5. The most ethical option will be that which, while it affects relationships, minimizes the harm caused by the impact of the dilemma on those relationships. Accordingly, if most relationships are affected but the harm caused is minimized by a particular option, then this is the most ethical option under the ethic of care.

   After comparing options 1 and 2, it is evident that both options affect the relationships involved when action is taken to resolve the dilemma. However, it is evident that harms are maximized under the first option and minimized under the second. Accordingly, Option 2 is the most ethical choice of action because even though most relationships are affected, overall harms are minimized under this option.

Summary

Feminist approaches to moral philosophy have drawn attention to the importance of gender in ethical theory. Feminists have critiqued ethical theories for their emphasis on the individual, impartiality, and universality, arguing that a feminist approach would stress relationships, care, and connectiveness.

Research by Carol Gilligan and Lawrence Kohlberg has shown how moral development varies according to gender and, in particular, how gender shapes the focus of moral inquiry. Thus, women tend to see moral life in terms of care and responsibility, asking whether relationships were maintained or harm suffered, whereas men stress the application of rules in a fair, impartial, and equal manner. As well, men are concerned with individual rights and autonomy and whether the rules have been followed, whereas women are more likely to resolve issues by applying solutions that affirm relationships and minimize harm. It is important to appreciate, however, that women should not be seen as creatures of emotion or as somehow deficient in taking a different moral approach from that of men, because it is social conditioning and not sex roles that creates gender boundaries. Also, women do not claim a monopoly on the ethic of care; men may also follow this ethic rather than applying the ethical perspective generally shared by men.

There are a number of problems with the ethic of care, including in particular whether it is capable of standing on its own as a philosophical theory. Some argue that it is best seen as a supplement to virtue ethics. Another problem with the ethic of care is the extent of the obligation to honor relationships and to show care. While it is easy to see how an ethic of care can be applied in close family relationships, philosophers dispute the boundaries of the ethic, asking, for example, whether the duty can extend to the needy throughout the world. Some see the obligation to the family as absolute and other obligations as secondary if only a potential rather than an actual relationship exists. Others stress the importance of the depth of a relationship and the extent to which the depth varies according to the closeness between the caregiver and a third person. Some argue that the ethic of care can be extended to include one's identity in a communal sense, such as membership of an ethnic group.

Robin West has suggested that caring should be a focus of public and legal virtues and at the core of legal justice. She believes that an ethic of care should be allied with the ethic of justice so that public institutions exercise compassion or care while applying legal justice. According to West, this would avoid injustice, because the law would be read and interpreted compassionately so as to take account, for example, of the life circumstances of an accused in a death penalty case.

Peacemaking has close connections with the ethic of care but is advocated as a separate philosophy variously called peacemaking, peacekeeping, or peacemaking criminology. In a general way, all these concepts emphasize relationships, caring, and mindfulness (thinking about our actions and the needs of others in the long term). Peacemaking also identifies nonviolence as a fundamental principle, advocating that violence and coercion in such forms as capital punishment and excessive force should be eradicated from the criminal justice system. Peacemaking advocates come from many different persuasions and positions, including Christian ethics and Buddhism. As a concept, peacemaking, although attractive with its emphasis on connectiveness and caring, seems to lack theoretical rigor and to be in need of greater definitional specificity.

DISCUSSION CASE

Practical Jokes, Initiation, Hazing, or Discrimination?

Mary Bloom is a chief of police. She worked her way up through the ranks, starting as a patrol officer at a time when women police officers were not taken seriously and were allocated tasks like doing secretarial work, acting as matrons, or working with juveniles. In those days the idea that a woman police officer could go on patrol like a male officer was considered laughable. Male officers, on the other hand, were assumed capable of being patrolmen, and no one used the term "patrol woman."

As a new recruit Mary was the victim of practices that can variously be described as practical jokes, hazing, initiation rituals, or discrimination. One time her field training officer (FTO) told her to inventory the contents of a squad car, and when she opened the door there was a large snake there! She recognized it as a harmless species, picked it up, and brought it to her FTO, whose turn it now was to be startled. She noted that other recruits were also subjected to these antics, such as being sent to the maintenance section for a sawdust pump, being told to fetch a "group tightener" to place on the end of a service weapon to improve aim, or finding shaving cream in their hats just before inspection.

Those officers who just accepted these jokes and didn't complain were accepted, but the complaining officers were not. Mary opted not to make a fuss, and after a while the jokes diminished and she became accepted. Later, she herself participated in these antics with the rookie police. As she climbed through the ranks, she noticed that these practices did not interfere with the daily police work because they happened during slow periods or after especially stressful events, when officers needed some relaxation and amusement.

Being promoted to police chief put Mary in charge of a large metropolitan area. She was the first female police chief, and one issue that she needed to pay attention to, following a request from the city manager, was the under representation of minorities in the police department—minority officers made up only 3% of the force, and among the 300 officers, only 2 sergeants were minorities. As well, she was the only female above the rank of patrol officer. Responding to the need to bring in minorities, Mary went on a recruitment drive, and after 4 years there was adequate minority representation. However, the issue was not dead.

Members of the African-American Law Enforcement Officers Association (AALEOA) and the Hispanic-American Law Enforcement Officers Association (HALEOA) were not satisfied. They claimed there existed an undercurrent of racism among command officers and supervisors, and at least one independent study confirmed this. They wanted this issue addressed, and Mary responded by

(Continued)

(Continued)

organizing a series of seminars concerned with cultural diversity and sensitization. Every officer completed at least 16 hours of this training. In spite of this, the AALEOA and HALEOA members continued to voice their concerns and now began to allege being victims of "pranks" organized by senior officers. Mary's command officers have told her that these pranks are not racially motivated. They are a ritual that all new recruits undergo, but the minority associations' members remain unconvinced and believe the practices are discriminatory and racially based.

After analyzing this issue applying an ethic of care approach, consider what Chief Bloom can do to resolve the situation.

SOURCE: Adapted from Close and Meier 1995: 531–532.

DISCUSSION QUESTIONS

1. What linkages do you see between an ethic of care and virtue ethics? Explain with examples.

2. Explain how moral development is differentiated according to gender.

3. "Applying the ethic of care to the criminal justice system would bring about a more compassionate system." Discuss three examples of areas within the criminal justice system where compassion might influence decision making.

4. Explain how a peacemaking approach can be applied to our system of corrections.

References

Chapter 1 References

Arrington, Robert. 1983. "A Defense of Ethical Relativism." *Metaphilosophy* 14: 225–239.

BBC News. 2006, October 6. "Jack Straw in the Lancashire Evening Telegraph." Retrieved March 24, 2007 (http://news.bbc.co.uk/2/hi/uk_news/politics/5413470.stm).

Bell, Dan. 2006. "Netherlands Moves Toward Total Ban on Muslim Veils." *The Guardian,* November 11. Retrieved April 23, 2007 (http://www.guardian.co.uk/religion/Story/ 0,,1945461,00.html).

Bunting, Harry. 1996. "A Single True Morality? The Challenge of Relativism." Pp. 73–85 in *Philosophy and Pluralism,* edited by David Archard. Cambridge, England: Cambridge University Press.

CNN. 2003, December 17. "Chirac: Ban Headscarves in Schools." Retrieved March 23, 2007 (http://www.cnn.com/2003/WORLD/europe/12/17/france.headscarves/index.html).

Cook, John. 1999. *Morality and Cultural Differences.* New York: Oxford University Press.

Death Penalty Information Center. 2007. "Ohio Inmate Becomes the 119th Innocent Person Freed From Death Row." Washington, DC: Death Penalty Information Center. Retrieved April 7, 2007 (http://truthinjustice.org/jamison.htm).

Felkenes, George. 1987. "Ethics in the Graduate Criminal Justice Curriculum." *Teaching Philosophy* 10 (1): 23–26.

Glover, Jonathan. 1999. "Capital Punishment." Pp. 245–253 in *The Right Thing to Do: Basic Readings in Moral Philosophy* (2nd ed.), edited by James Rachels. Boston: McGraw-Hill.

Hare, Richard M. 1987. "Moral Conflicts." Pp. 205–238 in *Moral Dilemmas,* edited by Christopher Gowans. New York: Oxford University Press.

Hinman, Lawrence. 1998. *Ethics: A Pluralistic Approach to Moral Theory.* Fort Worth, TX: Harcourt Brace.

Holmes, Robert. 1998. *Basic Moral Philosophy* (4th ed.). Belmont, CA: Wadsworth.

Human Rights Watch. 1998. "New Orleans: Recent History." New York: Human Rights Watch. Retrieved March 1, 2008 (http://www.hrw.org/reports98/police/uspo93.htm# TopOfPage).

Kane, Robert. 1996. *Through the Moral Maze: Searching for Absolute Values in a Pluralistic World.* Armonk, NY: North Castle Books.

Ladd, John. 1973. *Ethical Relativism.* Belmont, CA: Wadsworth.

Rachels, James. 1991. "Subjectivism." Pp. 432–441 in *A Companion to Ethics,* edited by Peter Singers. Cambridge, MA: Blackwell Press.

Roper v. Simmons, 543 U.S. 541 (2005).

Singer, Peter. 1995. *How Are We to Live? Ethics in an Age of Self-Interest.* Amherst, NY: Prometheus Books.

Womack, Mari. 1995. "Studying Up and the Issue of Cultural Relativism." *NAPA Bulletin* 16: 48.

Chapter 2 References

Alemika, Etannibi E. O. 2003. "Police, Policing and Rule of Law in Transitional Countries." Pp. 63–102 in *Human Rights and the Police in Transitional* Countries, edited by Leone Lindhot, Paulo de Mesquita Neto, Danny Titus, and Etannibi E. Alemika. The Hague/London/New York: The Danish Institute for Human Rights and Kluwer Law International.

Alpert, Geoffrey P. and Roger G. Dunham. 2004. *Understanding Police Use of Force: Officers, Suspects, and Reciprocity.* Cambridge, England: Cambridge University Press.

Barker, Tom. 1996. *Police Ethics: Crisis in Law Enforcement.* Springfield, IL: Charles C Thomas.

Barker, Tom and David Carter. 1995. "Police Lies and Perjury: A Motivation-Based Taxonomy." Pp. 254–262 in *Morality in Criminal Justice: An Introduction to Ethics,* edited by Daryl Close and Nicholas Meier. Belmont, CA: Wadsworth.

Bayley, David. 1994. *Police for the Future.* New York: Oxford University Press.

Beckett, Katherine and Theodore Sasson. 2000. *The Politics of Injustice: Crime and Punishment in America.* Thousand Oaks, CA: Pine Forge Press.

Bittner, Egon. 1967. "The Capacity to Use Force as the Core of the Police Role." Pp. 36–47 in *The Functions of Police in Modern Society,* edited by Egon Bittner. Washington, DC: National Institute of Mental Health.

Catlin, Dennis and James R. Maupin. 2004. "A Two Cohort Study of the Ethical Orientations of State Police Officers." *Policing: An International Journal of Police Strategies & Management* 27 (3): 289–301.

Center for the Study of Ethics in the Professions. 2003. "Law Enforcement Code of Ethics." Chicago: Illinois Institute of Technology. Retrieved August 31, 2003 (http://www.iit.edu/departments/csep/PublicWWW/codes/coe/International_Association_of_Chiefs_of_Police_Law_Enforcement_Code_of_ Ethics_1989.html).

Chan, Janet. 1997. *Changing Police Culture: Policing in a Multicultural Society.* Cambridge, England: Cambridge University Press.

Chevigny, Paul G. 1999. "Police Accountability in Hemispheric Perspective." Pp. 69–88 in *Democratic Policing and Accountability: Global Perspectives,* edited by Errol Mendes, Joaquin Zuckerberg, Susan Lecorre, Anne Gabriel, and Jeffrey Clark. Aldershot, England: Ashgate.

Closs, William and Paul McKenna. 2006. "Profiling a Problem in Canadian Police Leadership: The Kingston Police Data Collection Project." *Canadian Public Administration* 49 (2): 143–161.

CNN.com/Travel. 2001, October 3. "Airlines, Passengers Confront Racial Profiling." Retrieved April 3, 2007 (http://archives.cnn.com/2001/TRAVEL/NEWS/10/03/rec.airlines.profiling/index.html).

Cohen, Howard. 1996. "Police Discretion and Police Objectivity." Pp. 91–106 in *Handled With Discretion: Ethical Issues in Police Decision Making,* edited by John Kleinig. Lanham, MD: Rowman & Littlefield.

Coleman, Stephen. 2004. "When Police Should Say 'No!' to Gratuities." *Criminal Justice Ethics* Winter/Spring: 33–41.

Commission to Investigate Allegations of Corruption and Anti-Corruption Procedures of the Police Department, City of New York. 1994. *Commission Report.* New York: Author.

Crank, John. 1998. *Understanding Police Culture.* Cincinnati, OH: Anderson.

Crank, John and Michael Caldero. 2000. *Police Ethics: The Corruption of Noble Cause.* Cincinnati, OH: Anderson.

Delattre, Edwin. 1989. *Character and Cops: Ethics in Policing.* Washington, DC: American Enterprise Institute for Public Policy Research.

Del Pozo, Brandon. 2005. "One Dogma of Police Ethics: Gratuities and the 'Democratic Ethos' of Policing." *Criminal Justice Ethics* Summer/Fall: 25–46.

Dershowitz, Alan. 1983. *The Best Defense.* New York: Vintage Books.

Dershowitz, Alan. 1996. *Reasonable Doubts: The O. J. Simpson Case and the Criminal Justice System.* New York: Touchstone Books.

Doyle, Arthur. 2000. "From the Inside Looking Out: Twenty-Nine Years in the New York Police Department." Pp. 171–186 in *Police Brutality: An Anthology,* edited by Jill Nelson. New York: Norton.

Eck, John E. and Edward R. Maguire. 2005. "Have Changes in Policing Reduced Crime?: An Assessment of the Evidence." Pp. 207–265 in *The Crime Drop in America,* edited by Alfred Blumstein and Joel Wallman. New York: Cambridge University Press.

Eijkman, Quirine. 2006. "To Be Held Accountable: Police Accountability in Costa Rica." *Police Practice and Research* 7 (5): 411–430.

Ericson, Richard. 1992. "The Police as Reproducers of Order." Pp. 163–208 in *Understanding Policing,* edited by K. R. E. McCormick and L. A. Visano. Toronto, ON: Canadian Scholar's Press.

Feldberg, Michael. 1985. "Gratuities, Corruption, and the Democratic Ethos of Policing: The Case of the Free Cup of Coffee." Pp. 267–276 in *Moral Issues in Police Work,* edited by Frederick Elliston and Michael Feldberg. Totowa, NJ: Rowan & Allanheld.

Felknes, George. 1984. "Attitudes of Police Officers Toward Their Professional Ethics." *Journal of Criminal Justice* 12 (3): 211–220.

Ferge v. State. 764 N.E. 2d 268, 270 (Ind. Ct. App. 2002).

Fernando, Basil. 2003. "Police and the Rule of Law in Asia." Pp. 29–49 in *Human Rights and the Police in Transitional Countries,* edited by Leone Lindhot, Paulo de Mesquita Neto, Danny Titus, and Etannibi E. Alemika. The Hague/London/New York: The Danish Institute for Human Rights, Kluwer Law International.

Fyfe, James. 1996. "Structuring Police Discretion." Pp. 183–205 in *Handled With Discretion: Ethical Issues in Police Decision Making,* edited by John Kleinig. Lanham, MD: Rowman & Littlefield.

Goldsmith, Andrew. 1999. "Better Policing, More Human Rights: Lessons From Civilian Oversight." Pp. 33–68 in *Democratic Policing and Accountability: Global Perspectives,* edited by Errol Mendes, Joaquin Zuckerberg, Susan Lecorre, Anne Gabriel, and Jeffrey Clark. Aldershot: Ashgate.

Goldstein, Herman. 1977. *Policing in a Free Society.* Cambridge, MA: Ballinger.

Government Accounting Office. 1998. *Report to the Honorable Charles B. Rangel, House of Representatives, Law Enforcement: Information on Drug Related Police Corruption.* Washington, DC: Author.

Haller, Mark. 1996. "Historical Roots of Police Behaviors: Chicago, 1890–1925." Pp. 7–26 in *Classics in Policing,* edited by Steven Brandl and David Barlow. Cincinnati, OH: Anderson.

Hays, Tom. 2000. "Cop Gets 15 Years in Torture Case." *Infobeat.* Retrieved January 15, 2001 (http://www.infobeat.com/stories/cgi/story.cgi?id=2567684838-eb5).

Hays, Tom. 2007. "Would-Be NY Subway Bomber Gets 30 Years." *The Washington Post,* January 8. Retrieved April 9, 2007 (http://www.washingtonpost.com/wp-dyn/content/article/2007/01/08/AR2007010800158.html).

Herbert, Steve. 2006. *Citizens, Cops, and Power: Recognizing the Limits of Community.* Chicago and London: University of Chicago Press.

Hickman, Matthew. 2006. *Citizen Complaints About Police Use of Force.* Bureau of Justice Statistics Special Report. Washington, DC: U.S. Department of Justice.

Huberts, Leo, Terry Lamboo, and Maurice Punch. 2003. "Police Integrity in the Netherlands and the United States: Awareness and Alertness." *Police Practice and Research* 4 (3): 217–232.

Ivkovic, Sanja Kutnjak. 2005a. *Fallen Blue Knights: Controlling Police Corruption.* New York: Oxford University Press.

Ivkovic, Sanja Kutnjak. 2005b. "Police (Mis)behavior: A Cross-Cultural Study of Corruption Seriousness." *Policing: An International Journal of Police Strategies & Management* 28 (3): 546–566.

Ivkovic, Sanja Kutnjak and Tara O'Connor Shelley. 2005. "The Bosnian Police and Police Integrity: A Continuing Story." *European Journal of Criminology* 2 (4): 428–464.

Jackman, Tom. 2006. "Spotsylvania Deputies Receive Sex Services in Prostitution Cases." *The Washington Post,* February 13. Retrieved April 8, 2007 (http://www.washington post.com/wp-dyn/content/article/2006/02/12/AR2006021200943.html).

Jobard, Fabien. 2003. "Counting Violence Committed by the Police: Raw Facts and Narratives." *Policing and Society* 13 (4): 423–428.

Johnston, M. 1995. "Police Corruption." Pp. 285–313 in *Morality in Criminal Justice: An Introduction to Ethics,* edited by Daryl Close and Nicholas Meier. Belmont, CA: Wadsworth.

Kania, Richard. 2004. "The Ethical Acceptability of Gratuities: Still Saying "Yes" After All These Years." *Criminal Justice Ethics* Winter/Spring: 54–63.

Kelling, George and Mark Moore. 1996. "The Evolving Strategy of Policing." Pp. 71–95 in *Classics in Policing,* edited by Steven Brandl and David Barlow. Cincinnati, OH: Anderson.

Kennedy, Randall. 1991. *Race, Crime, and the Law.* New York: Vintage Books.

Kleinig, John. 1996. *The Ethics of Policing.* New York: Cambridge University Press.

Klockars, Carl. 1980. "The Dirty Harry Problem." *The Annals of the American Academy of Political and Social Science* 451: 33–47.

Lawrence, Regina. 2000. *The Politics of Force: Media and the Construction of Police Brutality.* Berkeley: University of California Press.

Manning, Peter. 1996. "The Police: Mandate, Strategies Appearances." Pp. 215–243 in *Classics in Policing,* edited by Steven Brandl and David Barlow. Cincinnati, OH: Anderson.

Manning, Peter. 1997. *Police Work: The Social Organization of Policing.* Prospect Heights, IL: Waveland Press.

Marx, Gary. 1985. "'Who Really Gets Stung?' Some Issues Raised by the New York Undercover Work." Pp. 99–128 In *Moral Issues in Police Work,* edited by Frederick A. Elliston and Michael Feldberg. Totowa, NJ: Rowan & Allanheld.

Marx, Gary. 2001. "Under-the-Covers Undercover Investigations: Some Reflections on the State's Use of Sex and Deception in Law Enforcement." Pp. 262–274 In *Criminal Justice Ethics,* edited by Paul Leighton and Jeffrey Reiman. Upper Saddle River, NJ: Prentice-Hall.

Mendes, Errol P. 1999. "Raising the Social Capital of Policing and Nations: How Can Professional Policing and Civilian Oversight Weaken the Circle of Violence." Pp. 13–32 in *Democratic Policing and Accountability: Global Perspectives,* edited by Errol Mendes, Joaquin Zuckerberg, Susan Lecorre, Anne Gabriel, and Jeffrey Clark. Aldershot, England: Ashgate.

Mesquita Neto, Paulo and Adrianna Loche. 2003. "Policing Community Partnerships in Brazil." In *Crime and Violence in Latin America: Citizen Security, Democracy, and the State,* edited by Hugo Fruhling, Joseph Tulchin, and Heather Golding. Washington/Baltimore/London: Woodrow Wilson Center Press and The John Hopkins University Press.

Miethe, Terance. 1999. *Whistleblowing at Work: Tough Choices in Exposing Fraud, Waste, and Abuse on the Job.* Boulder, CO: Westview Press.

Miller, Joel. 2003. "Police Corruption in England and Wales: An Assessment of Current Evidence." London: Home Office: Research Development and Statistics Directorate. Retrieved March 19, 2007 (http://www.homeoffice.gov.uk/rds/pdfs2/rdsolr1103.pdf).

Miller, Seumas, John Blackler, and Andrew Alexandra. 1997. *Police Ethics.* Sydney, Australia: Allen and Unwin.

Miranda v. Arizona, 384 U.S. 436, 86 S. Ct. 1602, 16 L.Ed.2d 694 (1966).

More, Harry. 1998. *Special Topics in Policing* (2nd ed.). Cincinnati, OH: Anderson.

Muir, William K. 1977. *Police: Streetcorner Politicians.* Chicago: University of Chicago Press.

Newsome, Yvonne. 2003. "Border Patrol: The U.S. Customs Service and the Racial Profiling of African American Women." *Journal of African American Studies* 7 (3): 31–57.

Neyroud, Peter and Alan Beckley. 2001. *Policing, Ethics and Human Rights.* Cullompton, England: Willan.

Perlmutter, David. 2000. *Policing and the Media: Street Cops and Public Perceptions of Law Enforcement.* Thousand Oaks, CA: Sage.

The Pittsburgh Channel. 2000, December 28. "Wilkinsburg Police Officers Punished: Is Move Whistleblowing Retaliation?" Retrieved April 26, 2003 (http://www.thepittsburgchannel.com/station/218765/detail.html).

Parent, Rick. 2006. "The Police Use of Deadly Force: International Comparisons." *The Police Journal* 79: 230–237.

Pollock-Byrne, Joycelyn. 1998. *Ethics in Crime and Justice: Dilemmas and Decisions.* Pacific Grove, CA: Brooks/Cole.

Prenzler, Tim and Carol Ronken. 2003. "A Survey of Innovations in the Development and Maintenance of Ethical Standards by Australian Police Departments." *Police Practice and Research* 4 (2): 149–161.

Punch, Maurice. 2003. "Rotten Orchards: 'Pestilence,' Police Misconduct and System Failure." *Policing and Society* 13 (2): 171–196.

Rahtz, Howard. 2003. *Understanding Police Use of Force.* Monsey, NY: Criminal Justice Press.

Reiman, Jeffrey. 1996. "Is Police Discretion Justified in a Free Society?" Pp. 71–83 in *Handled With Discretion: Ethical issues in police decision making,* edited by John Kleinig. Lanham, MD: Rowman & Littlefield.

Reiner, Robert. 1985. "The Police and Race Relations." Pp. 149–187 in *Police: The Constitution and the Community,* edited by John Baxter and Laurence Koffman. London: Professional Books.

Rochin v. California, 342 U.S. 165 (1952).

Roebuck, Julian and Thomas Barker. 1974. "A Typology of Police Corruption." *Social Problems* 21 (3): 423–437.

Rokeach, Milton, Martin Miller, and John Snyder. 1977. "The Value Gap Between Police and the Policed." *Journal of Social Issues* 27 (2): 155–171.

Ruiz, Jim and Christine Bono. 2004. "At What Price a "Freebie"? The Real Cost of Police Gratuities." *Criminal Justice Ethics* Winter/Spring: 44–53.

Schafer, Joseph A., Beth M. Huebner, and Timothy Bynum. 2003. "Citizen Perceptions of Police Services: Race, Neighborhood Context, and Community Policing." *Police Quarterly* 6 (4): 440–468.

Scheingold, Stuart. 1984. *The Politics of Law and Order.* New York: Longman.

Sherman, Lawrence. 1982. "Learning Police Ethics." *Criminal Justice Ethics* 1 (1): 10–19.

Sherman, Lawrence. 1985. "Becoming Bent." Pp. 253–266 in *Moral Issues in Police Work,* edited by Frederick A. Elliston and Michael Feldberg. Totowa, NJ: Rowman & Allanheld.

Sherman v. the United States 356 U.S. 369 (1958).

Skolnick, Jerome. 1966. *Justice Without Trial.* New York: Wiley.

Skolnick, Jerome. 1982. "Deception by Police." *Criminal Justice Ethics* 1 (2): 40–54.

Skolnick, Jerome and James Fyfe. 1993. *Above the Law: Police and the Excessive Use of Force.* New York: The Free Press.

Slobogin, Christopher. 1996. "Testilying: Police Perjury and What To Do About It." *University of Colorado Law Review* 67 (4): 1037–1060.

Smith, Erica and Matthew Durose. 2006, June. "Characteristics of Drivers Stopped by Police, 2002." Bureau of Justice Statistics publication NCJ 211471. Washington, DC: Department of Justice.

Smulovitz, Catalina. 2003. "Citizen Insecurity and Fear: Public and Private Responses in Argentina." In *Crime and Violence in Latin America: Citizen Security, Democracy, and the State,* edited by Hugo Fruhling, Joseph Tulchin, and Heather Golding. Washington, DC, Baltimore, and London: Woodrow Wilson Center Press and The John Hopkins University Press.

Stitt, B. Grant and Gene G. James. 1985. "Entrapment: An Ethical Analysis." Pp. 129–146 in *Moral Issues in Police Work,* edited by Frederick A. Elliston and Michael Feldberg. Totowa, NJ: Rowan & Allanheld.

Tobar, Hector. 1998. "An Ugly Stain on a City's Bright and Shining Plan." *Los Angeles Times,* December 28, A1.

Walker, Samuel. 1996. "A Critical History of Police Reform: The Emergence of Professionalism—Introduction." Pp. 27–35 in *Classics in Policing,* edited by Steven Brandl and David Barlow. Cincinnati, OH: Anderson.

Walker, Samuel. 2001. *Police Accountability: The Role of Citizen Oversight.* Belmont, CA: Wadsworth.

Walker, Samuel. 2005. *The New World of Police Accountability.* Thousand Oaks, CA: Sage.

Walker, Samuel and Betsy Wright Kreisel. 1996. "Varieties of Citizen Review: The Implications of Organizational Features of Complaint Review Procedures for Accountability of the Police." *American Journal of Police* XV (3): 65–88.

Walker, Samuel, Cassia Spohn, and Miriam DeLone. 2000. *The Color of Justice: Race, Ethnicity and Crime in America.* Belmont, CA: Wadsworth.

Warren, Patricia, Donald Tomaskovic-Devey, William Smith, Matthew Zingraff, and Marcinda Mason. 2006. "Driving While Black: Bias Processes and Racial Disparity in Police Stops." *Criminology* 44 (3): 709–738.

Westmarland, Louise. 2001. "Blowing the Whistle on Police Violence." *British Journal of Criminology* 41: 523–535.

Westmarland, Louise. 2005. "Police Ethics and Integrity: Breaking the Blue Code of Silence." *Policing and Society* 15 (2): 145–165.

Wilson, James Q. 1968. *Varieties of Police Behavior.* Cambridge, MA: Harvard University Press.

Withrow, Brian and Jeffrey Dailey. 2004. "A Model of Circumstantial Corruptibility." *Police Quarterly* 7 (2): 159–178.

Zhao, Jihong Ni He and Nicholas P. Lovrich. 1998. "Individual Value Preferences Among American Police Officers." *Policing: An International Journal of Police Strategies & Management* 21 (1): 22–37.

Chapter 3 References

Aguirre, Adalberto and David Baker. 1990. "Empirical Research on Racial Discrimination in the Imposition of the Death Penalty." *Criminal Justice Abstracts* 22: 135–153.

Albonetti, Celesta. 1990. "Race and the Probability of Pleading Guilty." *Journal of Quantitative Criminology* 6: 315–334.

Albonetti, Celesta, Robert Hauser, John Hagan, and Ilene Nagel. 1989. "Criminal Justice Decision Making as a Stratification Process: The Role of Race and Stratification Resources in Pretrial Release." *Journal of Quantitative Criminology* 5: 57–82.

Alvarez, A. 2000. "Unwelcome Citizens: Latinos and the Criminal Justice System." Pp. 85–98 in *Investigating Difference: Human and Cultural Relations in Criminal Justice*, edited by The Criminal Justice Collective of Northern Arizona University. Needham Heights, MA: Allyn & Bacon.

American Anthropological Association. 1997. *Race and Ethnic Standards for Federal Statistics and Administrative Reporting.* Arlington, VA: Author.

Baldus, David, George Woodward, and Charles Pulaski. 1990. *Equal Justice and the Death Penalty: A Legal and Empirical Analysis.* Boston: Northeastern University Press.

Banks, Cyndi. 2002. "Doing Time in Alaska: Women, Culture and Crime." Pp. 232–257 in *It's a Crime: Women and Justice* (3rd ed.), edited by R. Muraskin. Upper Saddle River, NJ: Prentice-Hall.

Banks, Richard and Jennifer Eberhardt. 1998. "Social Psychological Processes and the Legal Bases of Racial Categorization." Pp. 54–75 in *Confronting Racism: The Problem and the Response,* edited by Jennifer Eberhardt and Susan Fiske. Thousand Oaks, CA: Sage.

Banks, Richard, Jennifer Eberhardt, and Lee Ross. 2006. "Discrimination and Implicit Bias in a Racially Unequal Society." *California Law Review* 94: 1169–1190.

Barkan, Steven and Steven Cohn. 2005. "On Reducing White Support for the Death Penalty: A Pessimistic Appraisal." *Criminology & Public Policy* 4 (1): 39–44.

Batson v. Kentucky, 476 U.S. 79 (1986).

Beck, Allen and Paige Harrison. 2001. *Prisoners in 2000.* Bureau of Justice Statistics Bulletin NCJ 188207. Washington, DC: U.S. Department of Justice.

Beckett, Katherine, Kiris Nyrop, and Lori Pfingst. 2006. "Race, Drugs, and Policing: Understanding Disparities in Drug Delivery Arrests." *Criminology* 44 (1): 105–137.

Black, Donald and Albert Reiss. 1970. "Police Control of Juveniles." *American Sociological Review* 35: 63–77.

Blumstein, Alfred. 1982. "On the Racial Disproportionality of the U.S. States' Prison Population." *Journal of Criminal Law and Criminology* 73: 1259–1281.

Blumstein, Alfred. 1993. "Racial Disproportionality of U.S. Prison Populations Revisited." *University of Colorado Law Review* 64: 743–760.

Bright, Stephen and Patrick Keenan. 1995. "Judges and the Politics of Death: Deciding Between the Bill of Rights and the Next Election in Capital Cases." *Boston University Law Review* 75: 759–835.

Brod, Thomas M. 1975. "Alcoholism as a Mental Health Problem of Native Americans." *Archives of General Psychiatry* 32: 1385–1391.

Brown, Craig and Barbara Warner. 1995. "The Political Threat of Immigrant Groups and Police Aggressiveness in 1900." Pp. 82–98 in *Ethnicity, Race, and Crime: Perspectives Across Time and Place,* edited by Darnell Hawkins. Albany: State University of New York Press.

Brown, Robert and James Frank. 2006. "Race and Officer Decision Making: Examining Differences in Arrest Outcomes Between Black and White Officers." *Justice Quarterly* 23 (1): 86–126.

Brown v. Board of Education, 347 U.S. 483 (1954).

Building Blocks For Youth. April 2000. *Resources for Disproportionate Minority Confinement/ Overrepresentation of Youth of Color: Key Studies.* Retrieved April 8, 2007 (http://www .buildingblocksforyouth.org/issues/dmc/studies.html).

Byers, Bryan and Lori Spillane. 2000. "Hate Crime in Contemporary American Society: A Sociological Approach." Pp. 243–270 in *Multicultural Perspectives in Criminal Justice and Criminology,* edited by James Hendricks and Bryan Byers. Springfield, IL: Charles C Thomas.

Chambliss, William. 1995. "Crime Control and Ethnic Minorities: Legitimizing Racial Oppression by Creating Moral Panics." Pp. 235–258 in *Ethnicity, Race, and Crime: Perspectives Across Time and Space,* edited by Darnell Hawkins. Albany: State University of New York Press.

Chambliss, William and Robert Seidman. 1971. *Law, Order, and Power.* Reading, MA: Addison-Wesley.

DeNava-Walt, Carmen, Bernadette Proctor, and Cheryl Hill Lee. 2006. *Income, Poverty, and Health Insurance Coverage in the United States: 2005.* Washington, DC: U.S. Census Bureau.

DiIulio, John. 1996. "My Black Crime Problem, and Ours." *City Journal* 6: 14–28.

Fienup-Riordan, Ann. 1994. *Boundaries and Passages: Rule and Ritual in Yup'ik Eskimo Oral Tradition.* Norman: University of Oklahoma Press.

Fyfe, James. 1982. "Blind Justice: Police Shootings in Memphis." *Journal of Criminal Law and Criminology* 73: 707–722.

Georges-Abeyie, Daniel. 2001. "Petit Apartheid in Criminal Justice: The More 'Things' Change, The More 'Things' Remain The Same." Pp. ix–xiv in *Petit Apartheid in the U.S. Criminal Justice System,* edited by Dragan Milovanovic and Katheryn Russell. Durham, NC: Carolina Academic Press.

Greenfeld, Lawrence A. and Steven Smith. 1999. *American Indians and crime.* Bureau of Justice Statistics Publication NCJ 173386. Washington, DC: U.S. Department of Justice.

Grobsmith, Elizabeth. 1994. *Indians in Prison: Incarcerated Native Americans in Nebraska.* Lincoln: University of Nebraska Press.

Hagan, John and Kristin Bumiller. 1983. "Making Sense of Sentencing: A Review and Critique of Sentencing Research." Pp. 1–54 in *Research on Sentencing: The Search for Reform,* edited by Alfred Blumstein, Jacqueline Cohen, S. Martin, and Michael Tonry. Washington, DC: National Academy Press.

Harlow, Caroline W. 2005, November. *Hate Crime Reported by Victims and Police.* Bureau of Justice Statistics Bulletin NCJ 209911. Washington, DC: U.S. Department of Justice.

Harrison, Paige and Allen Beck. 2003, July. *Prisoners in 2002.* Bureau of Justice Statistics Bulletin NCJ 200248. Washington, DC: U.S. Department of Justice.

Harrison, Paige and Allen Beck. 2005, October. *Prisoners in 2004.* Bureau of Justice Statistics Bulletin NCJ 210677. Washington, DC: U.S. Department of Justice.

Harrison, Paige and Allen Beck. 2006, November. *Prisoners in 2005.* Bureau of Justice Statistics Bulletin NCJ 215092. Washington, DC: U.S. Department of Justice.

Hinman, Lawrence. 1998. *Ethics: A Pluralistic Approach to Moral Theory.* Fort Worth, TX: Harcourt Brace.

Independent Commission on the Los Angeles Police Department. 1991. *Report of the Independent Commission on the Los Angeles Police Department.* Los Angeles: City of Los Angeles.

Innocence Project. 2002. "Loren Santow and The Illinois Death Penalty Education Project." Retrieved January 17, 2003 (www.innocenceproject. org).

Klein, Stephen, Joan Petersilia, and Susan Turner. 1990. "Race and Imprisonment Decisions in California." *Science* 247: 812–816.

Knepper, Paul. 2000. "The Alchemy of Race and Crime Research." Pp. 15–30 in *The System in Black and White: Exploring the Connections Between Race, Crime, and Justice,* edited by Michael Markowitz and Delores Jones-Brown. Westport, CT: Praeger.

Kraus, Robert and Patricia Buffler. 1979. "Sociocultural Stress and the American Native in Alaska: An Analysis of Changing Patterns of Psychiatric Illness and Alcohol Abuse Among Alaska Natives." *Culture, Medicine and Psychiatry* 3: 111–151.

Lee, Catherine. 2006. "Hispanics and the Death Penalty: Discriminatory Charging Practices in San Joaquin County, California." *Journal of Criminal Justice* 35: 17–27.

Mast, Brent, Bruce Benson, and David Rasmussen. 2000. "Entrepreneurial Police and Drug Enforcement Policy." *Public Choice* 104: 285–308.

Mauer, Marc, Cathy Potler, and Richard Wolf. 1999. *Gender and Justice: Women, Drugs, and Sentencing Policy.* Washington, DC: The Sentencing Project.

Mauer, Marc and U.S. Sentencing Project. 1999. *Race to Incarcerate: The Sentencing Project.* New York: New Press.

May, Larry and Shari Sharratt. 1994. *Applied Ethics: A Multicultural Approach.* Englewood Cliffs, NJ: Prentice-Hall.

McDonald, Douglas and Kenneth Carlson. 1993, December. *Sentencing in the Federal Courts: Does Race Matter?* Bureau of Justice Statistics Publication NCJ 145332. Washington, DC:. U.S. Department of Justice.

Miethe, Terance and Charles Moore. 1986. "Racial Differences in Criminal Processing: The Consequences of Model Selection on Conclusions About Differential Treatment." *Sociological Quarterly* 27: 217–237.

Milovanovic, Dragan and Katheryn Russell (Eds.). 2001. *Petit Apartheid in the U.S. Criminal Justice System: The Dark Figure of Racism.* Durham, NC: Carolina Academic Press.

New York State Judicial Commission on Minorities. 1991. "Panel Says New York Courts Are 'Infested With Racism.'" *Criminal Justice Newsletter* 22 (12): 1–2.

Paternoster, Raymond, Robert Brame, Sarah Bacon, Andrew Ditchfield, David Biere, Karen Beckman, Deanna Perez, Michael Strauch, Nadine Frederique, Kristin Gawkoski, Daniel Zeigler, and Katheryn Murphy. 2003. "An Empirical Analysis of Maryland's Death Sentencing System With Respect to the Influence of Race and Legal Jurisdiction: Final Report." Retrieved March 21, 2007 (http://www.newsdesk.umd.edu/pdf/exec.pdf).

Perry, Steven. 2004. *American Indians and Crime: A BJS statistical profile, 1992–2002.* Bureau of Justice Statistics Publication NCJ 203097. Washington, DC: U.S. Department of Justice.

Petersilia, Joan. 1983. *Racial Disparities in the Criminal Justice System.* Santa Monica, CA: RAND.

Peterson, Ruth and John Hagan. 1984. "Changing Conceptions of Race: Towards an Account of Anomalous Findings of Sentencing Research." *American Sociological Review* 49: 56–70.

The Pew Center on the States. 2008. *One in 100: Behind Bars in America in 2008.* Washington, DC: Author. Retrieved March 27, 2008 (http://www.pewcenteronthestates.org/uploadedFiles/8015PCTS_Prison08_FINAL_2-1-1_FORWEB.pdf).

Phillips, Michael and Thomas Inui. 1986. "The Interaction of Mental Illness, Criminal Behavior and Culture: Native Alaskan Mentally Ill Criminal Offenders." *Culture, Medicine and Psychiatry* 10: 123–149.

Piliavin, Irving and Scott Briar. 1964. "Police Encounters With Juveniles." *American Journal of Sociology* 69: 206–214.

Pope, Carl and William Feyerherm. 1990, June and September. "Minority Status and Juvenile Justice Processing: An Assessment of the Research Literature" (Parts 1 and 2). *Criminal Justice Abstracts:* 327–335, 527–542.

Rachels, James. 1999. *The Elements f Moral Philosophy.* Boston: McGraw-Hill College.

Rimer, Sara. 2002. "In Dallas, Dismissal of Black Jurors Leads to Appeal by Death Row Inmate." *New York Times,* February 13. Retrieved January 15, 2003 (http://www.nytimes.com/2002/02/13/national/13DEAT.html).

Ross, Luana. 2000. "Imprisoned Native Women and the Importance of Native Traditions." Pp. 132–144 in *States of Confinement: Policing, Detention, and Prisons,* edited by J. James. New York: St. Martin's Press.

Russell-Brown, Katheryn. 1998. *The Color of Crime: Racial Hoaxes, White Fear, Black Protectionism, Police Harassment, and Other Macroaggressions.* New York: New York University Press.

Sampson, Robert and Janet Lauritsen. 1997. "Racial and Ethnic Disparities in Crime and Criminals in the United States." Pp. 311–374 in *Ethnicity, Crime and Immigration: Comparative and Cross-National Perspectives,* edited by Michael Tonry. Chicago: University of Chicago Press.

Schafer, N. E., Richard Curtis, and Cassie Atwell. 1997. *Disproportionate Representation of Minorities in the Alaska Juvenile Justice System: Phase 1 Report.* Anchorage: Justice Center, University of Alaska.

Smith, Brian. 2000. "Historical Injustices, Contemporary Inequalities: African Americans and Criminal Justice." Pp. 71–84 in *Investigating Difference: Human and Cultural Relations in Criminal Justice,* edited by The Criminal Justice Collective of Northern Arizona University. Boston: Allyn & Bacon.

Smith, Douglas. 1986. "The Neighborhood Context of Police Behavior." Pp. 313–341 in *Crime and Justice: A Review of Research: Vol. 8, Communities and Crime,* edited by Albert Reiss and Michael Tonry. Chicago: University of Chicago Press.

Snell, Tracy. 2006. *Capital Punishment, 2005.* Bureau of Justice Statistics Bulletin NCJ 215083. Washington, DC: U.S. Department of Justice.

Soss, Joe, Laura Langbein, and Alan Metelko. 2003. "Why Do White Americans Support the Death Penalty?" *The Journal of Politics* 65: 397–421.

Spohn, Cassia, John Gruhl, and Susan Welch. 1987. "The Impact of the Ethnicity and Gender of Defendants on the Decision to Reject or Dismiss Felony Charges." *Criminology* 25: 175–192.

Strauder v. West Virginia, 100 U.S. 303 (1880).

Strom, Kevin. 2001, September. *Hate Crimes Reported in NIBRS, 1997–99.* Bureau of Justice Statistics Bulletin NCJ 186765. Washington, DC: U.S. Department of Justice.

Tonry, Michael. 1995. *Malign Neglect: Race, Crime, and Punishment in America.* Oxford, England: Oxford University Press.

Tonry, Michael. 1998. "Racial Politics, Racial Disparities, and the War on Crime." Pp. 41–57 in *The Criminal Justice System: Politics and Policies,* edited by George Cole and Marc Gertz. Belmont, CA: West/Wadsworth.

Walker, Samuel, Cassia Spohn, and Miriam DeLone. 2000. *The Color of Justice: Race, Ethnicity and Crime in America.* Belmont, CA: Wadsworth.

Weitzer, Ronald. 1996. "Racial Discrimination in the Criminal Justice System: Findings and the Problems in the Literature." *Journal of Criminal Justice* 24 (4): 309–322.

Wice, Paul. 1985. *Chaos in the Courthouse: The Inner Workings of the Urban Municipal Courts.* New York: Praeger.

Wilbanks, William. 1987. *The Myth of a Racist Criminal Justice System.* Monterey, CA: Brooks/Cole.

Zatz, Marjorie and Coramae Mann. 1998. "The Power of Images." Pp. 1–12 in *Images of Color, Images of Crime: Readings,* edited by Coramae Mann and Marjorie Zatz. Los Angeles: Roxbury.

Chapter 4 References

Allen, Francis. 1985. "A Serendipitous Trek Through the Advance-Sheet Jungle: Criminal Justice in the Courts of Review." *Iowa Law Review:* 311–341.

American Bar Association. Standing Committee on Ethics and Professional Responsibility. 1999. *ABA Model Code of Judicial Conduct.* Chicago: Author.

American Bar Association. 1993. *ABA Standards for Criminal Justice: The Prosecution Function.* Chicago: Author.

American Bar Association and Center for Professional Responsibility. 1998. *Model Rules of Professional Conduct.* Chicago: Author.

Averett, Steve. 2004. "Judicial Ethics in Utah." *BYU Journal of Public Law* 18: 695–707.

Babcock, Barbara. 1983. "Defending the Guilty." *Cleveland State Law Review* 32: 175–187.

Baker, Al. 2004. "Judge Censured for Conduct Unbecoming His Authority." *New York Times,* December 11, B5.

Berger v. United States, 295 U.S. 78 (1935).

Brady v. Maryland, 373 U.S. 83 (1963).

Bureau of Justice Statistics. 2002. *Sourcebook of Criminal Justice Statistics–2002.* Washington, DC: U.S. Department of Justice.

Comisky, Marvin, Phillip Patterson, and William Taylor. 1987. *The Judiciary—Selection, Compensation, Ethics, and Discipline.* New York: Quorum Books.

Dodd v. Florida Bar, 118 So.2d 17 (Fla. 1960).

Etienne, Margareth. 2005. "The Ethics of Cause Lawyering: An Empirical Examination of Criminal Defense Lawyers as Cause Lawyers." *The Journal of Criminal Law & Criminology* 95 (4): 1195–1260.

Faretta v. California, 422 U.S. 806 (1975); 95 S. Ct. 2525 (1975).

Fisher, Stanley. 1988. "In Search of the Virtuous Prosecutor: A Conceptual Framework." *American Journal of Criminal Law* 197: 198–199.

Frankel, Marvin. 1975. "The Search for Truth: An Umpireal View." *University of Pennsylvania Law Review* 123: 1031–1059.

Freedman, Monroe. 1966. "Professional Responsibility of the Criminal Defense Lawyer: The Three Hardest Questions." *Michigan Law Review* 64: 1469–1484.

Freedman, Monroe. 1975a. "Judge Frankel's Search for the Truth," *University of Pennsylvania Law Review* 123: 1060–1082.

Freedman, Monroe. 1975b. *Lawyers' Ethics in an Adversary System.* Indianapolis, IN: Bobbs-Merrill.

Fried, Charles. 1994. "The Lawyer as Friend: The Moral Foundations of the Lawyer-Client Relation." Pp. 97–126 in *The Ethics of Lawyers,* edited by David Luban. New York: New York University Press.

Gerber, Rudolph. 1999. *Cruel and Unusual: Our Criminal Injustice System.* Westport, CT: Praeger.

Gershman, Bennett. 1986. "Why Prosecutors Misbehave." *Criminal Law Bulletin* 22 (2): 131–143.

Gershman, Bennett. 1987. *Prosecutorial Misconduct.* New York: C. Boardman.

Gershman, Bennett. 2001. "The Prosecutor's Duty to Truth." *Georgetown Journal of Legal Ethics* 14: 309–354.

Gier, Kelly. 2006. "Prosecuting Injustice: Consequences of Misconduct." *American Journal of Criminal Law* 33 (2): 191–222.

Glaberson, William. 2002. "Prosecutor Says Tape Shows Brooklyn Judge Took a Bribe." *New York Times,* February 9. Retrieved June 27, 2003 (http://www.nytimes.com/2002/02/09/nyregion/09JUDG.html).

Gottfredson, Michael and Don Gottfredson. 1988. *Decision Making in Criminal Justice: Toward the Rational Exercise of Discretion* (2nd ed.). New York: Plenum Press.

Greenhouse, Linda. 2006. "Federal Judges Take Steps to Improve Accountability." *The New York Times,* September 19, A20.

Hansen, Mark. 2005. "Hand It Over." *ABA Journal* 91 (12): 30–32.

Haskell, Paul G. 1998. *Why Lawyers Behave as They Do, New Perspectives on Law, Culture, and Society.* Boulder, CO: Westview Press.

Hazard, Geoffrey and William Hodes. 2002. *The Law of Lawyering* (3rd ed., Vol. 1). Gaithersburg, MD: Aspen Law & Business.

Herzog, Sergio. 2004. "Plea Bargaining Practices: Less Covert, More Public Support?" *Crime & Delinquency* 50 (4): 590–614.

In re Friedman, 392 N.E.2d 1333, 1336 (1979).

"Judges Might Go on Ballot in Maricopa County." 2008. *East Valley Tribune,* March 24. Retrieved March 30, 2008 (http://www.msnbc.msn.com/id/23774435/from/ET/).

Kipnis, Kenneth. 1986. *Legal Ethics.* Englewood Cliffs, NJ: Prentice-Hall.

Kipnis, Kenneth. 2001. "Criminal Justice and the Negotiated Plea." Pp. 362–371 in *Criminal Justice Ethics,* edited by Paul Leighton and Jeffrey Reiman. Upper Saddle River, NJ: Prentice-Hall.

Levine, Susan and Lori Montgomery. 2003. "Large Racial Disparity Found in Study of Md. Death Penalty." *Washington Post,* January 8, A01.

Liptak, Adam. 2006. "Reprimand for a Justice Who Met With Inmates." *New York Times,* 27 October, A12.

Luban, David. 1984. "The Sources of Legal Ethics: A German-American Comparison of Lawyers' Professional Duties." *Rabels Zeitschift* 48: 245–288.

Luban, David. 1988. *Lawyers and Justice: An Ethical Study.* Princeton, NJ: Princeton University Press.

Luban, David. 1990. "Partnership, Betrayal and Autonomy in the Lawyer-Client Relationship: A Reply to Stephen Ellmann." *Columbia Law Review* 90: 1004–1043.

McDonough, Chris, Diana McDonough, and Raymond Keenan. 2000. "The Ethical Obligations of the Criminal Prosecutor." Pp. 50–64 in *Morality and the Law,* edited by Roslyn Muraskin and Matthew Muraskin. Upper Saddle River, NJ: Prentice-Hall.

McKissick v. United States, 379 F.2d 754 (5th Cir. 1967).

Miller v. Pate, 386 U.S. 1 (1967).

Mitchell, John. 1980. "The Ethics of the Criminal Defense Attorney—New Answers to Old Questions." *Stanford Law Review* 32: 293–337.

Morrell v. State, P.2d 1200: Alaska Supreme Court (1978).

Newman, Andy. 2004. "Played in Court, Tapes Show Judge Coaching Lawyer and Taking Cash." *New York Times,* August 19, B1.

Nix v. Whiteside, 475 U.S. 157, 106 S. Ct. 988 (1986).

Noonan, John. 1966. "The Purposes of Advocacy and the Limits of Confidentiality." *Michigan Law Review* 64: 1485–1492.

Papke, David. 1986. "The Legal Profession and Its Legal Responsibilities: A History." Pp. 29–49 in *Ethics and the Legal Profession,* edited by Michael Davis and Frederick Elliston. Buffalo, NY: Prometheus Books.

Pepinsky, Hal. 2000. "Prosecuting for Safety's Sake." Pp. 65–78 in *Morality and the Law,* edited by Roslyn Muraskin and Matthew Muraskin. Upper Saddle River, NJ: Prentice-Hall.

Pepper, Stephen. 1994. "The Lawyer's Amoral Ethical Role: A Defense, A Problem, and Some Possibilities." Pp. 57–80 in *The Ethics of Lawyers,* edited by David Luban. New York: New York University Press.

Philips, Susan. 1998. *Ideology in the Language of Judges: How Judges Practice Law, Politics, and Courtroom Control.* Oxford, England: Oxford University Press.

Pool, J. 1979. "Defending the 'Guilty' Client." *Massachusetts Law Review* 64: 11–19.

Remington, Frank. 1993. "The Decision to Charge, the Decision to Convict on a Plea of Guilty, and the Impact of Sentence Structure on Prosecution Practices." Pp. 73–133 in *Discretion in Criminal Justice: The Tension Between Individualization and Uniformity,* edited by Lloyd Ohlin and Frank Remington. Albany: State University of New York Press.

Rimer, Sara. 2002. "Convict's DNA Sways Labs, Not a Determined Prosecutor. *New York Times,* February 6. Retrieved June 27, 2003 (http://www.nytimes.com/2002/02/06/national/06DNA.html).

Shaffer, Thomas. 1981. *On Being a Christian and a Lawyer.* Provo, UT: Brigham Young University Press.

Scheck, Barry, Peter Neufeld, and Jim Dwyer. 2000. *Actual Innocence: When Justice Goes Wrong and How to Make It Right.* New York: Signet.

Schoenfeld, Heather. 2005. "Violated Trust: Conceptualizing Prosecutorial Misconduct." *Journal of Contemporary Criminal Justice* 21 (3): 250–271.

Shaman, Jeffrey M., Steven Lubet, and James J. Alfini. 2000. *Judicial Conduct and Ethics.* Charlottesville, VA: Lexis Law.

Simon, William. 1988. "Ethical Discretion in Lawyering." *Harvard Law Review* 101 (6): 1083–1145.

Simon, William. 1994. "The Ideology of Advocacy: Procedural Justice and Professional Ethics." Pp. 179–296 in *The Ethics of Lawyers,* edited by David Luban. New York: New York University Press.

Subin, Harry. 1987. "The Criminal Lawyer's 'Different Mission': Reflections on the 'Right' to Present a False Defense. *Georgetown Journal of Legal Ethics* 1: 125–153.

Truth in Justice. 2001. "92nd Death Row Inmate Freed Since '73." *New York Times,* January 5. Retrieved March 12, 2008 (http://www.truthinjustice.org/no92.htm).

United States v. Agurs, 427 U.S. 97 (1976).

United States v. Perry, 643 F.2d 38 2d Cir. (1981).

Wasserstrom, Richard. 1975. "Lawyers as Professionals: Some Moral Issues." *Human Rights* 5: 1–24.

Wasserstrom, Richard. 1986. "Lawyers as Professionals: Some Moral Issues." Pp. 114–131 in *Ethics and the Legal Profession,* edited by Michael Davis and Frederick Elliston. Buffalo, NY: Prometheus Books.

Wolfram, Charles. 1986. *Modern Legal Ethics.* St. Paul, MN: West.

Chapter 5 References

American Friends Service Committee. 1971. *Struggle for Justice. A Report on Crime and Punishment in America.* New York: Hill and Wang.

Andenaes, Johannes. 1972. "Does Punishment Deter Crime?" Pp. 342–357 in *Philosophical Perspectives on Punishment,* edited by Gertrude Ezorsky. Albany: State University of New York Press.

Bazemore, Gordon and M. Dooley. 2001. "Restorative Justice and the Offender: The Challenge of Reintegration." Pp. 101–126 in *Restorative Community Justice: Repairing Harm and Transforming Communities,* edited by Gordon Bazemore and Mara Schiff. Cincinnati, OH: Anderson.

Bazemore, Gordon and Maria Schiff. 2001. "What and Why Now: Understanding Restorative Justice." Pp. 21–46 in *Restorative Community Justice: Repairing Harm and Transforming Communities,* edited by Gordon Bazemore and Mara Schiff. Cincinnati, OH: Anderson.

Bean, Philip. 1981. *Punishment: A Philosophical and Criminological Inquiry.* Oxford, England: Martin Robertson.

Blumstein, Alfred, Jaqueline Cohen, and Daniel. Nagin (Eds.). 1978. *Deterrence and Incapacitation: Estimating the Effects of Criminal Sanctions on Crime Rates.* Washington, DC: Panel on Research on Deterrent and Incapacitative Effects.

Braithwaite, John. 1998. "Restorative Justice." Pp. 323–344 in *Handbook of Crime and Punishment,* edited by Michael Tonry. New York: Oxford University Press.

Carawan, Edwin. 1998. *Rhetoric and the Law of Draco.* Oxford, England: Clarendon Press.

Carlen, Pat. 1994. "Crime, Inequality, and Sentencing." Pp. 306–332 in *A Reader on Punishment,* edited by Antony Duff and David Garland. Oxford, England: Oxford University Press.

Daly, Kathleen and Julie. Stubbs. 2007. "Feminist Theory, Feminist and Anti-Racist Politics, and Restorative Justice." Pp. 149–170 in edited by G. Johnstone and D. W. V. Ness. *Handbook of Restorative Justice,* Portland, OR: Willan.

Day, Andrew, Kylie Tucker, and Kevin Howells. 2004. "Coerced Offender Rehabilitation—A Defensible Practice?" *Psychology, Crime & Law* 10 (3): 259–269.

Duff, Antony and David Garland. 1994. "Introduction: Thinking About Punishment." Pp. 1–43 in *A Reader on Punishment,* edited by Antony Duff and David Garland. Oxford, England: Oxford University Press.

Duff, R. 1999. "Punishment, Communication, and Community." Pp. 48–68 in *Punishment and Political Theory,* edited by Matt Matravers. Portland, OR: Hart.

Feinberg, Joel. 1994. "The Expressive Function of Punishment." Pp. 71–91 in *A Reader on Punishment,* edited by Antony Duff and David Garland. Oxford, England: Oxford University Press.

Foucault, Michael 1977. *Discipline and Punish: The Birth of Prison.* London: Penguin Books.

Frankel, Marvin. 1972. *Criminal Sentences: Law without Order.* New York: Hill and Wang.

Furman v. Georgia, 408 U.S. 238, 308, 342, 394 (1972).

Gaes, Gerald., Timothy. Flanagan, Lawrence. Motiuk, and Lynn. Stewart. 1999. "Adult Correctional Treatment." Pp. 361–426 in *Prisons,* edited by Michael Tonry and Joan Petersilia. Chicago: University of Chicago Press.

Gallo, E. and V. Ruggiero. 1991. "The 'Immaterial' Prison: Custody as a Factory for the Manufacture of Handicaps." *International Journal of the Sociology of Law* 19 (3): 273–291.

Garland, David. 1990. *Punishment and Modern Society.* Oxford, England: Oxford University Press.

Gregg v. Georgia, 428 U.S. 153, 184 (1976).

Howe, Adrian. 1994. *Punish and Critique: Towards a Feminist Analysis of Penality.* London: Routledge.

Hudson, Barbara. 1996. *Understanding Justice: An Introduction to Ideas, Perspectives and Controversies in Modern Penal Theory.* Buckingham, England: Open University Press.

Kleinig, John. 1973. *Punishment and Desert.* The Hague, Netherlands: Martinus Nijhoff.

Martinson, Robert. 1974 "What Works?—Questions and Answers About Prison Reform." *The Public Interest* 35: 22–54.

Matthews, Roger. 1989. "Alternatives to and in Prisons: A Realistic Approach." Pp. 128–150 in *Paying for Crime,* edited by Pat Carlen and D. Cook. Milton Keynes, England: Open University Press.

Morris, Herbert. 1994. "A Paternalistic Theory of Punishment." Pp. 92–111 in *A Reader on Punishment,* edited by Antony Duff and David Garland. Oxford, England: Oxford University Press.

Morris, Norval. 1974. *The Future of Imprisonment.* Chicago: University of Chicago Press.

Murphy, Jeffrey. G. 1994. "Marxism and Retribution." Pp. 44–70 in *A Reader on Punishment,* edited by Antony Duff and David Garland. Oxford, England: Oxford University Press.

Nagin, Daniel. 1998. "Deterrence and Incapacitation." Pp. 345–368 in *The Handbook of Crime and Punishment,* edited by Michael Tonry. Oxford, England: Oxford University Press.

Nozick, Robert. 1981. *Philosophical Explanations.* Cambridge, MA: Harvard University Press.

Nygaard, Richard. 2000. *Sentencing As I See It.* Incline Village, NV: Copperhouse.

Reiman, Jeffrey. 1985. "Justice, Civilization, and the Death Penalty: Answering Van Den Haag." *Philosophy and Public Affairs* 14: 115–148.

Rotman, Edgardo. 1994. "Beyond Punishment." Pp. 281–305 in *A Reader on Punishment,* edited by Antony Duff and David Garland. Oxford, England: Oxford University Press.

Ten, C. L. 1987. *Crime, Guilt, and Punishment: A Philosophical Introduction.* Oxford, England: Clarendon Press.

Tonry, Michael. 1994. "Proportionality, Parsimony, and Interchangeability of Punishments." Pp. 133–160 in *A Reader on Punishment*, edited by Antony Duff and David Garland. Oxford, England: Oxford University Press.

Travis, Lawrence, III. 2002. "Criminal Sentencing: Honesty, Prediction, Discrimination and Ethics." Pp. 175–187 in *Justice, Crime and Ethics* (4th ed.), edited by M. Braswell, B. R. McCarthy, and B. J. McCarthy. Cincinnati, OH: Anderson.

Tullock, Gordon. 1974. "Does Punishment Deter Crime?" *The Public Interest* 36: 103–111.

van den Haag, Ernest. 1975. *Punishing Criminals: Concerning a Very Old and Painful Question*. New York: Basic Books.

Van Ness, Dan and Karen Heetderks Strong. 1997. *Restoring Justice*. Cincinnati, OH: Anderson.

Volpe, Maria R. 1991. "Mediation in the Criminal Justice System: Process, Promises, Problems." Pp. 194–206 in *Criminology as Peacemaking*, edited by H. E. Pepinsky and R. Quinney. Bloomington: Indiana University Press.

von Hirsch, Andrew. 1994. "Censure and Proportionality." Pp. 112–132 in *A Reader on Punishment*, edited by Antony Duff and David Garland. Oxford, England: Oxford University Press.

von Hirsch, Andrew. 1998. "Penal Theories." Pp. 659–682 in *The Handbook of Crime & Punishment*, edited by Michael Tonry. New York: Oxford University Press.

Walker, Nigel. 1991. *Why Punish?* Oxford, England: Oxford University Press.

Zimring, Franklin. 1976. "Punishing Homicide in Philadelphia: Perspectives on the Death Penalty." *University of Chicago Law Review* 43 (2): 227–252.

Zimring, Franklin. 1994. "Making the Punishment Fit the Crime: A Consumer's Guide to Sentencing Reform." Pp. 161–173 in *A Reader on Punishment*, edited by Antony Duff and David Garland. Oxford, England: Oxford University Press.

Chapter 6 References

Abadinsky, Howard. 1982. *Probation and Parole: Theory and Practice*. Chicago: Nelson-Hall.

American Correctional Association. 1990. "American Correctional Association Code of Ethics." Retrieved April 3, 2008 (http://www.aca.org/pastpresentfuture/ethics.asp).

American Probation and Parole Association. n.d. "Code of Ethics." Retrieved August 30, 2003 (http://www.appa-net.org/about%20appa/codeof.htm).

Austin, James and John Irwin. 2001. *It's About Time: America's Imprisonment Binge* (3rd ed.). Belmont, CA: Wadsworth.

Banks, Cyndi, Paul Rector, and Mary Jackson. 2005. *Coconino County Juvenile Court Probation Officer Attitudes Toward Safety and Carrying Weapons Study*. Unpublished Report Prepared for Coconino County Juvenile Court. Flagstaff, Arizona.

Berger, Joseph. 1994. "10 Jail Guards Are Charged in Smuggling." *New York Times*, April 21, B1.

Brookes, Derek. 2001. "The Possibility of a Correctional Ethic." Pp. 39–68 in *Discretion, Community, and Correctional Ethics*, edited by John Kleinig and Margaret Leland Smith. Lanham, MA: Rowman & Littlefield.

Carroll, Leo. 1998. *Lawful Order: A Case Study of Correctional Crisis and Reform*. New York: Garland.

Champion, Dean. 1996. *Probation, Parole and Community Corrections* (2nd ed.). Upper Saddle River, NJ: Prentice-Hall.

Clark v. Evans, 840 F.2d 876 11th Cir. (1988).

Clemmer, Donald. 1940. *The Prison Community*. New York: Rinehart.

Conover, Ted. 2001. *Newjack: Guarding Sing Sing*. New York: Vintage.

Conrad, John P. 1973. "Corrections and Simple Justice." *Journal of Criminal Law and Criminology* 64: 208–217.

Conrad, John P. 1982. "Can Corrections Be Rehabilitated?" *Federal Probation* 46 (2): 3–8.

Crouch, Ben. 1980a. "The Guard in a Changing Prison World." Pp. 5–48 in *The Keepers: Prison Guards and Contemporary Corrections,* edited by Ben Crouch. Springfield, IL: Charles C Thomas.

Crouch, Ben. 1980b. *The Keepers: Prison Guards and Contemporary Corrections.* Springfield, IL: Charles C Thomas.

Crouch, Ben and J. Marquart. 1980. "On Becoming a Prison Guard." Pp. 63–110 in *The Keepers: Prison Guards and Contemporary Corrections,* edited by Ben Crouch. Springfield, IL: Charles C Thomas.

del Carmen, Rolando., Maldine Beyh Barnhill, Gene Bonham, Lance Hignite, and Todd Jermstad. 2001. *Civil Liabilities and Other Legal Issues for Probation/Parole Officers and Supervisors* (3rd ed.). Washington, DC: U.S. Department of Justice.

Domurad, Frank. 2000. "Who Is Killing Our Probation Officers? The Performance Crisis in Community Corrections." *Corrections Management Quarterly* 4 (2): 41–51.

Dreyer v. Jalet, 349 F. Supp, 452 S.D. Texas (1972).

"Ex–S.C. Correctional Officer Sentenced." 2001. Retrieved May 7, 2003 (http://database .corrections.com/news/results2.asp?ID?1503).

Farmer v. Brennan, 511 U.S. 825 (1994).

Gifford, Sidra Lee. 2002. *Justice Expenditure and Employment in the United States, 1999.* Bureau of Justice Statistics Bulletin NCJ 191746. Washington, DC: U.S. Department of Justice.

Gilbert, Michael. 1999. "The Illusion of Structure." Pp. 263–277 in *The Administration and Management of Criminal Justice Organizations: A Book of Readings,* edited by Stan Stojkovic, John Klofas, and David Kalinich. Prospect Heights, IL: Waveland Press.

Glaser, Daniel and Lincoln Fry. 1987. "Corruption of Prison Staff in Inmate Discipline." *Journal of Offender Counseling, Services and Rehabilitation* 12 (1): 27–38.

Glaze, Lauren. 2002, August. *Probation and Parole in the United States, 2001.* Bureau of Justice Statistics Bulletin NCJ 195669. Washington, DC: U.S. Department of Justice.

Glaze, Lauren. 2006, August. *Probation and Parole in the United States, 2005.* Bureau of Justice Statistics Bulletin NCJ 215091. Washington, DC: U.S. Department of Justice.

Goffman, Erving. 1959. *Asylums: Essays on the Social Situation of Mental Patients and Other Inmates,* New York, London, Toronto: Anchor Books.

Goffman, Erving. 1961. "On the Characteristics of Total Institutions: The Inmate World." Pp. 15–67 in *The Prison: Studies in Institutional Organization and Change,* edited by D. Cressey. New York: Holt, Rinehart, and Winston

Guenther, Anthony and Mary Quinn Guenther. 1980. "Screws vs. Thugs." Pp. 162–182 in *The Keepers: Prison Guards and Contemporary Corrections,* edited by Ben Crouch. Springfield, IL: Charles C Thomas.

Hamm, Mark. 1995. "Whistleblowing in Corrections." Pp. 202–209 in *Morality in Criminal Justice: An Introduction to Ethics,* edited by Daryl Close and Nicholas Meier. Belmont, CA: Wadsworth.

Harrison, Paige and Allen Beck. 2003, July. *Prisoners in 2002.* Bureau of Justice Statistics Bulletin NCJ 200248. Washington, DC: U.S. Department of Justice.

Harrison, Paige and Allen Beck. 2006, November. *Prisoners in 2005.* Bureau of Justice Statistics Bulletin NCJ 215092. Washington, DC: U.S. Department of Justice.

Henriques, Z. W. 2001. "The Path of Least Resistance: Sexual Exploitation of Female Offenders as an Unethical Corollary to Retributive Ideology and Correctional Practice."

Pp. 193–201 in *Discretion, Community, and Correctional Ethics,* edited by John Kleinig and Margaret Leland Smith. Lanham, MA: Rowman & Littlefield.

Hensley, Christopher, Mary Koscheski, and Richard Tewksbury. 2003. "The Impact of Institutional Factors on Officially Reported Sexual Assaults in Prisons." *Sexuality & Culture* 7 (4): 16–26.

Hensley, Christopher and Richard Tewksbury. 2005. "Wardens' Perceptions of Prison Sex." *The Prison Journal* 85 (2): 186–197.

Hepburn, James. 1985. "The Exercise of Power in Coercive Organizations: A Study of Prison Guards." *Criminology* 23 (1): 145–164.

Hepburn, James. 1989. "Prison Guards as Agents of Social Control." Pp. 191–206 in *The American Prison: Issues in Research and Policy,* edited by Lynne Goodstein and Doris Layton MacKenzie. New York: Plenum Press.

Hudson v. McMillian, 503 U.S. 1 (1992).

Hughes, Kristen. April 2006. *Justice Expenditure and Employment in the United States, 2003.* Bureau of Justice Statistics Bulletin NCJ 212260. Washington, DC: U.S. Department of Justice.

Human Rights Watch. 2001. *No Escape: Male Rape in U.S. Prisons.* New York: Human Rights Watch.

In re Tyrell, 876 P.2d 445 (Cal. 1998).

Jacobs, J. 1977. *Statesville: The Penitentiary in Mass Society.* Chicago: University of Chicago Press.

Jones 'El and Others v. Berge and Litscher, 164 F.2d 1096 (2001).

Jones, James and Daniel. Carlson. 2001. *Reputable Conduct: Ethical Issues in Policing and Corrections.* Upper Saddle River, NJ: Prentice-Hall.

Kauffman, Kelsey. 1988. *Prison Officers and Their World.* Cambridge, MA: Harvard University Press.

Kenny v. Indiana Youth Center, 950 F.2d 462 (1991).

Kleinig, John. 2001. "Professionalizing Incarceration." Pp. 1–15 in *Discretion, Community, and Correctional Ethics,* edited by John Kleinig and Margaret Leland Smith. Lanham, MA: Rowman & Littlefield.

Klofas, John. 1984. "Reconsidering Prison Personnel: New Views of the Correctional Officer Subculture." *International Journal of Offender Therapy and Comparative Criminology* 28 (3): 169–175.

Lippke, Richard. 2007. *Rethinking Imprisonment.* Oxford, England: Oxford University Press.

Lombardo, Lucien. 1989. *Guards Imprisoned: Correctional Officers at Work* (2nd ed.). Cincinnati, OH: Anderson.

Mair, Julie Samia, Shannon Frattaroli, and Stephen Teret. 2003. "New Hope for Victims of Sexual Assault." *Journal of Law: Medicine & Ethics* 31: 602–606.

Marquart, James. 1986. "Prison Guards and the Use of Physical Coercion as a Mechanism of Prisoner Control." *Criminology* 24 (2): 347–366.

May, Edgar. 1980. "Prison Guards in America—The Inside Story." Pp. 138–149 in *The Keepers: Prison Guards and Contemporary Corrections,* edited by Ben Crouch. Springfield, IL: Charles C Thomas.

McCarthy, Bernard. 1995. "Patterns of Prison Corruption." Pp. 280–285 in *Morality in Criminal Justice: An Introduction to Ethics,* edited by Daryl Close and Nicholas Meier. Belmont, CA: Wadsworth.

McCarthy, Bernard. 2002. "Keeping an Eye on the Keeper: Prison Corruption and Its Control." Pp. 253–266 in *Justice, Crime and Ethics* (4th ed.), edited by M. Braswell, B. R. McCarthy and B. J. McCarthy. Cincinnati, OH: Anderson.

McCullough v. Cady, 640 F. Supp. 1012, E.D. Mich. (1986).

Melby, Todd. September 2006. "Convicted Once, Punished Twice." in *Contemporary Sexuality* 40 (9): 1, 4–6.

National Institute of Justice. 2006. "NIJ's Response to the Prison Rape Elimination Act" *Corrections Today* 68 (1): 60–61.

Owen, Barbara. 1998. *"In the Mix": Struggle and Survival in a Women's Prison.* Albany: State University of New York Press.

Petersilia, Joan. 1999. "Parole and Prisoner Reentry in the United States." Pp. 479–529 in *Prisons,* edited by Michael Tonry and Joan Petersilia. Chicago: University of Chicago Press.

Pew Charitable Trusts. 2008. *One in 100: Behind Bars in America in 2008.* Washington, DC: Author. Retrieved March 27, 2008 (http://www.pewcenteronthestates.org/uploaded Files/8015PCTS_Prison08_FINAL_2-1-1_FORWEB.pdf).

Poole, Eric and Robert Regoli. 1980. "Role Stress, Custody Orientation, and Disciplinary Actions: A Study of Prison Guards." *Criminology* 18 (2): 215–226.

Public Safety Performance Project. 2007. *Public Safety, Public Spending: Forecasting America's Prison Population 2007–2011.* Washington, DC: Pew Charitable Trusts. Retrieved March 19, 2007 (http://wwwpewtrustsorg/Reports/Statebased_policy/PSPP_prison_projections_0207.pdf).

Rosecrance, John. 1986. "Probation Supervision: Mission Impossible." *Federal Probation* 50 (1): 25–31.

Rudovsky, D., A. Bronstein, E. Koren, and J. Cade. 1988. *The Rights of Prisoners.* Carbondale: Southern Illinois University Press.

Silverman, Mitchell. 1993. "Ethical Issues in the Field of Probation." *International Journal of Offender Therapy and Comparative Criminology* 37 (1): 85–94.

Small, Shawn and Sam Torres. 2001. "Arming Probation Officers: Enhancing Public Confidence and Officer Safety." *Federal Probation* 65 (3): 24–28.

Smith, Margaret Leland. 2001. "The Shimmer of Reform: Prospects for a Correctional Ethic." Pp. 17–37 in *Discretion, Community, and Correctional Ethics,* edited by John Kleinig and Margaret Leland Smith. Lanham, MA: Rowman & Littlefield.

Steen, Sara and Rachel Bandy. 2007. "When the Policy Becomes the Problem: Criminal Justice and the New Millennium." *Punishment & Society* 9 (1): 5–26.

Stephan, James. 2004, June. *State Prison Expenditures, 2001.* Bureau of Justice Statistics Bulletin NCJ 202949. Washington, DC: U.S. Department of Justice.

Stop Prisoner Rape. 2006. *In the Shadows: Sexual Violence in U.S. Detention Facilities, A Shadow Report to the U.N. Committee Against Torture.* Los Angeles, CA: Author. Retrieved March 22, 2007 (http://www.spr.org/pdf/in_the_shadows.pdf).

Stop Prisoner Rape. 2007. *Stories From Inside: Prisoner Rape and the War on Drugs.* Los Angeles, CA: Author. Retrieved March 23, 2007 (http://www.spr.org).

Studt, Eliot. 1973. *Surveillance and Service in Parole: A Report of the Parole Action Study.* Washington, DC: National Institute of Corrections.

Sykes, Gresham. 1999. *The Society of Captives: A Study of a Maximum Security Prison.* Princeton, NJ: Princeton University Press. (Original work published 1958)

U.S. Department of Justice, Bureau of Prisons. 2000. "Quick Facts and Statistics." Retrieved August 30, 2003 (www.bop.gov/fact0598.html).

U.S. v. Nix, 501 F.2d 516 7th Cir. (1974).

Vaughn, Michael S. (1996). "Prison Civil Liability for Inmate-Against-Inmate Assault and Breakdown/Disorganization Theory." *Journal of Criminal Justice* 24 (2): 139–152.

Walker, Jaffrey. 1996. "Police and Correctional Use of Force: Legal and Policy Standards and Implications." *Crime and Delinquency* 42 (1): 144–156.

Webb, G. L. and D. Morris. 1980. "Prison Guard Conceptions." Pp. 150–161 in *The Keepers: Prison Guards and Contemporary Corrections,* edited by Ben Crouch. Springfield, IL: Charles C Thomas.

Wheeler, Stanton. 1961. "Socialization in Correctional Communities." *American Sociological Association* 26 (5): 697–712.

Whitley v. Albers, 475 U.S. 312 (1986).

Worley, Robert, James Marquart, and Janet Mullings. 2003. "Prison Guard Predators: An Analysis of Inmates Who Established Inappropriate Relations With Prison Staff, 1995–1998." *Deviant Behavior: An Interdisciplinary Journal* 24: 175–194.

Wyatt, Rachel. (2006). "Male Rape in U.S. Prisons: Are Conjugal Visits the Answer?" *Case Western Reserve Journal of International Law* 37: 579–614.

Chapter 7 References

Adcox, Seanna. 2007. "S. C. Considers Cutting Prison Time for Inmates who Donate Organs." Retrieved March 13, 2007 (http://www.thestate.com/mld/thestate/news/local/16861780.htm).

Amy, Douglas. 1987. "Can Policy Analysis Be Ethical?" Pp. 45–69 in *Confronting Values in Policy Analysis: The Politics of Criteria,* edited by Frank Fischer and John Forester. Newbury Park, CA: Sage.

Anderson, Charles. 1987. "Political Philosophy, Practical Reason, and Policy Analysis." Pp. 22–44 in *Confronting Values in Policy Analysis: The Politics of Criteria,* edited by Frank Fischer and John Forester. Newbury Park, CA: Sage.

Austin, James and John Irwin. 2001. *It's About Time: America's Imprisonment Binge* (3rd ed.). Belmont, CA: Wadsworth.

Banks, Cyndi. 2005. *Punishment in America: A Reference Handbook.* Santa Barbara, CA: ABC-Clio.

Baron, Jonathan. 1998. *Judgment Misguided: Intuition and Error in Public Decision Making.* New York: Oxford University Press.

Beckett, Katherine. 1997. *Making Crime Pay: Law and Order in Contemporary American Politics.* New York: Oxford University Press.

Bedau, Hugo A. 1996. "The United States of America." Pp. 45–76 in *Capital Punishment: Global Issues and Prospects,* edited by Peter Hodgkinson and Andrew Rutherford. Winchester, England: Waterside Press.

Bedau, Hugo A. 1997. "A Reply to Van Den Haag." Pp. 457–469 in *The Death Penalty in America: Current Controversies,* edited by Hugo Adam Bedau. New York: Oxford University Press.

Bedau, Hugo. A. 1999. "Abolishing the Death Penalty Even for the Worst Murderers." Pp. 40–59 in *The Killing State: Capital Punishment in Law, Politics, and Culture,* edited by Austin Sarat. Oxford, England: Oxford University Press.

Bennett, William, John DiIulio, and John Walters. 1999. *Body Count: Moral Poverty . . . and How to Win America's War Against Crime and Drugs.* New York: Simon & Schuster.

Bibas, Stephanos. 2004. "The Feeney Amendment and the Continuing Rise of Prosecutorial Power to Plea Bargain." *Journal of Criminal Law and Criminology* 94 (2): 295–308.

Brownstein, Henry. 2000. *The Social Reality of Violence and Violent Crime.* Boston: Allyn & Bacon.

Bush-Baskette, Stephanie. 1999. "The 'War on Drugs': A War Against Women." Pp. 211–229 in *Harsh Punishment: International Experiences of Women's Imprisonment,* edited by Sandy Cook and Susanne Davies. Boston: Northeastern University Press.

Christie, Nils. 2000. *Crime Control as Industry: Towards Gulags, Western Style?* London: Routledge.

Cohen, Stanley. 1972. *Folk Devils and Moral Panics: The Creation of the Mods and Rockers.* London: MacGibbon & Kee.

Cohen, Stanley and Jock Young. 1973. *The Manufacture of News: Social Problems, Deviance and the Mass Media.* London: Constable.

Cook, Philip and John Laub. 1998. "The Unprecedented Epidemic in Youth Violence." Pp. 27–64 in *Youth Violence* (Vol. 24), edited by Michael Tonry and Mark Moore. Chicago: University of Chicago Press.

Cullen, Francis, Bonnie Fisher, and Brandon Applegate. 2000. "Public Opinion About Punishment and Corrections." Pp. 1–79 in *Crime and Justice: A Review of Research,* edited by Michael Tonry. Chicago: University of Chicago Press.

Culver, John. 1999. "Capital Punishment Politics and Policies in the States, 1977–1997." *Crime, Law & Social Change* 32: 287–300.

Davey, Monica and Abby Goodnough. 2007. "Doubts Rise as States Detain Sex Offenders After Prison." *New York Times,* March 4. Retrieved March 4, 2007 (http://www.nytimes.com/2007/03/04/us/04civil.html?ei=5088&en=4b5d93af1ae8077f&ex=1330664400&partner=&pagewanted=print).

Department of Justice. 1998, November 25. "Report to the Attorney General: Inspection and Review of the Northeast Ohio Correctional Center." Retrieved September 1, 2003 (www.usdoj.gov/ag/youngstown/youngstown.htm).

DiIulio, John. 1990. "The Duty to Govern: A Critical Perspective on the Private Management of Prisons and Jails." Pp. 155–178 in *Private Prisons and the Public Interest,* edited by D. C. McDonald. New Brunswick, NJ: Rutgers University Press.

Feeley, Malcolm and Jonathan Simon. 1992. "The New Penology: Notes on the Emerging Strategy of Corrections and Its Implications." *Criminology* 30: 449–474.

Finkelstein, Katherine E. 2000. "New York to Offer Most Addicts Treatment Instead of Jail Terms." *New York Times,* June 23.

Finn, Peter. 1996. "No-Frills Prisons and Jails: A Movement in Flux." *Federal Probation* 60: 35–44.

Fischer, Frank and John Forester (Eds.). 1987. *Confronting Values in Policy Analysis: The Politics of Criteria.* Newbury Park, CA: Sage.

Furman v. Georgia, 408 U.S. 238 (1972).

Gaines, Larry and Peter Kraska (Eds.). 1997. *Drugs, Crime, and Justice.* Prospect Heights, IL: Waveland Press.

Gall v. United States, 200 U.S. 321 (2007).

Garland, David (Ed.). 2001. *Mass Imprisonment: Social Causes and Consequences.* London: Sage.

Geis, Gilbert. 1996. "A Base on Balls for White-Collar Criminals." Pp. 244–264 in *Three Strikes and You're Out: Vengeance as Public Policy,* edited by David Shichor and Dale Sechrest. Thousand Oaks, CA: Sage.

Glassner, Barry. 1999. *The Culture of Fear: Why Americans Are Afraid of the Wrong Things.* New York: Basic Books.

Glaze, Lauren and Thomas Bonczar. 2006, November. *Probation and Parole in the United States, 2005.* Bureau of Justice Statistics Bulletin NCJ 215091. Washington, DC: U.S. Department of Justice.

Glick, Henry and Amy Hutchinson. 2001. "Physician-Assisted Suicide: Agenda Setting and the Elements of Morality Policy." Pp. 55–70 in *The Public Clash of Private Values: The Politics of Morality Policy,* edited by Christopher Mooney. New York: Chatham House.

Goggin, Malcolm. and Christopher Mooney. 2001. "Congressional Use of Policy Information on Fact and Value Issues." Pp. 130–139 in *The Public Clash of Private Values: The Politics of Morality Policy,* edited by Christopher Mooney. New York: Chatham House.

Goode, Erich and Nachman Ben-Yehuda. 1994. Moral Panics: The Social Construction of Deviance. Oxford, England: Blackwell.

Gregg v. Georgia, 428 U.S. 153, 184 (1976).

Haines, Herbert. 1996. *Against Capital Punishment: The Anti–Death Penalty Movement in America, 1972–1994.* New York: Oxford University Press.

Hall, Stuart, Charles Critcher, Tony Jefferson, John Clarke, and Brian Roberts. 1978. *Policing the Crisis: Mugging, the State, and Law and Order.* New York: Holmes & Meier.

Harding, Richard. 1998. "Private Prisons." Pp. 626–655 in *The Handbook of Crime and Punishment,* edited by Michael Tonry. New York: Oxford University Press.

Harrison, Paige and Allen Beck. 2006, November. *Prisoners in 2005.* Bureau of Justice Statistics Bulletin NCJ 215092. Washington, DC: U.S. Department of Justice.

Heineman, Robert, William Bluhm, Steven Peterson, and Edward Kearny. 1997. *The World of the Policy Analyst.* Chatham, NJ: Chatham House.

Henry, Stuart and Dragan Milovanovic. 1996. *Constitutive Criminology: Beyond Postmodernism.* Thousand Oaks, CA: Sage.

Hood, Roger. 2001. "Capital Punishment: A Global Perspective." *Punishment & Society* 3 (3): 331–354.

Hood, Roger. 2002. *The Death Penalty: A Worldwide Perspective* (3rd ed.). Oxford, England: Oxford University Press.

James, A. 2001. "Capital Punishment: The Execution of Child Offenders in the United States." *Kluwer Law International* 9: 181–189.

Jenkins, Philip. 1998. *Moral Panic: Changing Concepts of the Child Molester in Modern America.* New Haven, CT: Yale University Press.

Kimbrough v. United States, U.S.—, 128 S. Ct. 558 (2007).

Kleinig, John and Kevin Murtagh. 2005. "Disenfranchising Felons." *Journal of Applied Philosophy* 22 (3): 217–239.

Lenz, Nygel. 2002. "'Luxuries' in Prison: The Relationship Between Amenity Funding and Public Support." *Crime & Delinquency* 48 (4): 499–525.

Lilly, J. Robert and Paul Knepper. 1992. "An International Perspective on the Privatization of Corrections." *Howard Journal* 31: 174–191.

Lippke, Richard. 1997. "Thinking About Private Prisons." *Criminal Justice Ethics* 16 (1): 26–38.

Logan, Charles. 1990. *Private Prisons: Cons and Pros.* New York: Oxford University Press.

Lynch, Mona. 2002. "Pedophiles and Cyber-Predators as Contaminating Forces: The Language of Disgust, Pollution, and Boundary Invasions in Federal Debates on Sex Offender Legislation." *Law & Social Inquiry* 27: 529–566.

Lyons, Donna. 2006. "Where on Earth Are Sex Offenders?" *State Legislatures* 32 (3): 14–15.

Maynard-Moody, Steven and Donald Stull. 1987. "The Symbolic Side of Policy Analysis: Interpreting Policy Change in a Health Department." Pp. 248–265 in *Confronting Values in Policy Analysis: The Politics of Criteria,* edited by Frank Fischer and John Forester. Newbury Park, CA: Sage.

Meehan, Eugene. 1990. *Ethics for Policymaking: A Methodological Analysis.* New York: Greenwood Press.

Merlo, Alida and Peter Benekos. 2000. *What's Wrong With the Criminal Justice System: Ideology, Politics, and the Media.* Cincinnati, OH: Anderson.

Mikkelsen, Randall. 2007, December 10. "Supreme Court Allows Lighter Crack Cocaine Terms." Retrieved April 9, 2008 (http://www.reuters.com/article/domesticNews/id USN1119916620071210).

Mooney, Christopher. 2001. "Introduction: The Public Clash of Private Values: The Politics of Morality Policy." Pp. 3–18 in *The Public Clash of Private Values: The Politics of Morality Policy,* edited by Christopher Mooney. New York: Chatham House.

Moore, Mark and Michael Tonry. 1998. "Youth Violence in America." Pp. 1–26 in *Youth Violence* (Vol. 24), edited by Michael Tonry. Chicago: University of Chicago Press.

Mumola, Christopher and Jennifer Karberg. October 2006. *Drug Use and Dependence, State and Federal Prisoners, 2004.* Bureau of Justice Statistics Special Bulletin NCJ 213530. Washington, DC: U.S. Department of Justice.

Nozick, Robert. 1974. *Anarchy, State, and Utopia.* New York: Basic Books.

Petersilia, Joan. 1999. "Parole and Prisoner Reentry in the United States." Pp. 479–529 in *Prisons,* edited by Michael Tonry and Joan Petersilia. Chicago: University of Chicago Press.

Reamer, Frederic. 1986. "Principles of Ethics and the Justification of Policy." Pp. 223–245 in *Policy Analysis: Perspectives, Concepts, and Methods,* edited by William Dunn. Greenwich, CT: Jai Press.

Reisig, Michael and Travis Pratt. 2000. "The Ethics of Correctional Privatization: A Critical Examination of the Delegation of Coercive Authority." *Prison Journal* 80 (2): 210–222.

Robinson, Matthew. 2002. *Justice Blind? Ideals and Realities of American Criminal Justice.* Upper Saddle River, NJ: Prentice-Hall.

Roper v. Simmons, 543 U.S. 551 (2005).

Russell-Brown, Katheryn. 1998. *The Color of Crime: Racial Hoaxes, White Fear, Black Protectionism, Police Harassment, and Other Macroaggressions.* New York: New York University Press.

Sarat, Austin. 1999. "Capital Punishment as a Legal, Political, and Cultural Fact: An Introduction." Pp. 3–23 in *The Killing State: Capital Punishment in Law, Politics, and Culture,* edited by Austin Sarat. New York: Oxford University Press.

Sarat, Austin. 2005. "Innocence, Error, and the 'New Abolitionism': A Commentary." *Criminology & Public Policy* 4 (1): 45–54.

Scheingold, Stuart. 1984. *The Politics of Law and Order.* New York: Longman.

The Sentencing Project. 2008. "Felony Disenfranchisement Laws in the United States." Retrieved April 10, 2008 (http://www.sentencingproject.org/Admin/Documents/publi cations/fd_bs_fdlawsinus.pdf).

Shichor, David. 1995. *Punishment for Profit: Private Prisons/Public Concerns.* Thousand Oaks, CA: Sage.

Shichor, David. 1999. "Three Strikes as a Public Policy: The Convergence of the New Penology and the McDonaldization of Punishment." Pp. 421–441 in *The Administration and Management of Criminal Justice Organizations: A Book of Readings,* edited by Stan Stojkovic, John Klofas, and David Kalinich. Prospect Heights, IL: Waveland Press.

Shichor, David. 2000. "Penal Policies at the Threshold of the Twenty-First Century." *Criminal Justice Review* 25 (1): 1–30.

Simon, Jonathan. 2000. "Symposium Introduction: Law, Democracy, and Society: Megan's Law: Crime and Democracy in Late Modern America." *Law & Social Inquiry* 25: 1111–1150.

Simon, Jonathan and Christina Spaulding. 1999. "Tokens of Our Esteem: Aggravating Factors in the Era of Deregulated Death Penalties." Pp. 81–116 in *The Killing State: Capital Punishment in Law, Politics, and Culture,* edited by Austin Sarat. New York: Oxford University Press.

Spohn, Cassia. 2002. *How Do Judges Decide? The Search for Fairness and Justice in Punishment.* Thousand Oaks, CA: Sage.

Stanford v. Kentucky, 492 U.S. 361 (1989).

Studlar, Dunley. 2001. "What Constitutes Morality Policy? A Cross-National Analysis." Pp. 38–51 in *The Public Clash of Private Values: The Politics of Morality Policy,* edited by Christopher Mooney. New York: Chatham House.

Tong, Rosemarie. 1986. *Ethics in Policy Analysis.* Englewood Cliffs, NJ: Prentice-Hall.

Tonry, Michael. 2001. "Unthought Thoughts: The Influence of Changing Sensibilities on Penal Policies." *Punishment & Society* 3 (1): 167–181.

Tonry, Michael. 2006. "Criminology, Mandatory Minimums, and Public Policy." *Criminology & Public Policy* 5 (1): 45–56.

United States. v. Quinones, 205 F. Supp.2d 256 (S.D.N.Y. 2002).

van den Haag, Ernest. 1985. "The Death Penalty Once More." *U. C. Davis Law Review* 18 (4): 957–972.

Vergari, Sheila. 2001. "Morality Politics and the Implementation of Abstinence-Only Sex Education: A Case of Policy Compromise." Pp. 201–210 in *The Public Clash of Private Values: The Politics of Morality Policy,* edited by Christopher Mooney. New York: Chatham House.

Walker, Samuel, Cassia Spohn, and Miriam DeLone. 2000. *The Color of Justice: Race, Ethnicity and Crime in America.* Belmont, CA: Wadsworth.

Weber, Max 1964. *The Theory of Social and Economic Organization.* New York: Free Press.

Zimring, Franklin, Gordon Hawkins, and Sam Kamin. 2001. *Punishment and Democracy: Three Strikes and You're Out in California.* New York: Oxford University Press.

Chapter 8 References

Ackerman, Bruce. 2004. "This Is Not a War." *Yale Law Journal* 113: 1871–1908.

Banks, Cyndi. 2004. *Criminal Justice Ethics: Theory and Practice* (1st ed.). Thousand Oaks, CA: Sage.

Bauhn, Per. 2005. "Political Terrorism and the Rules of Just War." Pp. 123–134 in *Ethics of Terrorism & Counter-Terrorism,* edited by Georg Meggle. Frankfurt, Germany: Ontos.

Coady, C. A. J. (Tony). 2005. "Terrorism, Just War and Right Response." Pp. 135–150 in *Ethics of Terrorism & Counter-Terrorism,* edited by Georg Meggle. Frankfurt, Germany: Ontos.

Corlett, J. Angelo. 2003. *Terrorism: A Philosophical Analysis.* Dordrecht/Boston: Kluwer.

Crank, John and Patricia Gregor. 2005. *Counter-Terrorism After 9/11: Justice, Security and Ethics Reconsidered.* Cincinnati, OH: LexisNexis and Anderson Publishing.

Dworkin, Ronald. 2006. *Is Democracy Possible Here?* Princeton, NJ: Princeton University Press.

Emcke, Carolyn. 2005. "War on Terrorism and the Crises of the Political." Pp. 227–244 in *Ethics of Terrorism & Counter-Terrorism,* edited by Georg Meggle. Frankfurt, Germany: Ontos.

Freeman, Michael. 2005. "Order, Rights and Threats: Terrorism and Global Justice." Pp. 37–56 in *Human Rights in the "War on Terror,"* edited by Richard Wilson. Cambridge, England: Cambridge University Press.

Frey, Raymond G. and Christopher Morris. 1991. "Violence, Terrorism, and Justice." Pp. 1–17 in *Violence, Terrorism, and Justice,* edited by R. G. Frey and Christopher Morris. Cambridge, England: Cambridge University Press.

Held, Virginia. 1991. "Terrorism, Rights, and Political Goals." Pp. 59–85 in *Violence, Terrorism, and Justice,* edited by R. G. Frey and Christopher Morris. Cambridge, England: Cambridge University Press.

Hoffman, Paul. 2004. "Human Rights and Terrorism." *Human Rights Quarterly* 26: 932–955.

Hooks, Gregory and Clayton Mosher. 2005. "Outrages Against Personal Dignity: Rationalizing Abuse and Torture in the War on Terror." *Social Forces* 83 (1): 1627–1646.

ICRC. 2006. The Geneva Conventions: The Core of International Humanitarian Law. Retrieved June 11, 2007 (http://www.icrc.org/Web/Eng/siteeng0.nsf/htmlall/genevaconventions).

Ignatieff, Michael. 2004. *The Lesser Evil: Political Ethics in an Age of Terror: The Gifford Lectures.* Princeton, NJ: Princeton University Press.

Kanstroom, Daniel. 2007. "'Unlawful Combatants' in the United States: Drawing the Fine Line Between Law and War." *Human Rights Magazine.* Retrieved June 12, 2007 (http://www.abanet.org/irr/hr/winter03/unlawful.html).

Kapitan, Tomis. 2005. "'Terrorism' as a Method of Terrorism." Pp. 21–38 in *Ethics of Terrorism & Counter-Terrorism*, edited by G. Meggle. Frankfurt, Germany: Ontos.

Khatchadourian, Haig. 2005. "Counter-Terrorism: Torture and Assassination." Pp. 177–196 in *Ethics of Terrorism & Counter-Terrorism*, edited by Georg Meggle. Frankfurt, Germany: Ontos.

Kleinig, John. 2005. "Ticking Bombs and Torture Warrants." *Deakin Law Review* 10 (2): 614–627.

Laqueur, Walter. 1987. *The Age of Terrorism*. Boston: Little, Brown.

Manning, Peter. 2006. "Reflections on Risk Analysis, Screening, and Contested Rationalities." *Canadian Journal of Criminology and Criminal Justice* 48: 453–469.

Massimino, Elisa. 2004. "Leading by Example? U.S. Interrogation of Prisoners in the War on Terror." *Criminal Justice Ethics* Winter/Spring: 73–76.

McEldowney, John. 2005. "Political Security and Democratic Rights." *Democratization* 12 (5): 766–782.

Mertens, Thomas. 2005. "Criminal Justice 9–11: ICC or Military Tribunals." Pp. 281–300 in *Ethics of Terrorism & Counter-Terrorism*, edited by Georg Meggle. Frankfurt, Germany: Ontos.

Messelken, Daniel. 2005. "Terrorism and Guerilla Warfare—A Comparative Essay." Pp. 51–68 in *Ethics of Terrorism & Counter-Terrorism*, edited by Georg Meggle. Frankfurt, Germany: Ontos.

Narveson, Jan. 1991. "Terrorism and Morality." Pp. 116–169 in *Violence, Terrorism, and Justice*, edited by R. G. Frey and Christopher Morris. Cambridge, England: Cambridge University Press.

Simpson, Peter. 2005. "The War on Terrorism: Its Justification and Limits." Pp. 197–206 in *Ethics of Terrorism & Counter-Terrorism*, edited by Georg Meggle. Frankfurt, Germany: Ontos.

Smith, Jeffrey. 2007. "Report Details Missteps in Data Collection." *Washington Post*, March 10. Retrieved April 12, 2007 (http://www.washingtonpost.com/wp-dyn/content/article/2007/03/09/AR2007030902353.html).

Steinhoff, Uwe. 2005. "The Ethics of Terrorism." Pp. 215–224 in *Ethics of Terrorism and Counter-Terrorism*, edited by Georg Meggle. Frankfurt, Germany: Ontos.

Teson, Fernando. 2005. "Liberal Security." Pp. 57–77 in *Human Rights in the "War on Terror,"* edited by Richard Wilson. Cambridge, England: Cambridge University Press.

Whittaker, David. 2003. *The Terrorism Reader* (2nd ed.). London/New York: Routledge.

Wilkinson, Paul. 2001. *Terrorism Versus Democracy: The Liberal State Response*. London/Portland, OR: Frank Cass.

Wilkinson, Paul. 2006. *Terrorism Versus Democracy: The Liberal State Response* (2nd ed.). London/New York: Routledge.

Wilson, Richard. 2005. "Human Rights in the 'War on Terror.'" Pp. 1–36 in *Human Rights in the "War on Terror,"* edited by Richard Wilson. Cambridge, England: Cambridge University Press.

Young, Alison. 1996. *Imagining Crime: Textual Outlaws and Criminal Conversations*. London/Thousand Oaks, CA: Sage.

Part II References

Atterton, Peter. 2002. "Emmanuel Levinas." Pp. 231–238 in *Postmodernism: The Key Figures*, edited by Hans Bertens and Joseph Natoli. Oxford, England: Blackwell.

Bauman, Zygmunt. 1993. *Postmodern Ethics*. Oxford, England: Blackwell.

Davis, Nancy. 1991. "Contemporary Deontology." Pp. 205–218 in *A Companion to Ethics*, edited by Peter Singer. Cambridge, MA: Blackwell.

Hinman, Lawrence. 1998. *Ethics: A Pluralistic Approach to Moral Theory*. Fort Worth, TX: Harcourt Brace.

Kagan, Shelly. 1998. *Normative Ethics.* Boulder, CO: Westview Press.

Kekes, John. 2000. *Pluralism in Philosophy: Changing the Subject.* Ithaca, NY: Cornell University Press.

Kopperi, Marjaanna. 1999. *Right Actions and Good Persons: Controversies Between Eudaimonistic and Deontic Moral Theories.* Aldershot, England: Ashgate.

Rachels, James. 1997. *Can Ethics Provide Answers? And Other Essays in Moral Philosophy.* Lanham, MD: Rowman & Littlefield.

Rainsford, Dominic and Tim Woods (Eds.). 1999. *Critical Ethics: Text, Theory and Responsibility.* London: MacMillan Press.

Rumana, Richard. 2000. *On Rorty.* Belmont, CA: Wadsworth.

Scarre, Geoffrey. 1996. *Utilitarianism.* London: Routledge.

Sharples, Robert. W. 1996. *Stoics, Epicureans and Sceptics: An Introduction to Hellenistic Philosophy.* London: Routledge.

Wallace, James. 1996. *Ethical Norms, Particular Cases.* Ithaca, NY: Cornell University Press.

Chapter 9 References

Benn, Piers. 1998. *Ethics: Fundamentals of Philosophy.* Montreal, QC: McGill-Queen's University Press.

Dancy, Jonathan. 1991. "An Ethic of Prima Facie Duties." Pp. 219–229 in *A Companion to Ethics,* edited by Peter Singer. Cambridge, MA: Blackwell.

Giannetti, William. 2003. "Policing the Brass: A Case Study in Command Malfeasance." *Criminal Justice Ethics* Summer/Fall: 32–50.

Hill, Thomas E. 2000. *Respect, Pluralism, and Justice: Kantian Perspectives.* Oxford, England: Oxford University Press.

Hinman, Lawrence. 1998. *Ethics: A Pluralistic Approach to Moral Theory.* Fort Worth, TX: Harcourt Brace.

Holmes, Robert. 1998. *Basic Moral Philosophy* (2nd ed.). Belmont, CA: Wadsworth.

Jones, John and Daniel Carlson (Eds.). 2001. *Reputable Conduct: Ethical Issues in Policing and Corrections.* Upper Saddle River, NJ: Prentice-Hall.

O'Neill, Onora. 1991. "Kantian Ethics." Pp. 175–185 in *A Companion to Ethics,* edited by Peter Singer. Cambridge, MA: Blackwell.

Rachels, James. 1999. *The Elements of Moral Philosophy* (3rd ed.). Boston: McGraw-Hill College.

Schneewind, J. B. 1992. "Autonomy, Obligation, and Virtue: An Overview of Kant's Moral Philosophy." Pp. 309–341 in *The Cambridge Companion to Kant,* edited by Paul Guyer. Cambridge, England: Cambridge University Press.

Scruton, Roger. 2001. *Kant: A Very Short Introduction.* Oxford, England: Oxford University Press.

Chapter 10 References

Benn, Piers. 1998. *Ethics: Fundamentals of Philosophy.* Montreal, QC: McGill-Queen's University Press.

Close, Daryl and Nicholas Meier. 1995. *Morality in Criminal Justice: An Introduction to Ethics.* Belmont, CA: Wadsworth.

Darwall, Stephen. 1998. *Philosophical Ethics.* Boulder, CO: Westview Press.

Goodin, Robert. 1991. "Utility and the Good." Pp. 241–248 in *A Companion to Ethics,* edited by Peter Singer. Cambridge, MA: Blackwell.

Hinman, Lawrence. 1998. *Ethics: A Pluralistic Approach to Moral Theory.* Fort Worth, TX: Harcourt Brace.

Holmes, Robert. 1998. *Basic Moral Philosophy* (2nd ed.). Belmont, CA: Wadsworth.

Rachels, James. 1999a. *The Elements of Moral Philosophy* (3rd ed.). Boston: McGraw-Hill College.

Rachels, James. 1999b. *The Right Thing to Do: Basic Readings in Moral Philosophy* (2nd ed.). Boston: McGraw-Hill College.

Rashbaum, William. 2000. "Officer Accused of False Testimony Kills Himself, Police Say." *New York Times*, March 15. Retrieved May 15, 2007 (http://query.nytimes.com/gst/fullpage.html? sec=health&res=9B0CE7DF1E3BF936A25750C0A9669C8B63).

Scarre, Geoffrey. 1996. *Utilitarianism.* London: Routledge.

Shaw, William. 1999. *Contemporary Ethics: Taking Account of Utilitarianism.* Oxford, England: Blackwell.

Singer, Peter. 1979. "Famine, Affluence, and Morality." Pp. 263–278 in *Moral Problems* (3rd ed.), edited by James Rachels. New York: Harper and Row.

Chapter 11 References

Benn, Piers. 1998. *Ethics: Fundamentals of Philosophy.* Montreal, QC: McGill-Queen's University Press.

Blum, Lawrence. 1996. "Community and Virtue." Pp. 231–250 in *How Should One Live? Essays on the Virtues,* edited by Roger Crisp. Oxford, England: Clarendon Press.

Cassidy, Michael. 2006. "Character and Context: What Virtue Theory Can Teach Us About a Prosecutor's Ethical Duty to 'Seek Justice.'" *Notre Dame Law Review* 82 (2): 100–161.

Darwall, Stephen. 1998. *Philosophical Ethics.* Boulder, CO: Westview Press.

Goodman, Debbie. 1998. *Enforcing Ethics: A Scenario-Based Workbook for Police and Corrections Recruits and Officers.* Upper Saddle River, NJ: Prentice-Hall.

Hinman, Lawrence. 1998. *Ethics: A Pluralistic Approach to Moral Theory.* Fort Worth, TX: Harcourt Brace.

Hinman, Lawrence. 2003. *Ethics: A Pluralistic Approach to Moral Theory* (3rd ed.). Belmont, CA: Thomson/Wadsworth.

Holmes, Robert. 1998. *Basic Moral Philosophy* (2nd ed.). Belmont, CA: Wadsworth.

Hursthouse, Rosalind. 1999. *On Virtue Ethics.* Oxford, England: Oxford University Press.

Kopperi, Marjaanna. 1999. *Right Actions and Good Persons: Controversies Between Eudaimonistic and Deontic Moral Theories.* Aldershot, England: Ashgate.

MacIntyre, Alasdair. 1984. *After Virtue: A Study in Moral Theory.* Notre Dame, IN: University of Notre Dame Press.

Okin, Susan Moller. 1996. "Feminism, Moral Development, and the Virtues." Pp. 211–229 in *How Should One Live? Essays on the Virtues,* edited by Roger Crisp. Oxford, England: Clarendon Press.

Pincoffs, Edmund. 1998. "Quandary Ethics." Pp. 435–453 in *Ethical Theory,* edited by James Rachels. Oxford, England: Oxford University Press.

Prior, William. 1991. *Virtue and Knowledge: An Introduction to Ancient Greek Ethics.* London: Routledge.

Rachels, James. 1999. *The Elements of Moral Philosophy* (3rd ed.). Boston: McGraw-Hill College.

Tessitore, Aristide. 1996. *Reading Aristotle's Ethics: Virtue, Rhetoric, and Political Philosophy.* Albany: State University of New York Press.

Chapter 12 References

Baier, Kurt. 1991. "Egoism." Pp. 197–204 in *A Companion to Ethics,* edited by Peter Singer. Cambridge, MA: Blackwell.

Becker, Lawrence. 1998. *A New Stoicism.* Princeton, NJ: Princeton University Press.

Feldman, Fred. 1997. *Utilitarianism, Hedonism, and Desert: Essays in Moral Philosophy.* New York: Cambridge University Press.

Hinman, Lawrence. 1998. *Ethics: A Pluralistic Approach to Moral Theory.* Fort Worth, TX: Harcourt Brace.

Prior, William. 1991. *Virtue and Knowledge: An Introduction to Ancient Greek Ethics.* London: Routledge.

Rachels, James. 1999. *The Elements of Moral Philosophy* (3rd ed.). Boston: McGraw-Hill College.

Sharples, Robert W. 1996. *Stoics, Epicureans and Sceptics: An Introduction to Hellenistic Philosophy.* London: Routledge.

Chapter 13 References

Alejandro, Roberto. 1998. *The Limits of Rawlsian Justice.* Baltimore: The John Hopkins University Press.

Benn, Piers. 1998. *Ethics: Fundamentals of Philosophy.* Montreal, QC: McGill-Queen's University Press.

Blocker, H. Gene and Elisabeth H. Smith (Eds.). 1980. *John Rawls' Theory of Social Justice: An Introduction.* Athens: Ohio University Press.

Darwall, Stephen. 1980. "Is There a Kantian Foundation for Rawlsian Justice?" Pp. 311–345 in *John Rawls' Theory of Social Justice: An Introduction,* edited by H. Gene Blocker and Elisabeth H. Smith. Athens: Ohio University Press.

Holmes, Robert. 1998. *Basic Moral Philosophy* (2nd ed.). Belmont, CA: Wadsworth.

Jones, Hardy. 1980. "A Rawlsian Discussion of Discrimination." Pp. 270–288 in *John Rawls' Theory of Social Justice: An Introduction,* edited by H. Gene Blocker and Elisabeth H. Smith. Athens: Ohio University Press.

Martin, Rex. 1985. *Rawls and Rights.* Lawrence: University Press of Kansas.

Okin, Susan. 2003. "Justice and Gender." Pp. 236–250 in *Justice: Alternative Political Perspectives* (4th ed.), edited by James Sterba. Belmont, CA: Thompson/Wadsworth.

Rawls, John. 1973. *A Theory of Justice.* Oxford, England: Oxford University Press.

Scanlon, T. M. 1989. "Rawls' Theory of Justice." Pp. 169–205 in *Reading Rawls: Critical Studies on Rawls' A Theory of Justice,* edited by Norman Daniels. Palo Alto, CA: Stanford University Press.

Chapter 14 References

Benhabib, Seyla. 1987. "The Generalized and the Concrete Other: The Kohlberg-Gilligan Controversy and Moral Theory." Pp. 154–177 in *Women and Moral Theory,* edited by Eva Feder Kittay and Diana Meyers. Totowa, NJ: Rowman & Littlefield.

Blum, Lawrence. 1994. *Moral Perception and Particularity.* Cambridge, England: Cambridge University Press.

Braswell, Michael, John Fuller, and Bo Lozoff. 2001. *Corrections, Peacemaking, and Restorative Justice: Transforming Individuals and Institutions.* Cincinnati, OH: Anderson.

Braswell, Michael and Jeffrey Gold. 1998. "Peacemaking, Justice and Ethics." Pp. 25–39 in *Justice, Crime and Ethics* (3rd ed.), edited by Michael Braswell, Belinda McCarthy, and Bernard McCarthy. Cincinnati, OH: Anderson.

Close, Daryl and Nicholas Meier. 1995. *Morality in Criminal Justice: An Introduction to Ethics.* Belmont, CA: Wadsworth.

Darwall, Stephen. 1998. *Philosophical Ethics.* Boulder, CO: Westview Press.

Flanagan, Owen and Kathryn Jackson. 1993. "Justice, Care, and Gender: The Kohlberg–Gilligan Debate Revisited." Pp. 69–86 in *An Ethic of Care: Feminist and Interdisciplinary Perspectives,* edited by Mary Jeanne Larrabee. New York: Routledge.

Fuller, John. 1998. *Criminal Justice: A Peacemaking Perspective.* Boston: Allyn & Bacon.

Gilligan, Carol. 1982. *In a Different Voice: Psychological Theory and Women's Development.* Cambridge, MA: Harvard University Press.

Gilligan, Carol. 1993. *In a Different Voice* (2nd ed.). Cambridge, MA: Harvard University Press.

Grimshaw, Jean. 1991. "The Idea of a Female Ethic." Pp. 491–499 in *A Companion to Ethics,* edited by Peter Singer. Cambridge, MA: Blackwell.

Held, Virginia. 1987. "Feminism and Moral Theory." Pp. 111–128 in *Women and Moral Theory,* edited by Eva Kittay and Diana Meyers. Totowa, NJ: Rowman & Littlefield.

Hinman, Lawrence. 1998. *Ethics: A Pluralistic Approach to Moral Theory.* Fort Worth, TX: Harcourt Brace.

Holmes, Robert. 1998. *Basic Moral Philosophy* (2nd ed.). Belmont, CA: Wadsworth.

Nicholson, Linda. 1993. "Women, Morality, and History." Pp. 87–101 in *An Ethic of Care: Feminist and Interdisciplinary Perspectives,* edited by Mary Jeanne Larrabee. New York: Routledge.

Noddings, Nel. 1984. *Caring: A Feminine Approach to Ethics and Education.* Berkeley: University of California Press.

Pepinsky, Hal. 1999. "Peacemaking Criminology and Social Justice." Pp. 51–70 in *Social Justice/Criminal Justice: The Maturation of Critical Theory in Law, Crime, and Deviance,* edited by Bruce Arrigo. Belmont, CA: Wadsworth.

Rachels, James. 1999. *The Elements of Moral Philosophy* (3rd ed.). Boston: McGraw-Hill College.

Slote, Michael. 1998. "The Justice of Caring." Pp. 171–195 in *Virtue and Vice,* edited by Ellen Paul, Fred Miller, and Jeffrey Paul. Cambridge, England: Cambridge University Press.

Sterba, James. 2001. *Three Challenges to Ethics: Environmentalism, Feminism, and Multiculturalism.* Oxford, England: Oxford University Press.

West, Robin. 1997. *Caring for Justice.* New York: New York University Press.

Index

About the Author

Cyndi Banks is Professor of Criminology and Criminal Justice at Northern Arizona University. She teaches courses on a range of subjects with a special focus on criminal justice ethics, juvenile justice, gender and crime, as well as comparative criminology. As well as being an accomplished academic, Dr. Banks in an expert consultant for overseas development projects in the justice sector and, in that capacity, has worked in Papua New Guinea, Bangladesh, Iraq and, most recently, as a juvenile justice specialist with UNICEF in Sudan. In additional to this text, she is the author of four other books and has a new book in press concerned with the experience of institutionalization for juveniles in an institution in Alaska.